Gunnerkrigg Court

Orientation

by Tom Siddell

Gunnerkrigg Court
Written & Illustrated by
Tom Siddell

Published by
Archaia Studios Press
586 Devon Street
Kearny, NJ 07032
www.aspcomics.com

Mark Smylie & Aki Liao, *Publishers*
Joseph Illidge, *Comics Editor*
Pauline Beney, *Art Director*
Brian Petkash & Lys Fulda,
Marketing

Write to:
editorial@aspcomics.com

Gunnerkrigg Court. July 2008
FIRST PRINTING
10 9 8 7 6 5 4 3 2 1

ISBN 1-932386-34-3
IBSN 13: 98-1-932386-34-9

Printed in China.

Gunnerkrigg Court

Orientation

my name is antimony carver.
I would like to share with
you the strange events that
took place while I attended
school at...

Gunnerkrigg Court

Chapter 1:

The Shadow and The Robot

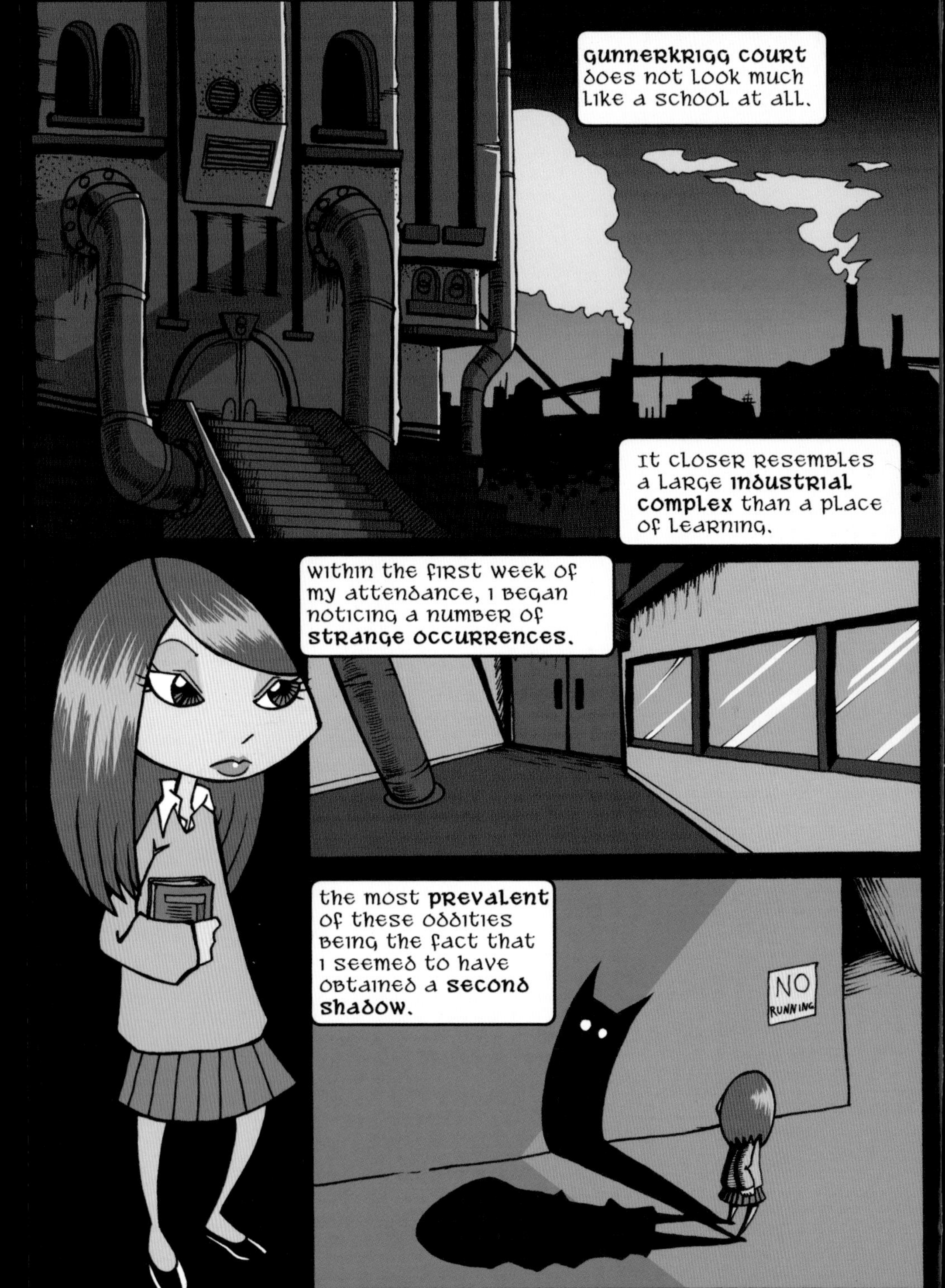
Gunnerkrigg Court does not look much like a school at all.
It closer resembles a large industrial complex than a place of learning.
Within the first week of my attendance, I began noticing a number of strange occurrences.
The most prevalent of these oddities being the fact that I seemed to have obtained a second shadow.
NO RUNNING

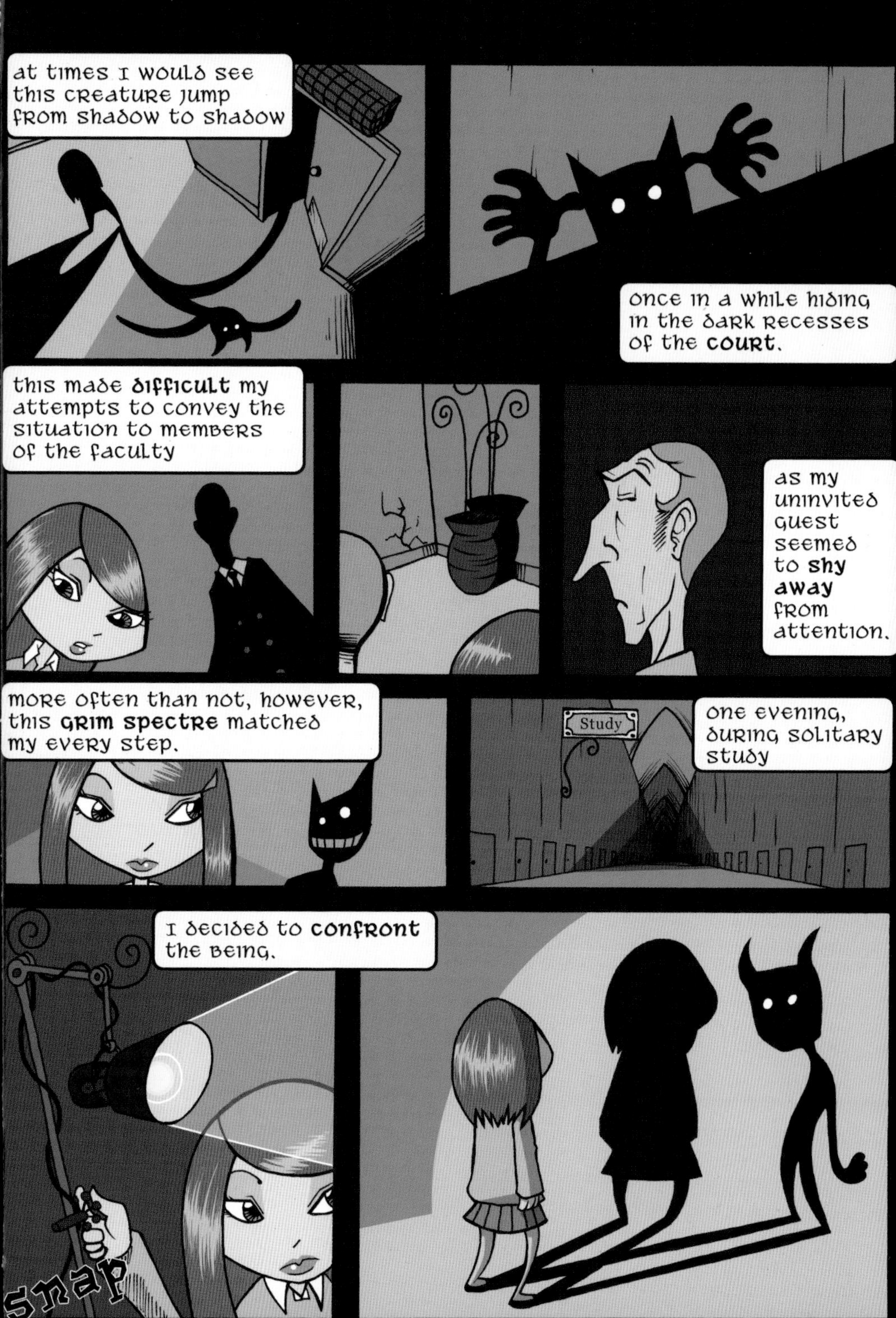
at times I would see this creature jump from shadow to shadow
once in a while hiding in the dark recesses of the **court**.
this made **difficult** my attempts to convey the situation to members of the faculty
as my uninvited guest seemed to **shy away** from attention.
more often than not, however, this **grim spectre** matched my every step.
Study
one evening, during solitary study
I decided to **confront** the being.
snap

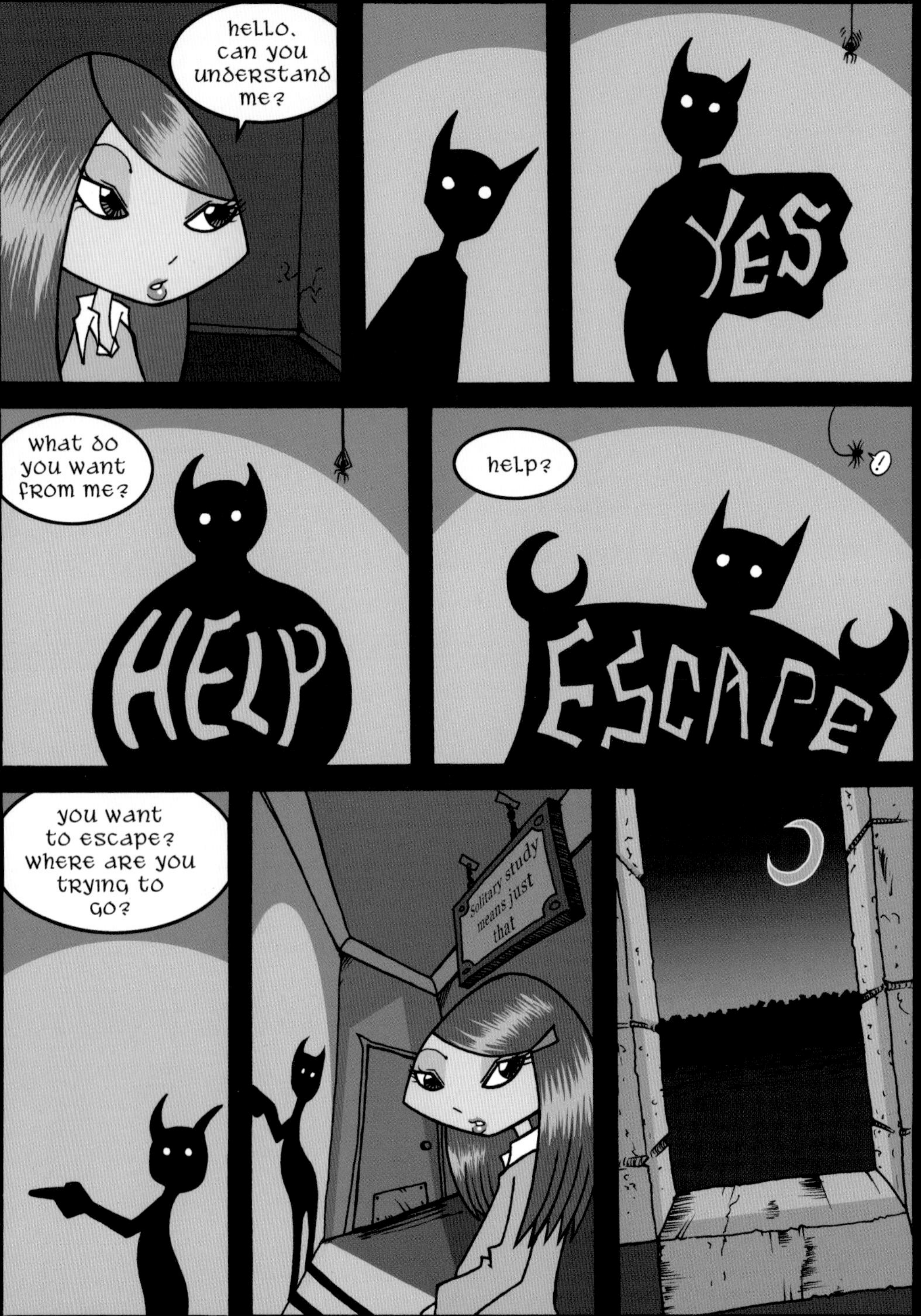
hello. can you understand me?
YES
what do you want from me?
HELP
help?
!
ESCAPE
you want to escape? where are you trying to go?
Solitary study means just that

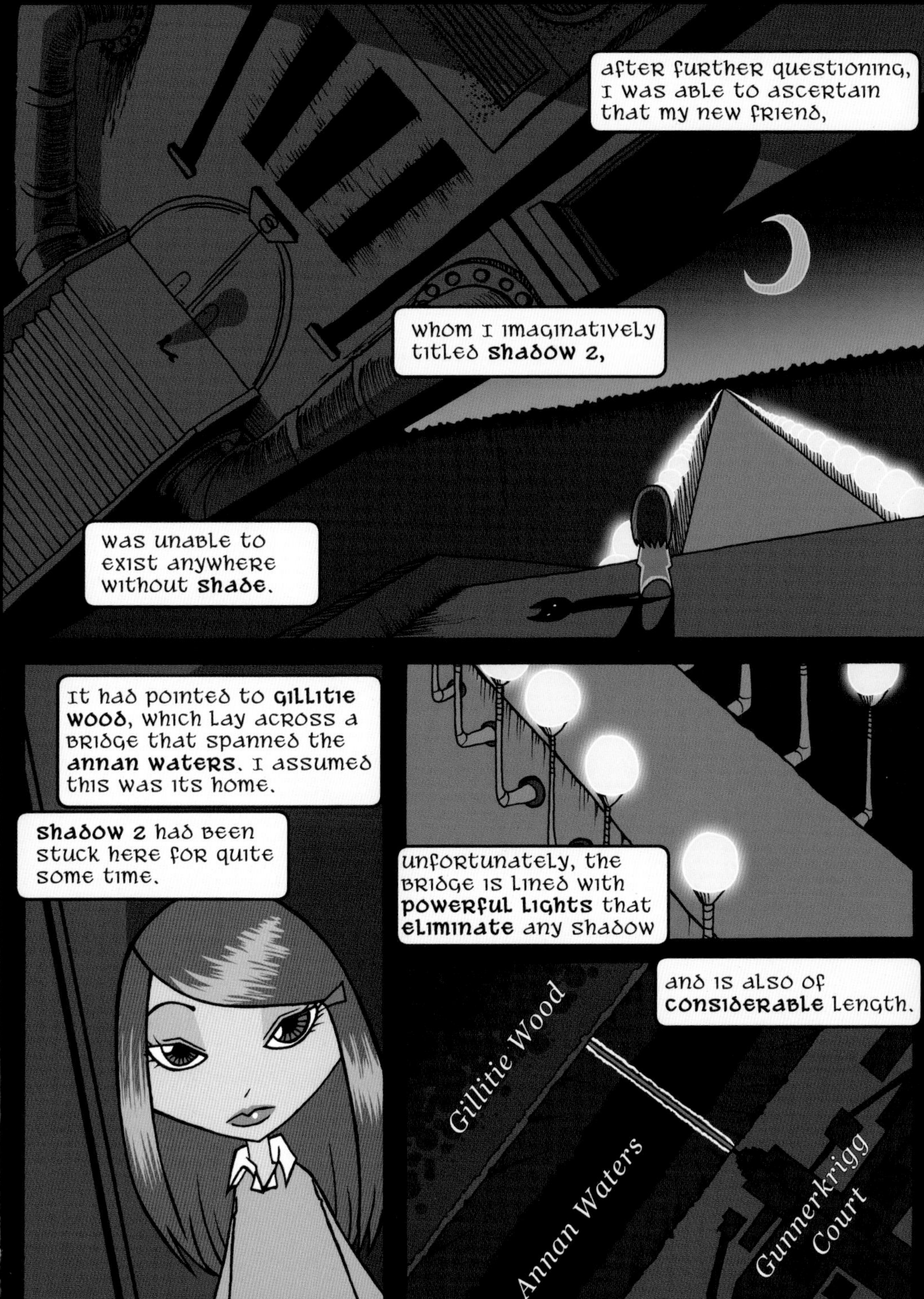
after further questioning, I was able to ascertain that my new friend,
whom I imaginatively titled shadow 2,
was unable to exist anywhere without shade.
It had pointed to gillitie wood, which lay across a bridge that spanned the annan waters. I assumed this was its home.
shadow 2 had been stuck here for quite some time.
unfortunately, the bridge is lined with powerful lights that eliminate any shadow
and is also of considerable length.
Gillitie Wood
Annan Waters
Gunnerkrigg Court

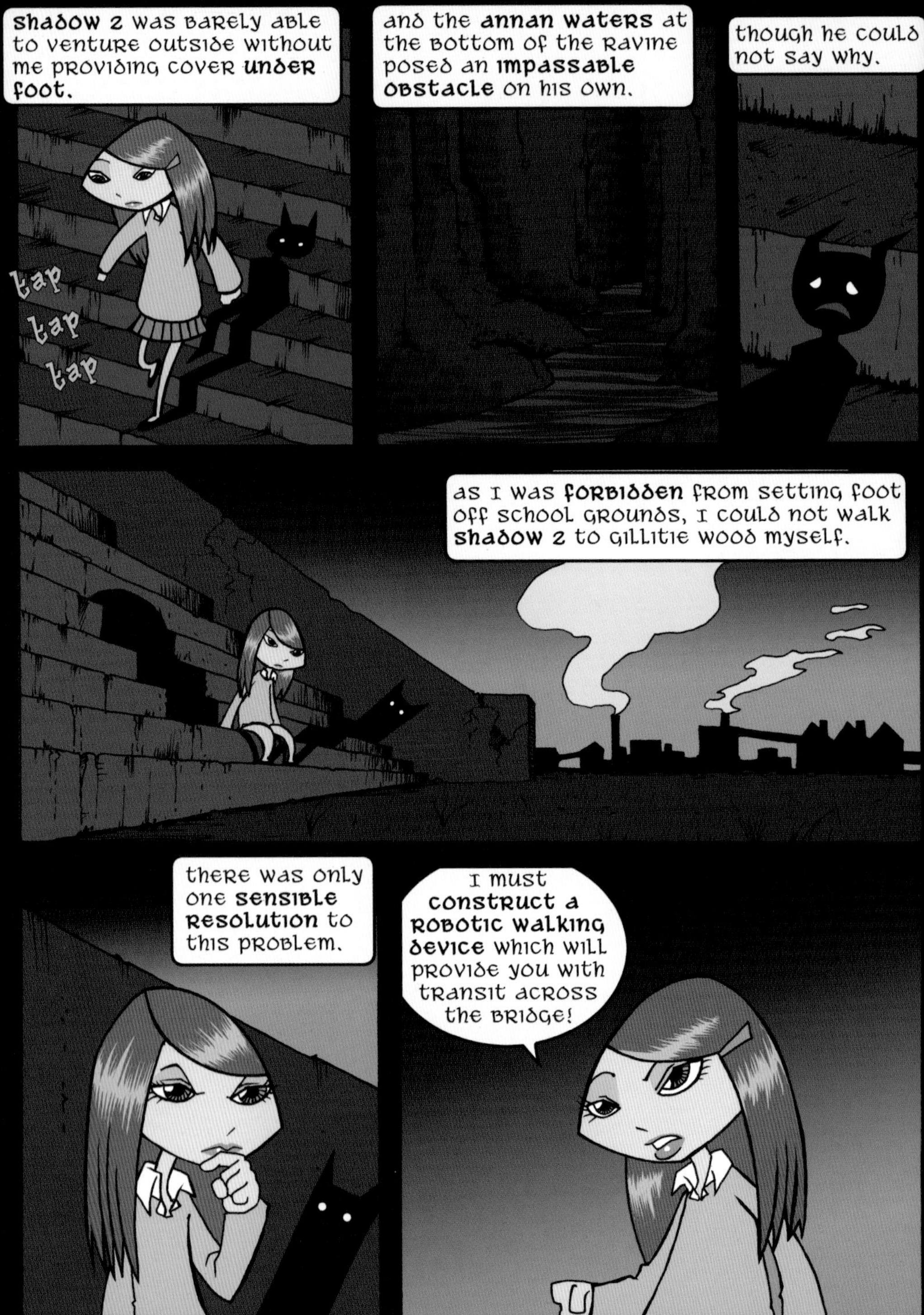
shadow 2 was barely able to venture outside without me providing cover under foot.
tap
tap
tap
and the annan waters at the bottom of the ravine posed an impassable obstacle on his own.
though he could not say why.
as I was forbidden from setting foot off school grounds, I could not walk shadow 2 to gillitie wood myself.
there was only one sensible resolution to this problem.
I must construct a robotic walking device which will provide you with transit across the bridge!

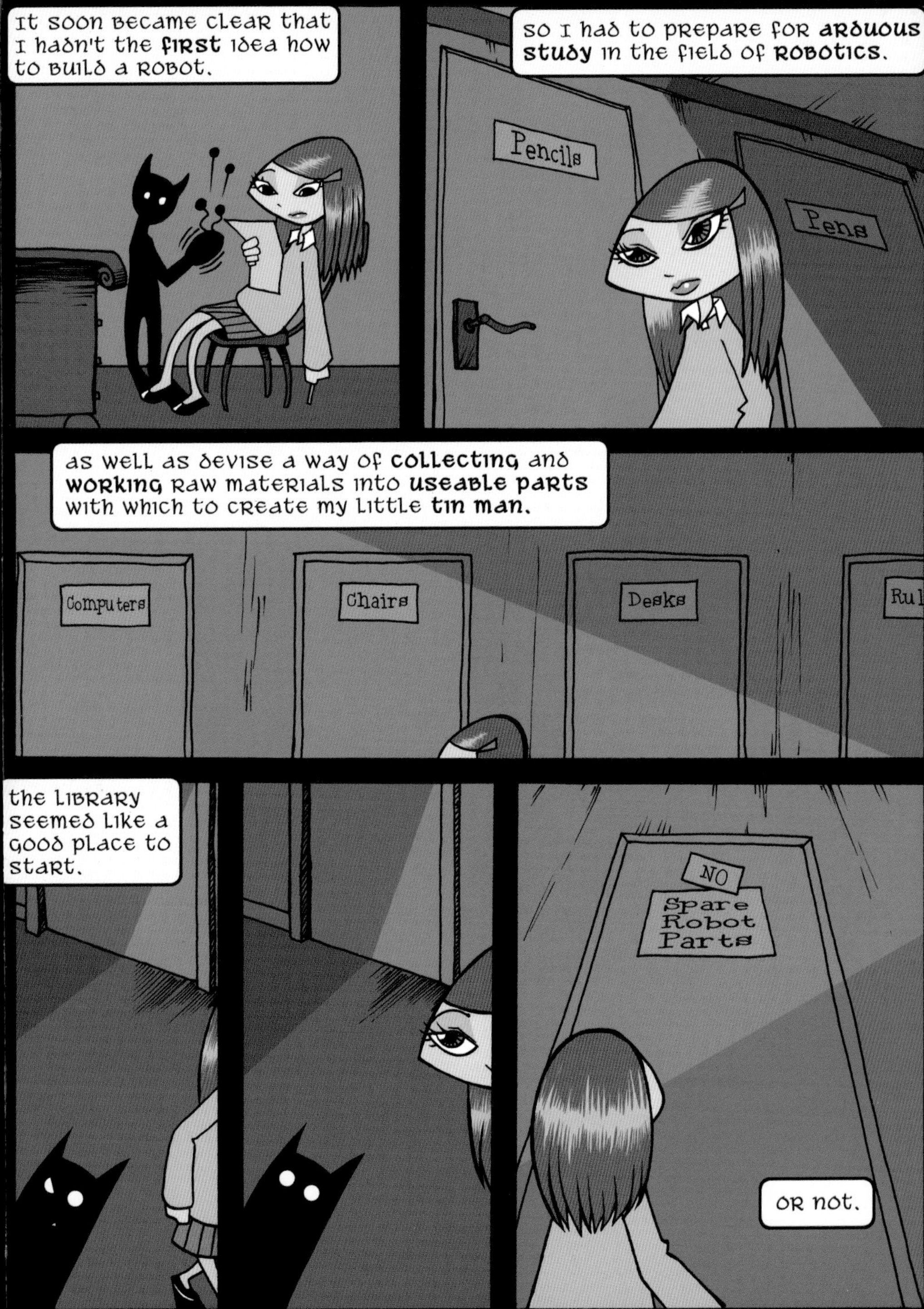
It soon became clear that I hadn't the **first** idea how to build a robot.
So I had to prepare for **arduous study** in the field of **robotics**.
Pencils
Pens
as well as devise a way of **collecting** and **working** raw materials into **useable parts** with which to create my little **tin man**.
Computers
Chairs
Desks
The library seemed like a good place to start.
NO
Spare Robot Parts
Or not.

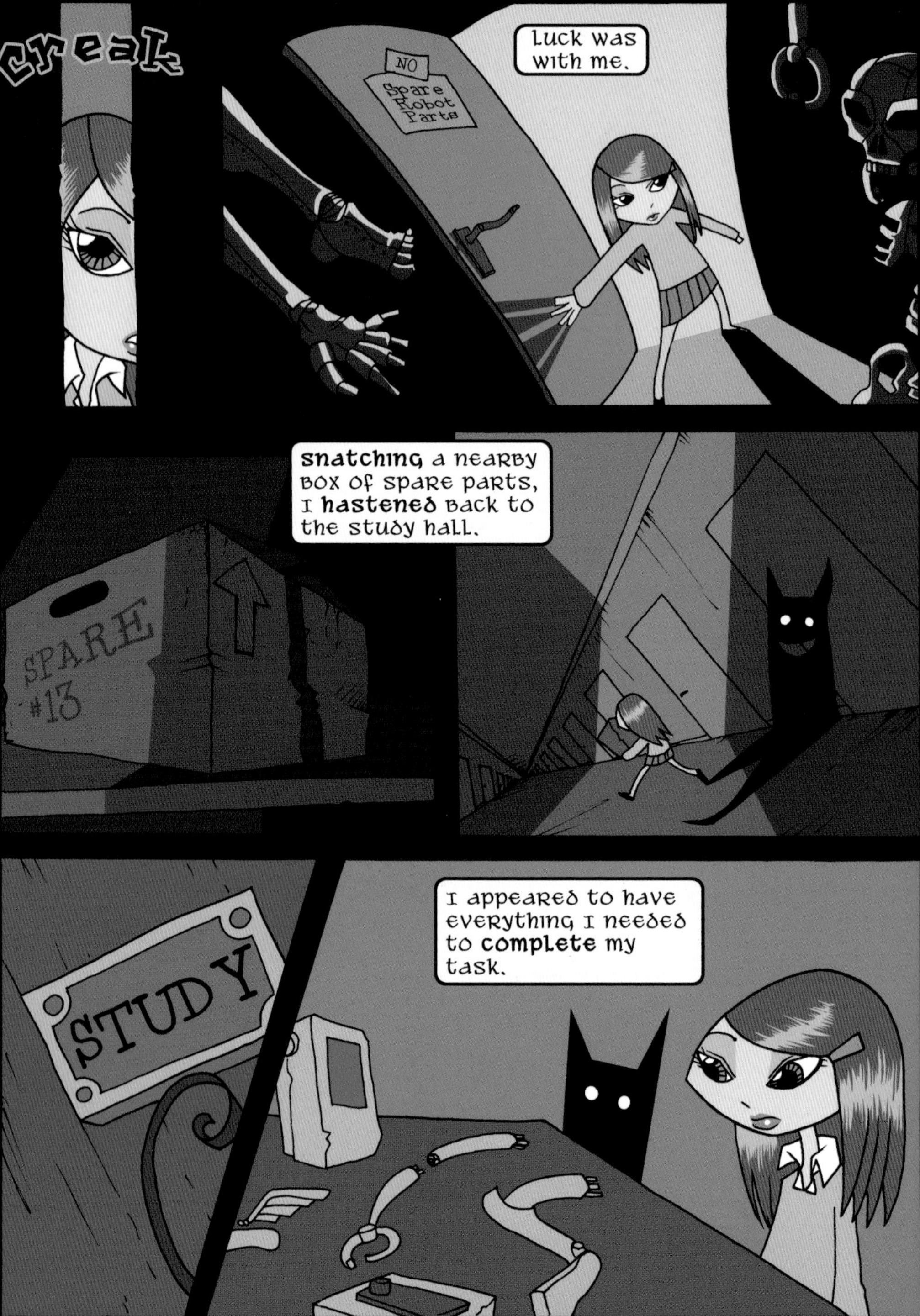
creak
NO
Spare Robot Parts
Luck was with me.
snatching a nearby box of spare parts, I hastened back to the study hall.
SPARE #13
STUDY
I appeared to have everything I needed to complete my task.

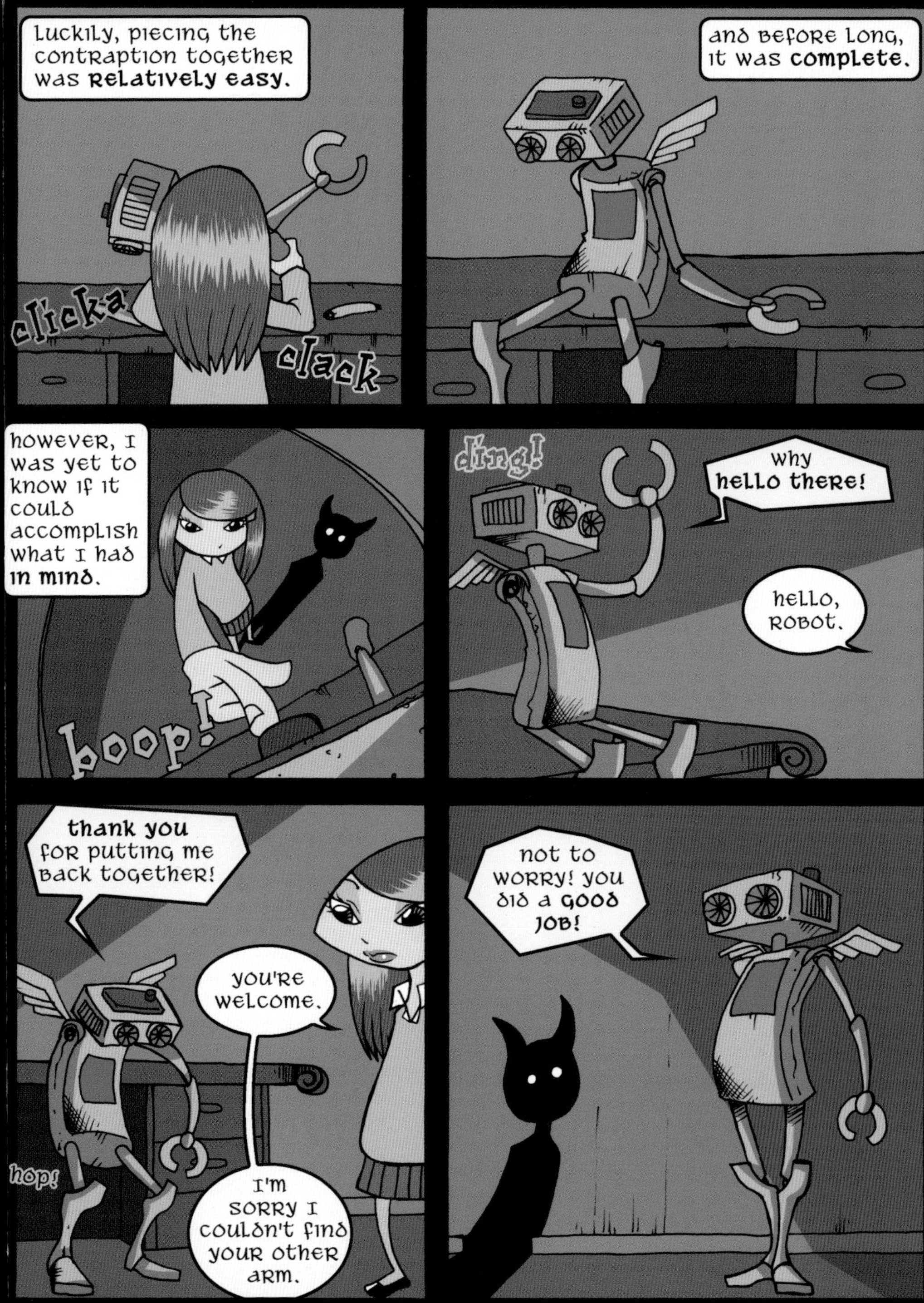

Luckily, piecing the contraption together was relatively easy.
clicka
clack
and before long, it was complete.
however, I was yet to know if it could accomplish what I had in mind.
boop!
ding!
why hello there!
hello, robot.
thank you for putting me back together!
you're welcome.
hop!
I'm sorry I couldn't find your other arm.
not to worry! you did a good job!

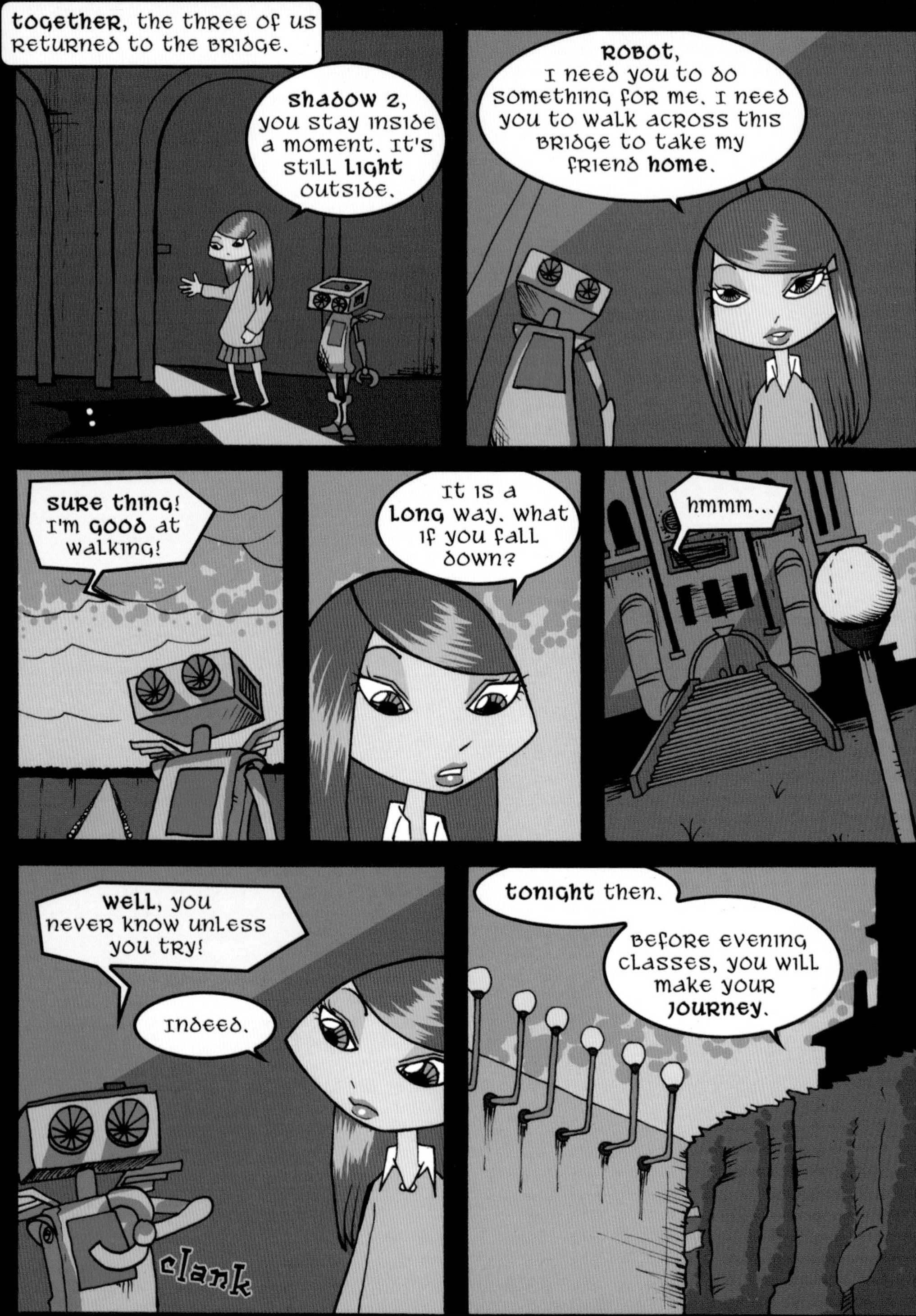
together, the three of us returned to the bridge.
Shadow 2, you stay inside a moment. It's still light outside.
Robot, I need you to do something for me. I need you to walk across this bridge to take my friend home.
Sure thing! I'm good at walking!
It is a long way. What if you fall down?
hmmm...
Well, you never know unless you try!
Indeed.
clank
tonight then.
Before evening classes, you will make your journey.

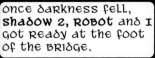

Once darkness fell, **Shadow 2, Robot** and I got ready at the foot of the bridge.

So I just walk straight?

that's right.

Do I have to come back?

...

Only if you want to.

Okay Shadow 2, you can finally go home. I hope your journey finds you well.

Well, let's be off!

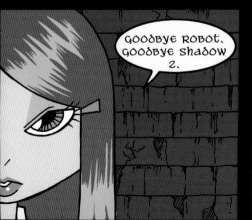

Goodbye Robot. Goodbye Shadow 2.

Bye mommy!

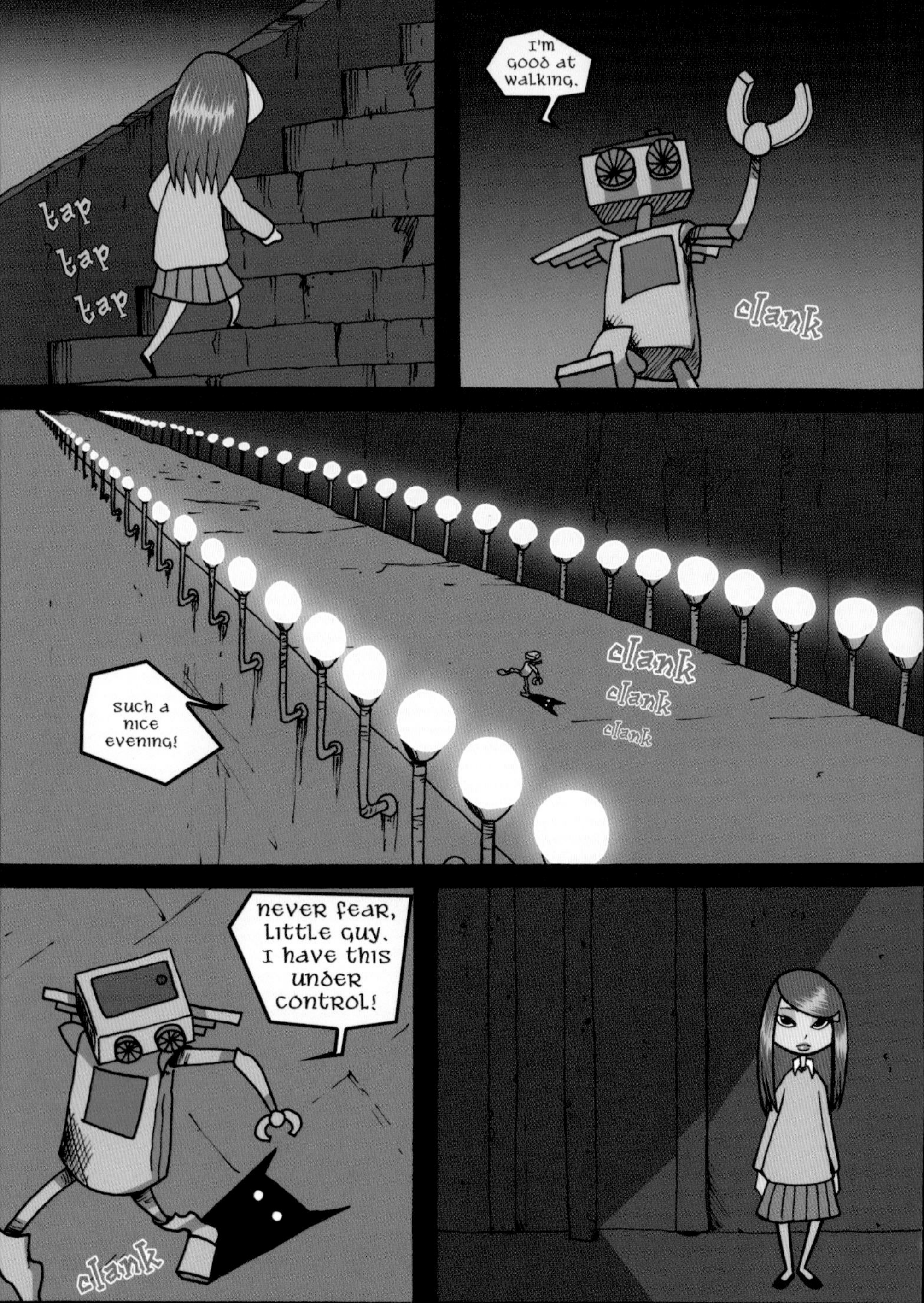
tap
tap
tap
I'm good at walking.
clank
clank
clank
clank
such a nice evening!
never fear, little guy. I have this under control!
clank

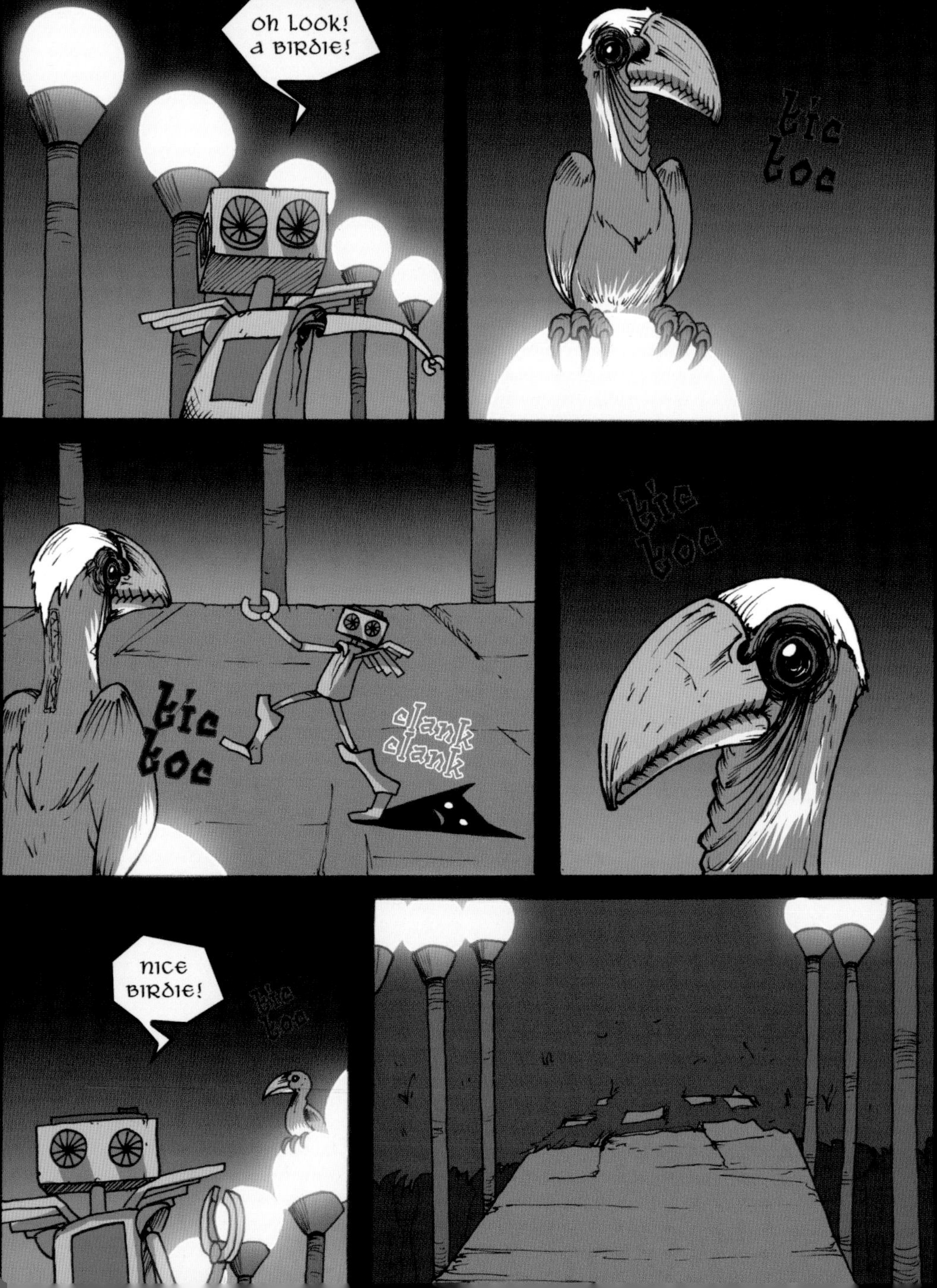
OH LOOK!
A BIRDIE!
tic toc
tic toc
tic toc
clank clank
NICE BIRDIE!
tic toc

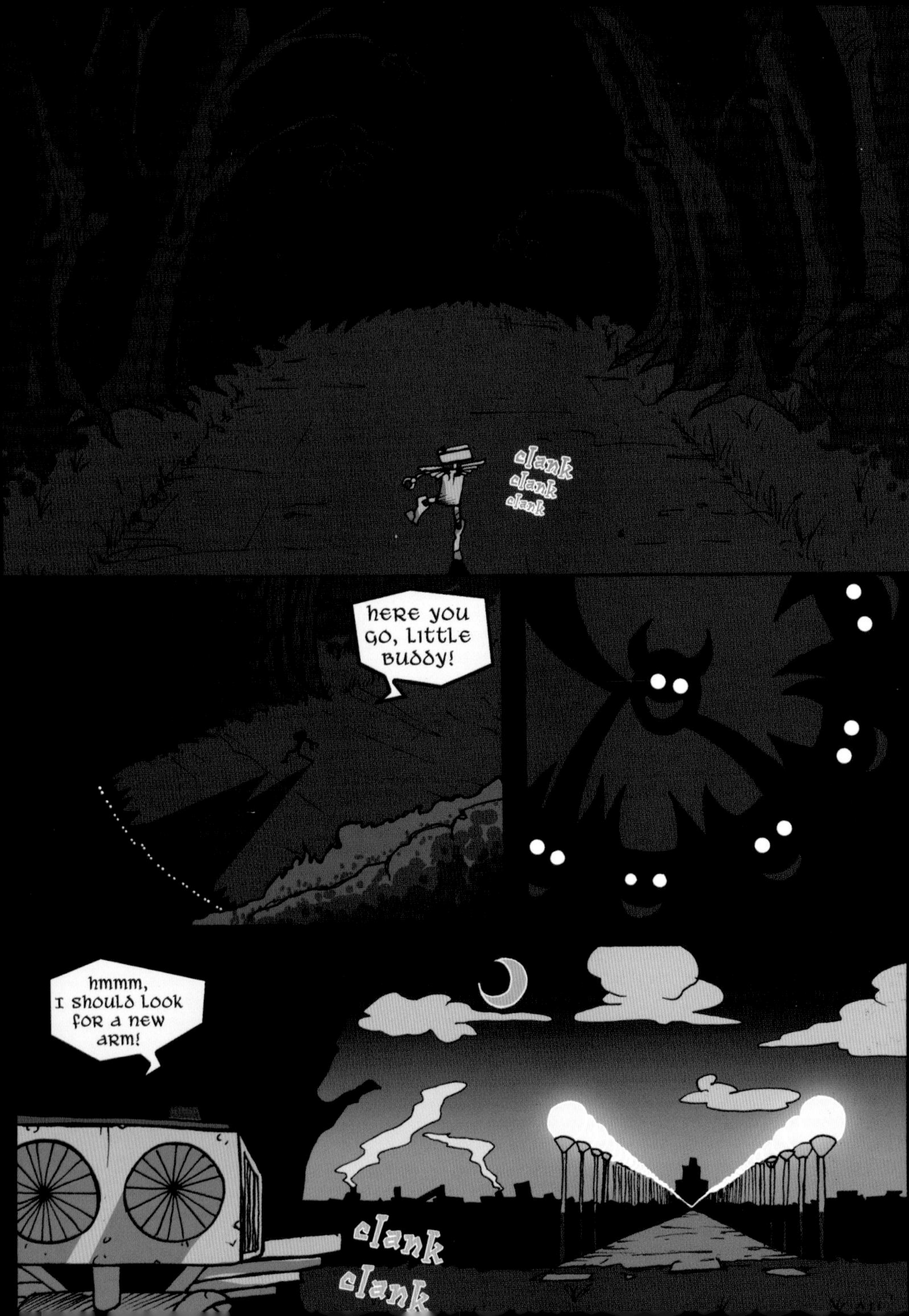
clank
clank
clank
HERE YOU GO, LITTLE BUDDY!
hmmm, I SHOULD LOOK FOR A NEW ARM!
clank
clank

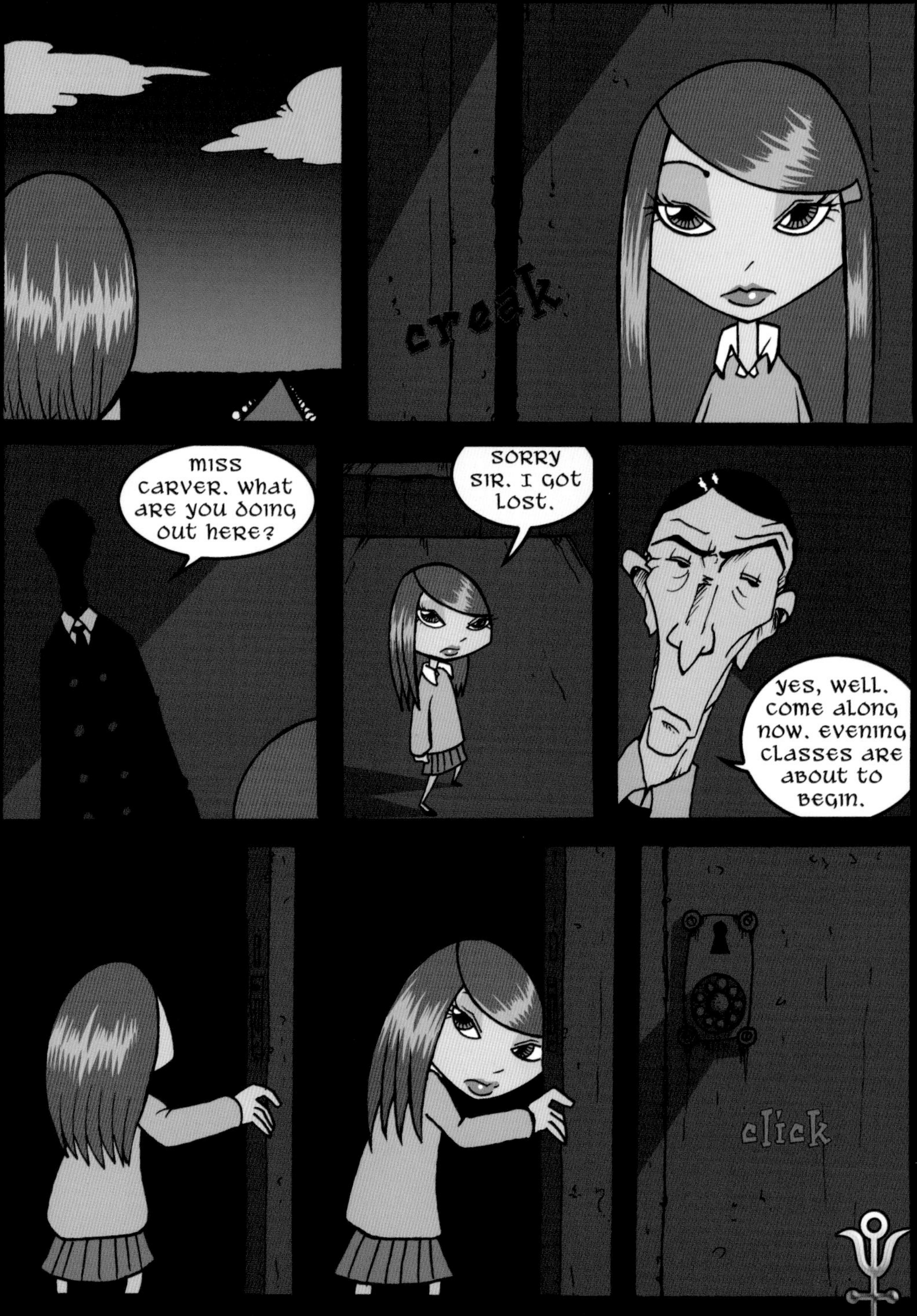
creak
MISS CARVER. WHAT ARE YOU DOING OUT HERE?
SORRY SIR. I GOT LOST.
YES, WELL. COME ALONG NOW. EVENING CLASSES ARE ABOUT TO BEGIN.
click

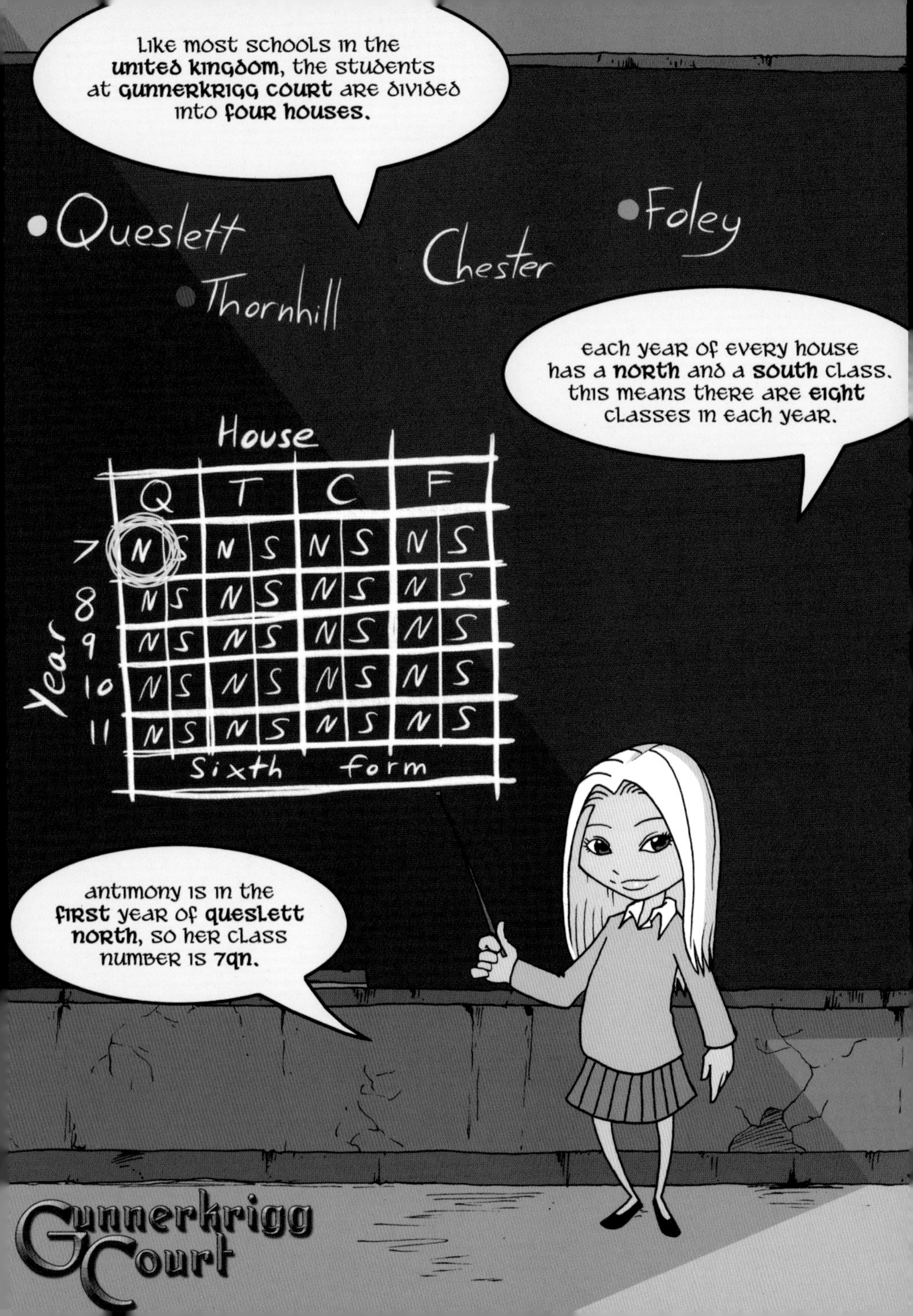
Like most schools in the united kingdom, the students at gunnerkrigg court are divided into four houses.
Queslett
Thornhill
Chester
Foley
each year of every house has a north and a south class. this means there are eight classes in each year.
House
Q T C F
N S N S N S N S
Year
7
8
9
10
11
Sixth form
antimony is in the first year of queslett north, so her class number is 7qn.
Gunnerkrigg Court

Gunnerkrigg Court

Chapter 2:

Schoolyard Myths

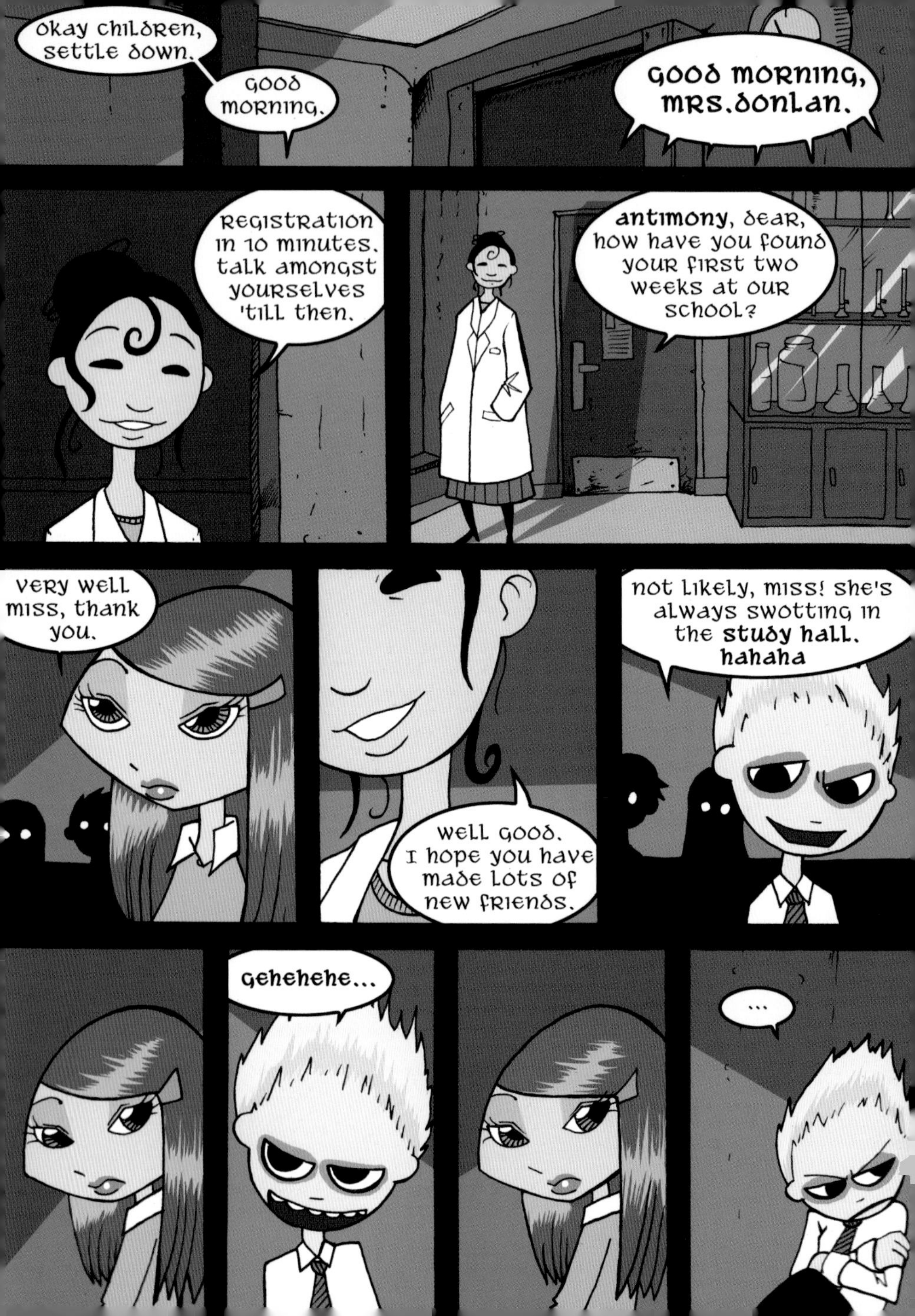

Okay children, settle down.
Good morning.
GOOD MORNING, MRS.DONLAN.
Registration in 10 minutes. talk amongst yourselves 'till then.
antimony, dear, how have you found your first two weeks at our school?
very well miss, thank you.
well good. I hope you have made lots of new friends.
not likely, miss! she's always swotting in the study hall. hahaha
gehehehe...
...

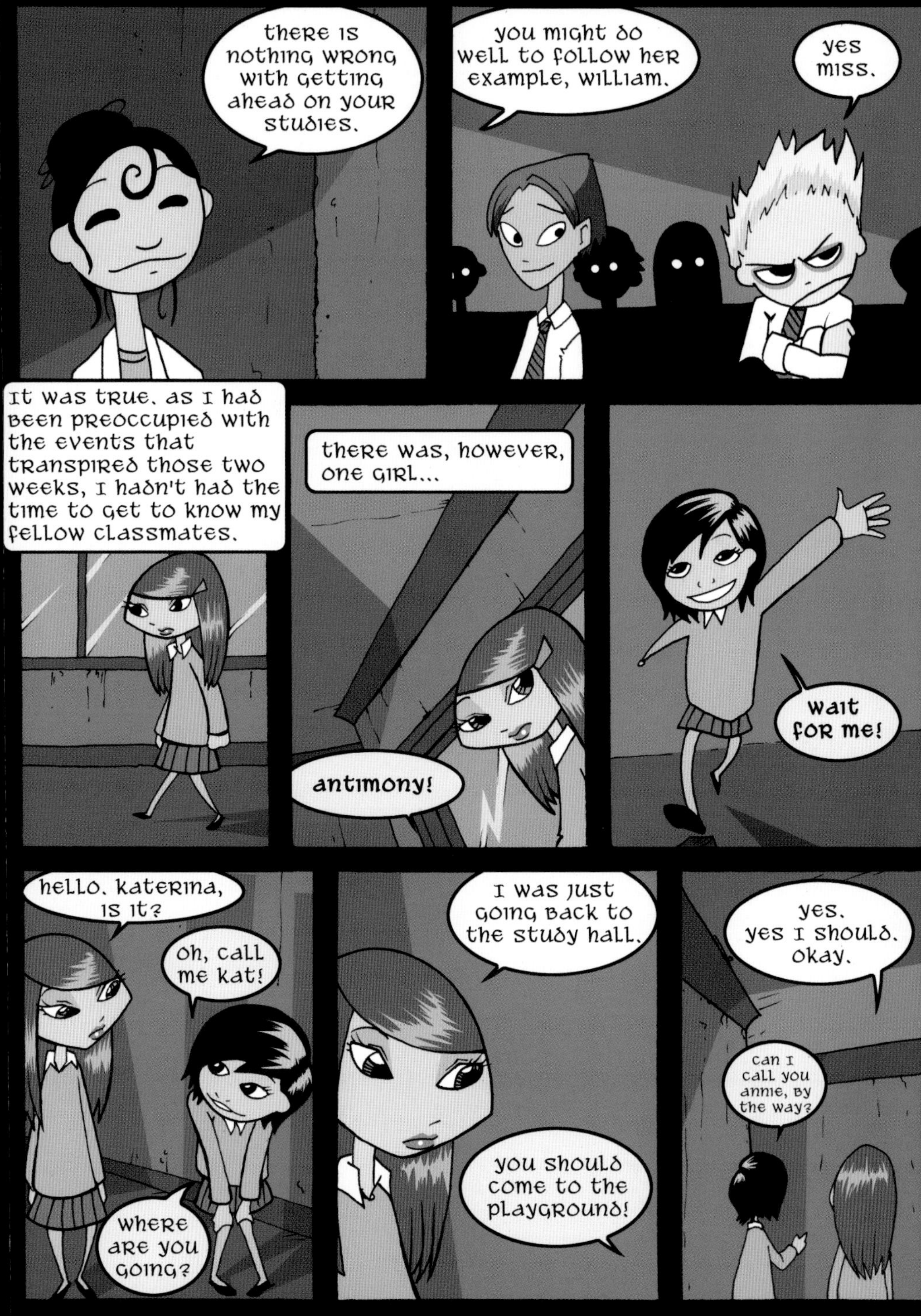
there is nothing wrong with getting ahead on your studies.
you might do well to follow her example, william.
yes miss.
It was true. as I had been preoccupied with the events that transpired those two weeks, I hadn't had the time to get to know my fellow classmates.
there was, however, one girl...
antimony!
wait for me!
hello. katerina, is it?
Oh, call me kat!
where are you going?
I was just going back to the study hall.
you should come to the playground!
yes. yes I should. okay.
can I call you annie, by the way?

Later that day.

ZZZ

and **that** concludes a brief exposition on the **creation of mythology**.

zzz

zzz

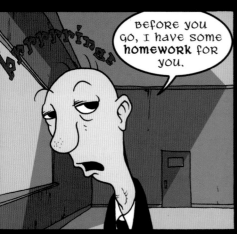

brrrrring!

before you go, I have some **homework** for you.

I want you all to go away in pairs and find as much information as you can on a **mythical figure** of your choice.

zzz .. wuh?

tomorrow you will present your findings in front of the class.

crick

we should work together!

I'd like that.

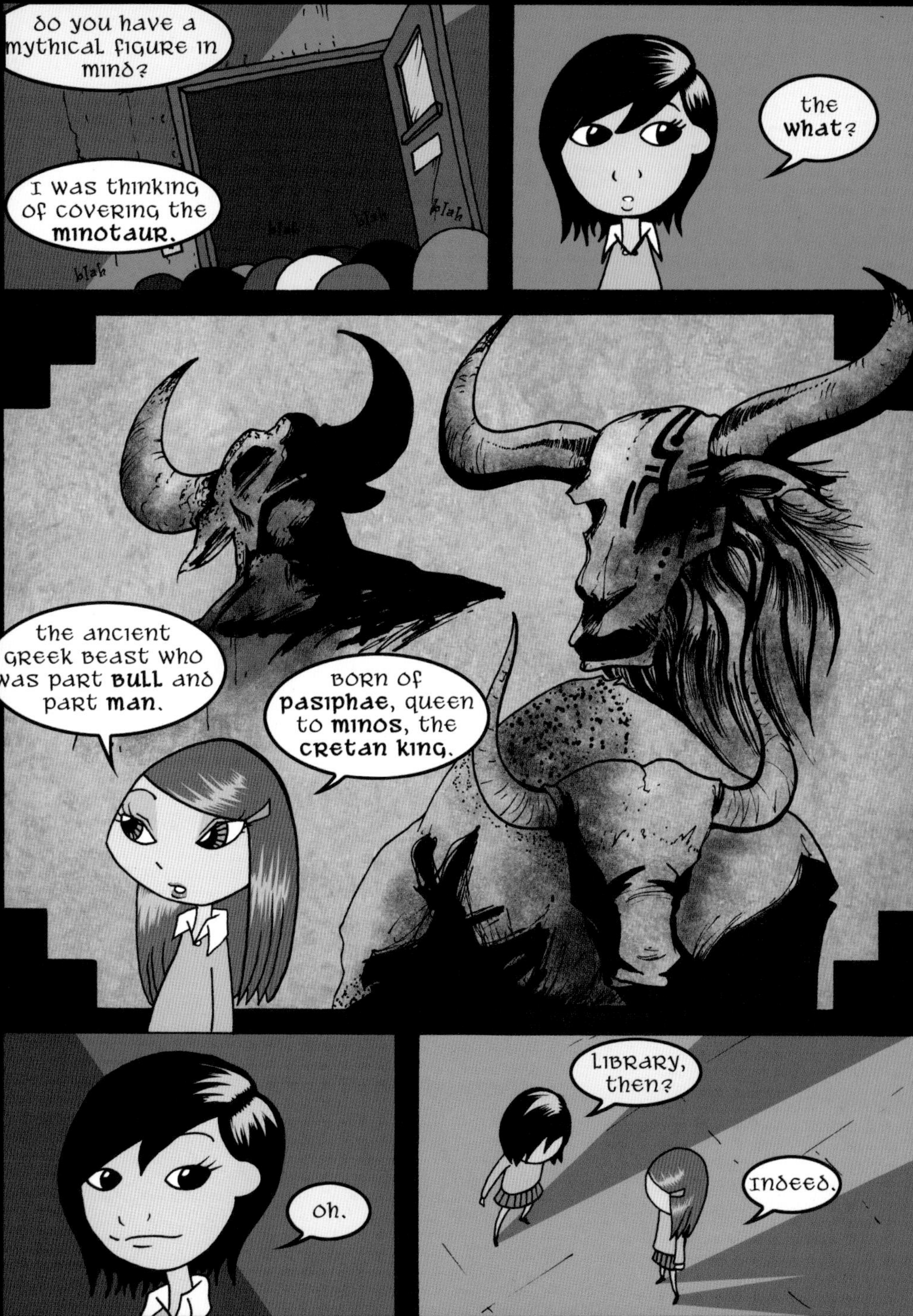
do you have a mythical figure in mind?
I was thinking of covering the **minotaur.**
blah
blah
blah
blah
the **what?**
the ancient greek beast who was part **BULL** and part **man.**
BORN of **pasiphae,** queen to **minos,** the **cretan king.**
oh.
LIBRARY, then?
Indeed.

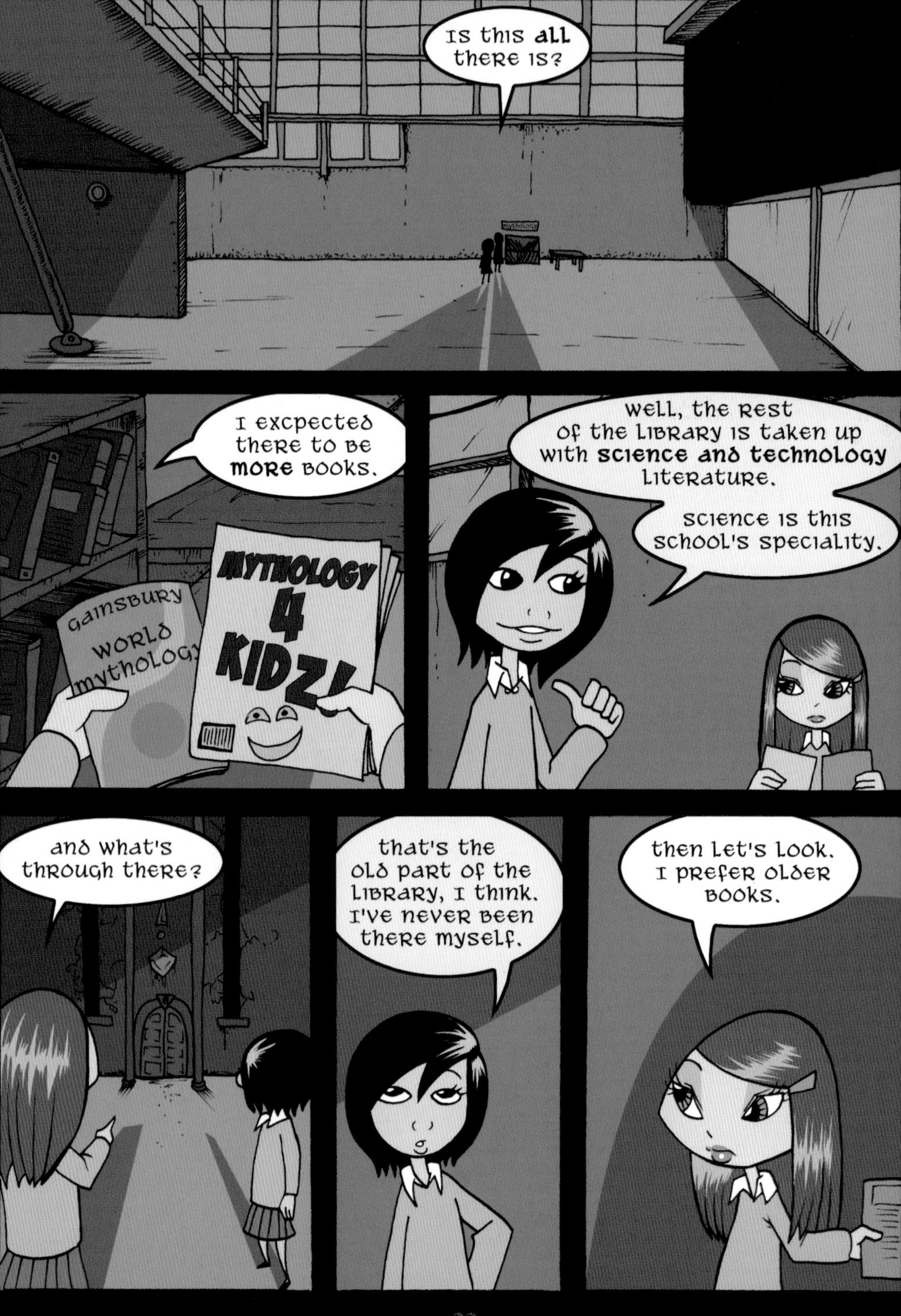
mythology
IS THIS ALL THERE IS?
I EXCPECTED THERE TO BE MORE BOOKS.
GAINSBURY
WORLD mythology
MYTHOLOGY 4 KIDZ!
WELL, THE REST OF THE LIBRARY IS TAKEN UP WITH SCIENCE AND TECHNOLOGY LITERATURE.
SCIENCE IS THIS SCHOOL'S SPECIALITY.
AND WHAT'S THROUGH THERE?
THAT'S THE OLD PART OF THE LIBRARY, I THINK. I'VE NEVER BEEN THERE MYSELF.
THEN LET'S LOOK. I PREFER OLDER BOOKS.

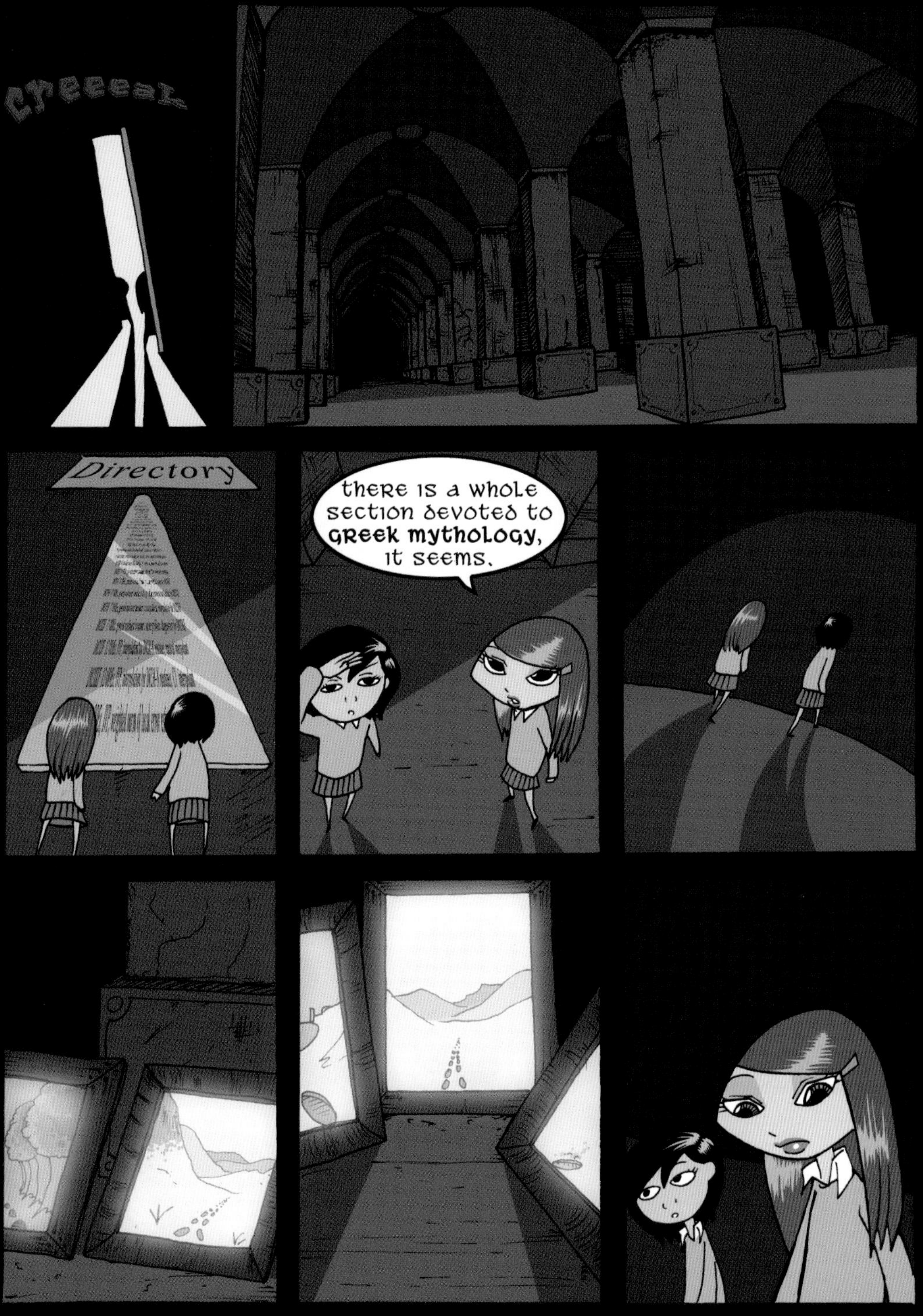
Creeeak
Directory
there is a whole section devoted to GREEK mythology, it seems.

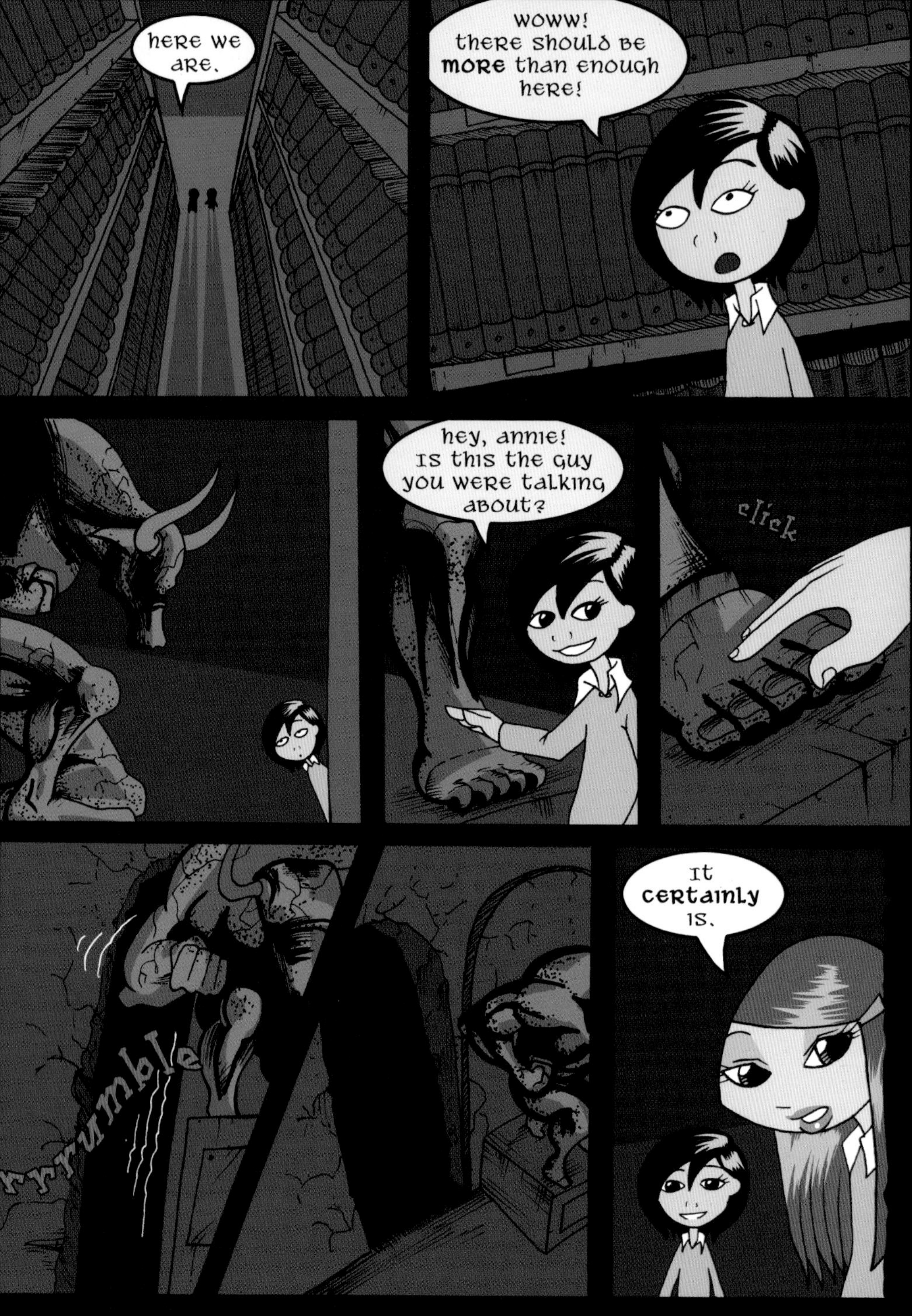

here we are.
WOWW! there should be MORE than enough here!
hey, annie! is this the guy you were talking about?
click
rrrumble
It certainly is.

IS that a **map**?

YES, FOR a **CRETAN LABYRINTH**, JUST LIKE the one on **KNOSSOS**, WHERE the MINOTAUR LIVED.

SO WE WON'T GET LOST IF WE WENT IN, BECAUSE THERE ARE NO **DEADENDS**, LIKE IN a MAZE.

that's RIGHT. a MAN NAMED **THESEUS** WENT INTO the LABYRINTH on KNOSSOS to **SLAY** the MINOTAUR, AND USED a **THREAD** to FIND HIS WAY BACK OUT.

BUT he DIDN'T REALLY NEED ONE, SINCE THERE IS ONLY **ONE PATH** to TAKE.

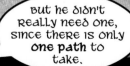

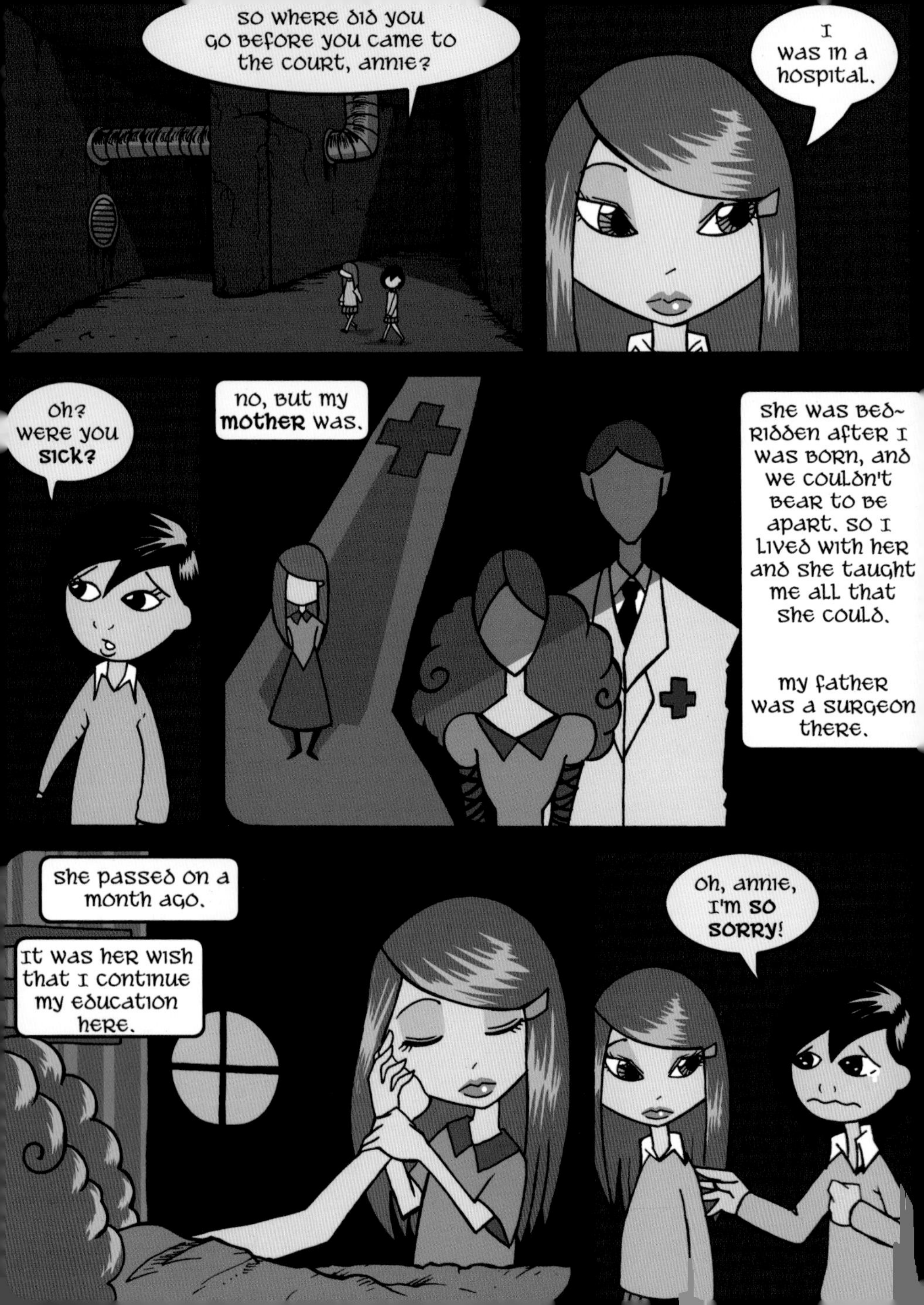
SO WHERE DID YOU GO BEFORE YOU CAME TO THE COURT, ANNIE?
I WAS IN A HOSPITAL.
OH? WERE YOU SICK?
NO, BUT MY MOTHER WAS.
SHE WAS BED-RIDDEN AFTER I WAS BORN, AND WE COULDN'T BEAR TO BE APART. SO I LIVED WITH HER AND SHE TAUGHT ME ALL THAT SHE COULD.
MY FATHER WAS A SURGEON THERE.
SHE PASSED ON A MONTH AGO.
IT WAS HER WISH THAT I CONTINUE MY EDUCATION HERE.
OH, ANNIE, I'M SO SORRY!

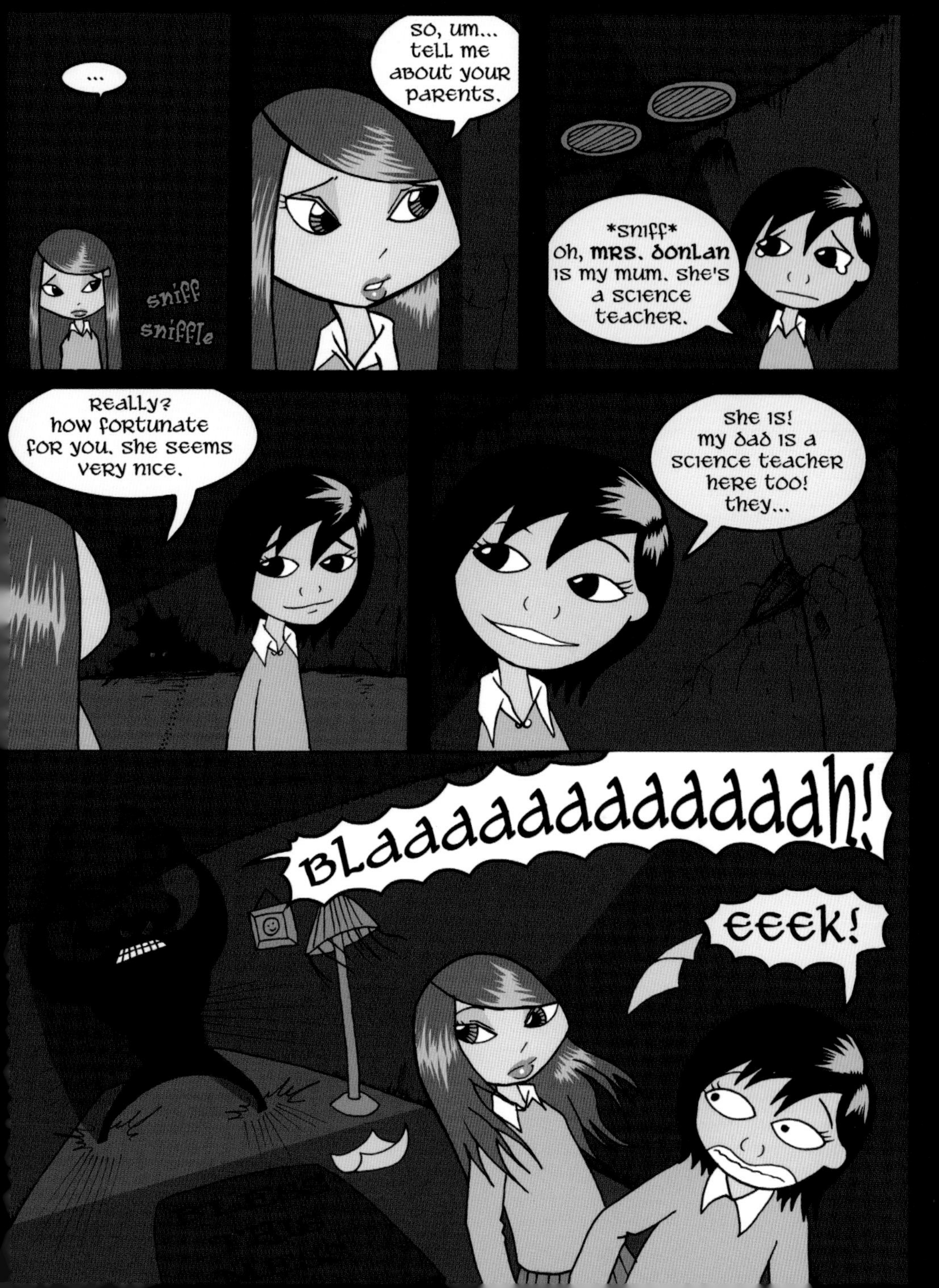
...
sniff
sniffle
so, um... tell me about your parents.
sniff oh, mrs. donlan is my mum. she's a science teacher.
really? how fortunate for you. she seems very nice.
she is! my dad is a science teacher here too! they...
BLAAAAAAAAAAAAH!
EEEK!

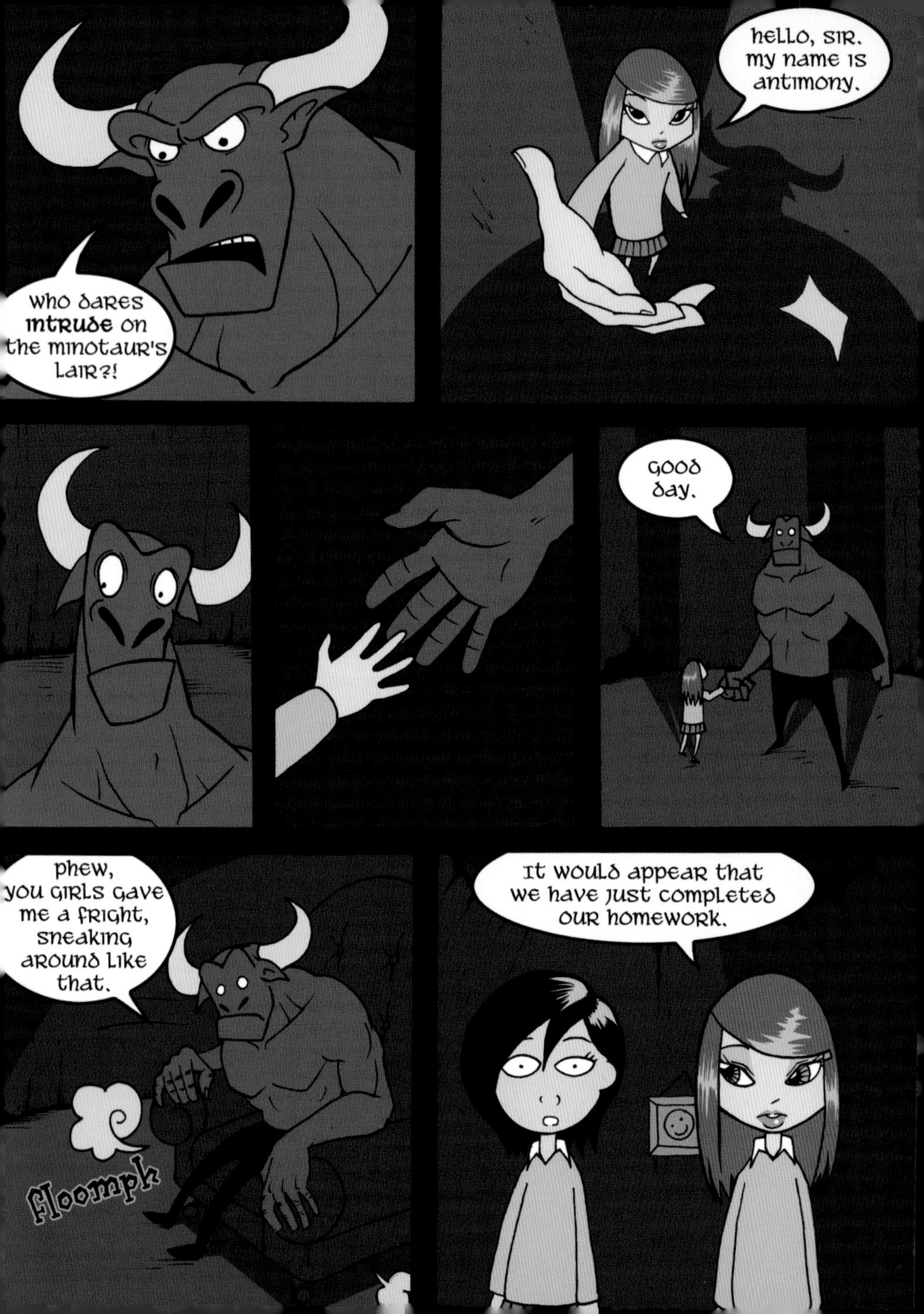
who dares **intrude** on the minotaur's lair?!
hello, sir. my name is antimony.
good day.
phew, you girls gave me a fright, sneaking around like that.
floomph
It would appear that we have just completed our homework.

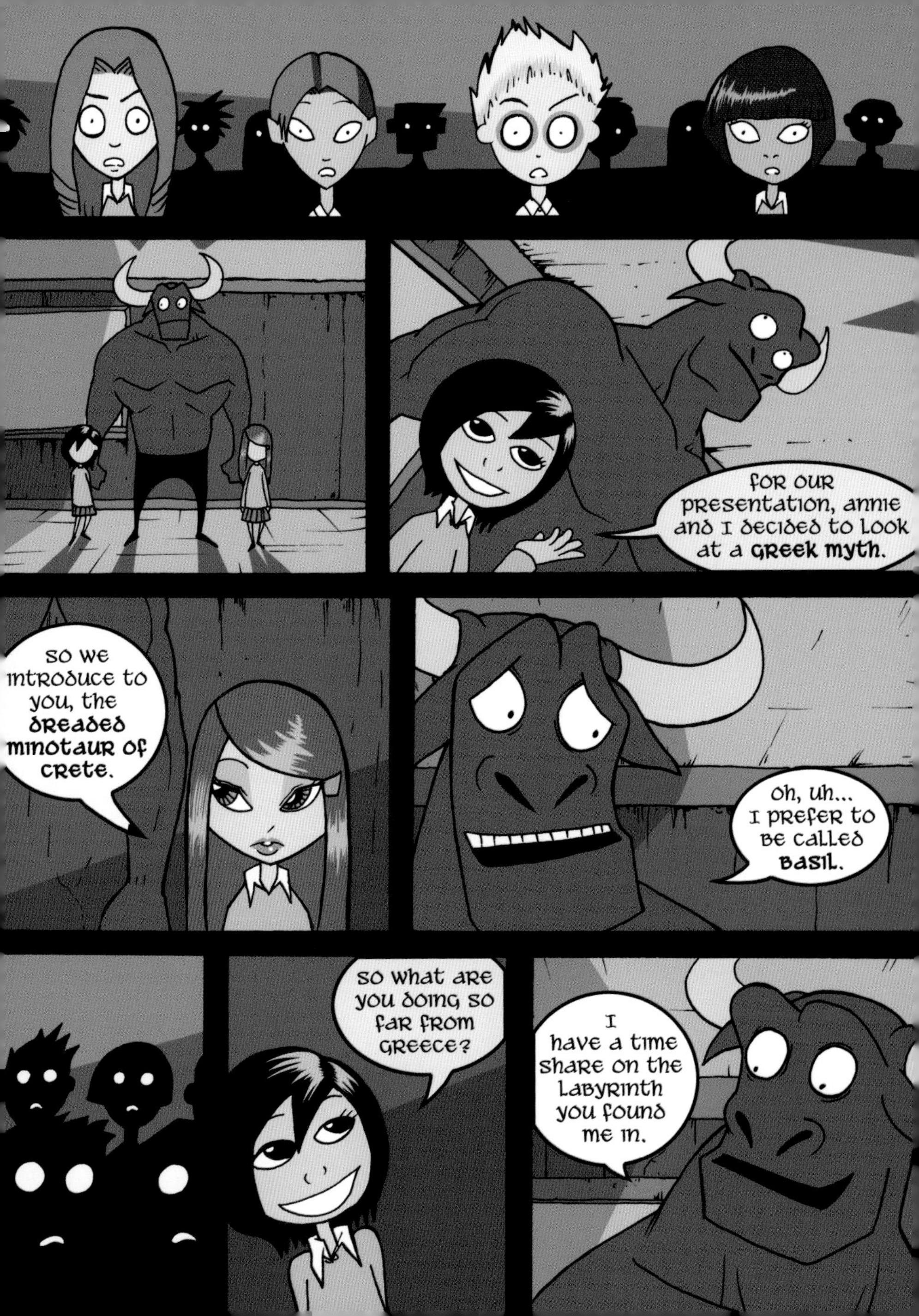
for our presentation, annie and I decided to look at a greek myth.
so we introduce to you, the dreaded minotaur of crete.
oh, uh... I prefer to be called basil.
so what are you doing so far from greece?
I have a time share on the labyrinth you found me in.

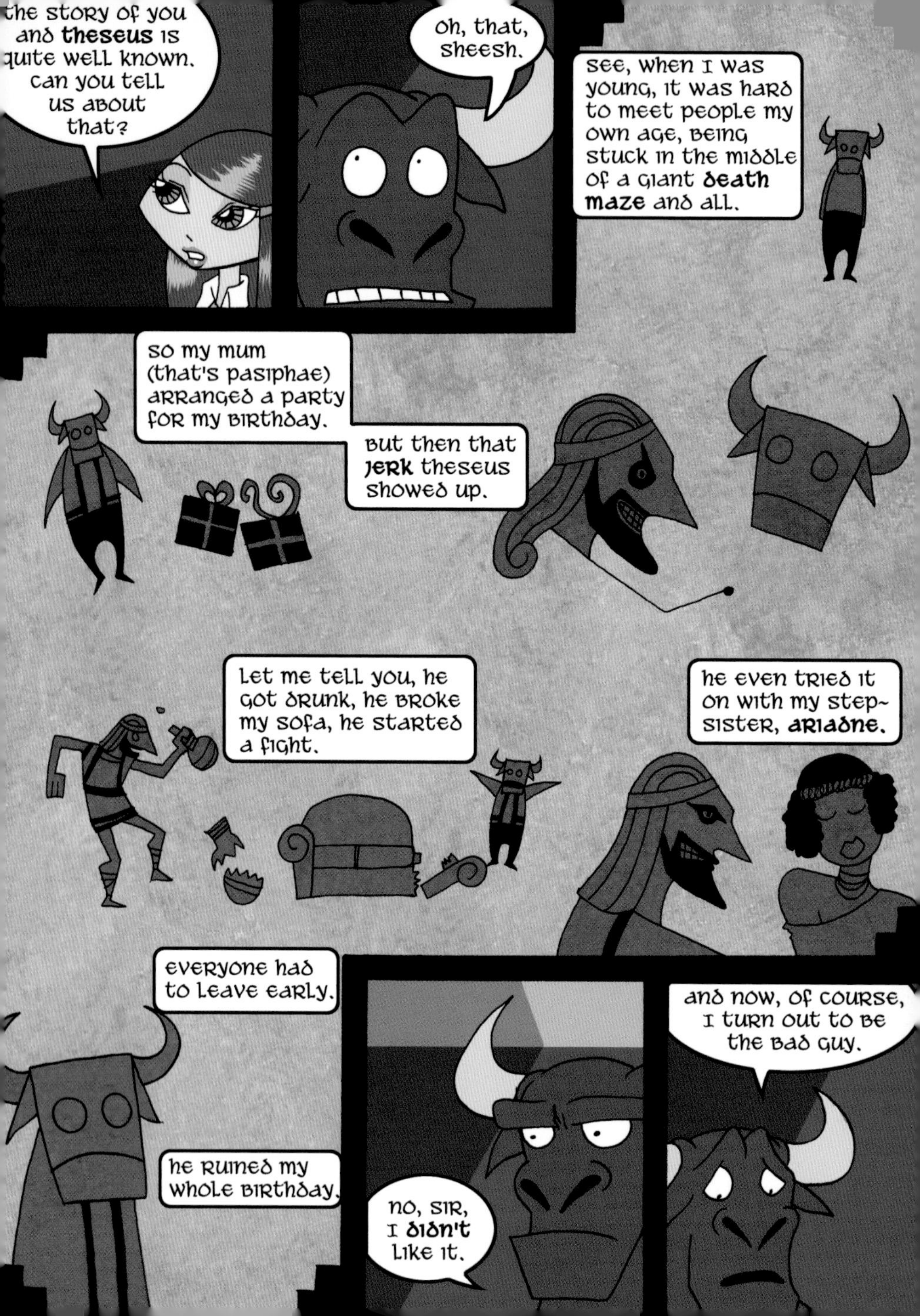
the story of you and theseus is quite well known. can you tell us about that?
oh, that, sheesh.
see, when I was young, it was hard to meet people my own age, being stuck in the middle of a giant death maze and all.
so my mum (that's pasiphae) arranged a party for my birthday.
but then that JERK theseus showed up.
let me tell you, he got drunk, he broke my sofa, he started a fight.
he even tried it on with my step-sister, ariadne.
everyone had to leave early.
he ruined my whole birthday.
no, sir, I didn't like it.
and now, of course, I turn out to be the bad guy.

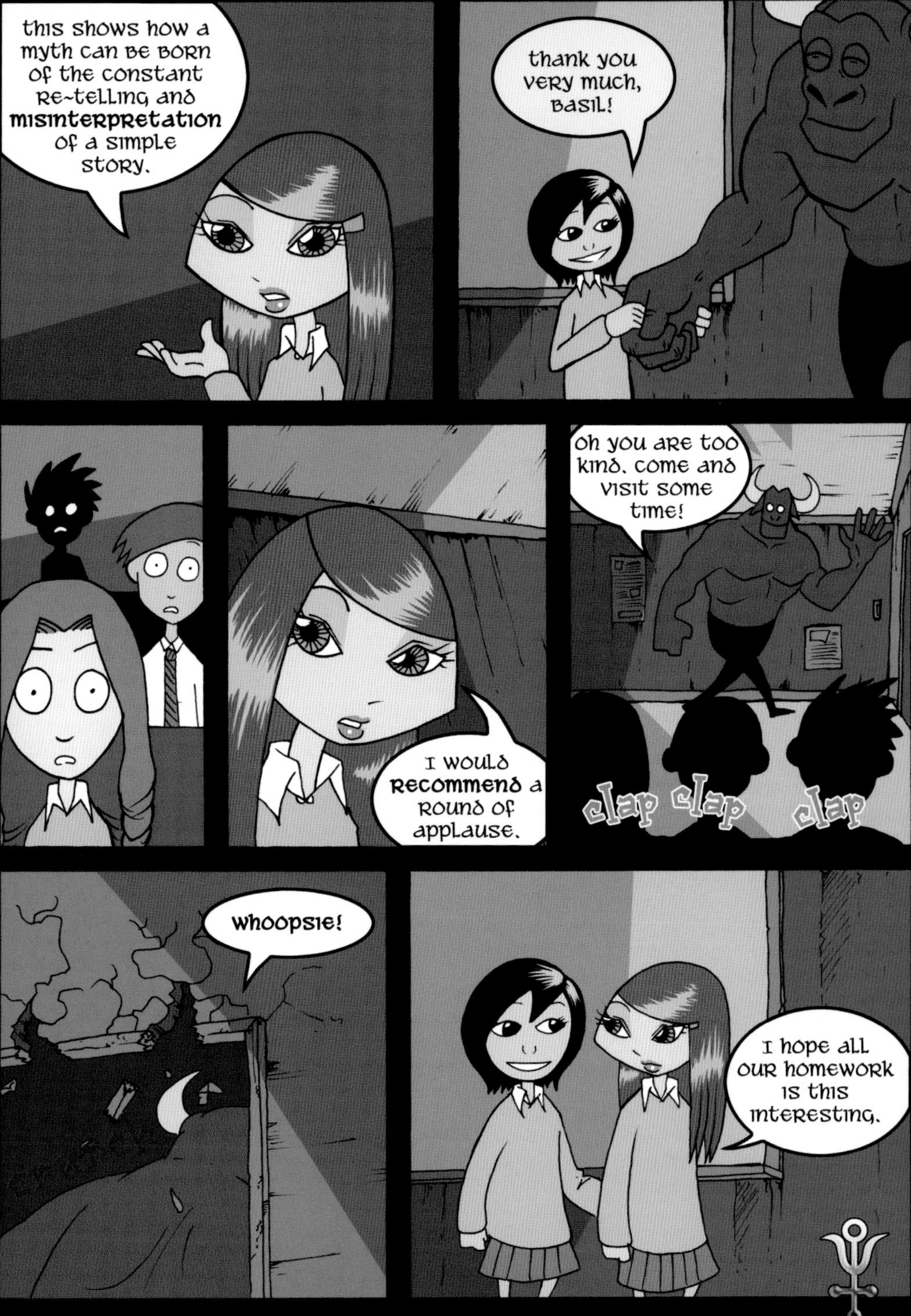
this shows how a myth can be born of the constant re-telling and misinterpretation of a simple story.
thank you very much, basil!
I would recommend a round of applause.
oh you are too kind. come and visit some time!
clap clap clap
whoopsie!
I hope all our homework is this interesting.

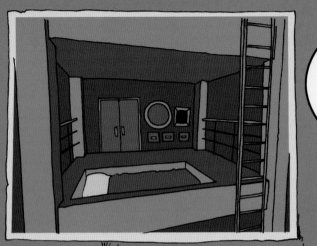

each student in **year 7** sleeps in their own individual bunk. these are fully equipped with a bed, wardrobe, mirror, drawer space and communications terminal.

each house has a male and female dorm which hold the 30 students from the north and south classes. the bunks are stacked on top of eachother.

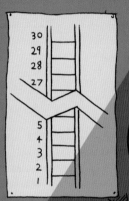

as antimony started the school year late, the only available bunk was **number 30**, which is at the very top of the queslett girl's dorm.

each year the accommodation changes.

Gunnerkrigg Court

Chapter 3:

Reynardine

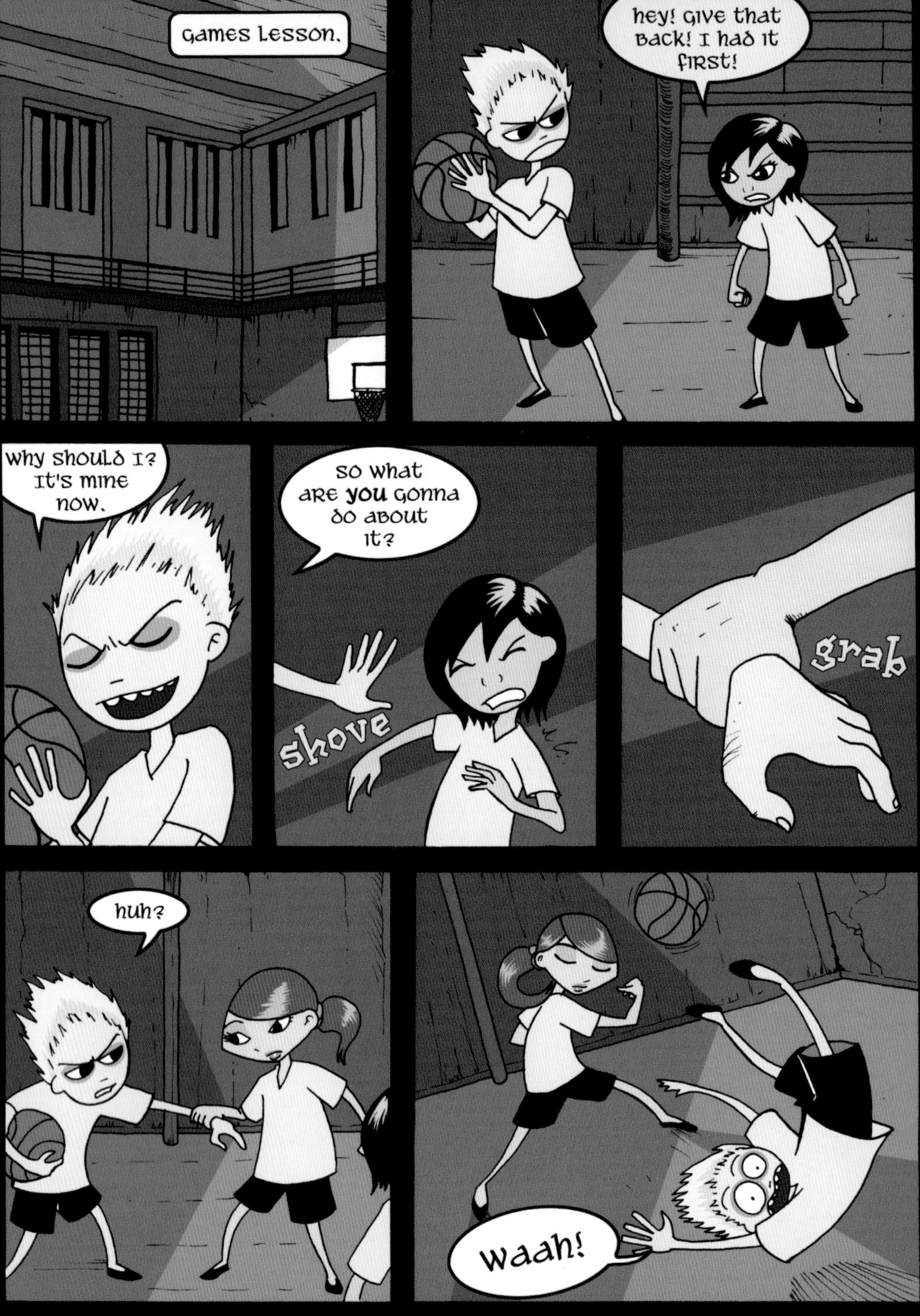
Games lesson.
hey! Give that back! I had it first!
Why should I? It's mine now.
So what are **you** gonna do about it?
shove
grab
huh?
Waah!

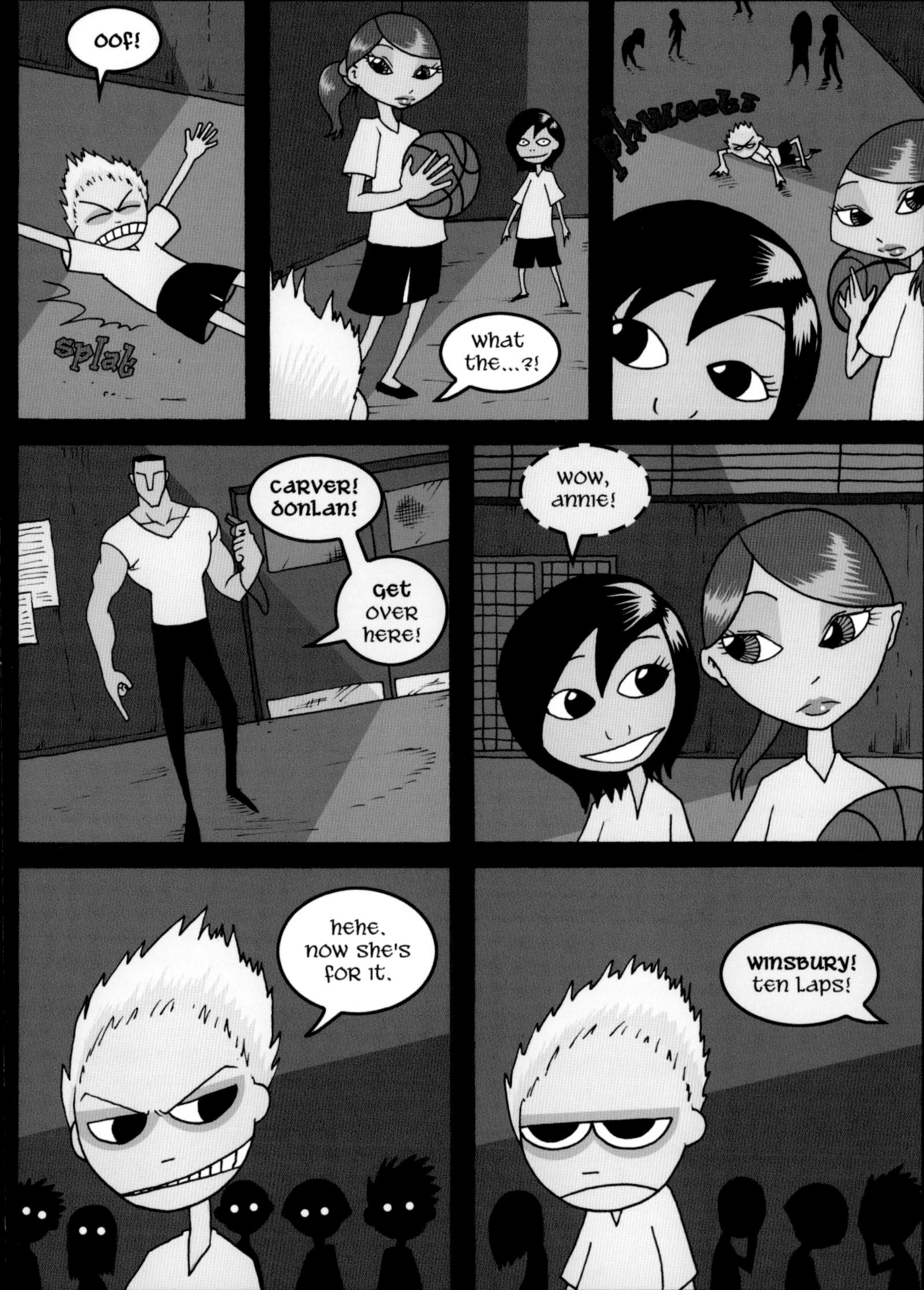
oof!
splat
What the...?!
phweet!
CARVER! DONLAN!
GET OVER HERE!
WOW, ANNIE!
hehe. now she's for it.
WINSBURY! ten Laps!

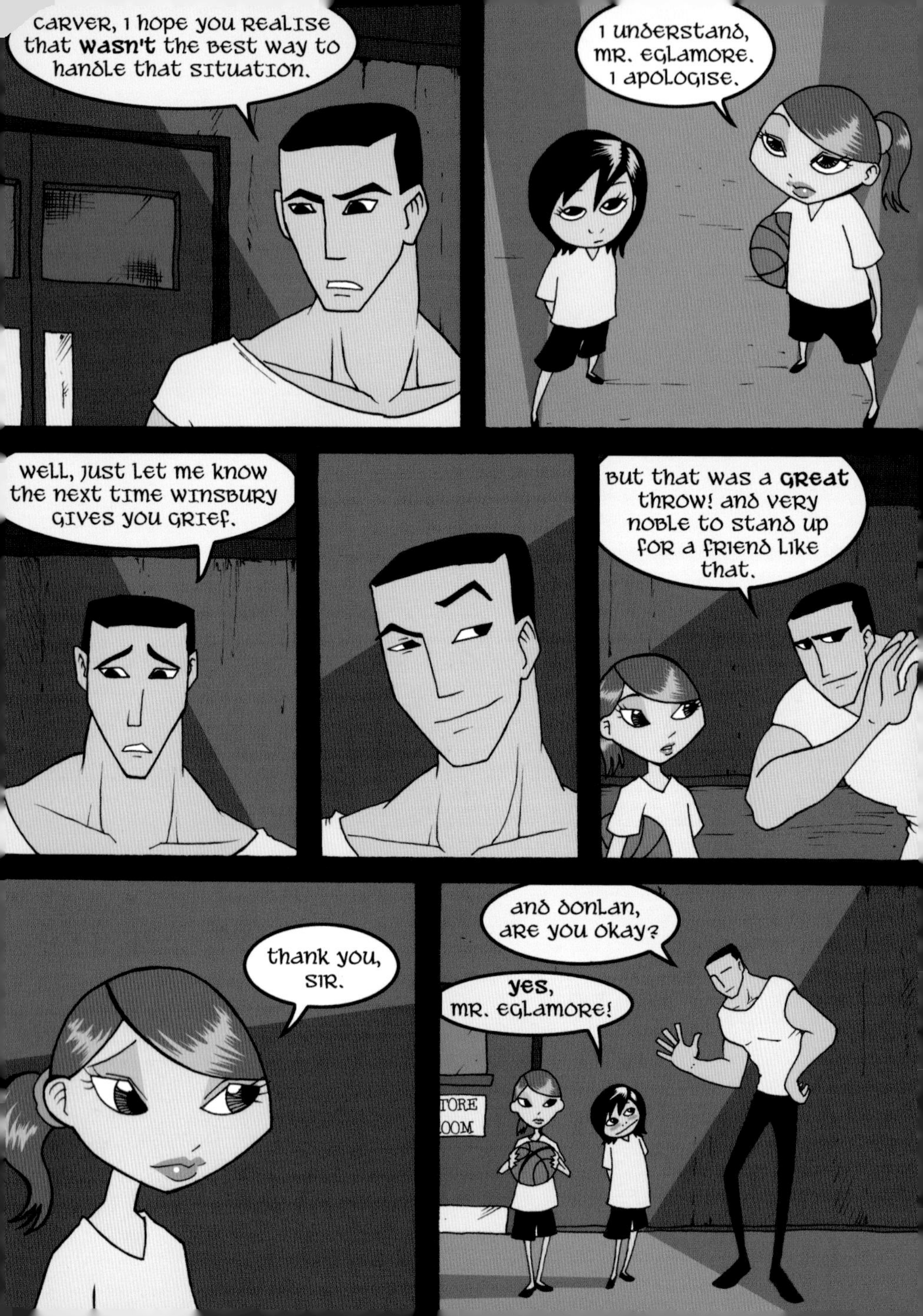
CARVER, I HOPE YOU REALISE THAT **WASN'T** THE BEST WAY TO HANDLE THAT SITUATION.
I UNDERSTAND, MR. EGLAMORE. I APOLOGISE.
WELL, JUST LET ME KNOW THE NEXT TIME WINSBURY GIVES YOU GRIEF.
BUT THAT WAS A **GREAT** THROW! AND VERY NOBLE TO STAND UP FOR A FRIEND LIKE THAT.
THANK YOU, SIR.
AND DONLAN, ARE YOU OKAY?
YES, MR. EGLAMORE!
TORE
OOM

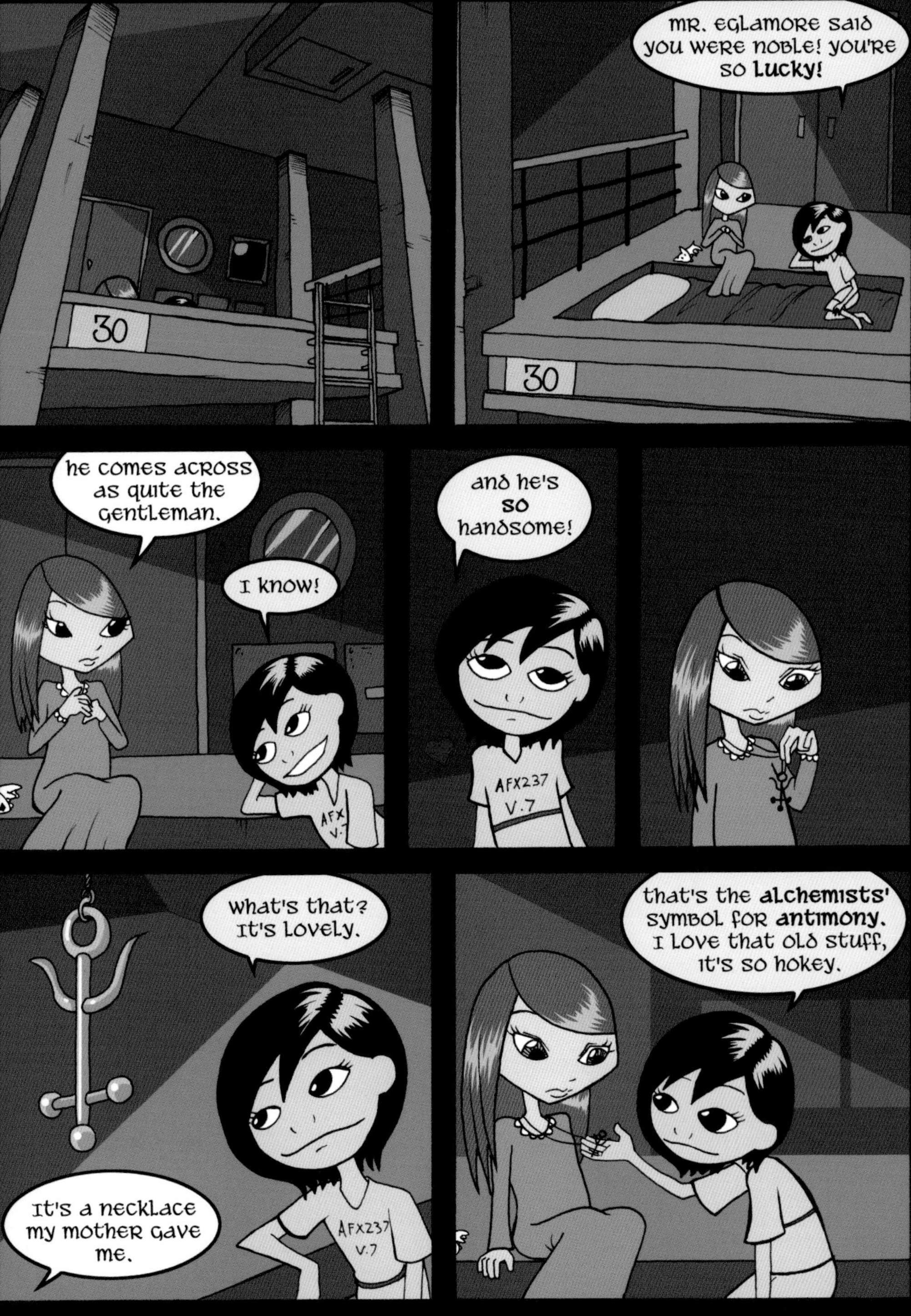

MR. EGLAMORE SAID YOU WERE NOBLE! YOU'RE SO LUCKY!
30
30
HE COMES ACROSS AS QUITE THE GENTLEMAN.
I KNOW!
AFX V.7
AND HE'S SO HANDSOME!
AFX237 V.7
WHAT'S THAT? IT'S LOVELY.
IT'S A NECKLACE MY MOTHER GAVE ME.
AFX237 V.7
THAT'S THE ALCHEMISTS' SYMBOL FOR ANTIMONY. I LOVE THAT OLD STUFF, IT'S SO HOKEY.

VOOOP VOOOP

TIME FOR BED!

NIGHT NIGHT!

SLEEP WELL.

LATER THAT NIGHT...

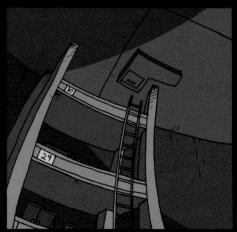

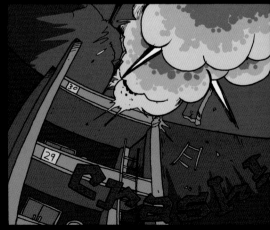

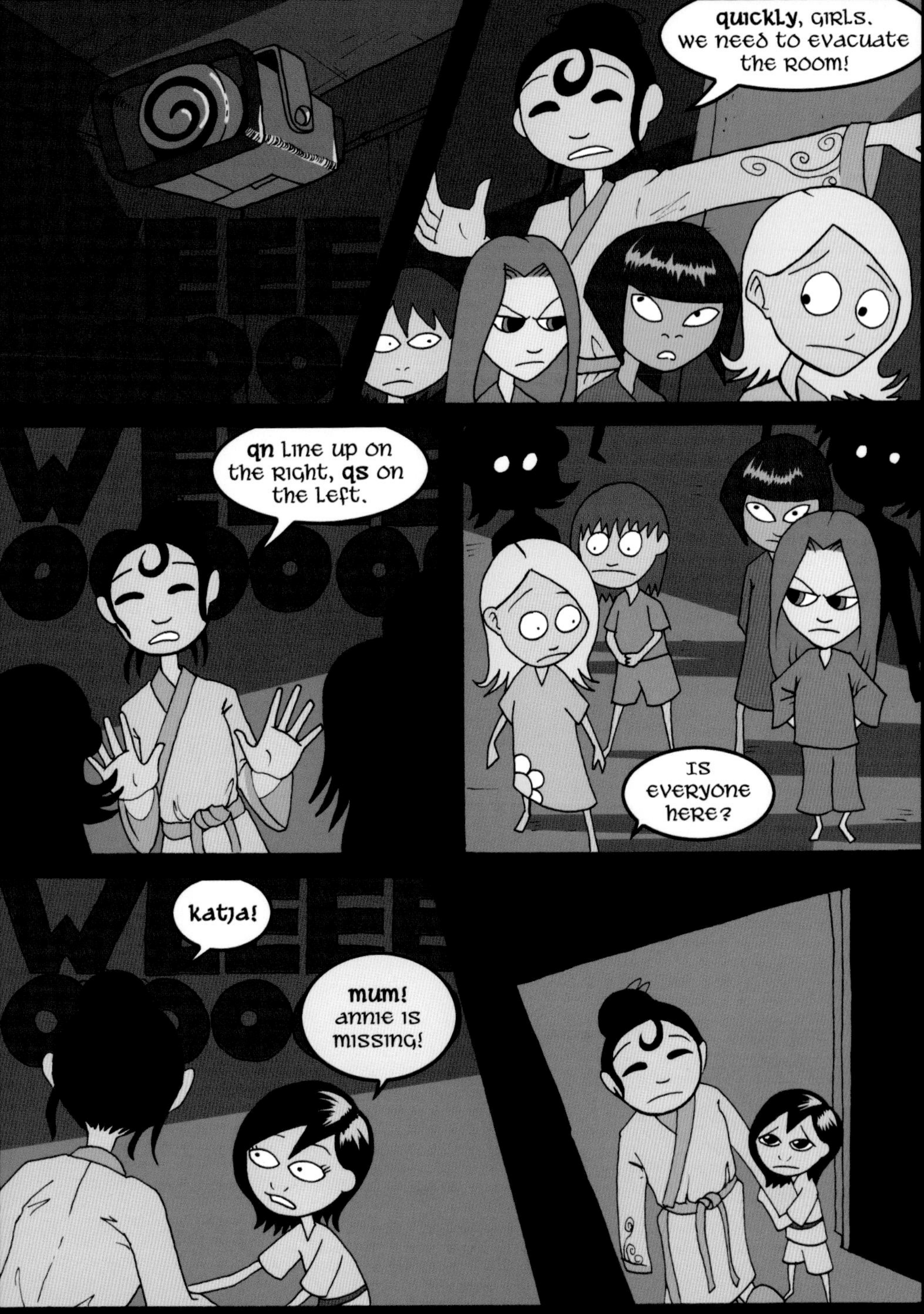
quickly, girls. we need to evacuate the room!
qn line up on the right, qs on the left.
is everyone here?
katja!
mum! annie is missing!

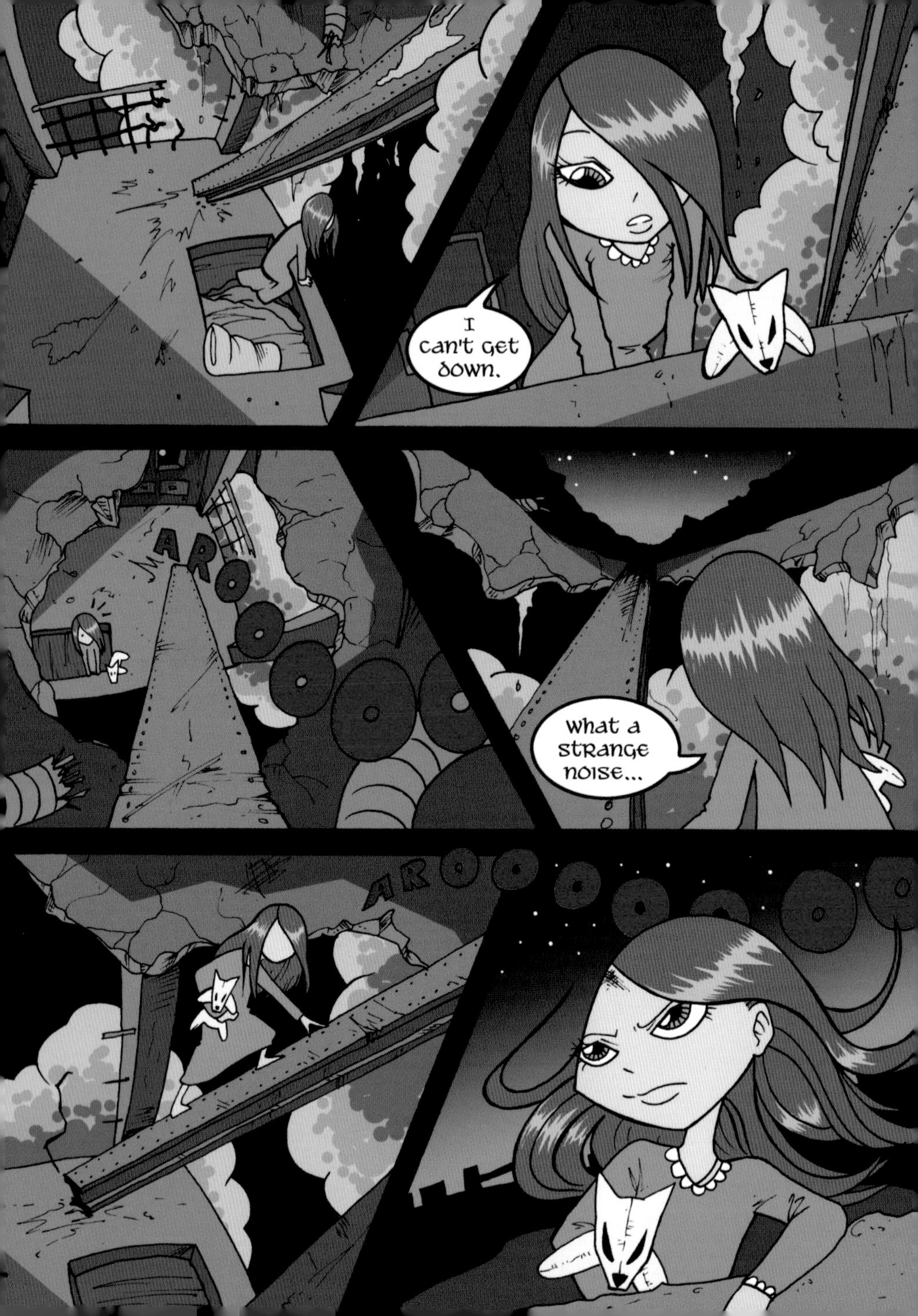
I can't get down.
AROOOOO
What a strange noise...
AROOOOOOOOO

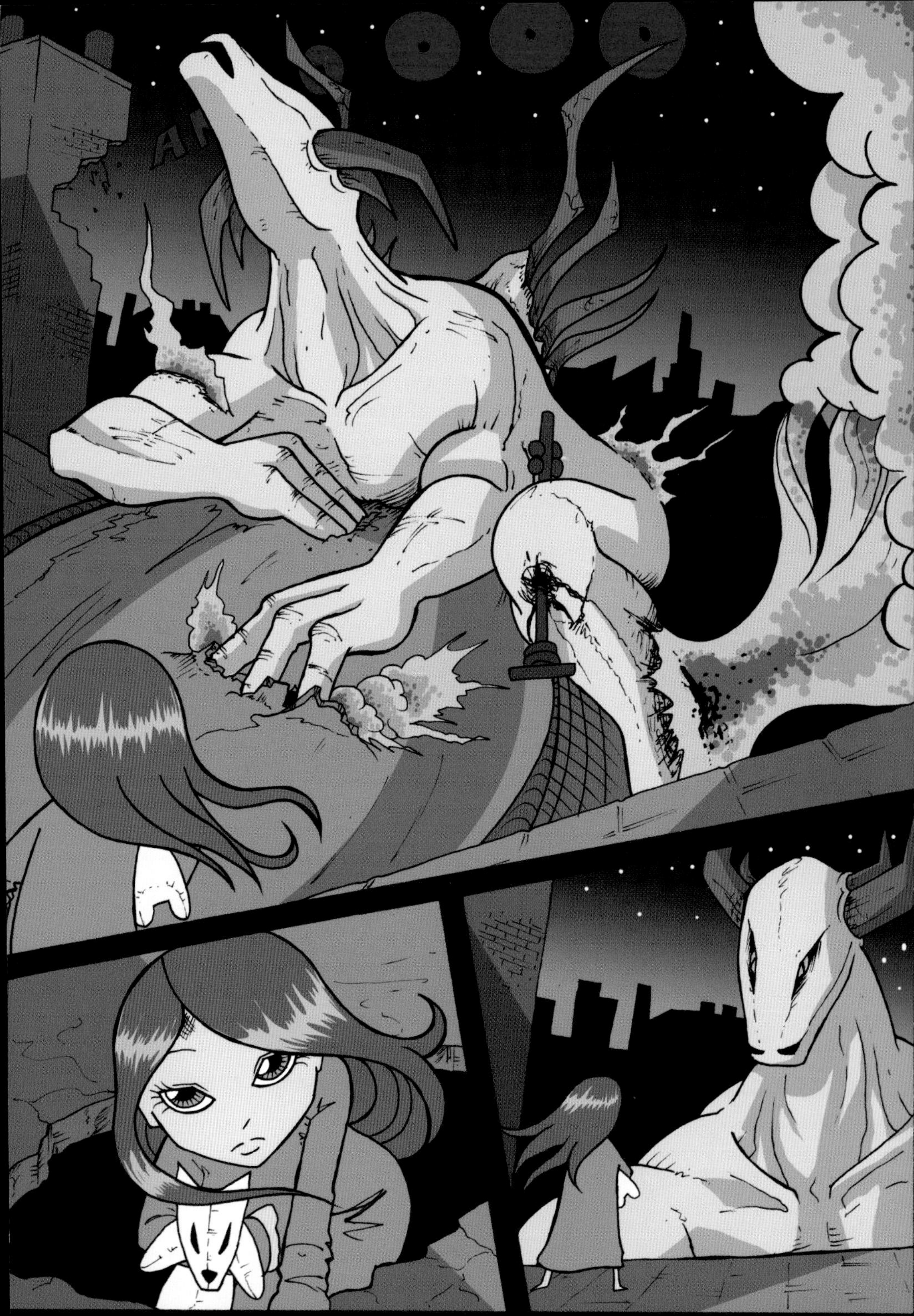

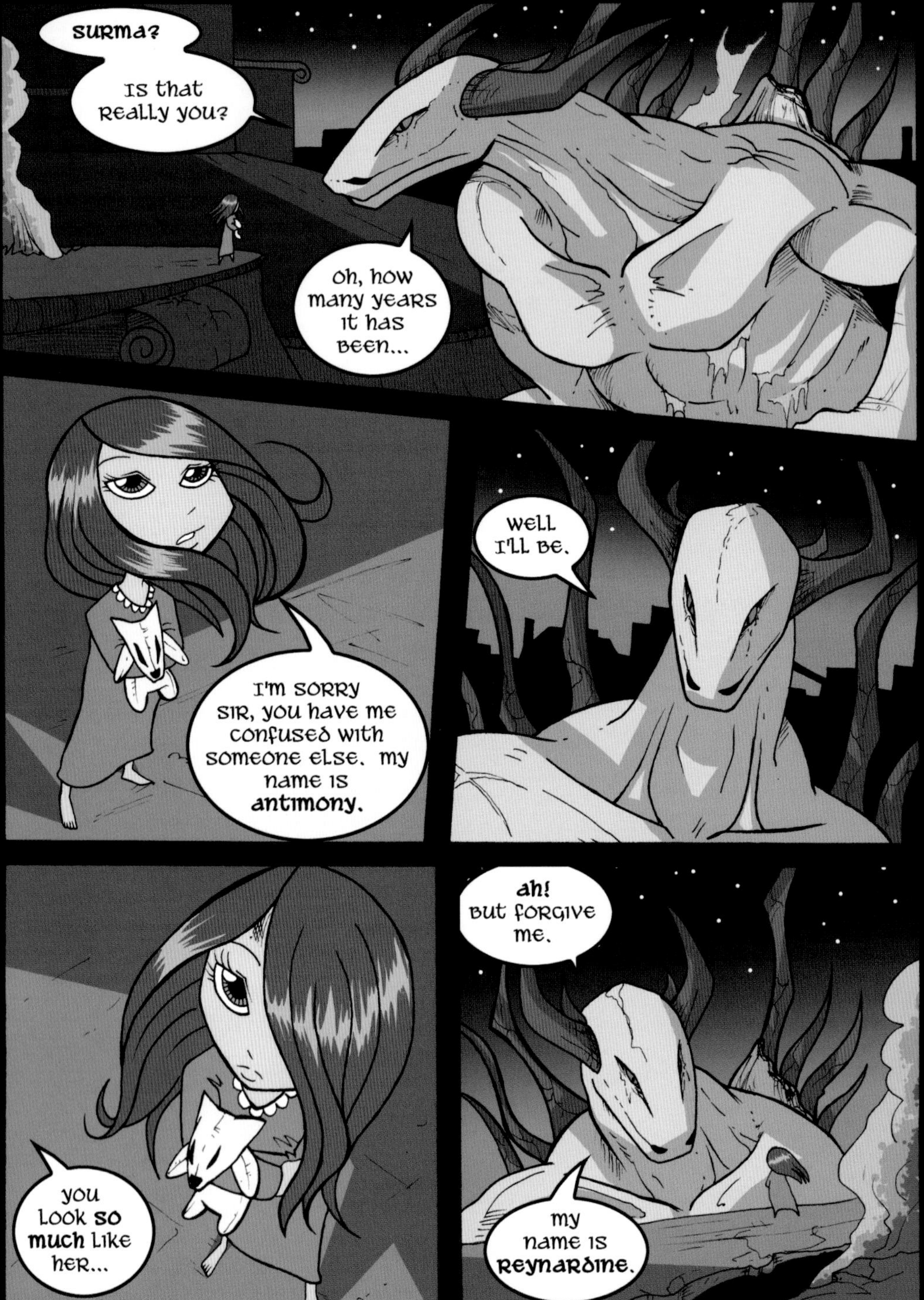

surma?
Is that really you?
oh, how many years it has been...
I'm sorry sir, you have me confused with someone else. my name is **antimony.**
well I'll be.
you look **so much** like her...
ah! but forgive me.
my name is **Reynardine.**

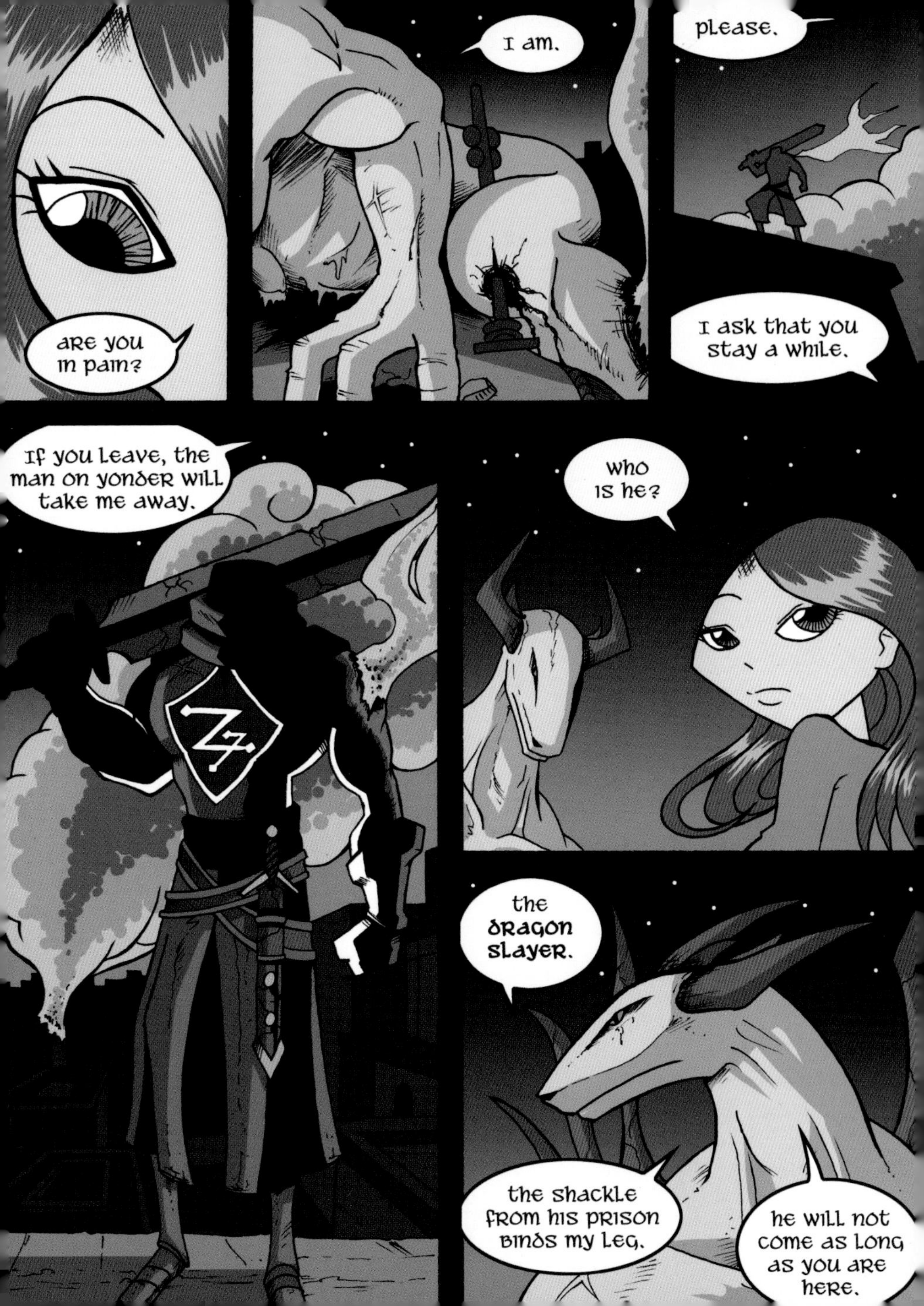
are you in pain?
I am.
please.
I ask that you stay a while.
If you leave, the man on yonder will take me away.
who is he?
the dragon slayer.
the shackle from his prison binds my leg.
he will not come as long as you are here.

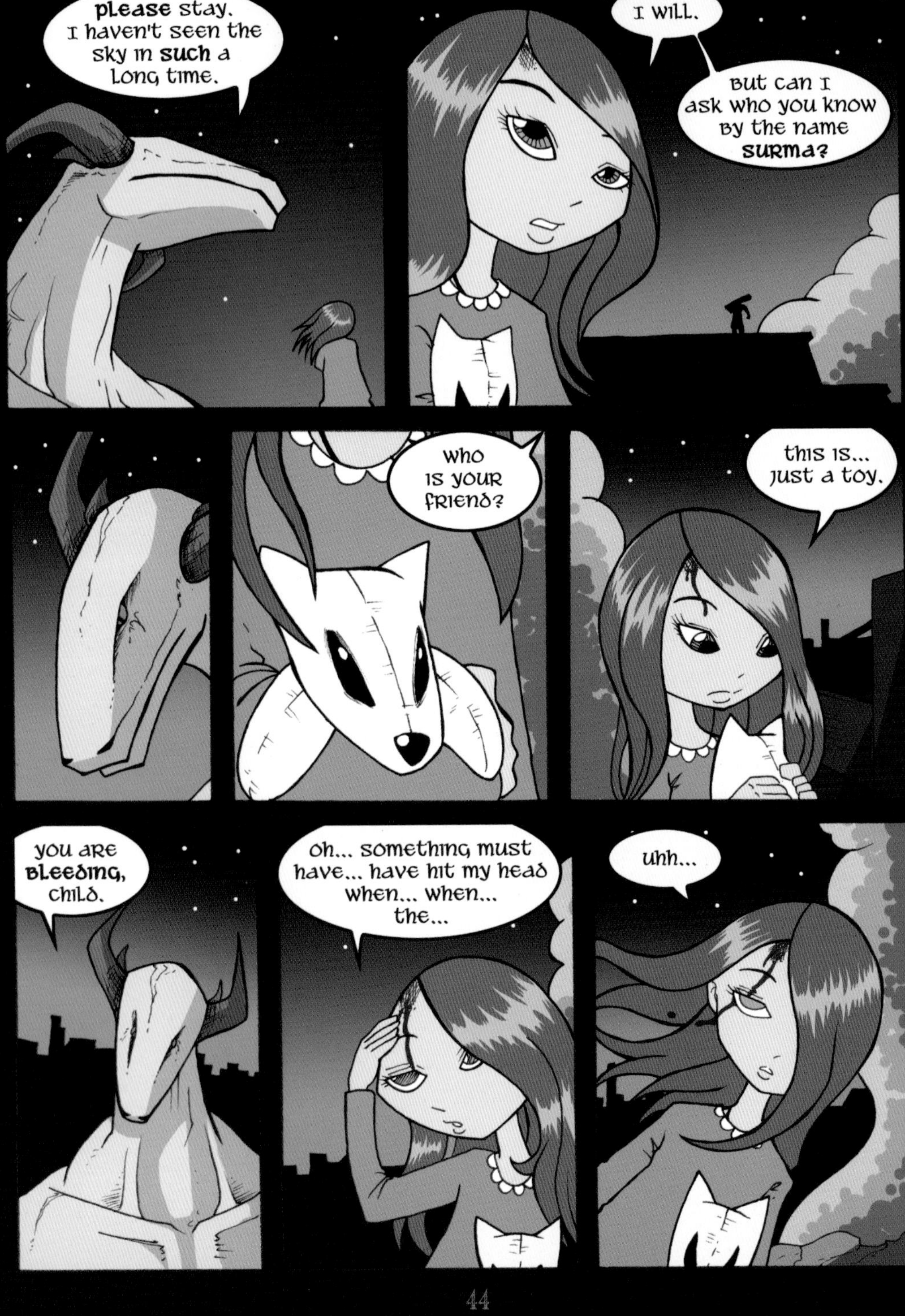
please stay. I haven't seen the sky in such a long time.
I will.
But can I ask who you know by the name Surma?
who is your friend?
this is... just a toy.
you are bleeding, child.
oh... something must have... have hit my head when... when... the...
uhh...

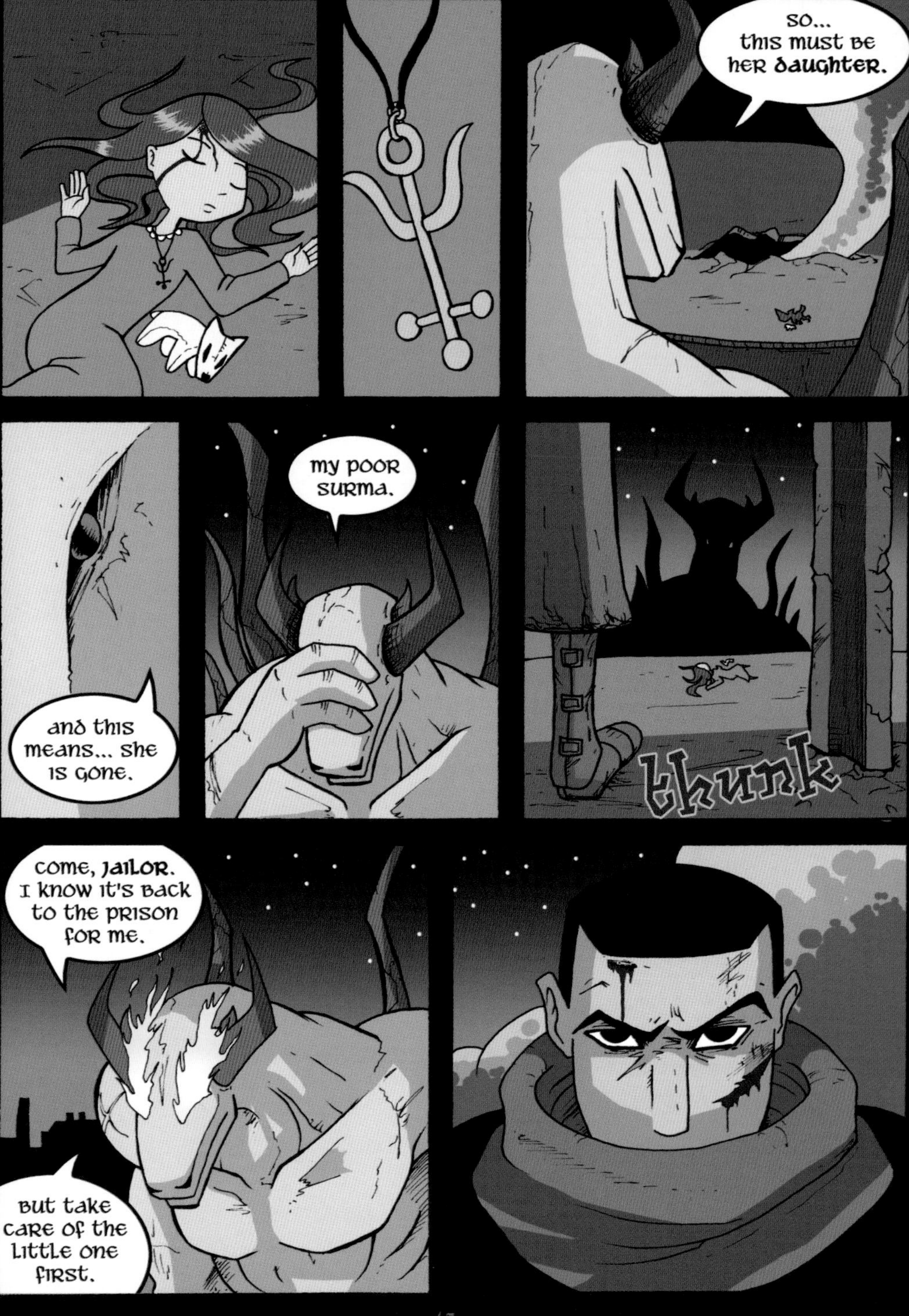
so... this must be her daughter.
my poor surma.
and this means... she is gone.
thunk
come, jailor. I know it's back to the prison for me.
but take care of the little one first.

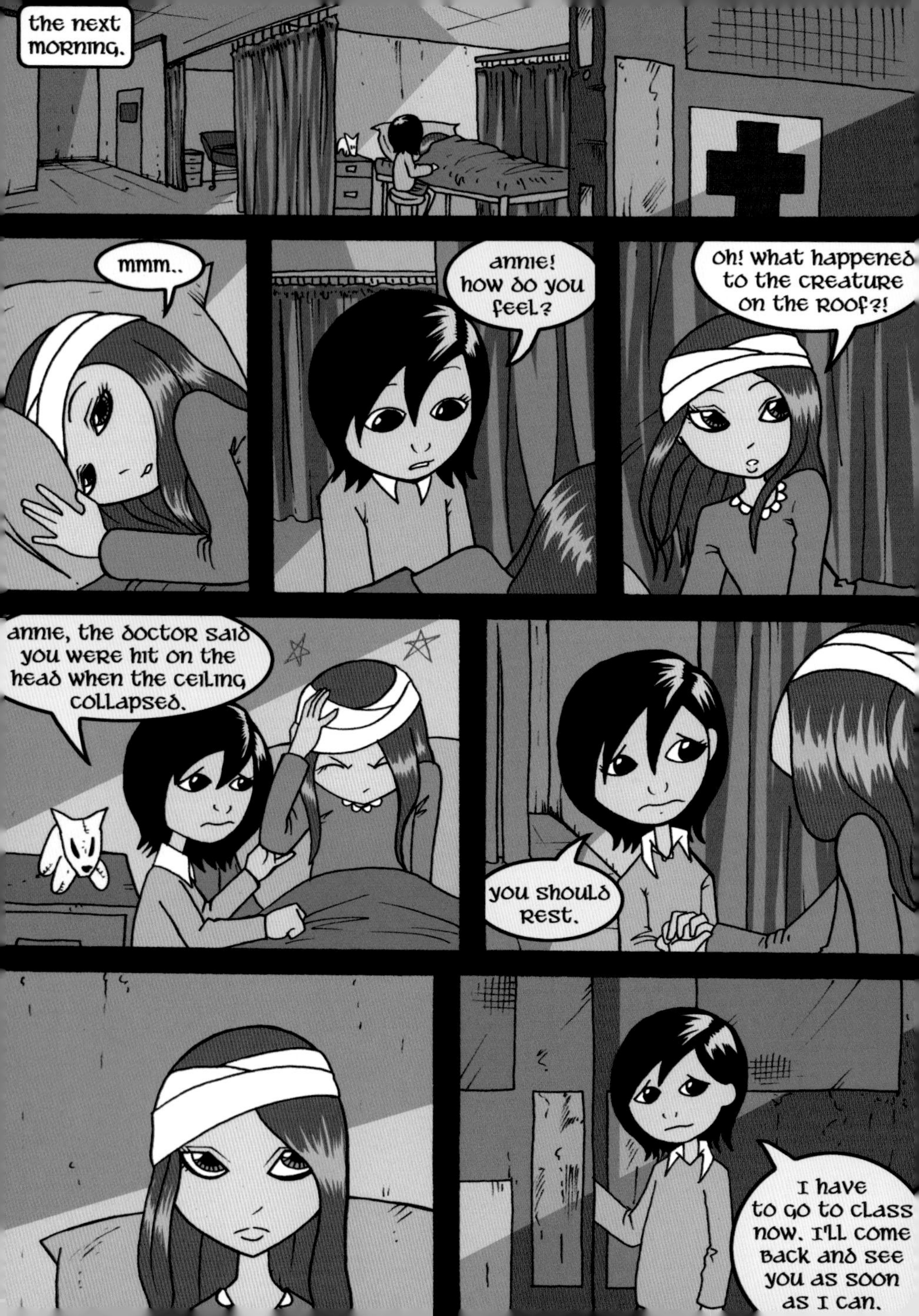
the next morning.
mmm..
annie! how do you feel?
oh! what happened to the creature on the roof?!
annie, the doctor said you were hit on the head when the ceiling collapsed.
you should rest.
I have to go to class now. I'll come back and see you as soon as I can.

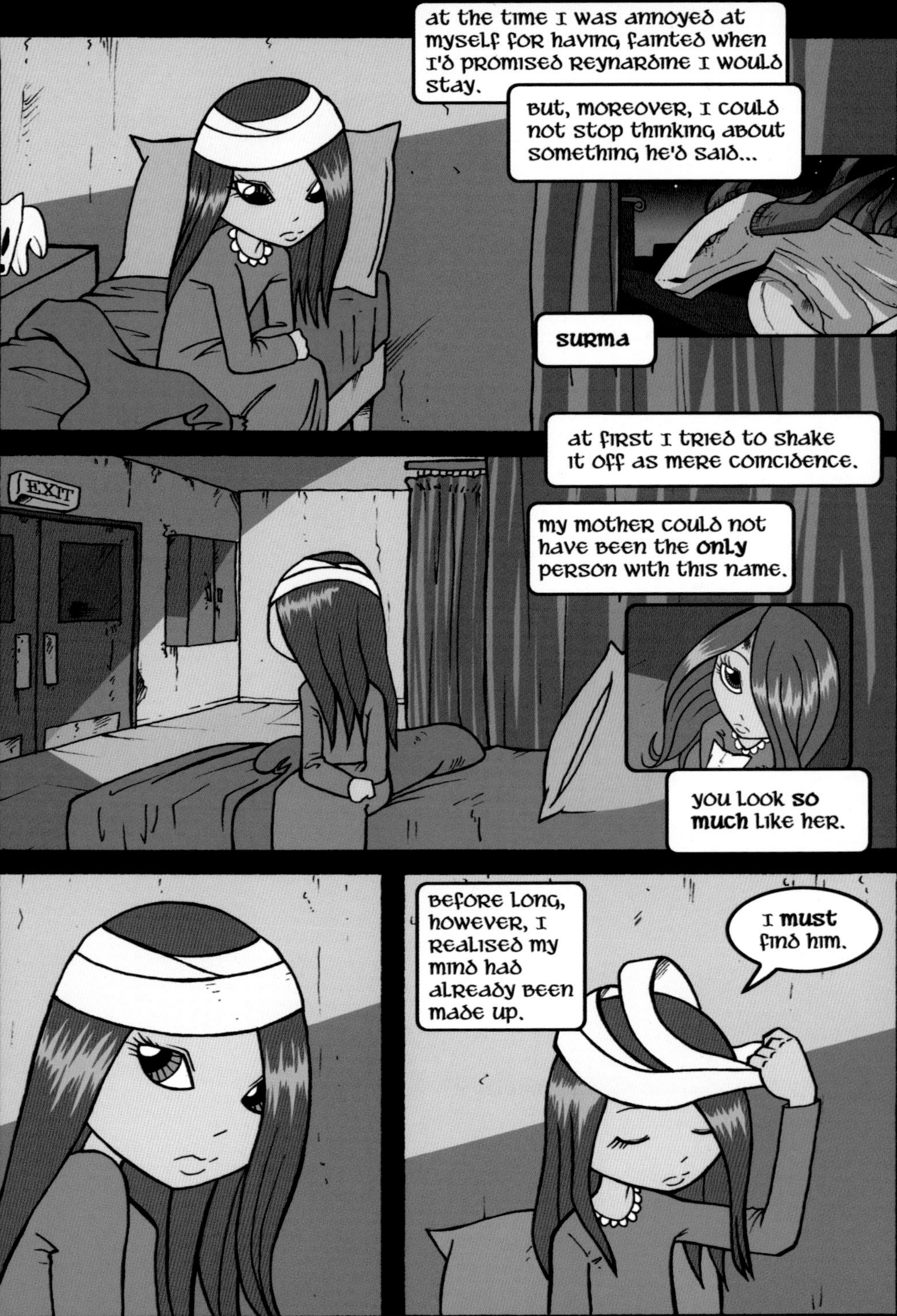
at the time I was annoyed at myself for having fainted when I'd promised Reynardine I would stay.
But, moreover, I could not stop thinking about something he'd said...
Surma
at first I tried to shake it off as mere coincidence.
EXIT
my mother could not have been the **only** person with this name.
you look **so much** like her.
Before long, however, I realised my mind had already been made up.
I **must** find him.

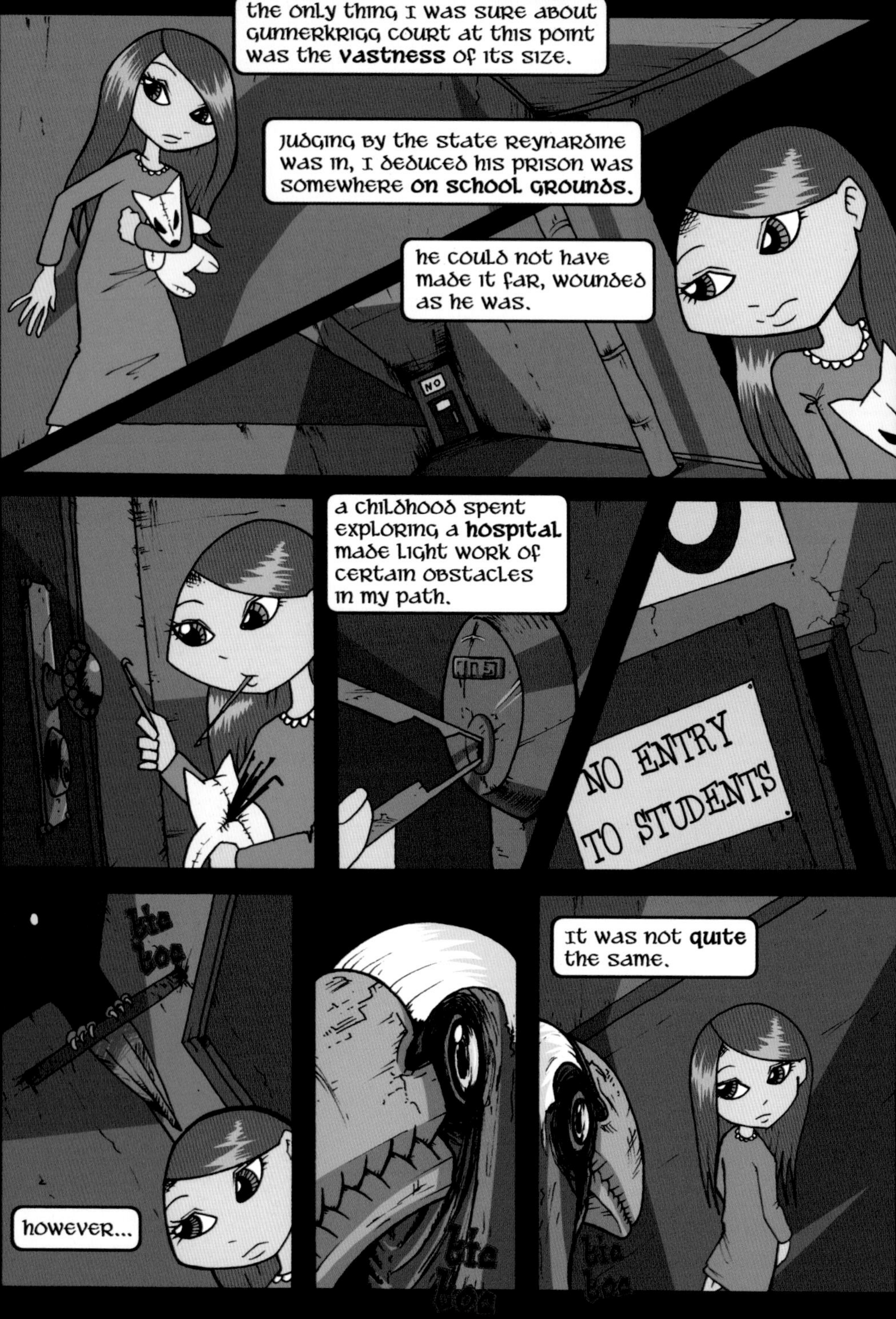

the only thing I was sure about Gunnerkrigg Court at this point was the **vastness** of its size.
Judging by the state Reynardine was in, I deduced his prison was somewhere **on school grounds.**
he could not have made it far, wounded as he was.
NO
a childhood spent exploring a **hospital** made light work of certain obstacles in my path.
NO ENTRY TO STUDENTS
however...
It was not **quite** the same.

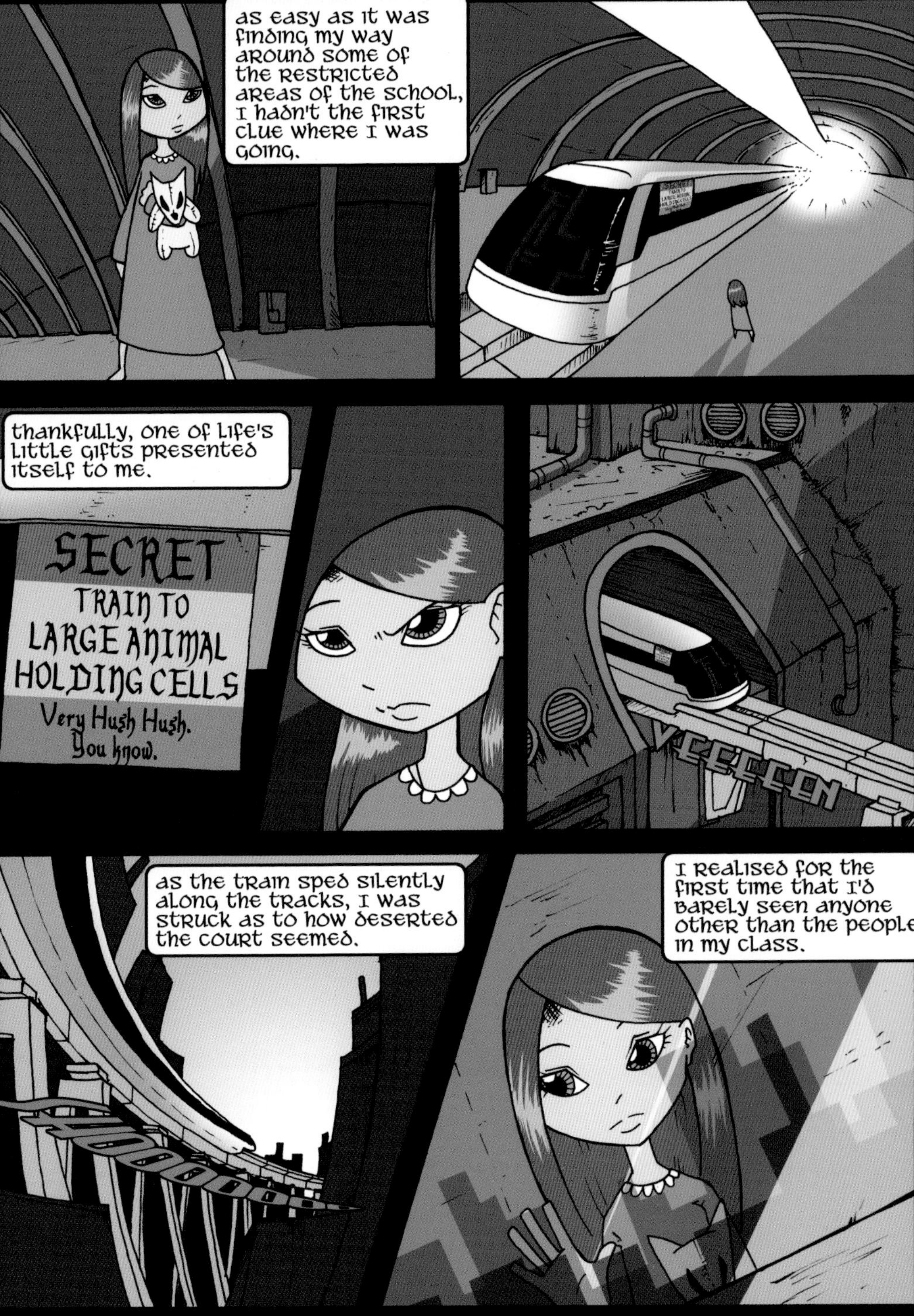
as easy as it was finding my way around some of the restricted areas of the school, I hadn't the first clue where I was going.
thankfully, one of life's little gifts presented itself to me.
SECRET
TRAIN TO
LARGE ANIMAL
HOLDING CELLS
Very Hush Hush.
You know.
as the train sped silently along the tracks, I was struck as to how deserted the court seemed.
I realised for the first time that I'd barely seen anyone other than the people in my class.

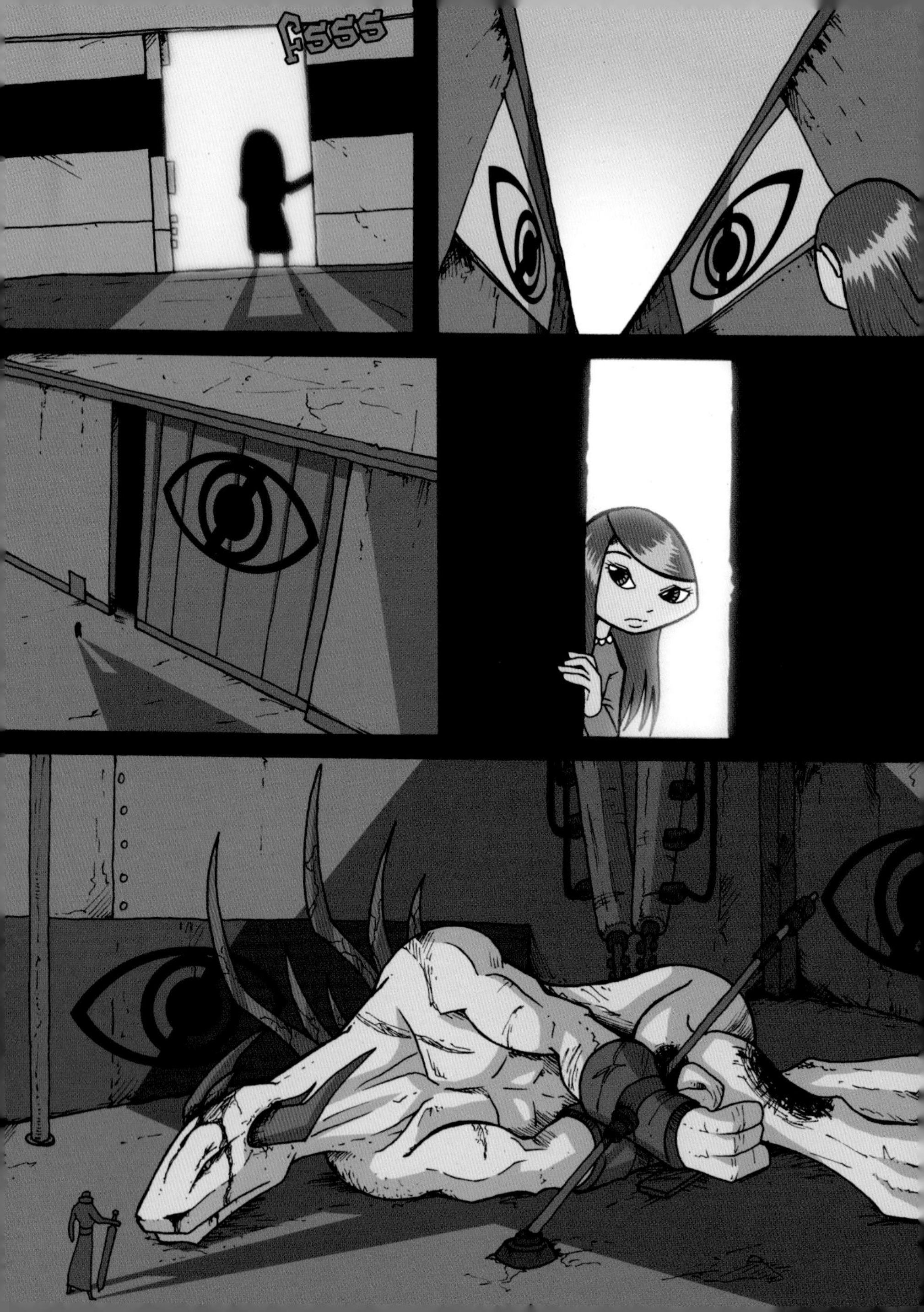
FSSS

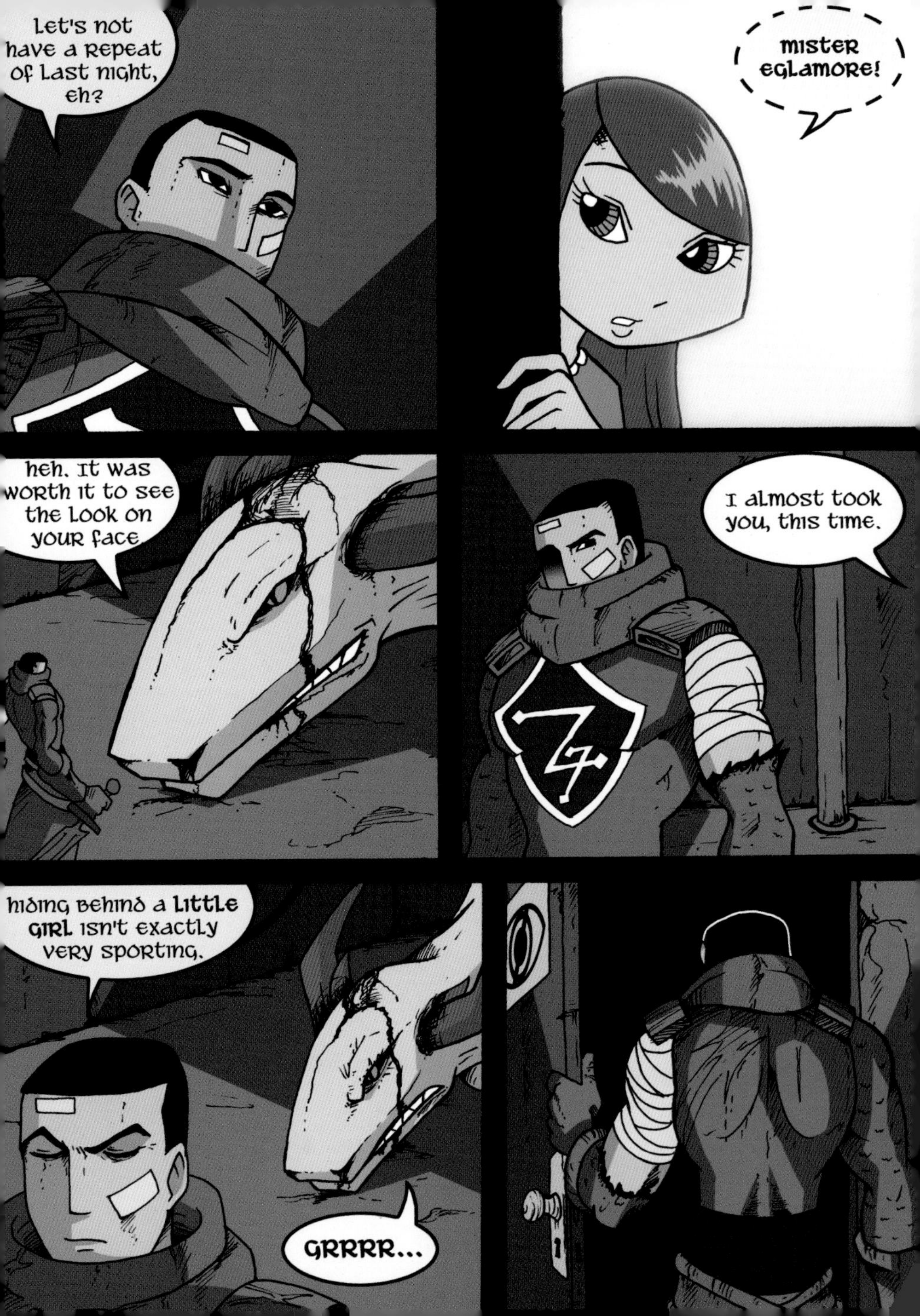
Let's not have a repeat of last night, eh?
mister eglamore!
heh. It was worth it to see the look on your face
I almost took you, this time.
hiding behind a little girl isn't exactly very sporting.
GRRRR...

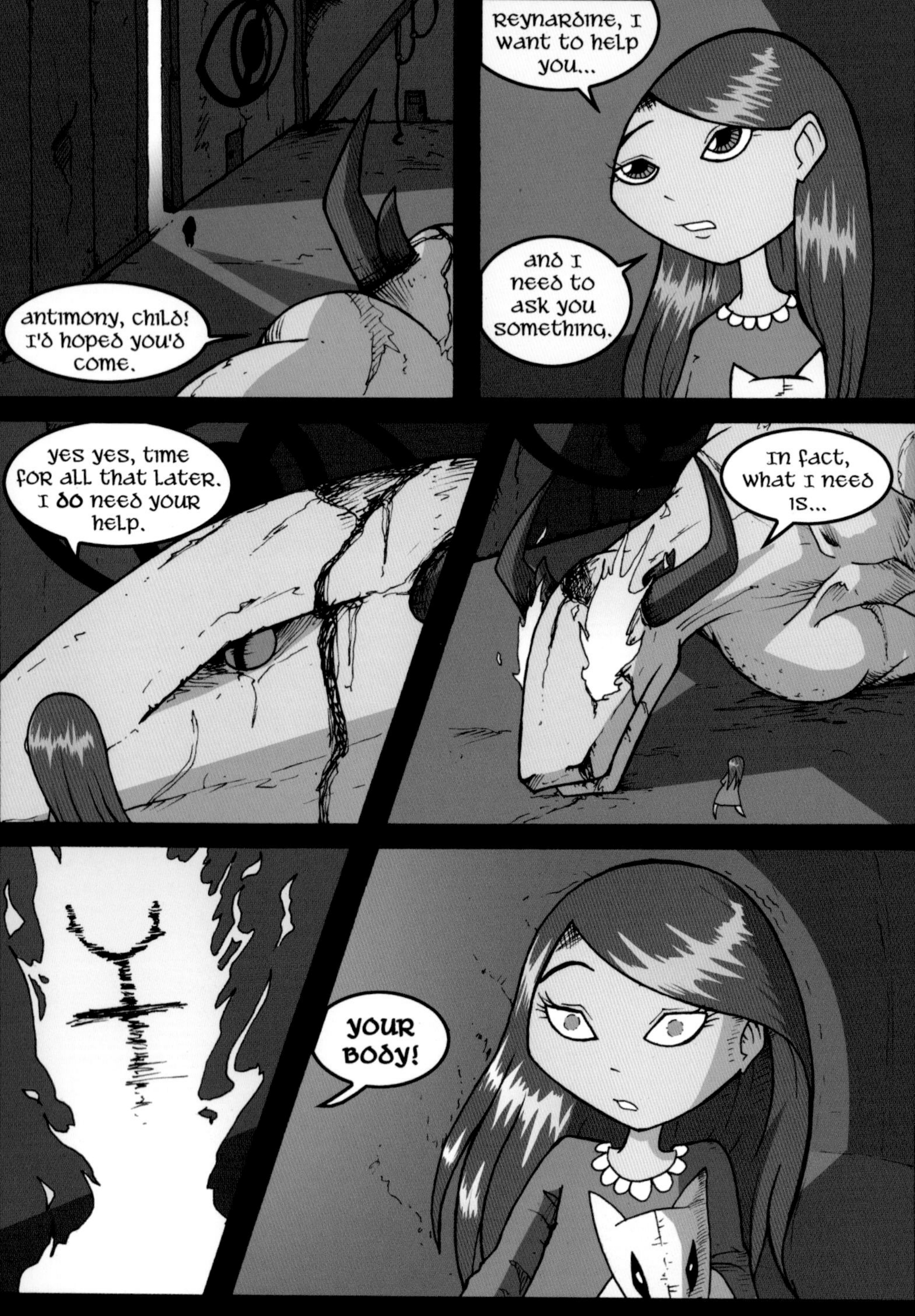
antimony, child! I'd hoped you'd come.
Reynardine, I want to help you...
and I need to ask you something.
yes yes, time for all that later. I **do** need your help.
In fact, what I need is...
your body!

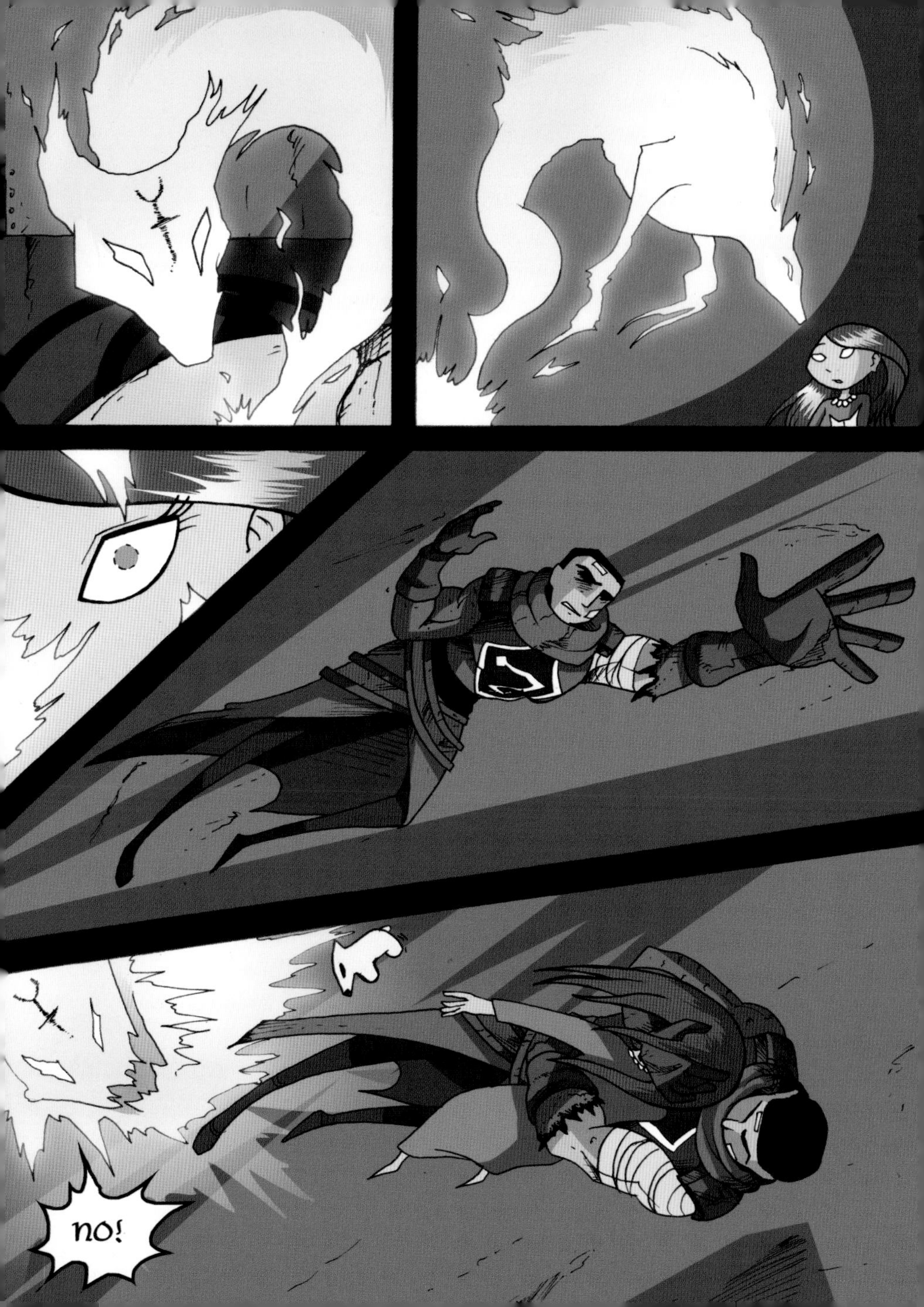
no!

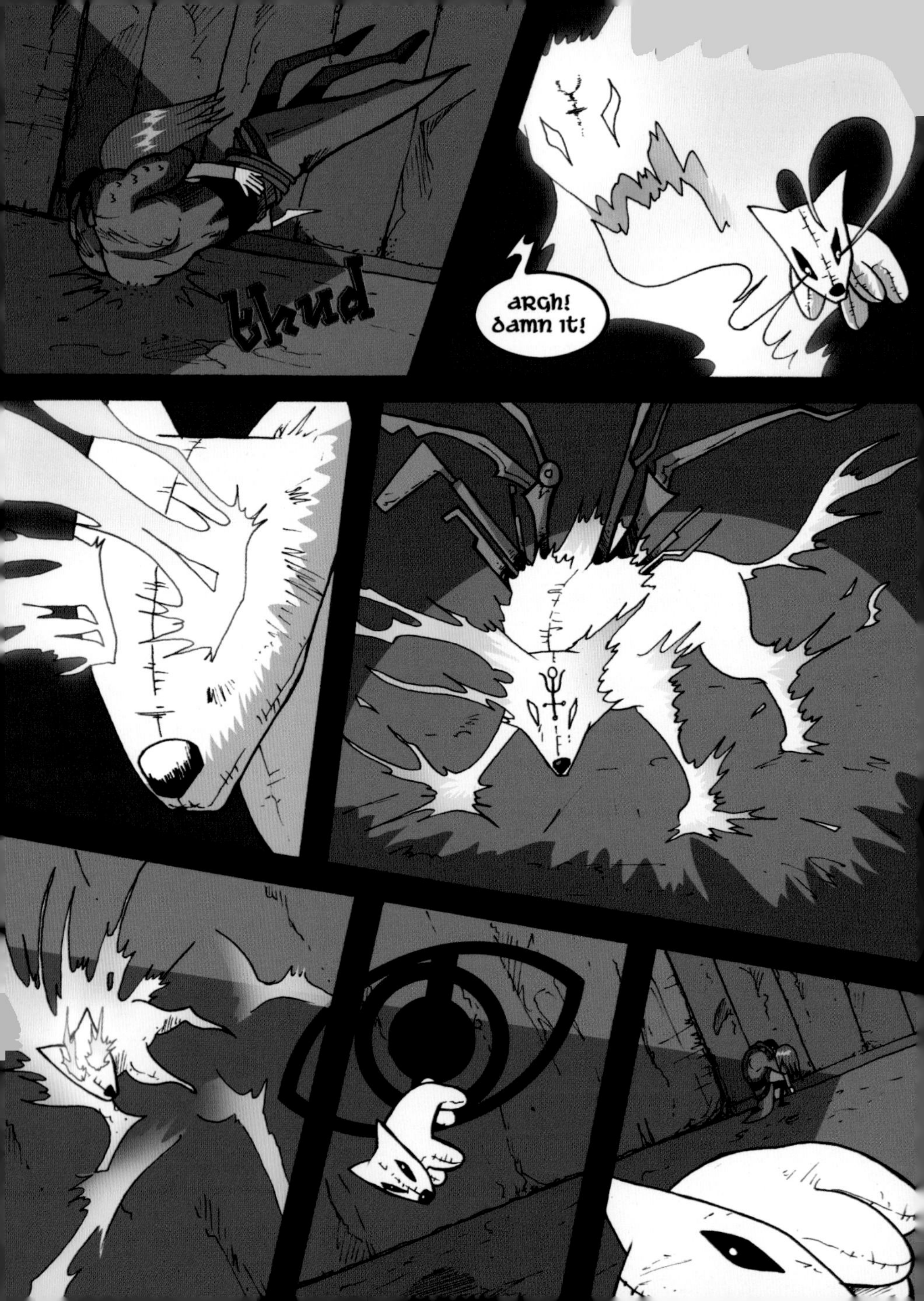

thud
argh! damn it!

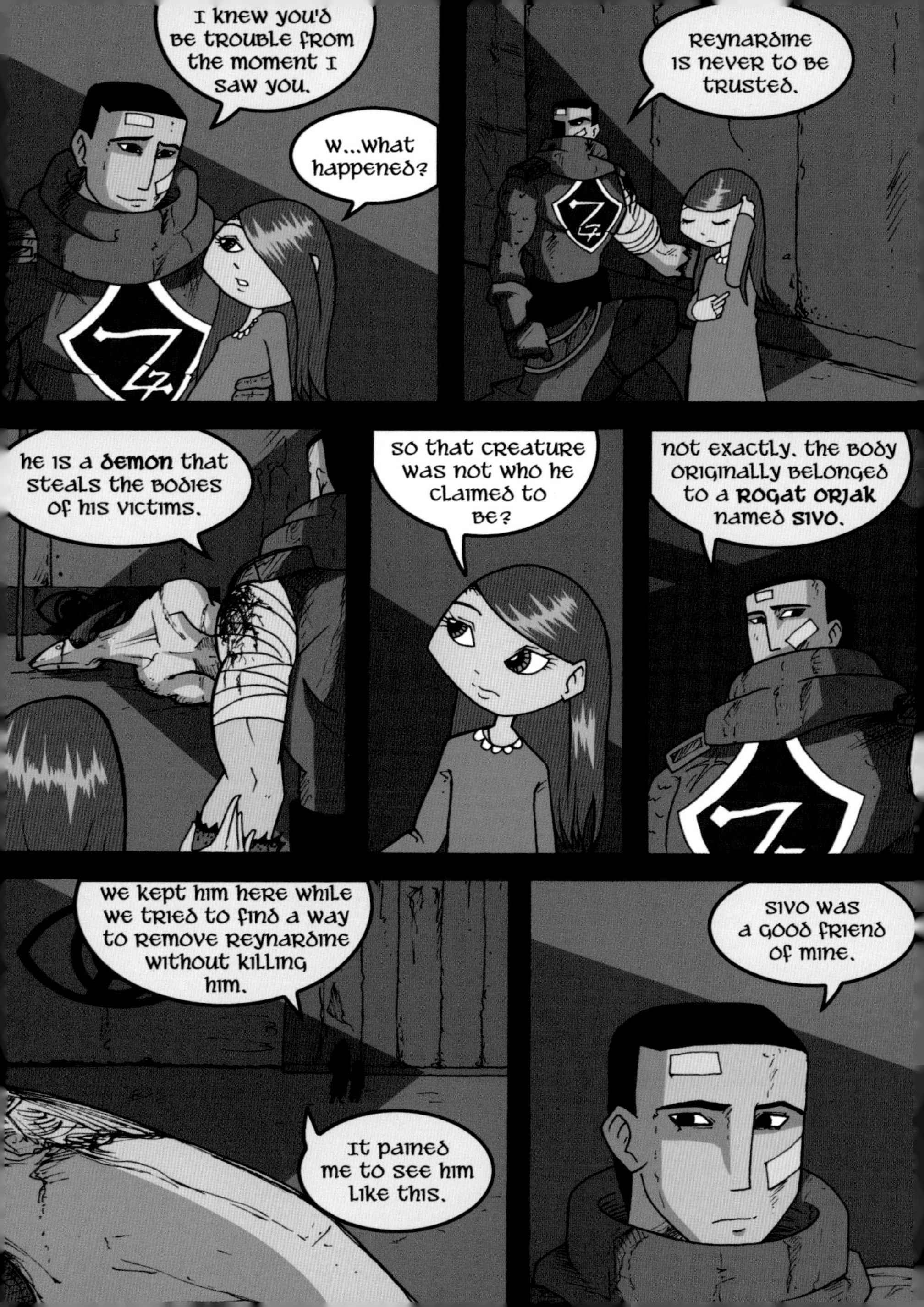
I knew you'd be trouble from the moment I saw you.
w...what happened?
Reynardine is never to be trusted.
he is a demon that steals the bodies of his victims.
so that creature was not who he claimed to be?
not exactly. the body originally belonged to a ROGAT ORJAK named SIVO.
we kept him here while we tried to find a way to remove Reynardine without killing him.
It pained me to see him like this.
SIVO was a good friend of mine.

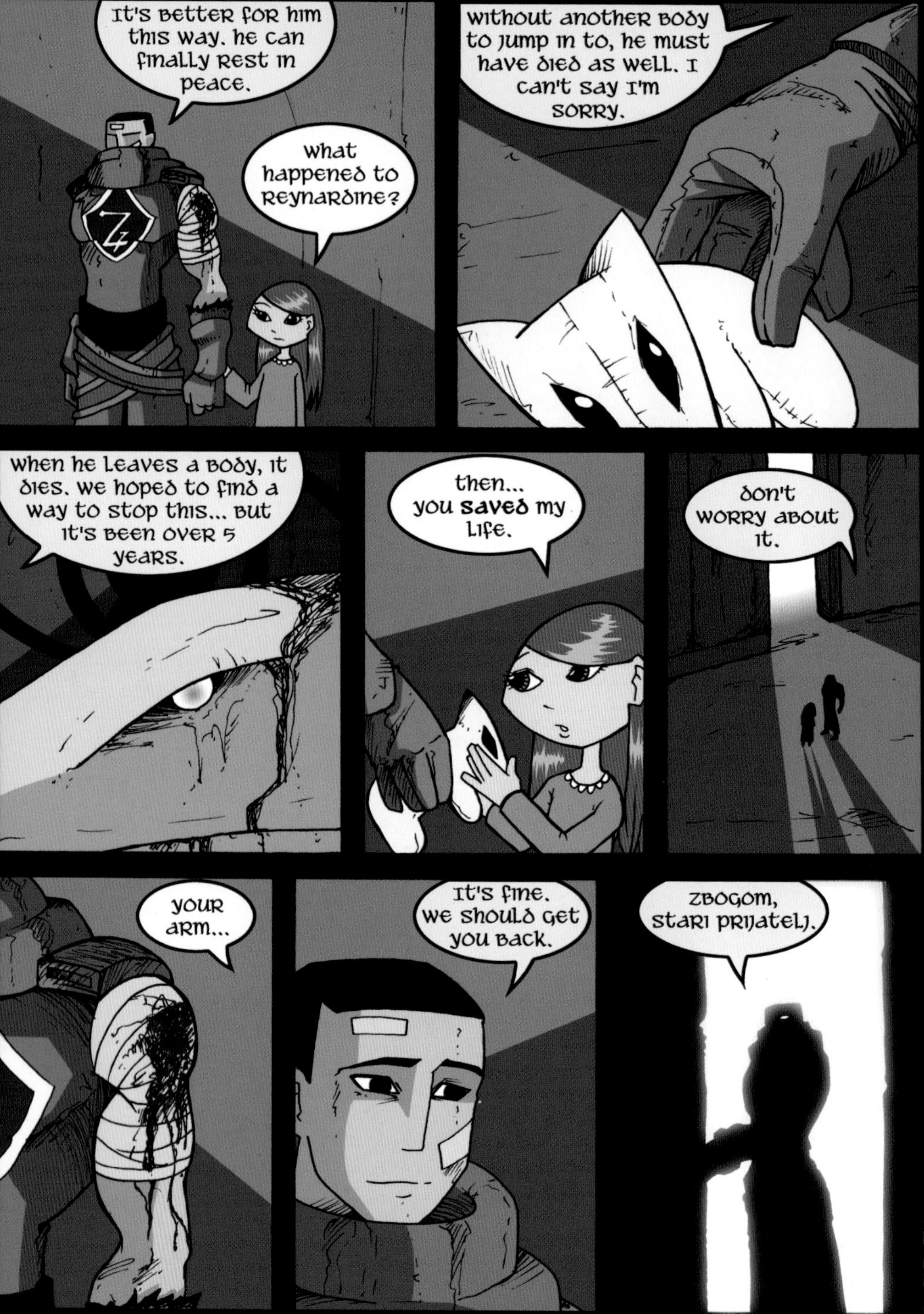
It's better for him this way. he can finally rest in peace.
what happened to Reynardine?
without another body to jump in to, he must have died as well. I can't say I'm sorry.
when he leaves a body, it dies. we hoped to find a way to stop this... but it's been over 5 years.
then... you **saved** my life.
don't worry about it.
your arm...
It's fine. we should get you back.
zbogom, stari prijatelj.

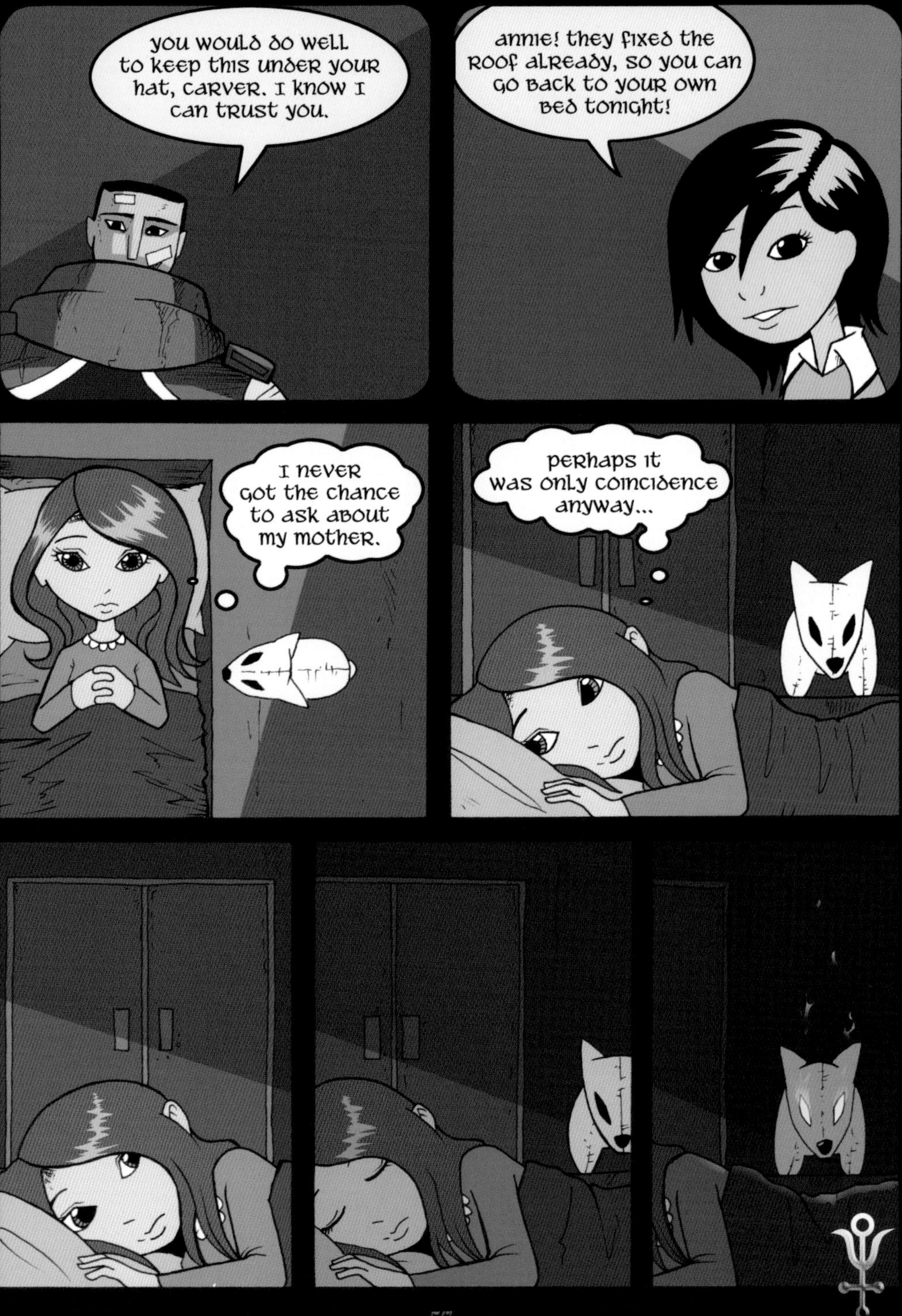
you would do well to keep this under your hat, carver. I know I can trust you.
annie! they fixed the roof already, so you can go back to your own bed tonight!
I never got the chance to ask about my mother.
perhaps it was only coincidence anyway...

Rogat Orjak

(Horned Giant)

Originally discovered in the Bovec mountains on the Slovenian/Italian border, the **Rogat Orjak** is native to most European regions. Rarely seen, these retiring creatures feed mainly on sheep and mountain goats. Sir Eugene Gould is credited with first human contact.

Possible depiction of an Orjak found, amongst others, near a cave in Trabzon, Turkey.

'I came upon [the creature] and he looked me square in the eyes, blood from a Bighorn dripping from its mouth. I was surprised, and relieved, when he offered me a leg.' - E. Gould.

Possessing a high level of intelligence and the ability to speak, the Orjak is generally found to be mild tempered and non-confrontational despite their large size. Upper torso musculature is surprisingly similar to human physique.

First reports of the Orjak date back to early 11th century while images of similar creatures predate these by many centuries.

A tooth currently on display at the Palaeontological Institute, Russian Academy of Science, Moscow. Originally procured by E.Gould. Later lost in a Poker match in Kursk.

'We like to keep a low profile. Best not to draw attention to ourselves, unlike those [common dragons]. And where are they now, eh?' - Kos, Orjak.

Sketch from E.Gould's field notebook.

Sketch from E.Gould's field notebook.

Possible depiction of an Orjak in a 16th Century manuscript.

Gunnerkrigg Court

Gunnerkrigg Court

Chapter 4:

Not Very Scary

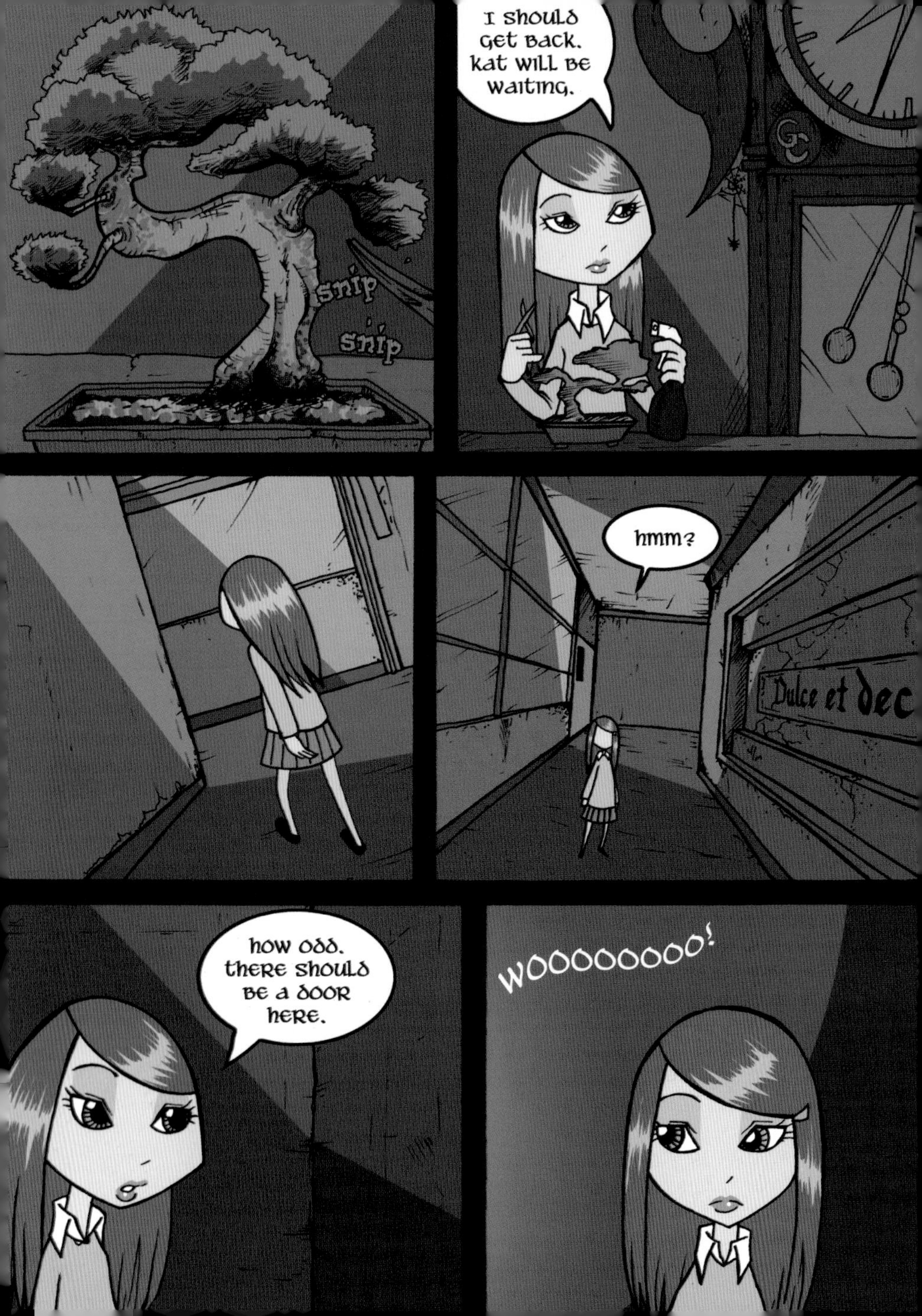
snip
snip
I should get back. kat will be waiting.
hmm?
Dulce et dec
how odd. there should be a door here.
WOOOOOOOO!

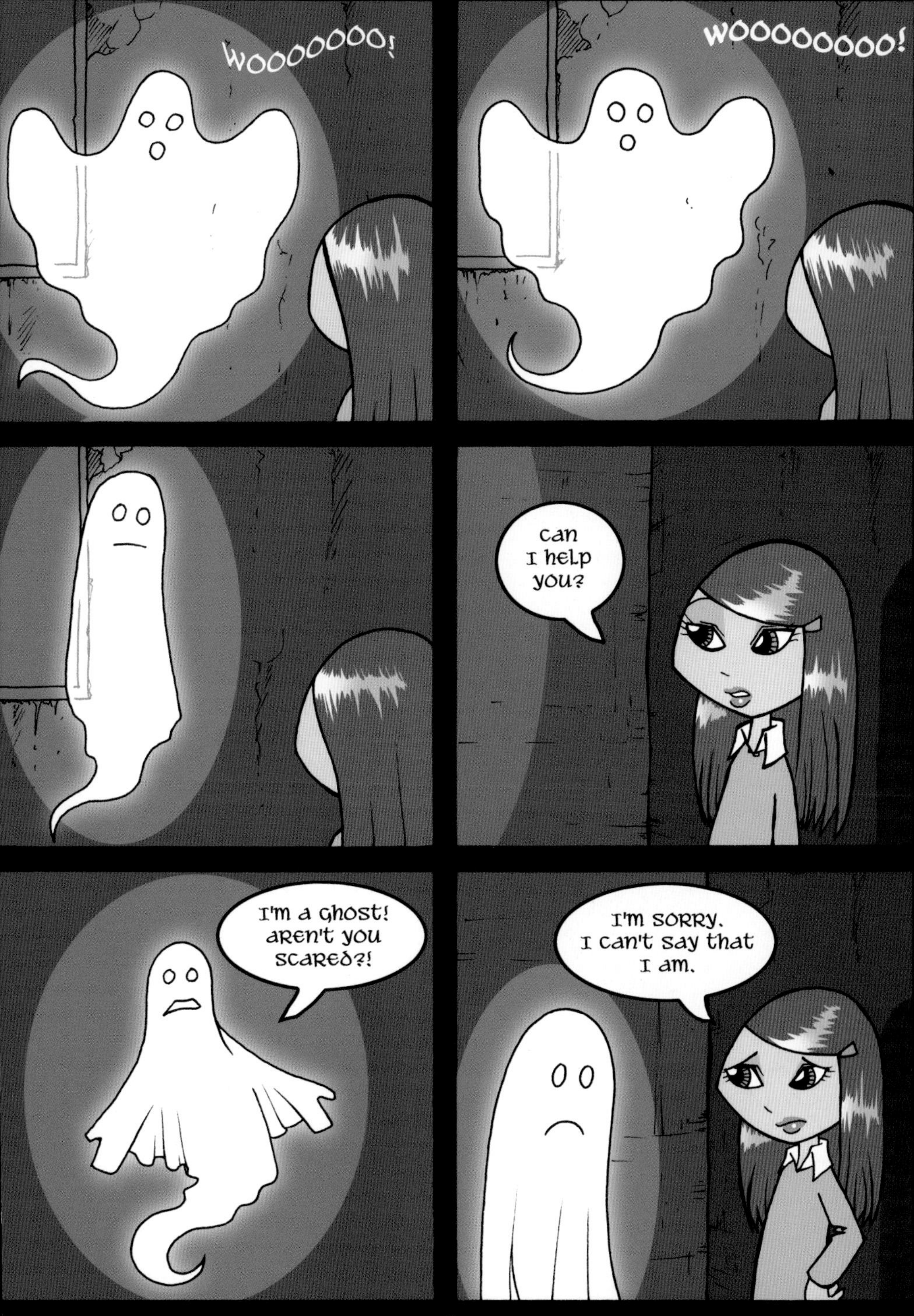
WOOOOOOO!
WOOOOOOOOO!
can I help you?
I'm a ghost! aren't you scared?!
I'm sorry. I can't say that I am.

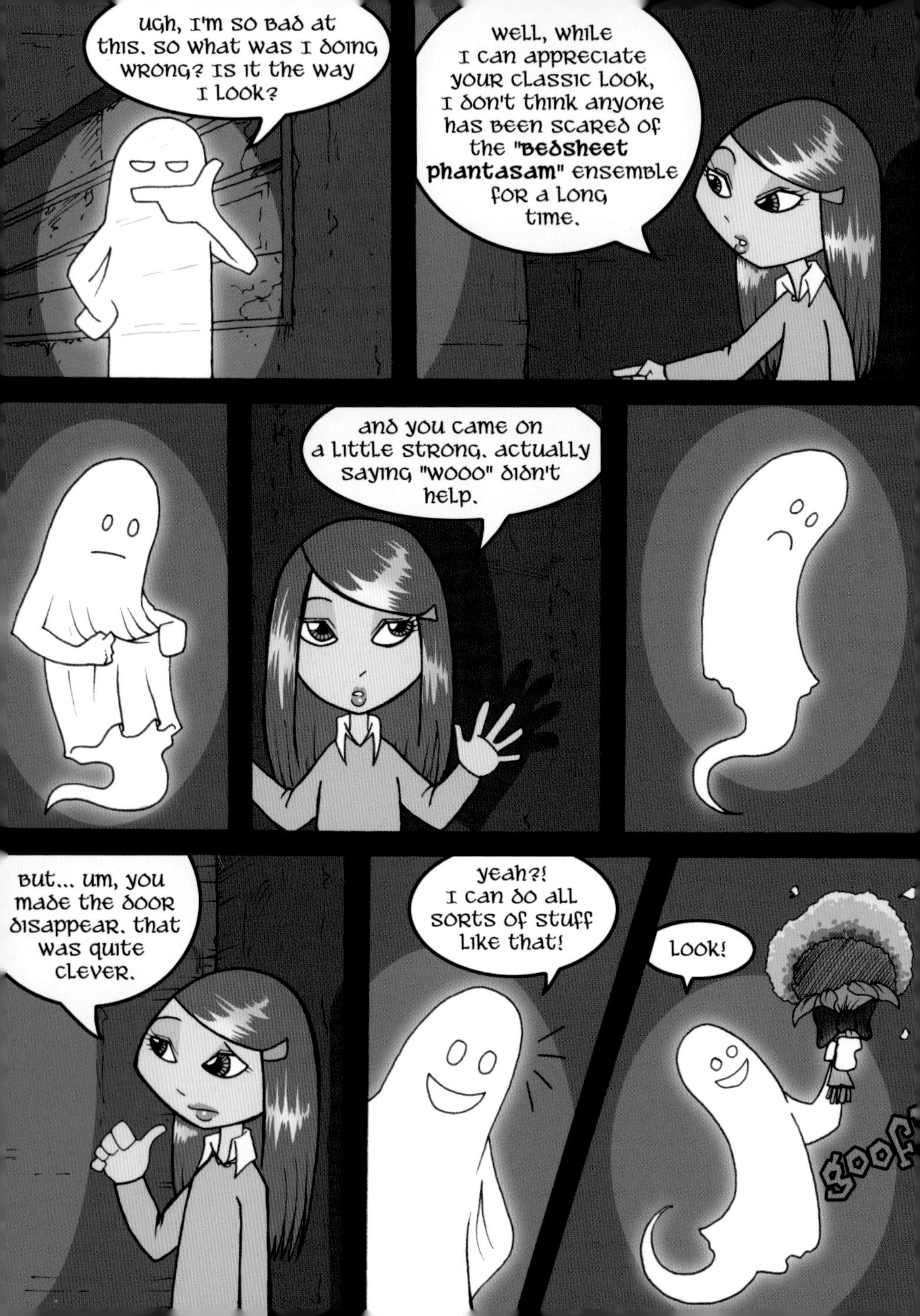
ugh, I'm so bad at this. so what was I doing wrong? is it the way I look?
well, while I can appreciate your classic look, I don't think anyone has been scared of the "**bedsheet phantasam**" ensemble for a long time.
and you came on a little strong. actually saying "wooo" didn't help.
but... um, you made the door disappear. that was quite clever.
yeah?! I can do all sorts of stuff like that!
look!

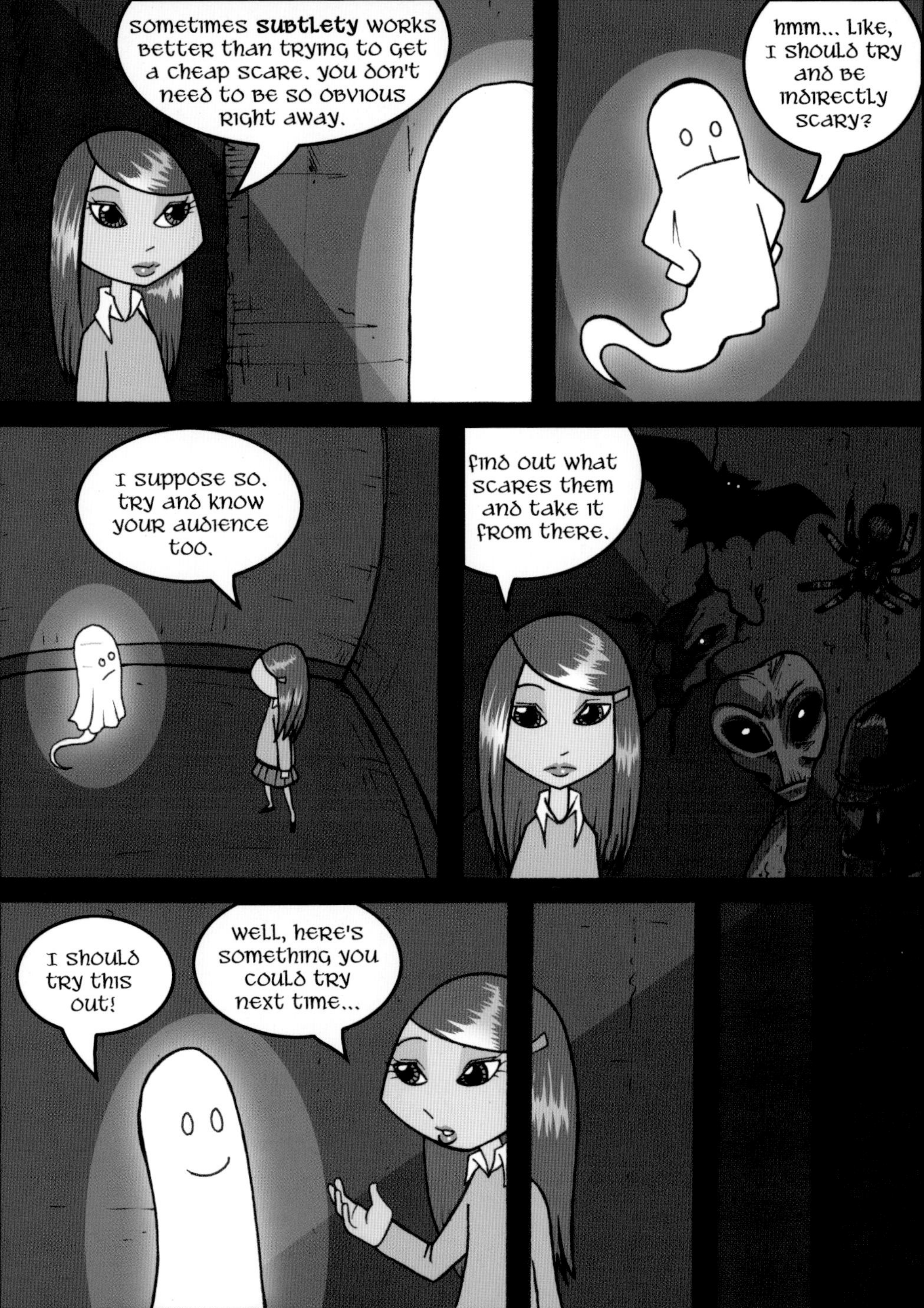
sometimes **subtlety** works better than trying to get a cheap scare. you don't need to be so obvious right away.
hmm... like, I should try and be indirectly scary?
I suppose so. try and know your audience too.
find out what scares them and take it from there.
I should try this out!
well, here's something you could try next time...

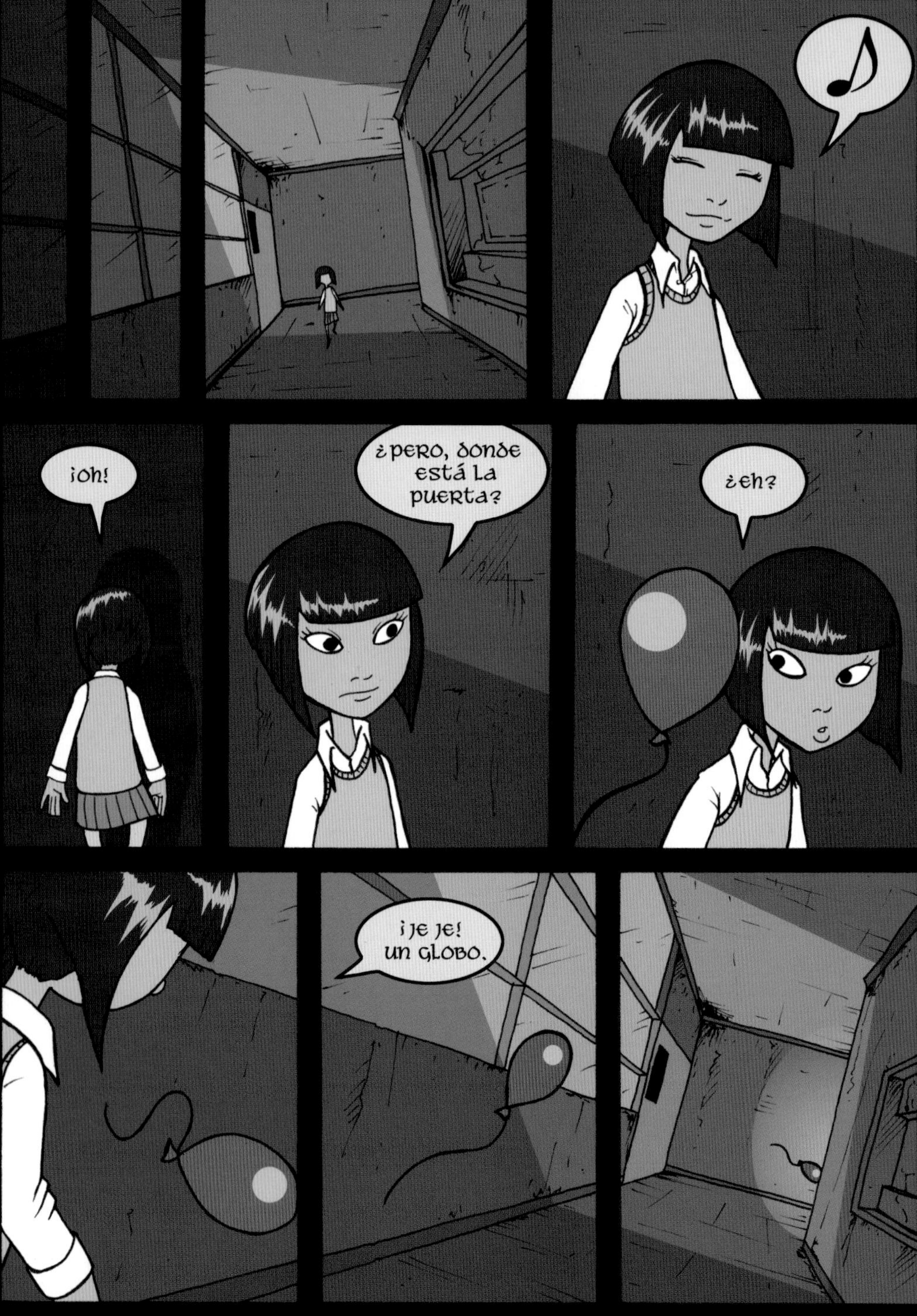
♪
¡OH!
¿PERO, DONDE ESTÁ LA PUERTA?
¿EH?
¡JE JE! UN GLOBO.

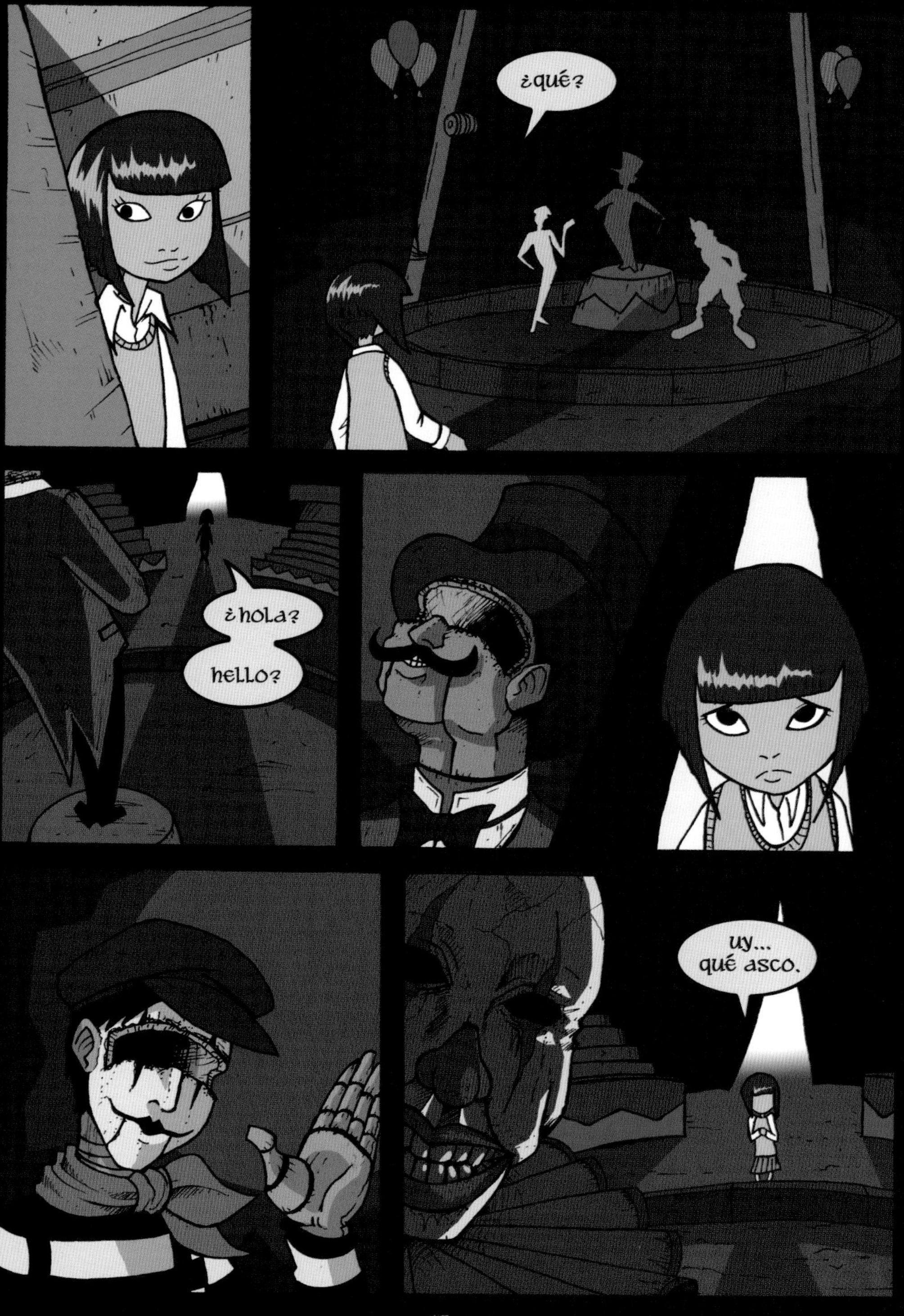
¿qué?
¿hola?
hello?
uy... qué asco.

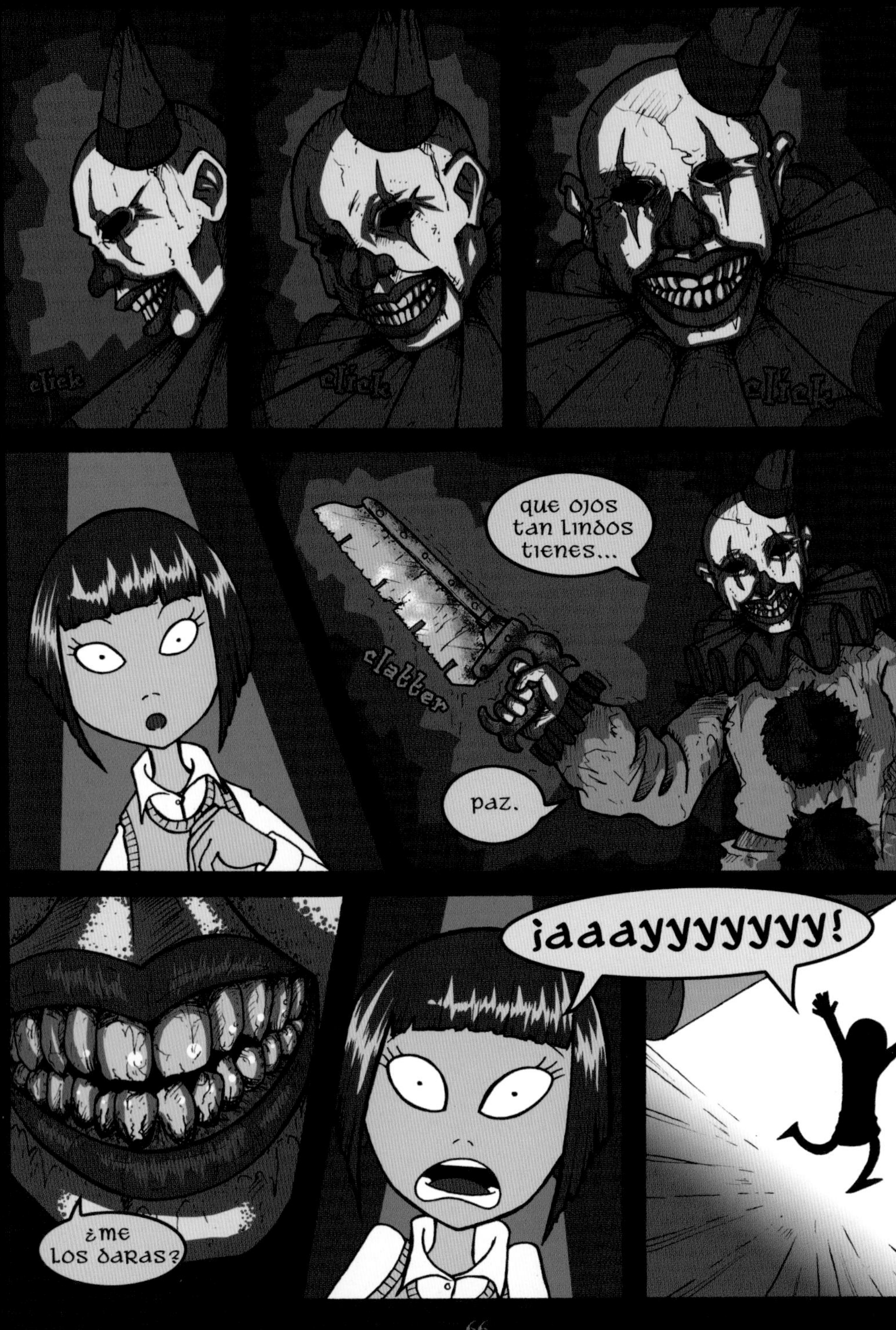
click
click
click
que ojos tan lindos tienes...
clatter
paz.
¿me los daras?
¡aaayyyyyyy!

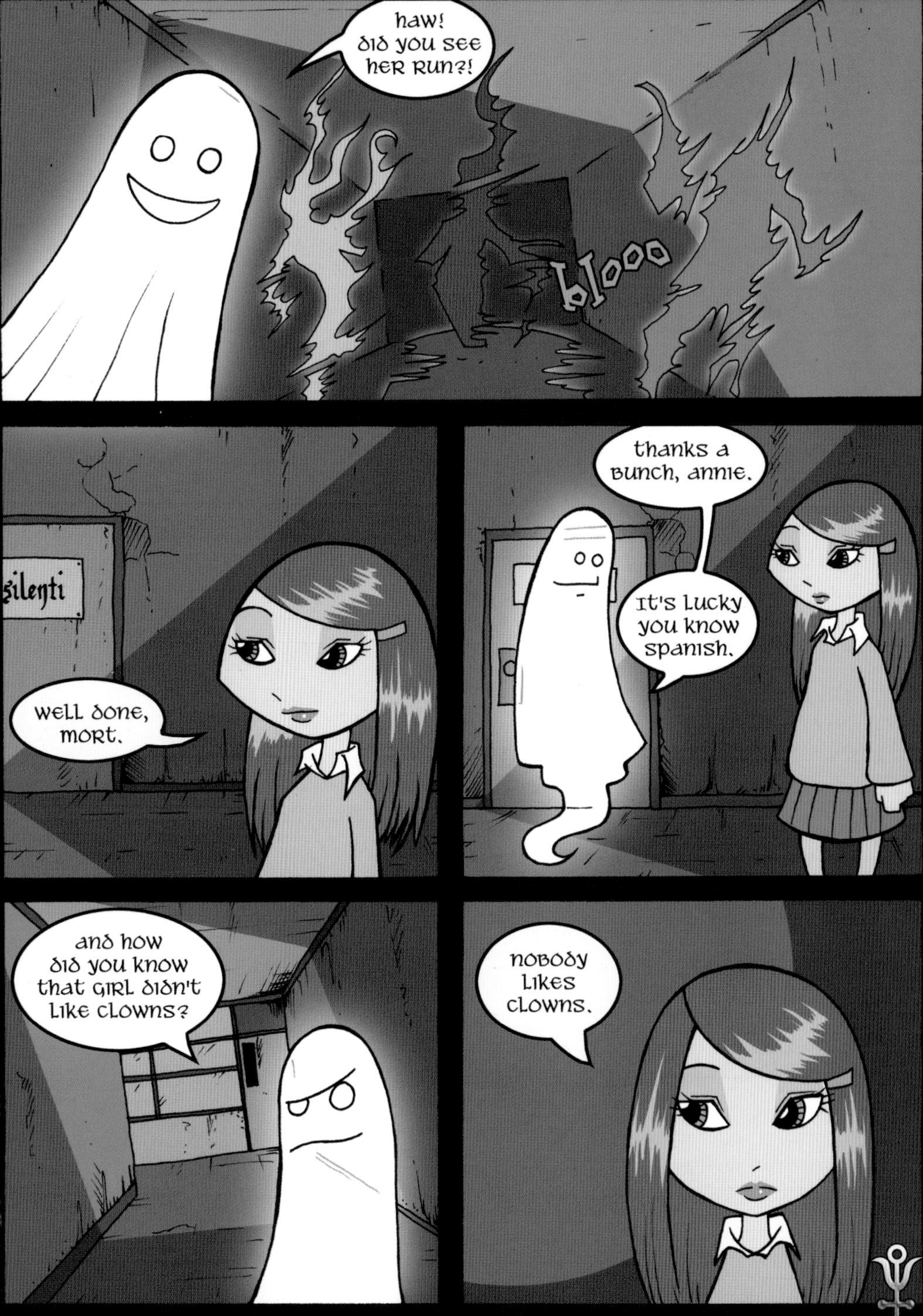
haw! did you see her run?!
blooo
silenti
well done, mort.
thanks a bunch, annie.
it's lucky you know spanish.
and how did you know that girl didn't like clowns?
nobody likes clowns.

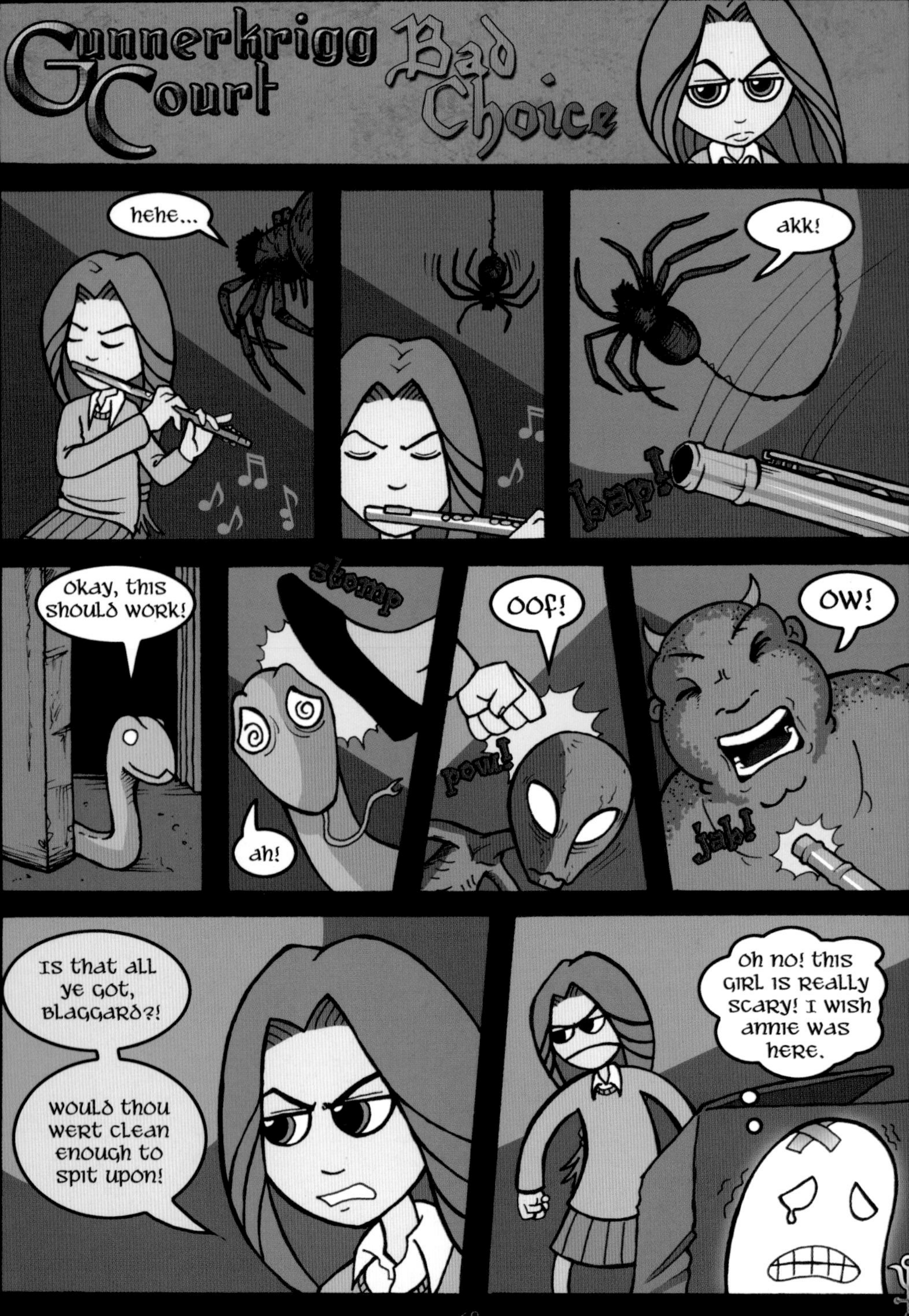
Gunnerkrigg Court
Bad Choice
hehe...
akk!
bap!
Okay, this should work!
stomp
ah!
OOF!
pow!
OW!
jab!
Is that all ye got, blaggard?!
Would thou wert clean enough to spit upon!
Oh no! this girl is really scary! I wish annie was here.

Gunnerkrigg Court

Chapter 5:

Two Strange Girls

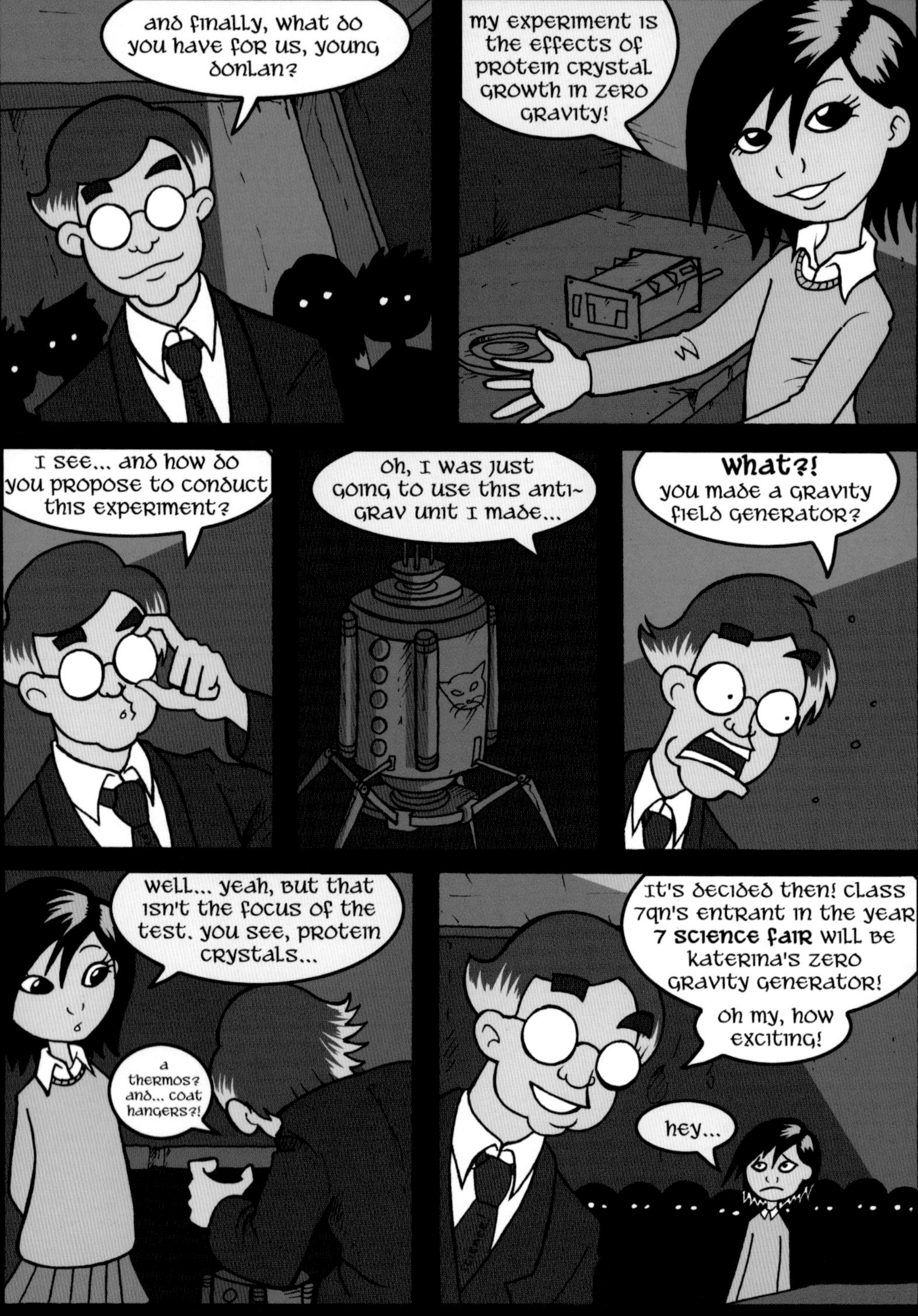
and finally, what do you have for us, young donlan?
my experiment is the effects of protein crystal growth in zero gravity!
I see... and how do you propose to conduct this experiment?
oh, I was just going to use this anti-grav unit I made...
what?! you made a gravity field generator?
well... yeah, but that isn't the focus of the test. you see, protein crystals...
a thermos? and... coat hangers?!
It's decided then! class 7qn's entrant in the year 7 science fair will be katerina's zero gravity generator!
oh my, how exciting!
hey...

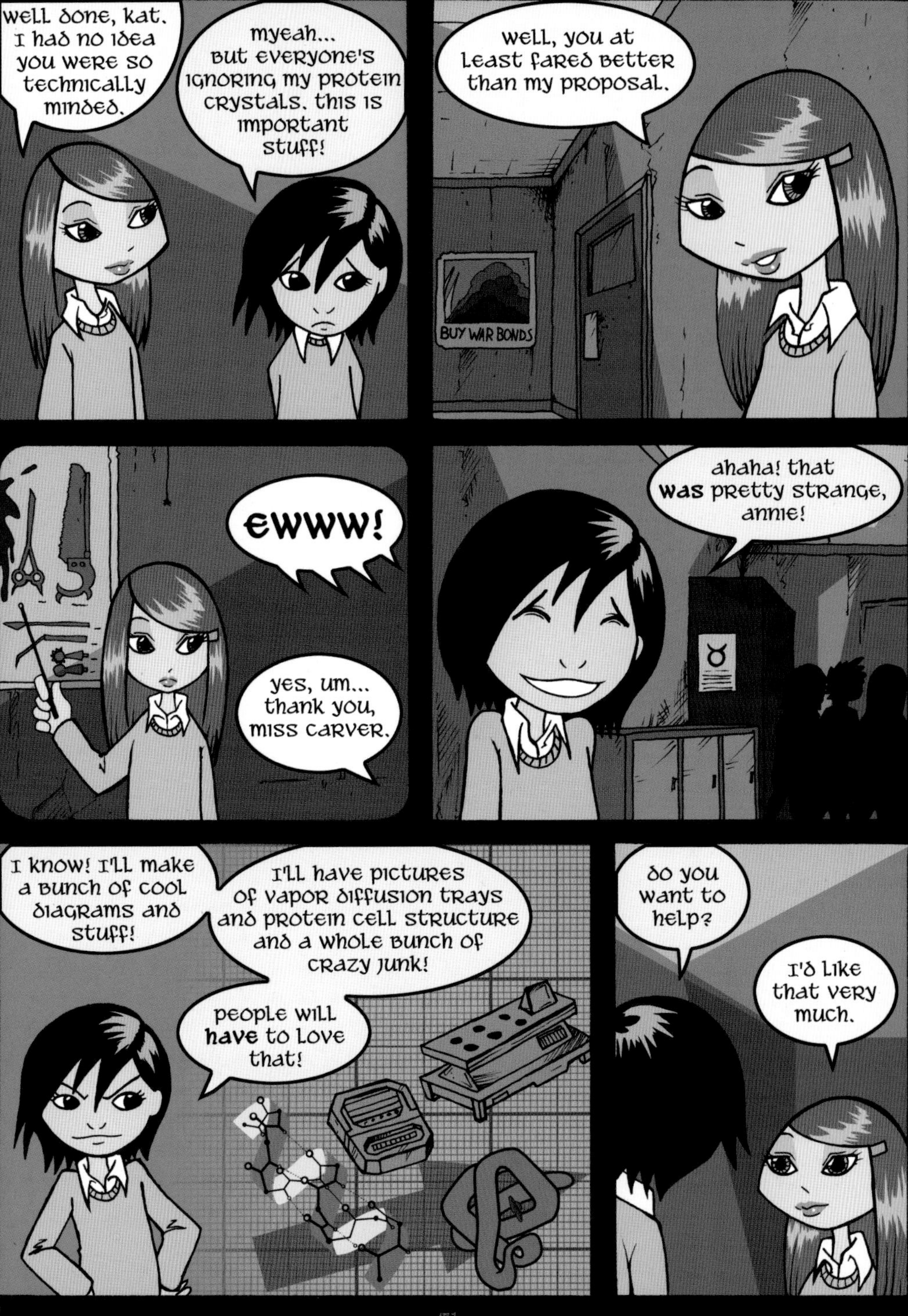

well done, kat. I had no idea you were so technically minded.
myeah... but everyone's ignoring my protein crystals. this is important stuff!
well, you at least fared better than my proposal.
BUY WAR BONDS
EWWW!
yes, um... thank you, miss carver.
ahaha! that **was** pretty strange, annie!
I know! I'll make a bunch of cool diagrams and stuff!
I'll have pictures of vapor diffusion trays and protein cell structure and a whole bunch of crazy junk!
people will **have** to love that!
do you want to help?
I'd like that very much.

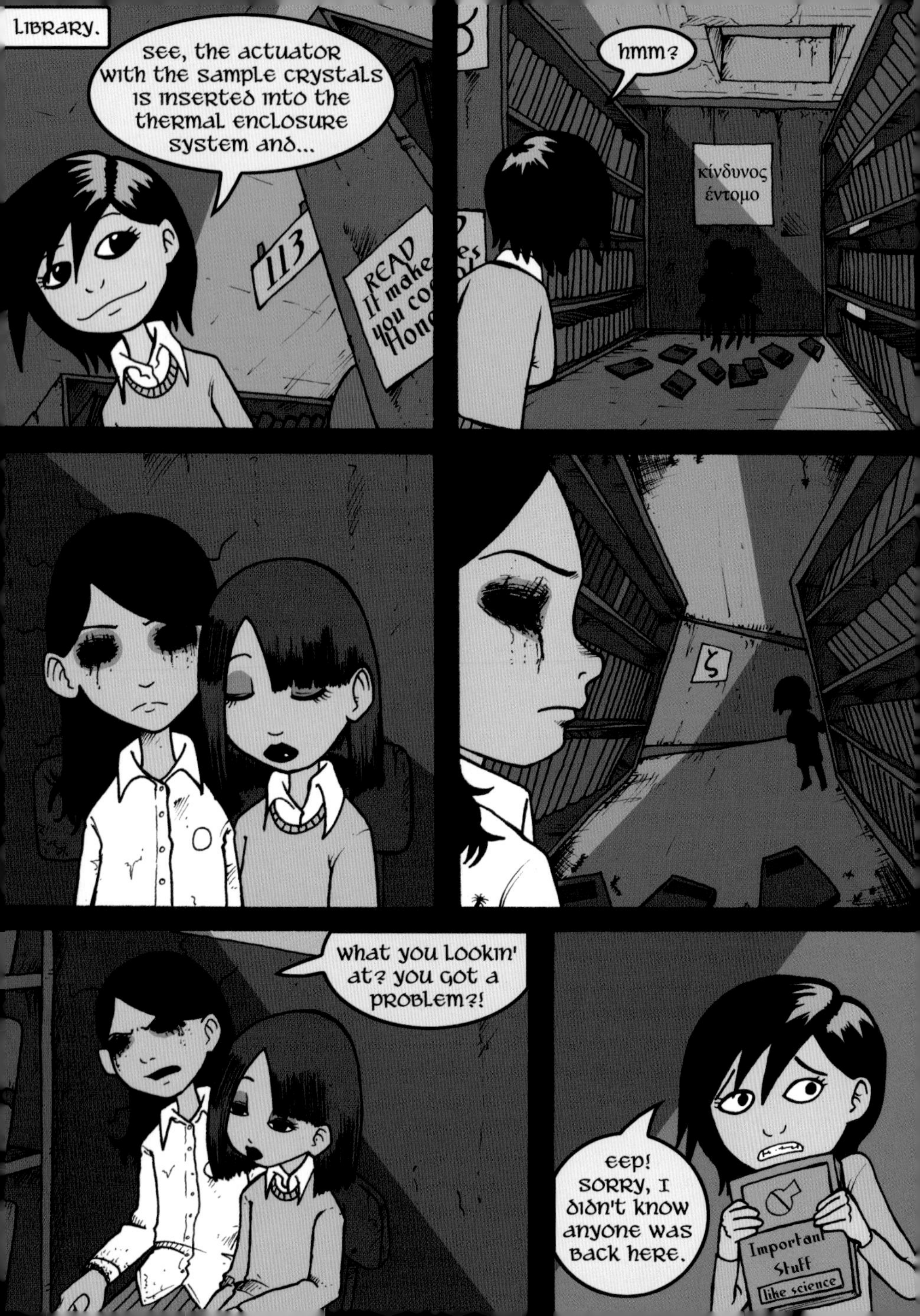
LIBRARY.
SEE, THE ACTUATOR WITH THE SAMPLE CRYSTALS IS INSERTED INTO THE THERMAL ENCLOSURE SYSTEM AND...
113
READ
HMM?
κίνδυνος
έντομο
ζ
WHAT YOU LOOKIN' AT? YOU GOT A PROBLEM?!
EEP! SORRY, I DIDN'T KNOW ANYONE WAS BACK HERE.
Important
Stuff
like science

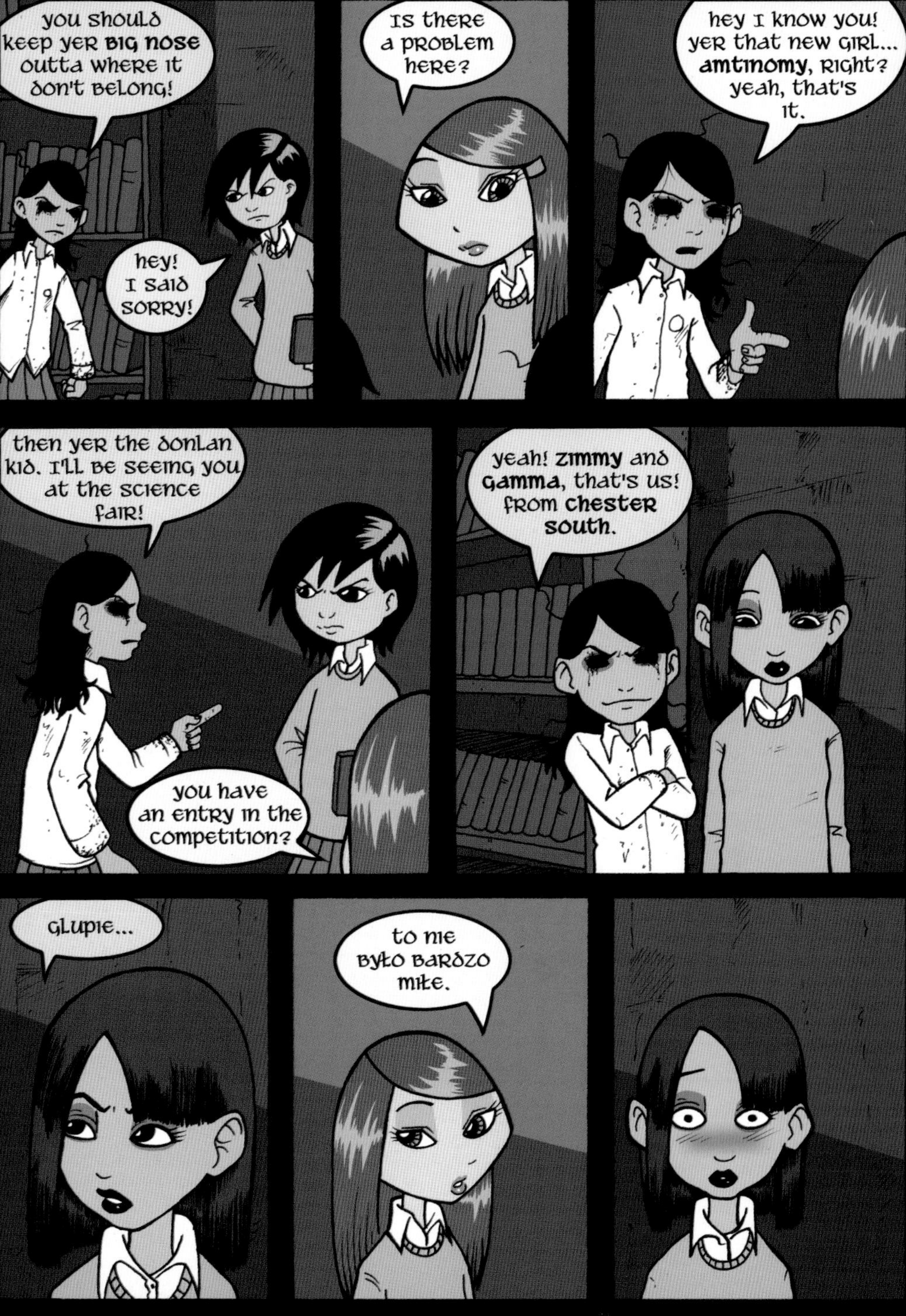
you should keep yer big nose outta where it don't belong!
hey! I said sorry!
is there a problem here?
hey I know you! yer that new girl... amtinomy, right? yeah, that's it.
then yer the donlan kid. I'll be seeing you at the science fair!
you have an entry in the competition?
yeah! zimmy and gamma, that's us! from chester south.
glupie...
to nie było bardzo miłe.

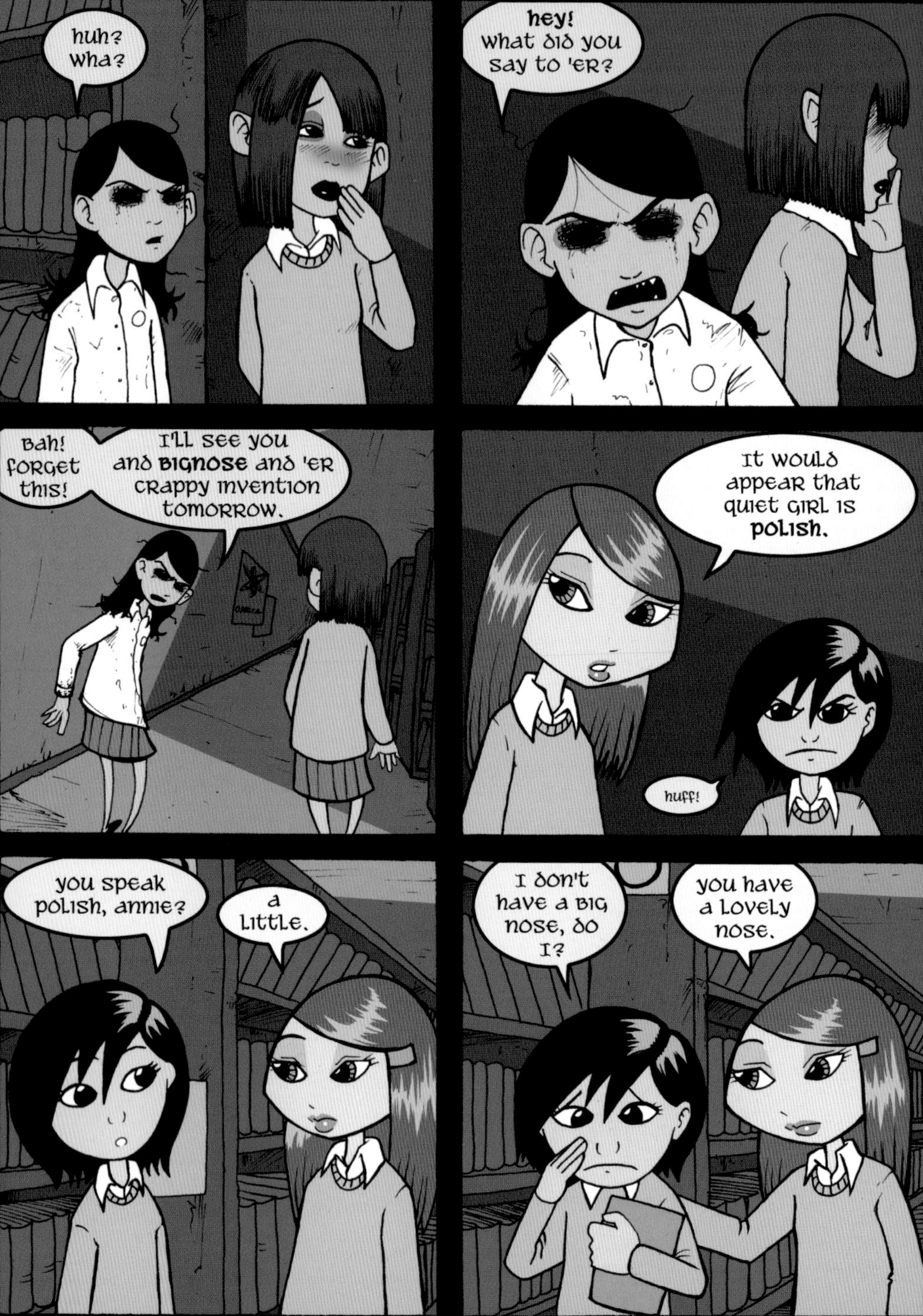
huh? wha?
hey! what did you say to 'er?
Bah! forget this!
I'll see you and BIGNOSE and 'er crappy invention tomorrow.
It would appear that quiet girl is polish.
huff!
you speak polish, annie?
a little.
I don't have a big nose, do I?
you have a lovely nose.

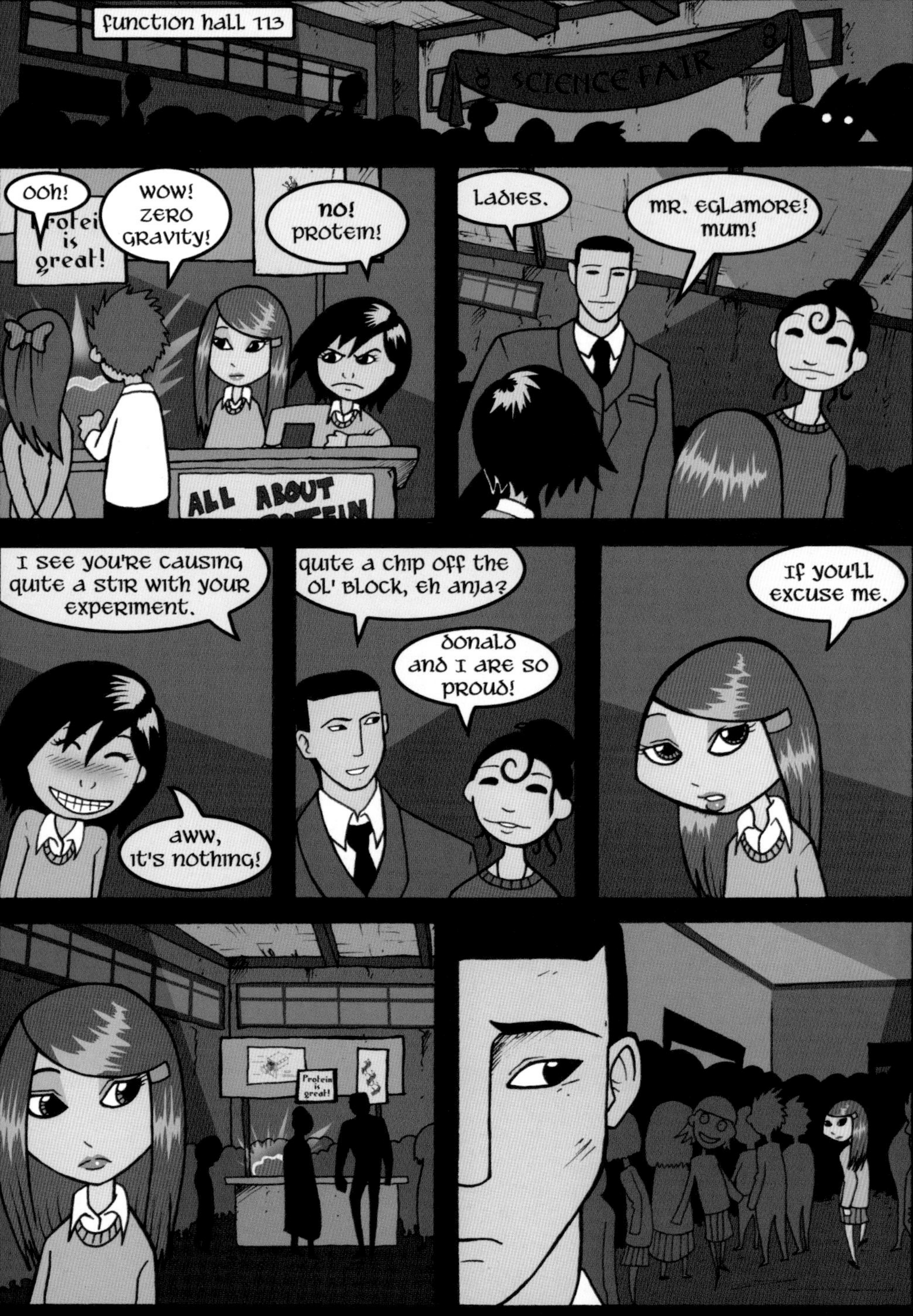
function hall 113
SCIENCE FAIR
OOH!
Protein is great!
WOW! ZERO GRAVITY!
no! PROTEIN!
ALL ABOUT
LADIES.
MR. EGLAMORE! MUM!
I SEE YOU'RE CAUSING QUITE A STIR WITH YOUR EXPERIMENT.
AWW, IT'S NOTHING!
QUITE A CHIP OFF THE OL' BLOCK, EH ANJA?
DONALD AND I ARE SO PROUD!
IF YOU'LL EXCUSE ME.
Protein is great!

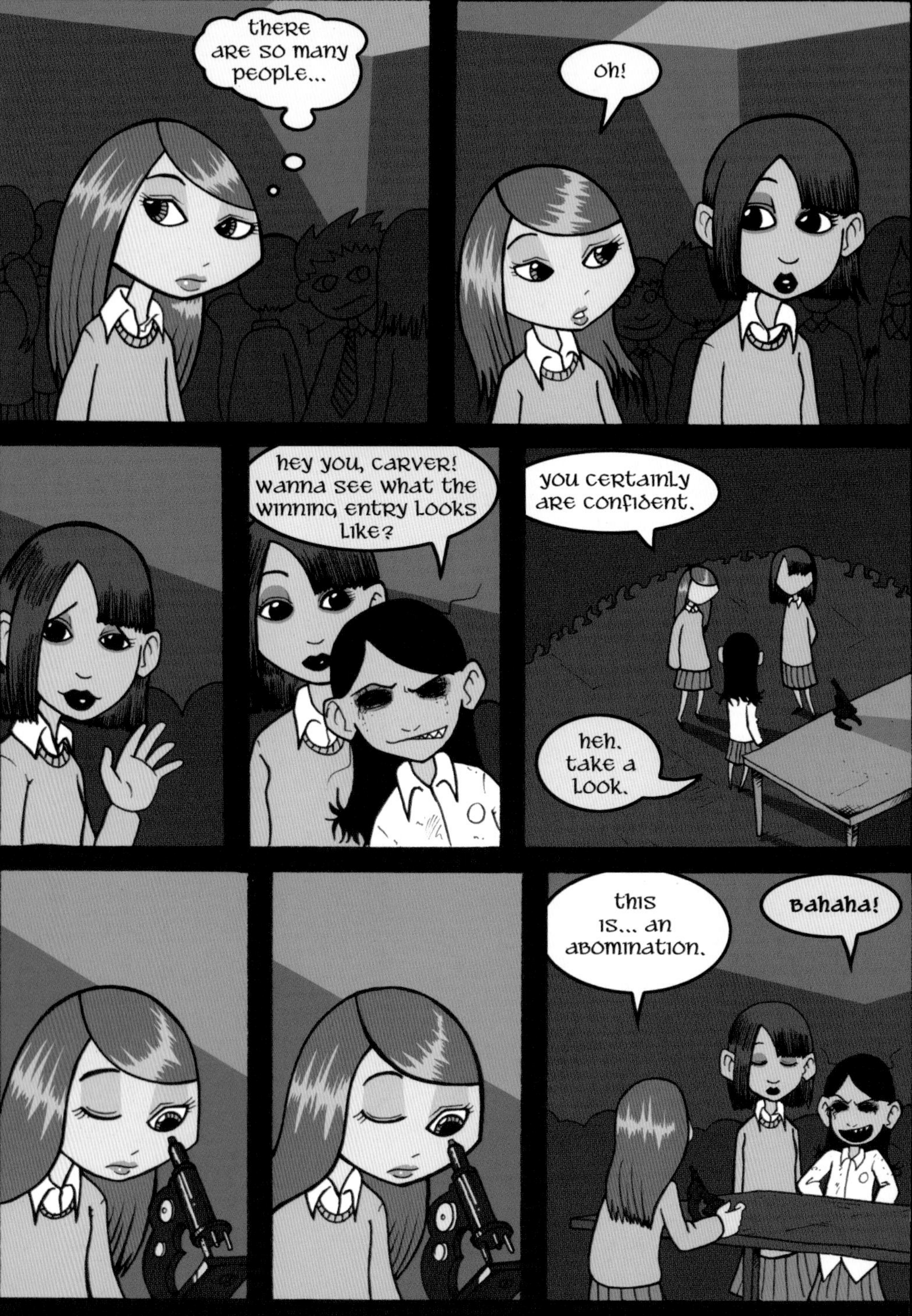
there are so many people...
oh!
hey you, carver! wanna see what the winning entry looks like?
you certainly are confident.
heh. take a look.
this is... an abomination.
Bahaha!

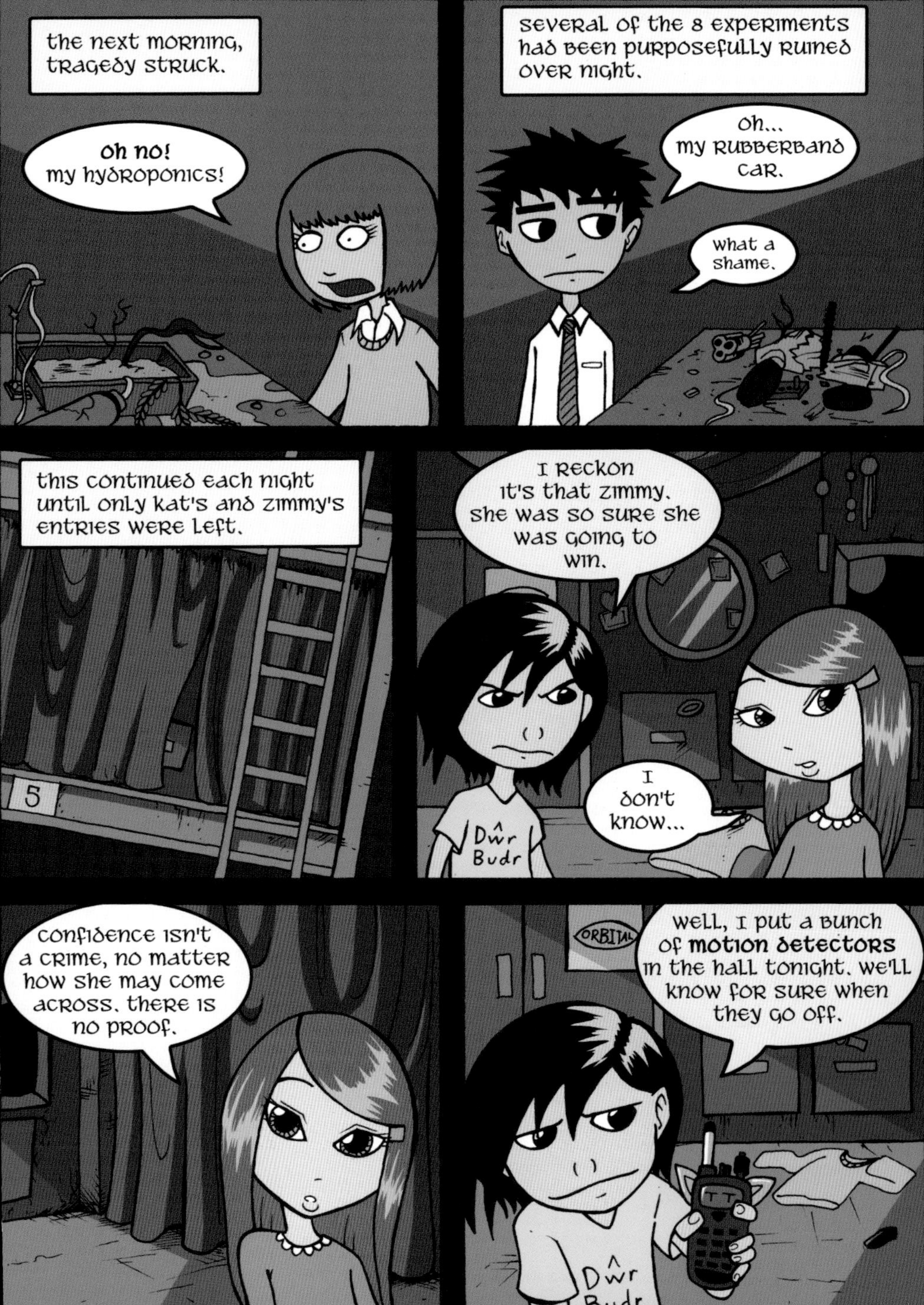
the next morning, tragedy struck.
oh no! my hydroponics!
several of the 8 experiments had been purposefully ruined over night.
oh... my rubberband car.
what a shame.
this continued each night until only kat's and zimmy's entries were left.
5
I reckon it's that zimmy. she was so sure she was going to win.
Dŵr Budr
I don't know...
confidence isn't a crime, no matter how she may come across. there is no proof.
ORBITAL
well, I put a bunch of **motion detectors** in the hall tonight. we'll know for sure when they go off.
Dŵr Budr

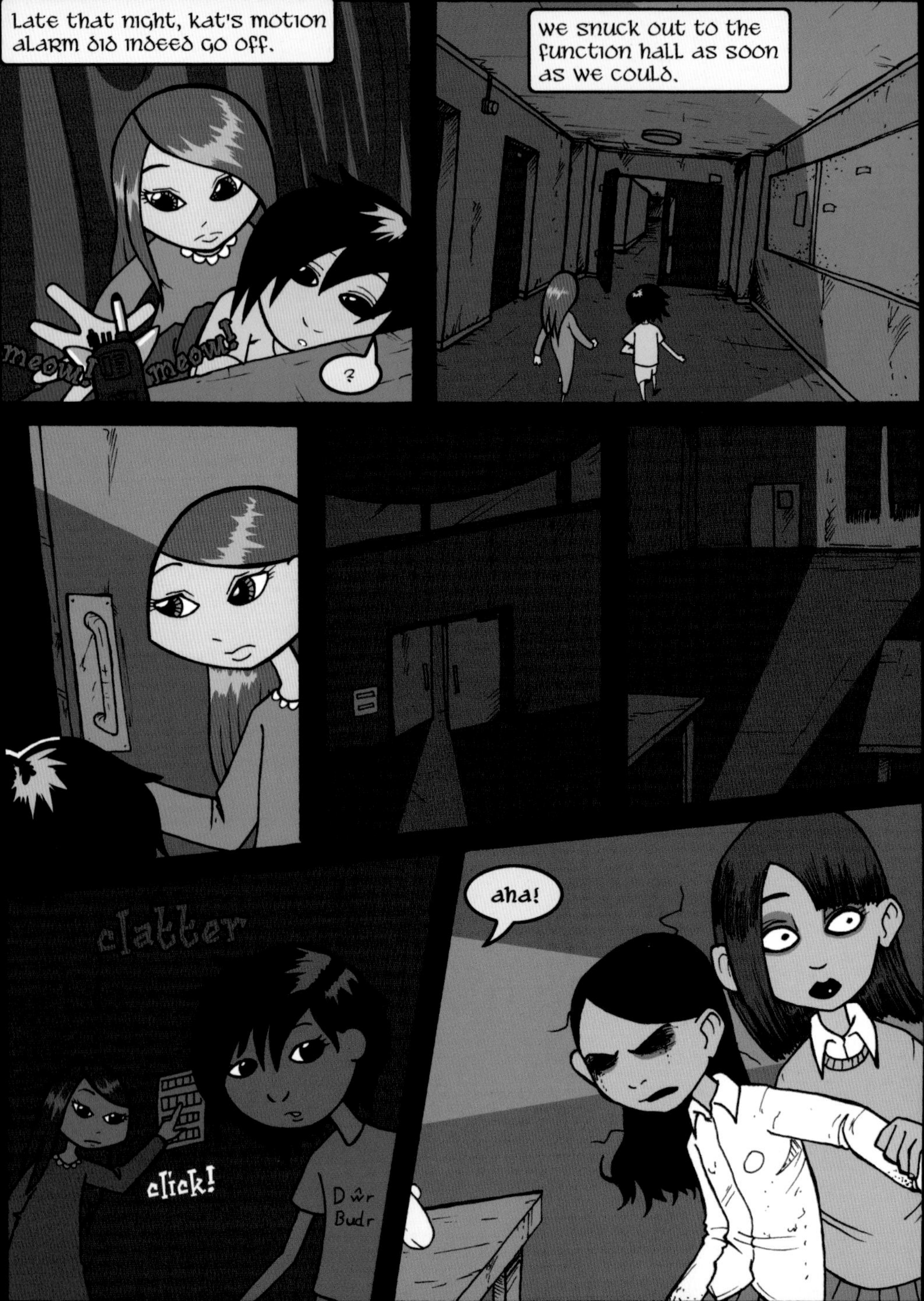
Late that night, kat's motion alarm did indeed go off.
meow! meow!
?
we snuck out to the function hall as soon as we could.
clatter
click!
aha!

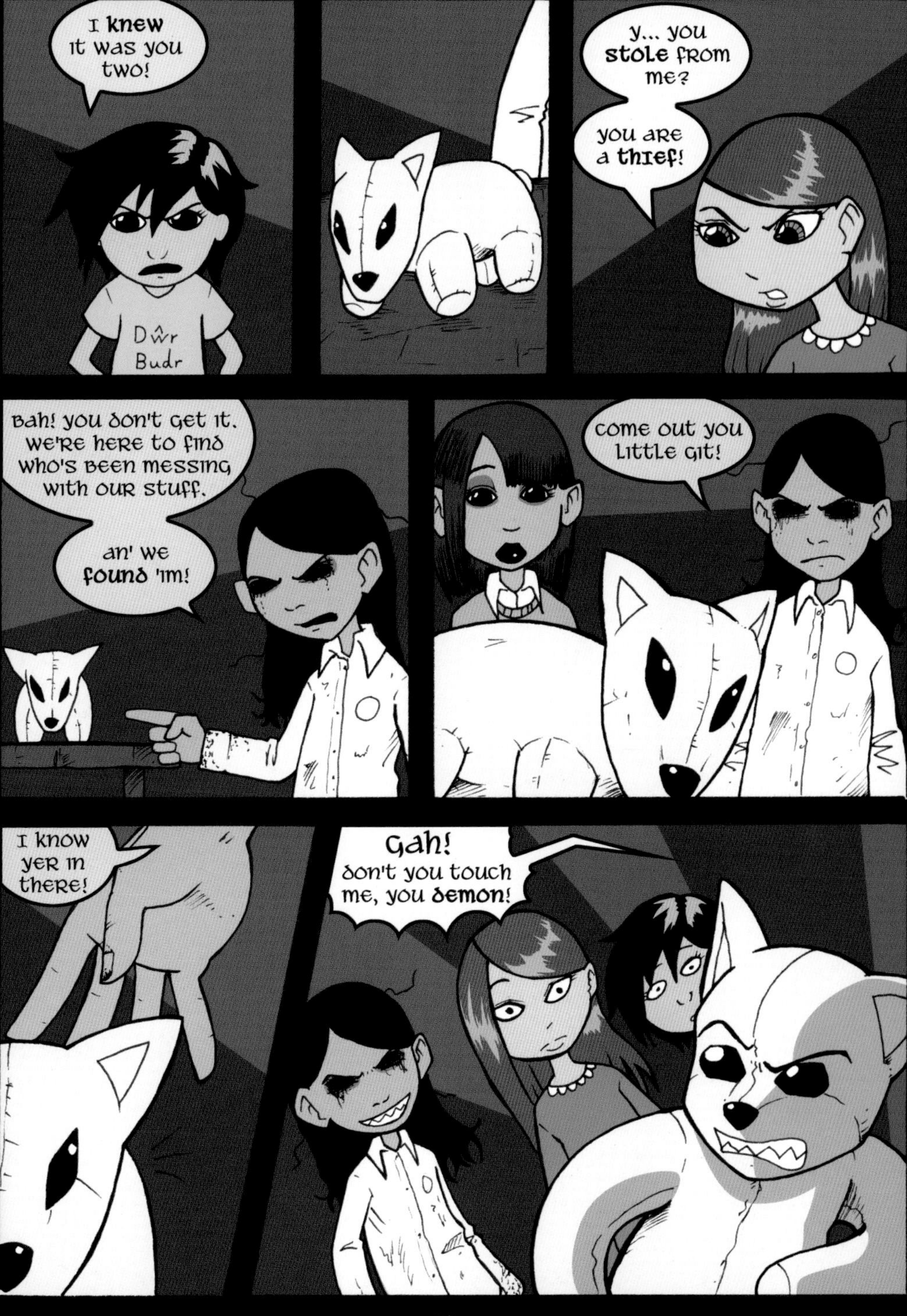
I knew it was you two!
Dŵr Budr
y... you stole from me?
you are a thief!
Bah! you don't get it. we're here to find who's been messing with our stuff.
an' we found 'im!
come out you little git!
I know yer in there!
Gah! don't you touch me, you demon!

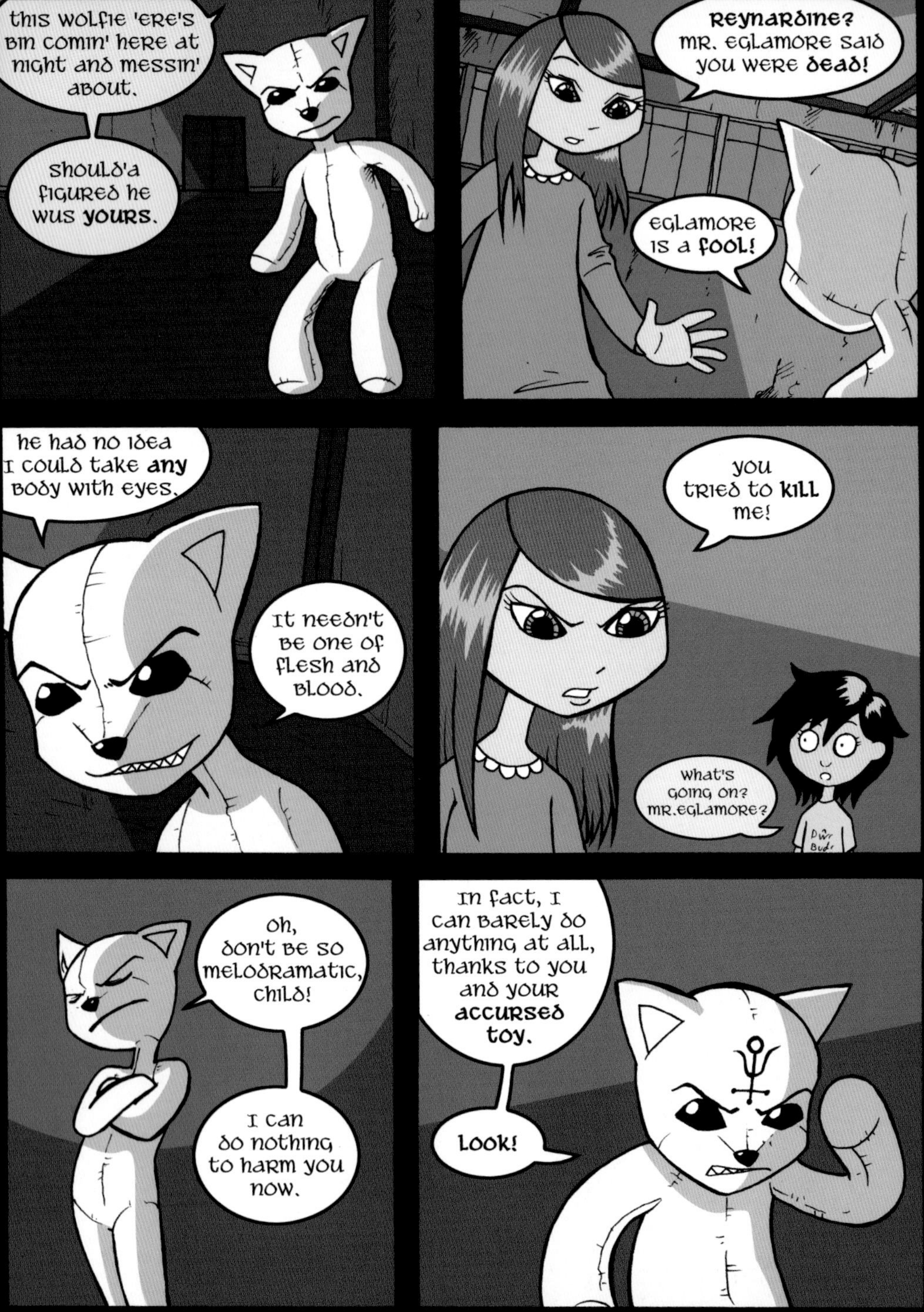
this wolfie 'ere's bin comin' here at night and messin' about.
should'a figured he wus **yours**.
Reynardine? mr. eglamore said you were **dead!**
eglamore is a **fool!**
he had no idea I could take **any** body with eyes.
It needn't be one of flesh and blood.
you tried to **kill** me!
what's going on? mr.eglamore?
oh, don't be so melodramatic, child!
I can do nothing to harm you now.
In fact, I can barely do anything at all, thanks to you and your **accursed toy.**
Look!

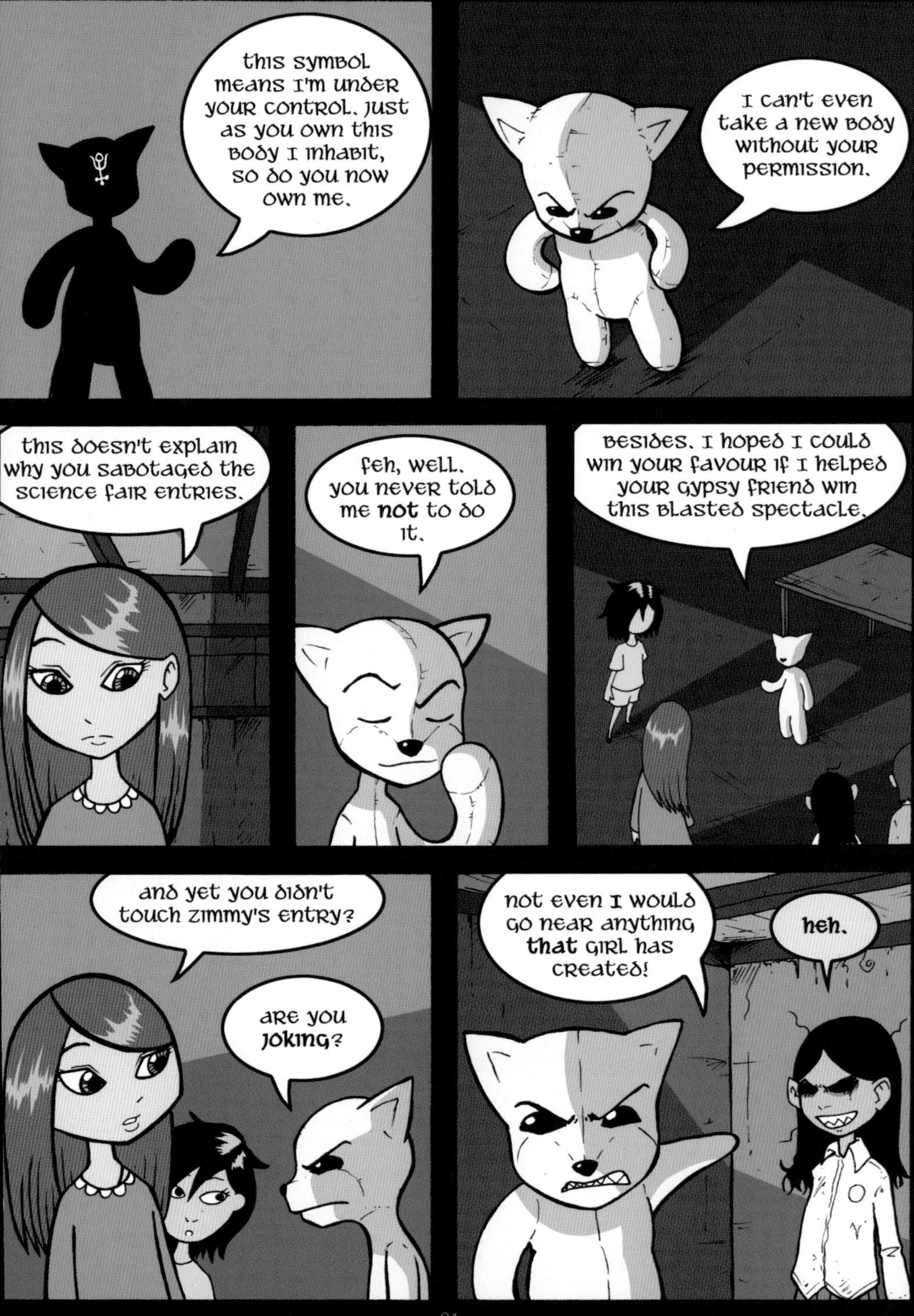
this symbol means I'm under your control. just as you own this body I inhabit, so do you now own me.
I can't even take a new body without your permission.
this doesn't explain why you sabotaged the science fair entries.
feh, well. you never told me **not** to do it.
besides. I hoped I could win your favour if I helped your gypsy friend win this blasted spectacle.
and yet you didn't touch zimmy's entry?
are you **joking**?
not even I would go near anything **that** girl has created!
heh.

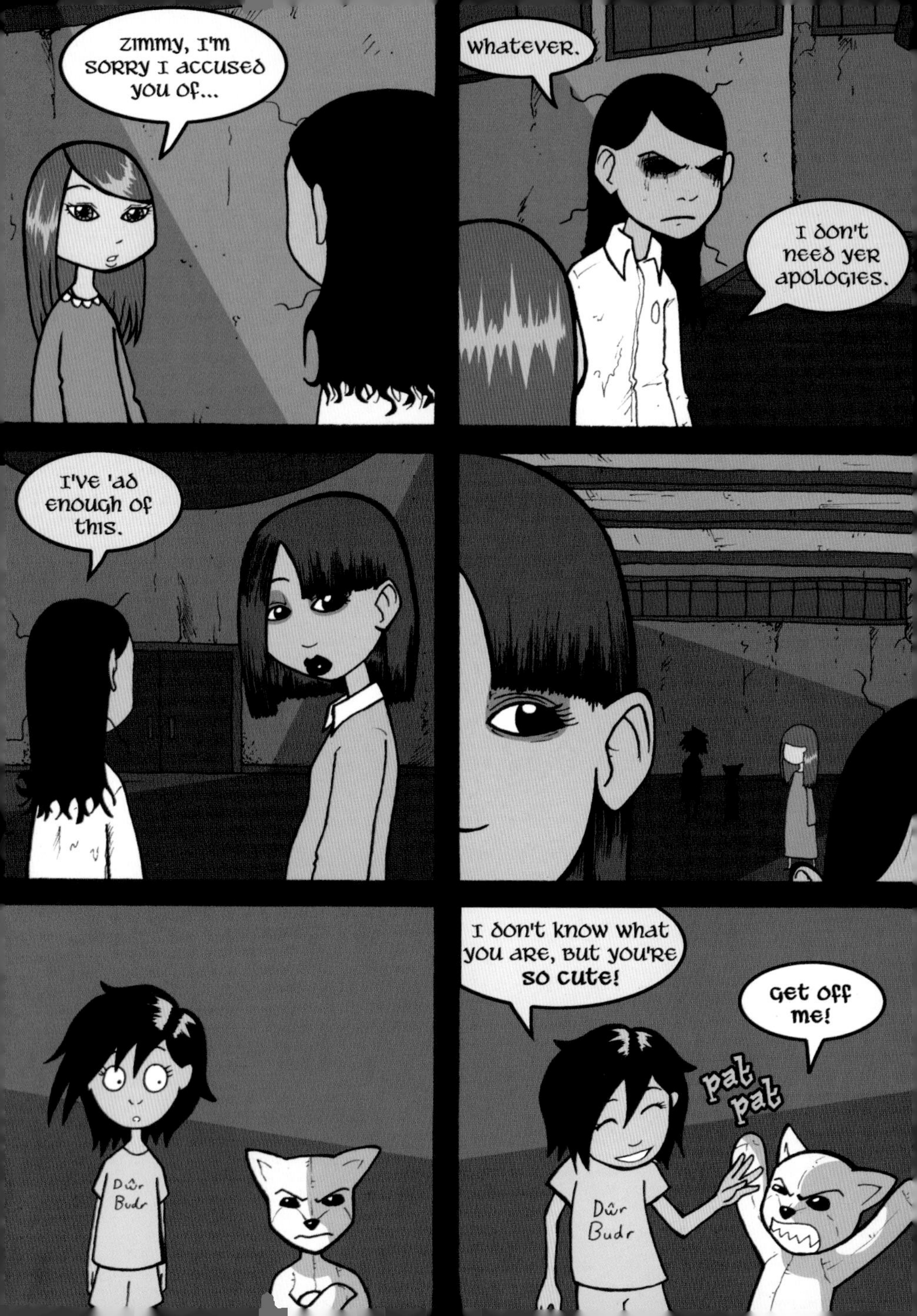

Zimmy, I'm sorry I accused you of...
Whatever.
I don't need yer apologies.
I've 'ad enough of this.
I don't know what you are, but you're so cute!
Get off me!
pat pat
Dŵr Budr

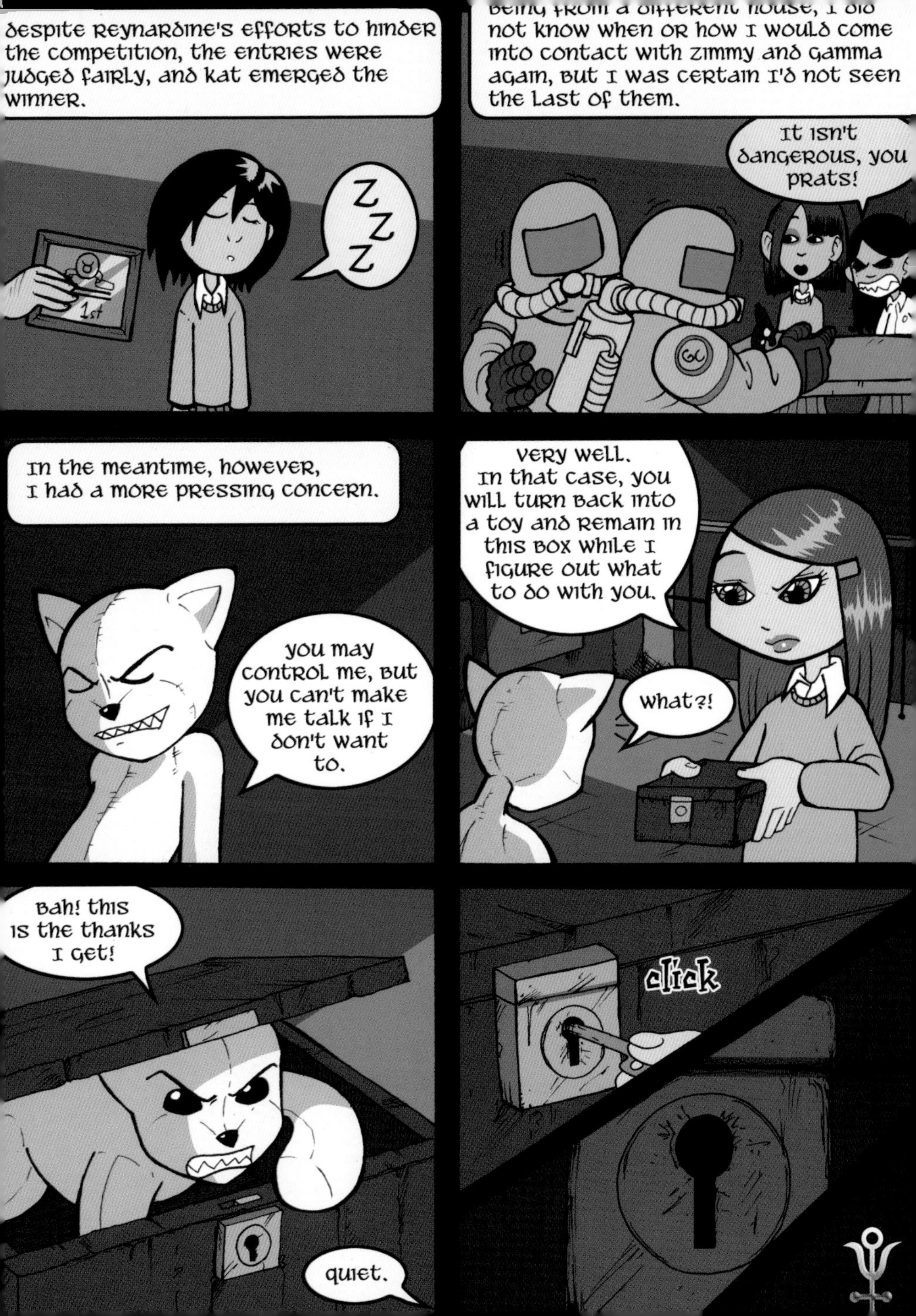
despite Reynardine's efforts to hinder the competition, the entries were judged fairly, and kat emerged the winner.
1st
Z Z Z
being from a different house, I did not know when or how I would come into contact with zimmy and gamma again, but I was certain I'd not seen the last of them.
It isn't dangerous, you prats!
In the meantime, however, I had a more pressing concern.
you may control me, but you can't make me talk if I don't want to.
very well. In that case, you will turn back into a toy and remain in this box while I figure out what to do with you.
What?!
Bah! this is the thanks I get!
quiet.
click

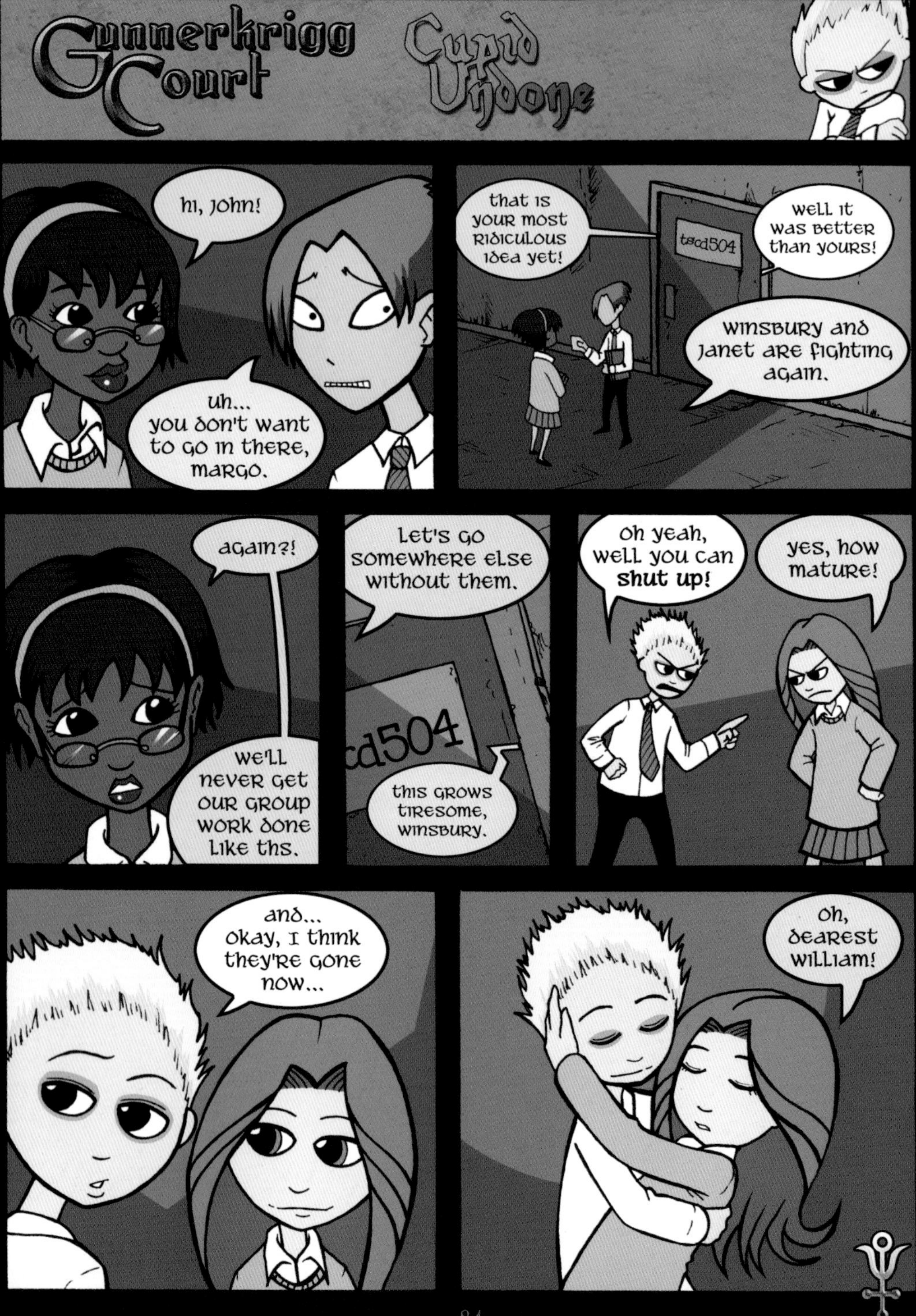
Gunnerkrigg Court
Cupid Undone
hi, John!
uh... you don't want to go in there, margo.
that is your most ridiculous idea yet!
tscd504
well it was better than yours!
winsbury and janet are fighting again.
again?!
we'll never get our group work done like ths.
let's go somewhere else without them.
cd504
this grows tiresome, winsbury.
oh yeah, well you can **shut up!**
yes, how mature!
and... okay, I think they're gone now...
oh, dearest william!

Gunnerkrigg Court

Chapter 6:

A Handful of Dirt

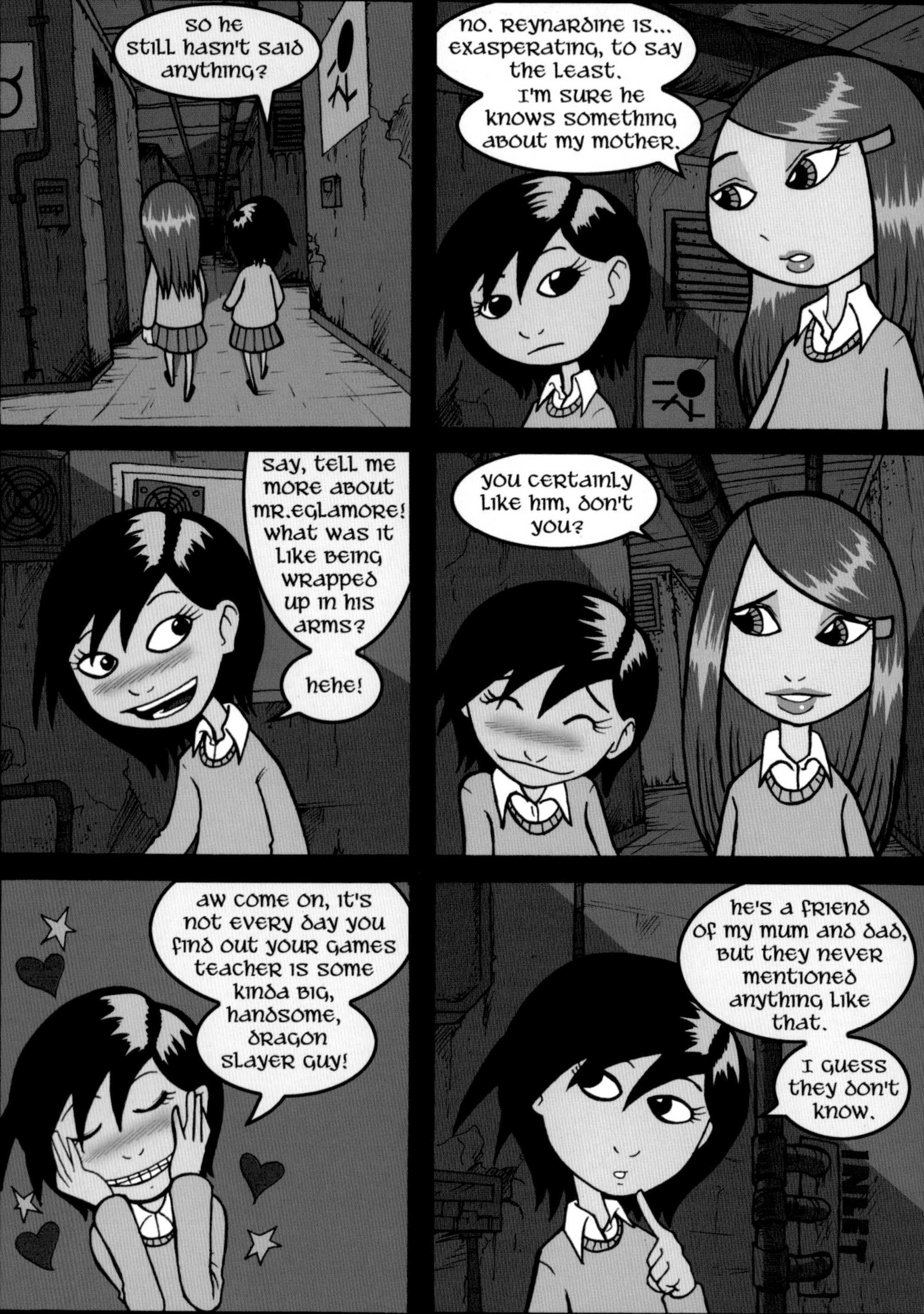
so he still hasn't said anything?
no. Reynardine is... exasperating, to say the least.
I'm sure he knows something about my mother.
say, tell me more about mr.eglamore! what was it like being wrapped up in his arms?
hehe!
you certainly like him, don't you?
aw come on, it's not every day you find out your games teacher is some kinda big, handsome, dragon slayer guy!
he's a friend of my mum and dad, but they never mentioned anything like that.
I guess they don't know.

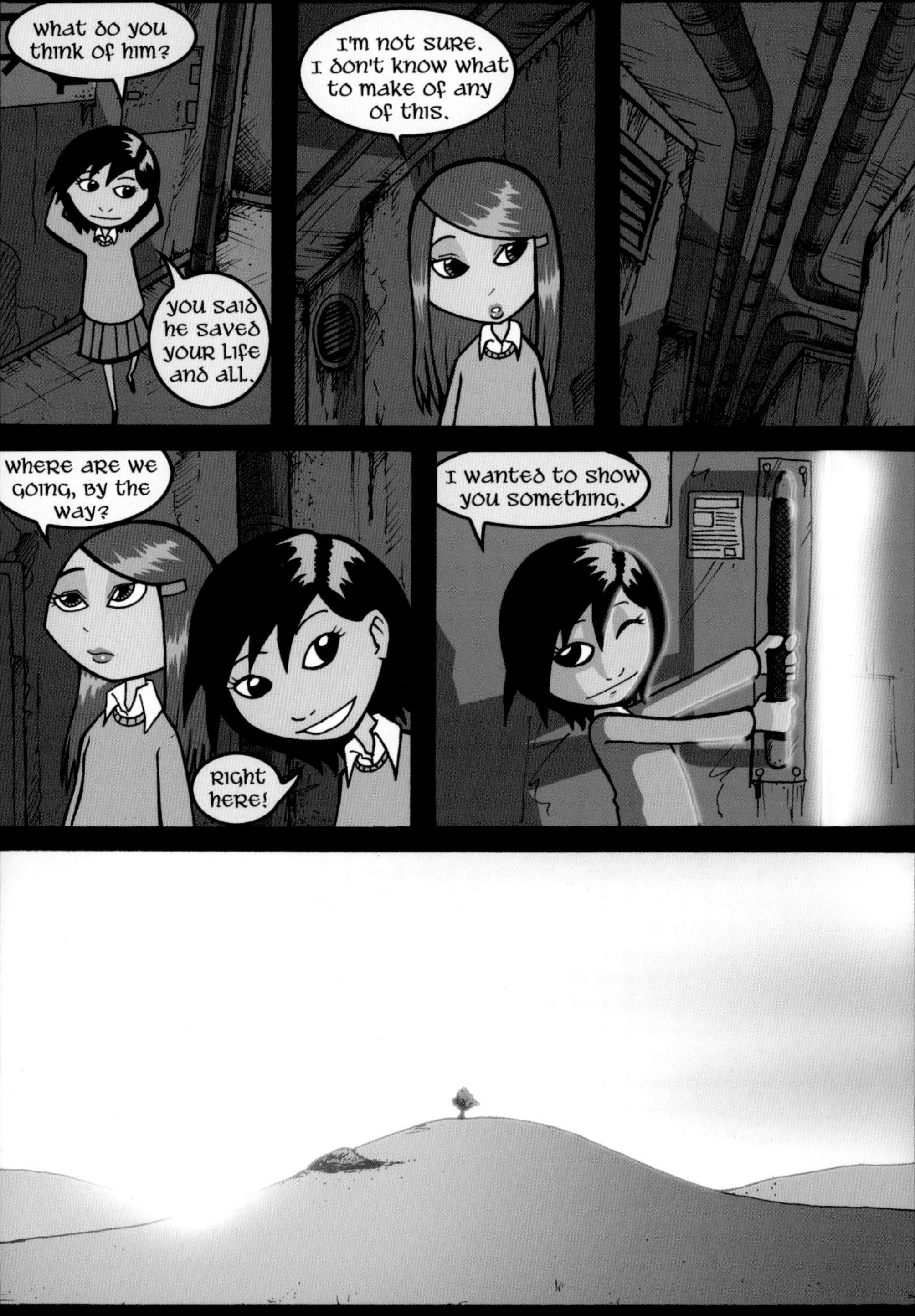
what do you think of him?
you said he saved your life and all.
I'm not sure. I don't know what to make of any of this.
where are we going, by the way?
Right here!
I wanted to show you something.

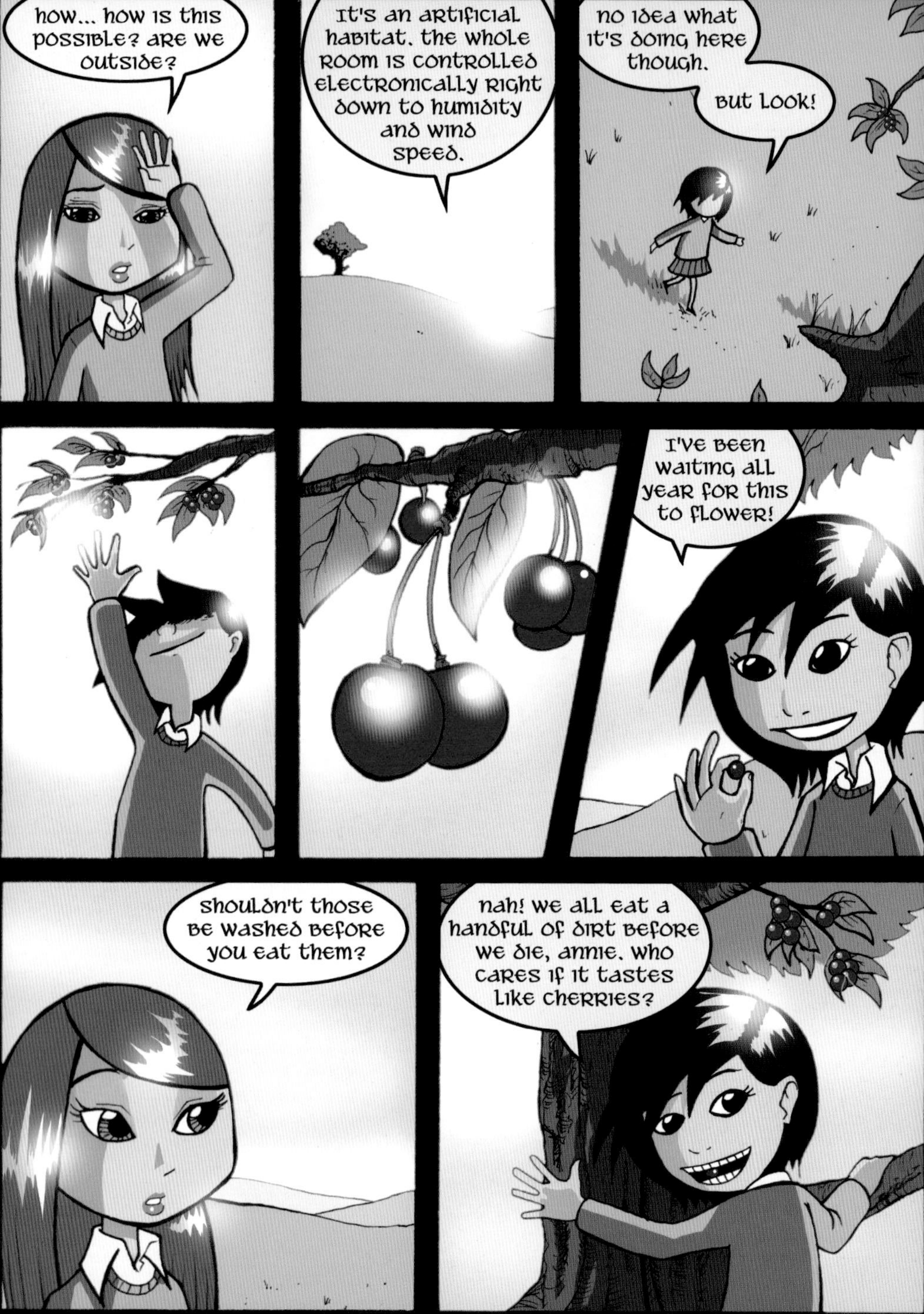
how... how is this possible? are we outside?
It's an artificial habitat. the whole room is controlled electronically right down to humidity and wind speed.
no idea what it's doing here though.
But look!
I've been waiting all year for this to flower!
shouldn't those be washed before you eat them?
nah! we all eat a handful of dirt before we die, annie. who cares if it tastes like cherries?

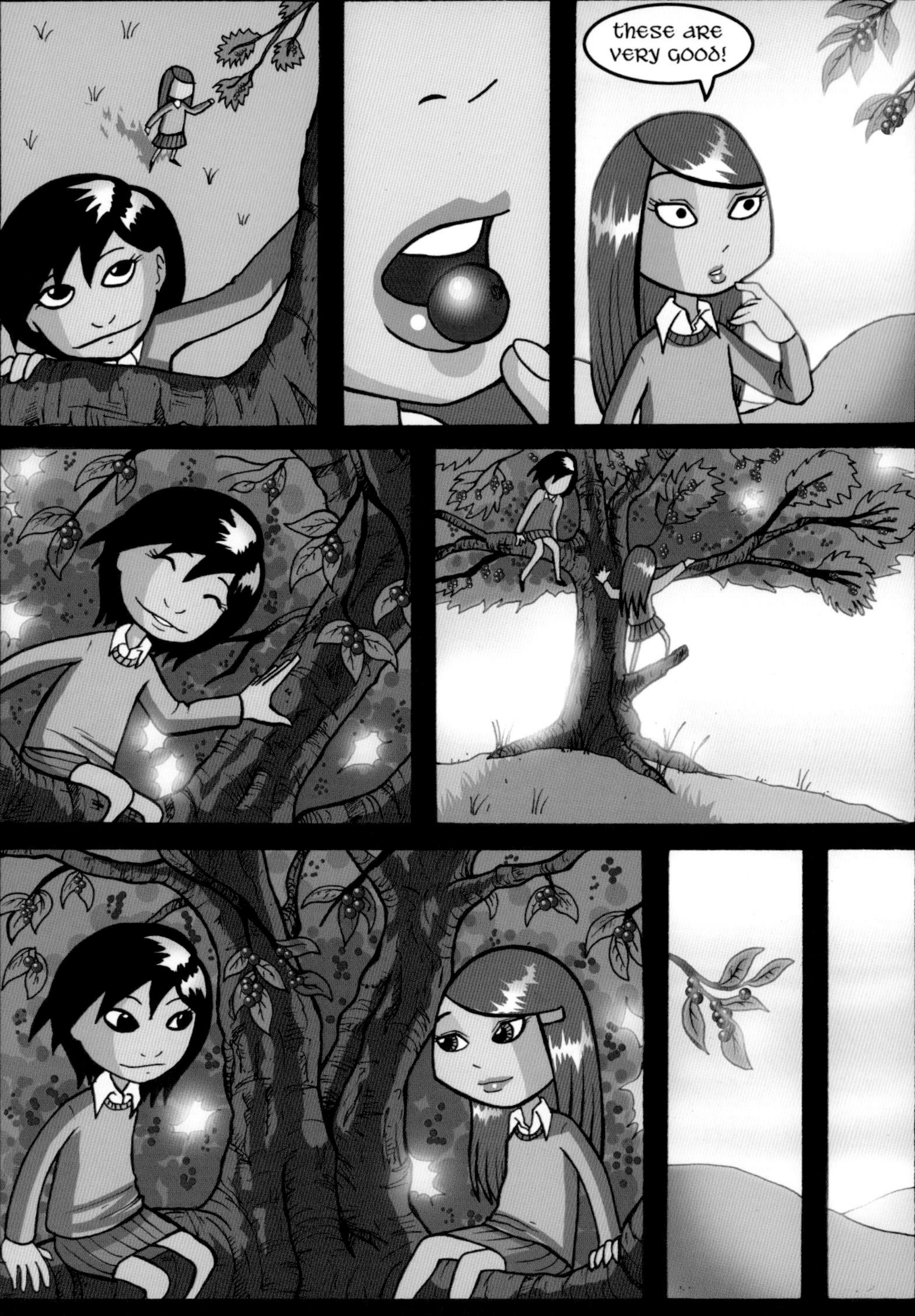
these are very good!

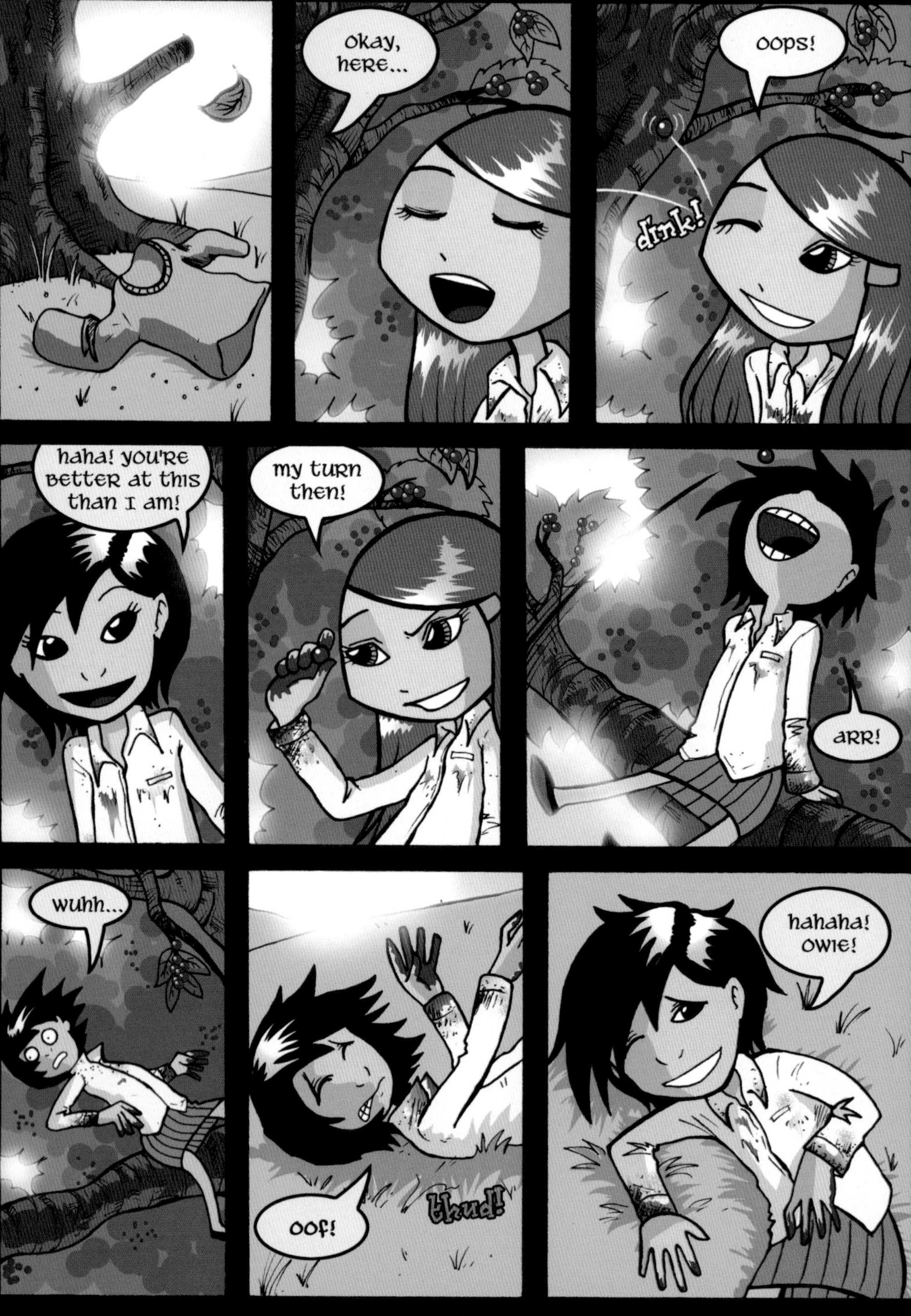
okay, here...
oops!
dink!
haha! you're better at this than I am!
my turn then!
arr!
wuhh...
oof!
thud!!
hahaha! owie!

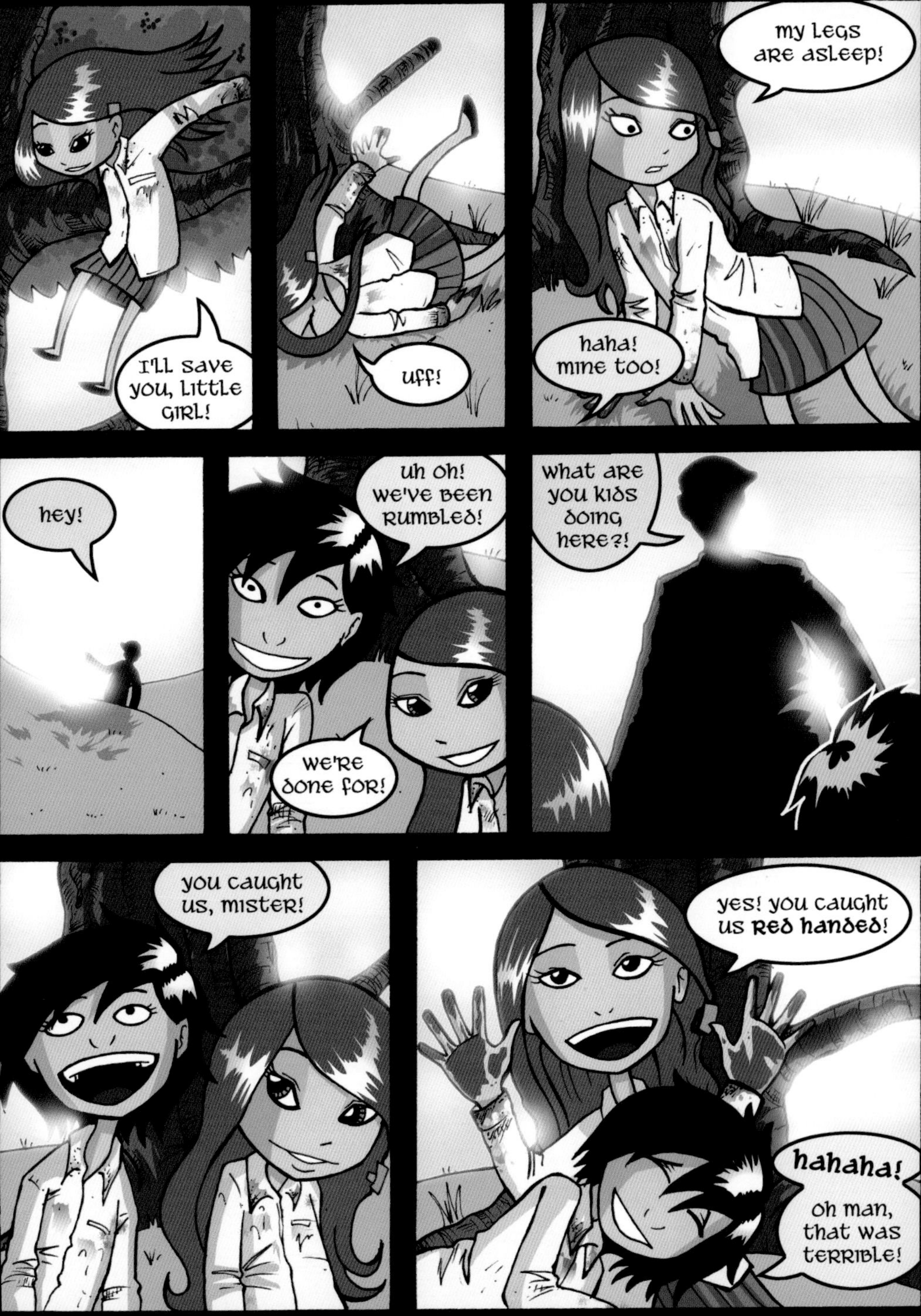
I'll save you, little girl!
uff!
my legs are asleep!
haha! mine too!
hey!
uh oh! we've been rumbled!
we're done for!
what are you kids doing here?!
you caught us, mister!
yes! you caught us red handed!
hahaha!
oh man, that was terrible!

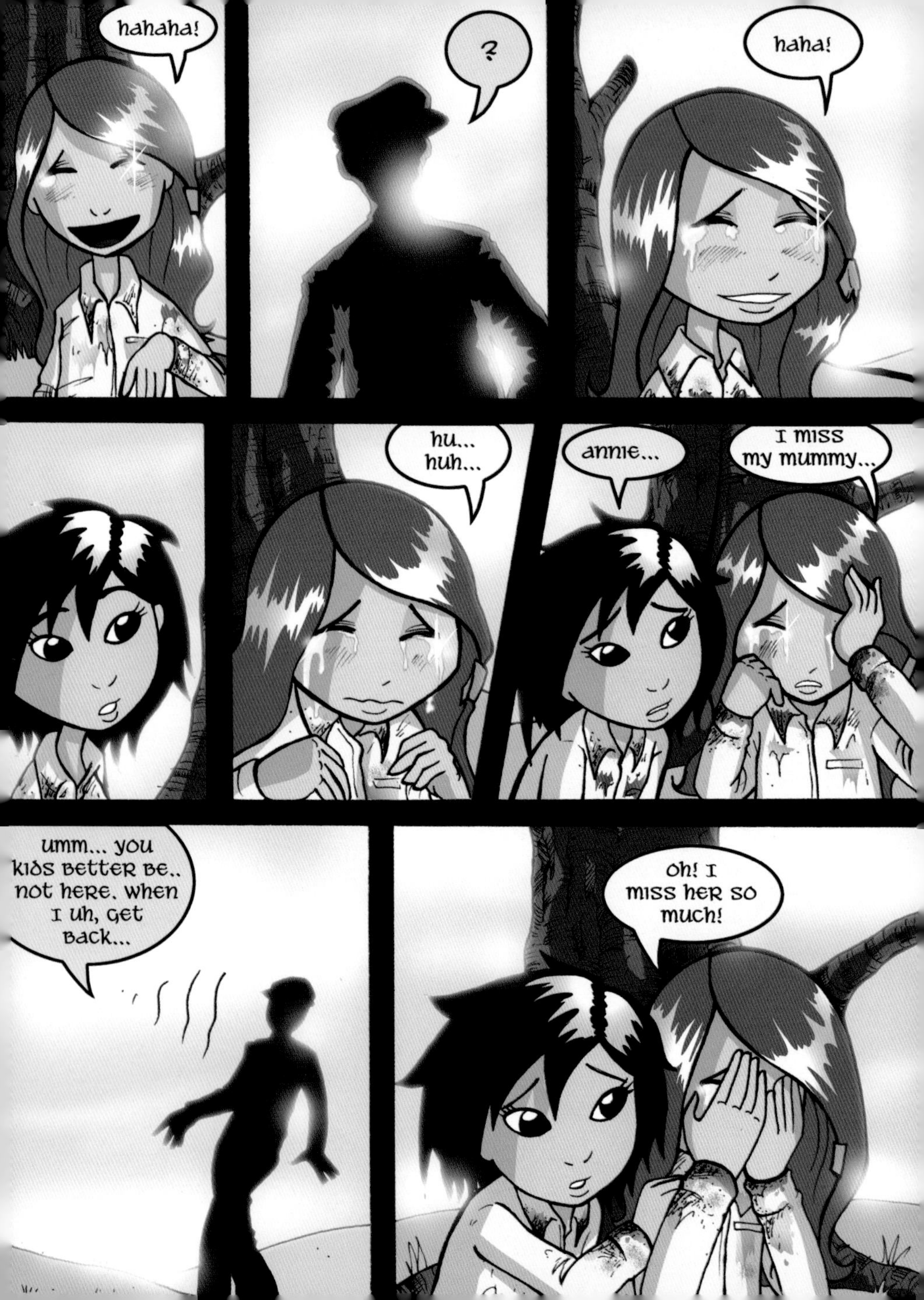
hahaha!
?
haha!
hu... huh...
annie...
I miss my mummy...
umm... you kids better be.. not here. when I uh, get back...
oh! I miss her so much!

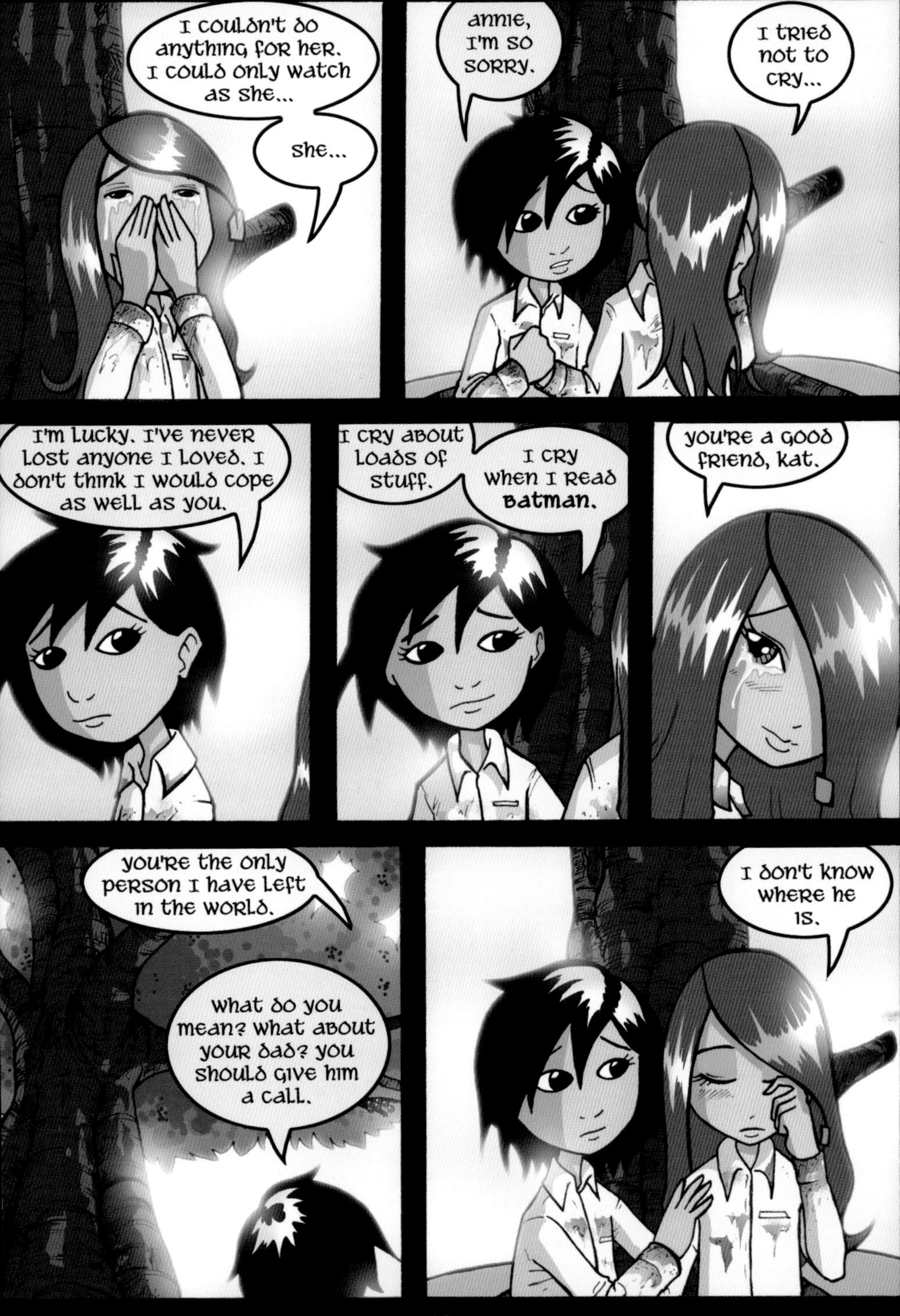
I couldn't do anything for her. I could only watch as she...
she...
annie, I'm so sorry.
I tried not to cry...
I'm lucky. I've never lost anyone I loved. I don't think I would cope as well as you.
I cry about loads of stuff.
I cry when I read Batman.
you're a good friend, kat.
you're the only person I have left in the world.
what do you mean? what about your dad? you should give him a call.
I don't know where he is.

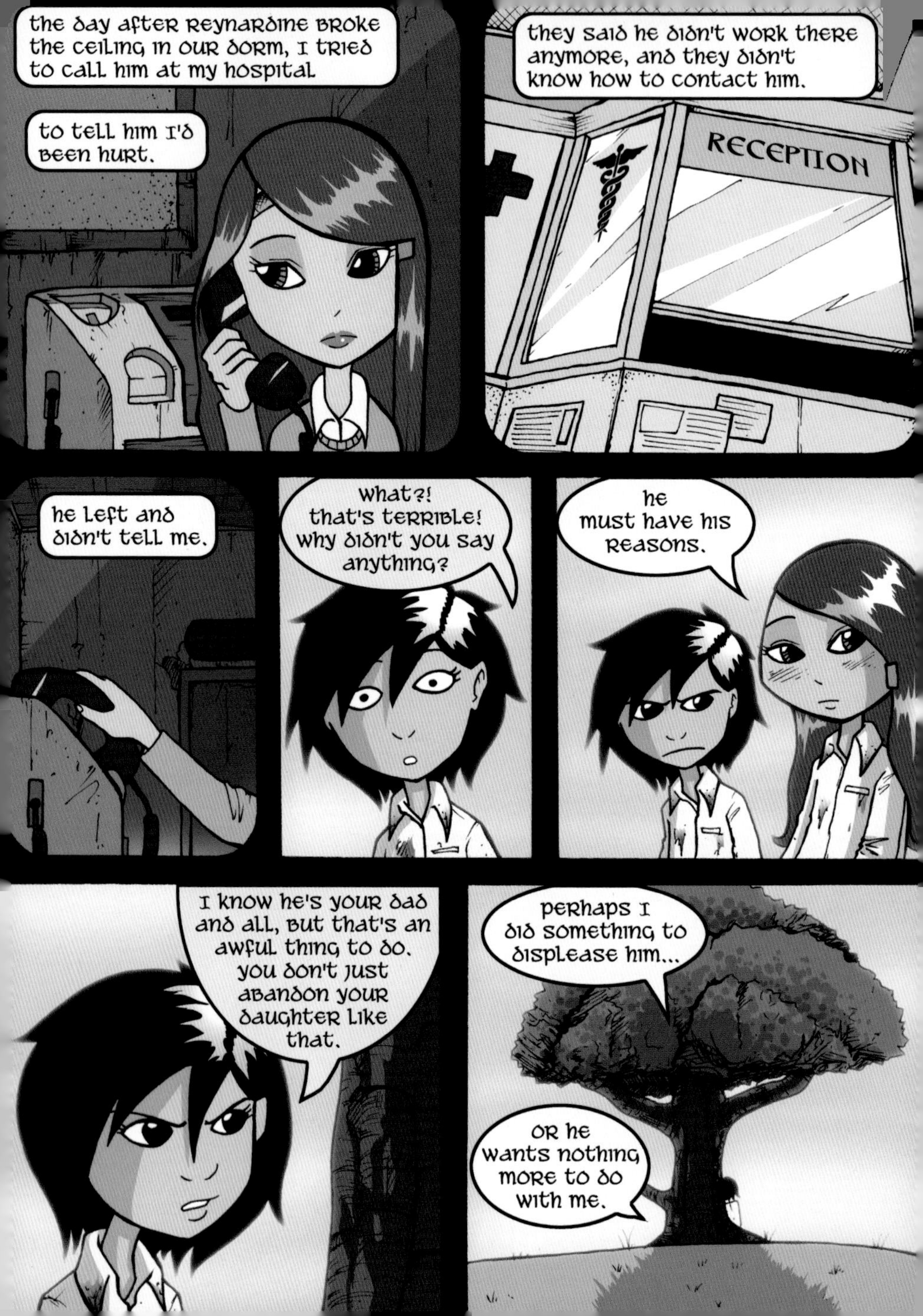
the day after Reynardine broke the ceiling in our dorm, I tried to call him at my hospital
to tell him I'd been hurt.
they said he didn't work there anymore, and they didn't know how to contact him.
RECEPTION
he left and didn't tell me.
What?! that's terrible! why didn't you say anything?
he must have his reasons.
I know he's your dad and all, but that's an awful thing to do. you don't just abandon your daughter like that.
perhaps I did something to displease him...
or he wants nothing more to do with me.

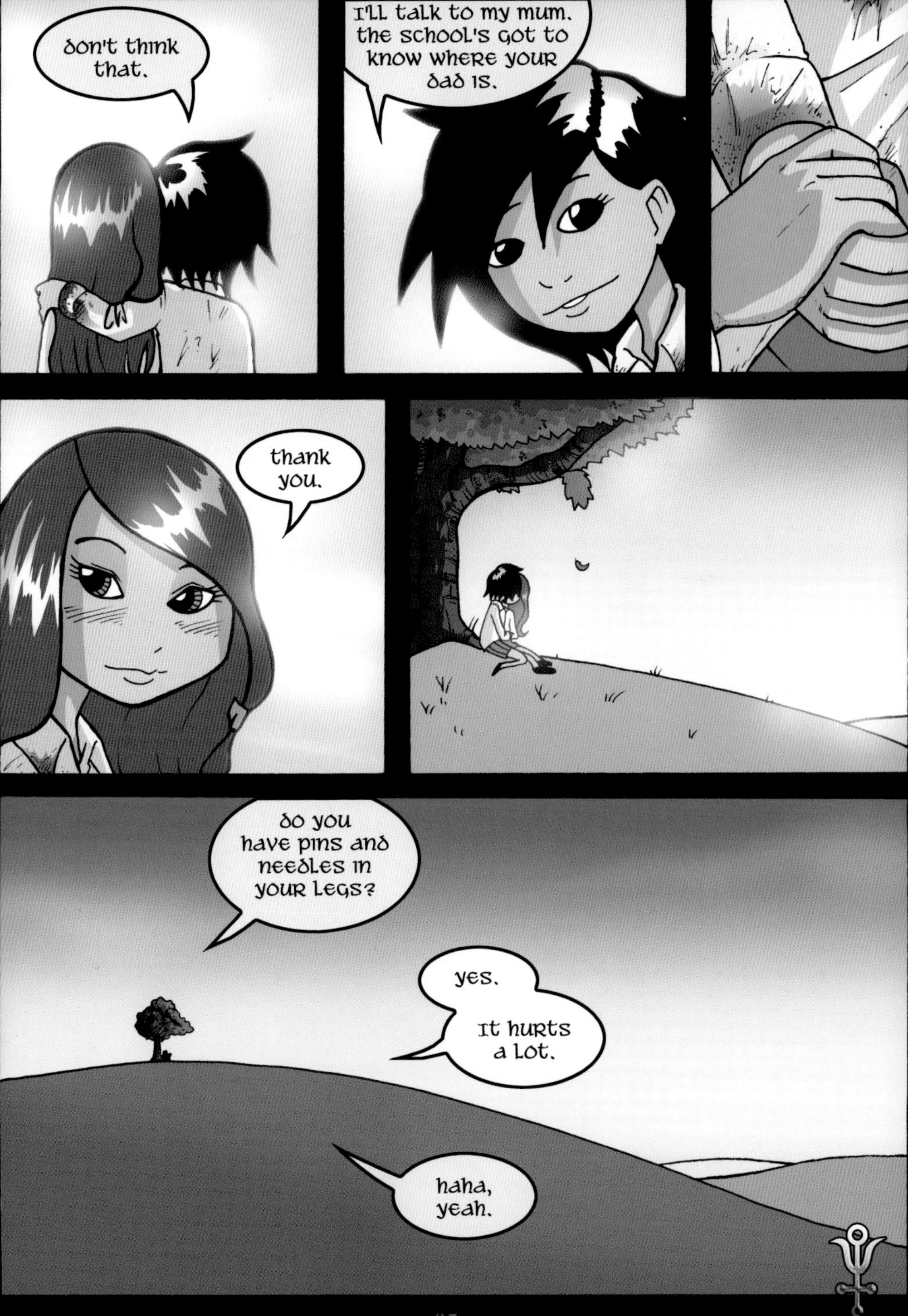
don't think that.
I'll talk to my mum. the school's got to know where your dad is.
thank you.
do you have pins and needles in your legs?
yes.
it hurts a lot.
haha, yeah.

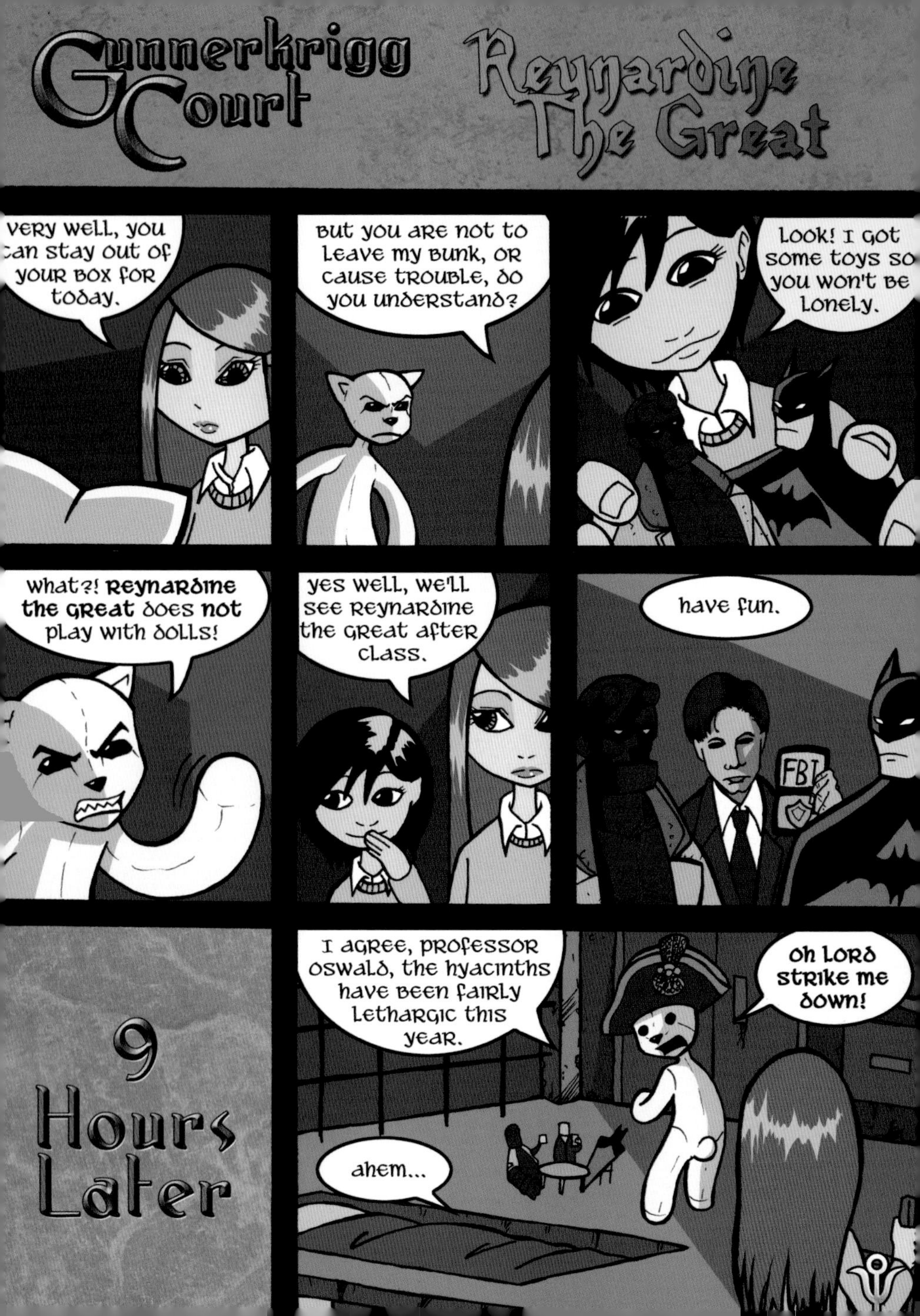
Gunnerkrigg Court
Reynardine The Great
very well, you can stay out of your box for today.
but you are not to leave my bunk, or cause trouble, do you understand?
Look! I got some toys so you won't be lonely.
what?! Reynardine the great does not play with dolls!
yes well, we'll see Reynardine the great after class.
have fun.
FBI
9 Hours Later
I agree, professor oswald, the hyacinths have been fairly lethargic this year.
Oh Lord strike me down!
ahem...

Gunnerkrigg Court

Chapter 7:

Of New And Old

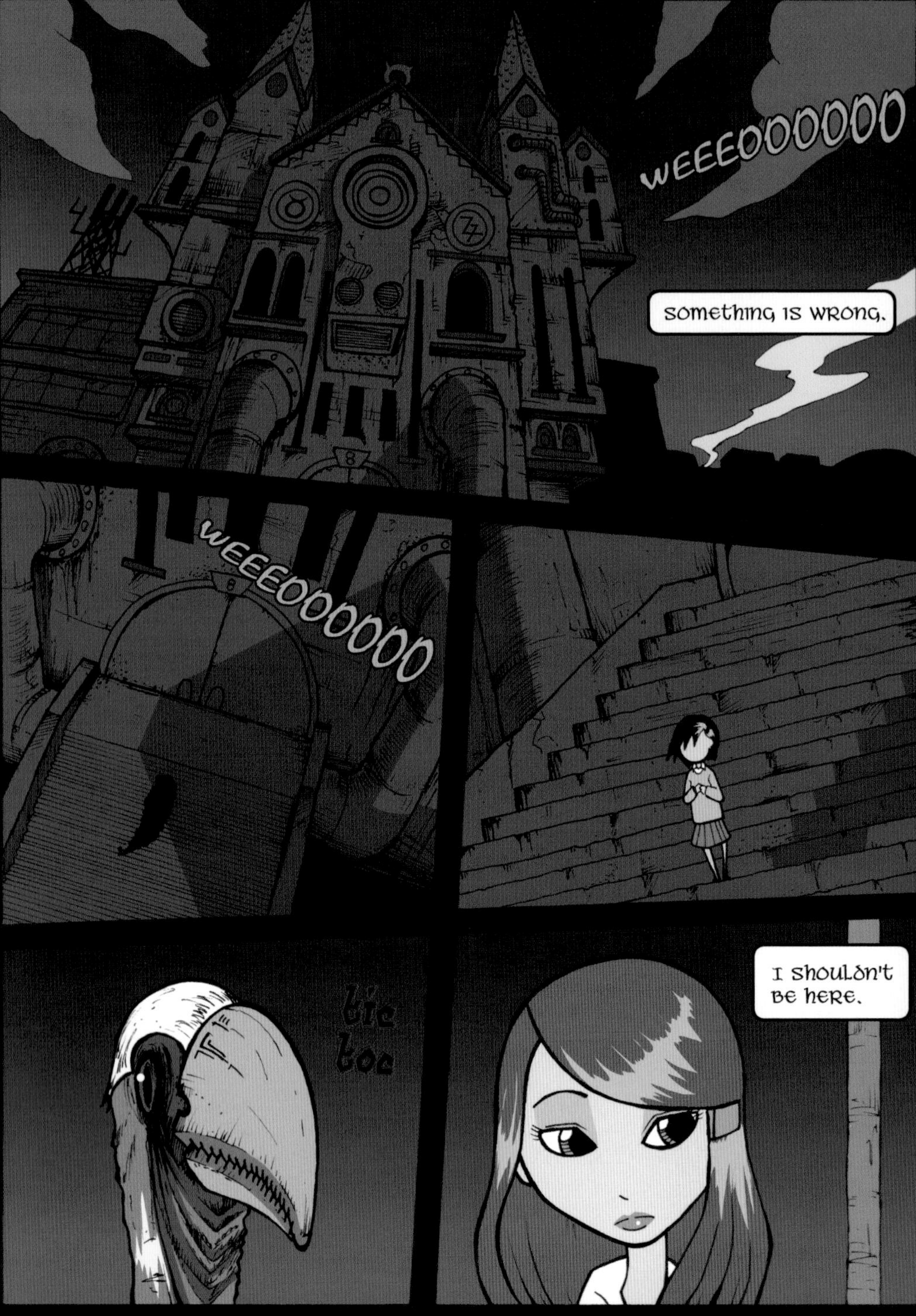
WEEEOOOOOO
something is wrong.
WEEEOOOOOO
tic
toc
I shouldn't be here.

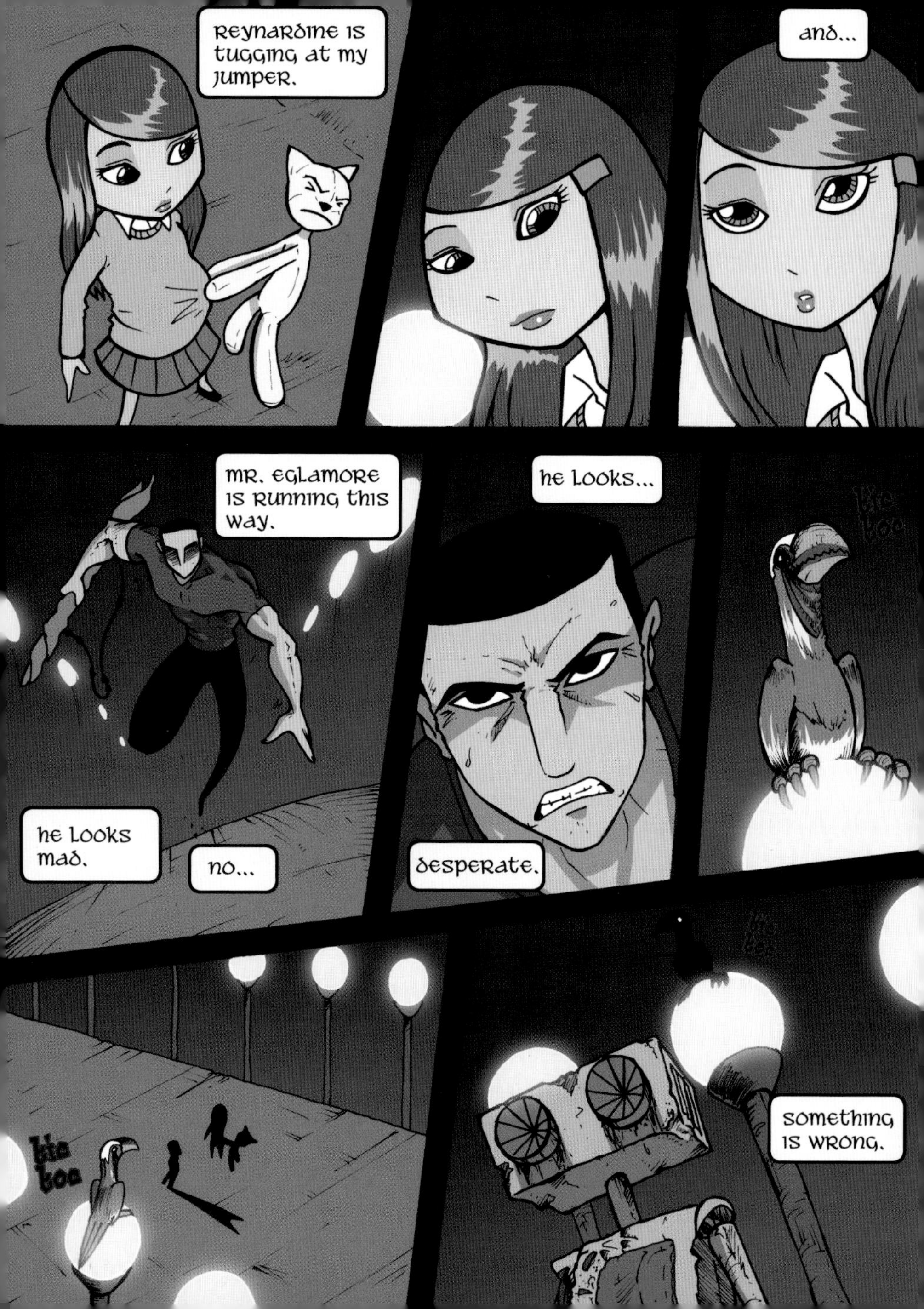
Reynardine is tugging at my jumper.
and...
Mr. Eglamore is running this way.
he looks...
he looks mad.
no...
desperate.
something is wrong.

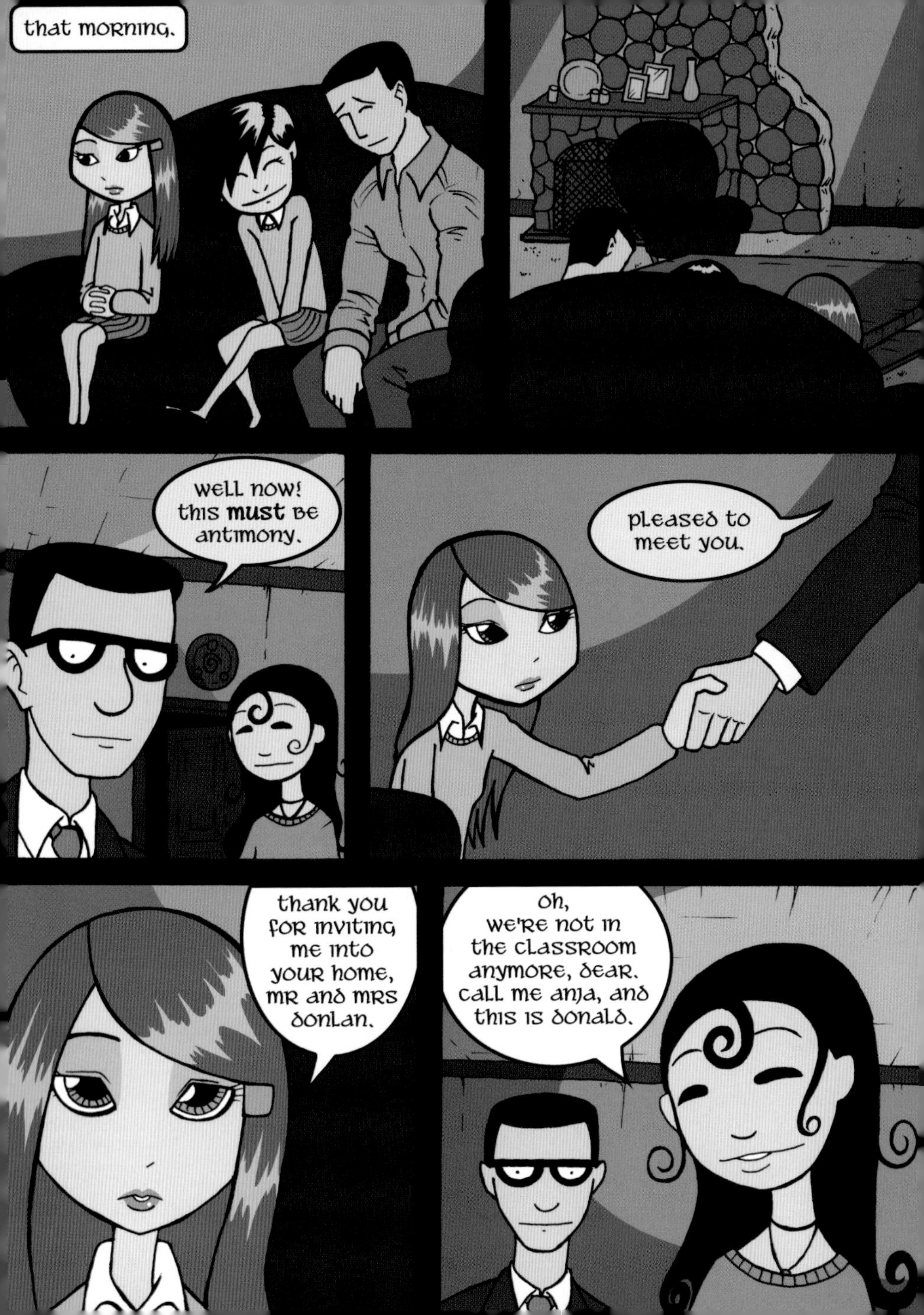
that morning.
well now! this **must** be antimony.
pleased to meet you.
thank you for inviting me into your home, mr and mrs donlan.
oh, we're not in the classroom anymore, dear. call me anja, and this is donald.

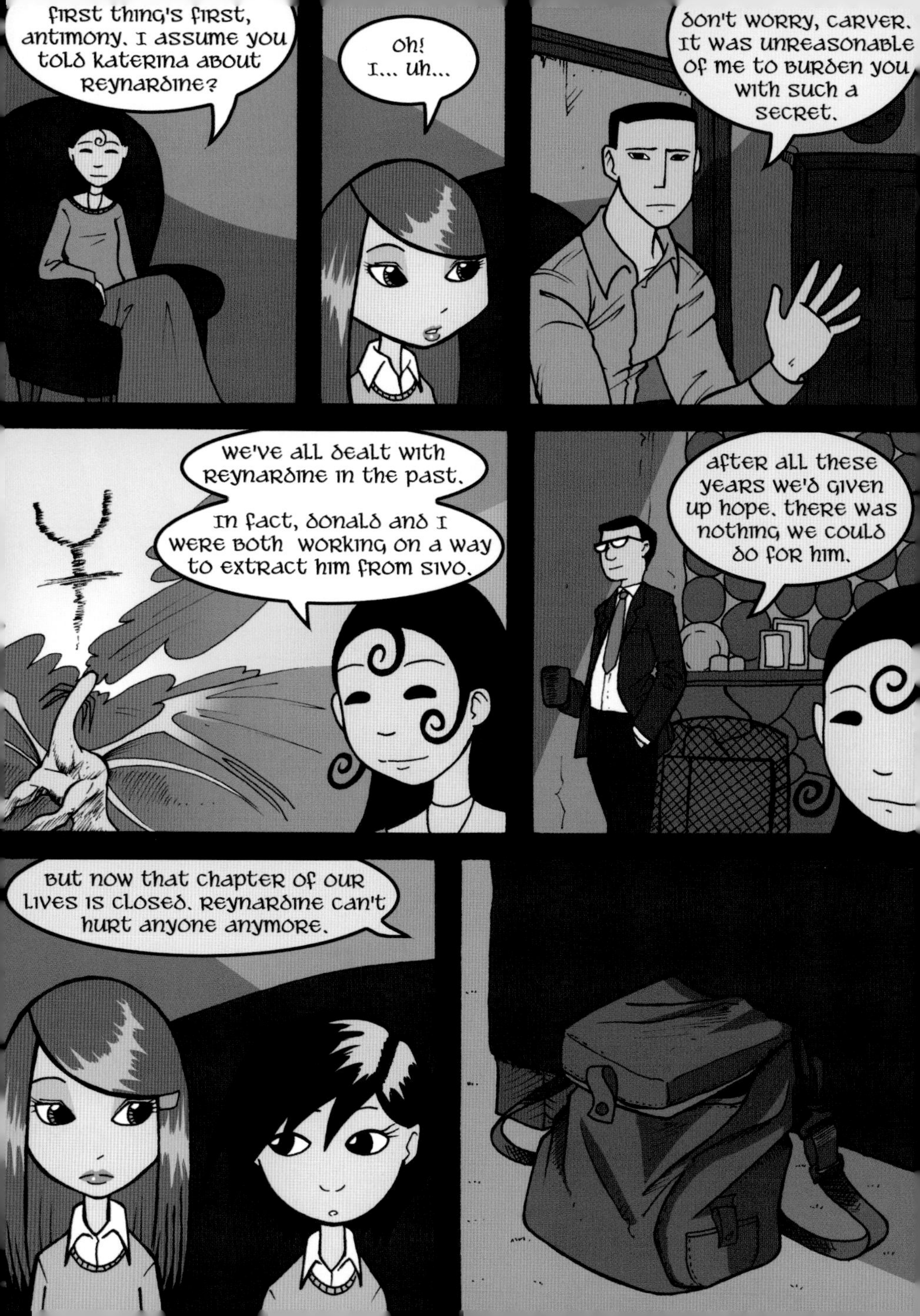
first thing's first, antimony. I assume you told katerina about Reynardine?
Oh! I... uh...
don't worry, carver. It was unreasonable of me to burden you with such a secret.
We've all dealt with Reynardine in the past.
In fact, donald and I were both working on a way to extract him from sivo.
after all these years we'd given up hope. there was nothing we could do for him.
But now that chapter of our lives is closed. Reynardine can't hurt anyone anymore.

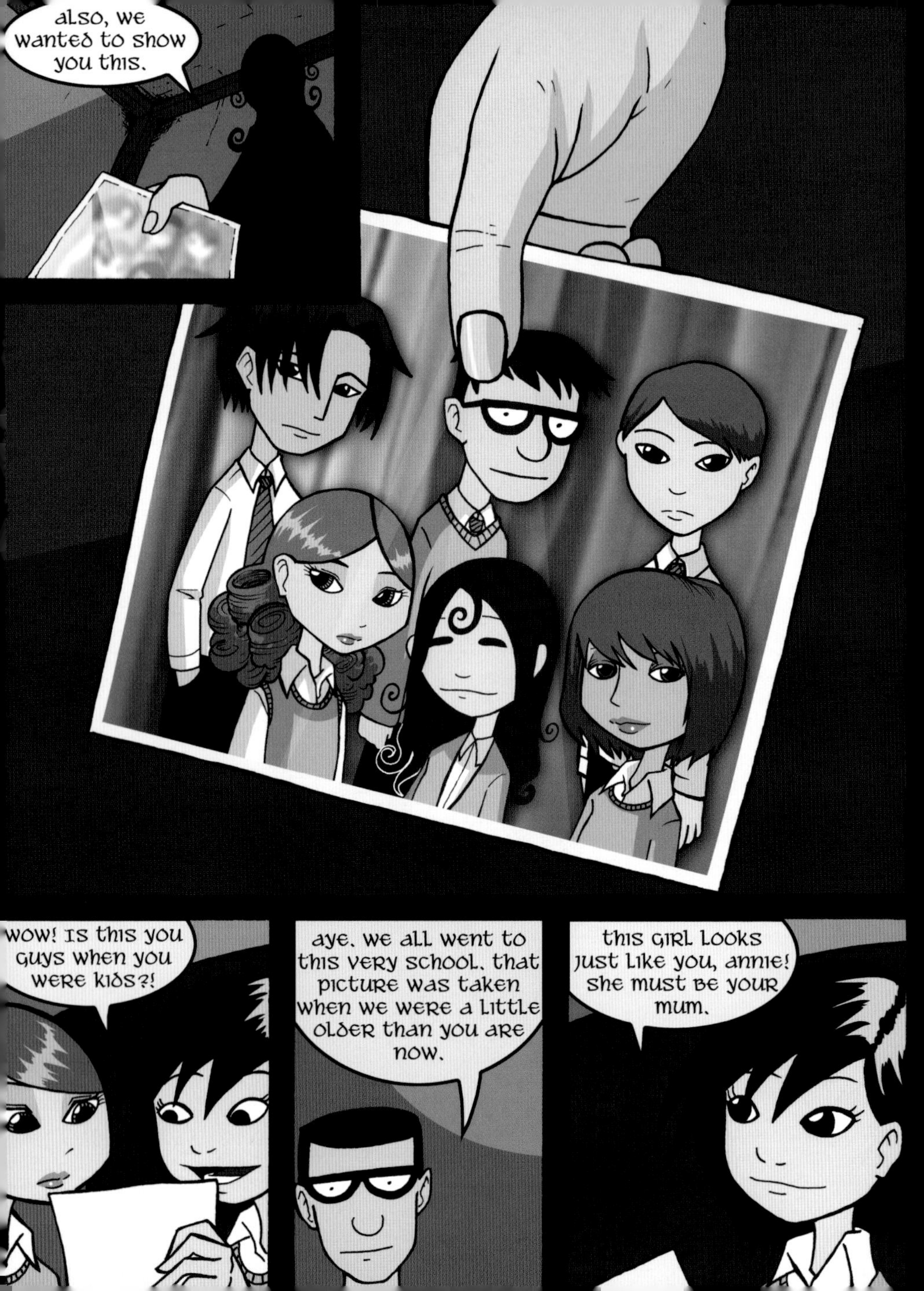
also, we wanted to show you this.
wow! is this you guys when you were kids?!
aye. we all went to this very school. that picture was taken when we were a little older than you are now.
this girl looks just like you, annie! she must be your mum.

Ooh, and who's this cute guy here?

That... that would be me.

Uh... oh...

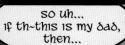
So uh... if th~this is my dad, then...

This must be annie's dad?

You knew my parents?

We did. I'm sorry, antimony, we should have told you sooner.

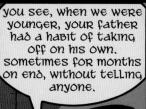
You see, when we were younger, your father had a habit of taking off on his own. Sometimes for months on end, without telling anyone.

It looks like he hasn't changed.

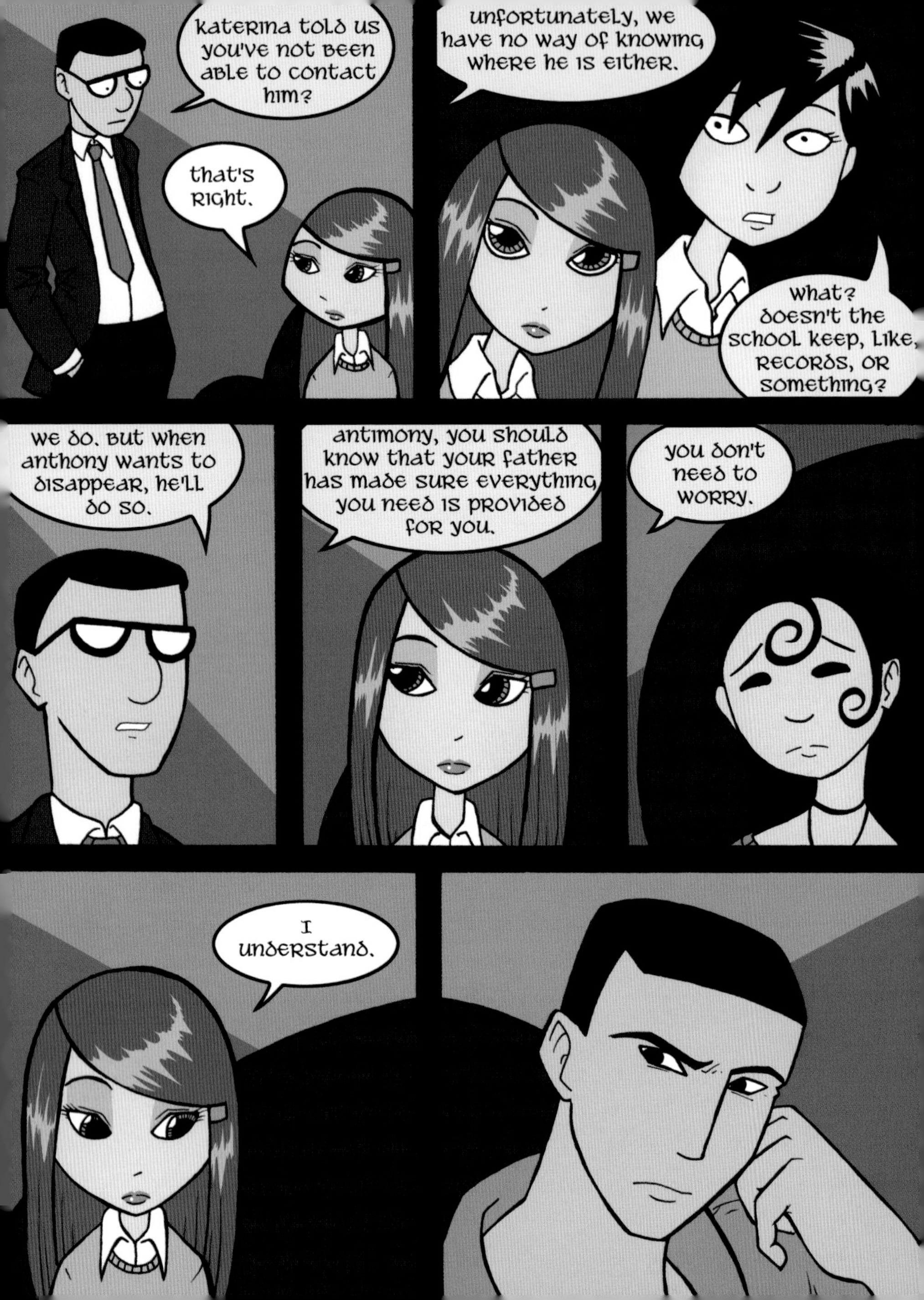
katerina told us you've not been able to contact him?
that's right.
unfortunately, we have no way of knowing where he is either.
what? doesn't the school keep, like, records, or something?
we do. but when anthony wants to disappear, he'll do so.
antimony, you should know that your father has made sure everything you need is provided for you.
you don't need to worry.
I understand.

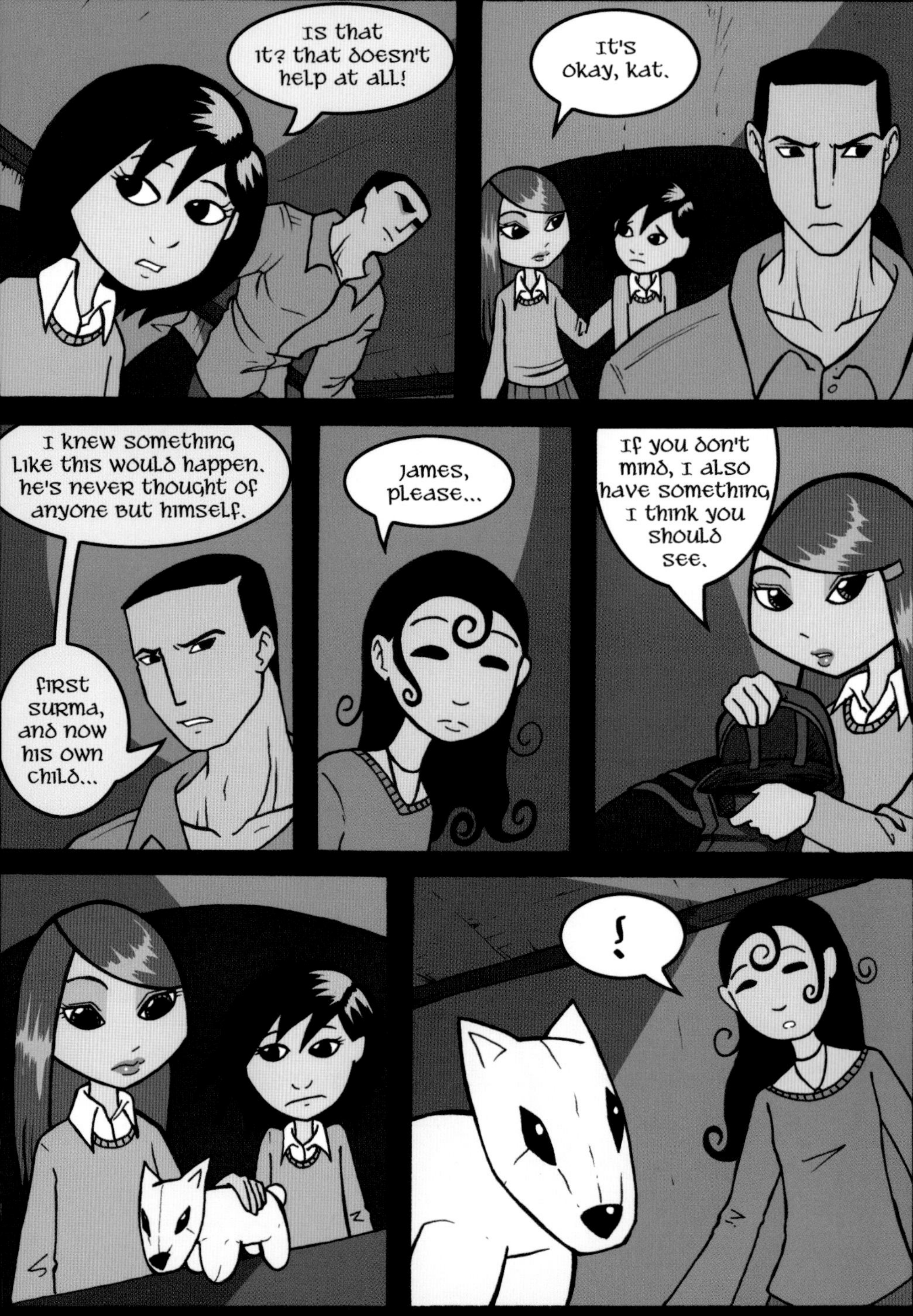
Is that it? that doesn't help at all!
It's okay, kat.
I knew something like this would happen. he's never thought of anyone but himself.
first surma, and now his own child...
James, please...
If you don't mind, I also have something I think you should see.
!

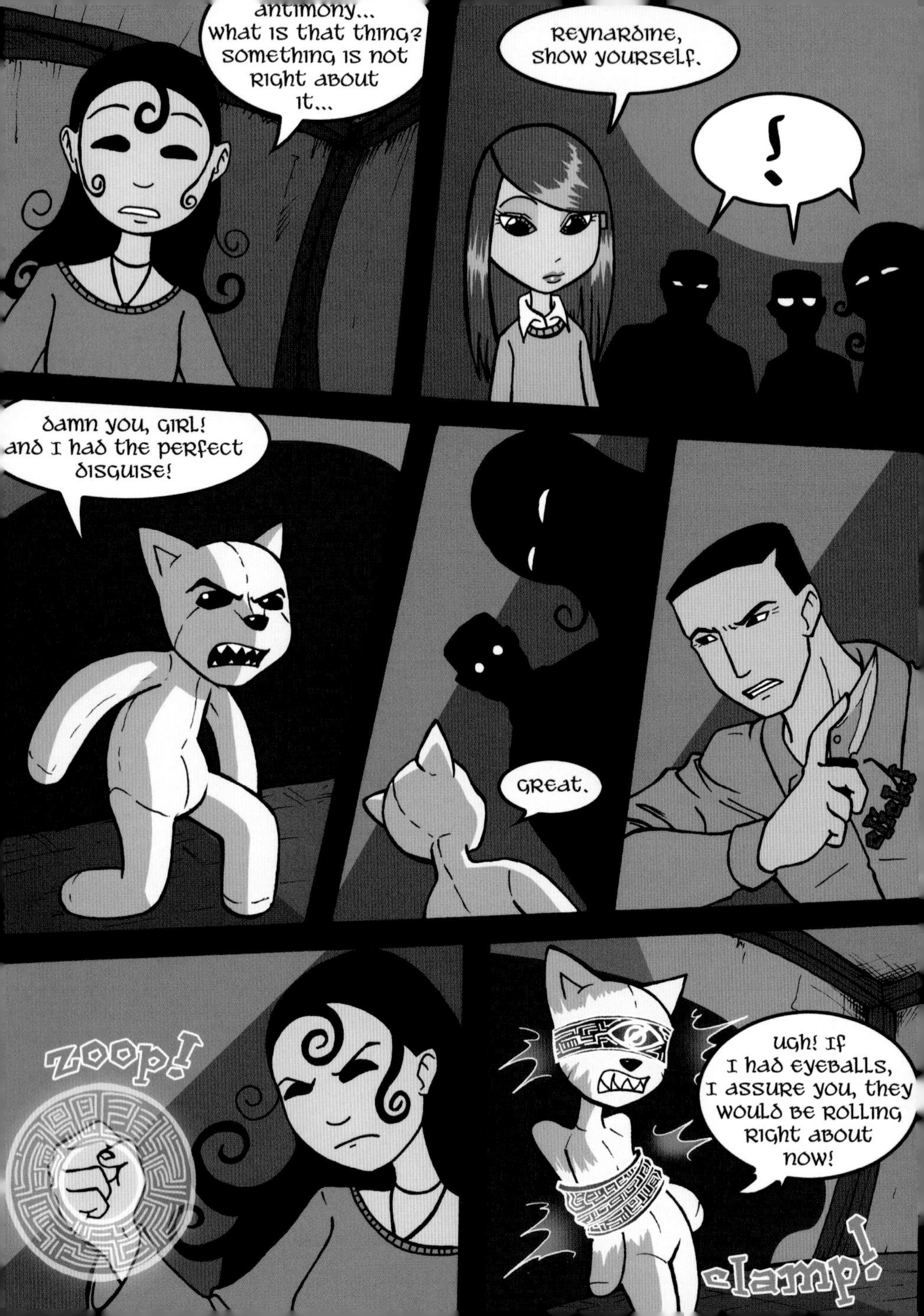
antimony...
what is that thing?
something is not
right about
it...
Reynardine,
show yourself.
?
damn you, girl!
and I had the perfect
disguise!
great.
zoop!
ugh! if
I had eyeballs,
I assure you, they
would be rolling
right about
now!
clamp!

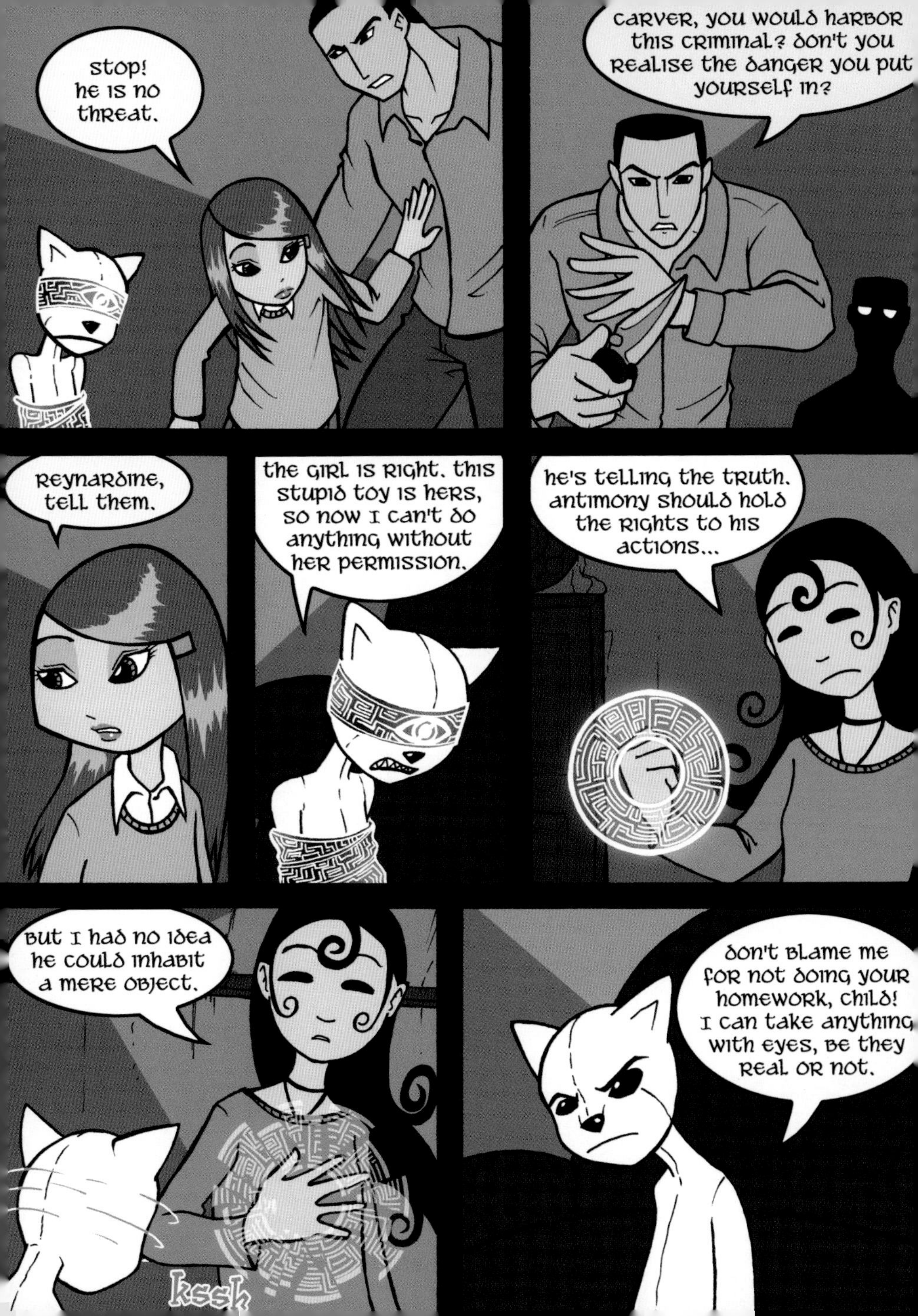
stop! he is no threat.
carver, you would harbor this criminal? don't you realise the danger you put yourself in?
reynardine, tell them.
the girl is right. this stupid toy is hers, so now I can't do anything without her permission.
he's telling the truth. antimony should hold the rights to his actions...
but I had no idea he could inhabit a mere object.
kssh
don't blame me for not doing your homework, child! I can take anything with eyes, be they real or not.

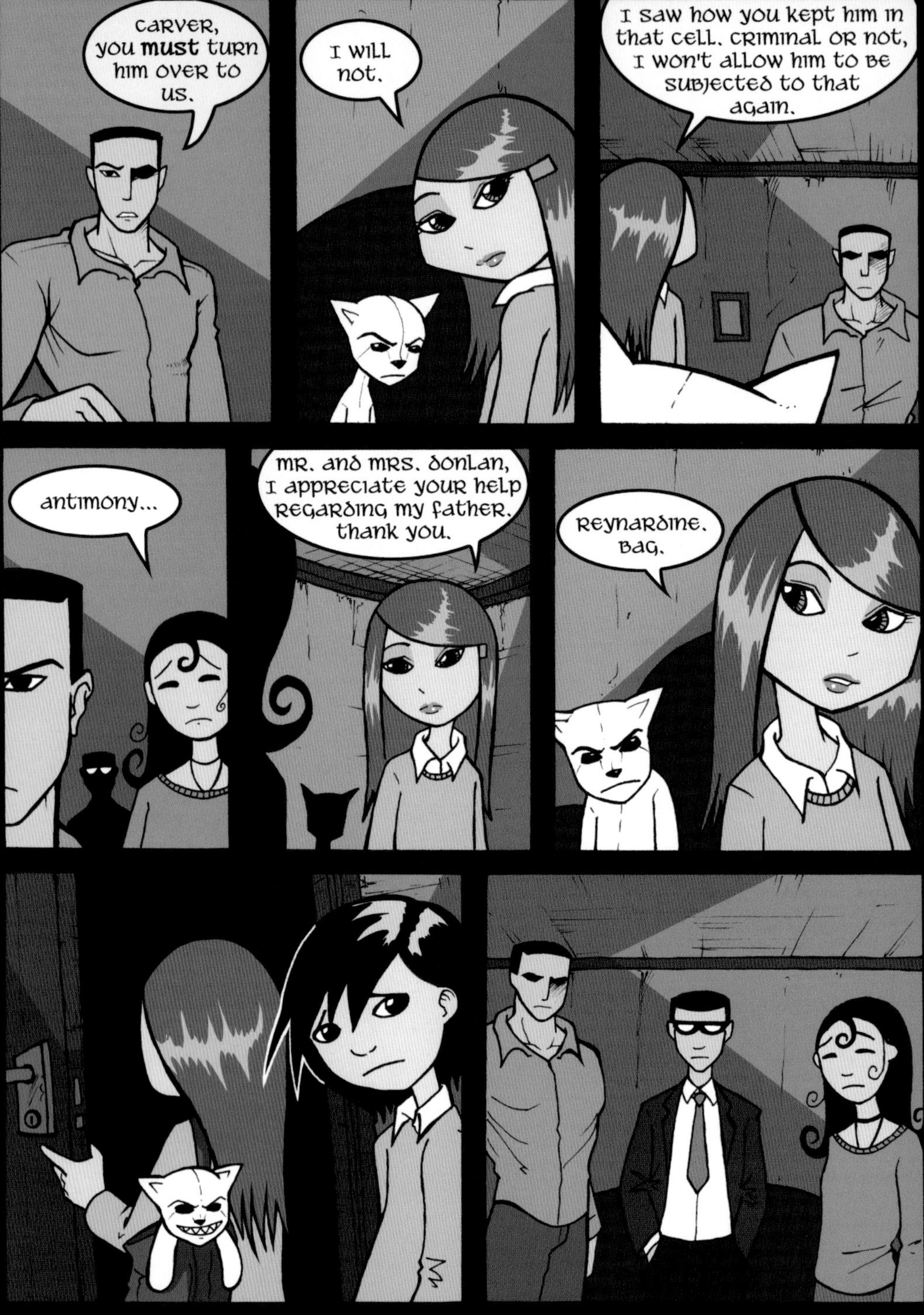
CARVER, YOU **MUST** TURN HIM OVER TO US.
I WILL NOT.
I SAW HOW YOU KEPT HIM IN THAT CELL. CRIMINAL OR NOT, I WON'T ALLOW HIM TO BE SUBJECTED TO THAT AGAIN.
ANTIMONY...
MR. AND MRS. DONLAN, I APPRECIATE YOUR HELP REGARDING MY FATHER. THANK YOU.
REYNARDINE. BAG.

WELL, THAT WAS UNEXPECTED.

IT'S AS IF SURMA HAS COME BACK TO US.

THIS IS MY FAULT.

I HANDED HER THE DAMN TOY AFTER SIVO DIED.

HOW COULD I BE SUCH A FOOL?

YOU WEREN'T TO KNOW, JAMES.

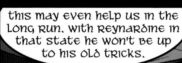

THIS MAY EVEN HELP US IN THE LONG RUN. WITH REYNARDINE IN THAT STATE HE WON'T BE UP TO HIS OLD TRICKS.

YOU STILL CARRY THAT THING, JIM?

James, with love, Surma.

ALWAYS.

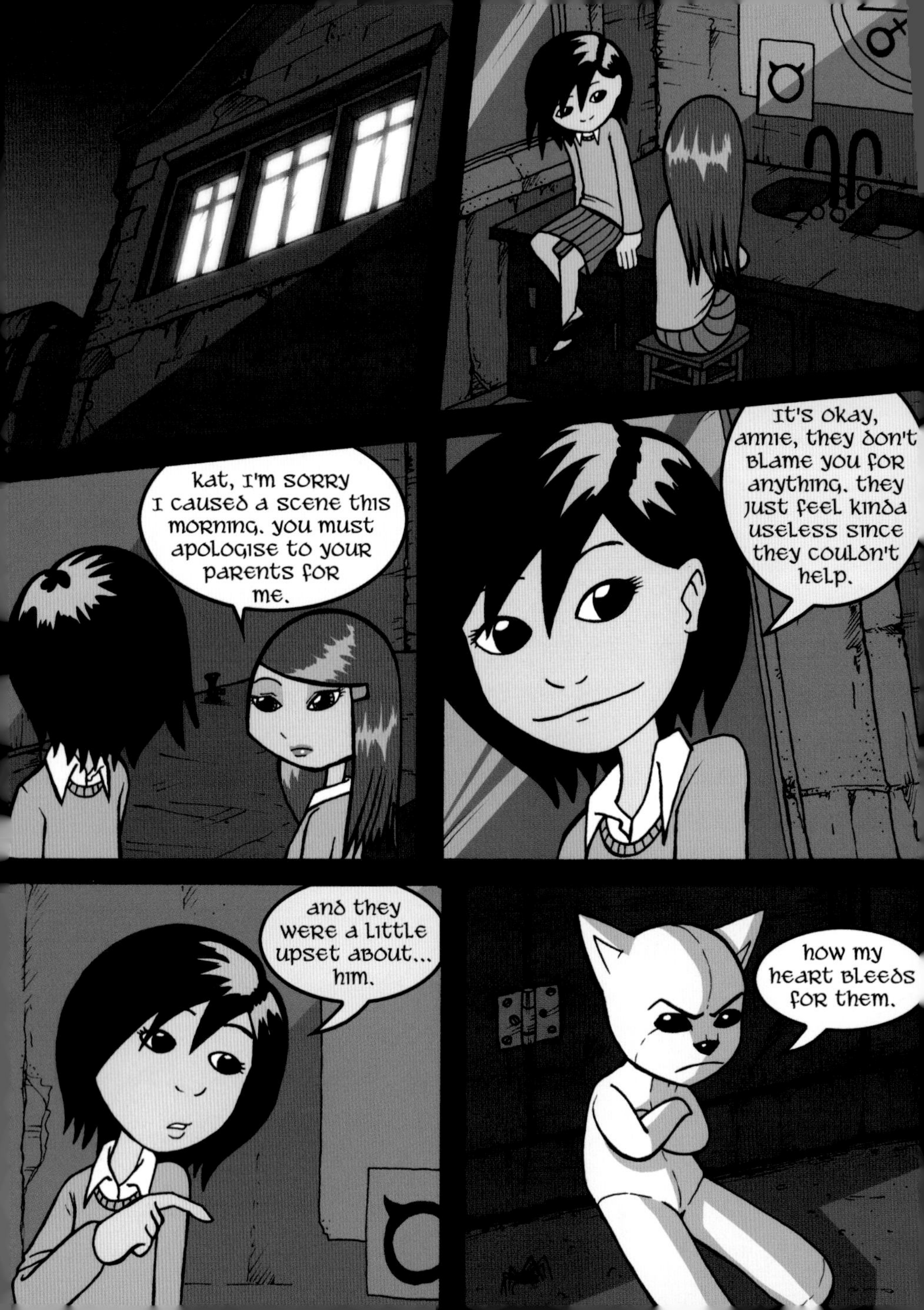
kat, I'm SORRY I caused a scene this morning. you must apologise to your parents for me.
It's okay, annie, they don't blame you for anything. they just feel kinda useless since they couldn't help.
and they were a little upset about... him.
how my heart bleeds for them.

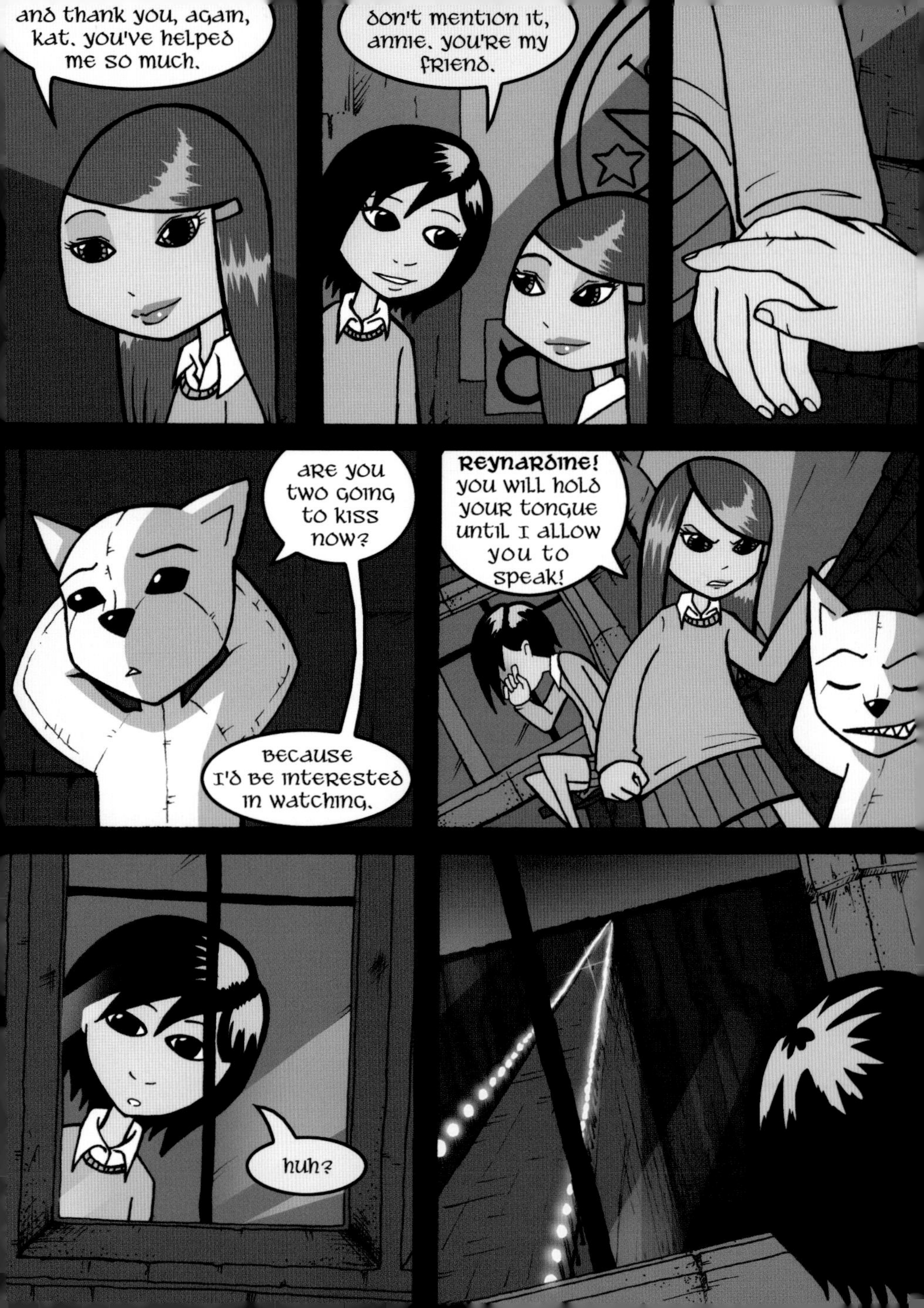
and thank you, again, kat. you've helped me so much.
don't mention it, annie. you're my friend.
are you two going to kiss now?
because I'd be interested in watching.
Reynardine! you will hold your tongue until I allow you to speak!
huh?

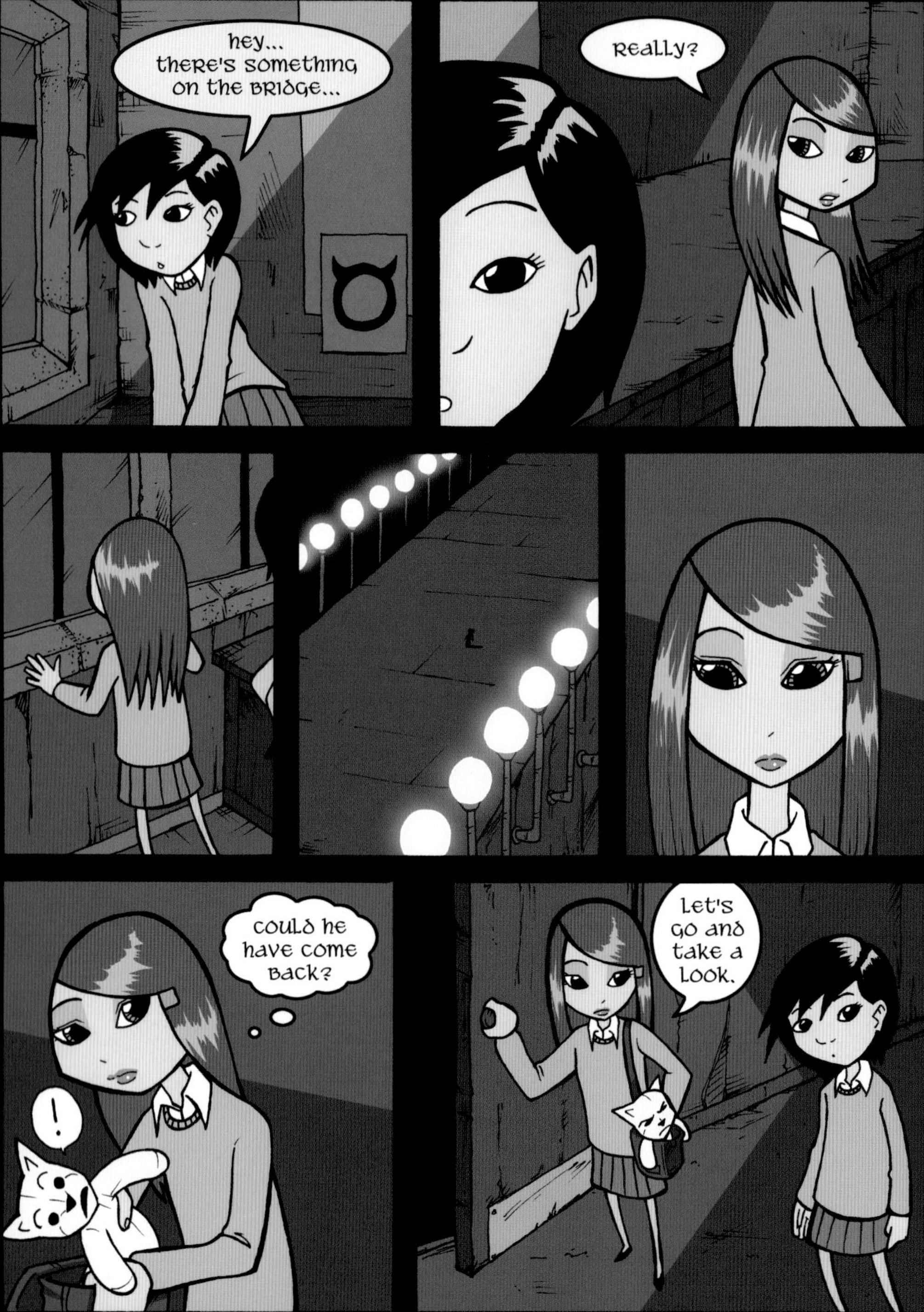
hey... there's something on the bridge...
Really?
could he have come back?
!
Let's go and take a look.

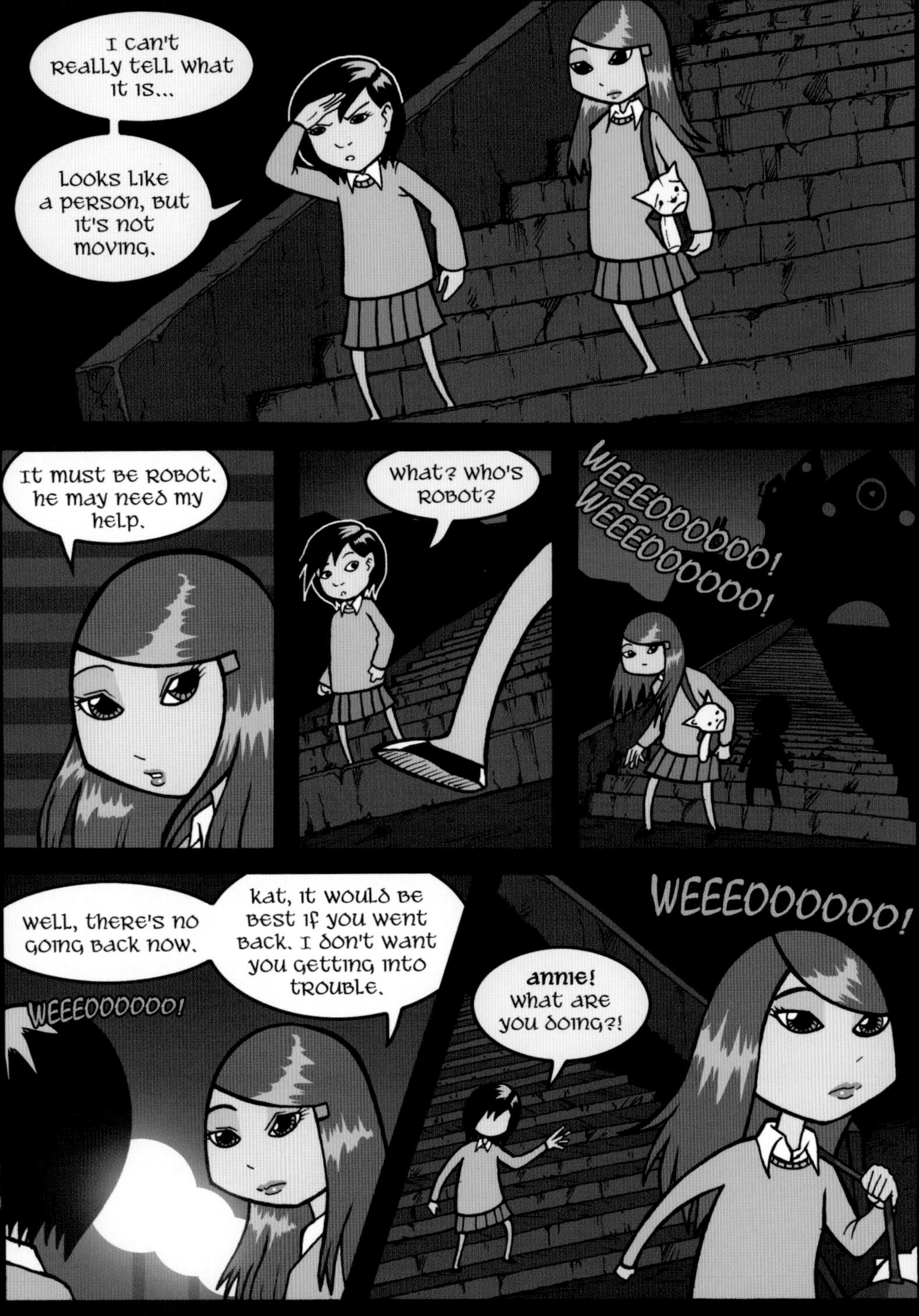
I can't really tell what it is...
Looks like a person, but it's not moving.
It must be Robot. He may need my help.
What? Who's Robot?
WEEEOOOOOOO! WEEEOOOOOOO!
Well, there's no going back now.
Kat, it would be best if you went back. I don't want you getting into trouble.
WEEEOOOOOO!
WEEEOOOOOOO!
Annie! What are you doing?!

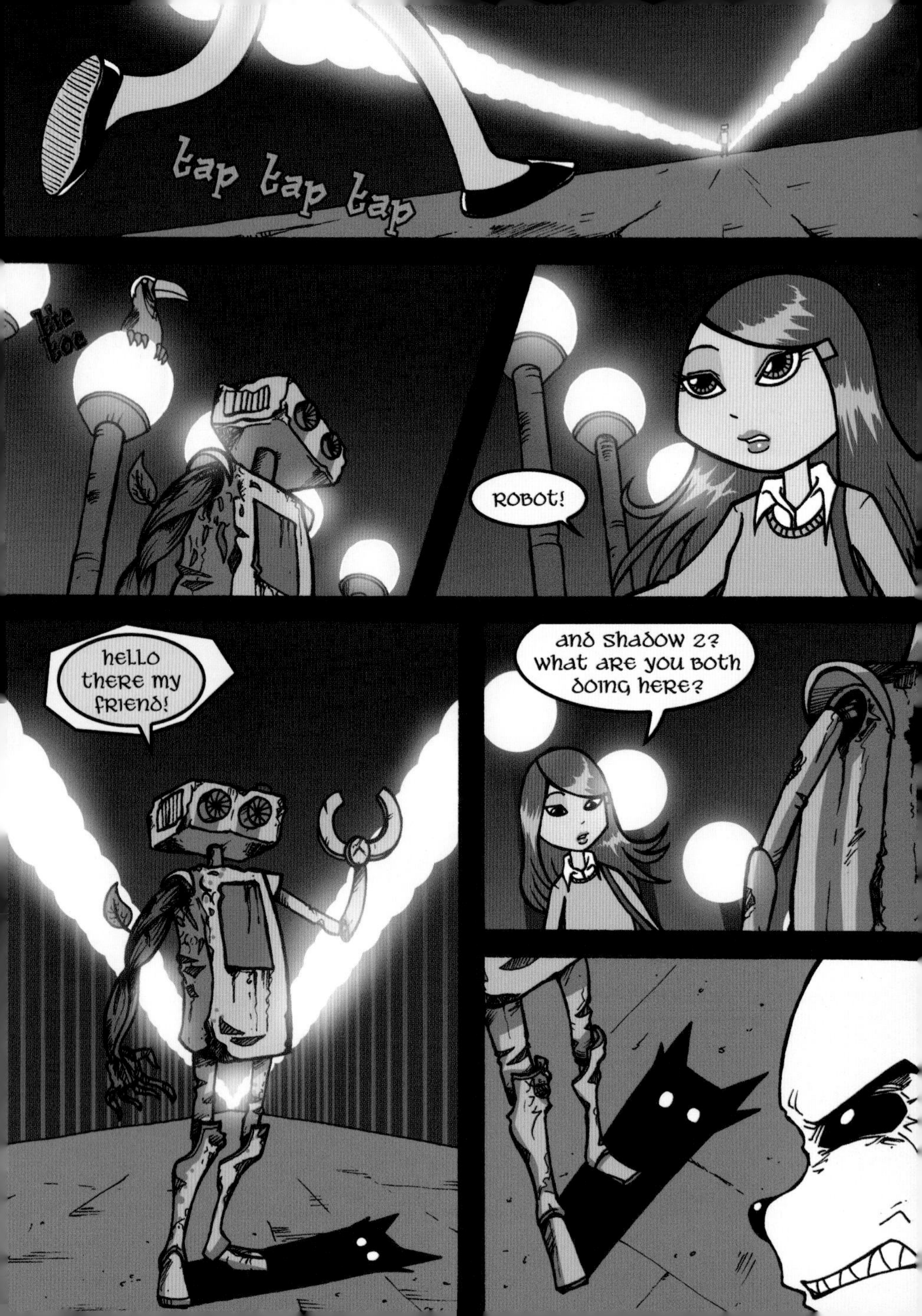
tap tap tap
tic toc
ROBOT!
hello there my friend!
and shadow 2? what are you both doing here?

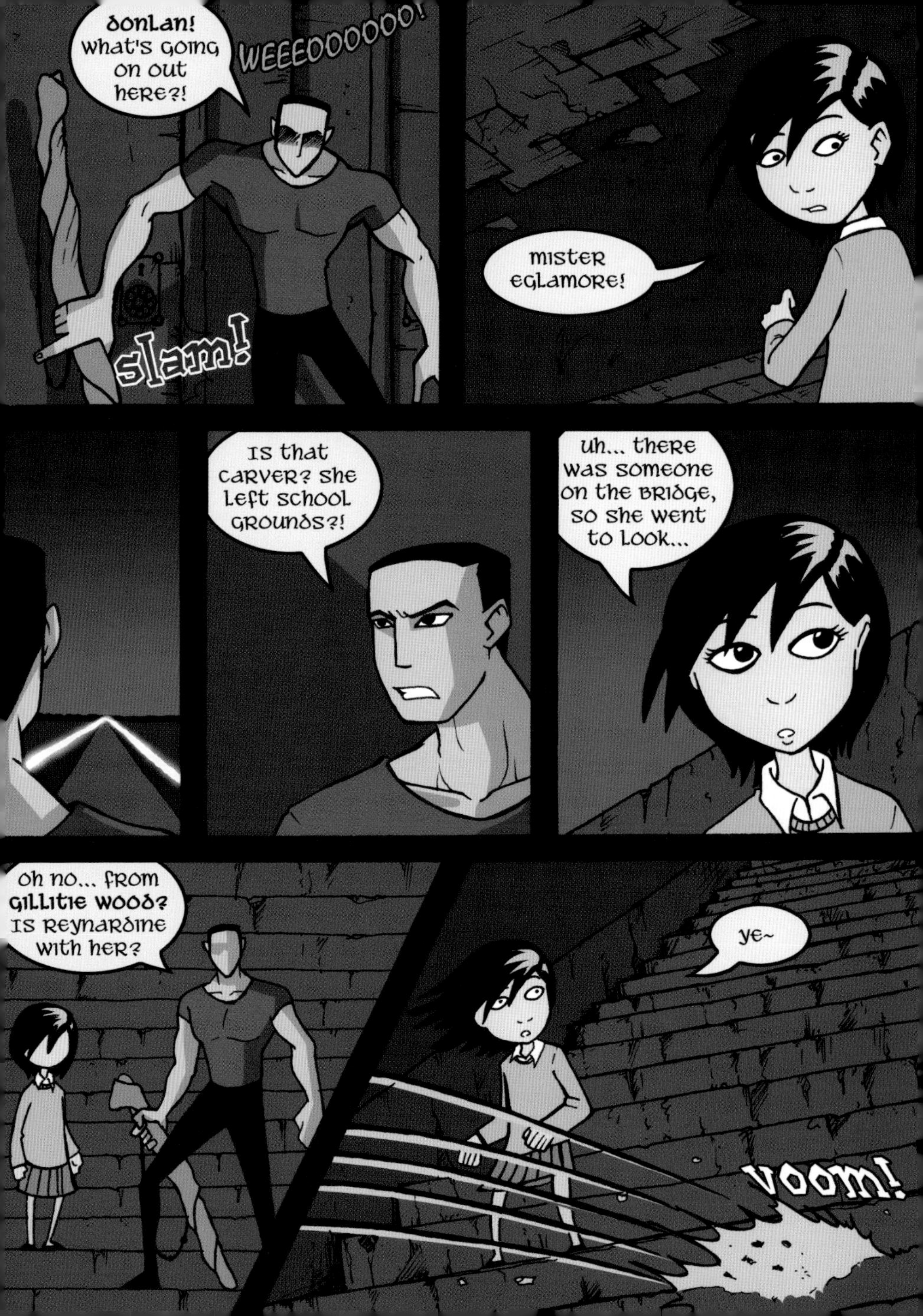
Donlan! What's going on out here?!
WEEEOOOOOO!
slam!
Mister Eglamore!
Is that Carver? She left school grounds?!
Uh... there was someone on the bridge, so she went to look...
Oh no... from Gillitie Wood? Is Reynardine with her?
ye~
VOOM!

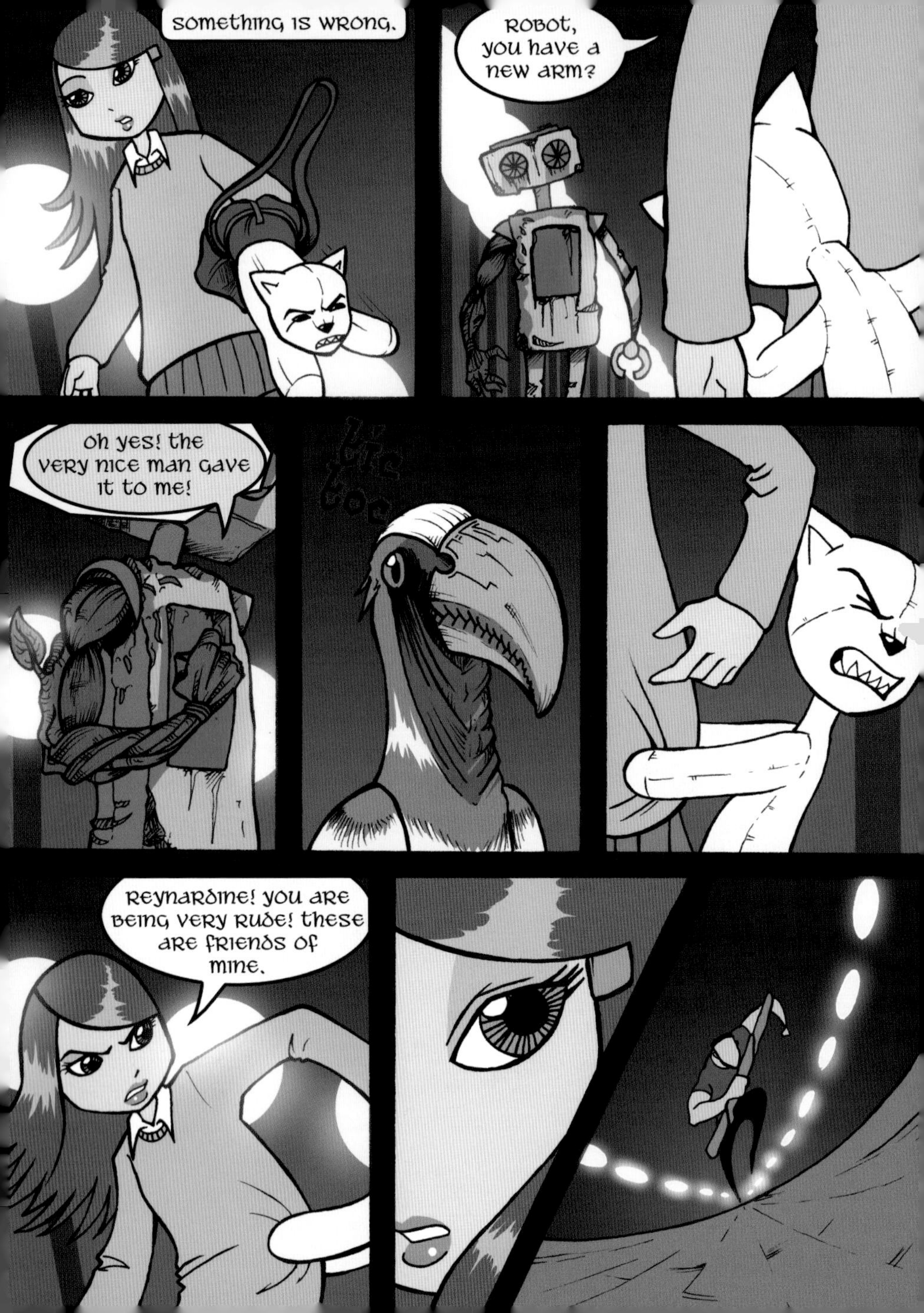
something is wrong.
Robot, you have a new arm?
oh yes! the very nice man gave it to me!
tic toc
Reynardine! you are being very rude! these are friends of mine.

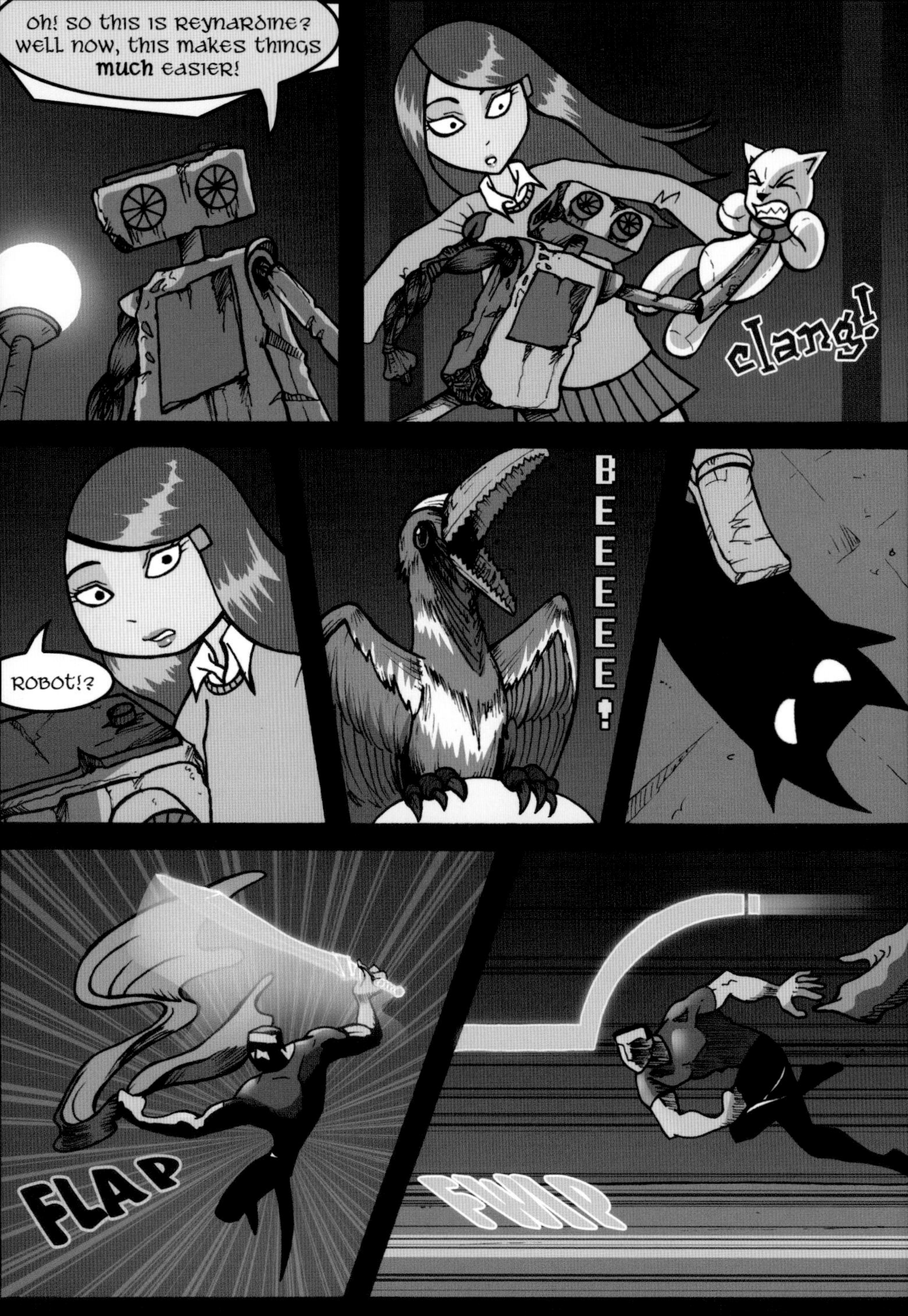

Oh! So this is Reynardine? Well now, this makes things much easier!
clang!
ROBOT!?
BEEEEEE!
FLAP
FWIP

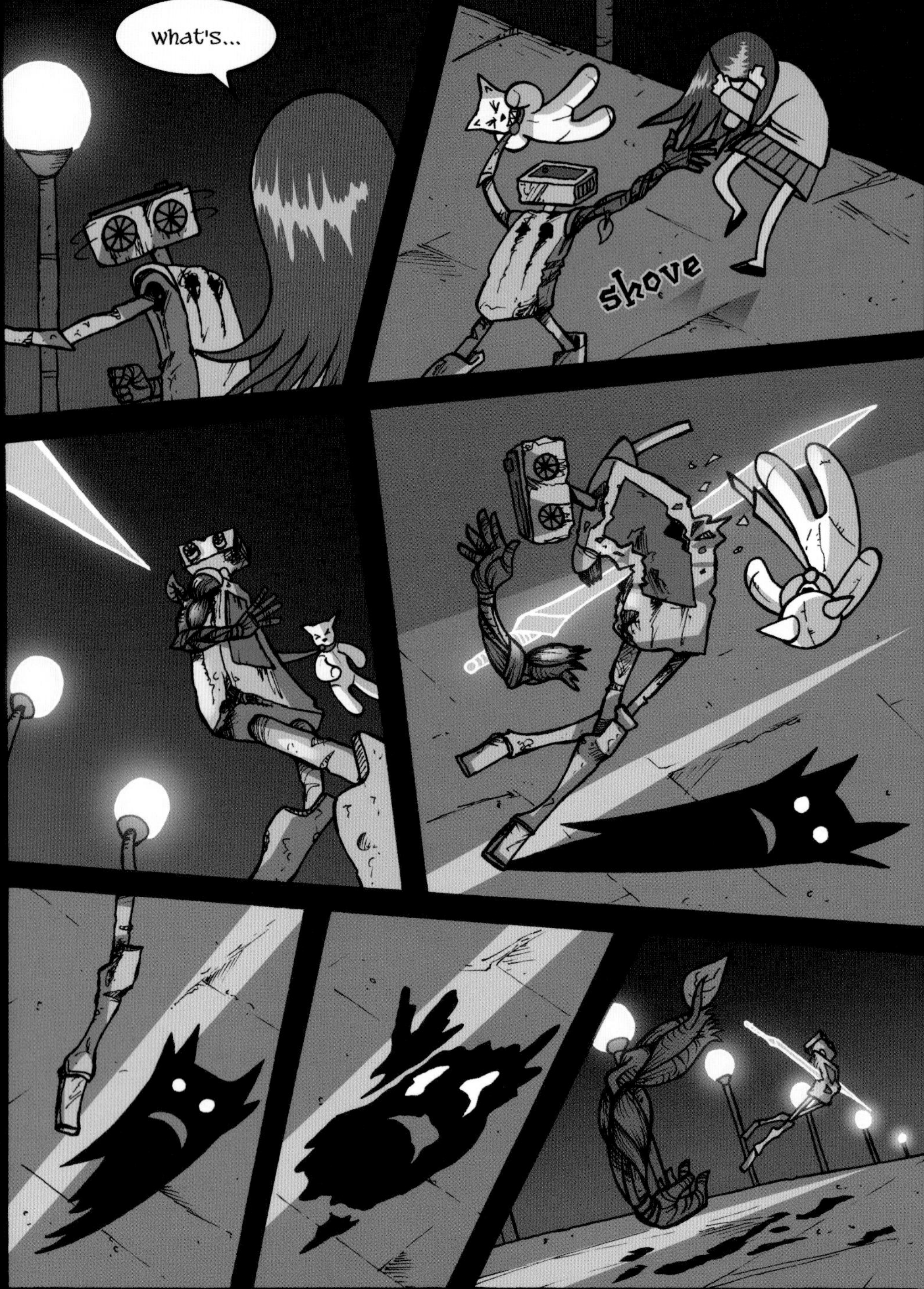
what's...
shove

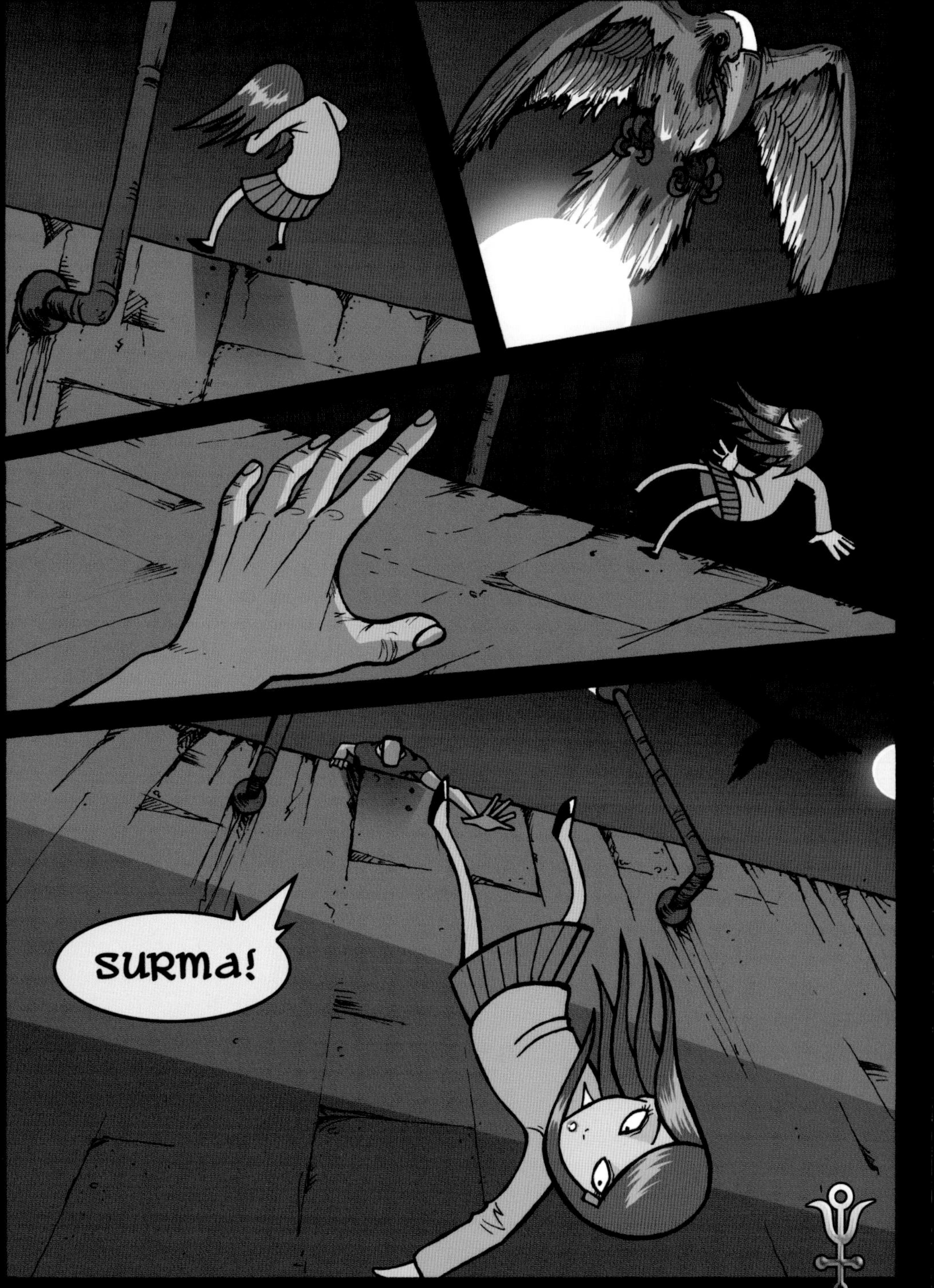
SURMA!

Ora Lege Relege Labora Et Invenies VII

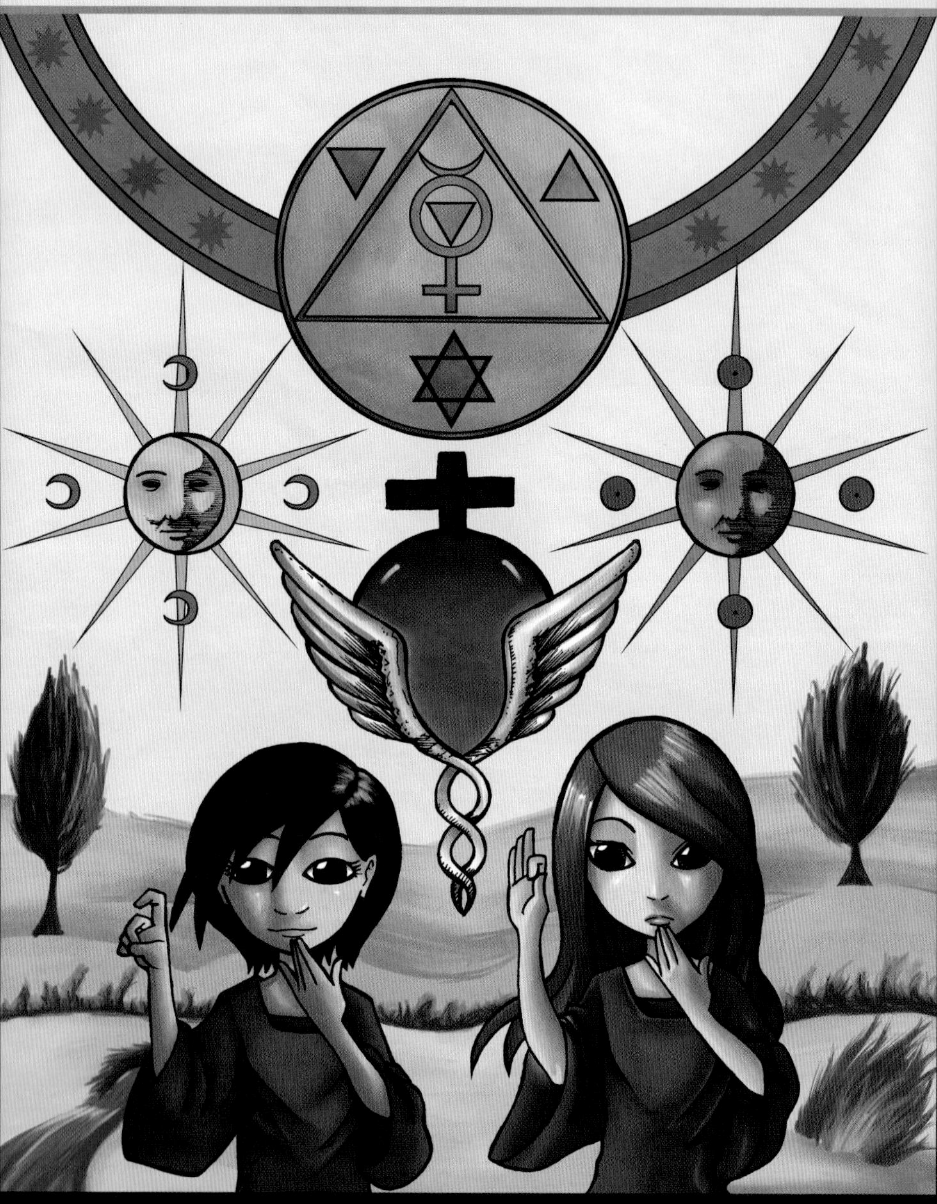

Gunnerkrigg Court

Gunnerkrigg Court

Chapter 8:

Broken Glass And Other Things

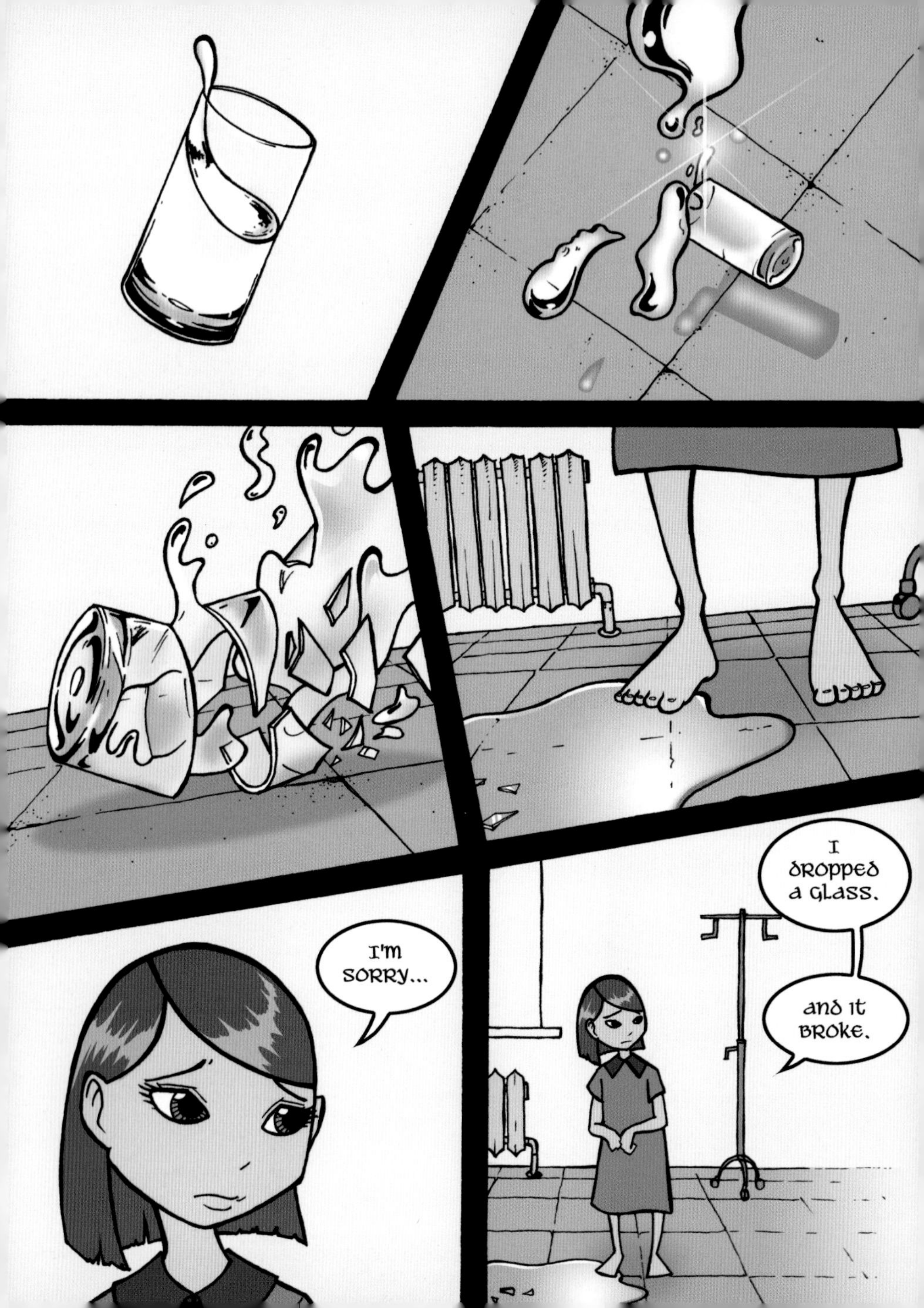
I'M SORRY...
I DROPPED A GLASS.
AND IT BROKE.

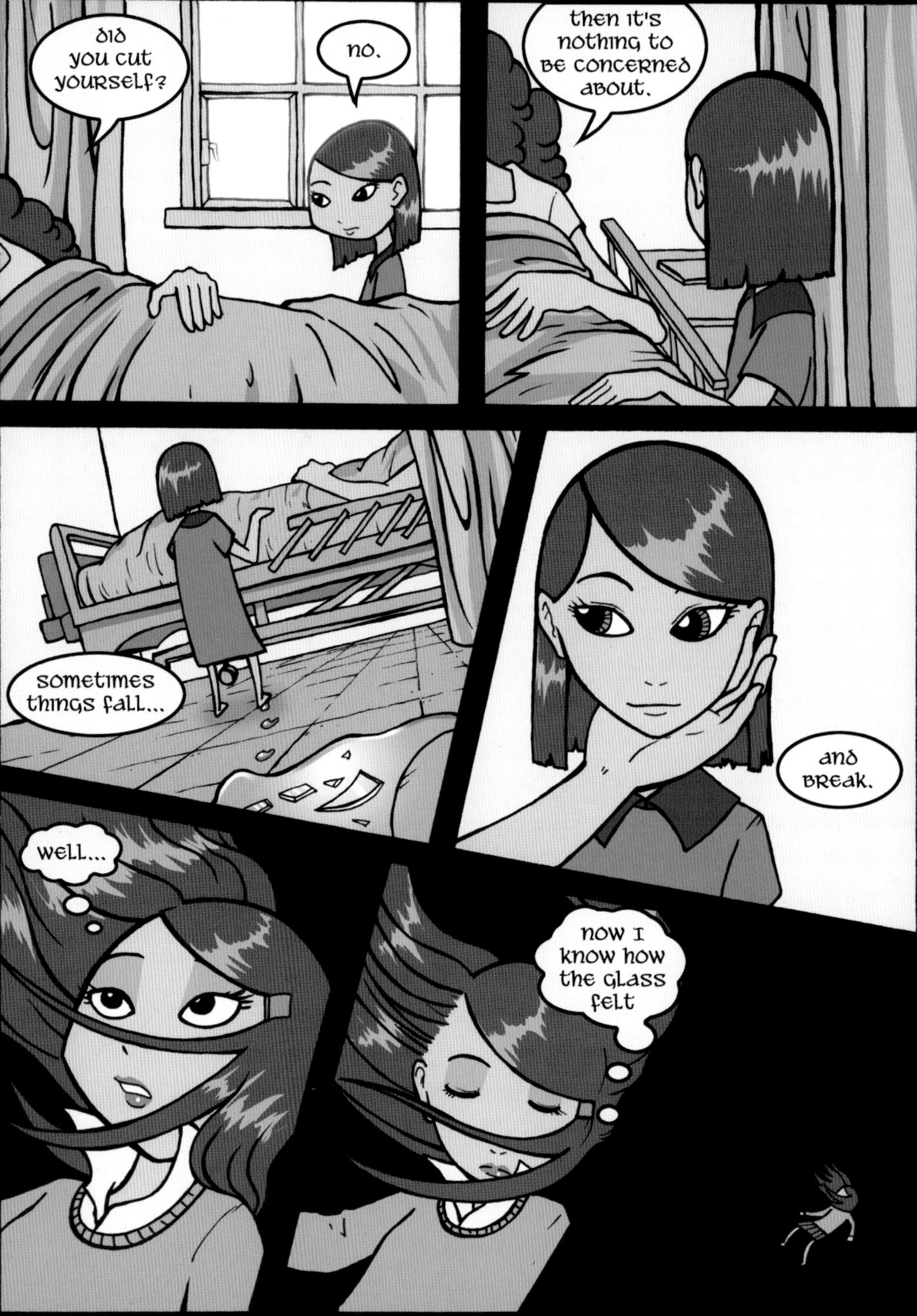
did you cut yourself?
no.
then it's nothing to be concerned about.
sometimes things fall...
and break.
well...
now I know how the glass felt

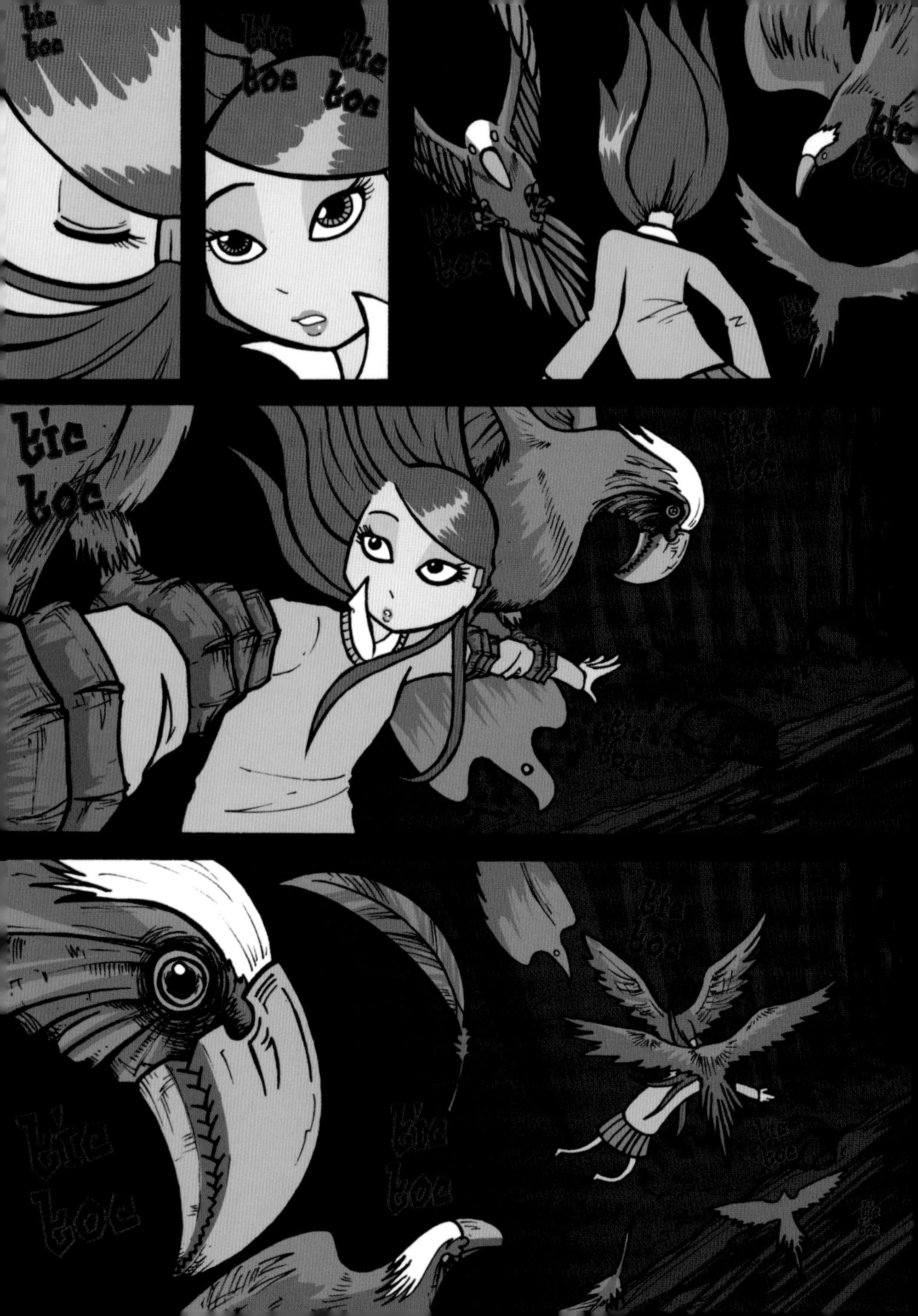
tic toc
tic toc
tic toc
tic toc
tic toc
tic toc
tic toc
tic toc
tic toc
tic toc
tic toc
tic toc
tic toc
tic toc

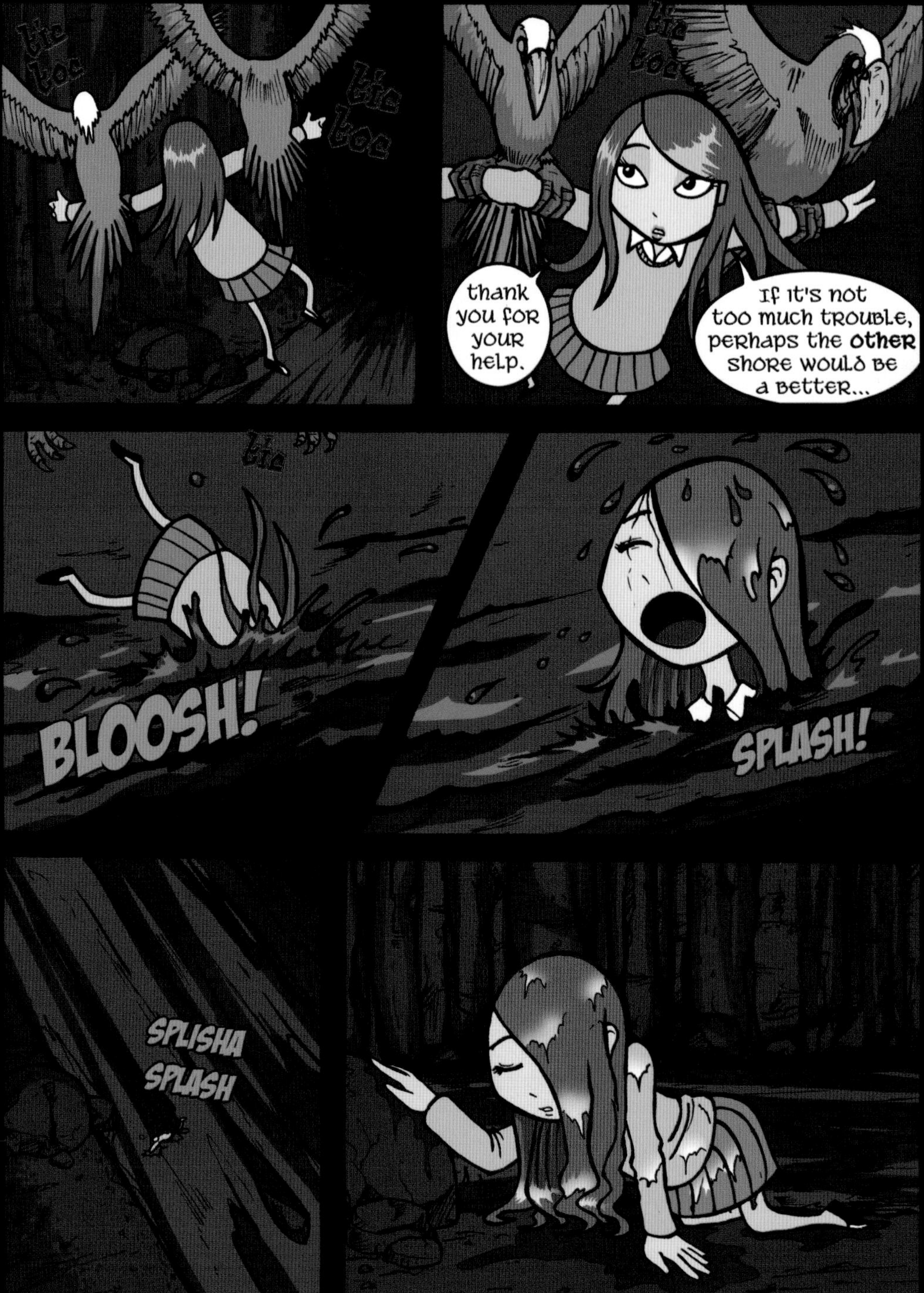
tic toc
tic toc
tic toc
thank you for your help.
If it's not too much trouble, perhaps the **other** shore would be a better...
tic
BLOOSH!
SPLASH!
SPLISHA SPLASH

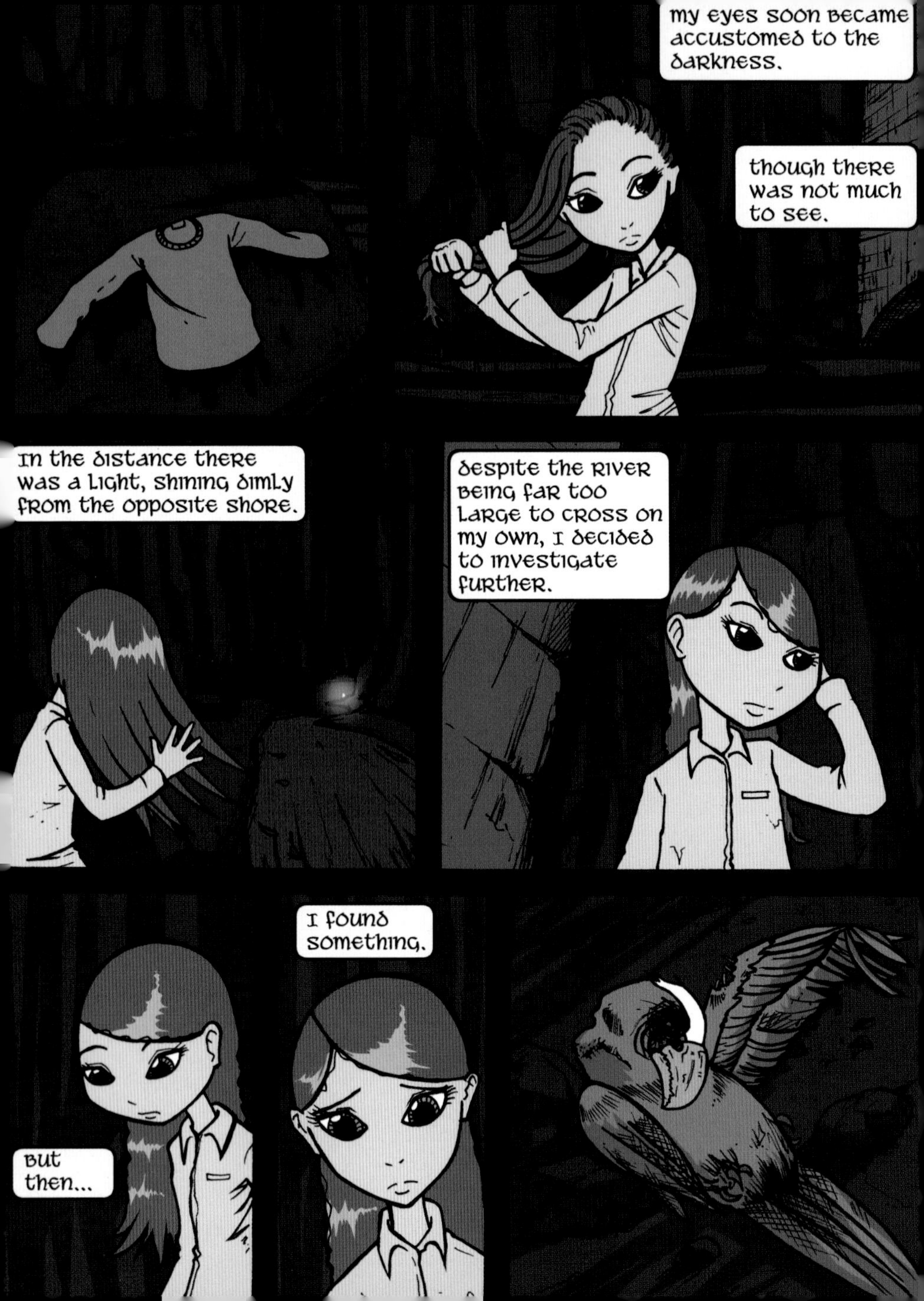
my eyes soon became accustomed to the darkness.
though there was not much to see.
In the distance there was a light, shining dimly from the opposite shore.
despite the river being far too large to cross on my own, I decided to investigate further.
But then...
I found something.

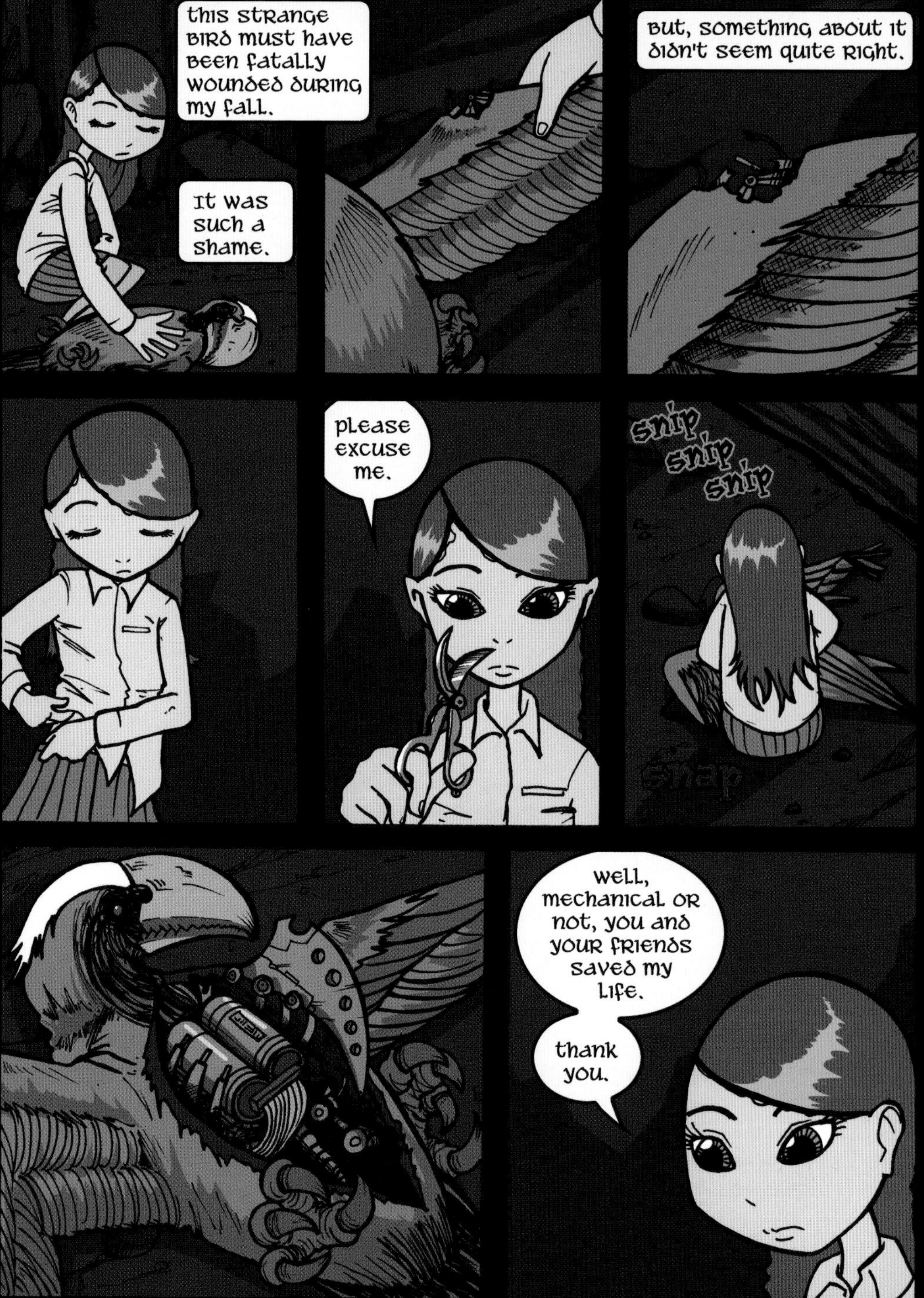
this strange bird must have been fatally wounded during my fall.
It was such a shame.
But, something about it didn't seem quite right.
please excuse me.
snip
snip
snip
snap
well, mechanical or not, you and your friends saved my life.
thank you.

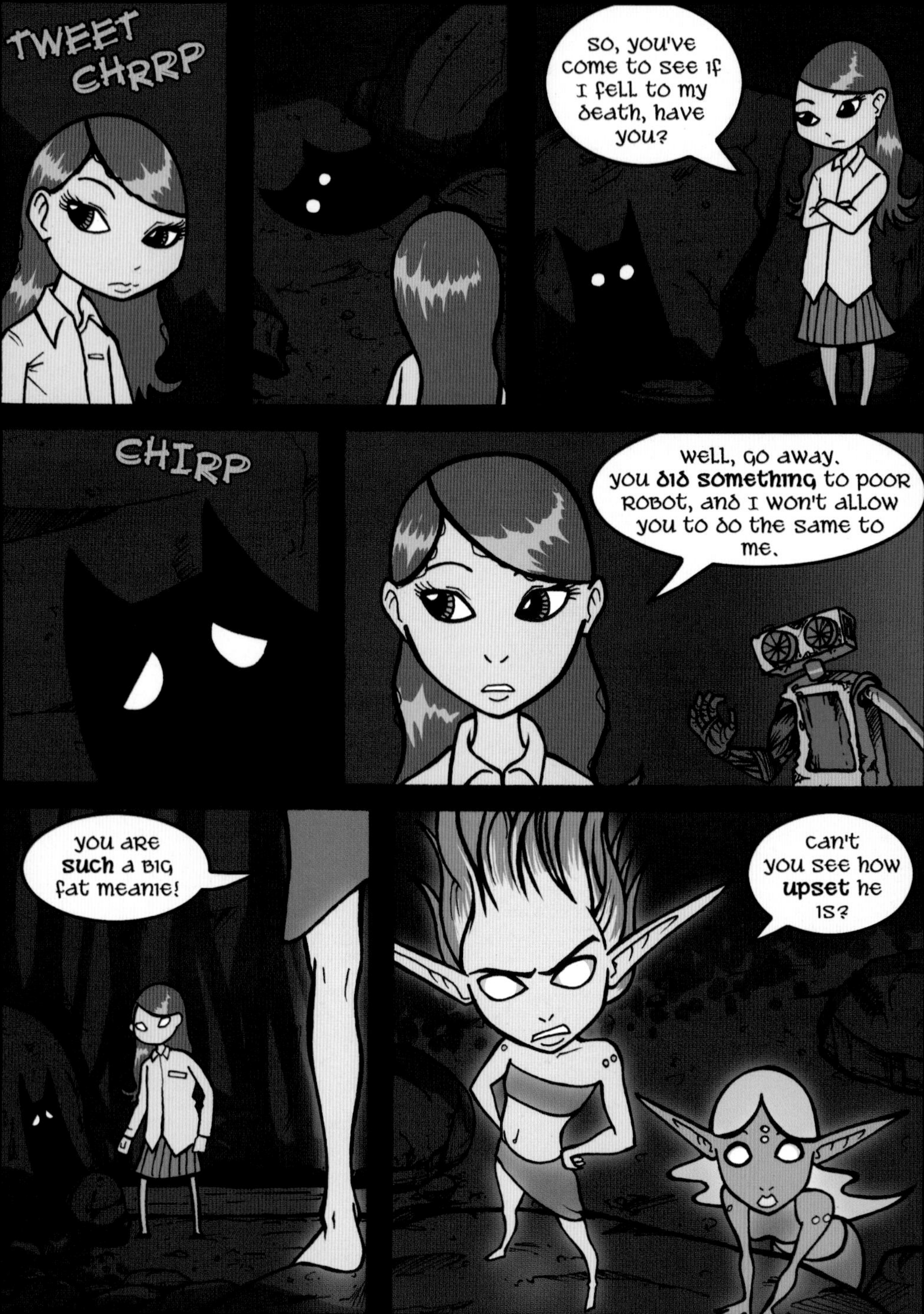
TWEET
CHRRP
so, you've come to see if I fell to my death, have you?
CHIRP
well, go away. you did something to poor ROBOT, and I won't allow you to do the same to me.
you are such a BIG fat meanie!
can't you see how upset he is?

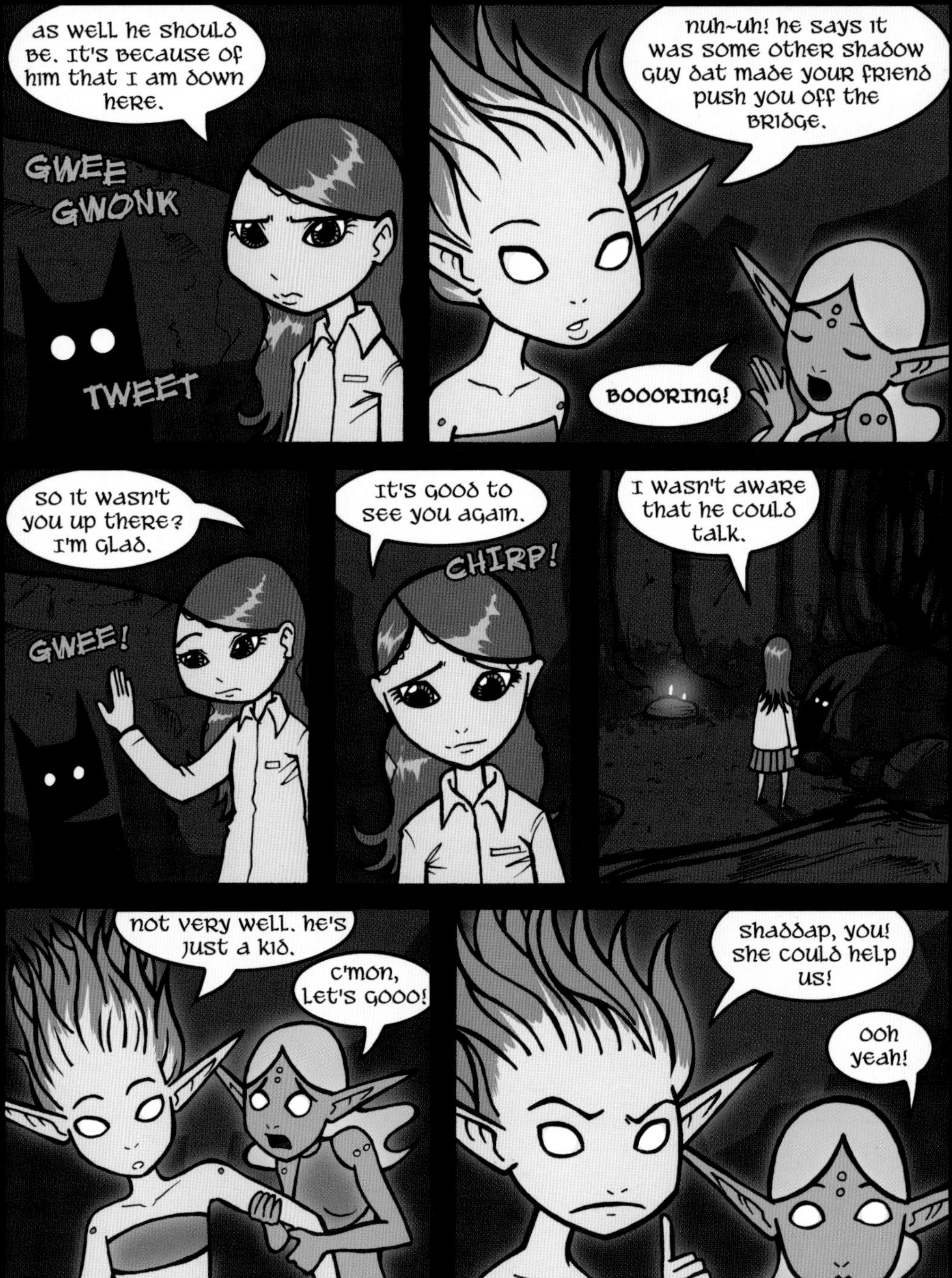
as well he should be. It's because of him that I am down here.
GWEE GWONK
TWEET
nuh~uh! he says it was some other shadow guy dat made your friend push you off the bridge.
BOOORING!
so it wasn't you up there? I'm glad.
GWEE!
It's good to see you again.
CHIRP!
I wasn't aware that he could talk.
not very well. he's just a kid.
c'mon, let's gooo!
shaddap, you! she could help us!
ooh yeah!

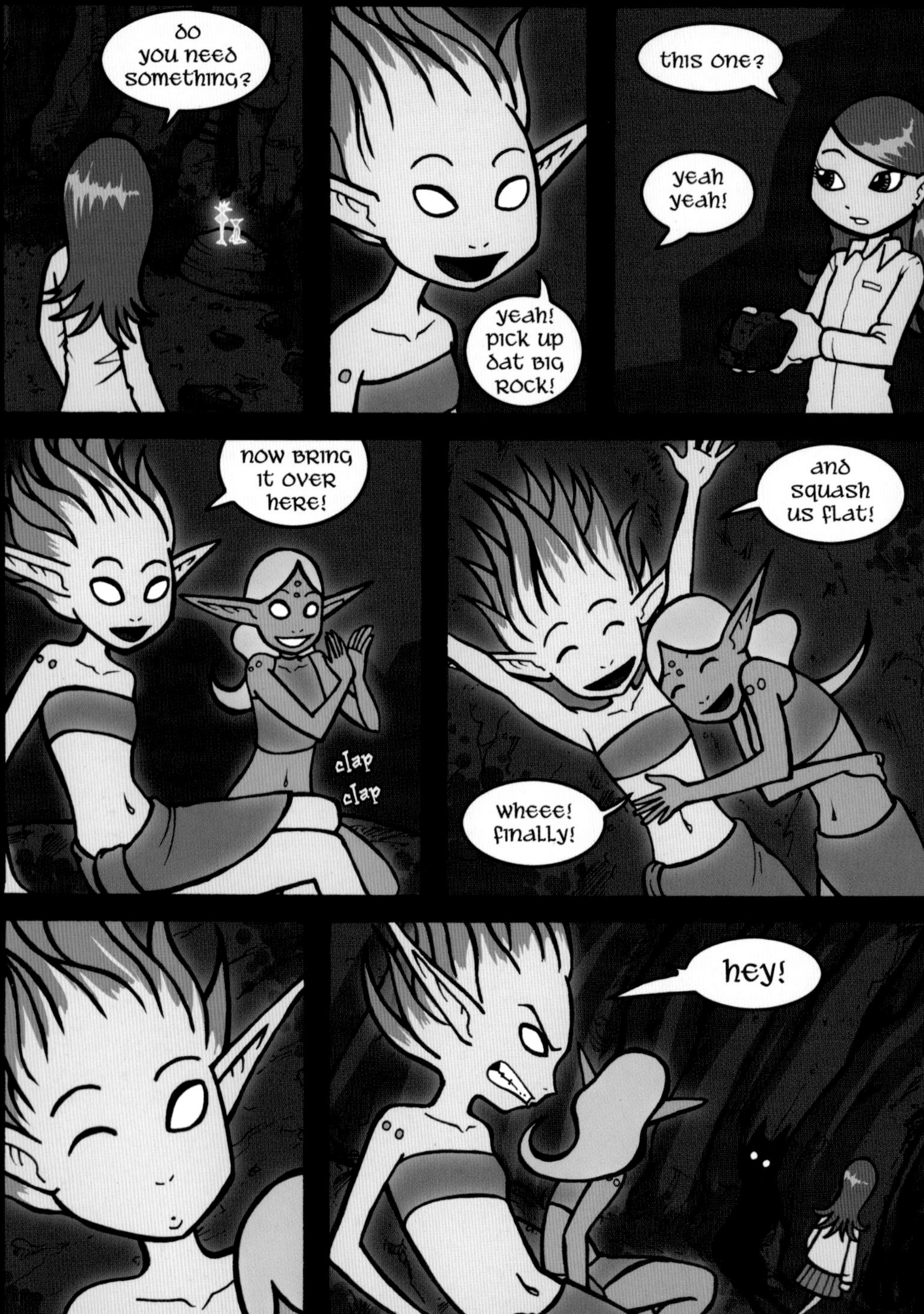
do you need something?
yeah! pick up dat big rock!
this one?
yeah yeah!
now bring it over here!
clap clap
and squash us flat!
wheee! finally!
hey!

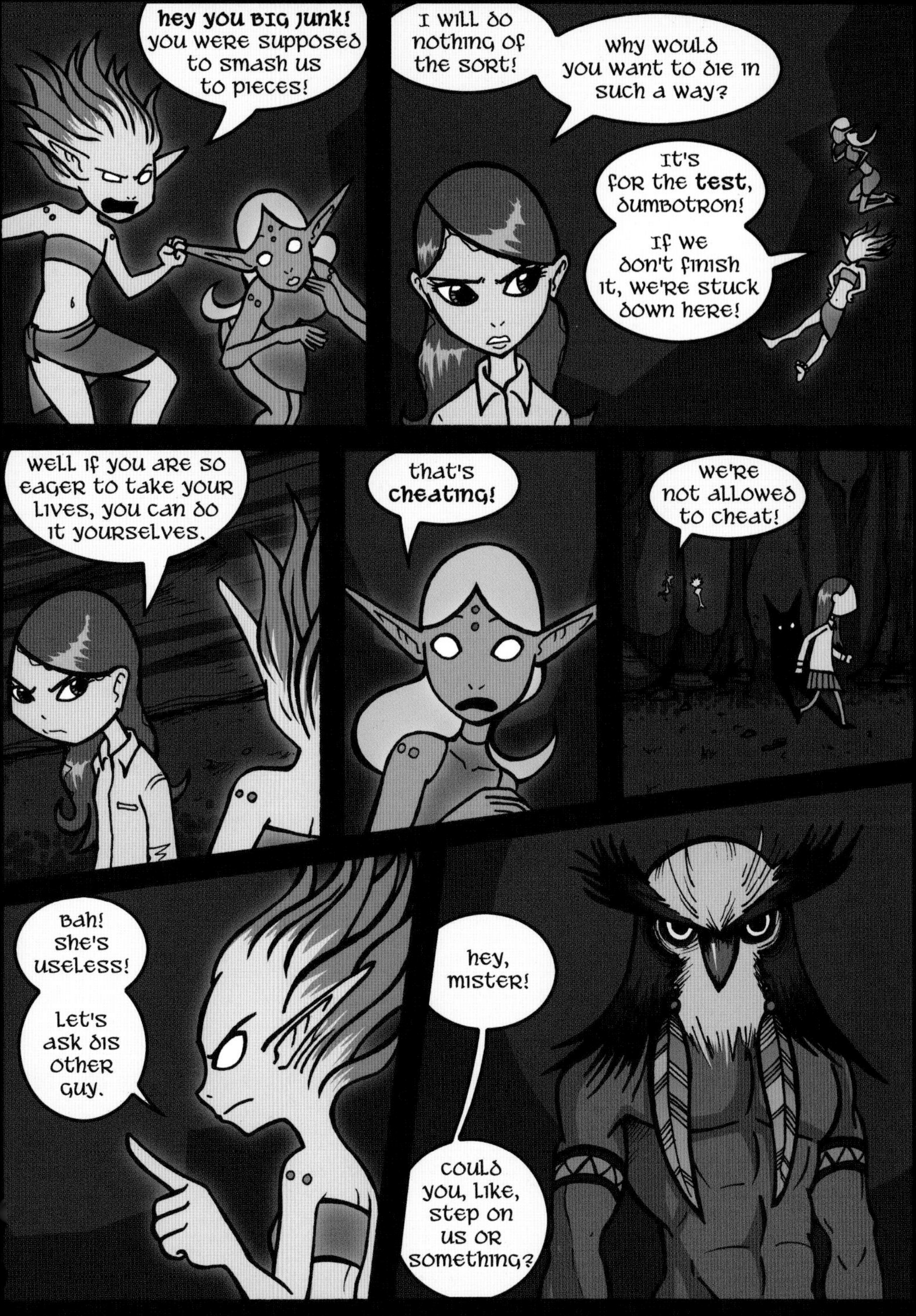

hey you BIG JUNK! you were supposed to smash us to pieces!
I will do nothing of the sort!
why would you want to die in such a way?
It's for the test, dumbotron!
If we don't finish it, we're stuck down here!
well if you are so eager to take your lives, you can do it yourselves.
that's cheating!
we're not allowed to cheat!
Bah! she's useless!
Let's ask dis other guy.
hey, mister!
could you, like, step on us or something?

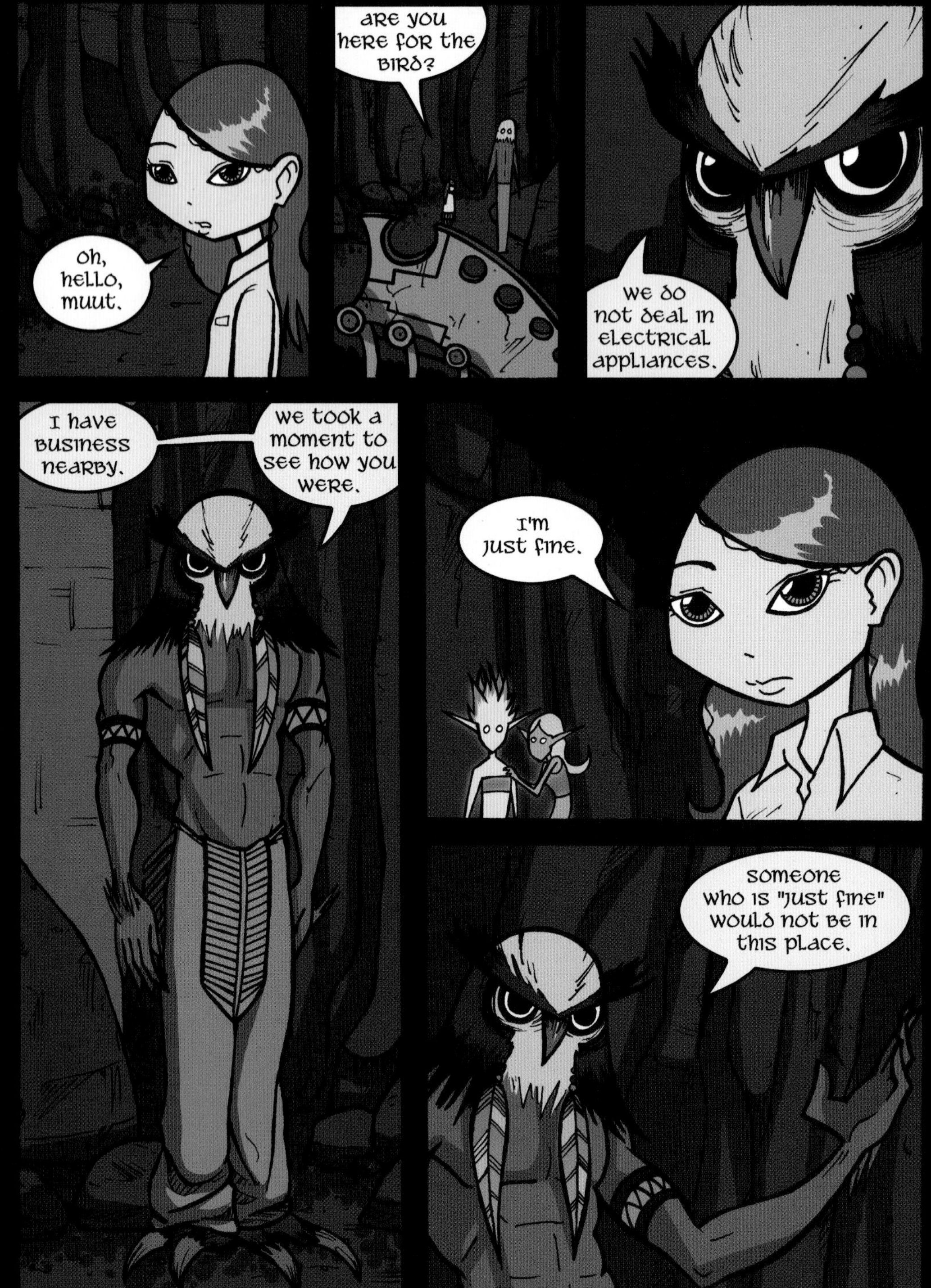
Oh, hello, muut.
Are you here for the bird?
We do not deal in electrical appliances.
I have business nearby.
We took a moment to see how you were.
I'm just fine.
Someone who is "just fine" would not be in this place.

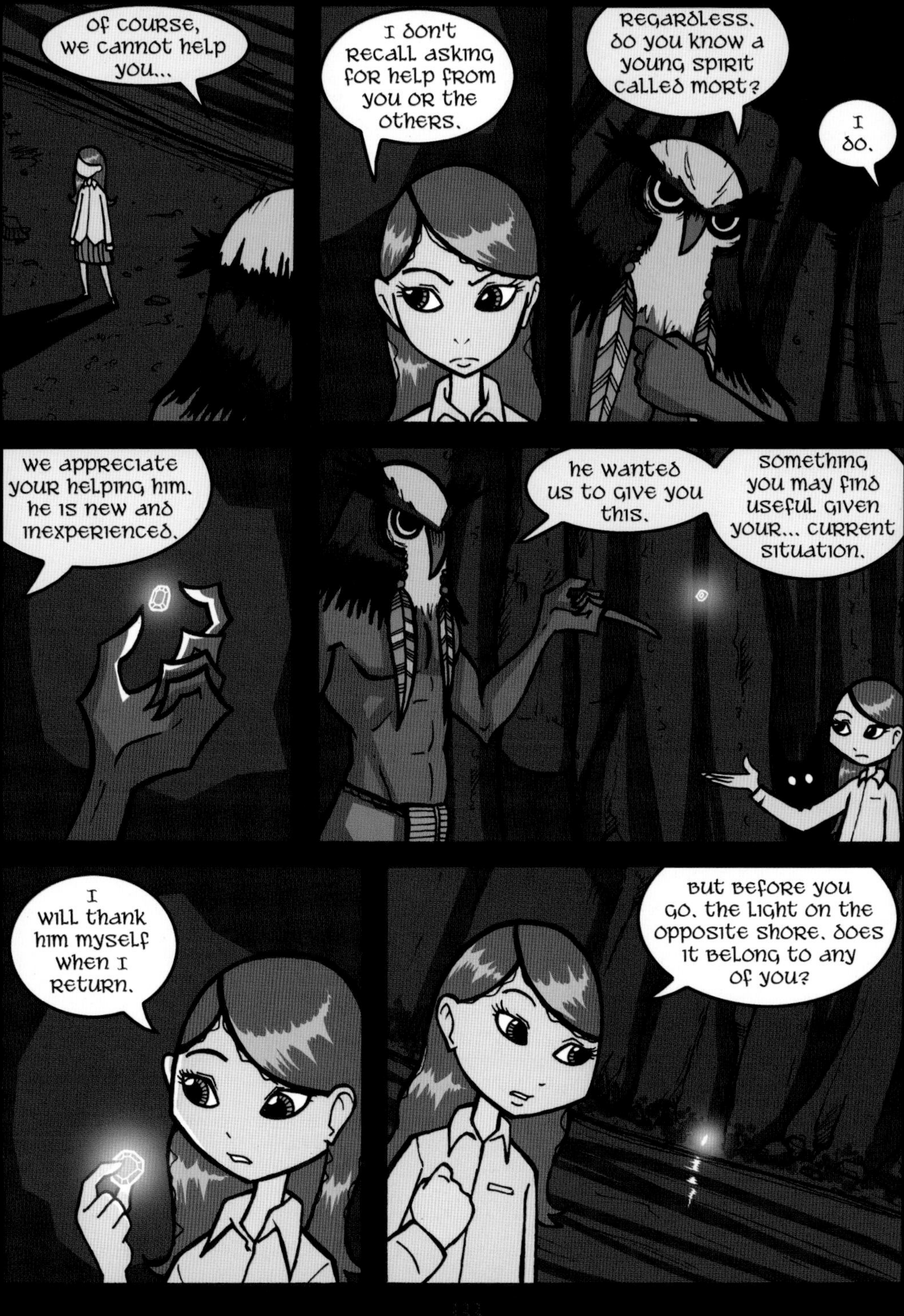
Of course, we cannot help you...
I don't recall asking for help from you or the others.
Regardless. Do you know a young spirit called Mort?
I do.
We appreciate your helping him. He is new and inexperienced.
He wanted us to give you this.
Something you may find useful given your... current situation.
I will thank him myself when I return.
But before you go, the light on the opposite shore, does it belong to any of you?

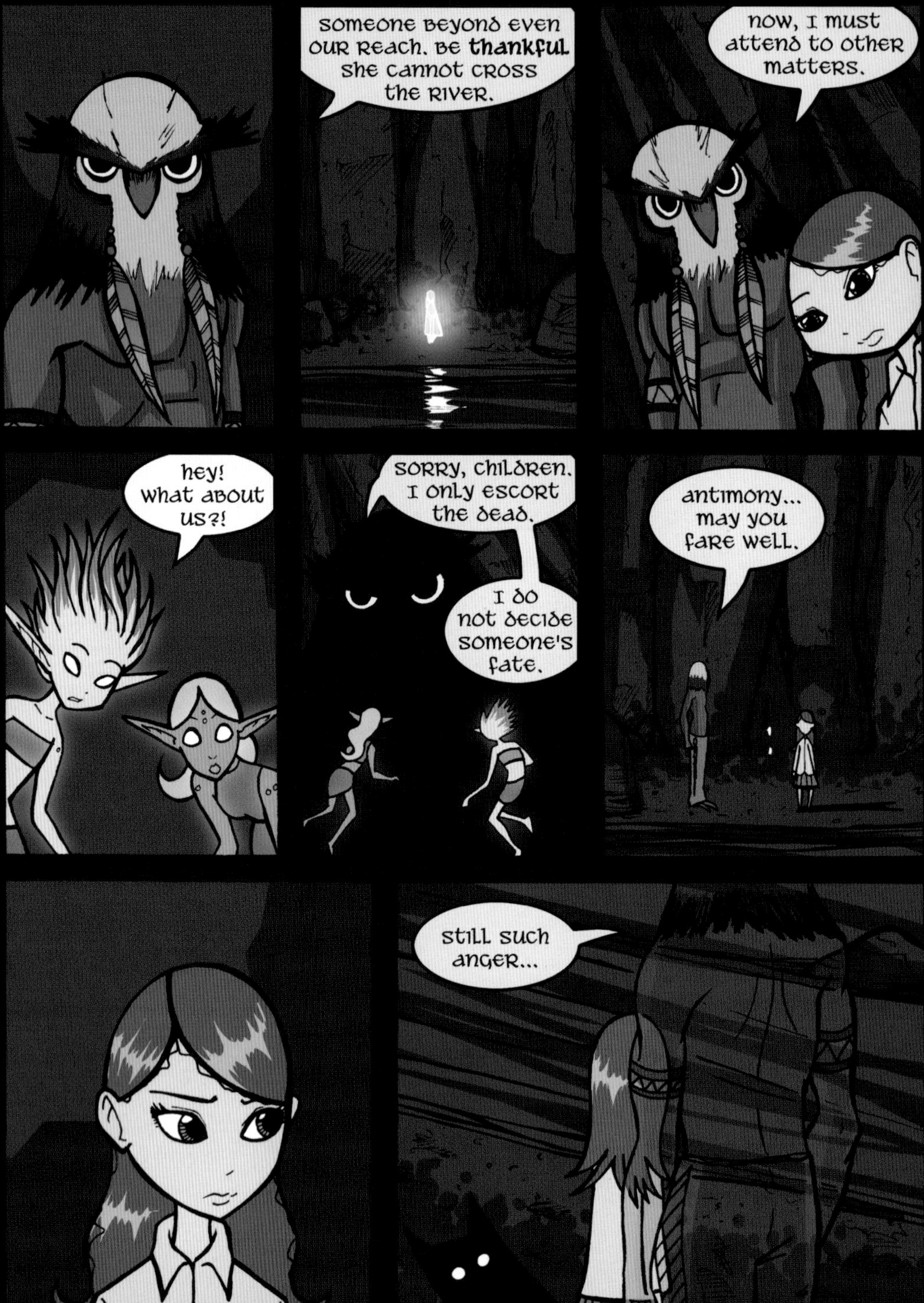
someone beyond even our reach. be **thankful** she cannot cross the river.
now, I must attend to other matters.
hey! what about us?!
sorry, children. I only escort the dead.
I do not decide someone's fate.
antimony... may you fare well.
still such anger...

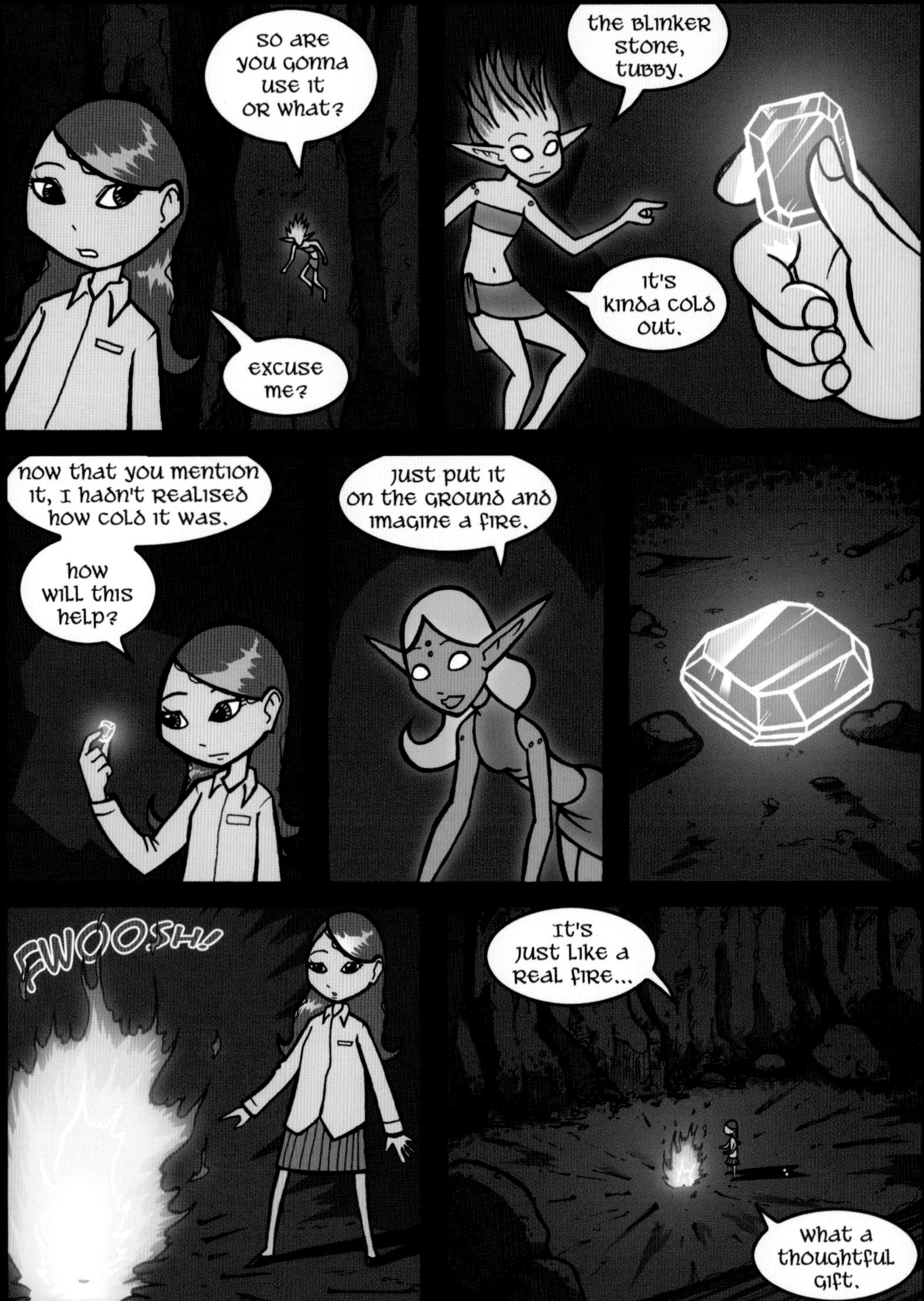
so are you gonna use it or what?
excuse me?
the blinker stone, tubby.
it's kinda cold out.
now that you mention it, I hadn't realised how cold it was.
how will this help?
just put it on the ground and imagine a fire.
FWOOSH!
it's just like a real fire...
what a thoughtful gift.

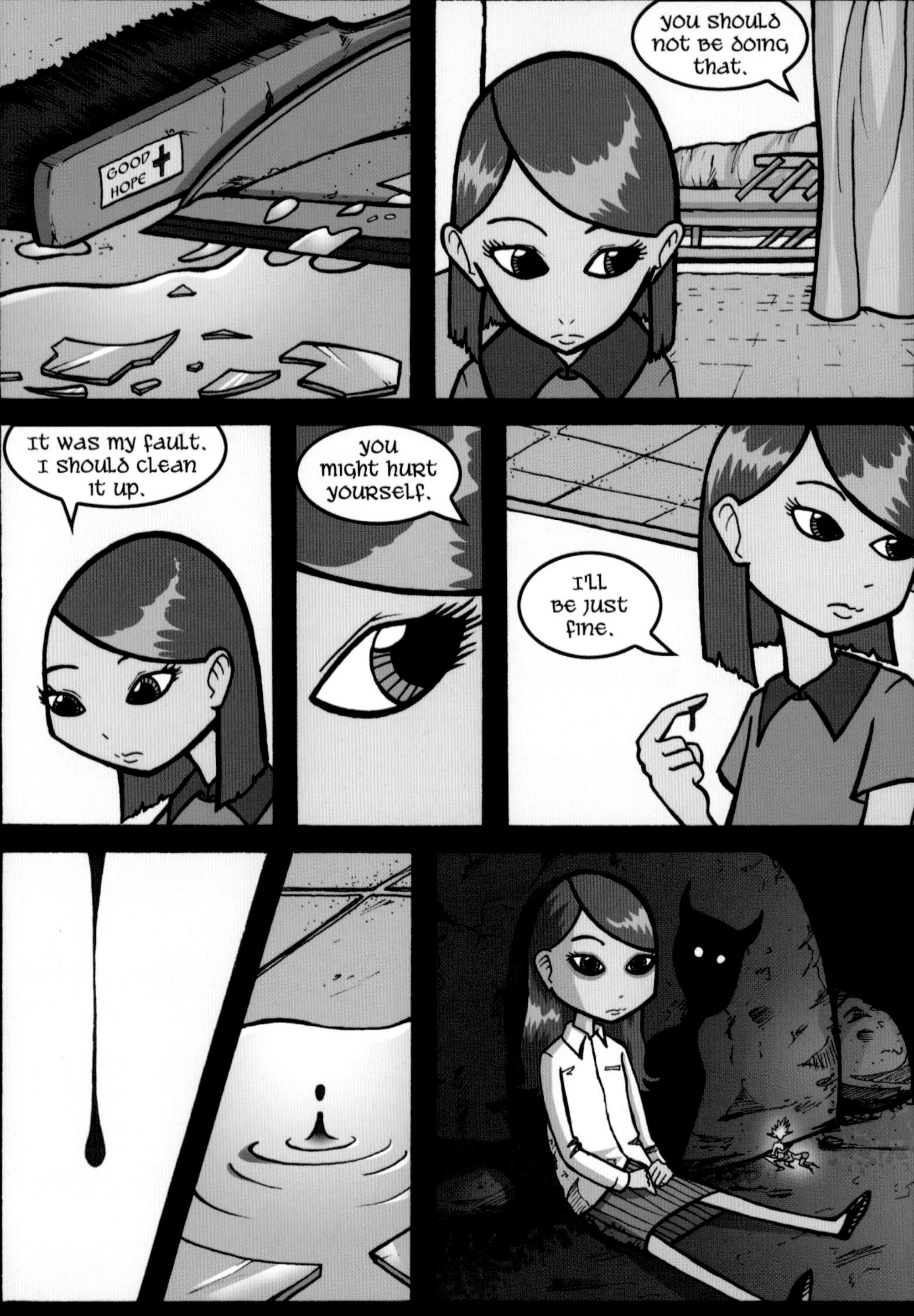
GOOD HOPE
you should not be doing that.
It was my fault. I should clean it up.
you might hurt yourself.
I'll be just fine.

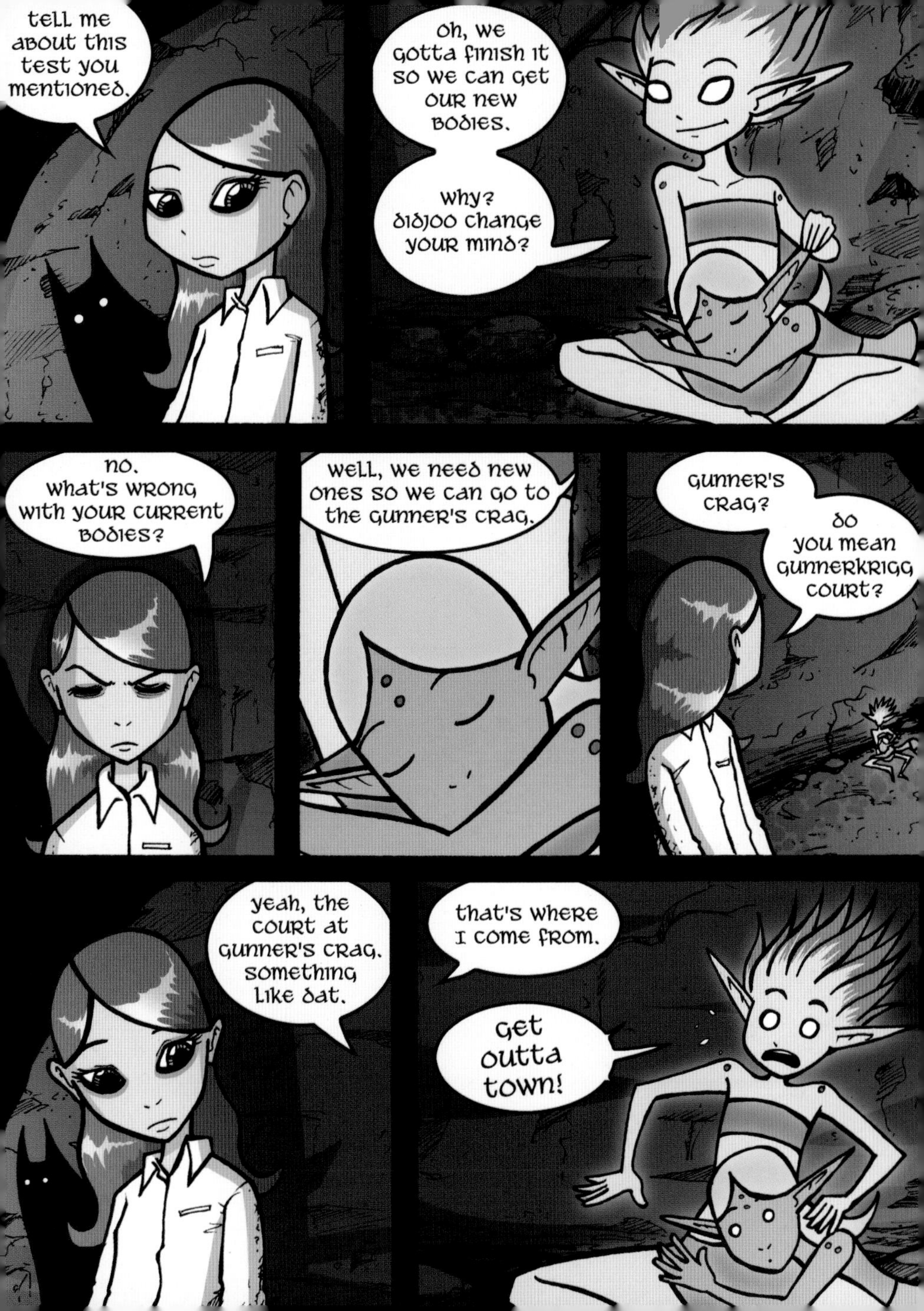
tell me about this test you mentioned.
Oh, we gotta finish it so we can get our new bodies.
Why? didjoo change your mind?
no. What's wrong with your current bodies?
Well, we need new ones so we can go to the Gunner's Crag.
Gunner's Crag?
do you mean Gunnerkrigg Court?
yeah, the court at Gunner's Crag. Something like dat.
that's where I come from.
Get outta town!

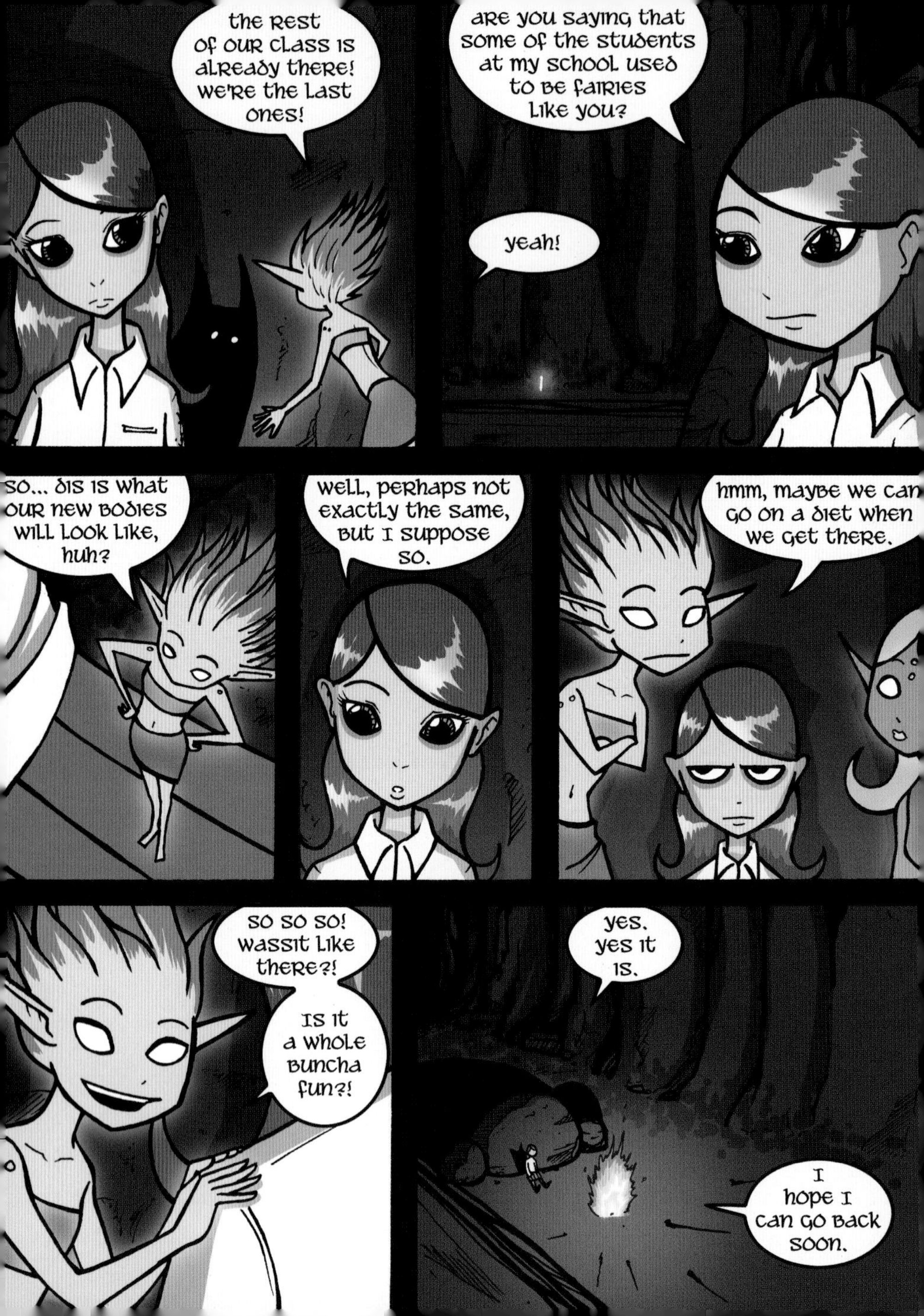
the rest of our class is already there! we're the last ones!
are you saying that some of the students at my school used to be fairies like you?
yeah!
so... dis is what our new bodies will look like, huh?
well, perhaps not exactly the same, but I suppose so.
hmm, maybe we can go on a diet when we get there.
so so so! wassit like there?!
Is it a whole buncha fun?!
yes. yes it is.
I hope I can go back soon.

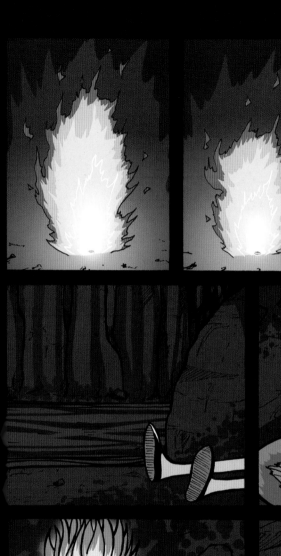

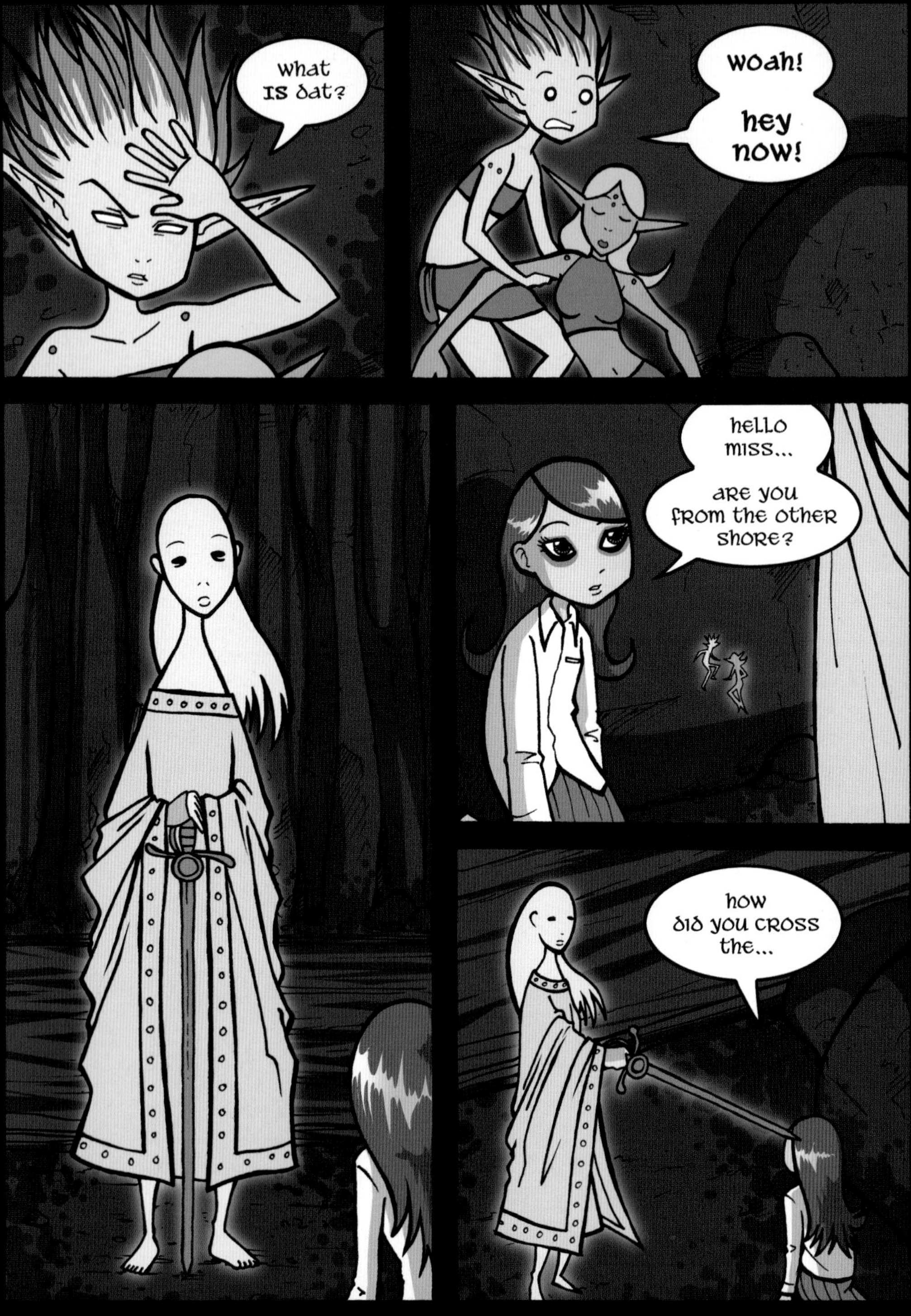
what IS dat?
woah!
hey now!
hello miss...
are you from the other shore?
how did you cross the...

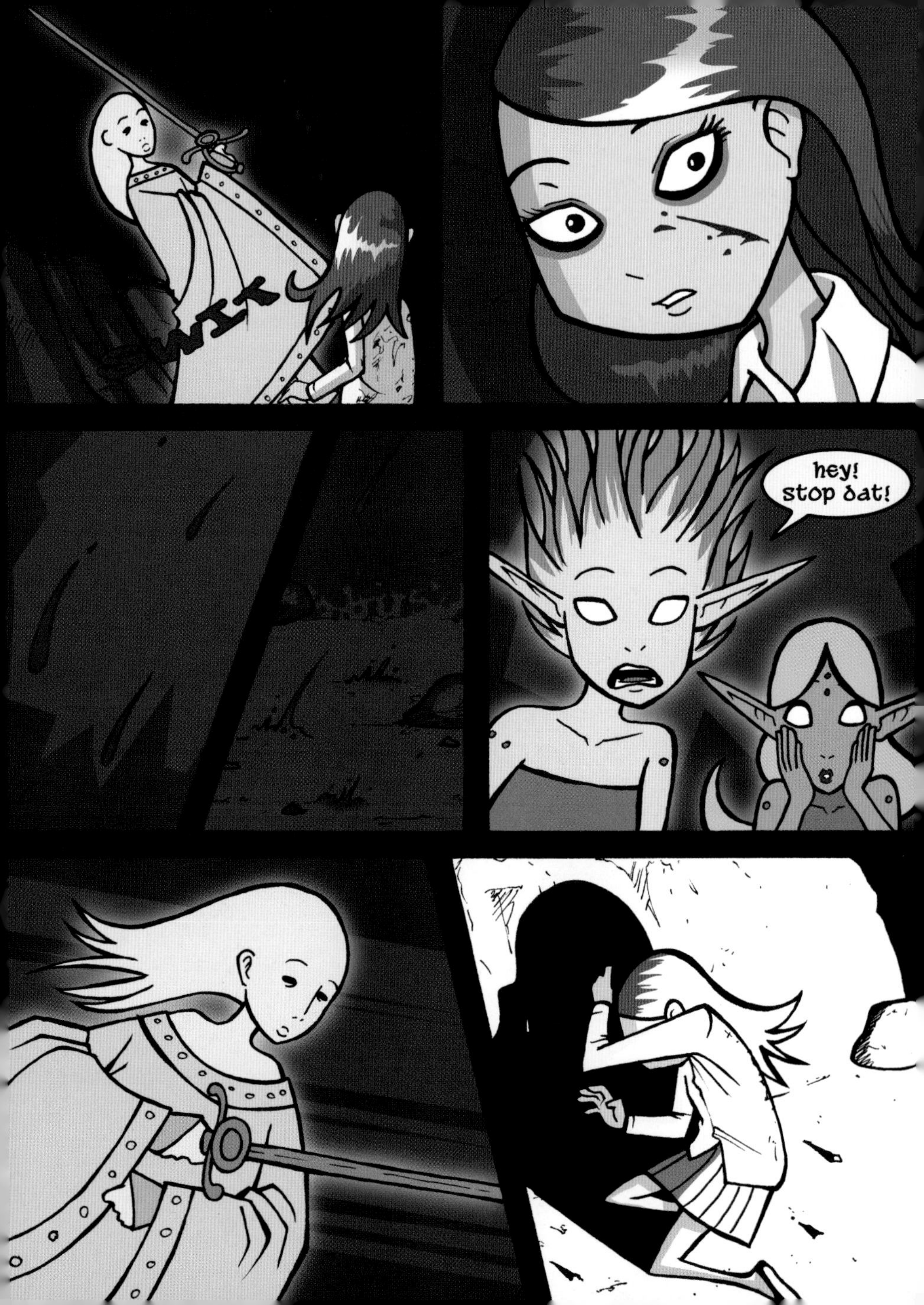
hey!
stop dat!

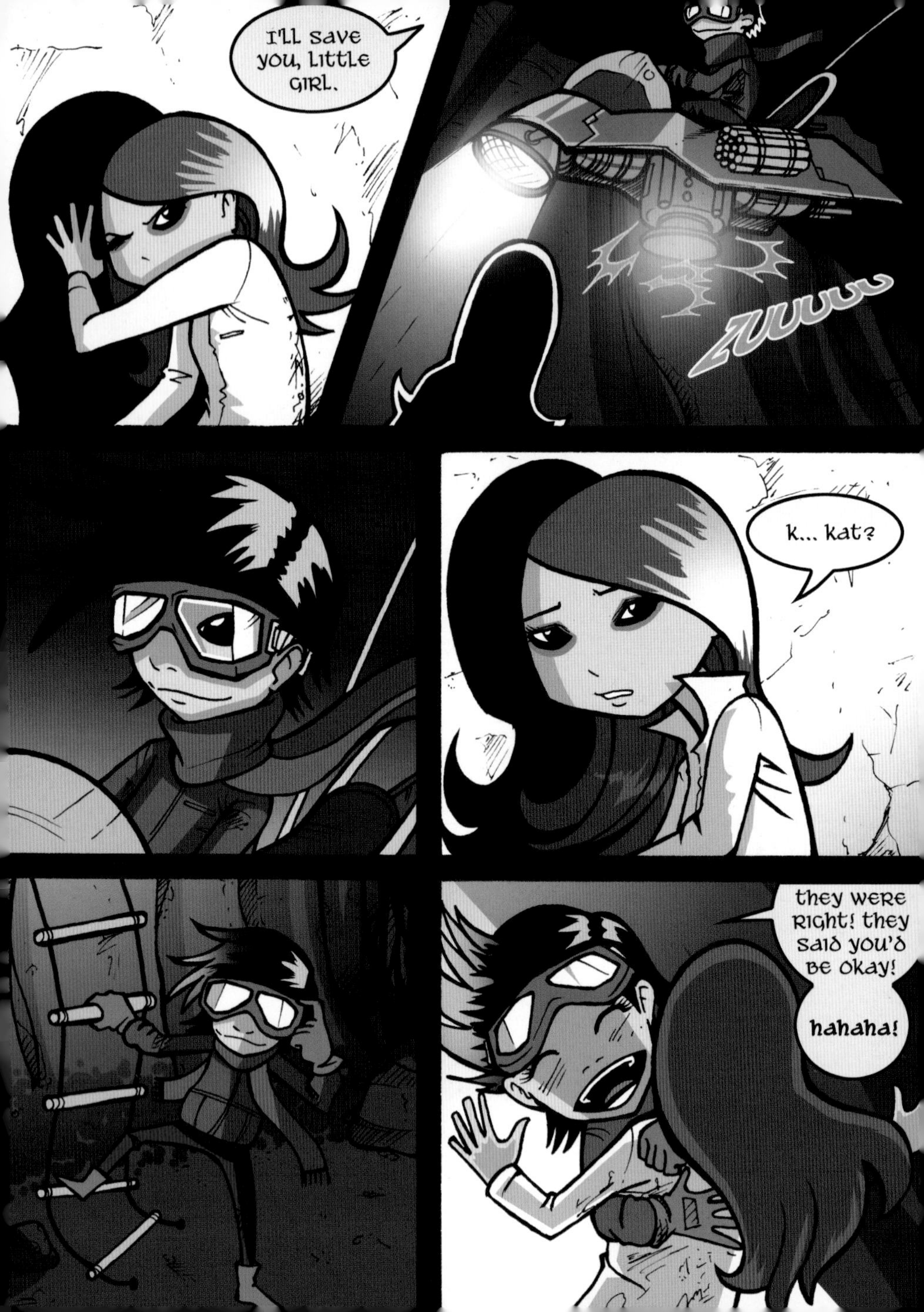
I'LL save you, little girl.
ZUUUUU
k... kat?
they were right! they said you'd be okay!
hahaha!

HOW DID YOU GET DOWN HERE?!

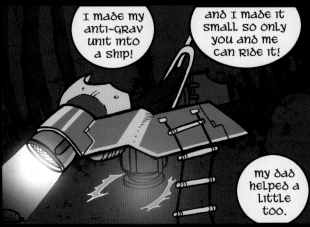

I MADE MY ANTI-GRAV UNIT INTO A SHIP!

AND I MADE IT SMALL SO ONLY YOU AND ME CAN RIDE IT!

MY DAD HELPED A LITTLE TOO.

I'M REALLY SORRY IT TOOK ME SO LONG, ANNIE. I SPENT LIKE THE FIRST HOUR BLUBBERING MY EYES OUT.

YOU DON'T NEED TO APOLOGISE, KAT...

C'MON, LET'S GET YOU HOME. ARE YOU OKAY?

I... I THINK SO, YES.

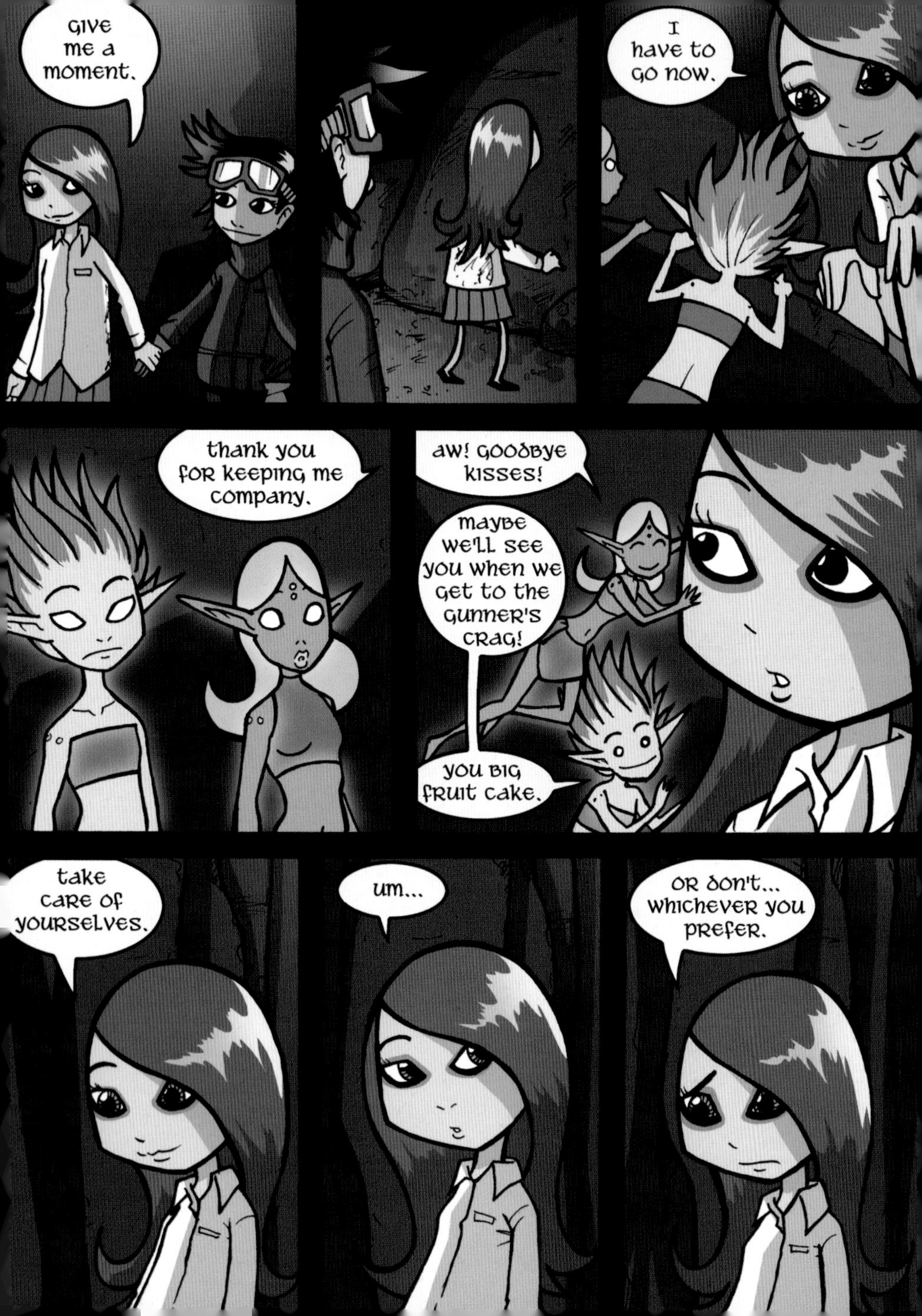
GIVE me a moment.
I have to go now.
thank you for keeping me company.
aw! GOODBYE KISSES!
maybe we'll see you when we get to the GUNNER'S CRAG!
you BIG fruit cake.
take care of yourselves.
um...
OR don't... whichever you prefer.

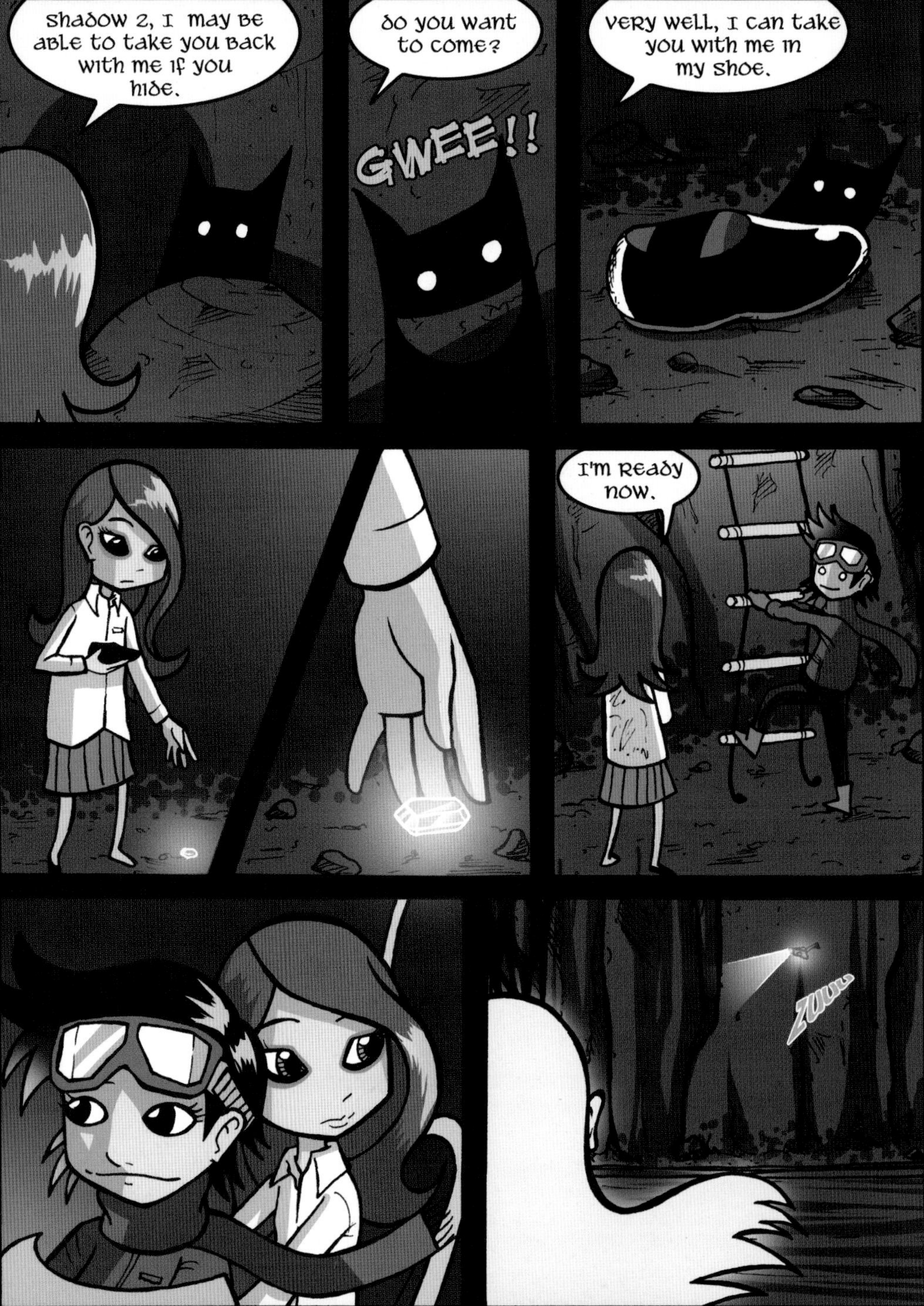
SHADOW 2, I MAY BE ABLE TO TAKE YOU BACK WITH ME IF YOU HIDE.
DO YOU WANT TO COME?
GWEE!!
VERY WELL, I CAN TAKE YOU WITH ME IN MY SHOE.
I'M READY NOW.
ZUUU

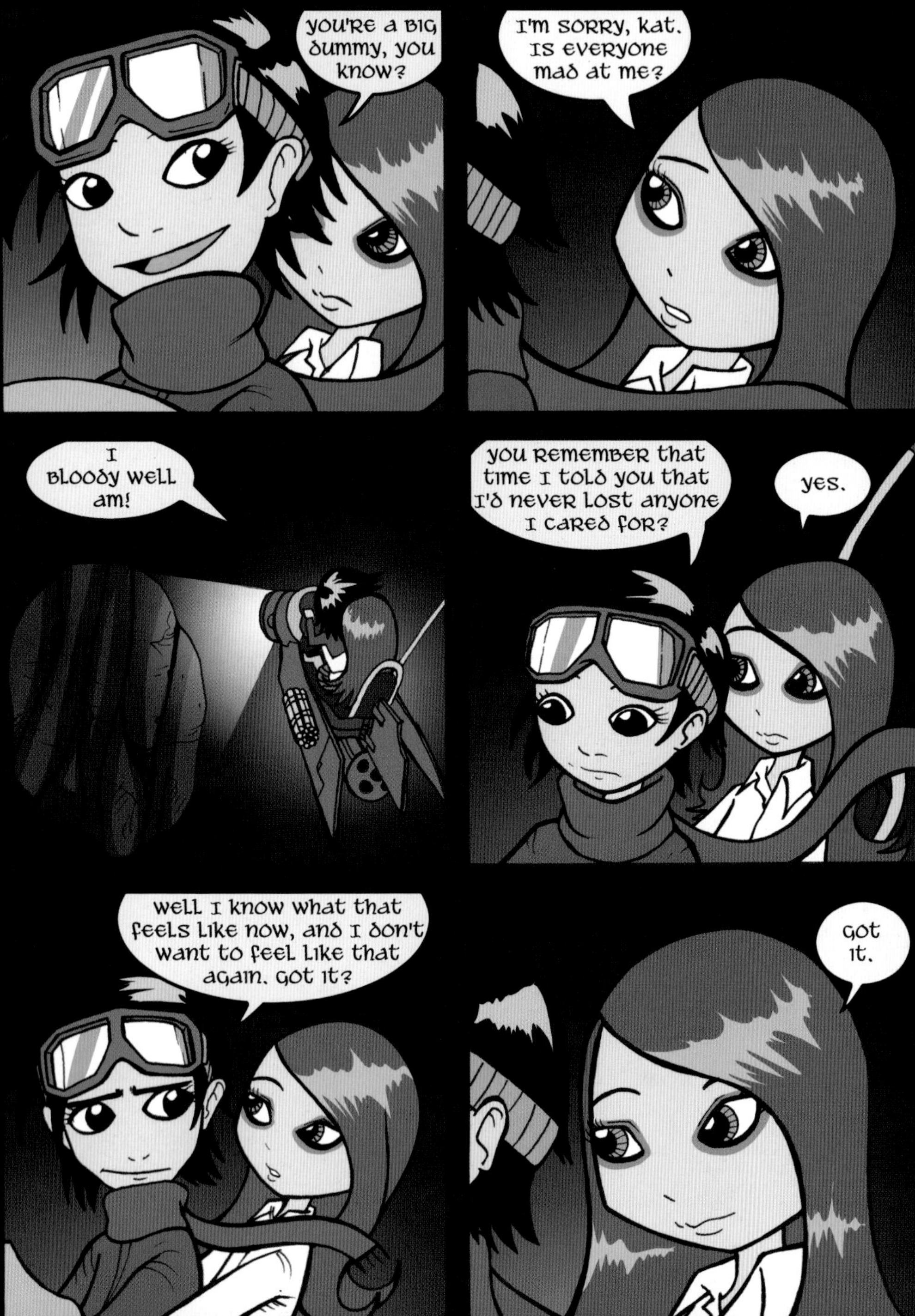
YOU'RE A BIG DUMMY, YOU KNOW?
I'M SORRY, KAT. IS EVERYONE MAD AT ME?
I BLOODY WELL AM!
YOU REMEMBER THAT TIME I TOLD YOU THAT I'D NEVER LOST ANYONE I CARED FOR?
YES.
WELL I KNOW WHAT THAT FEELS LIKE NOW, AND I DON'T WANT TO FEEL LIKE THAT AGAIN. GOT IT?
GOT IT.

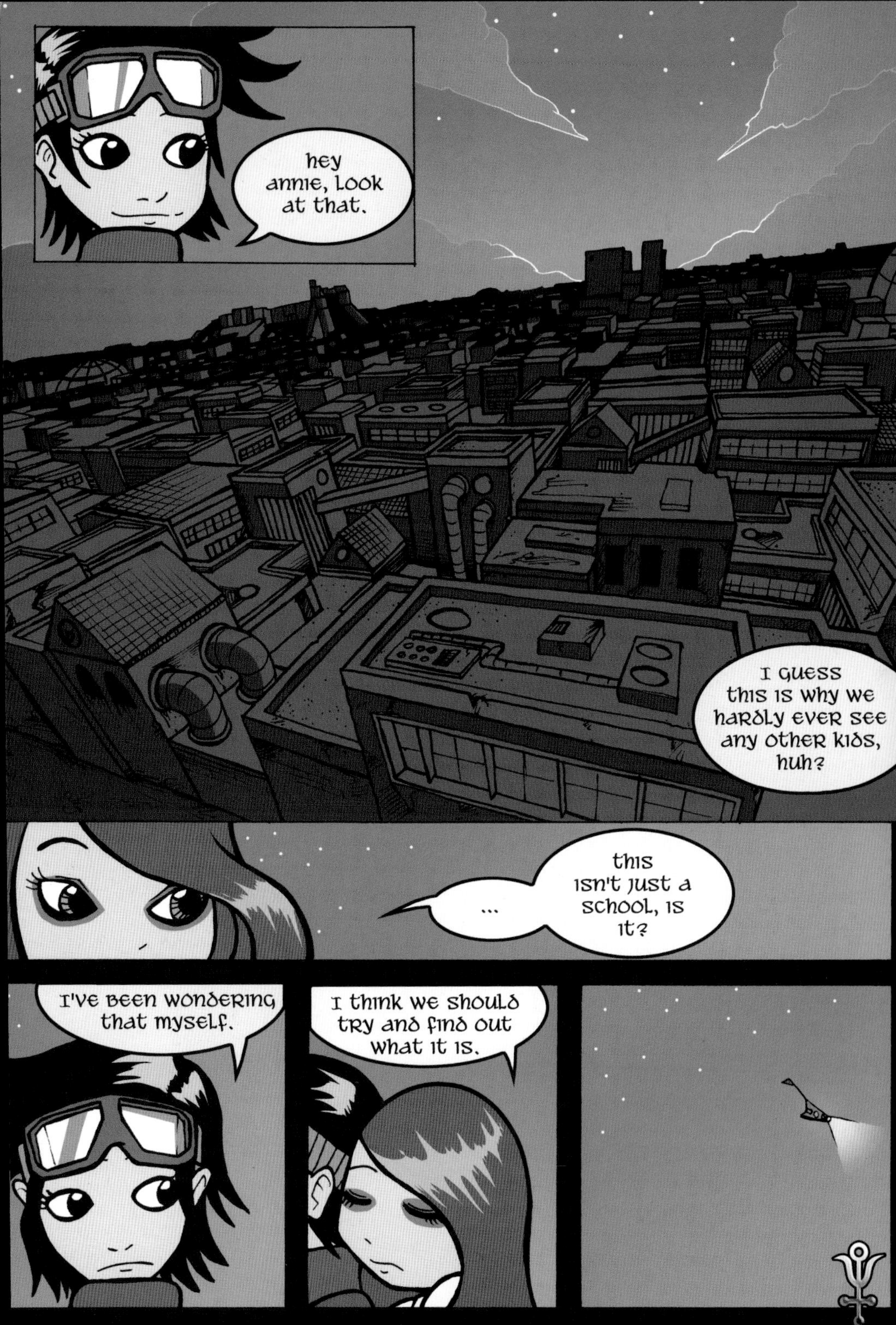
hey annie, look at that.
I guess this is why we hardly ever see any other kids, huh?
... this isn't just a school, is it?
I've been wondering that myself.
I think we should try and find out what it is.

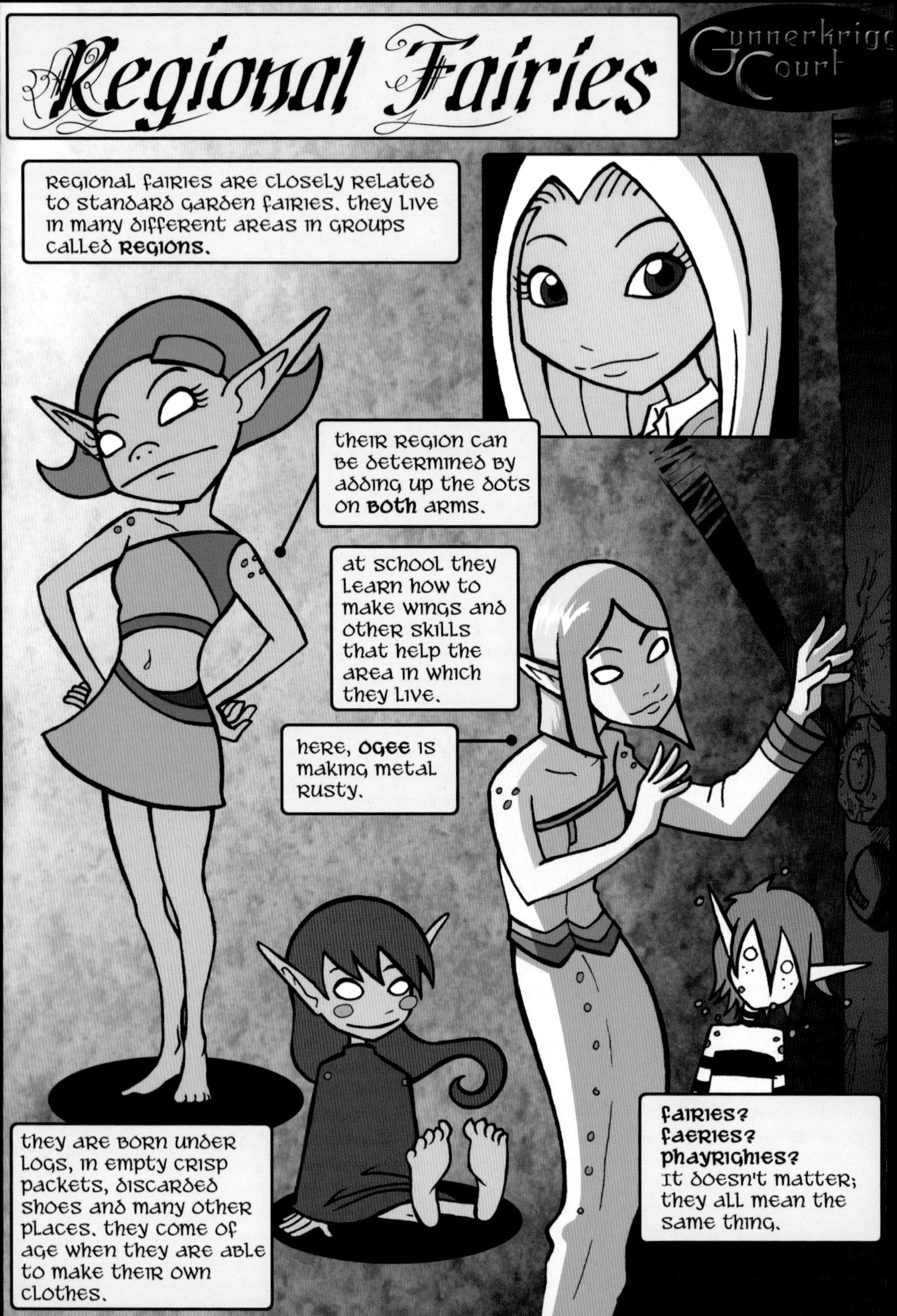
Regional Fairies
Gunnerkrigg Court
Regional fairies are closely related to standard garden fairies. they live in many different areas in groups called **Regions.**
their region can be determined by adding up the dots on **both** arms.
at school they learn how to make wings and other skills that help the area in which they live.
here, **Ogee** is making metal rusty.
they are born under logs, in empty crisp packets, discarded shoes and many other places. they come of age when they are able to make their own clothes.
fairies? faeries? phayrighies? It doesn't matter; they all mean the same thing.

Gunnerkrigg Court

Chapter 9:

Questions and Answers

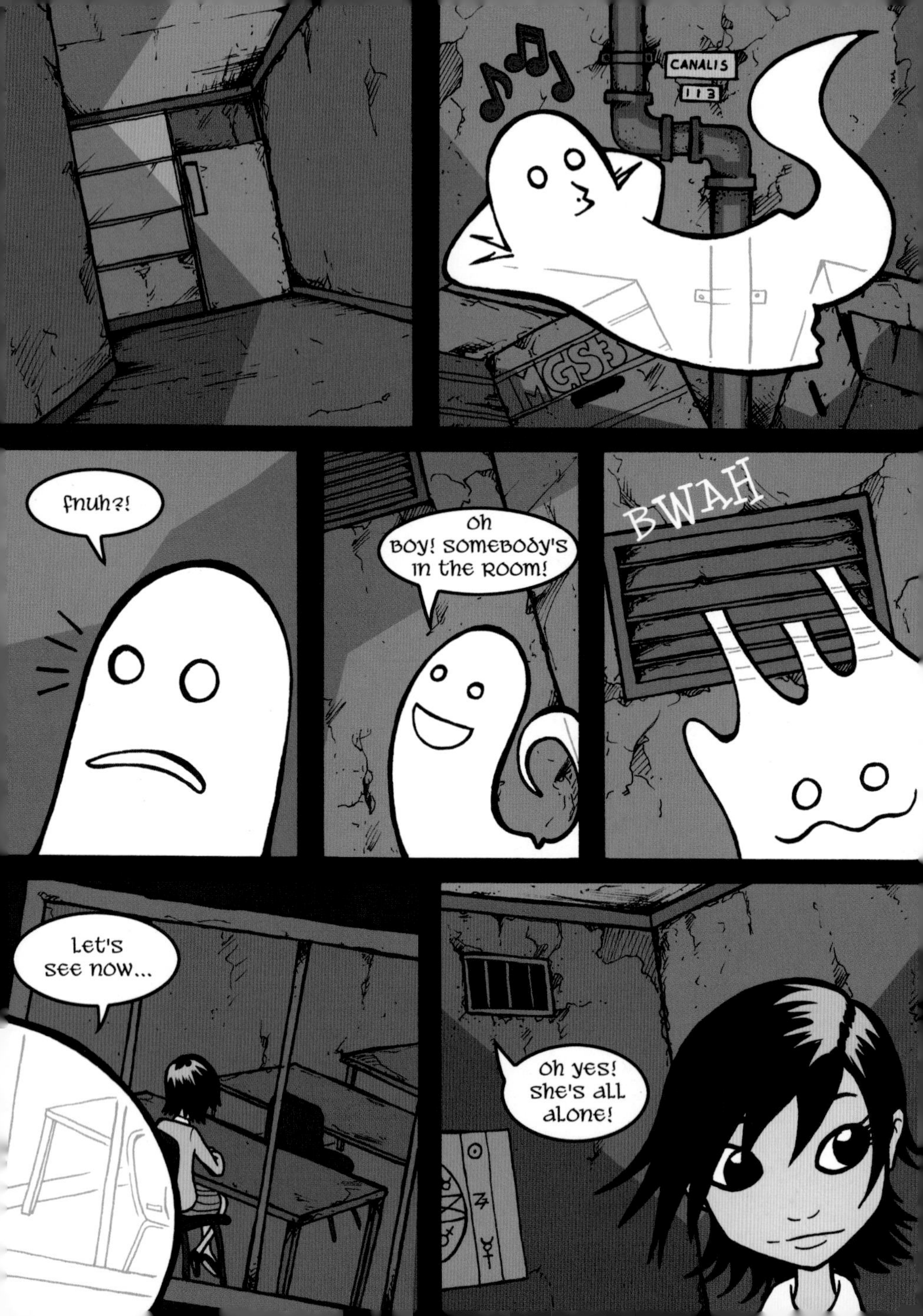
CANALIS
113
MGS3
fnuh?!
Oh BOY! SOMEBODY'S IN THE ROOM!
BWAH
Let's see now...
Oh yes! She's all alone!

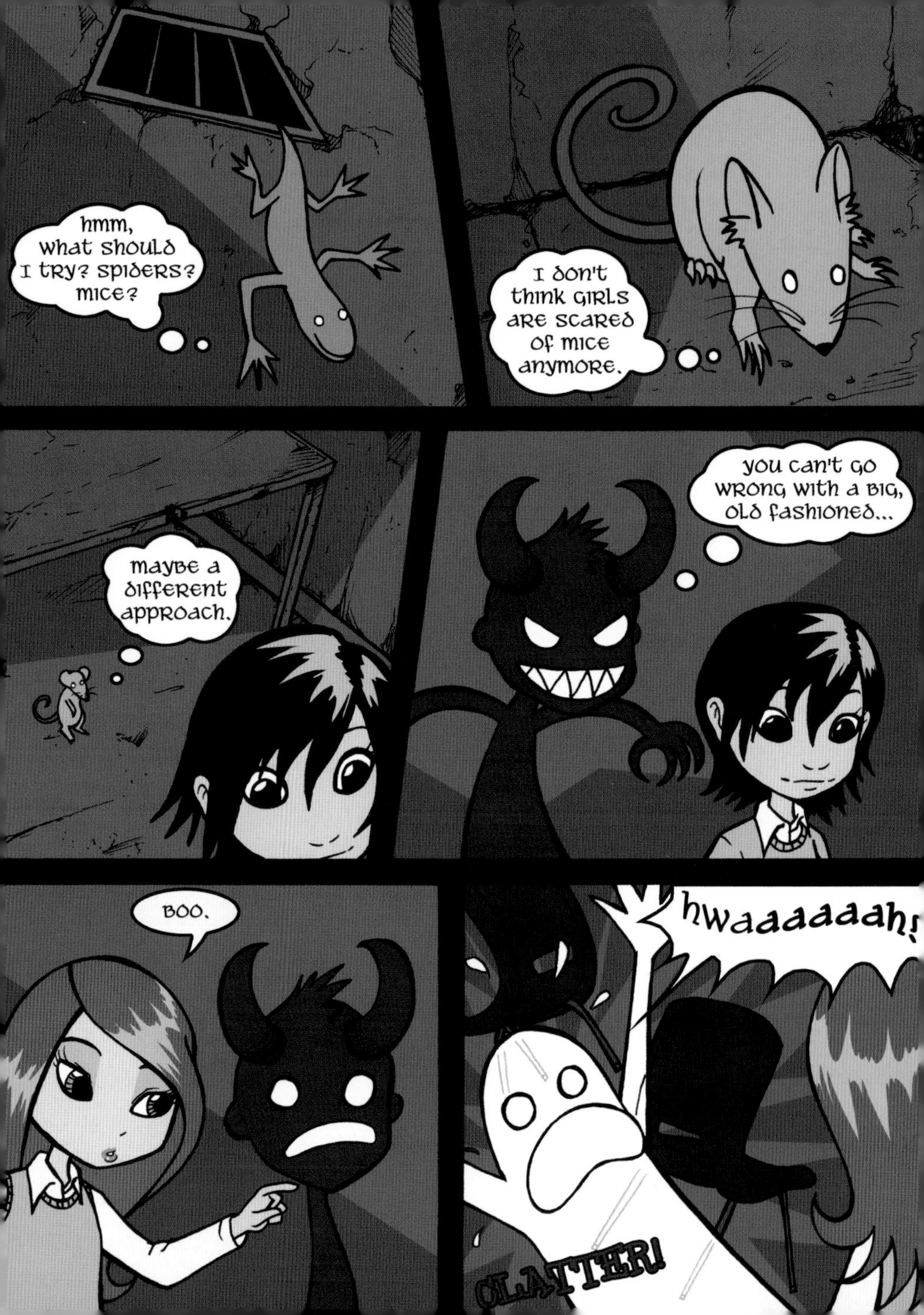
hmm, what should I try? spiders? mice?
I don't think girls are scared of mice anymore.
maybe a different approach.
you can't go wrong with a big, old fashioned...
BOO.
hwaaaaaah!
CLATTER!

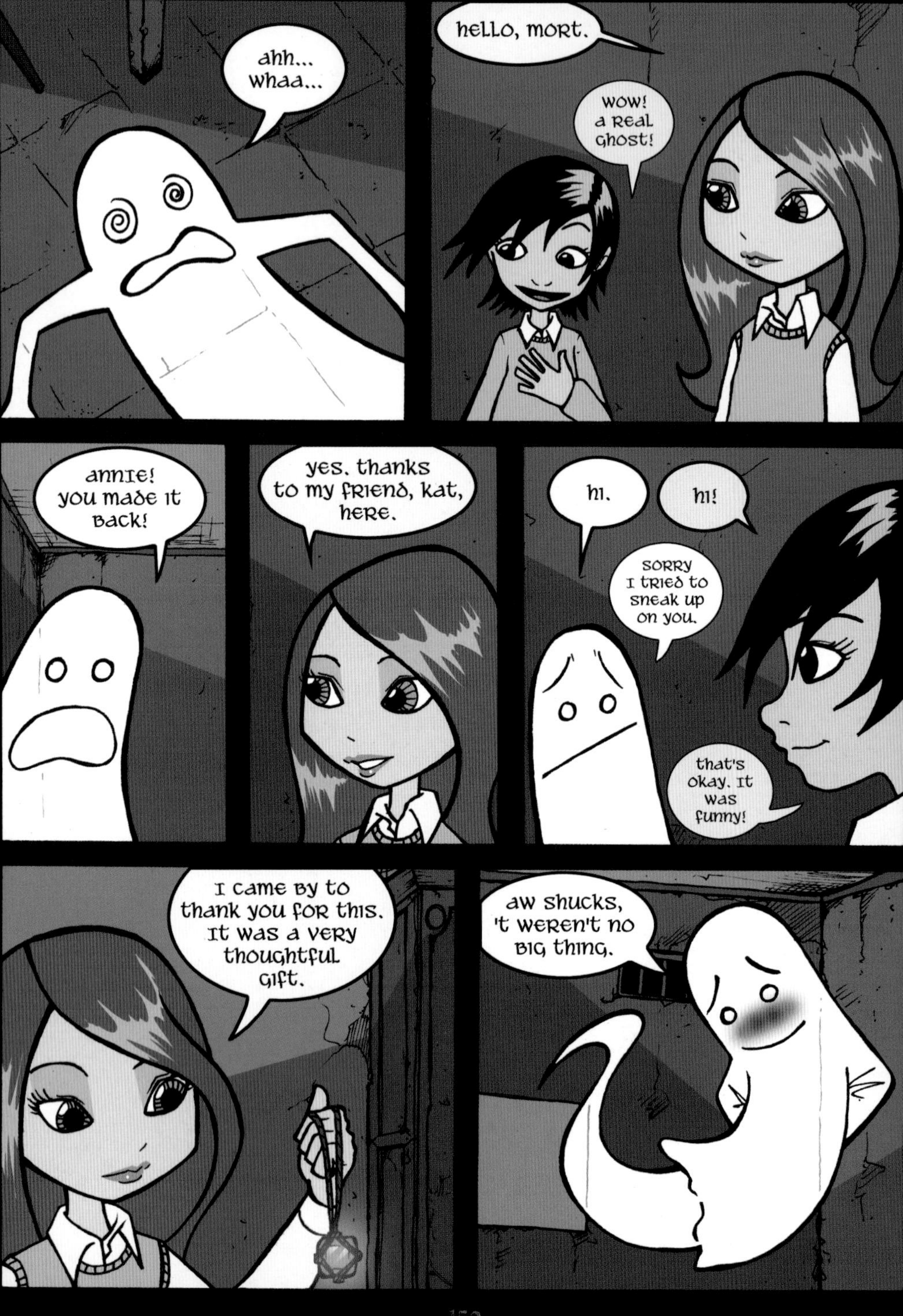
ahh... whaa...
hello, mort.
wow! a real ghost!
annie! you made it back!
yes. thanks to my friend, kat, here.
hi.
hi!
sorry I tried to sneak up on you.
that's okay. it was funny!
I came by to thank you for this. it was a very thoughtful gift.
aw shucks, 't weren't no big thing.

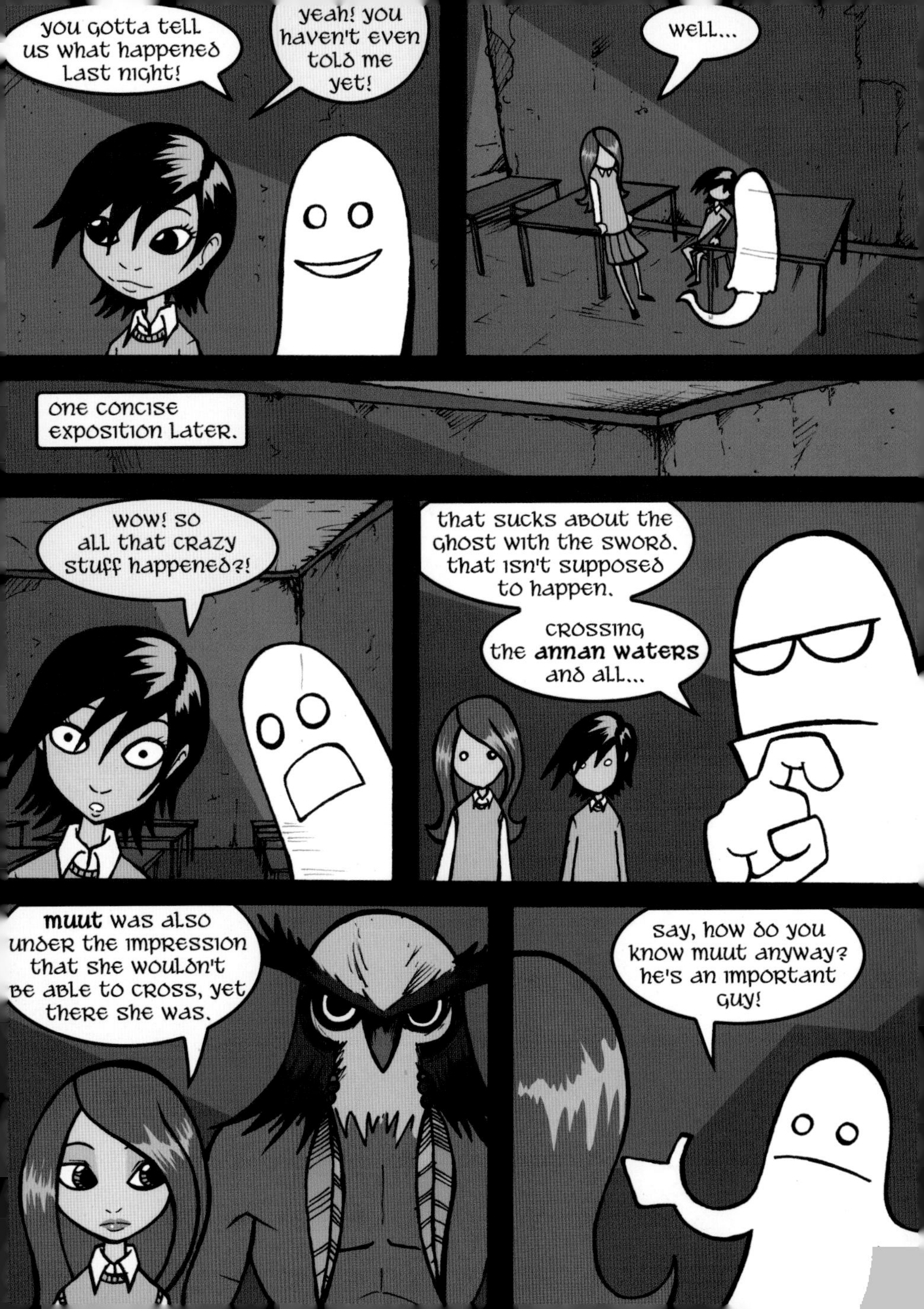
you gotta tell us what happened last night!
yeah! you haven't even told me yet!
well...
one concise exposition later.
wow! so all that crazy stuff happened?!
that sucks about the ghost with the sword. that isn't supposed to happen.
crossing the **annan waters** and all...
muut was also under the impression that she wouldn't be able to cross, yet there she was.
say, how do you know muut anyway? he's an important guy!

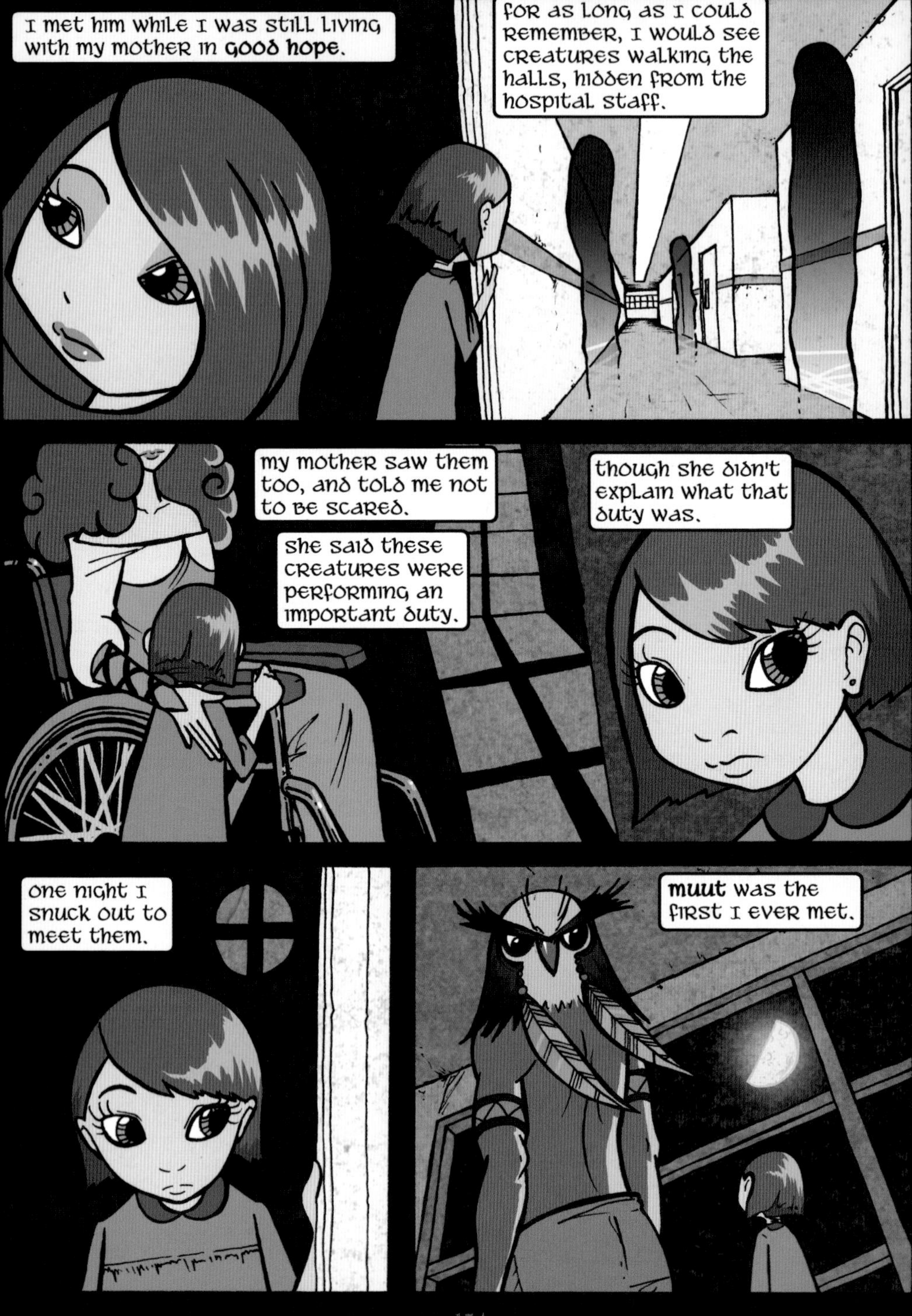
I met him while I was still living with my mother in GOOD HOPE.
For as long as I could remember, I would see creatures walking the halls, hidden from the hospital staff.
My mother saw them too, and told me not to be scared.
She said these creatures were performing an important duty.
Though she didn't explain what that duty was.
One night I snuck out to meet them.
MUUT was the first I ever met.

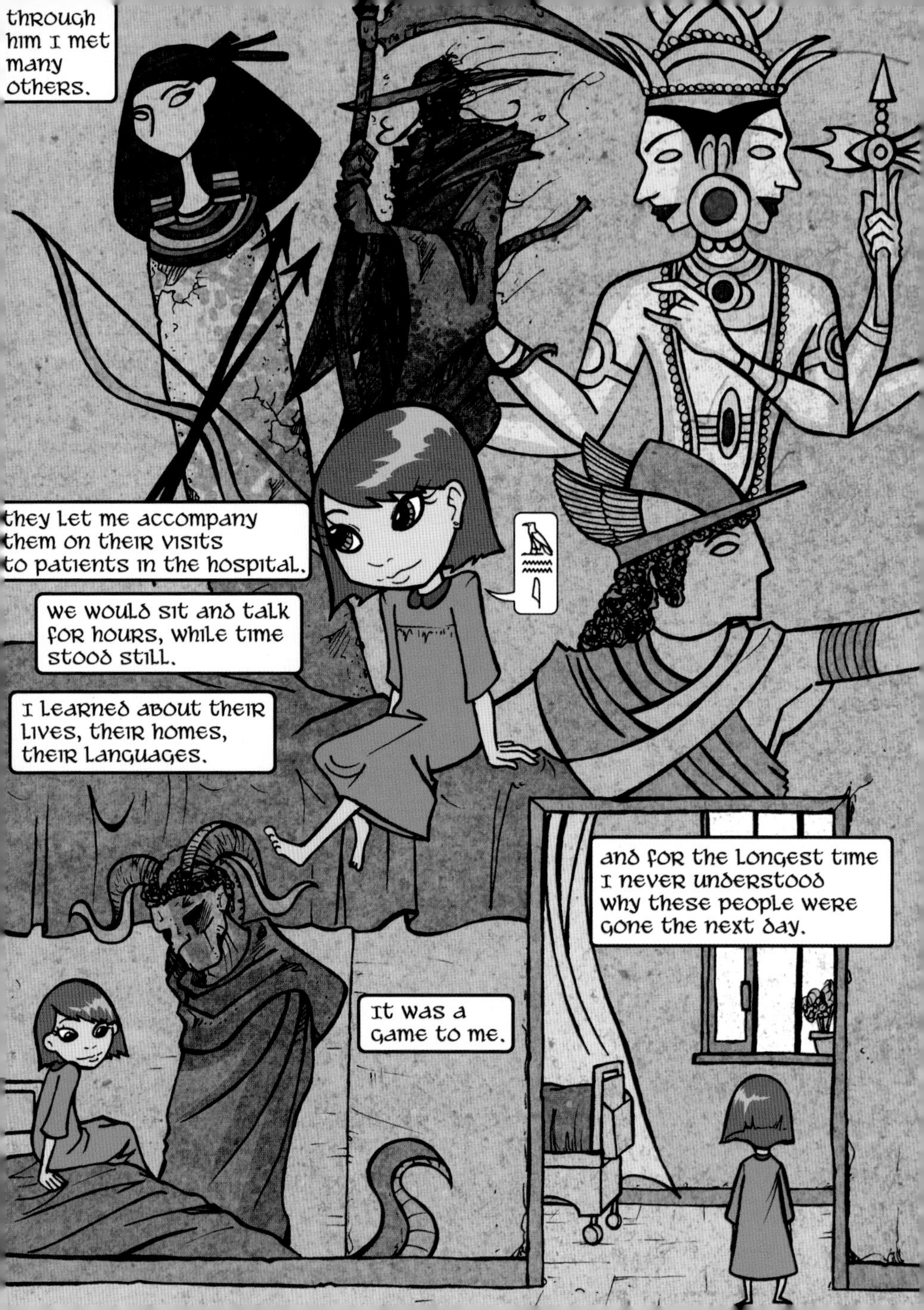
through him I met many others.
they let me accompany them on their visits to patients in the hospital.
we would sit and talk for hours, while time stood still.
I learned about their lives, their homes, their languages.
and for the longest time I never understood why these people were gone the next day.
It was a game to me.

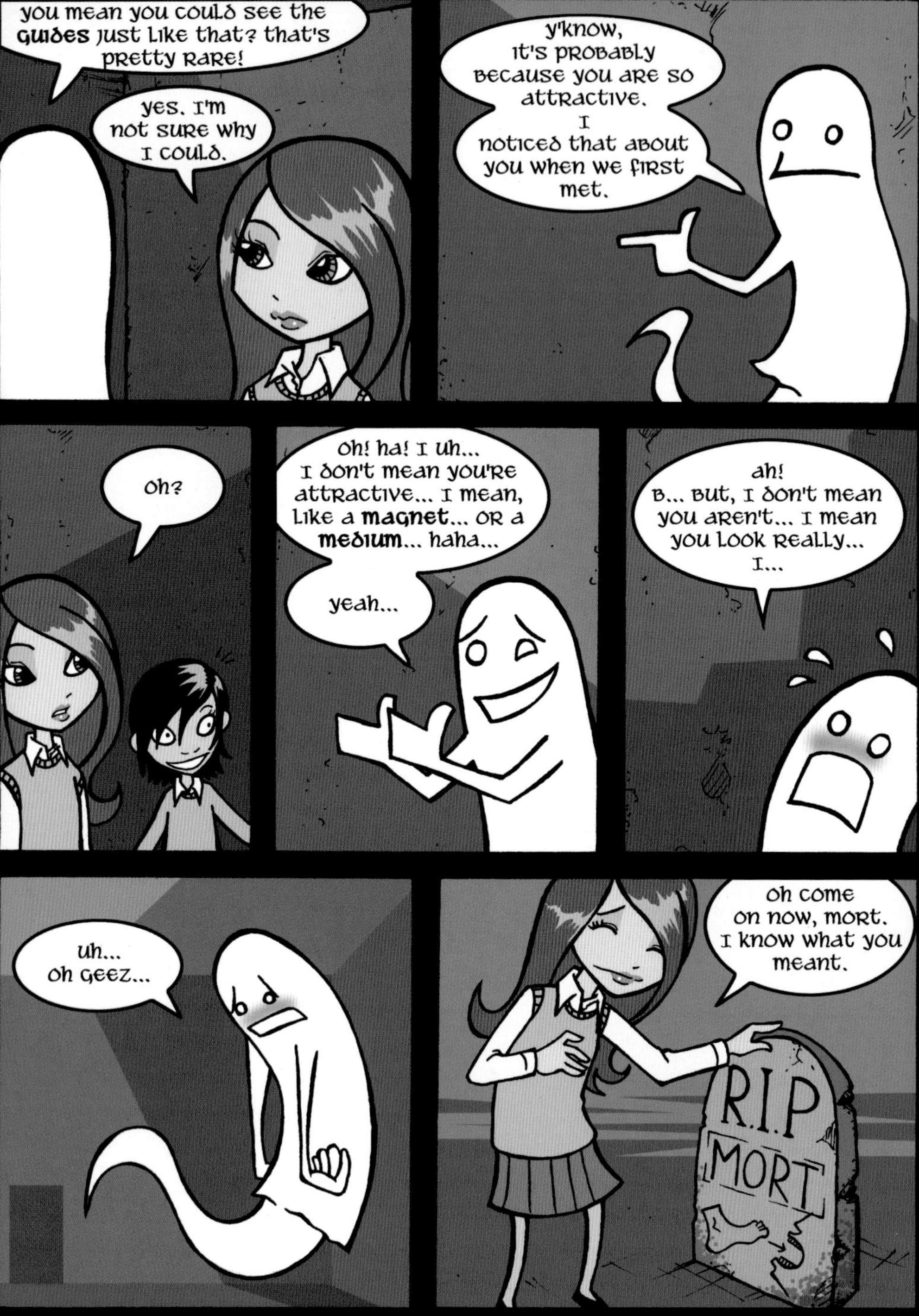
you mean you could see the guides just like that? that's pretty rare!
yes. I'm not sure why I could.
y'know, it's probably because you are so attractive.
I noticed that about you when we first met.
oh?
oh! ha! I uh... I don't mean you're attractive... I mean, like a magnet... or a medium... haha...
yeah...
ah! B... but, I don't mean you aren't... I mean you look really... I...
uh... oh geez...
oh come on now, mort. I know what you meant.
R.I.P
MORT

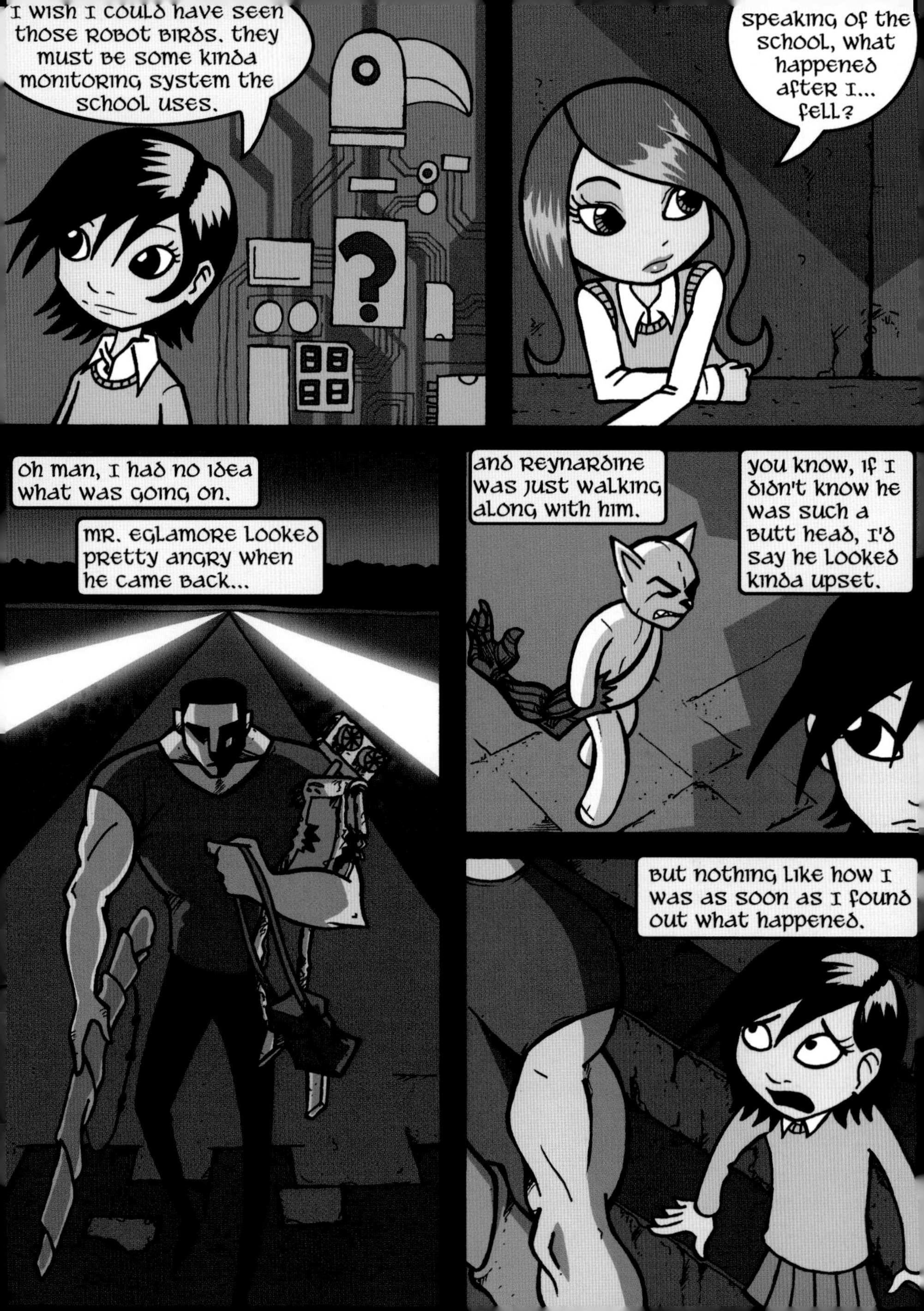
I wish I could have seen those robot birds. they must be some kinda monitoring system the school uses.
speaking of the school, what happened after I... fell?
oh man, I had no idea what was going on.
mr. eglamore looked pretty angry when he came back...
and reynardine was just walking along with him.
you know, if I didn't know he was such a butt head, I'd say he looked kinda upset.
but nothing like how I was as soon as I found out what happened.

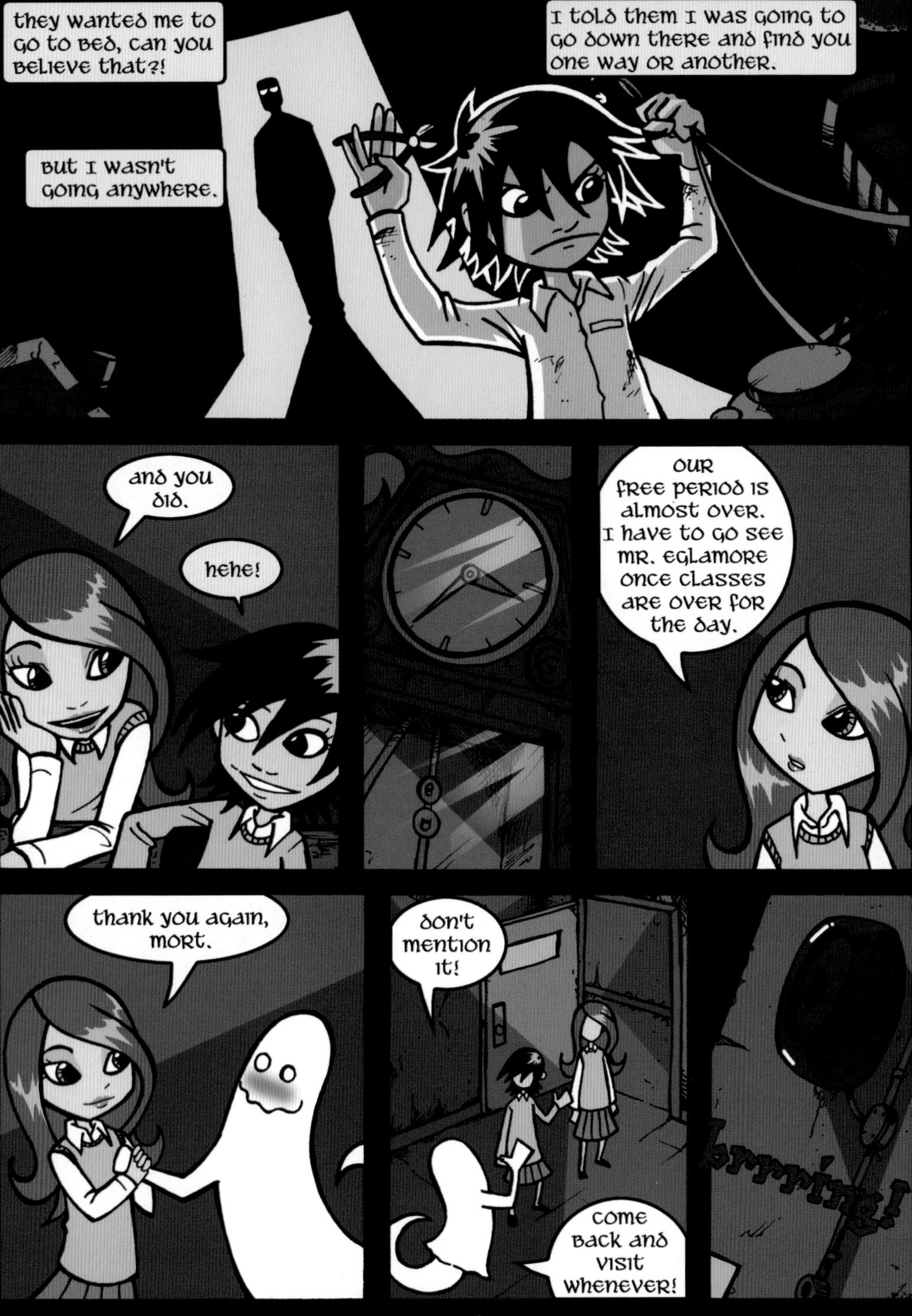
they wanted me to go to bed, can you believe that?!
I told them I was going to go down there and find you one way or another.
But I wasn't going anywhere.
and you did.
hehe!
our free period is almost over. I have to go see Mr. Eglamore once classes are over for the day.
thank you again, Mort.
don't mention it!
come back and visit whenever!
brrring!

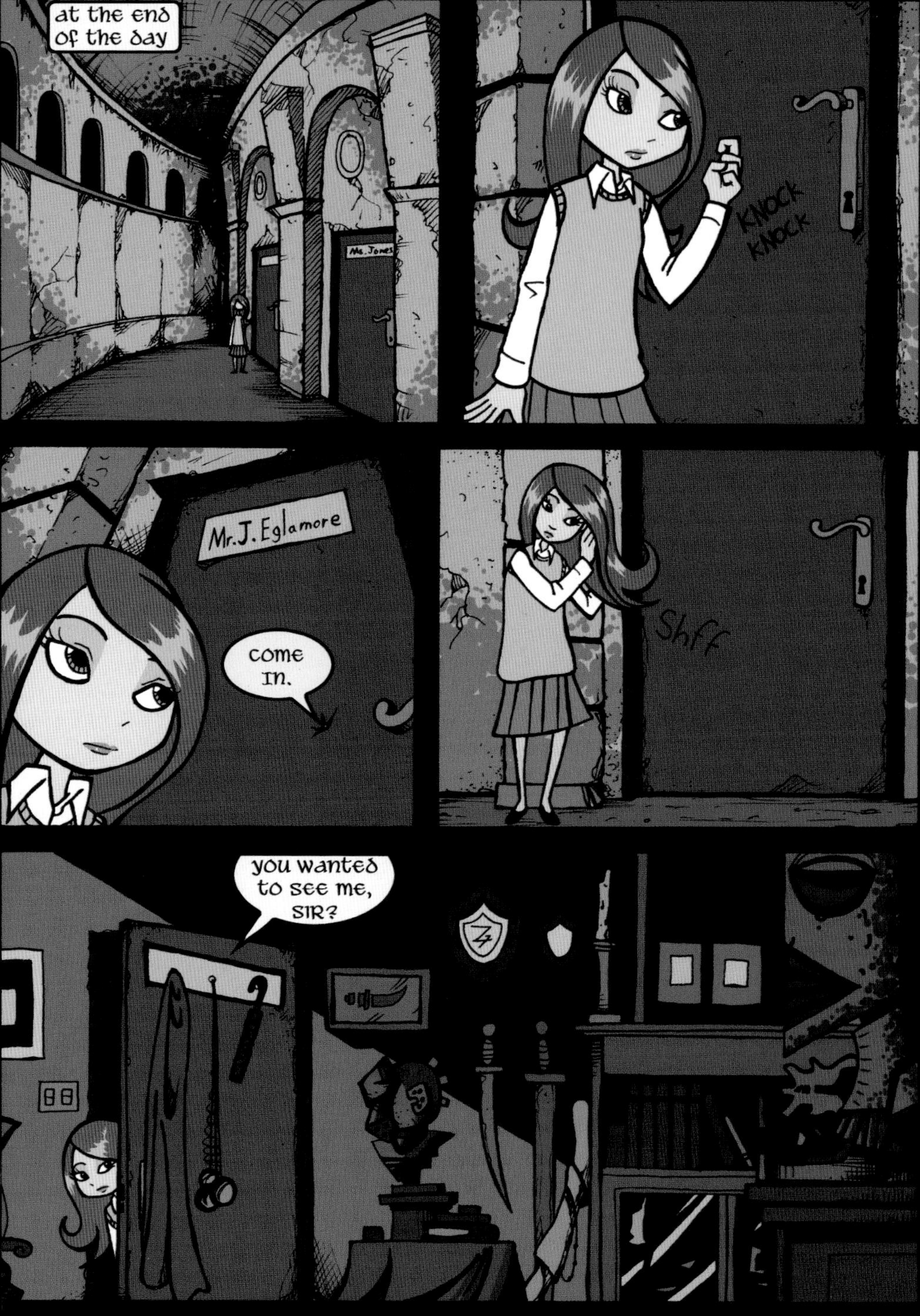
at the end of the day
Ms. Jones
KNOCK KNOCK
Mr. J. Eglamore
come in.
Shff
you wanted to see me, SIR?

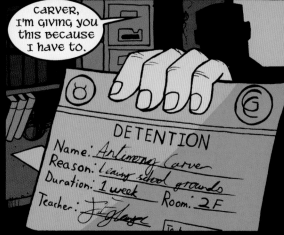

CARVER, I'M GIVING YOU THIS BECAUSE I HAVE TO.

DETENTION

Name: Antimony Carver
Reason: Leaving school grounds
Duration: 1 week   Room: 2F
Teacher:

WE HAVE RULES FOR A REASON.

FOR YOUR SAFETY.

AND IF YOU'RE GOING TO BREAK THEM, YOU SHOULD TRY HARDER TO NOT GET CAUGHT.

YOU KNOW, YOUR MOTHER NEVER GOT A SINGLE DAY'S DETENTION, BUT THAT DOESN'T MEAN SHE ALWAYS FOLLOWED THE RULES.

WELL I'M SORRY I'M NOT AS CLEVER AS MY MOTHER.

I DON'T THINK YOUR ADVICE IS VERY APPROPRIATE.

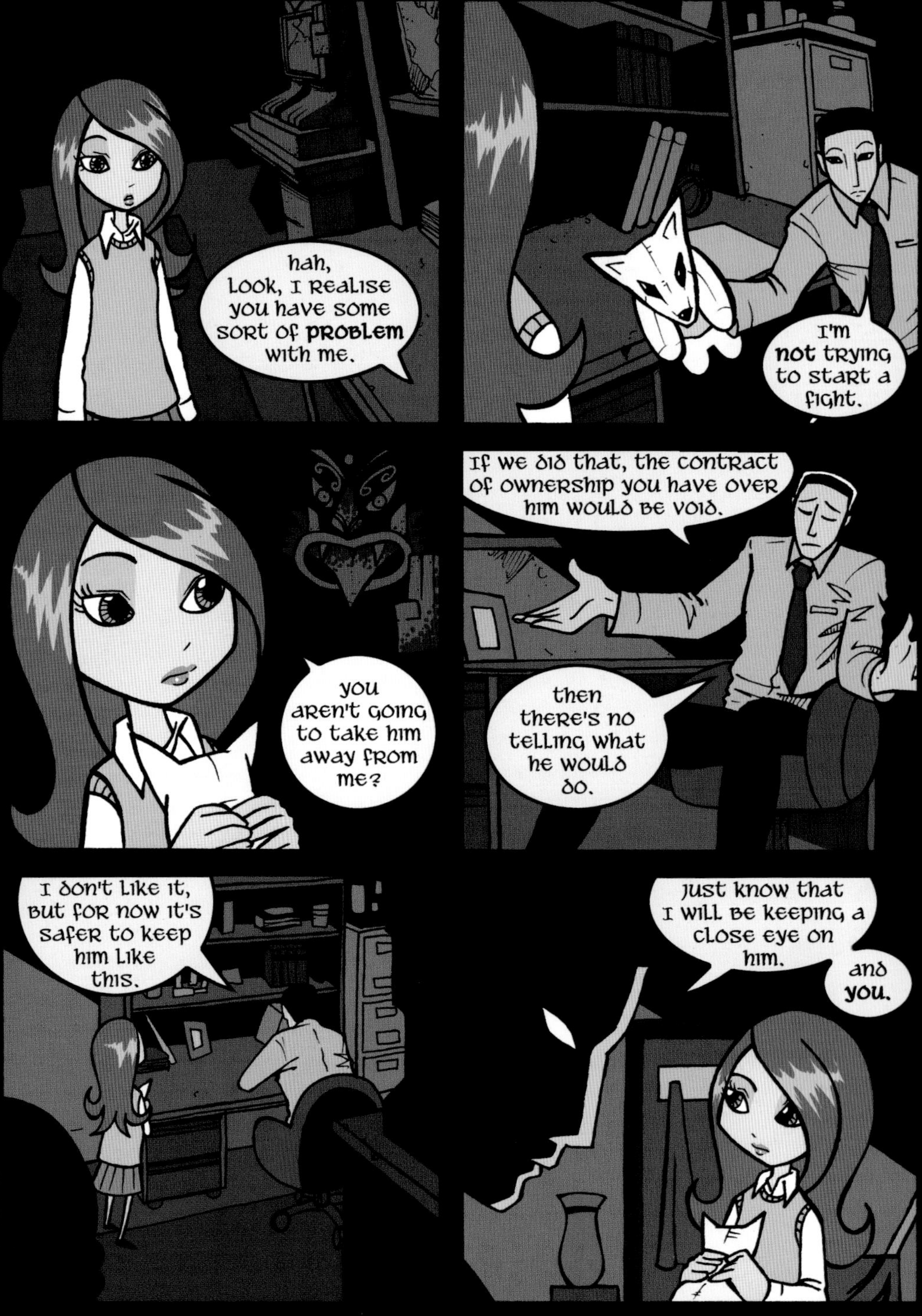
hah, look, I realise you have some sort of **problem** with me.
I'm **not** trying to start a fight.
you aren't going to take him away from me?
If we did that, the contract of ownership you have over him would be void.
then there's no telling what he would do.
I don't like it, but for now it's safer to keep him like this.
Just know that I will be keeping a close eye on him.
and **you.**

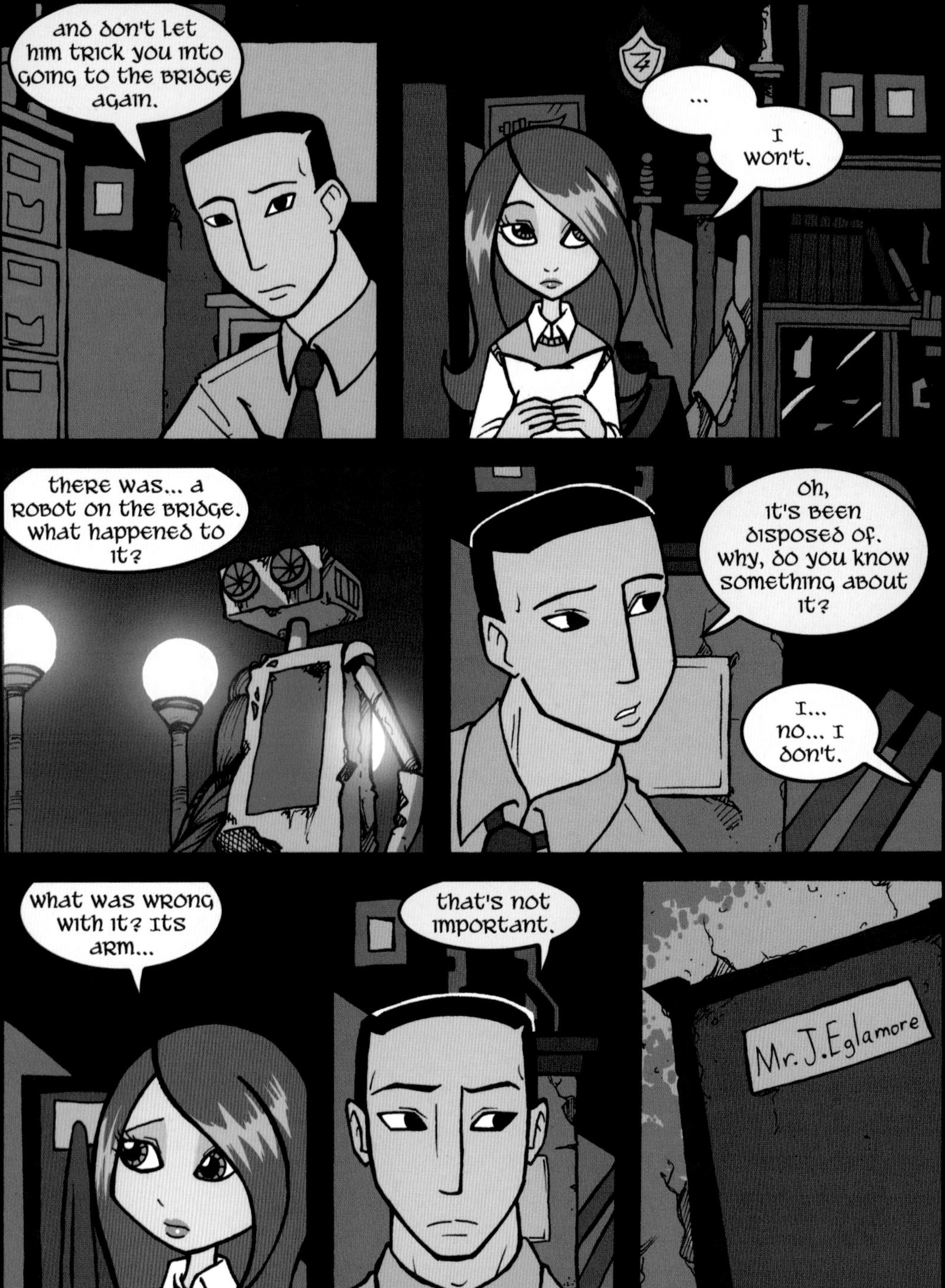
and don't let him trick you into going to the bridge again.
...
I won't.
there was... a robot on the bridge. what happened to it?
Oh, it's been disposed of. why, do you know something about it?
I... no... I don't.
what was wrong with it? its arm...
that's not important.
Mr. J. Eglamore

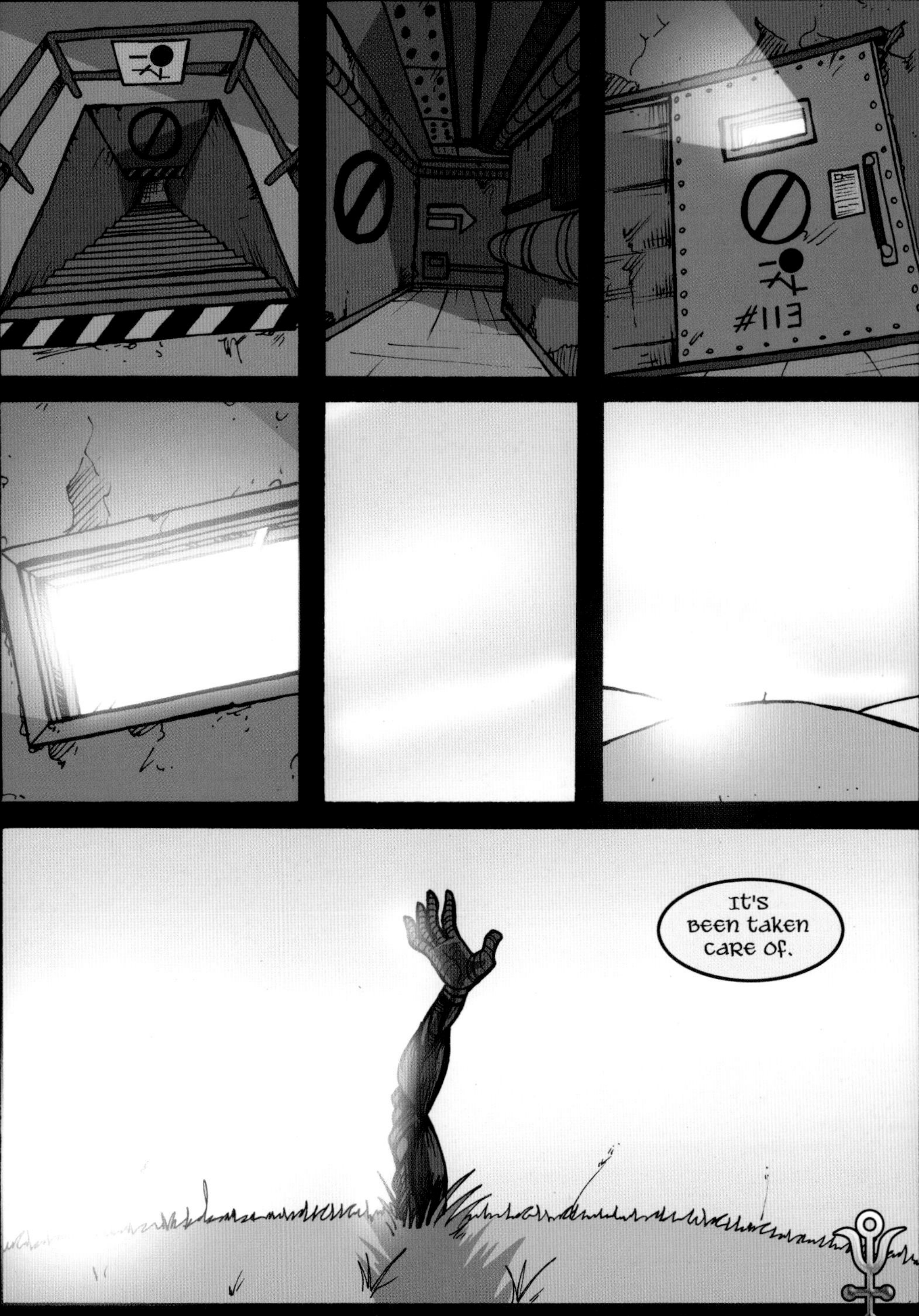
#113
It's been taken care of.

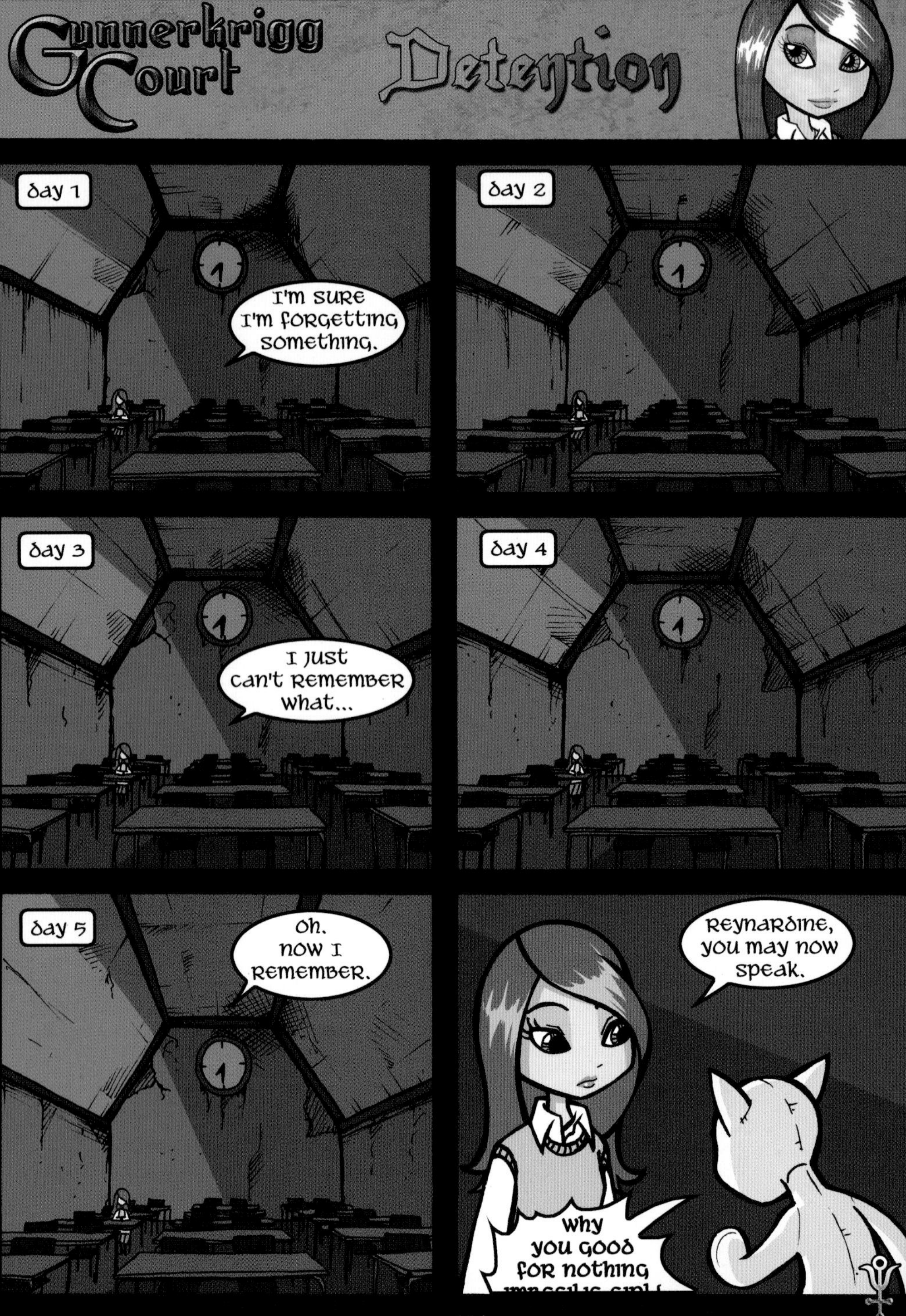
Gunnerkrigg Court
Detention
day 1
I'M SURE I'M FORGETTING SOMETHING.
day 2
day 3
I JUST CAN'T REMEMBER WHAT...
day 4
day 5
OH. NOW I REMEMBER.
REYNARDINE, YOU MAY NOW SPEAK.
WHY YOU GOOD FOR NOTHING

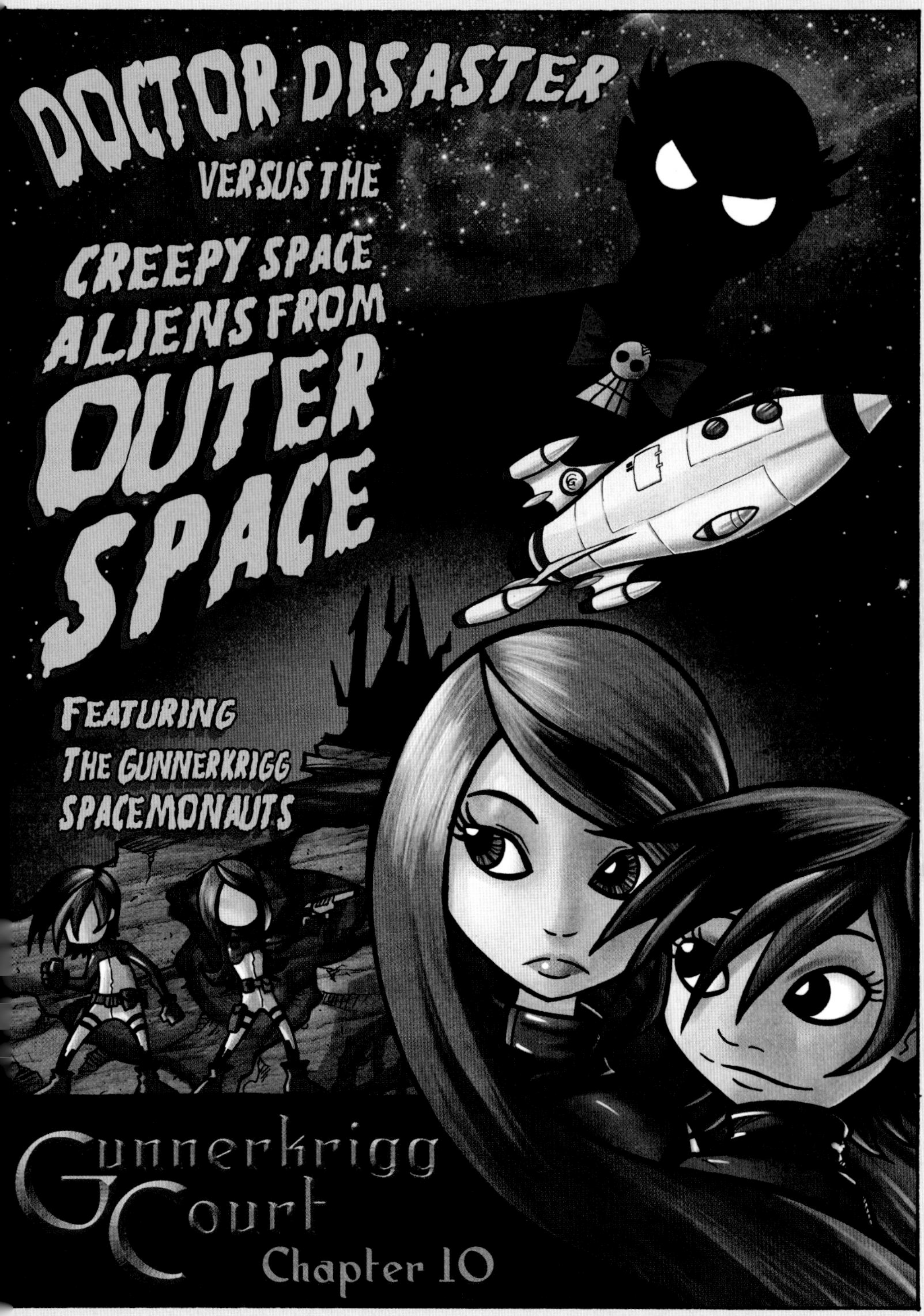
DOCTOR DISASTER
VERSUS THE
CREEPY SPACE
ALIENS FROM
OUTER
SPACE
FEATURING
THE GUNNERKRIGG
SPACEMONAUTS
Gunnerkrigg
Court
Chapter 10

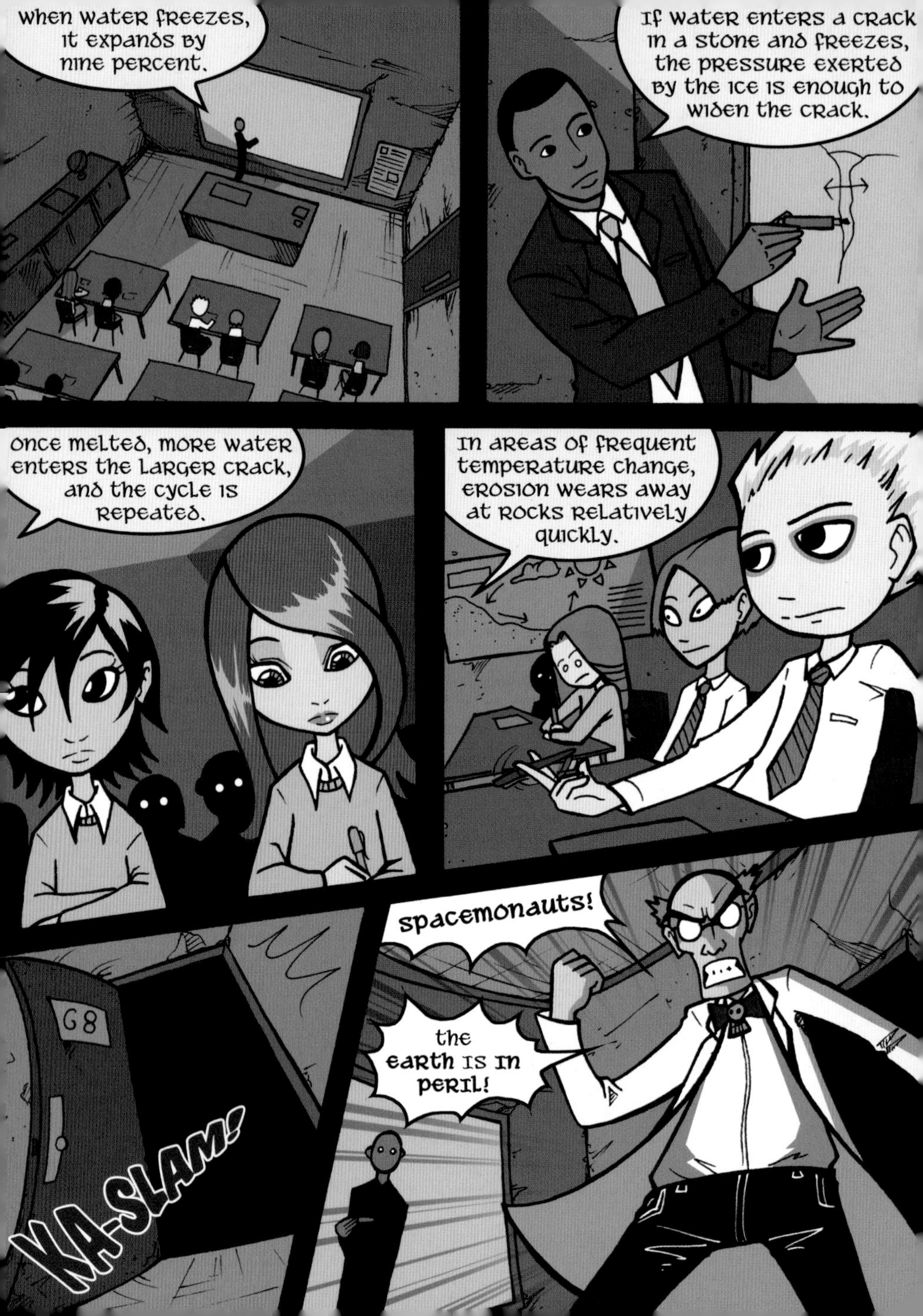
when water freezes, it expands by nine percent.
If water enters a crack in a stone and freezes, the pressure exerted by the ice is enough to widen the crack.
once melted, more water enters the larger crack, and the cycle is repeated.
In areas of frequent temperature change, erosion wears away at rocks relatively quickly.
G8
KA-SLAM!
spacemonauts!
the earth is in peril!

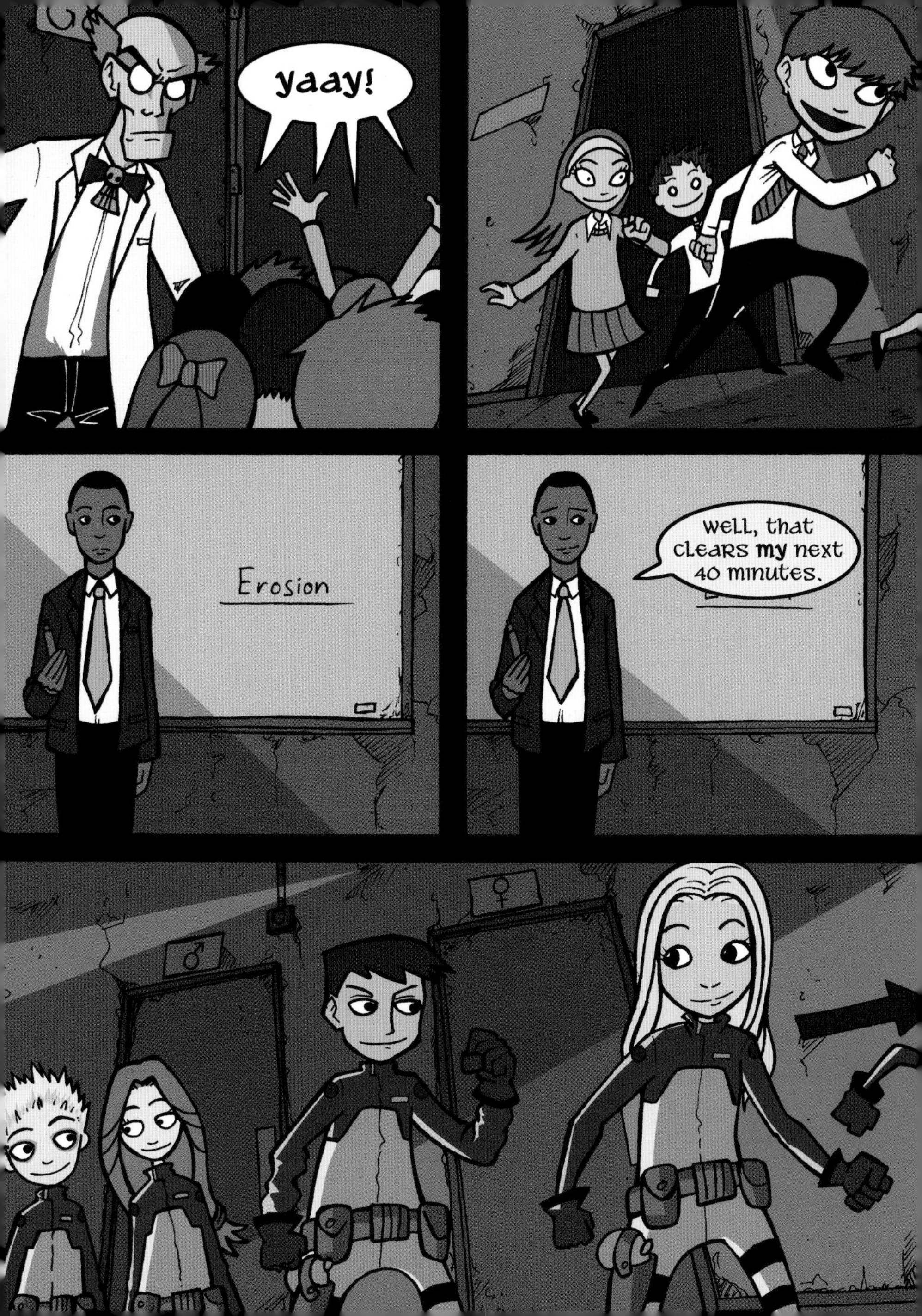
yaay!
Erosion
well, that clears my next 40 minutes.

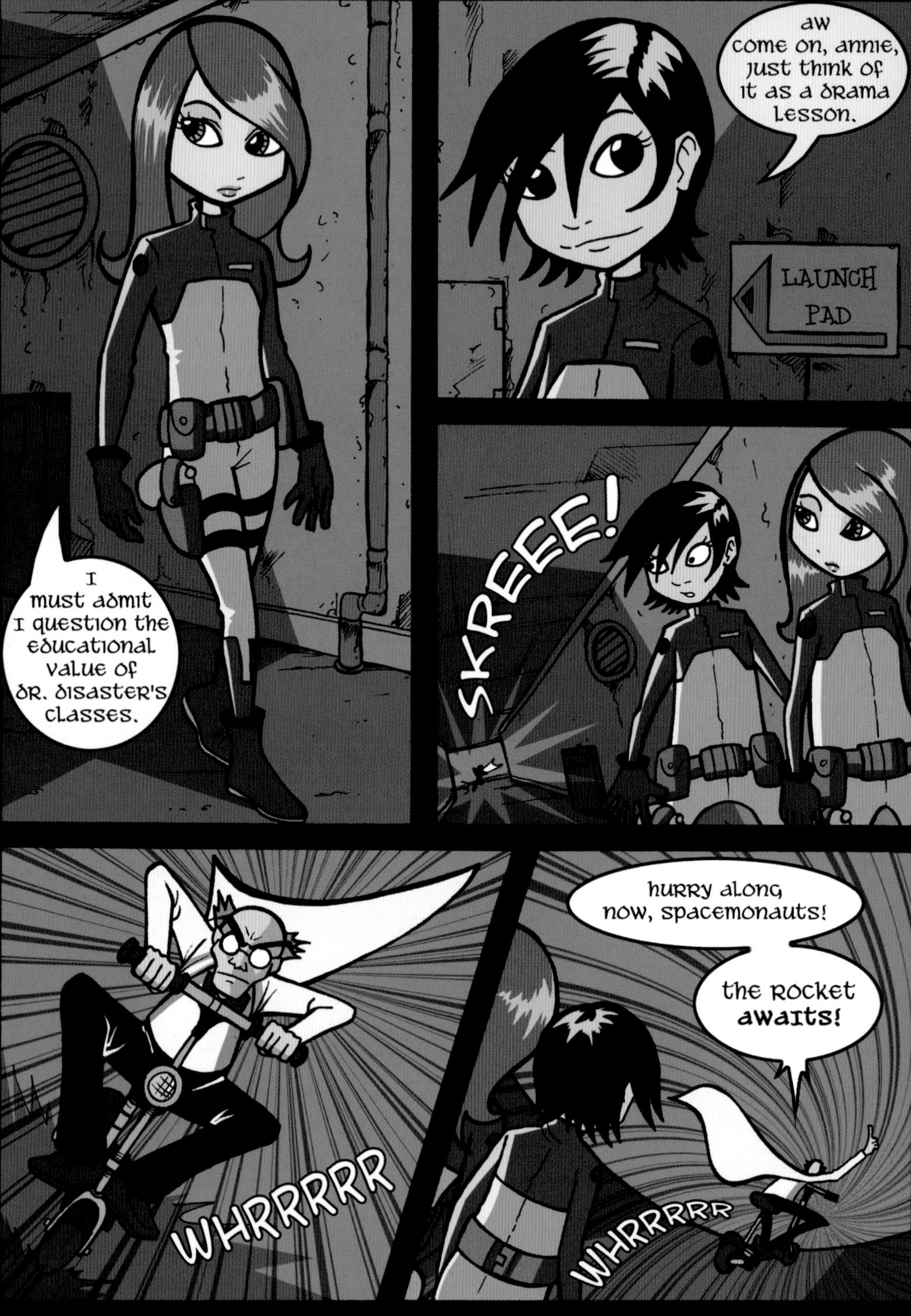
I must admit I question the educational value of dr. disaster's classes.
aw come on, annie, just think of it as a drama lesson.
LAUNCH PAD
SKREEE!
WHRRRRR
hurry along now, spacemonauts!
the rocket awaits!
WHRRRRR

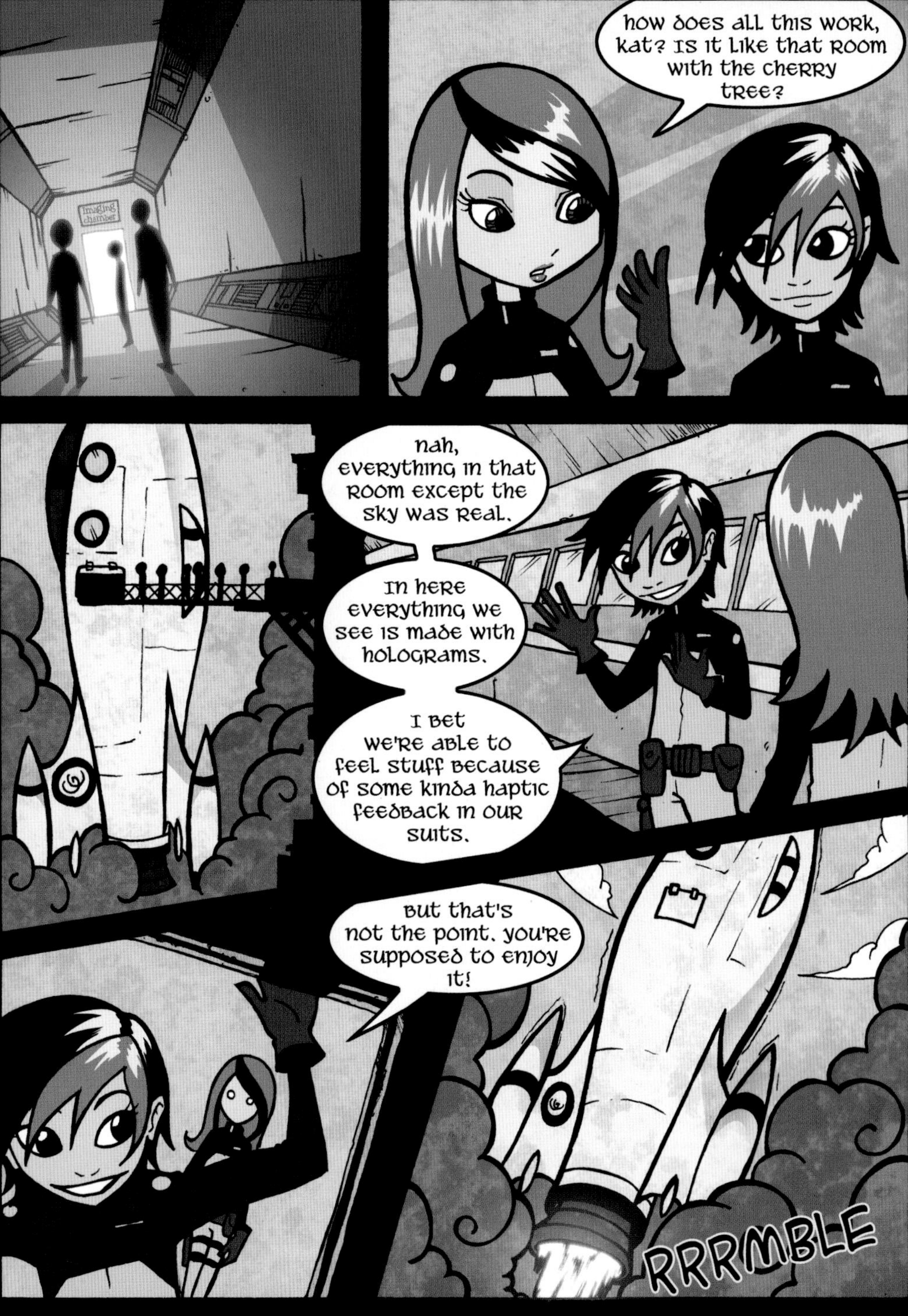
Imaging chamber
how does all this work, kat? is it like that room with the cherry tree?
nah, everything in that room except the sky was real.
in here everything we see is made with holograms.
I bet we're able to feel stuff because of some kinda haptic feedback in our suits.
but that's not the point. you're supposed to enjoy it!
RRRMBLE

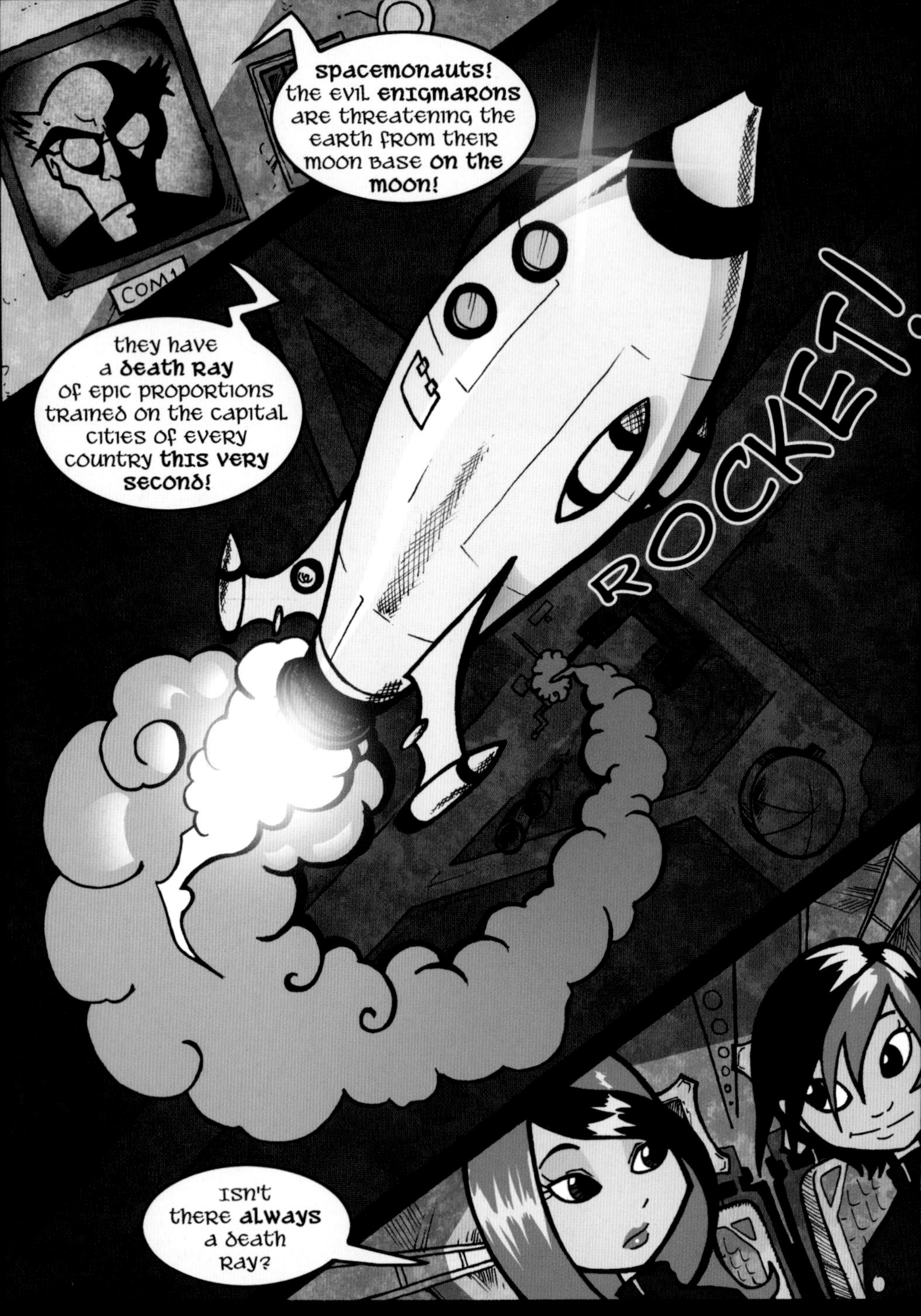

COM1
spacemonauts! the evil enigmarons are threatening the earth from their moon base on the moon!
they have a death ray of epic proportions trained on the capital cities of every country this very second!
ROCKET!
Isn't there always a death ray?

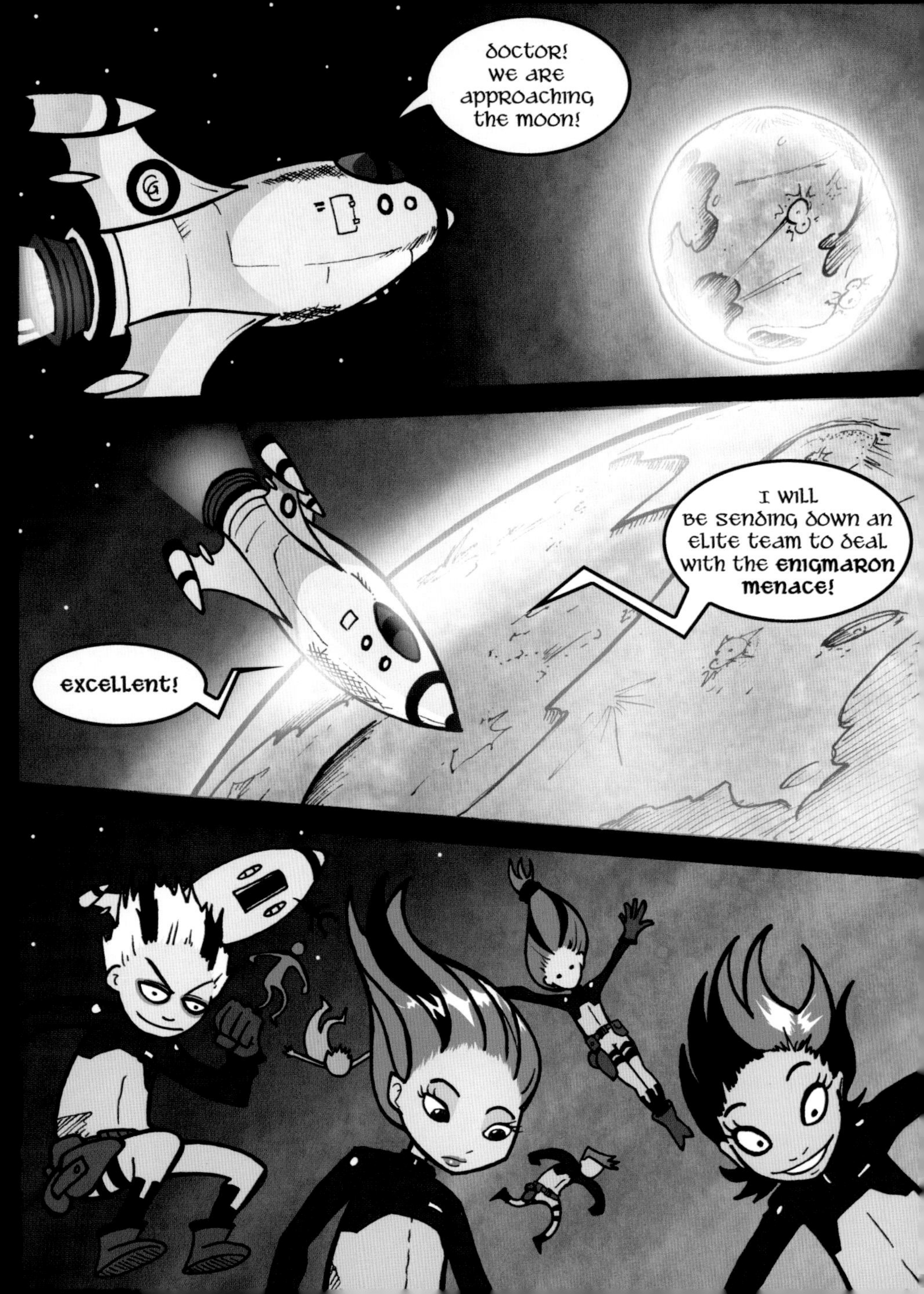
doctor! we are approaching the moon!
I will be sending down an elite team to deal with the enigmaron menace!
excellent!

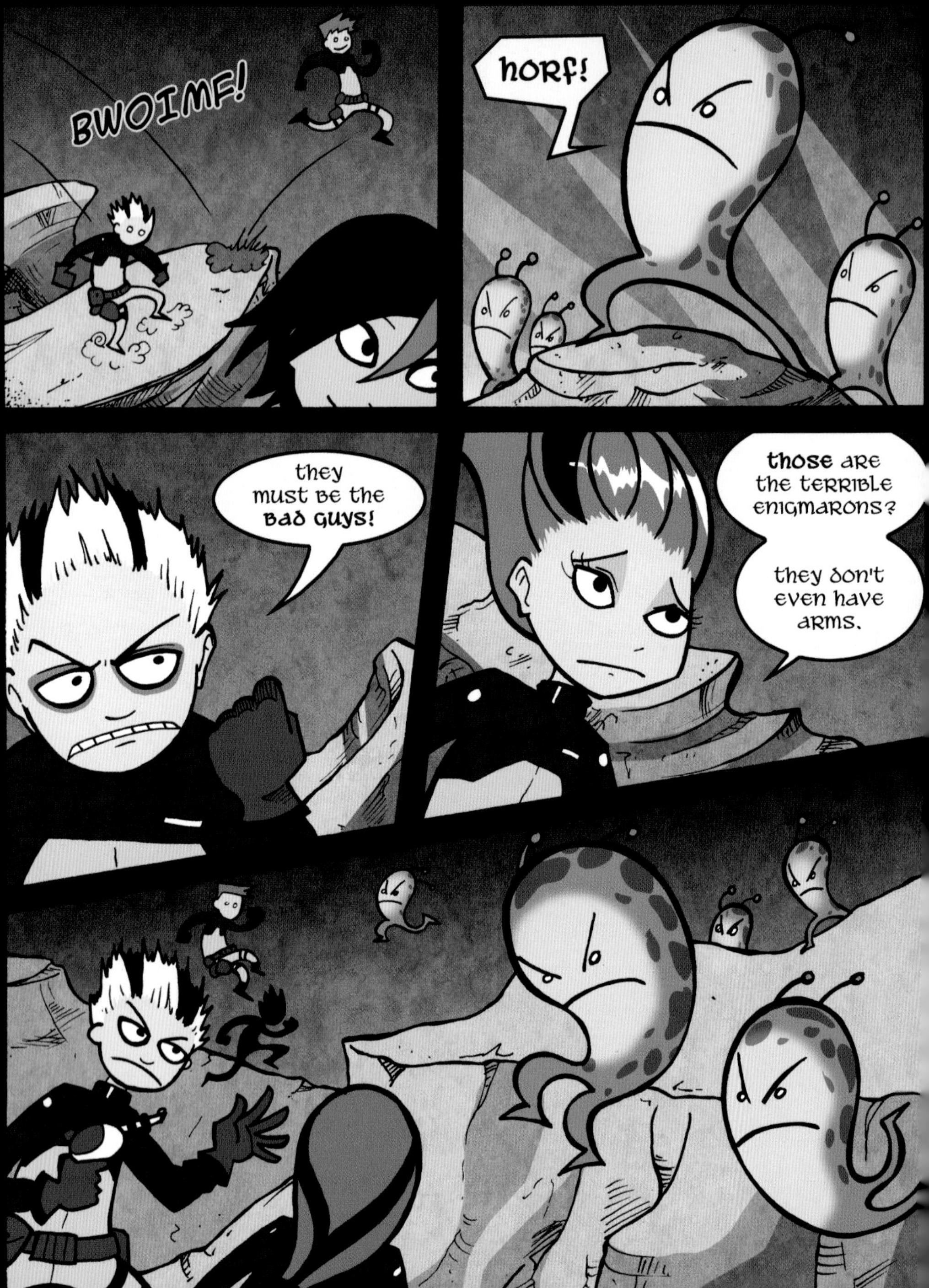
BWOIMF!
horf!
they must be the bad guys!
those are the terrible enigmarons?
they don't even have arms.

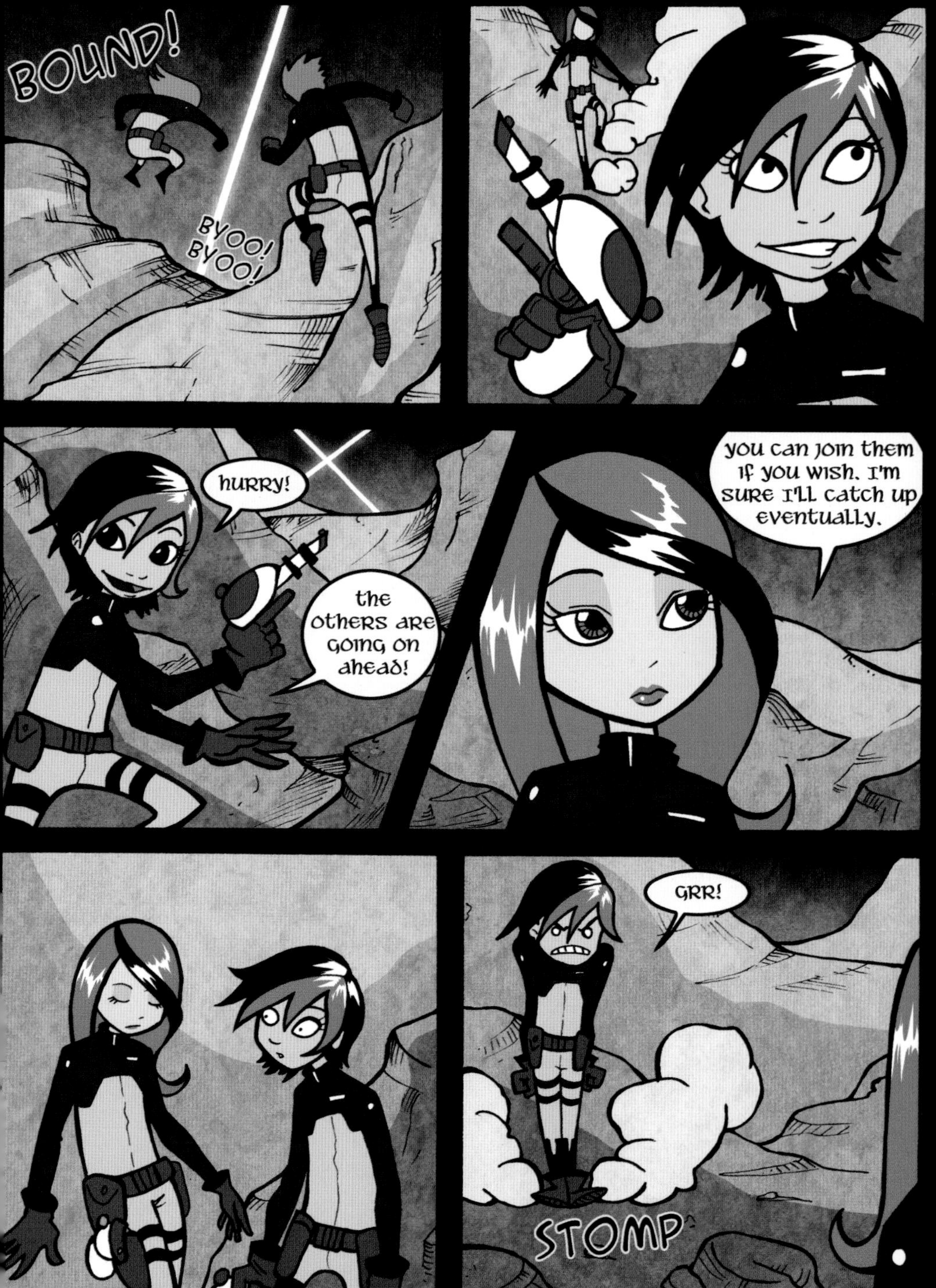
BOUND!
BYOO! BYOO!
hurry!
the others are going on ahead!
you can join them if you wish. I'm sure I'll catch up eventually.
GRR!
STOMP

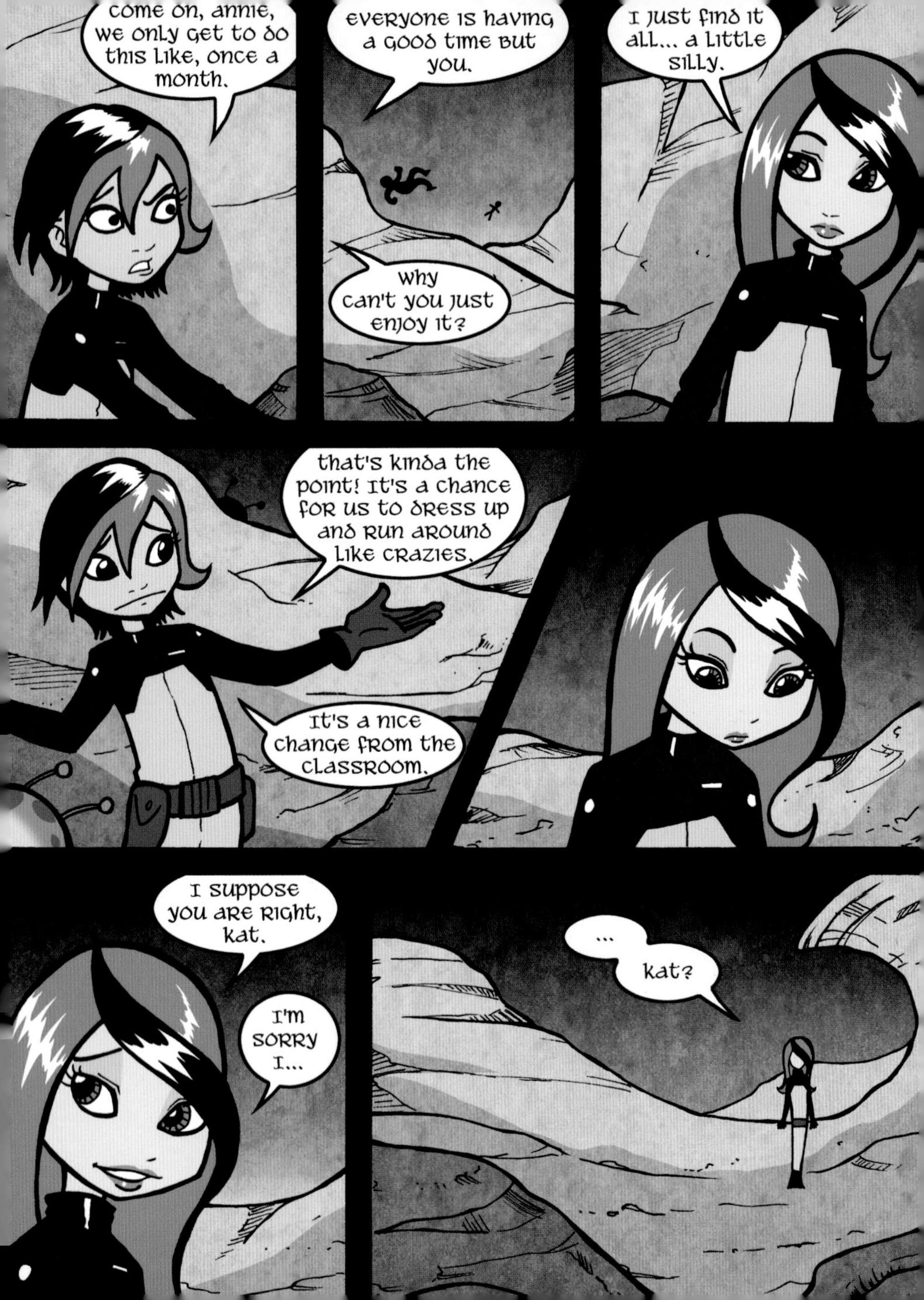
come on, annie, we only get to do this like, once a month.
everyone is having a good time but you.
why can't you just enjoy it?
I just find it all... a little silly.
that's kinda the point! it's a chance for us to dress up and run around like crazies.
it's a nice change from the classroom.
I suppose you are right, kat.
I'm sorry I...
...
kat?

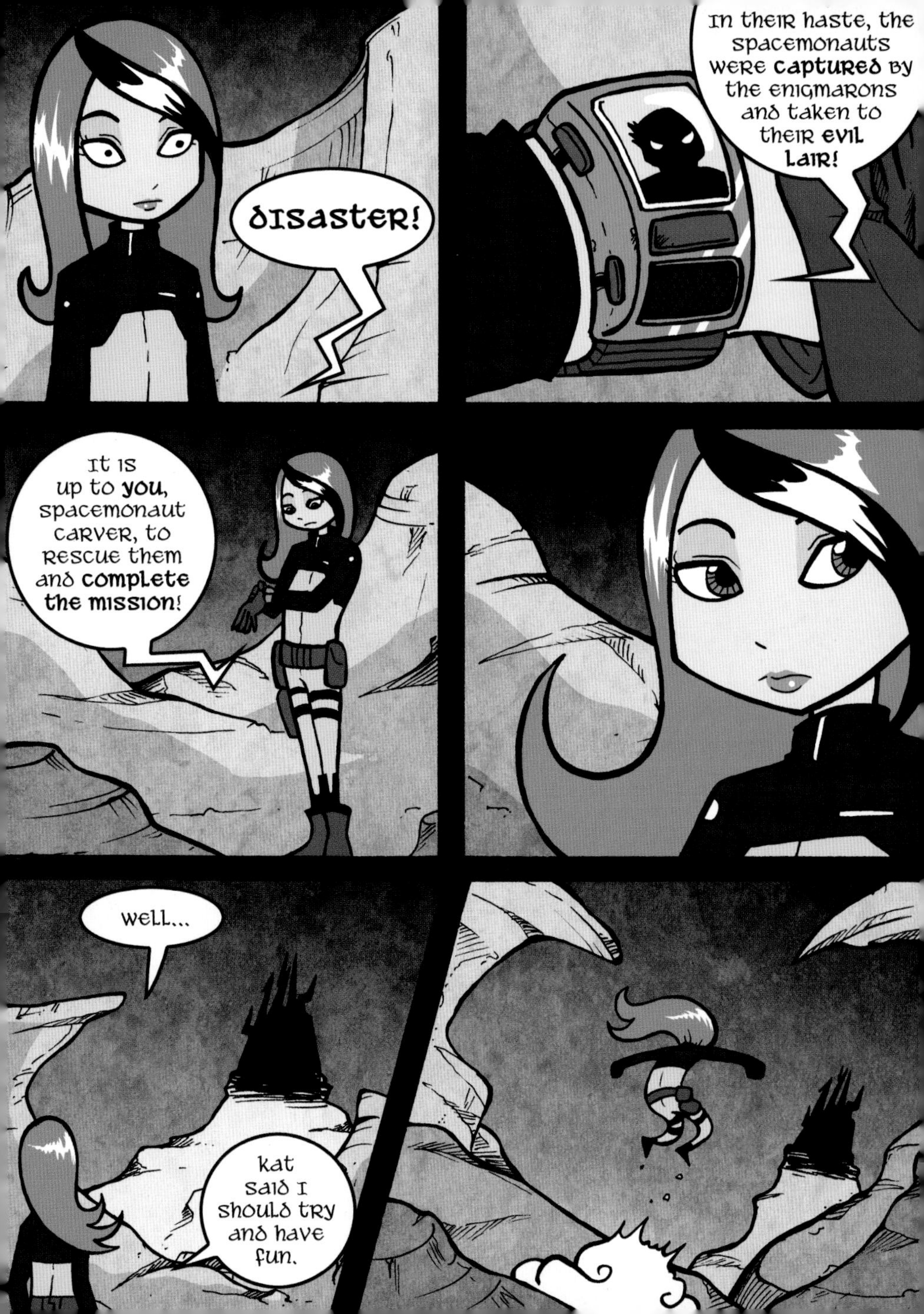
DISASTER!
In their haste, the spacemonauts were captured by the enigmarons and taken to their evil lair!
It is up to you, spacemonaut carver, to rescue them and complete the mission!
well...
kat said I should try and have fun.

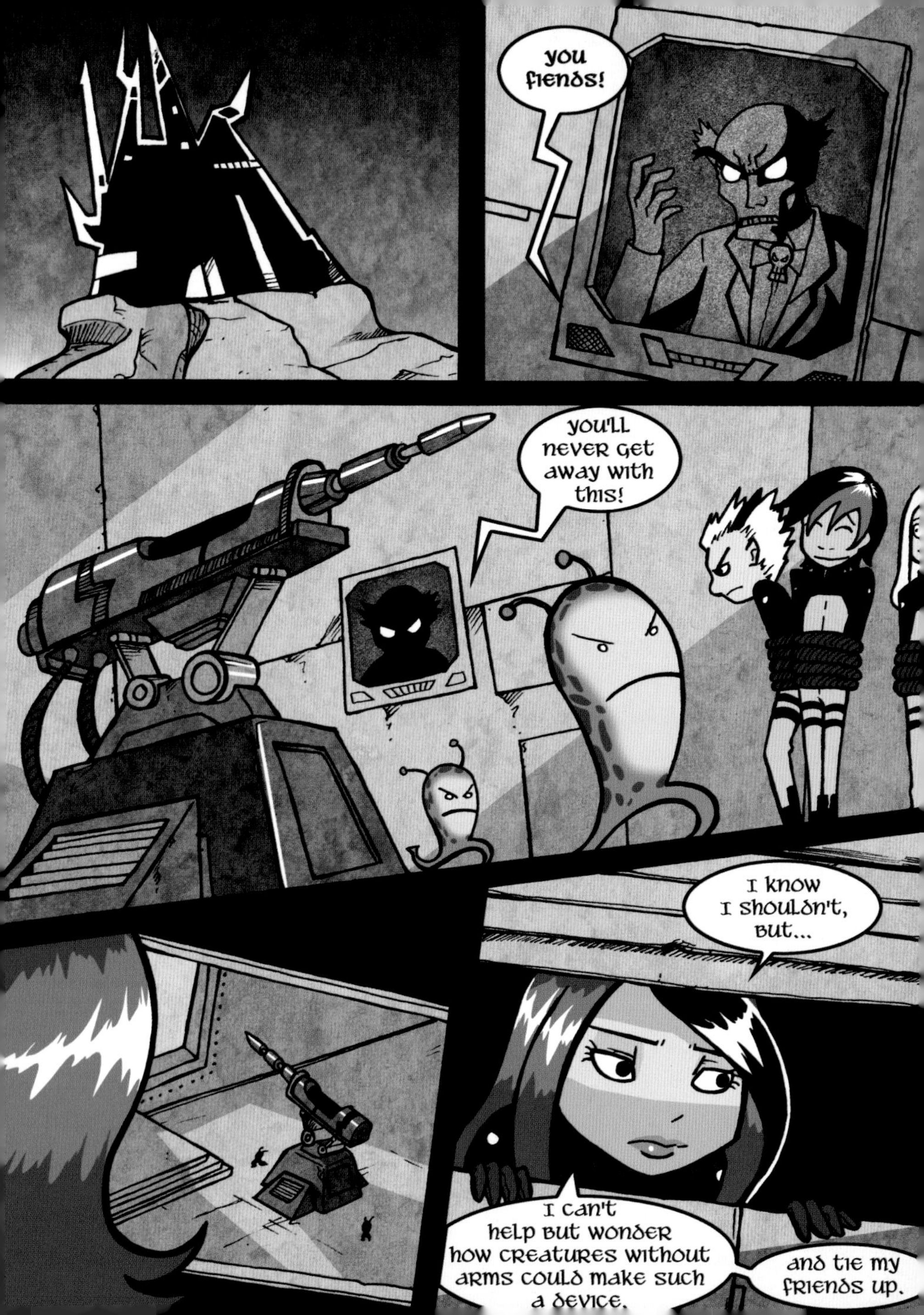
you fiends!
you'll never get away with this!
I know I shouldn't, but...
I can't help but wonder how creatures without arms could make such a device,
and tie my friends up.

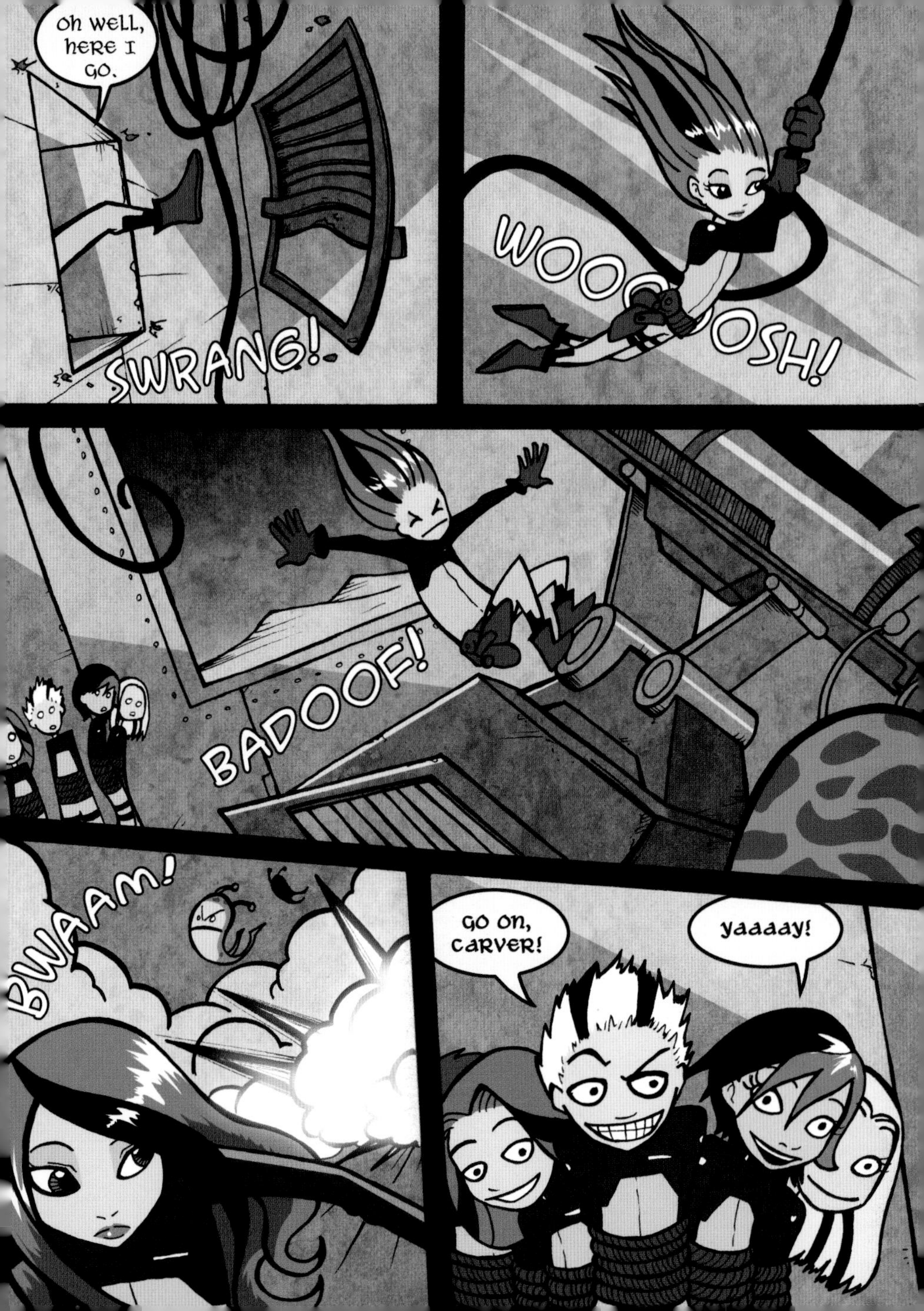
OH WELL, HERE I GO.
SWRANG!
WOOOOOOSH!
BADOOF!
BWAAAM!
GO ON, CARVER!
YAAAAY!

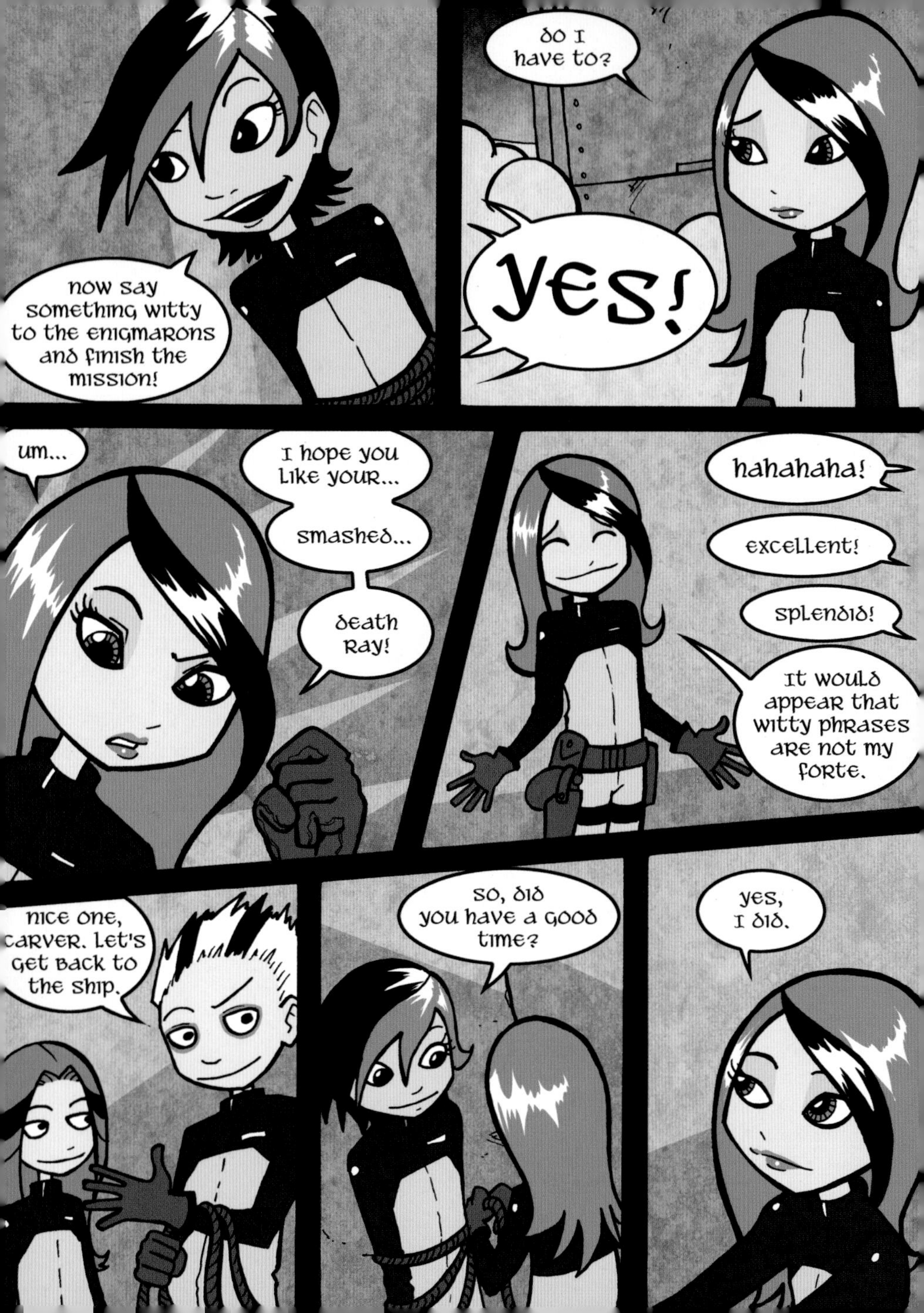
now say something witty to the enigmarons and finish the mission!
do I have to?
yes!
um...
I hope you like your...
smashed...
death ray!
hahahaha!
excellent!
splendid!
It would appear that witty phrases are not my forte.
nice one, carver. Let's get back to the ship.
so, did you have a good time?
yes, I did.

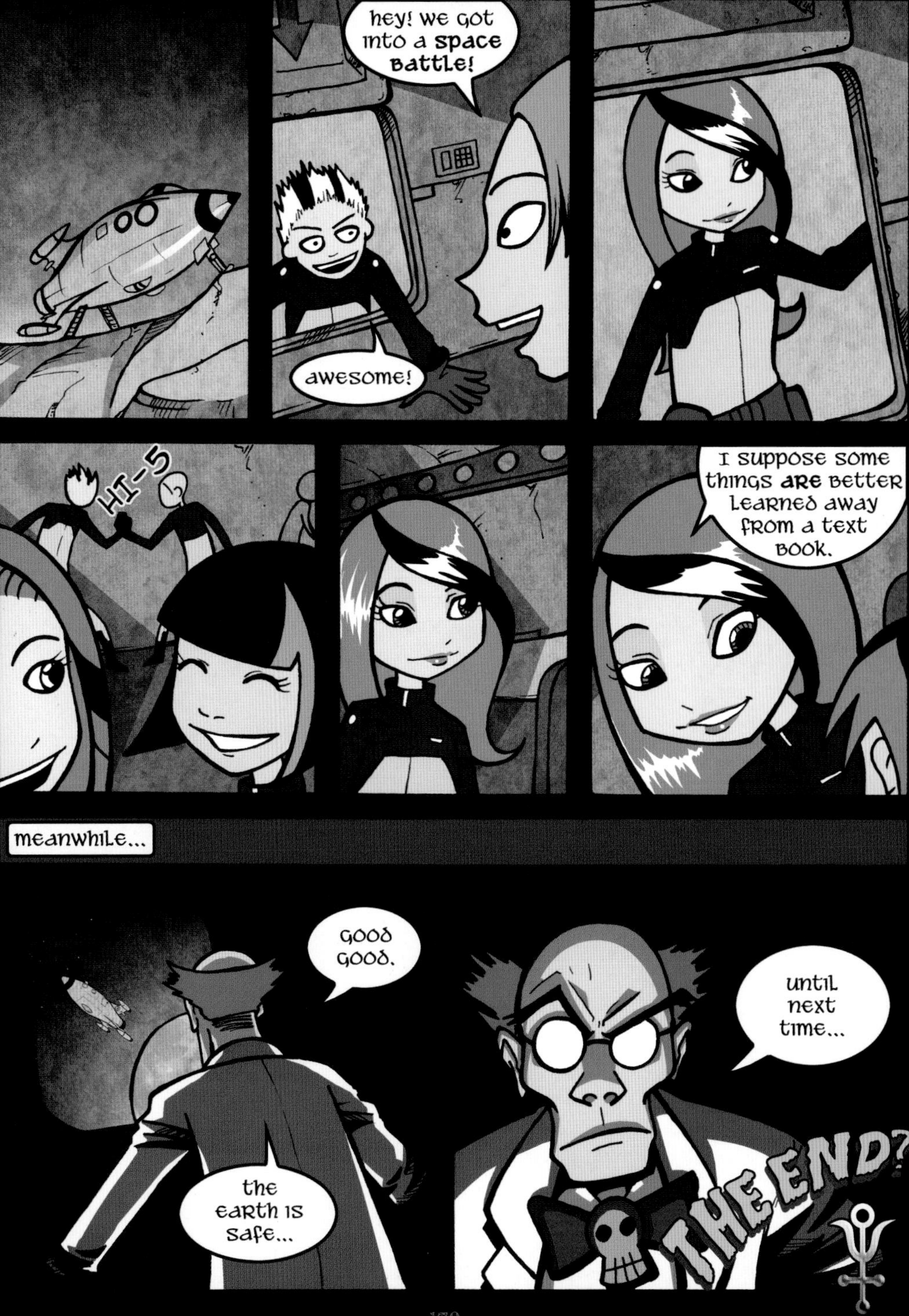
hey! we got into a space battle!
awesome!
HI-5
I suppose some things are better learned away from a text book.
meanwhile...
good good.
the earth is safe...
until next time...
THE END?

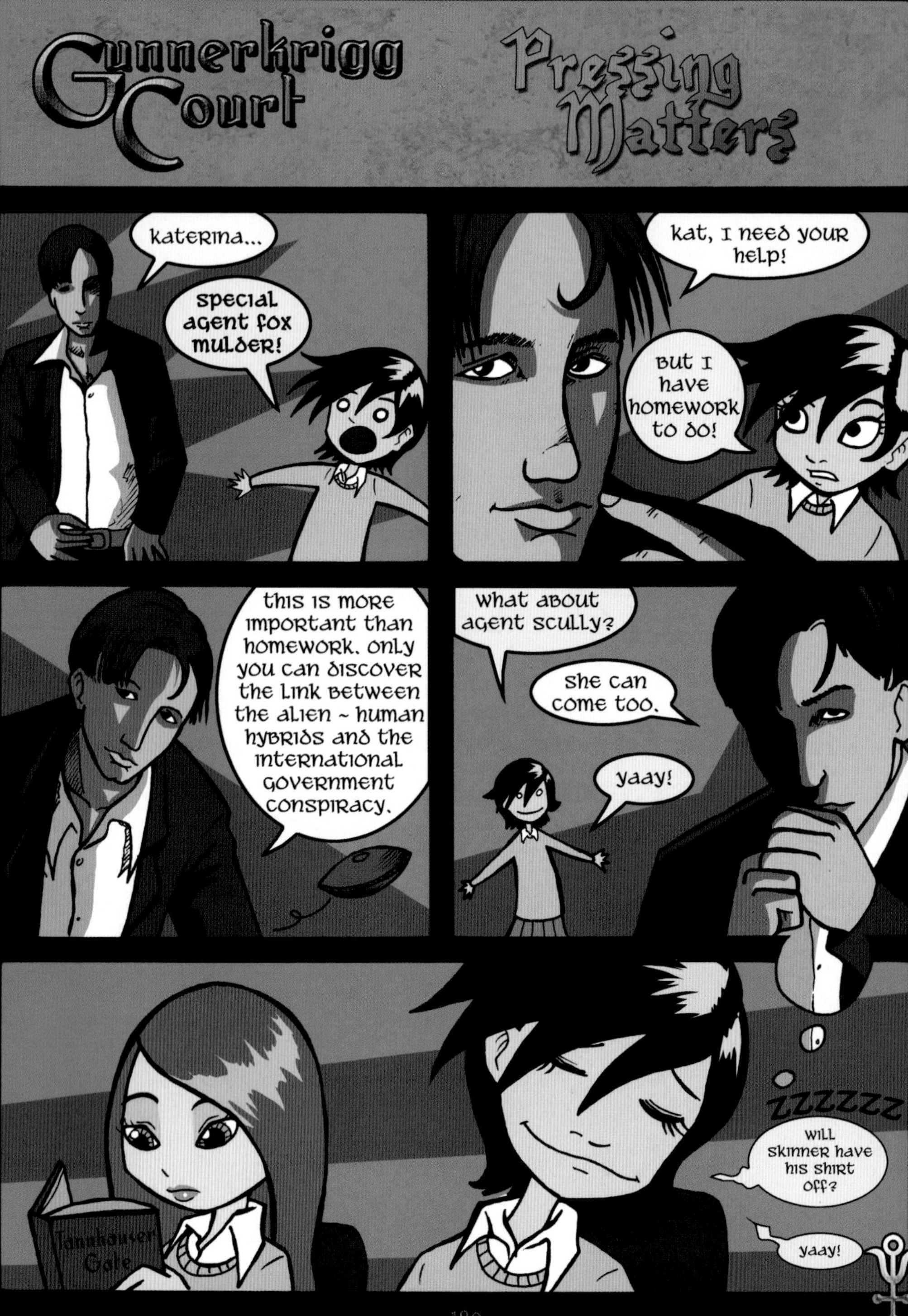
Gunnerkrigg Court
Pressing Matters
katerina...
special agent fox mulder!
kat, I need your help!
but I have homework to do!
this is more important than homework. only you can discover the link between the alien ~ human hybrids and the international government conspiracy.
what about agent scully?
she can come too.
yaay!
ZZZZZZ
will skinner have his shirt off?
yaay!
Tannhauser Gate

Gunnerkrigg Court

Chapter 11:

Dobranoc, Gamma

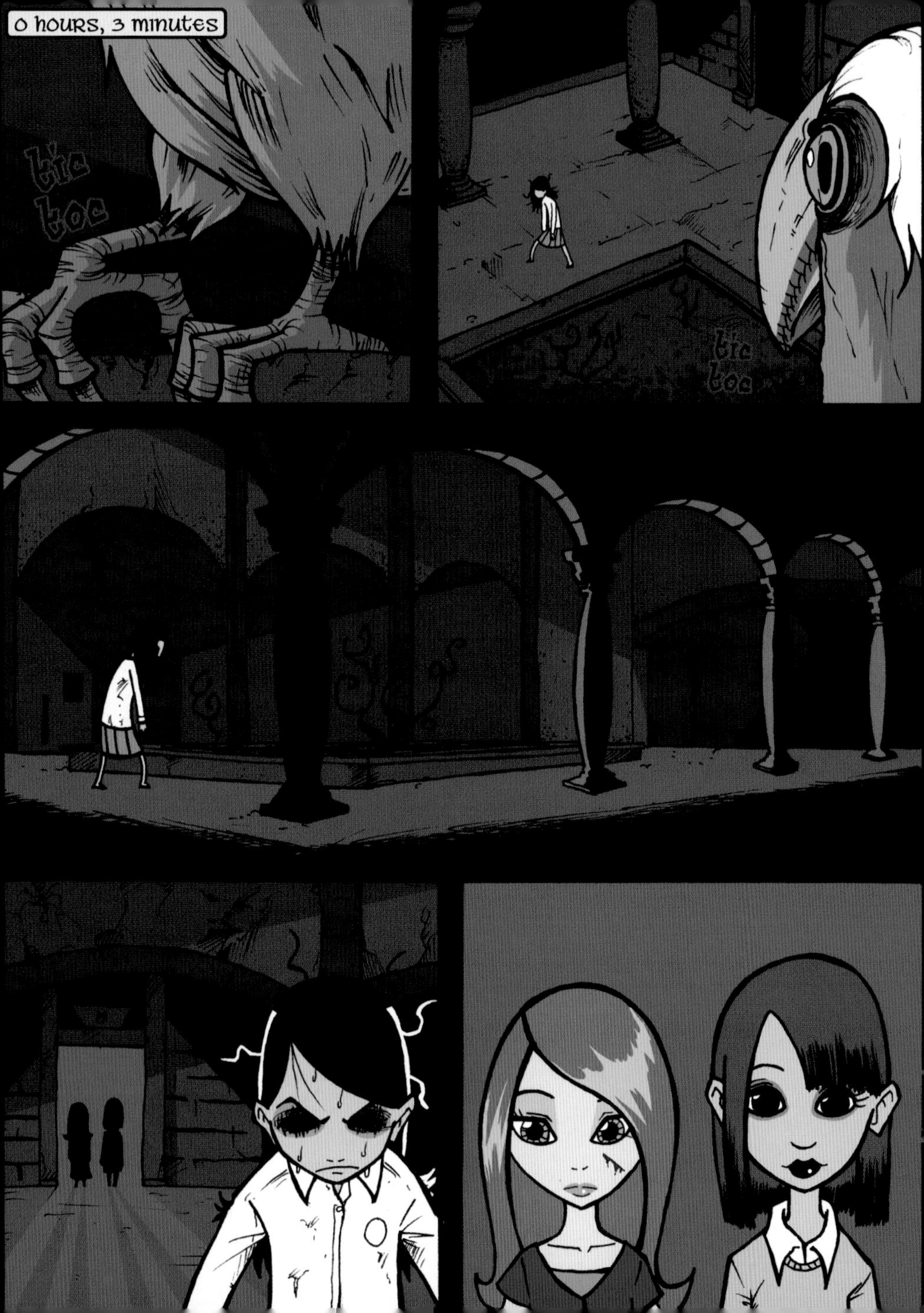
0 hours, 3 minutes
tic
toc
tic
toc

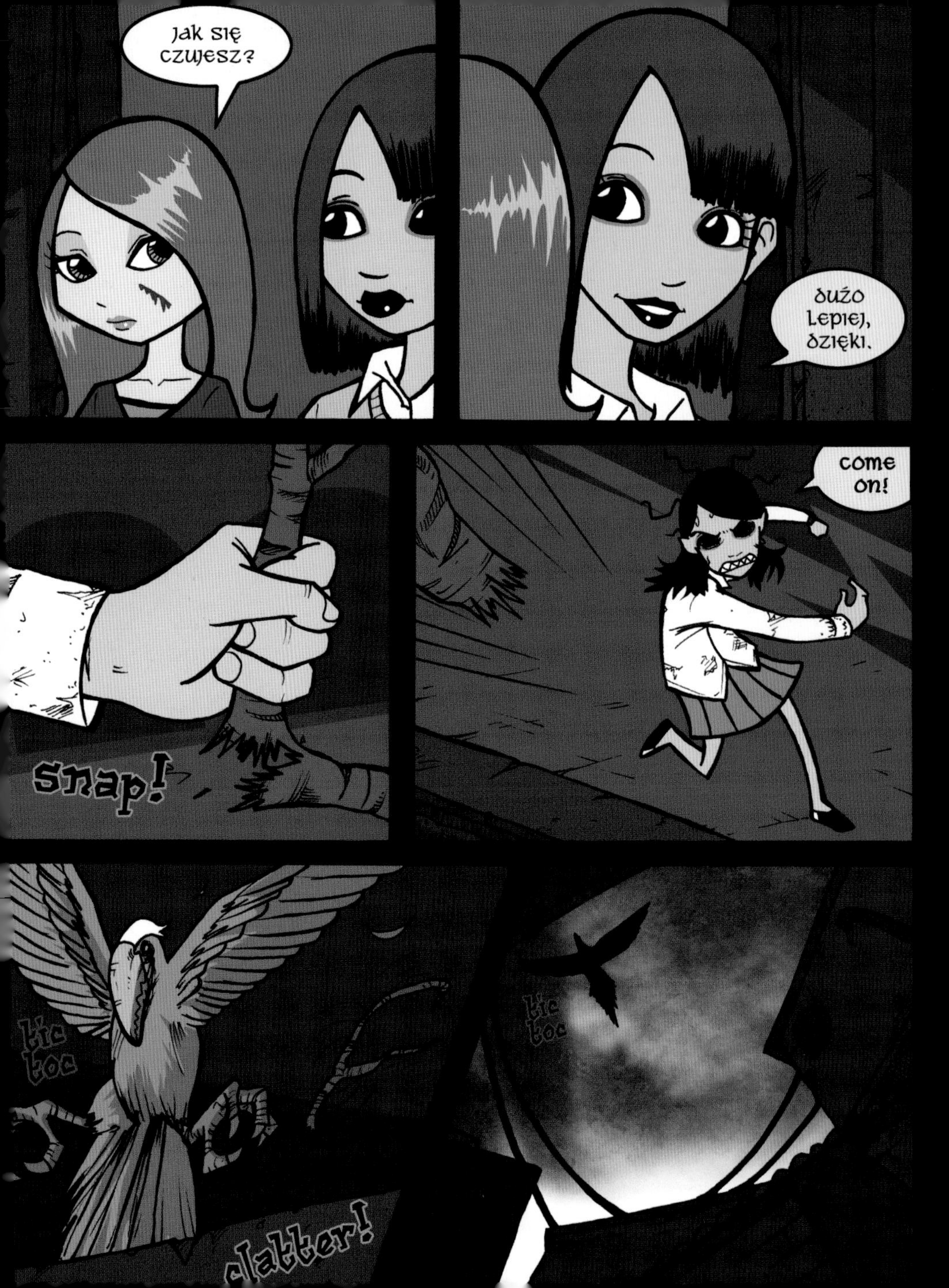
JAK SIĘ CZUJESZ?
DUŻO LEPIEJ, DZIĘKI.
snap!
come on!
tic toc
tic toc
clatter!

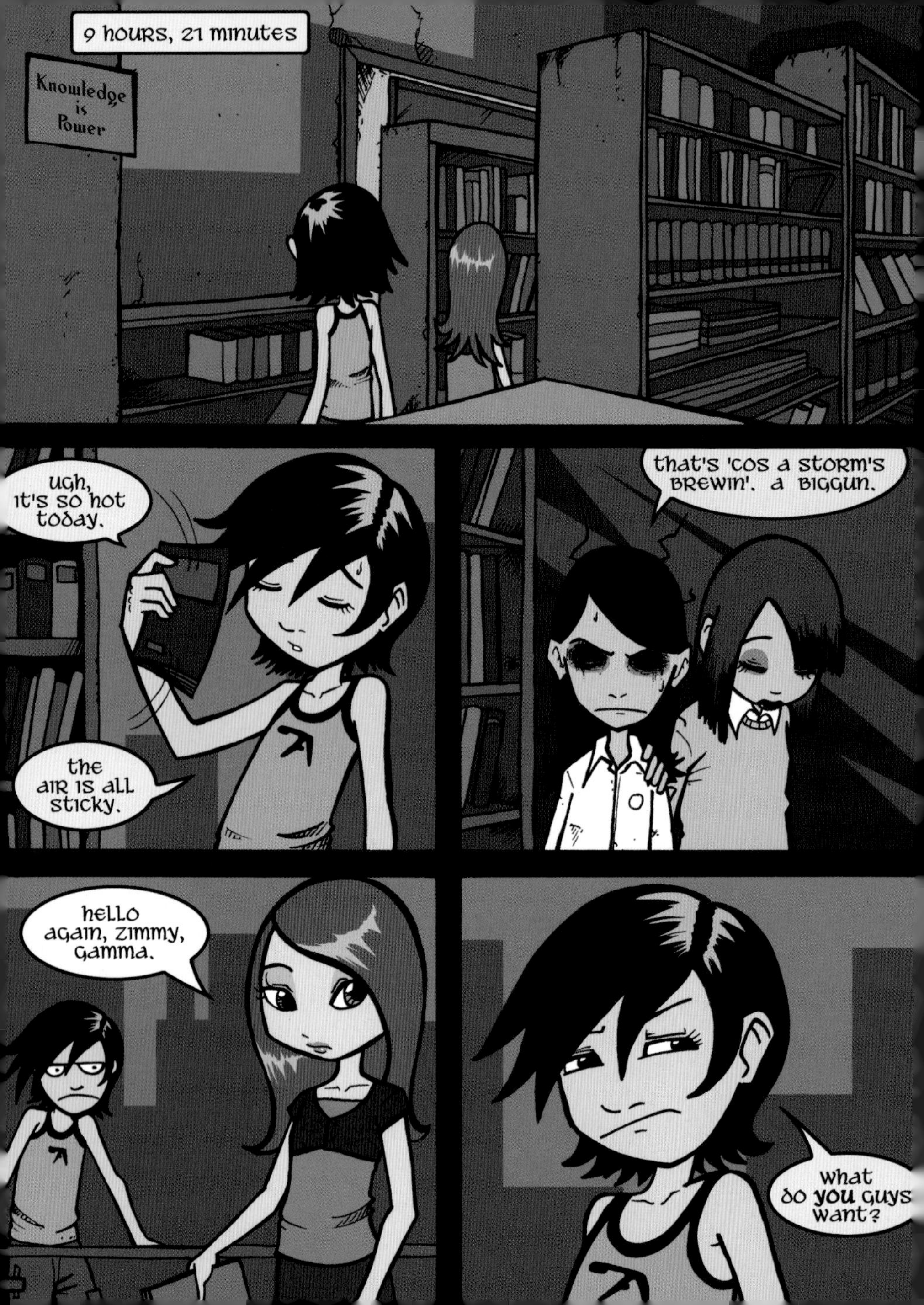
9 hours, 21 minutes
Knowledge is Power
ugh, it's so hot today.
the air is all sticky.
that's 'cos a storm's brewin'. a biggun.
hello again, zimmy, gamma.
what do **you** guys want?

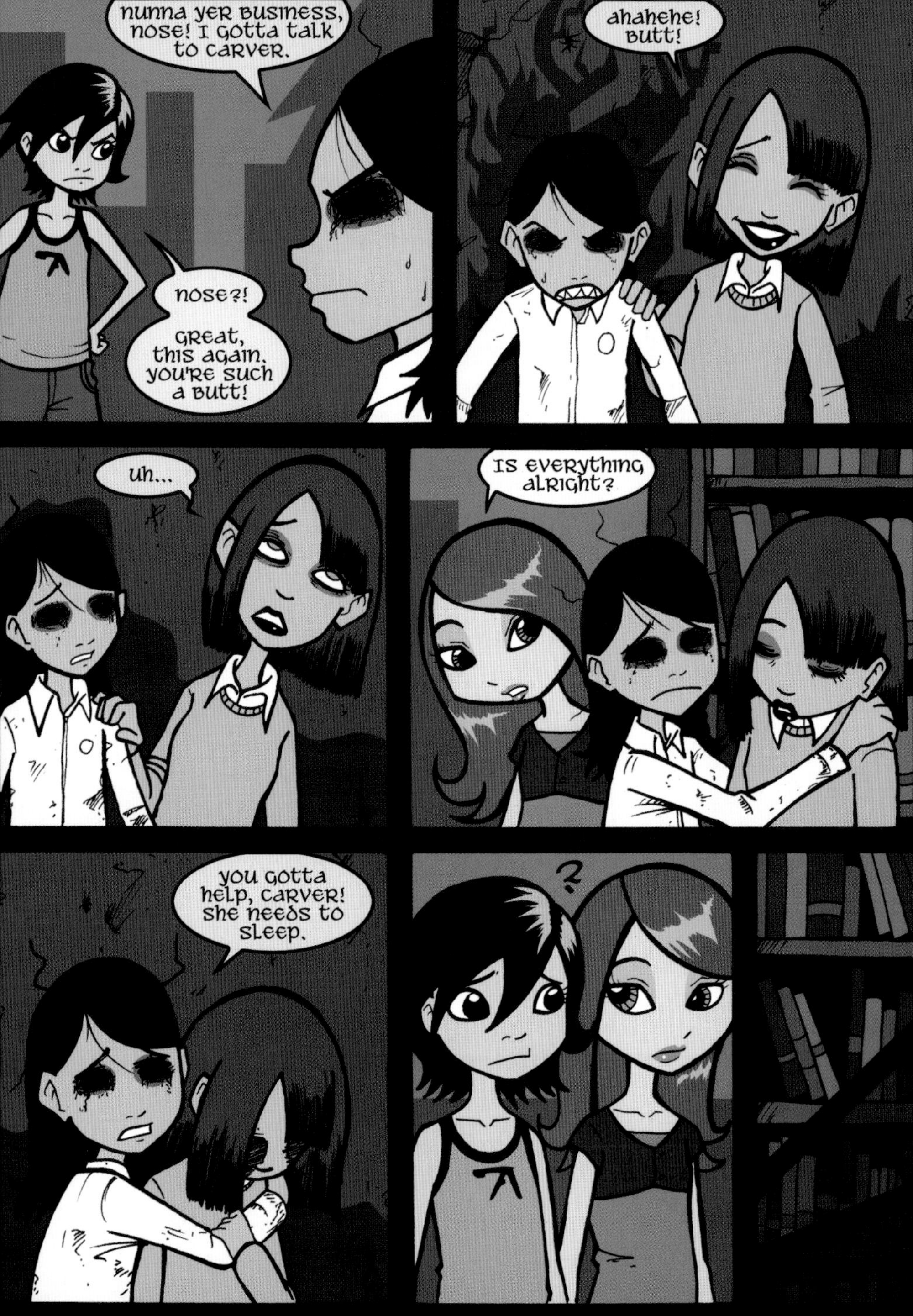
nunna yer business, nose! I gotta talk to carver.
nose?!
great, this again. you're such a butt!
ahahehe! butt!
uh...
is everything alright?
you gotta help, carver! she needs to sleep.
?

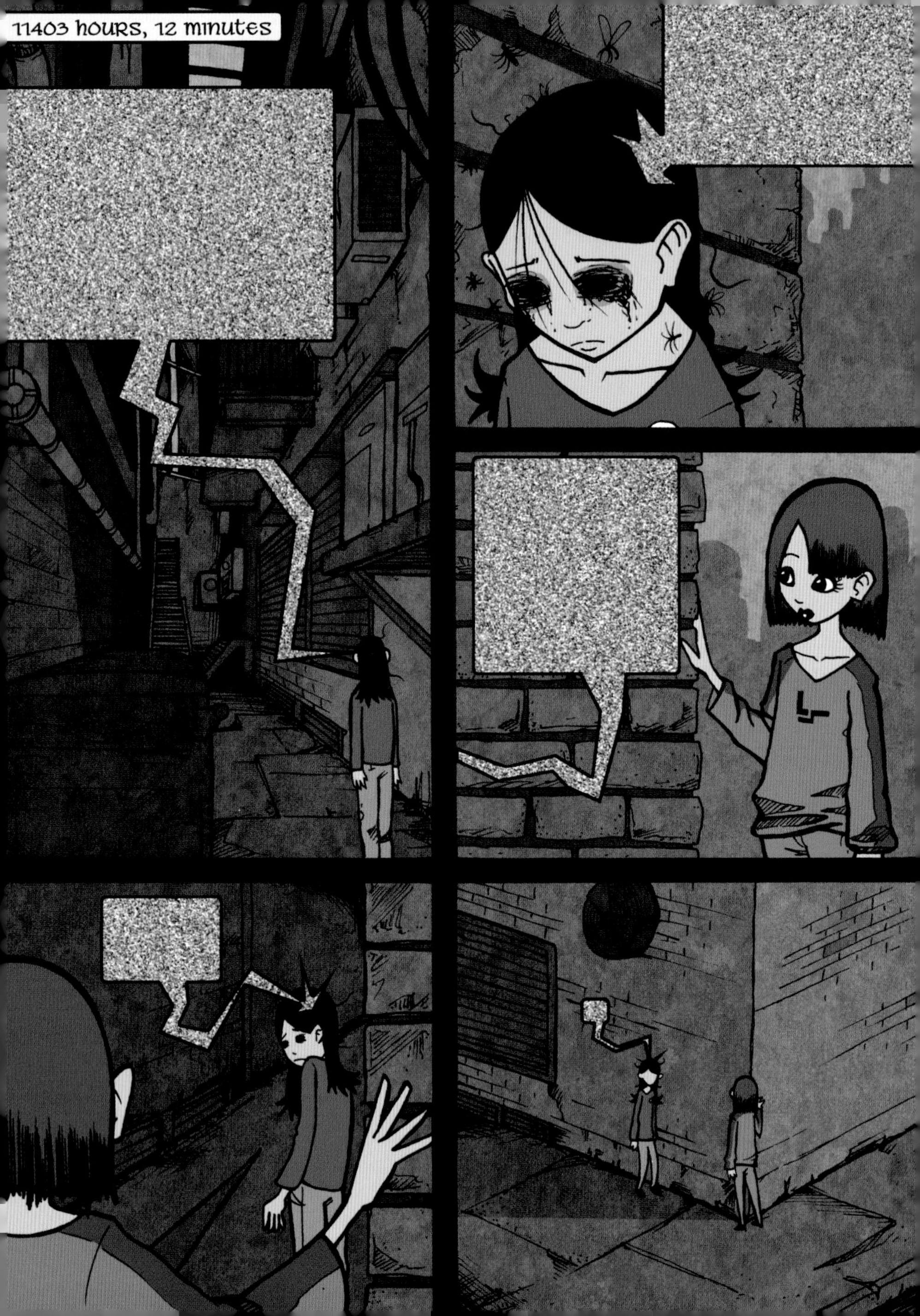
11403 HOURS, 12 MINUTES

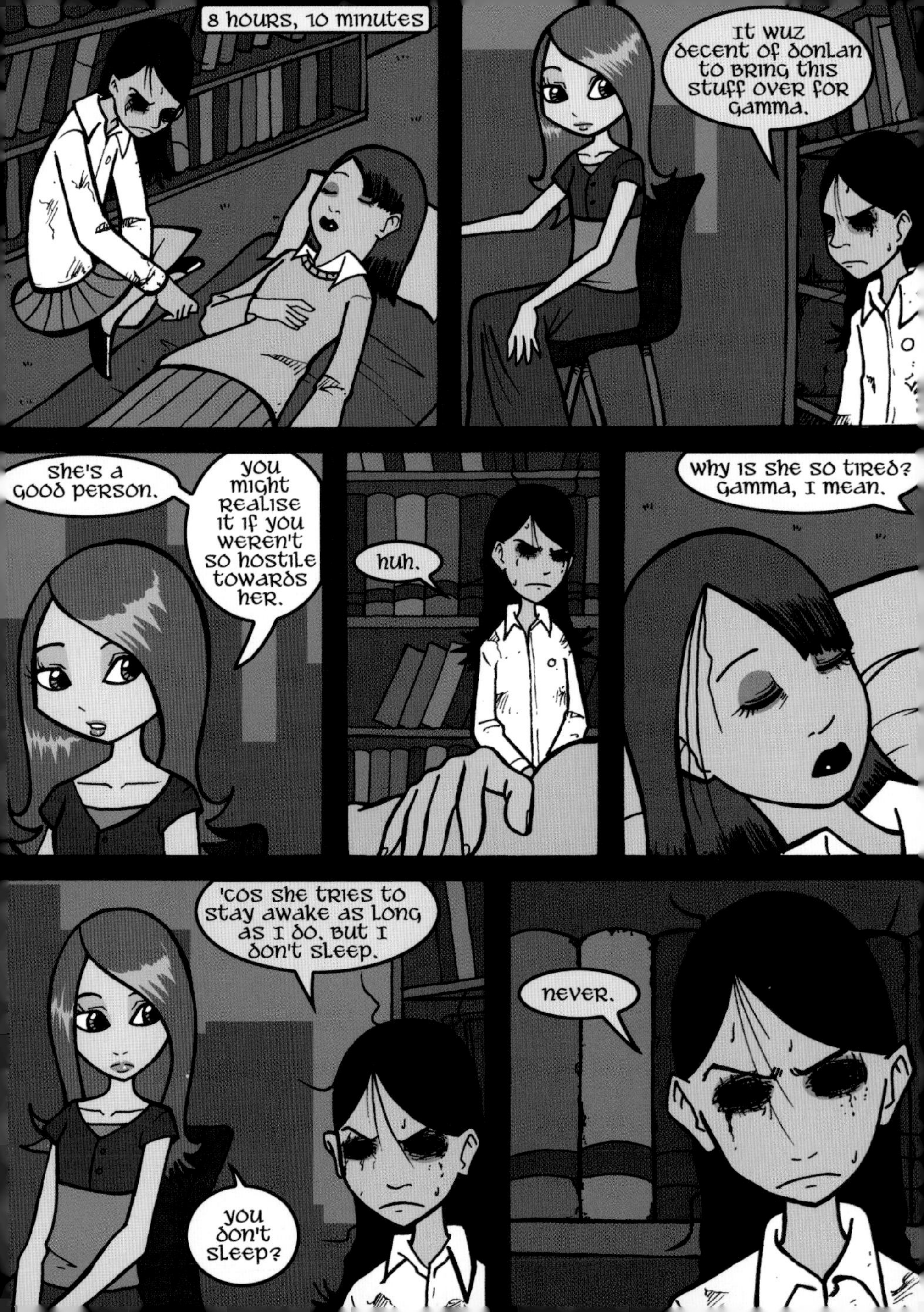
8 HOURS, 10 MINUTES
IT WUZ DECENT OF DONLAN TO BRING THIS STUFF OVER FOR GAMMA.
SHE'S A GOOD PERSON.
YOU MIGHT REALISE IT IF YOU WEREN'T SO HOSTILE TOWARDS HER.
HUH.
WHY IS SHE SO TIRED? GAMMA, I MEAN.
'COS SHE TRIES TO STAY AWAKE AS LONG AS I DO. BUT I DON'T SLEEP.
YOU DON'T SLEEP?
NEVER.

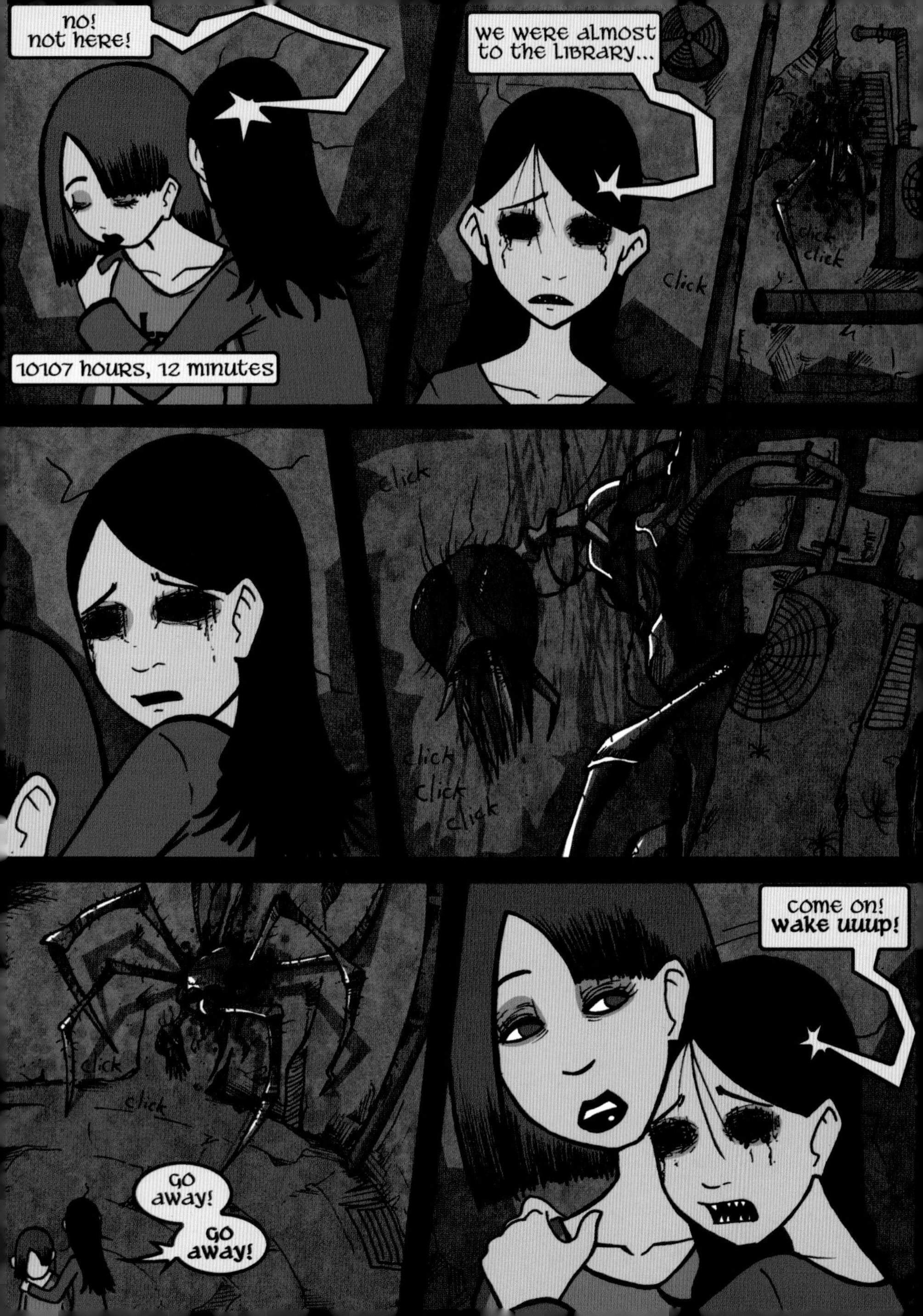
no! not here!
10107 hours, 12 minutes
we were almost to the library...
click
click
click
click
click
click
click
click
click
GO away!
GO away!
come on! wake uuup!

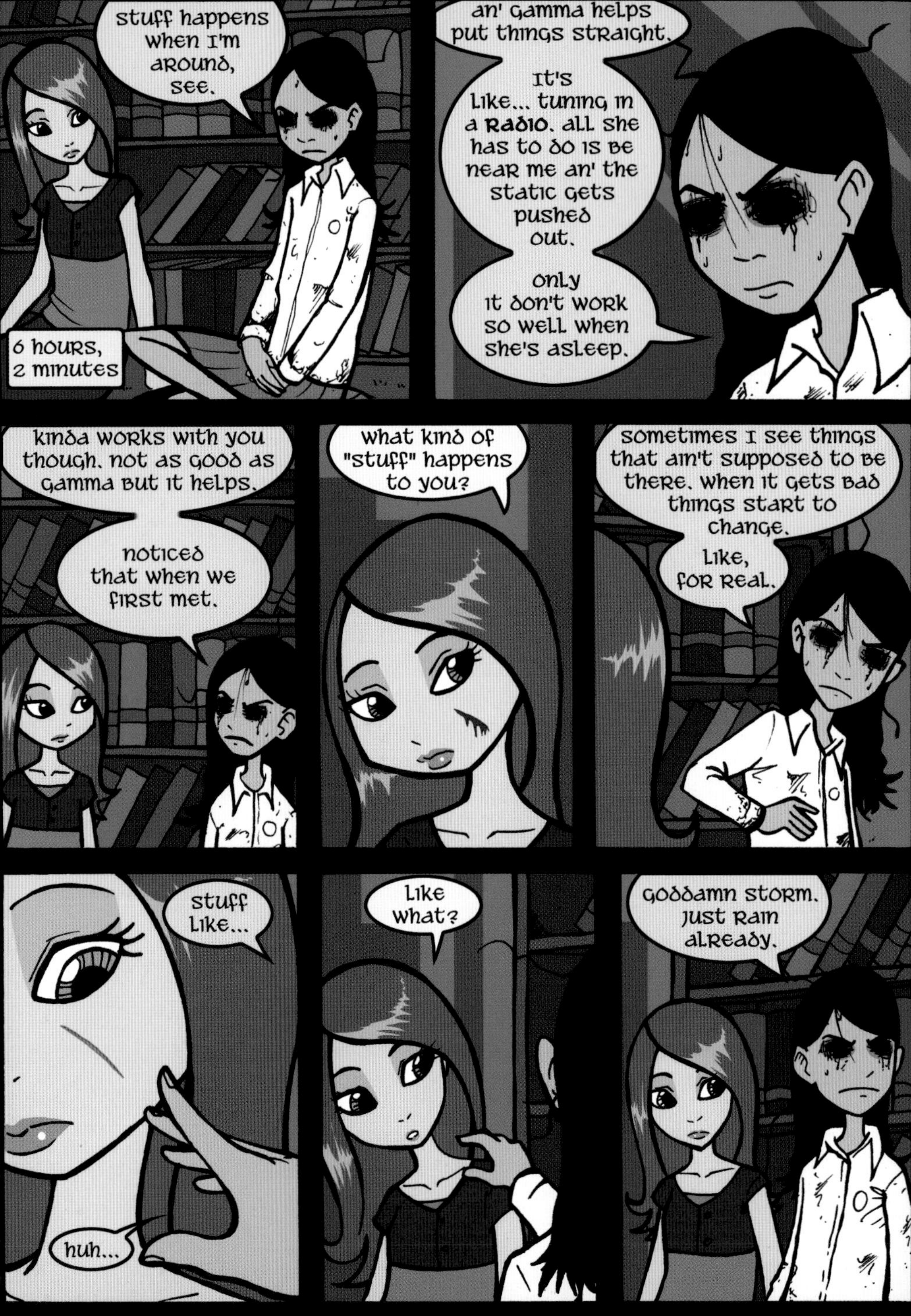

stuff happens when I'm around, see.
6 hours, 2 minutes
an' gamma helps put things straight.
It's like... tuning in a radio. all she has to do is be near me an' the static gets pushed out.
only it don't work so well when she's asleep.
kinda works with you though. not as good as gamma but it helps.
noticed that when we first met.
what kind of "stuff" happens to you?
sometimes I see things that ain't supposed to be there. when it gets bad things start to change.
like, for real.
stuff like...
huh...
like what?
goddamn storm. just rain already.

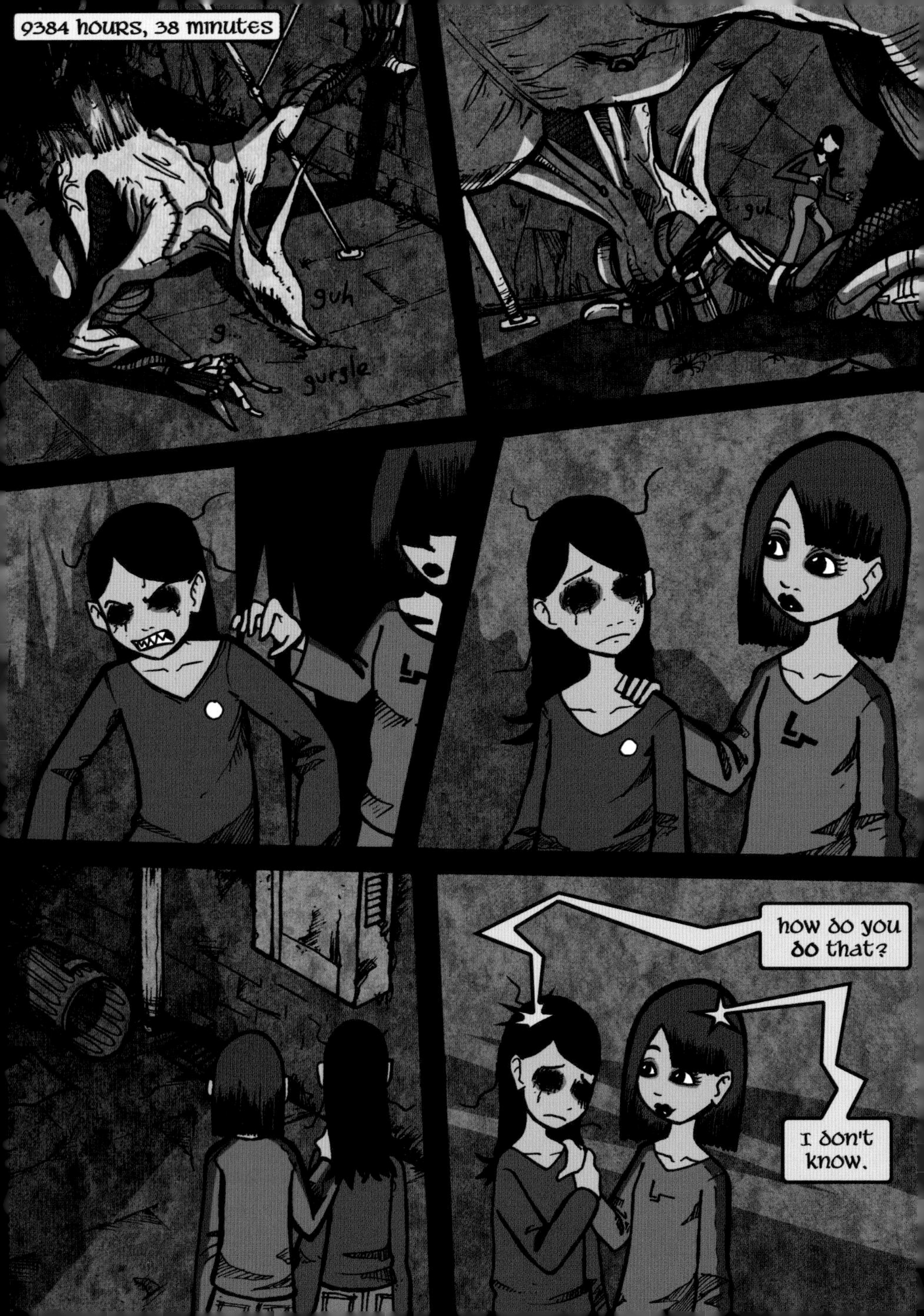
9384 HOURS, 38 MINUTES
guh
g..
gurgle
..guh..
how do you do that?
I don't know.

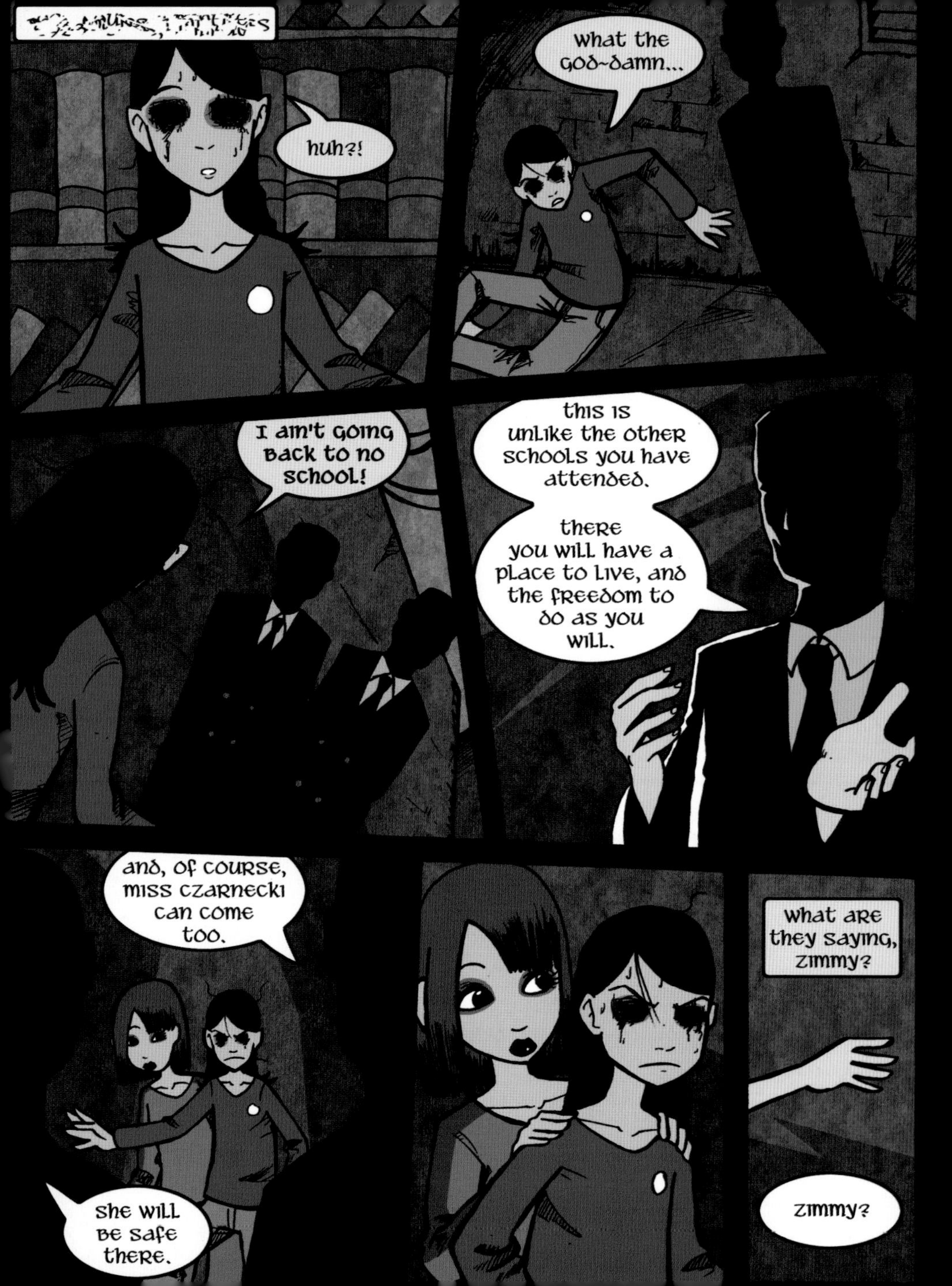
huh?!
What the God~damn...
I ain't going back to no school!
this is unlike the other schools you have attended.
there you will have a place to live, and the freedom to do as you will.
and, of course, miss Czarnecki can come too.
She will be safe there.
What are they saying, Zimmy?
Zimmy?

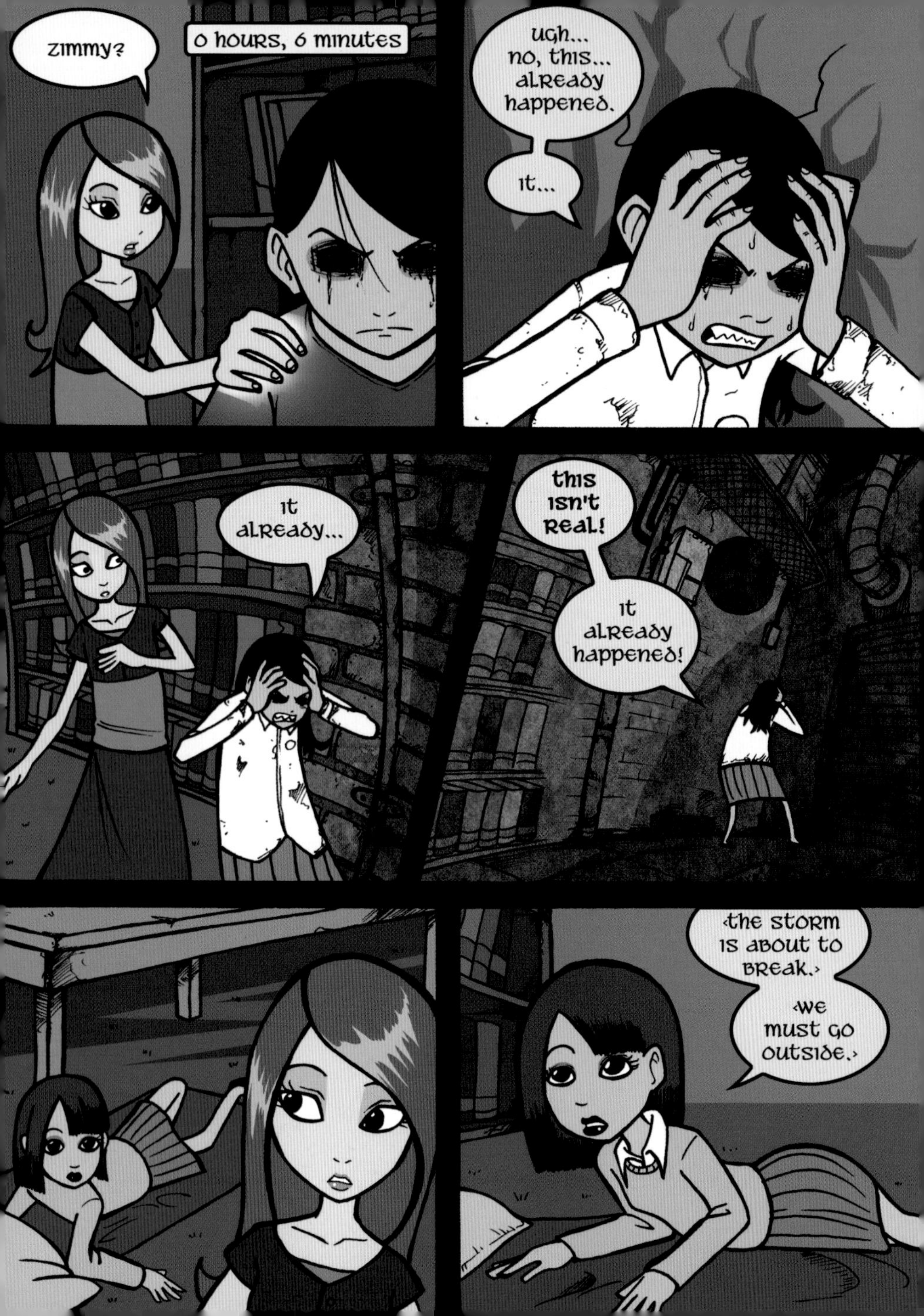
ZIMMY?
0 HOURS, 6 MINUTES
UGH... NO, THIS... ALREADY HAPPENED.
IT...
IT ALREADY...
THIS ISN'T REAL!
IT ALREADY HAPPENED!
‹THE STORM IS ABOUT TO BREAK.›
‹WE MUST GO OUTSIDE.›

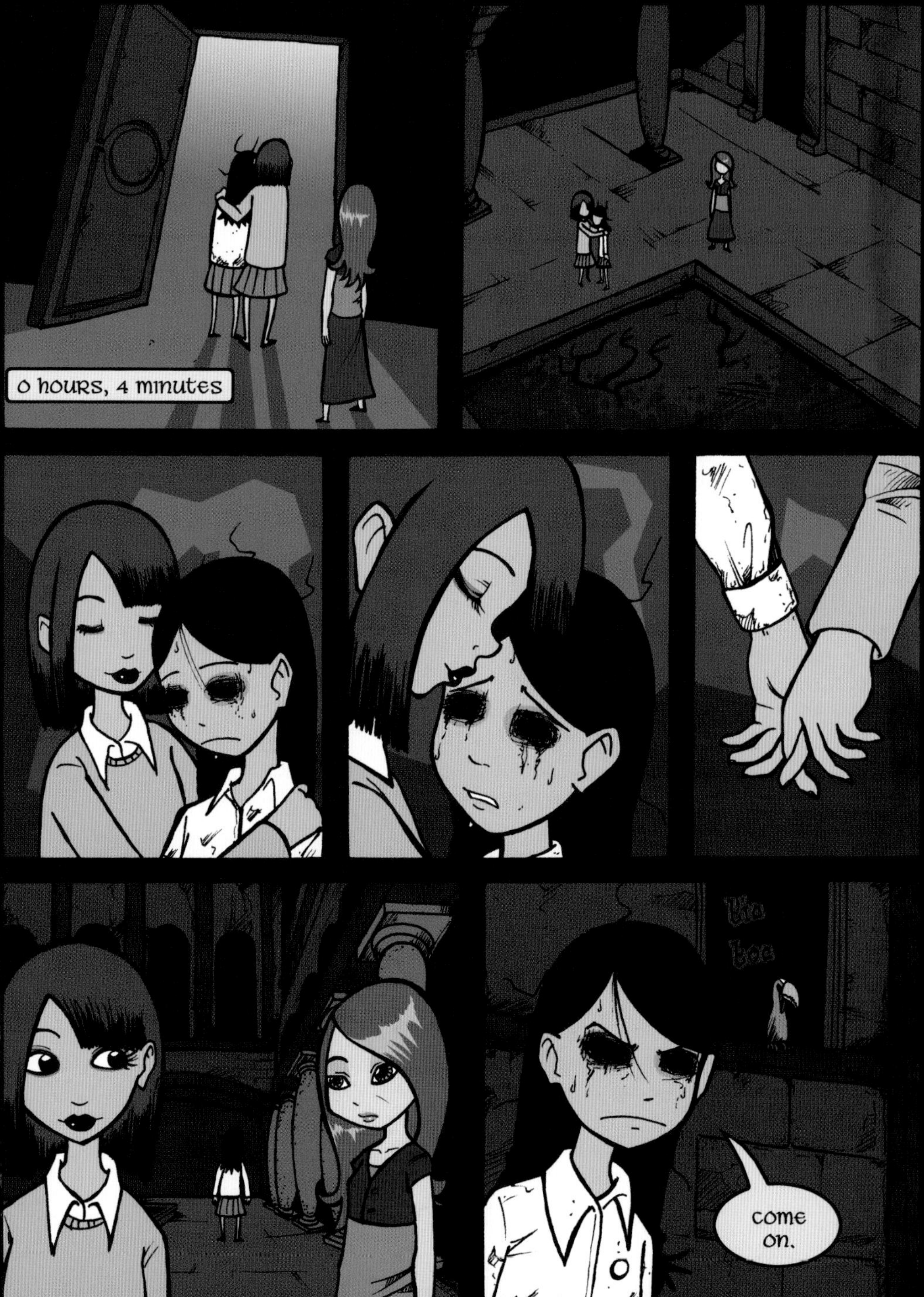
0 hours, 4 minutes
come on.

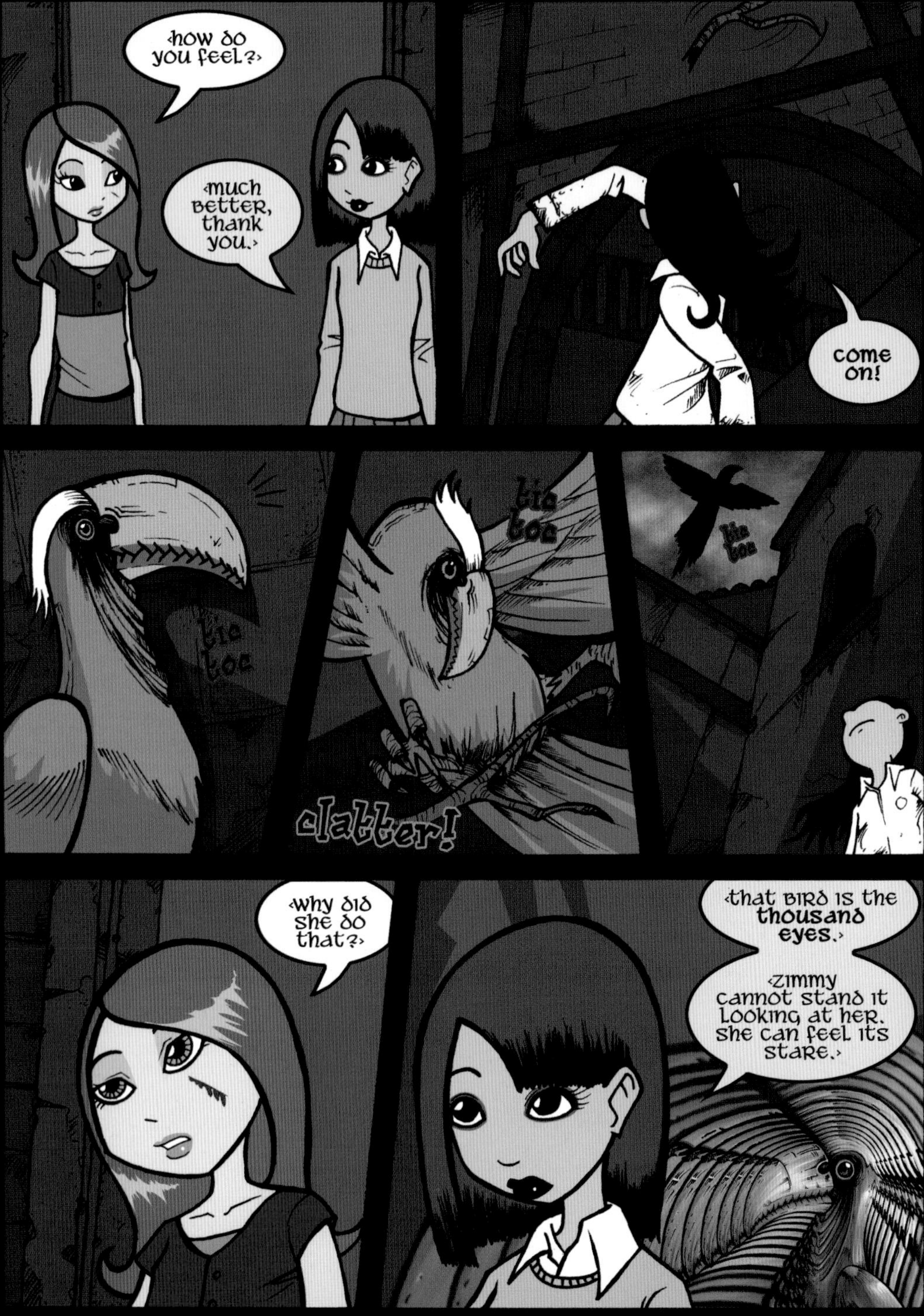
‹how do you feel?›
‹much better, thank you.›
come on!
tic toc
tic toc
tic toc
clabber!
‹why did she do that?›
‹that bird is the thousand eyes.›
‹zimmy cannot stand it looking at her. she can feel its stare.›

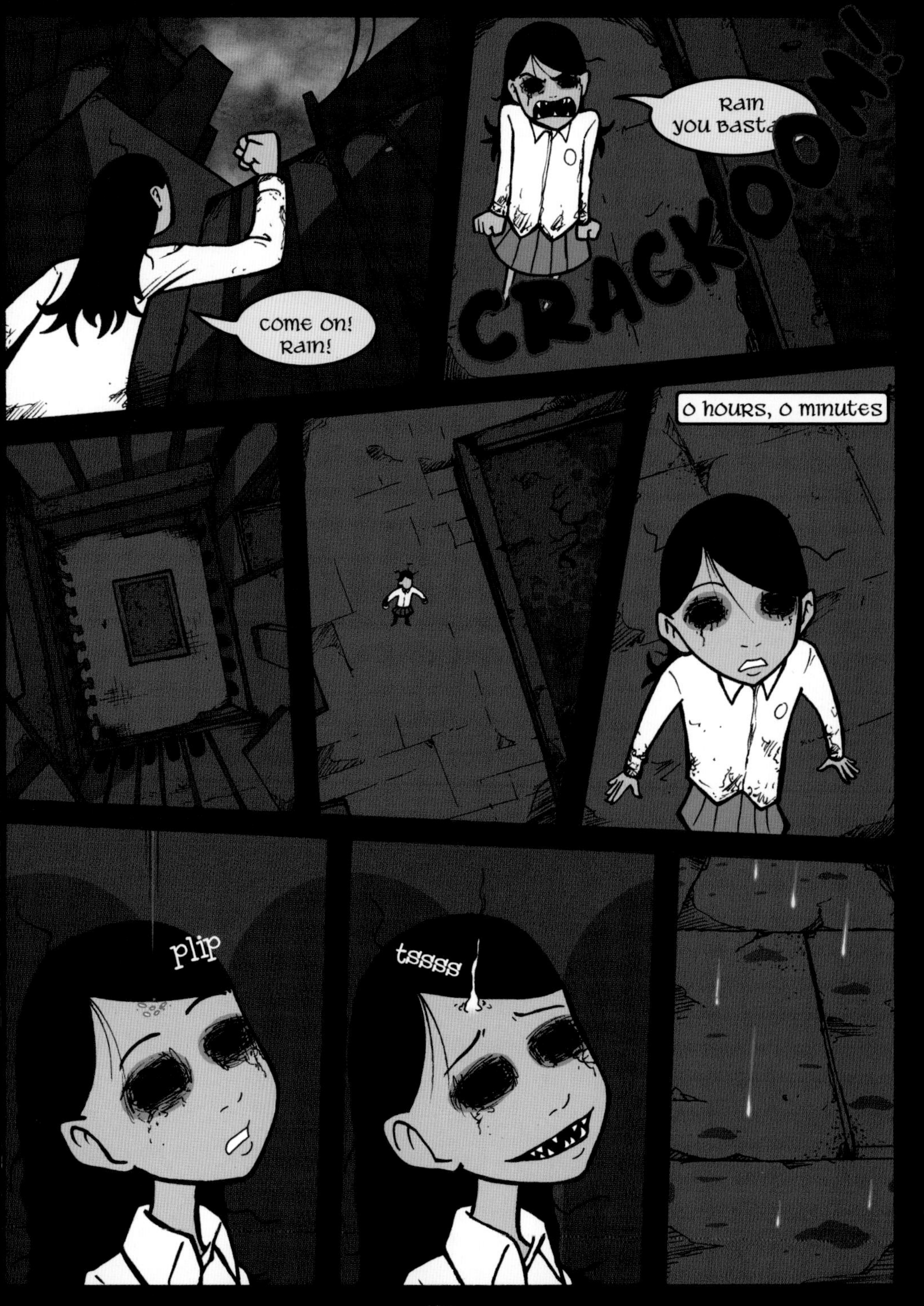
come on!
Rain!
Rain
you Basta
CRACKOOM!
0 hours, 0 minutes
plip
tssss

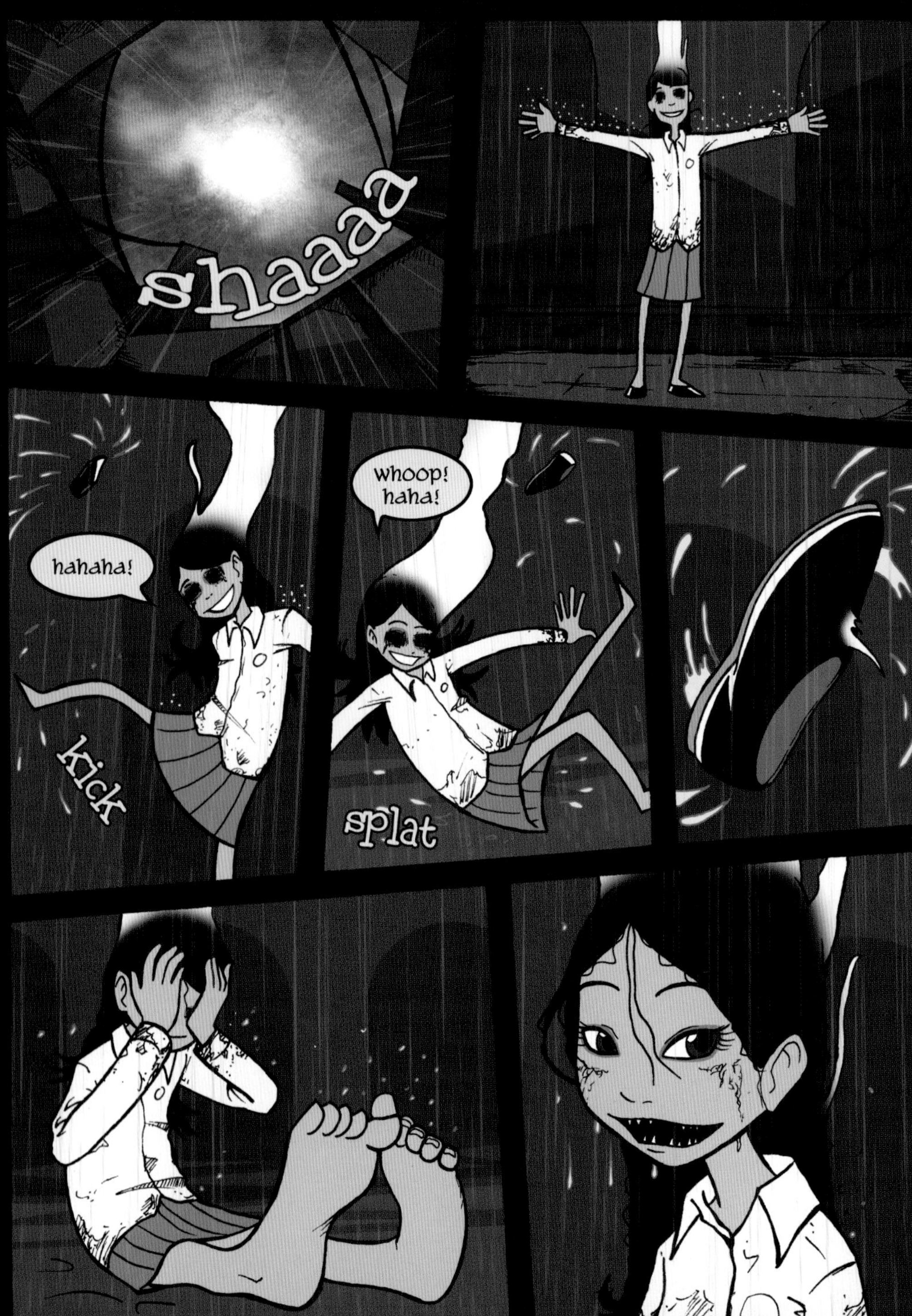
shaaaa
hahaha!
kick
whoop! haha!
splat

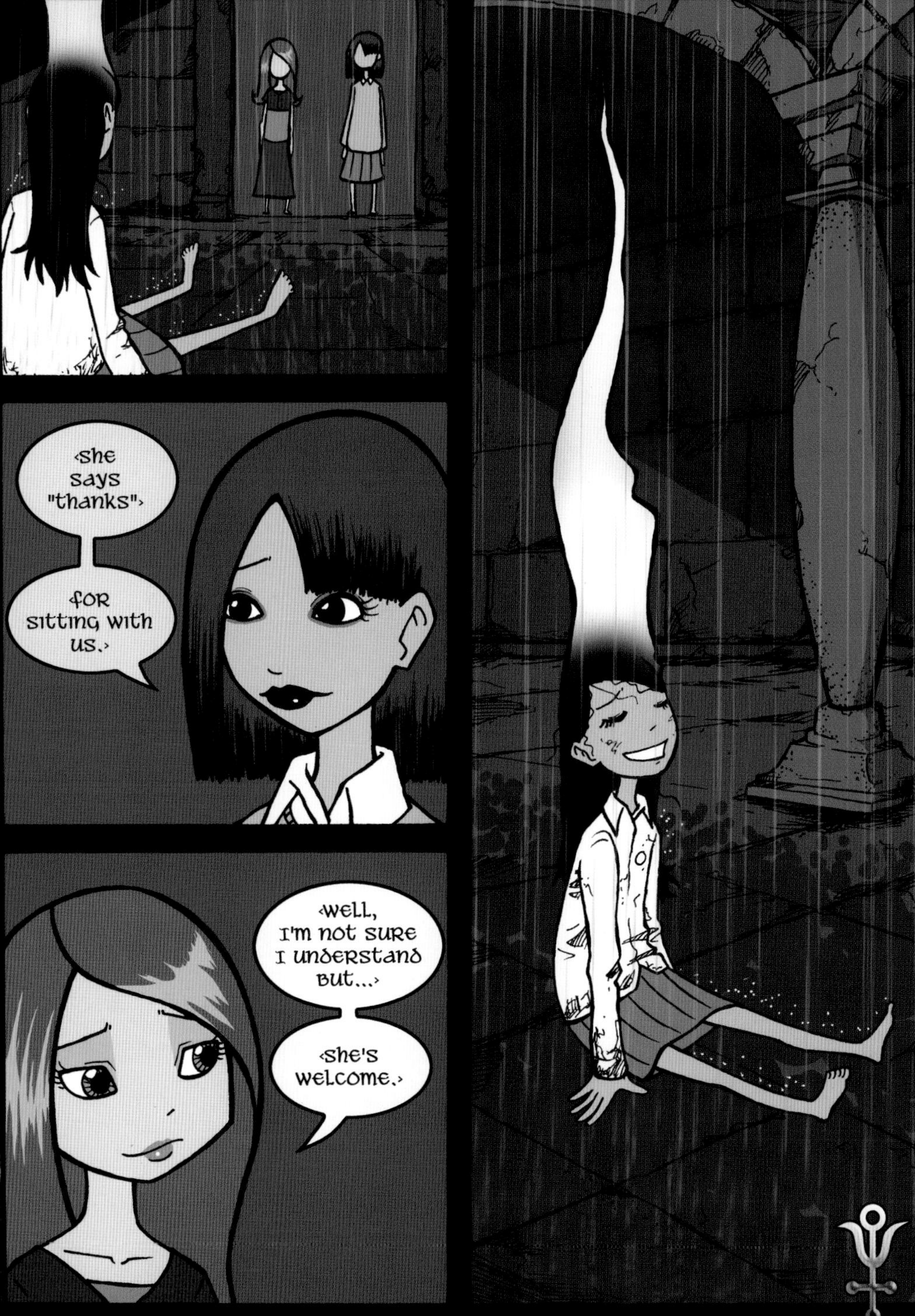
‹She says "thanks"›
‹for sitting with us.›
‹Well, I'm not sure I understand but...›
‹she's welcome.›

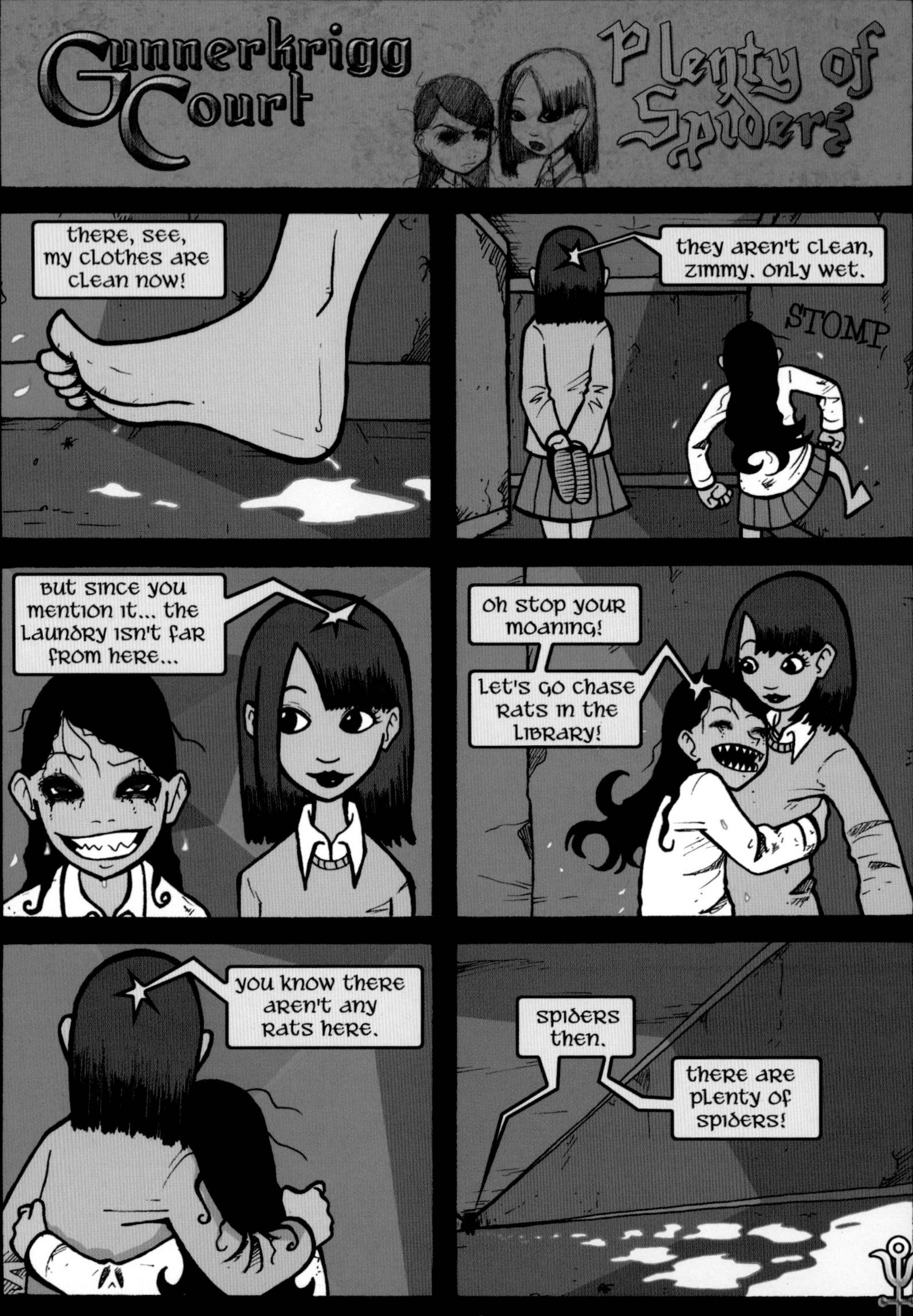
Gunnerkrigg Court
Plenty of Spiders
there, see, my clothes are clean now!
they aren't clean, zimmy. only wet.
STOMP
But since you mention it... the laundry isn't far from here...
oh stop your moaning!
let's go chase rats in the library!
you know there aren't any rats here.
spiders then.
there are plenty of spiders!

Gunnerkrigg Court

Chapter 12:

Mainly Involves Robots

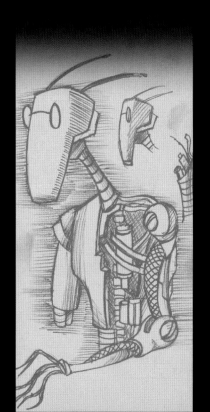

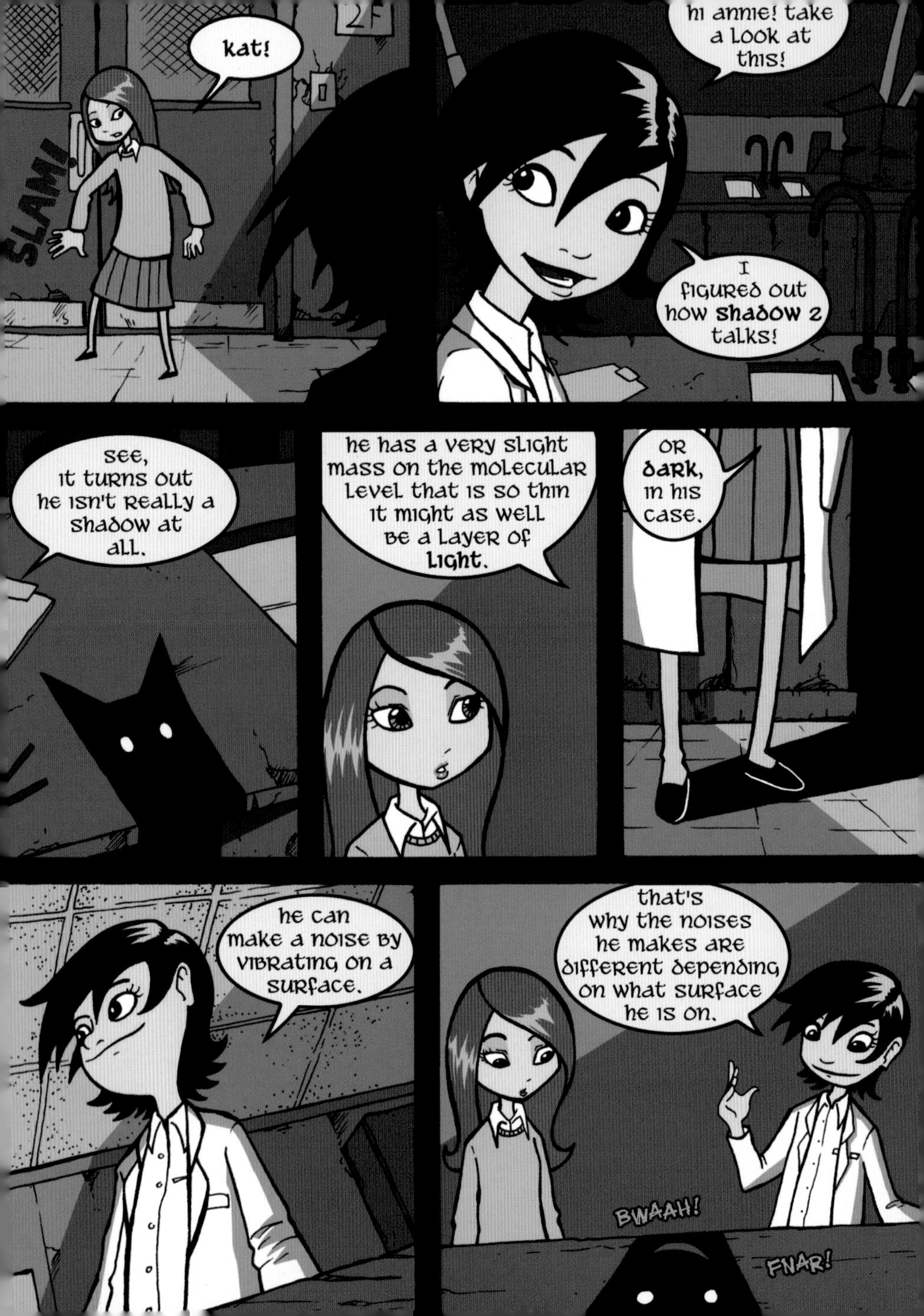

2F
kat!
SLAM!
hi annie! take a look at this!
I figured out how **shadow 2** talks!
see, it turns out he isn't really a shadow at all.
he has a very slight mass on the molecular level that is so thin it might as well be a layer of **light**.
or **dark**, in his case.
he can make a noise by vibrating on a surface.
that's why the noises he makes are different depending on what surface he is on.
BWAAH!
FNAR!

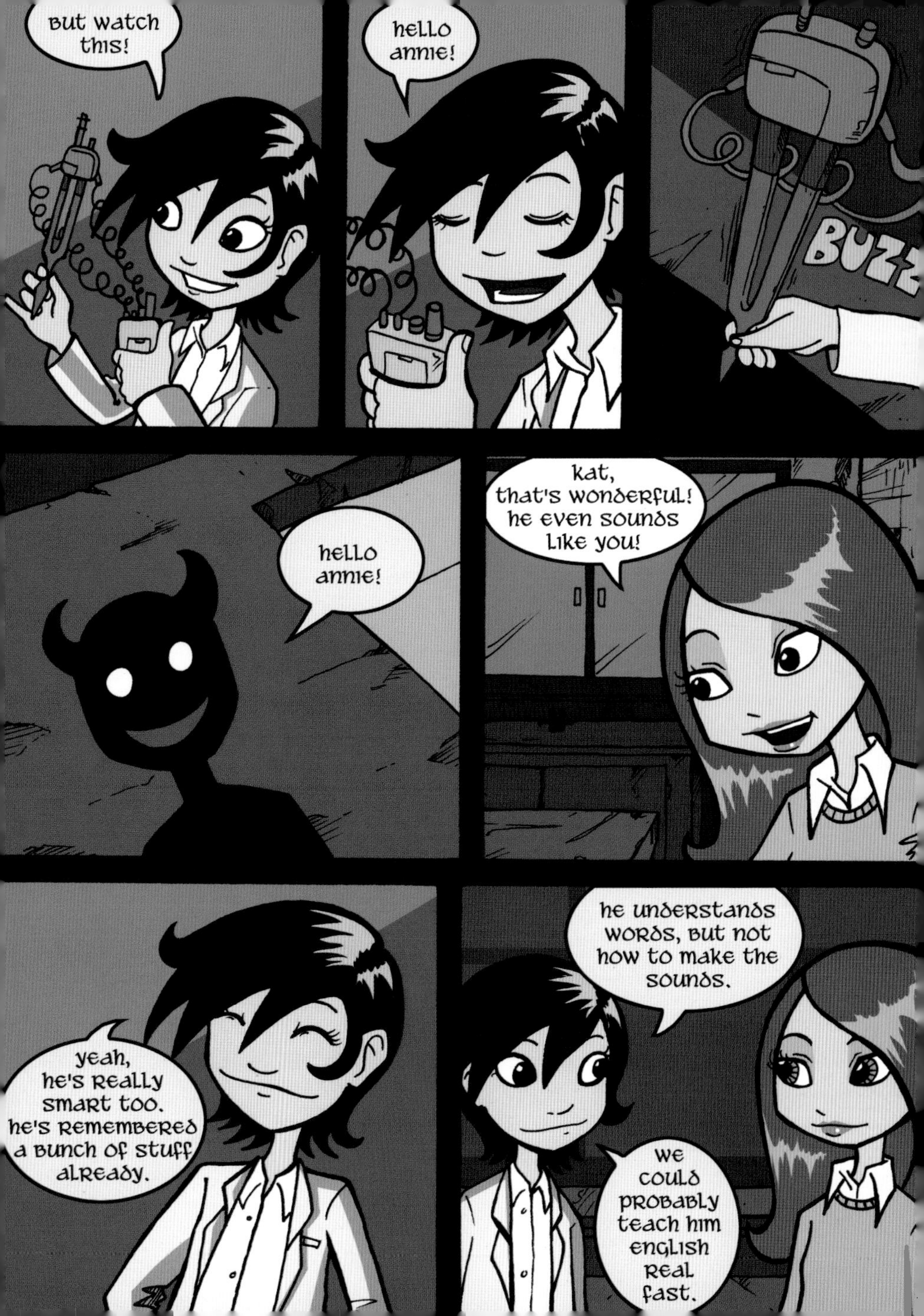

but watch this!
hello annie!
BUZZ
hello annie!
kat, that's wonderful! he even sounds like you!
yeah, he's really smart too. he's remembered a bunch of stuff already.
he understands words, but not how to make the sounds.
we could probably teach him english real fast.

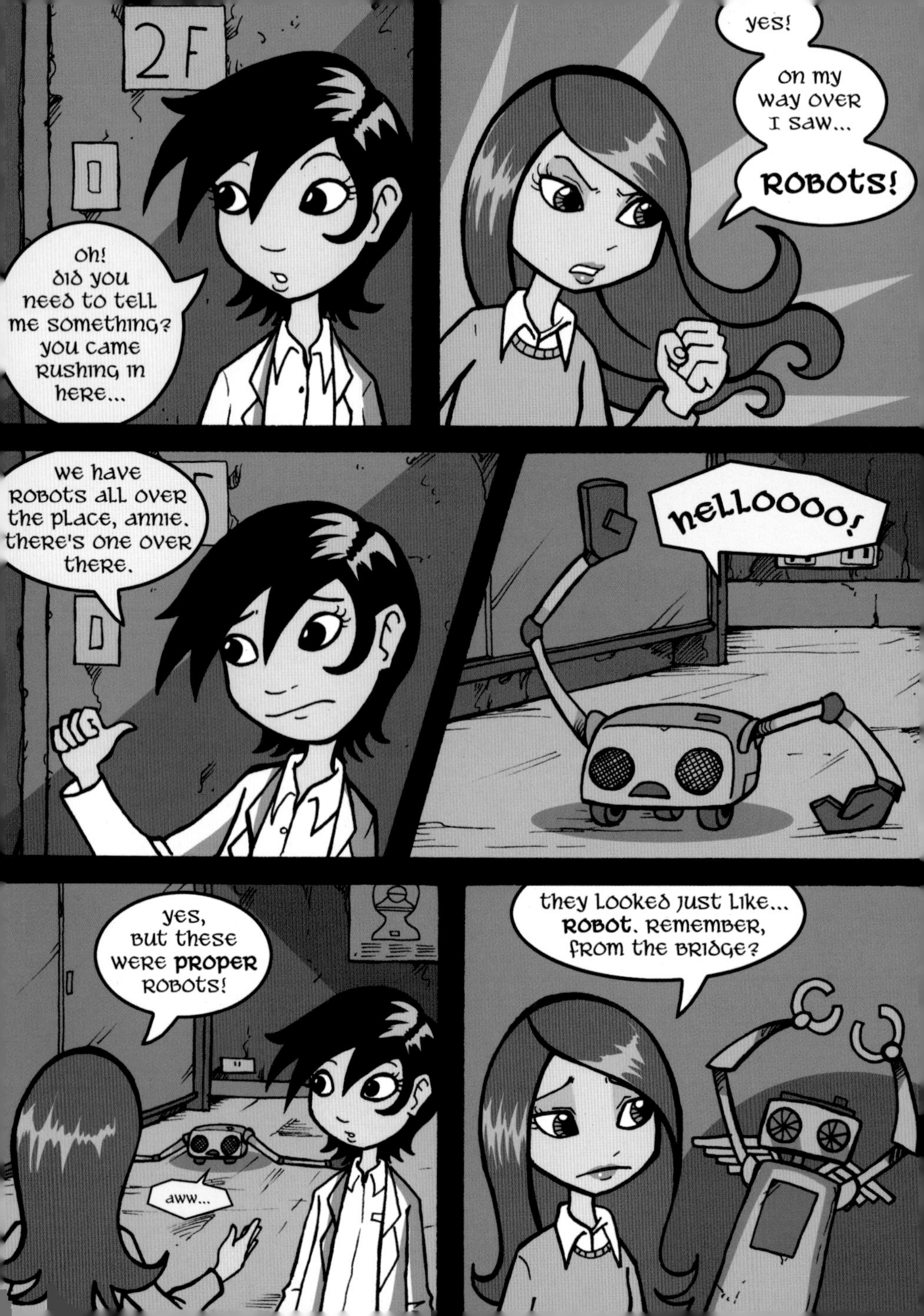
2F
oh! did you need to tell me something? you came rushing in here...
yes!
on my way over I saw...
ROBOTS!
we have robots all over the place, annie. there's one over there.
hellOOOO!
yes, but these were PROPER robots!
aww...
they looked just like... ROBOT. remember, from the bridge?

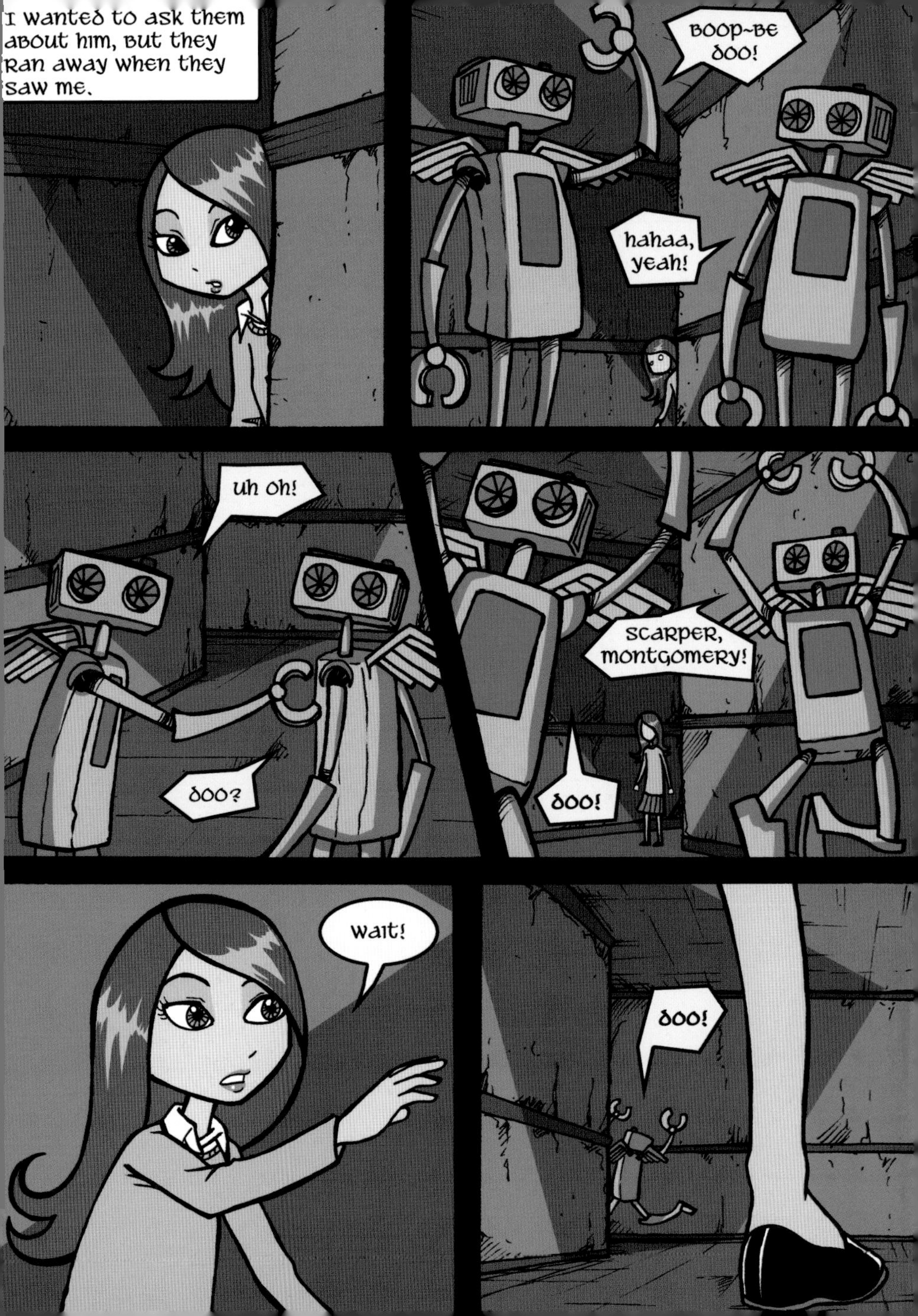
I wanted to ask them about him, but they ran away when they saw me.
BOOP~BE DOO!
hahaa, yeah!
uh oh!
DOO?
SCARPER, MONTGOMERY!
DOO!
Wait!
DOO!

THERE WAS NO HANDLE ON THE DOOR THROUGH WHICH THEY ESCAPED.

THEN, SUDDENLY...

ANOTHER ROBOT APPEARED!

WHAT?!

WADDA YOU WANT?!

I, UM... WOULD LIKE TO ENTER, PLEASE.

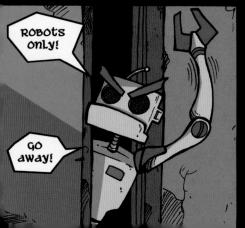

ROBOTS ONLY!

GO AWAY!

SLAM

BORING DOOR

HE WOULDN'T LET ME IN.

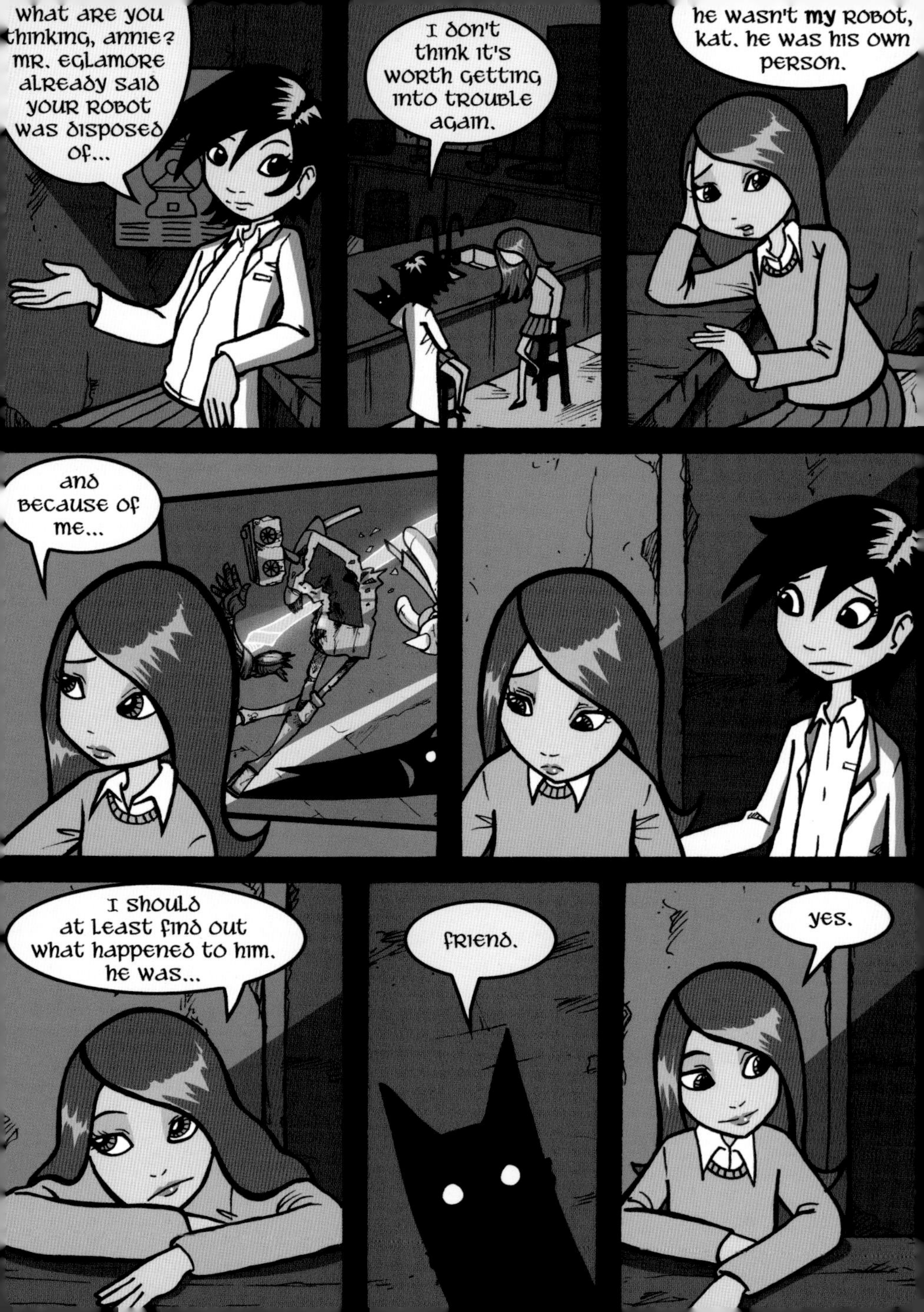
what are you thinking, annie? mr. eglamore already said your robot was disposed of...
I don't think it's worth getting into trouble again.
he wasn't **my** robot, kat. he was his own person.
and because of me...
I should at least find out what happened to him. he was...
friend.
yes.

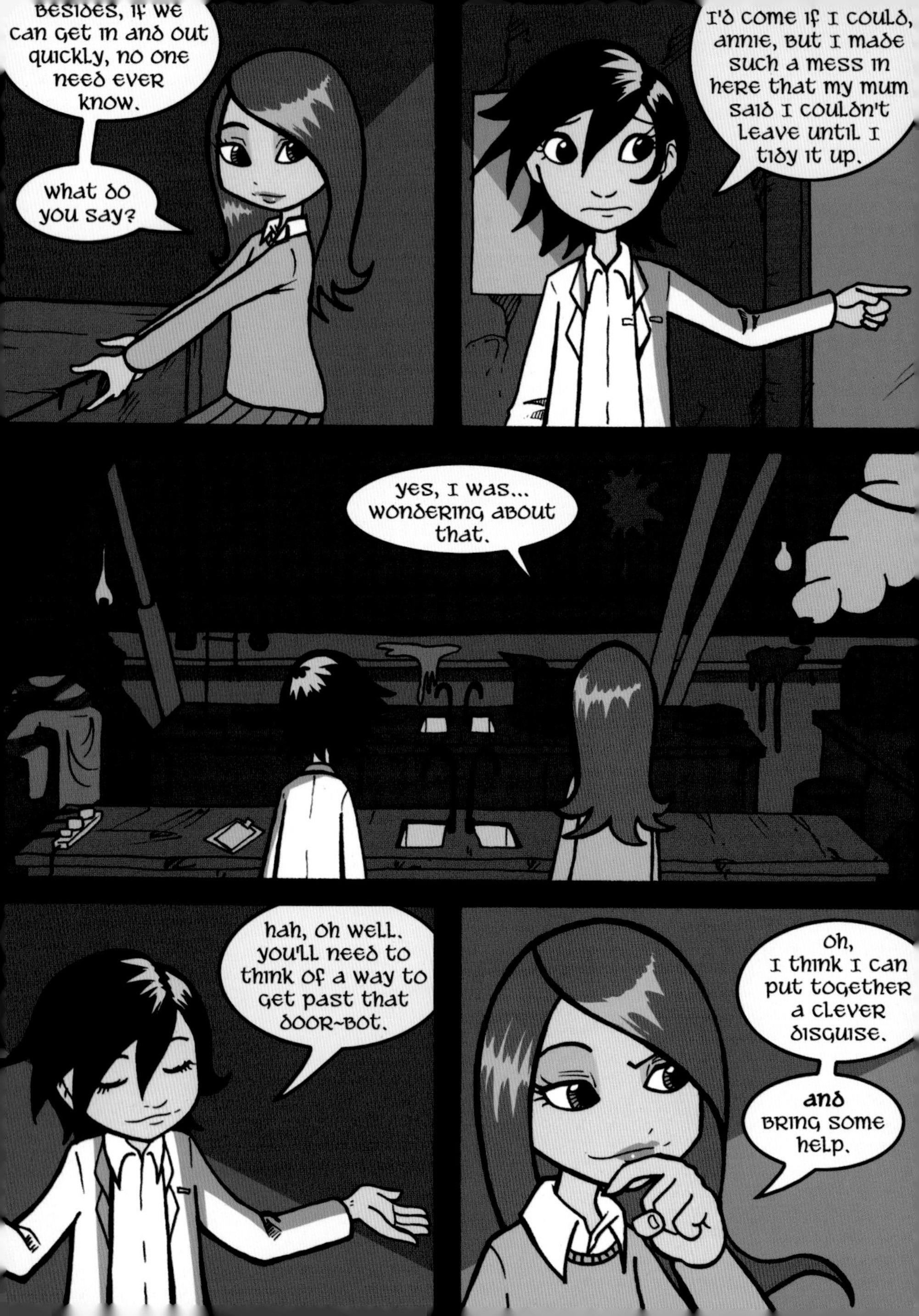
BESIDES, IF WE CAN GET IN AND OUT QUICKLY, NO ONE NEED EVER KNOW.
WHAT DO YOU SAY?
I'D COME IF I COULD, ANNIE, BUT I MADE SUCH A MESS IN HERE THAT MY MUM SAID I COULDN'T LEAVE UNTIL I TIDY IT UP.
YES, I WAS... WONDERING ABOUT THAT.
HAH, OH WELL. YOU'LL NEED TO THINK OF A WAY TO GET PAST THAT DOOR-BOT.
OH, I THINK I CAN PUT TOGETHER A CLEVER DISGUISE.
AND BRING SOME HELP.

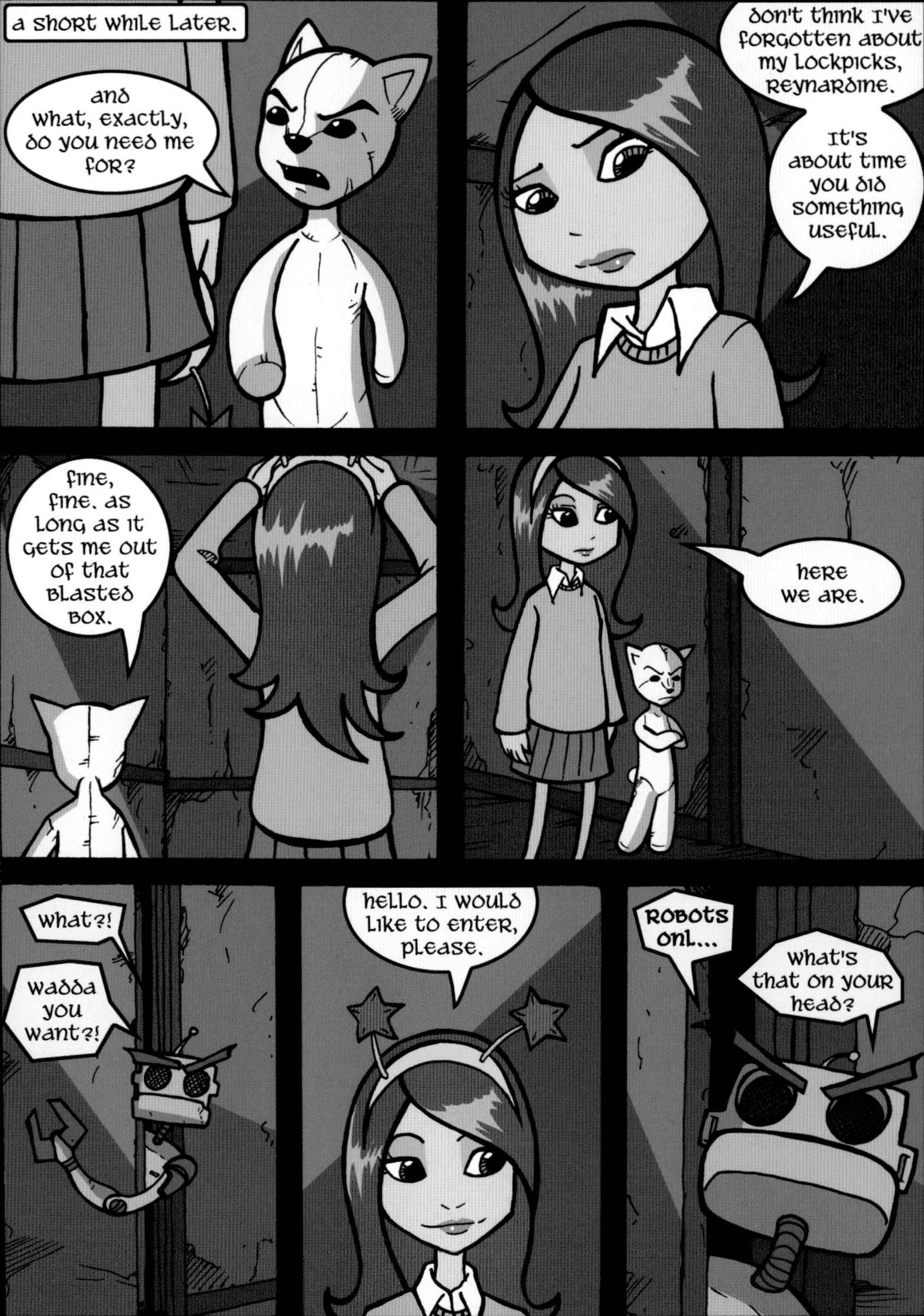
a short while later.
and what, exactly, do you need me for?
don't think I've forgotten about my lockpicks, Reynardine.
It's about time you did something useful.
fine, fine. as long as it gets me out of that blasted box.
here we are.
What?!
Wadda you want?!
hello. I would like to enter, please.
ROBOTS ONL...
What's that on your head?

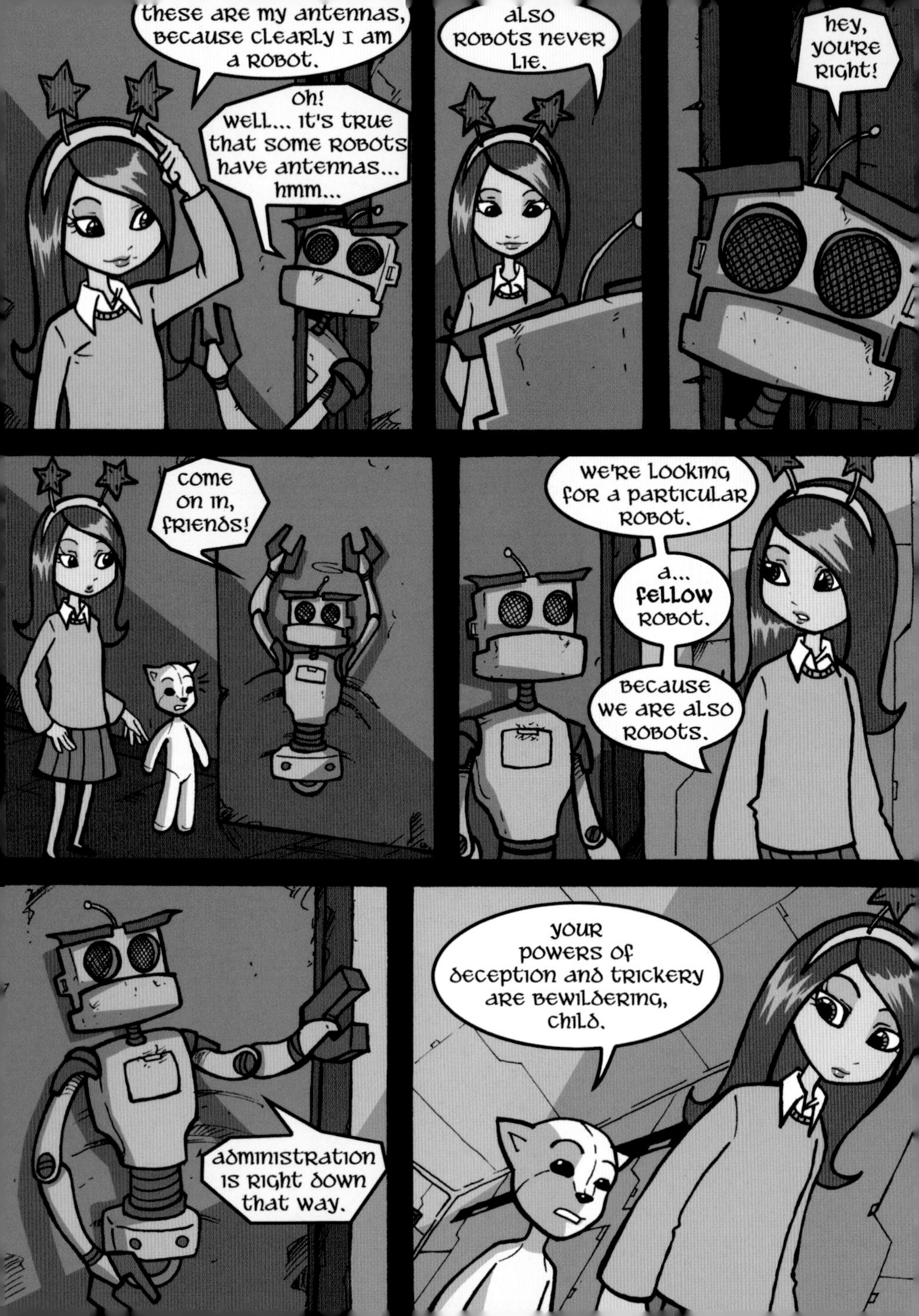
these are my antennas, because clearly I am a robot.
Oh! well... it's true that some robots have antennas... hmm...
also robots never lie.
hey, you're right!
come on in, friends!
we're looking for a particular robot.
a... **fellow** robot.
because we are also robots.
administration is right down that way.
your powers of deception and trickery are bewildering, child.

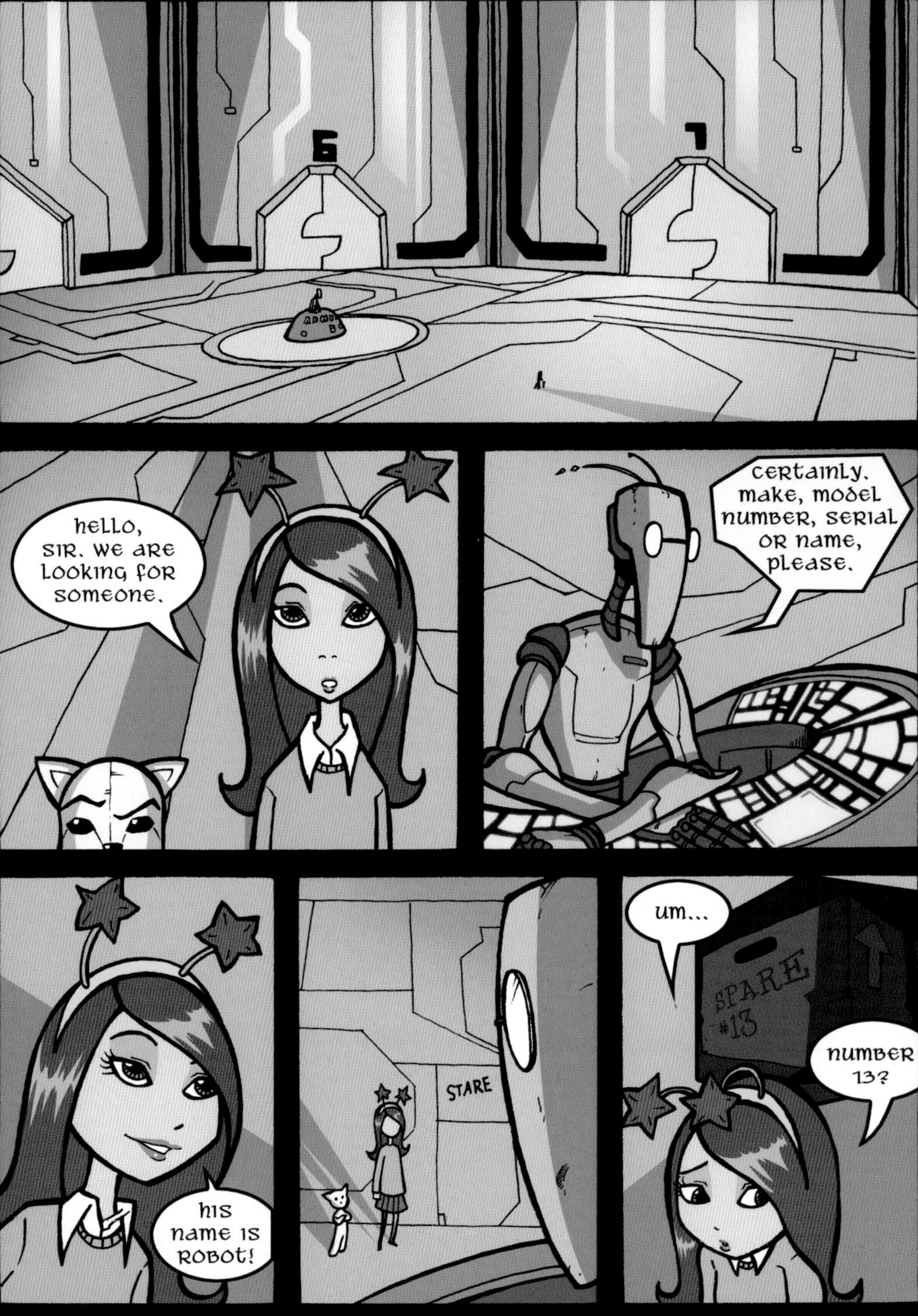
hello, sir. we are looking for someone.
certainly. make, model number, serial or name, please.
his name is robot!
STARE
um...
SPARE #13
number 13?

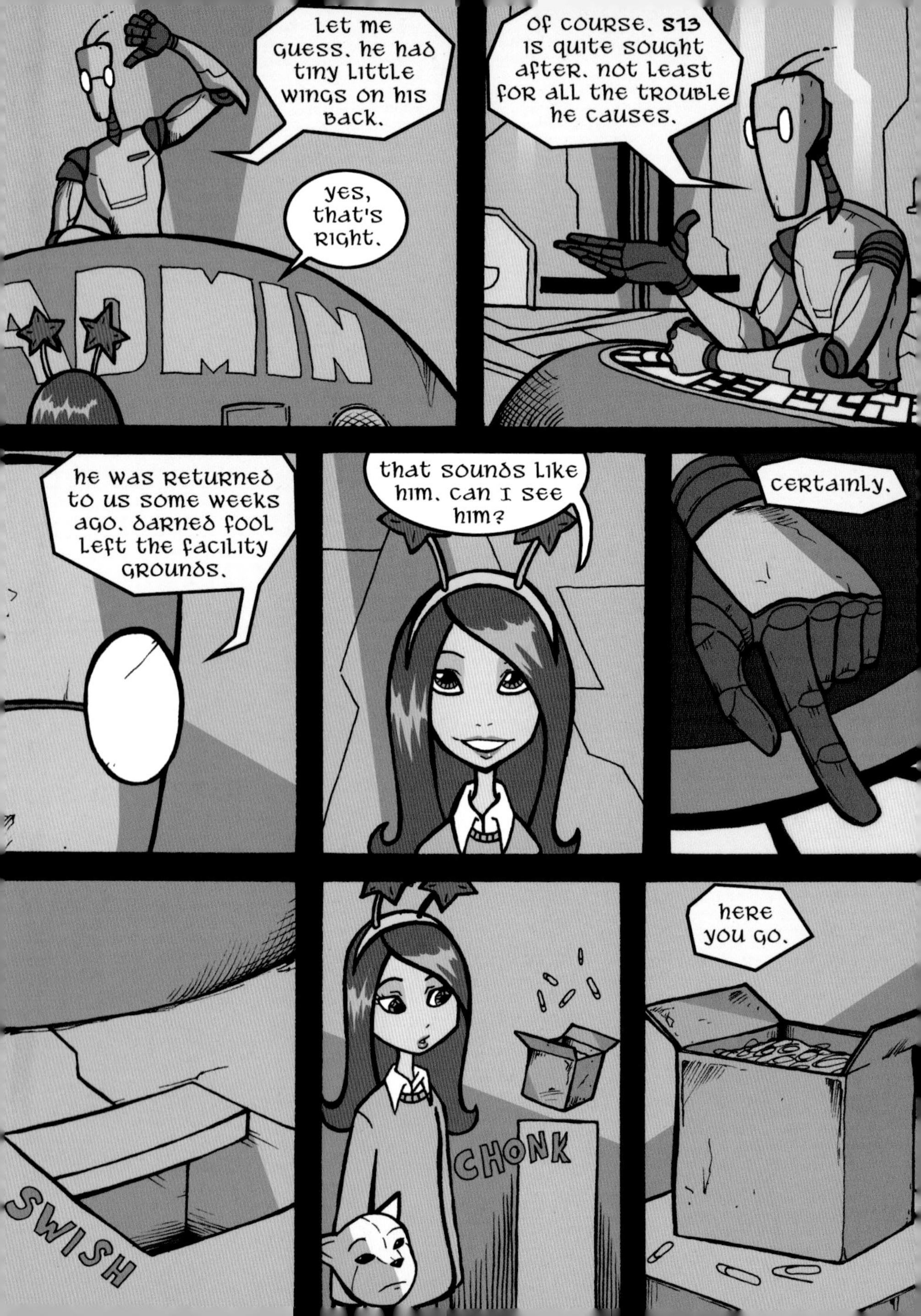
Let me guess. he had tiny Little wings on his back.
yes, that's right.
Of course. S13 is quite sought after. not least for all the trouble he causes.
he was returned to us some weeks ago. darned fool left the facility grounds.
that sounds like him. can I see him?
certainly.
SWISH
CHONK
here you go.

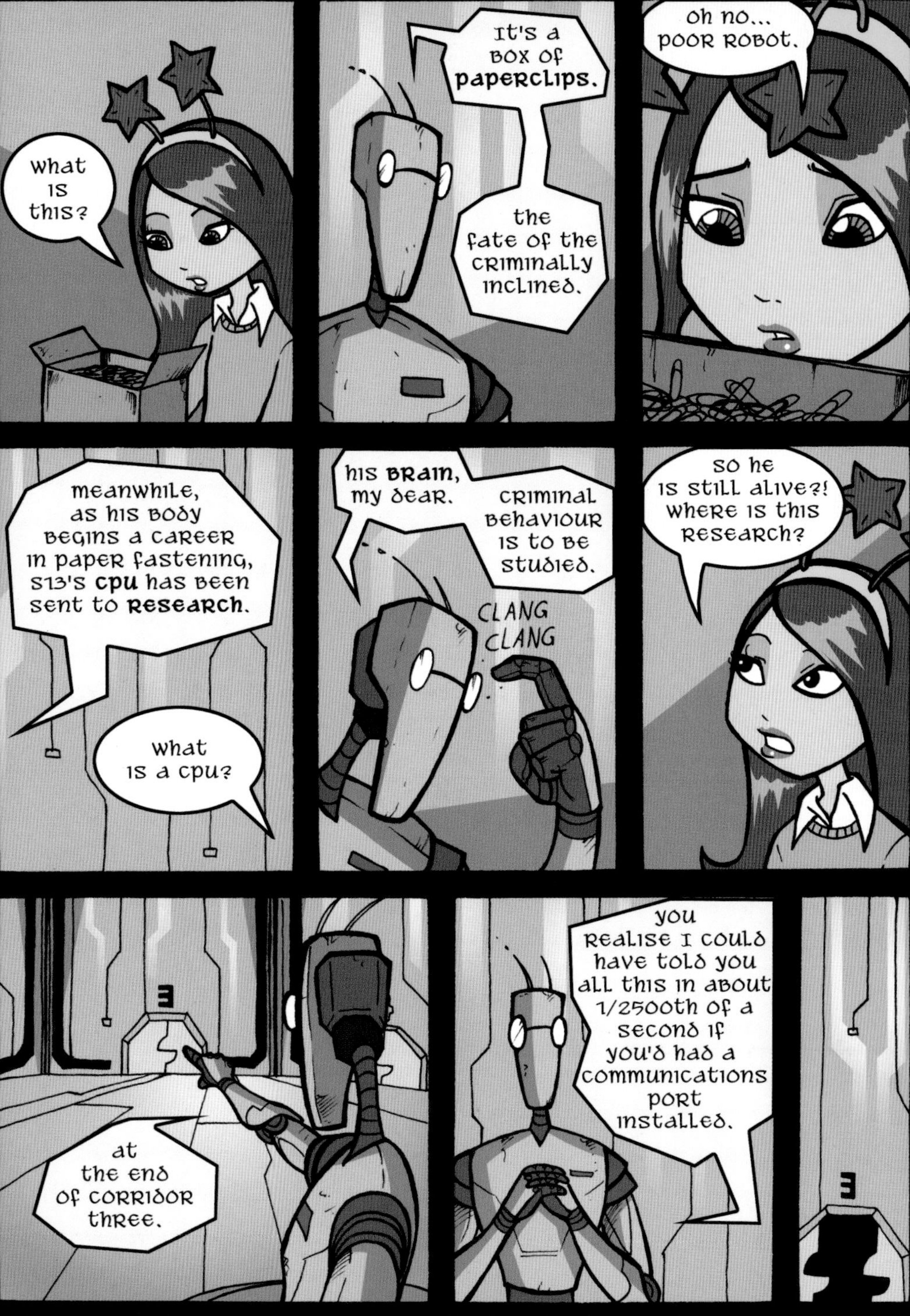
what is this?
It's a box of paperclips.
the fate of the criminally inclined.
oh no... poor robot.
meanwhile, as his body begins a career in paper fastening, S13's cpu has been sent to research.
what is a cpu?
his brain, my dear.
criminal behaviour is to be studied.
CLANG CLANG
so he is still alive?! where is this research?
at the end of corridor three.
you realise I could have told you all this in about 1/2500th of a second if you'd had a communications port installed.

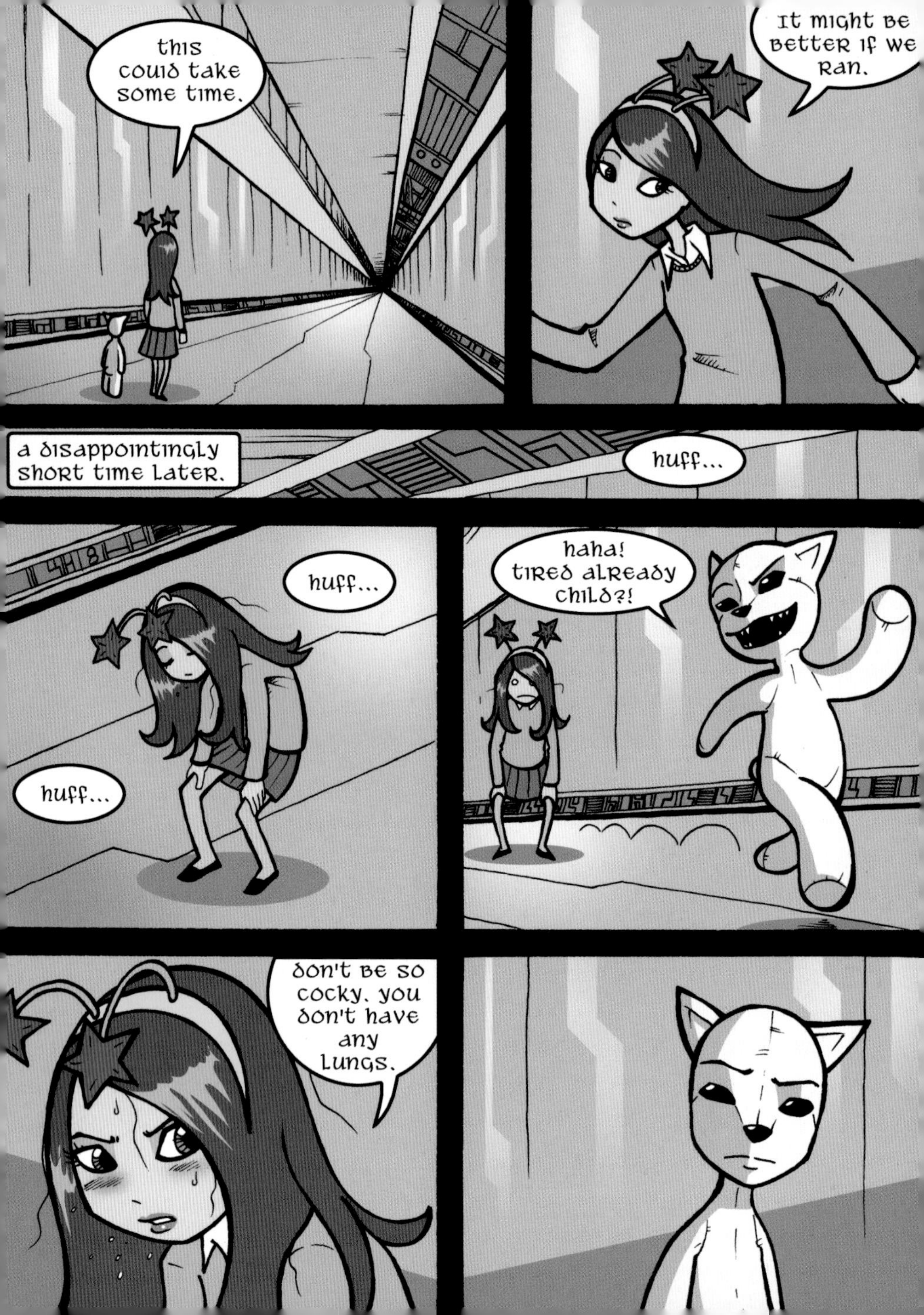
this could take some time.
It might be better if we ran.
a disappointingly short time later.
huff...
huff...
huff...
haha! tired already child?!
don't be so cocky. you don't have any lungs.

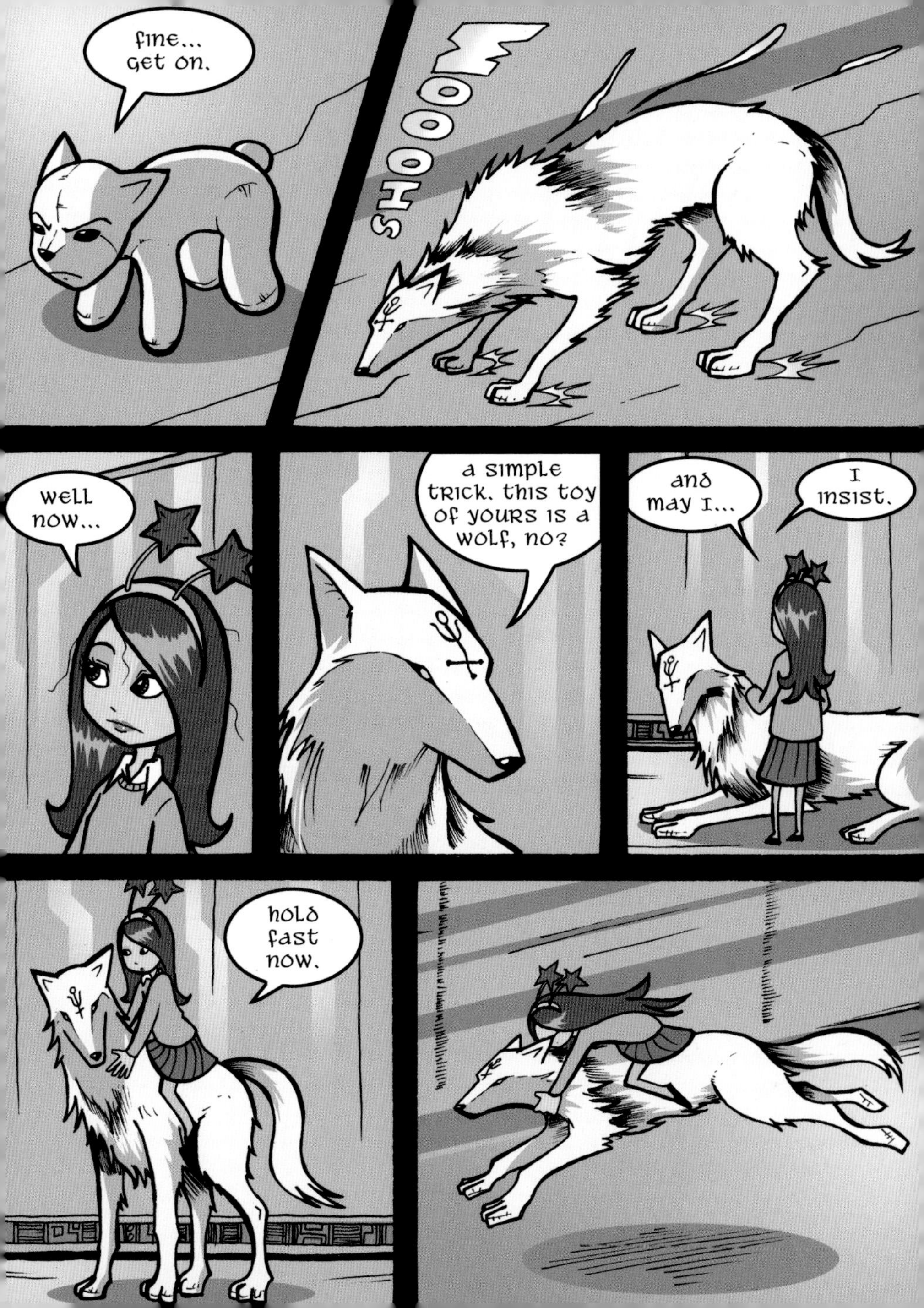
fine... get on.
SHOOOOM
well now...
a simple trick. this toy of yours is a wolf, no?
and may I...
I insist.
hold fast now.

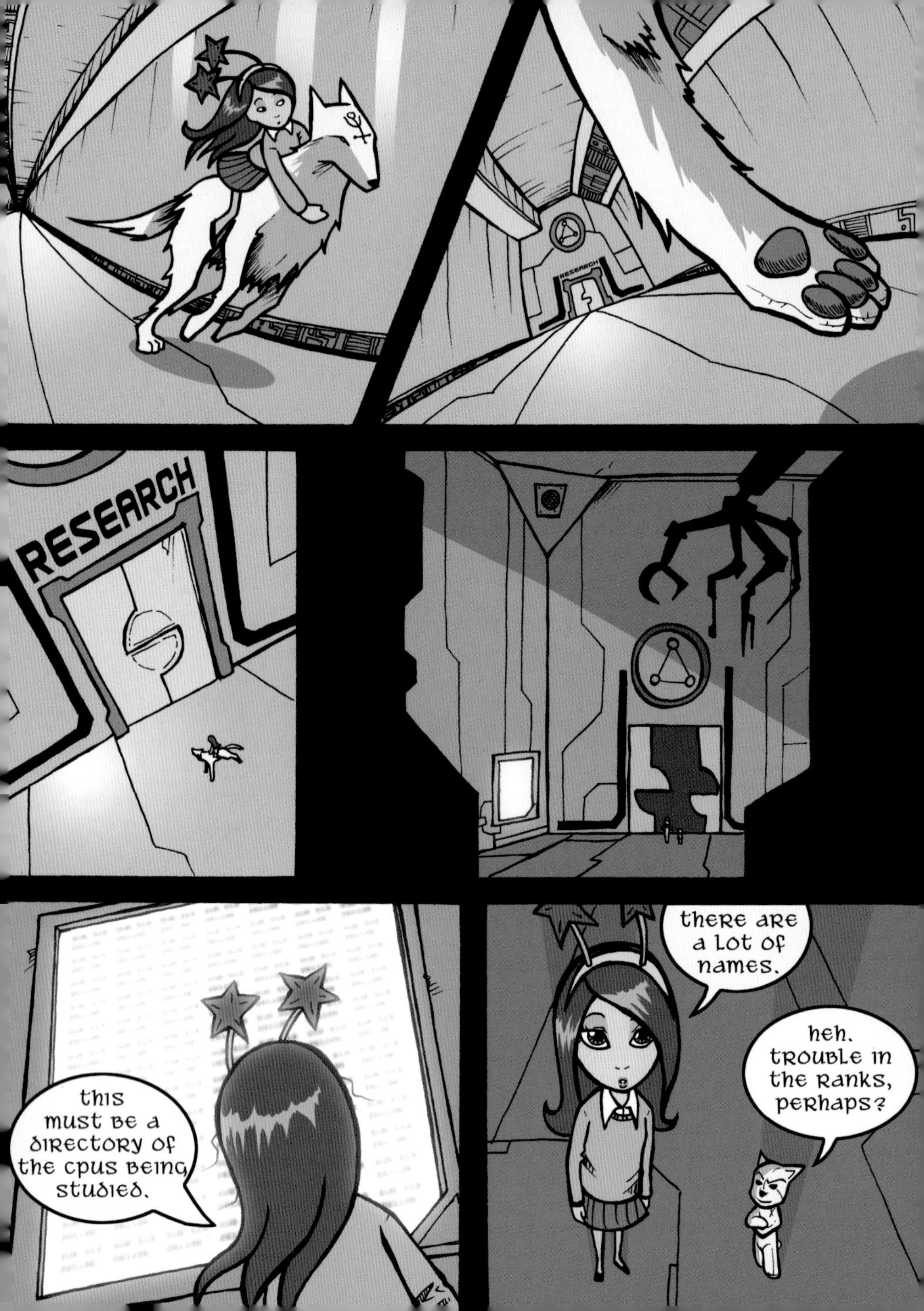
RESEARCH
RESEARCH
this must be a directory of the cpus being studied.
there are a lot of names.
heh. trouble in the ranks, perhaps?

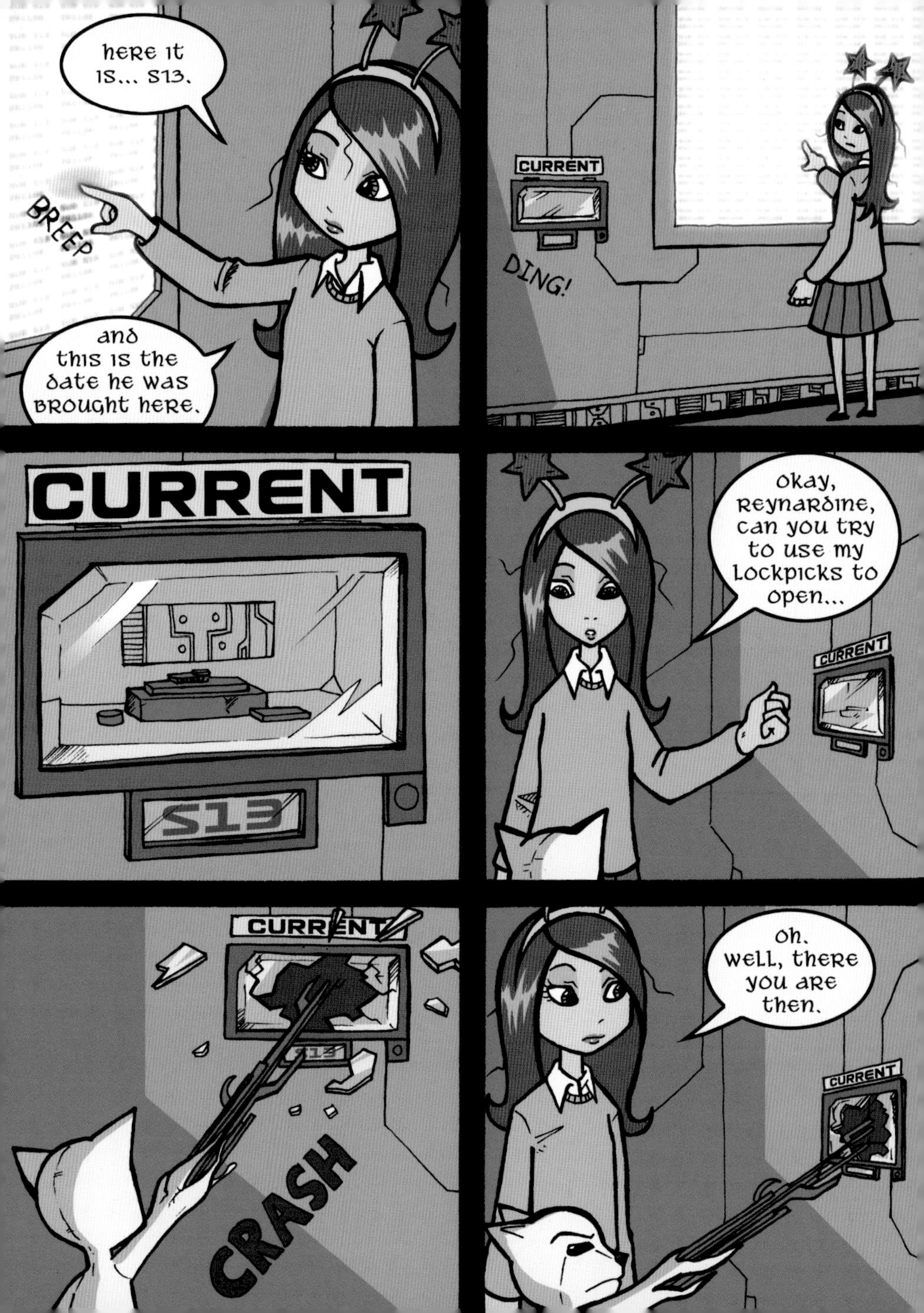
here it is... S13.
BREEP
and this is the date he was brought here.
CURRENT
DING!
CURRENT
S13
Okay, Reynardine, can you try to use my lockpicks to open...
CURRENT
CURRENT
CRASH
Oh. Well, there you are then.
CURRENT

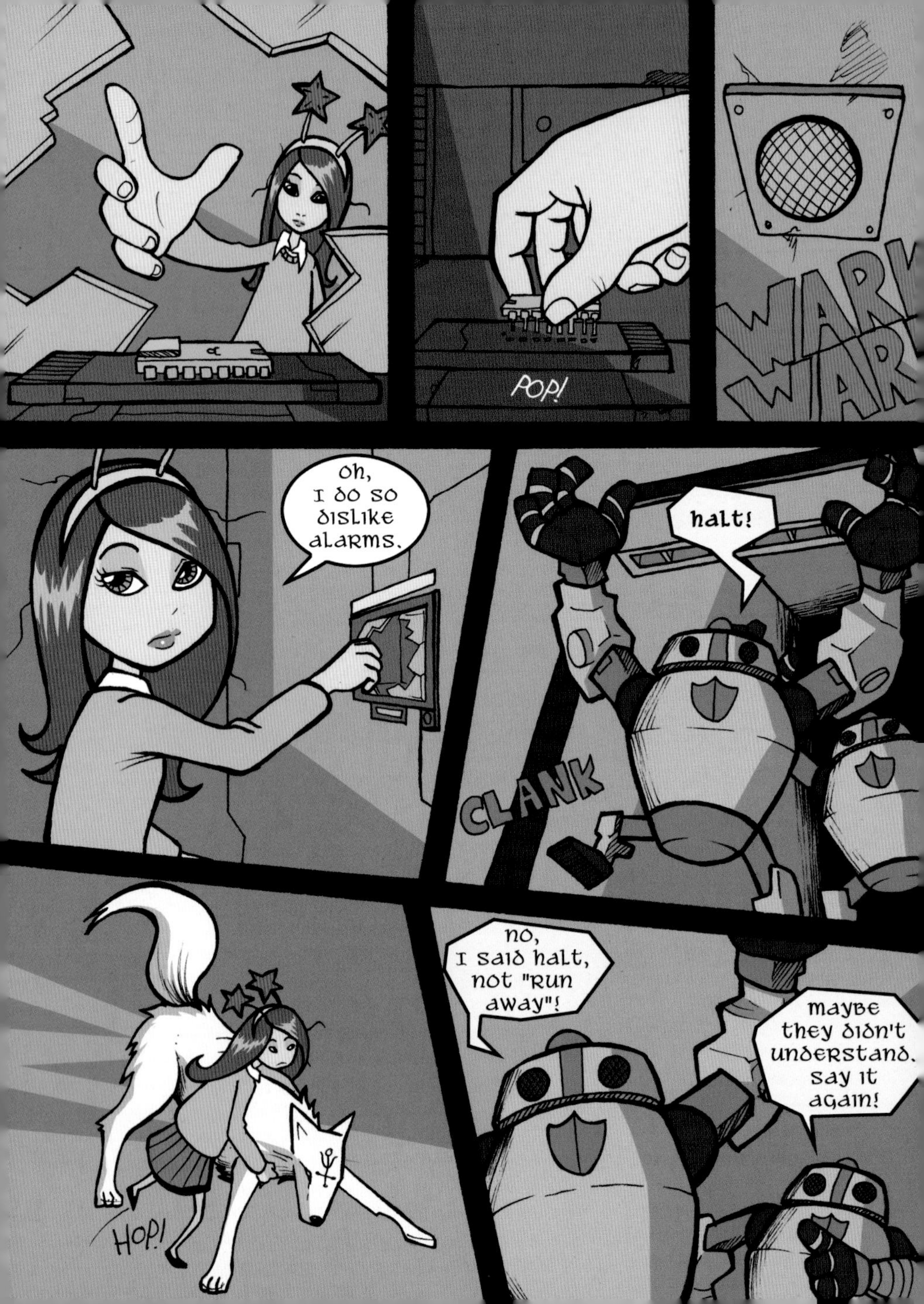
POP!
WARK
WARK
Oh, I do so dislike alarms.
halt!
CLANK
HOP!
no, I said halt, not "Run away"!
maybe they didn't understand. say it again!

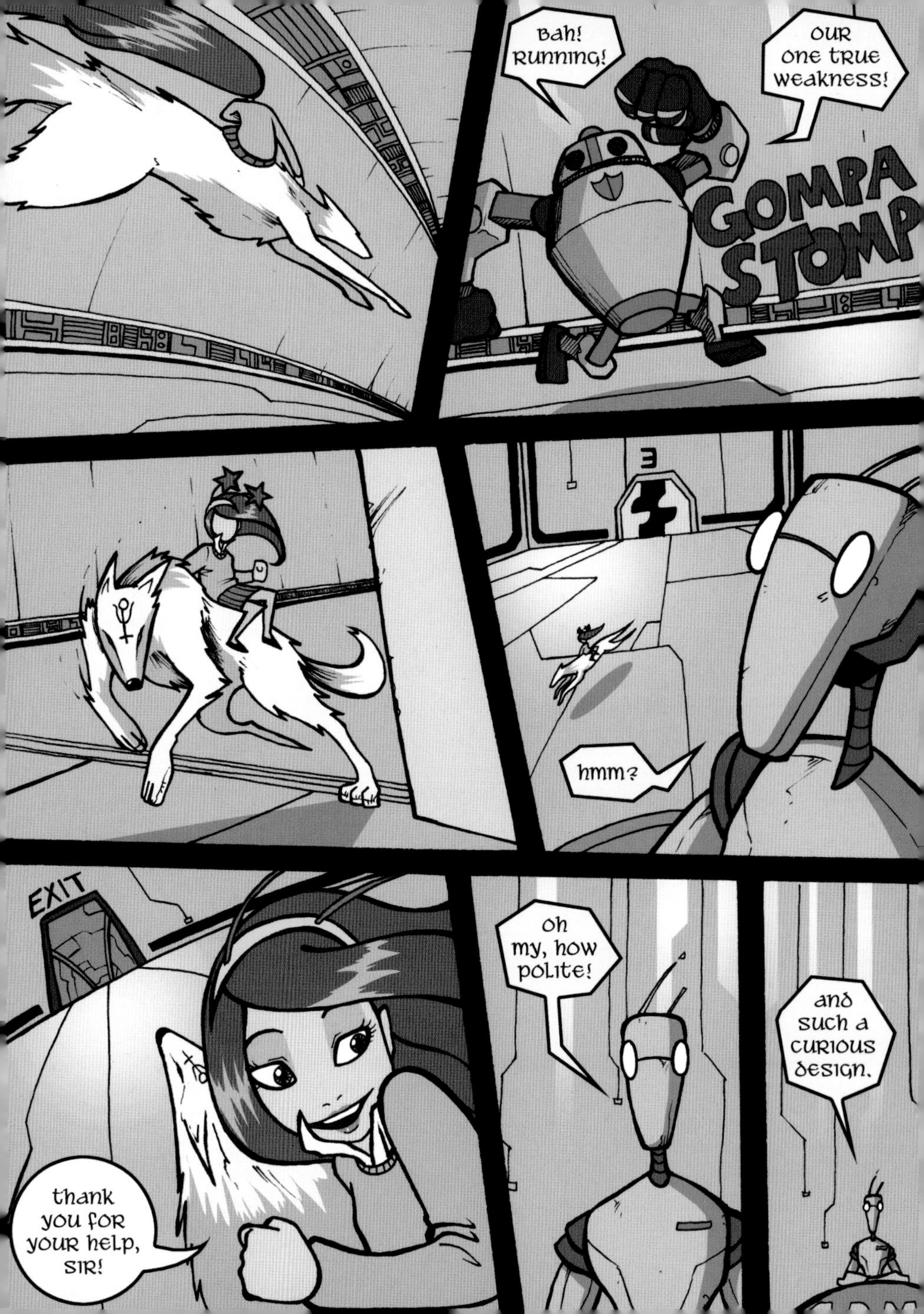
Bah! Running!
Our one true weakness!
GOMPA STOMP
3
hmm?
EXIT
thank you for your help, sir!
oh my, how polite!
and such a curious design.

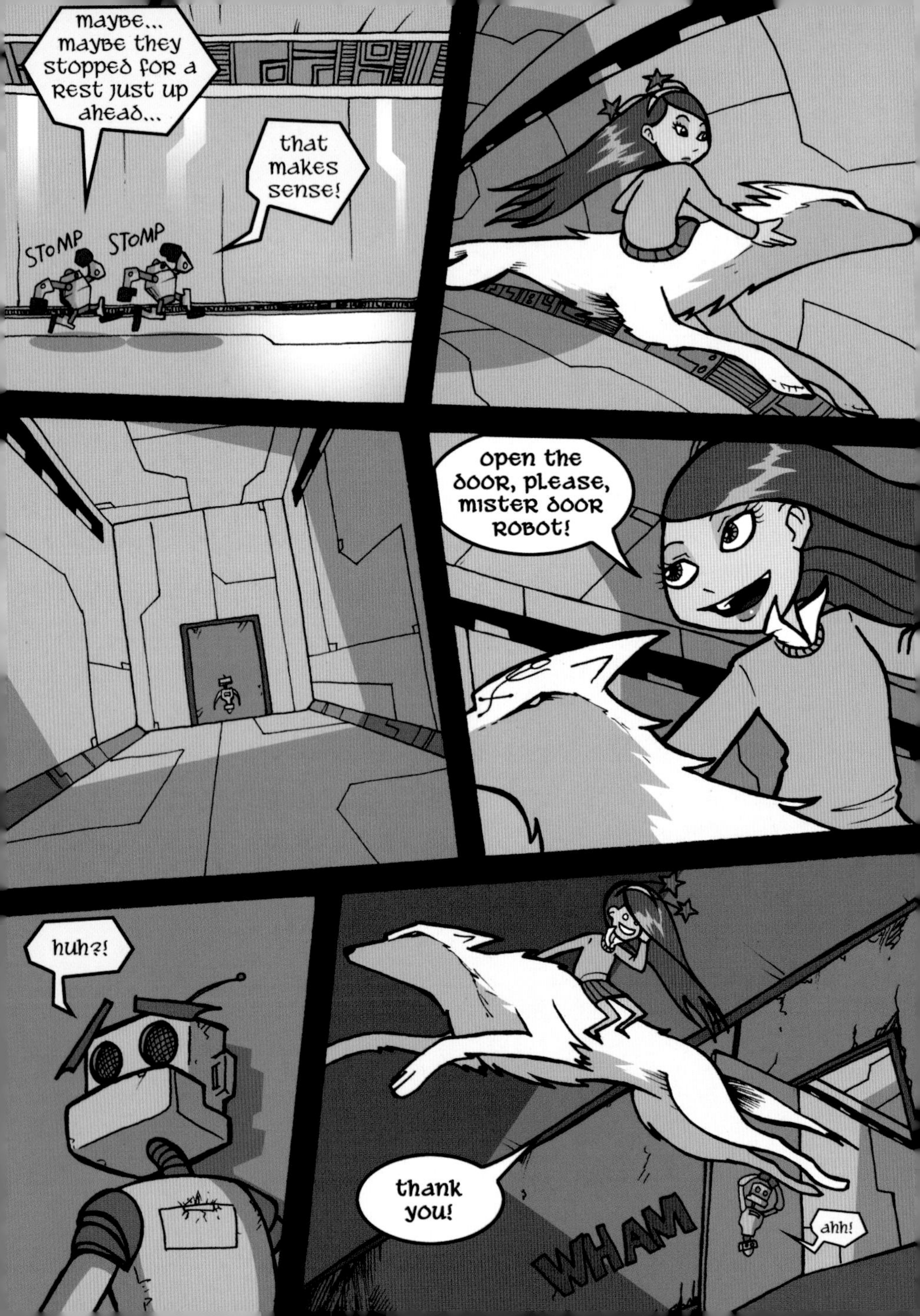
maybe... maybe they stopped for a rest just up ahead...
that makes sense!
STOMP STOMP
open the door, please, mister door robot!
huh?!
thank you!
WHAM
ahh!

BACK AT THE LAB.

BUT I DON'T KNOW WHAT THIS EXTRA PART IS.

LET'S SEE. WELL, IT LOOKS LIKE A NORMAL CPU...

TAP TAP

ANYWAY, I HAVE JUST THE THING!

THIS DOCKING STATION HAS A CAMERA, SPEAKER AND MICROPHONE, SO THE ROBOT WILL BE ABLE TO SEE, SPEAK AND HEAR.

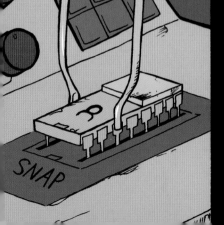

SNAP

~OOR MOMMY! HOW TERRIBLE I AM! SHE FELL OFF THE BRIDGE! WHAT DID I DO?!

WOAH!

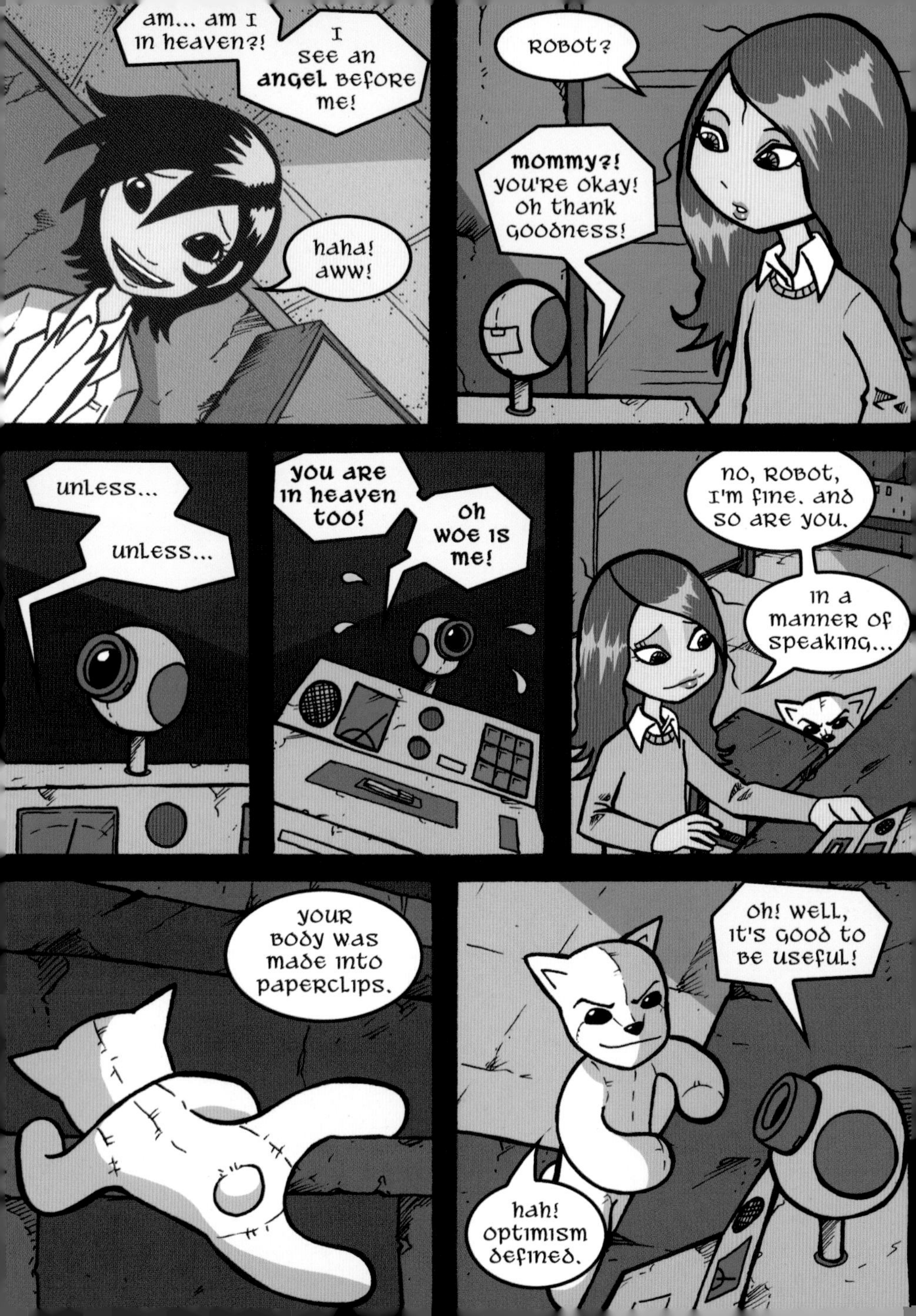
am... am I in heaven?!
I see an angel before me!
haha! aww!
Robot?
mommy?! you're okay! oh thank goodness!
unless...
unless...
you are in heaven too!
oh woe is me!
no, Robot, I'm fine. and so are you.
in a manner of speaking...
your body was made into paperclips.
oh! well, it's good to be useful!
hah! optimism defined.

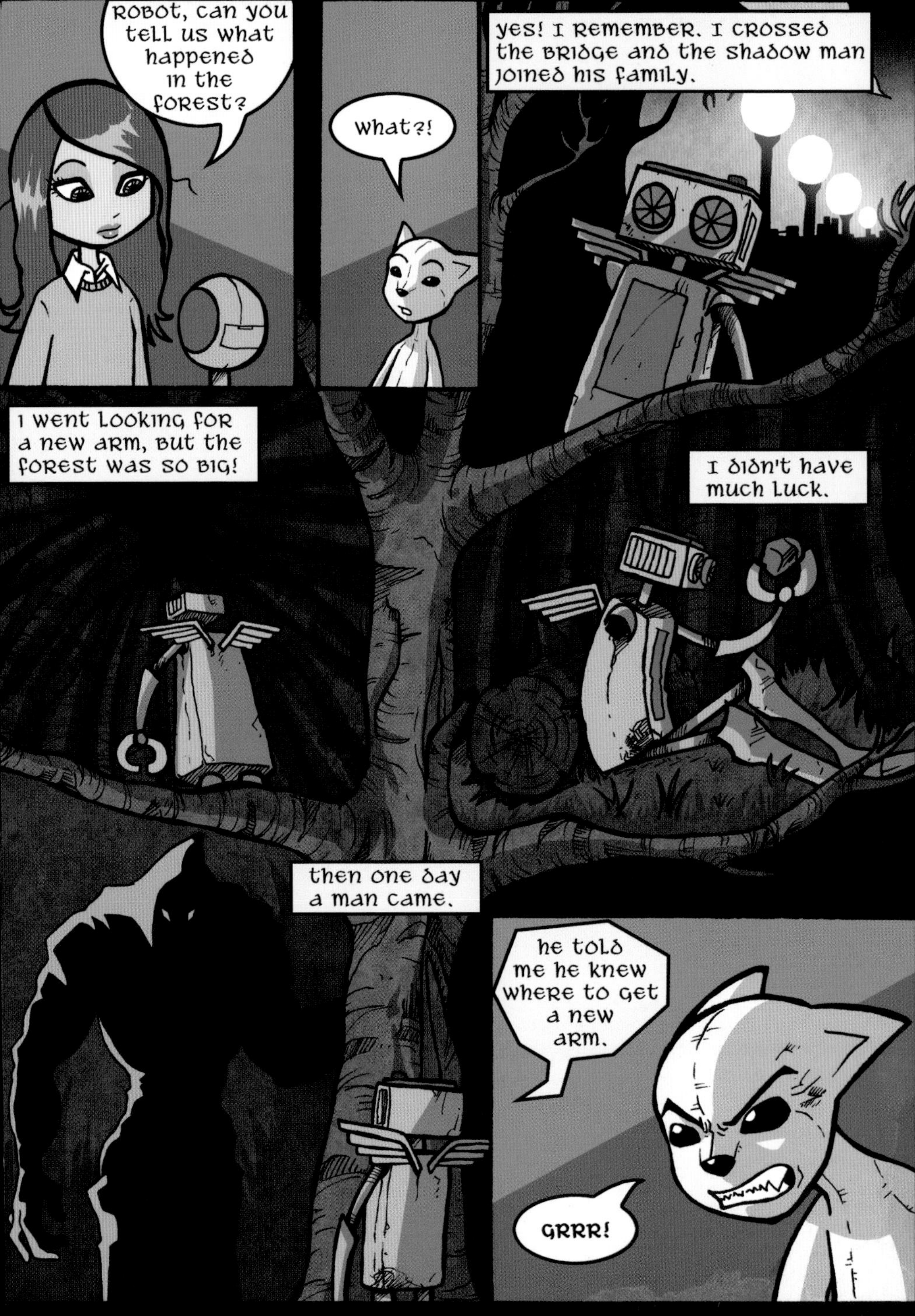
ROBOT, CAN YOU TELL US WHAT HAPPENED IN THE FOREST?
WHAT?!
YES! I REMEMBER. I CROSSED THE BRIDGE AND THE SHADOW MAN JOINED HIS FAMILY.
I WENT LOOKING FOR A NEW ARM, BUT THE FOREST WAS SO BIG!
I DIDN'T HAVE MUCH LUCK.
THEN ONE DAY A MAN CAME.
HE TOLD ME HE KNEW WHERE TO GET A NEW ARM.
GRRR!

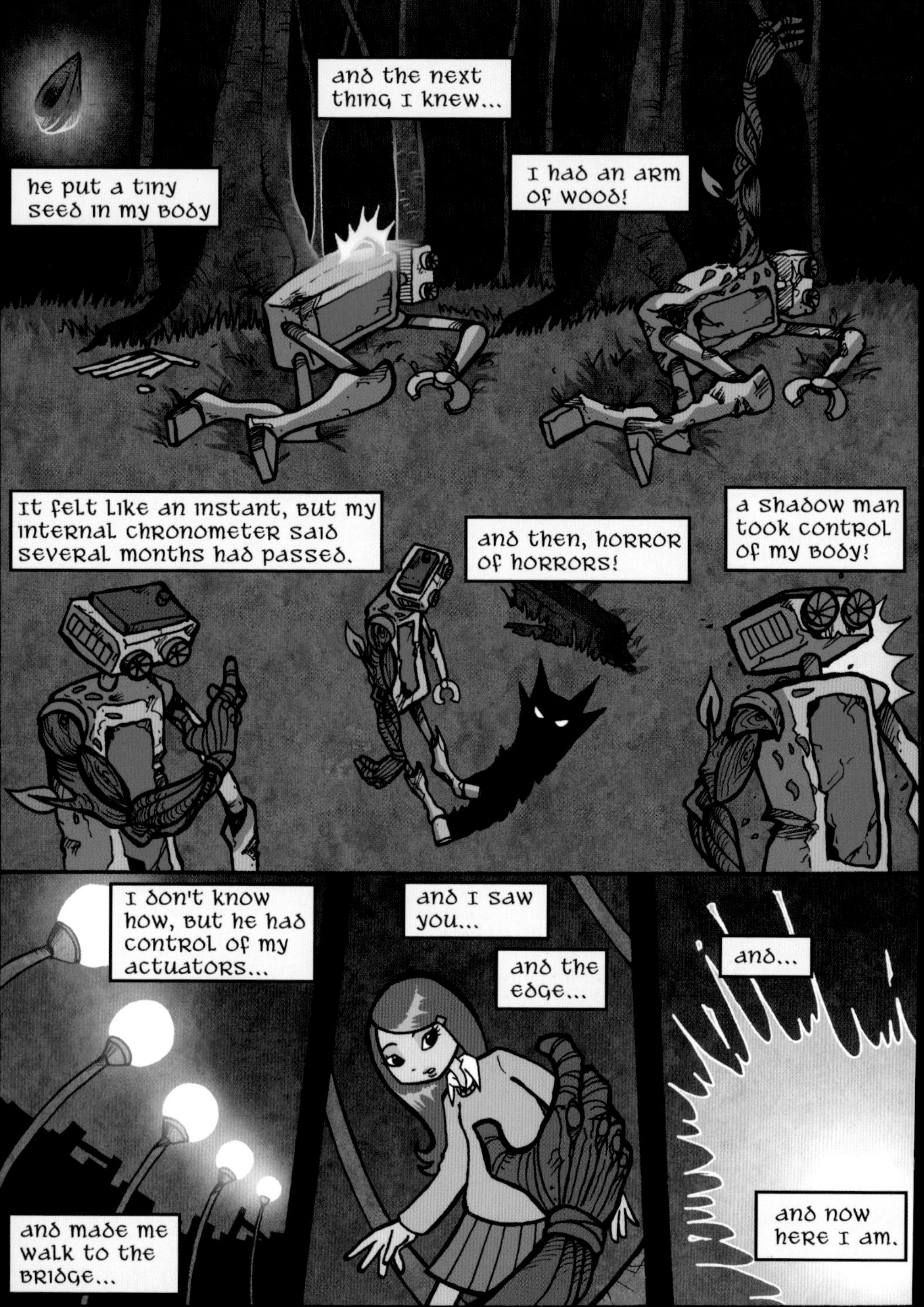
he put a tiny seed in my body
and the next thing I knew...
I had an arm of wood!
It felt like an instant, but my internal chronometer said several months had passed.
and then, horror of horrors!
a shadow man took control of my body!
I don't know how, but he had control of my actuators...
and made me walk to the bridge...
and I saw you...
and the edge...
and...
and now here I am.

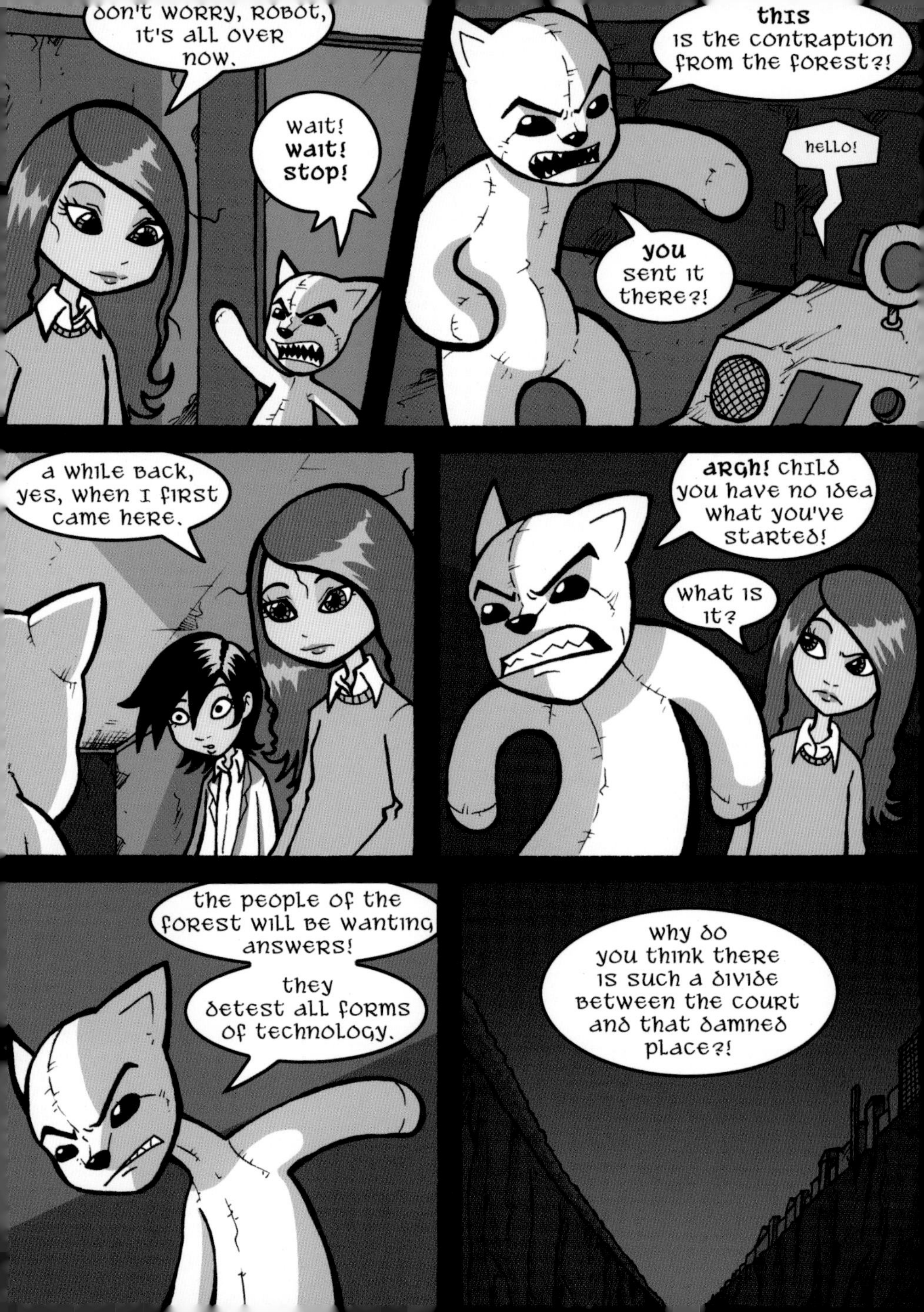
don't worry, robot, it's all over now.
wait! wait! stop!
this is the contraption from the forest?!
hello!
you sent it there?!
a while back, yes, when I first came here.
argh! child you have no idea what you've started!
what is it?
the people of the forest will be wanting answers!
they detest all forms of technology.
why do you think there is such a divide between the court and that damned place?!

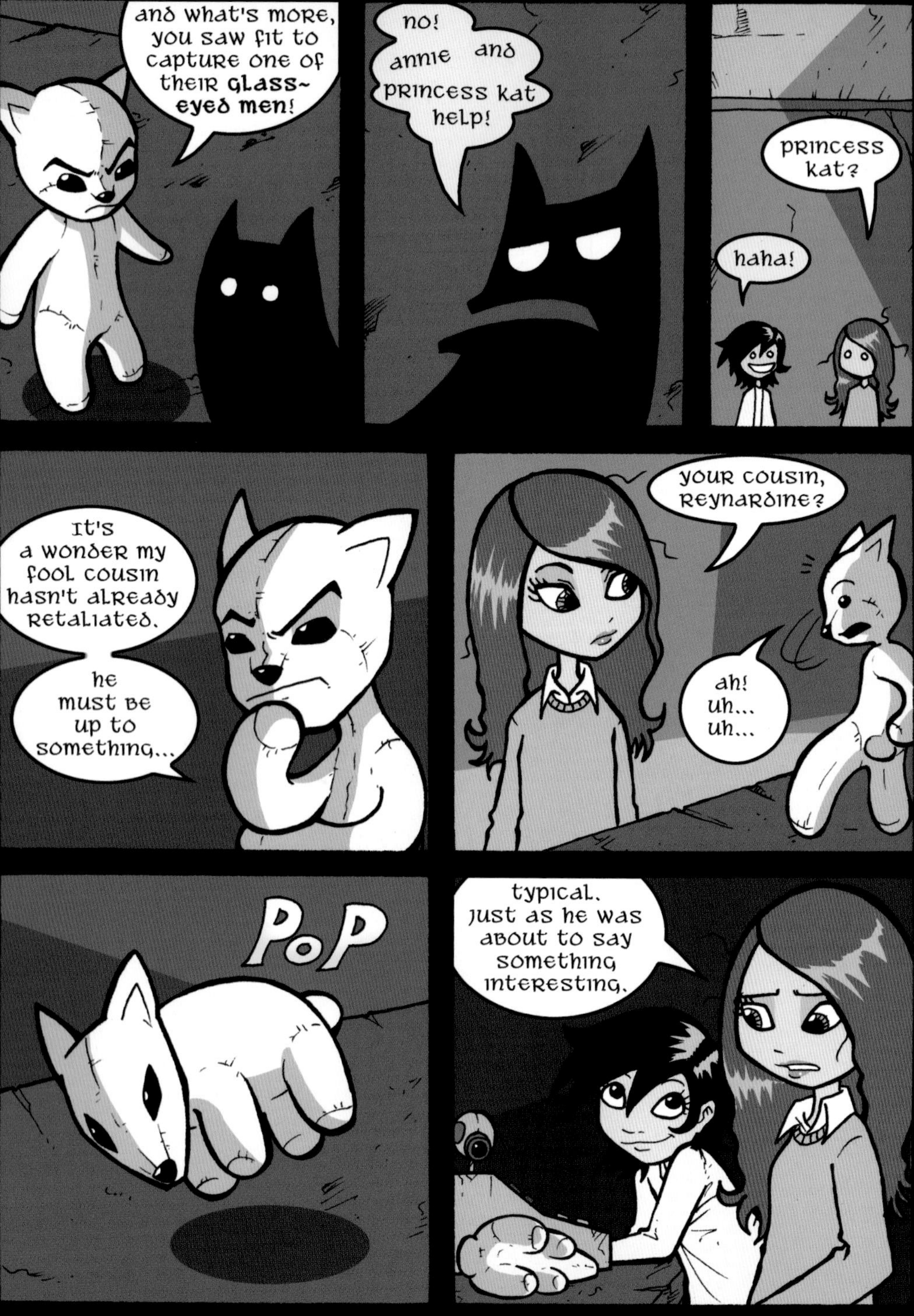
and what's more, you saw fit to capture one of their glass~eyed men!
no! annie and princess kat help!
princess kat?
haha!
It's a wonder my fool cousin hasn't already retaliated.
he must be up to something...
your cousin, Reynardine?
ah! uh... uh...
PoP
typical. just as he was about to say something interesting.

WELL, NOW THAT WE HAVE YOU BACK, ROBOT, WE SHOULD DO SOMETHING ABOUT YOUR BODY.

I think I can whip something up for him.

at Least something temporary while I get the parts to make a BETTER BODY.

thank you very much!

ROBOT, I'M SO SORRY I CAUSED YOU ALL THIS TROUBLE.

I should have told you to come back after you crossed the BRIDGE.

don't apologise.

you see, you gave me something I'D never had before.

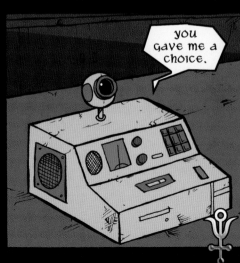

you gave me a choice.

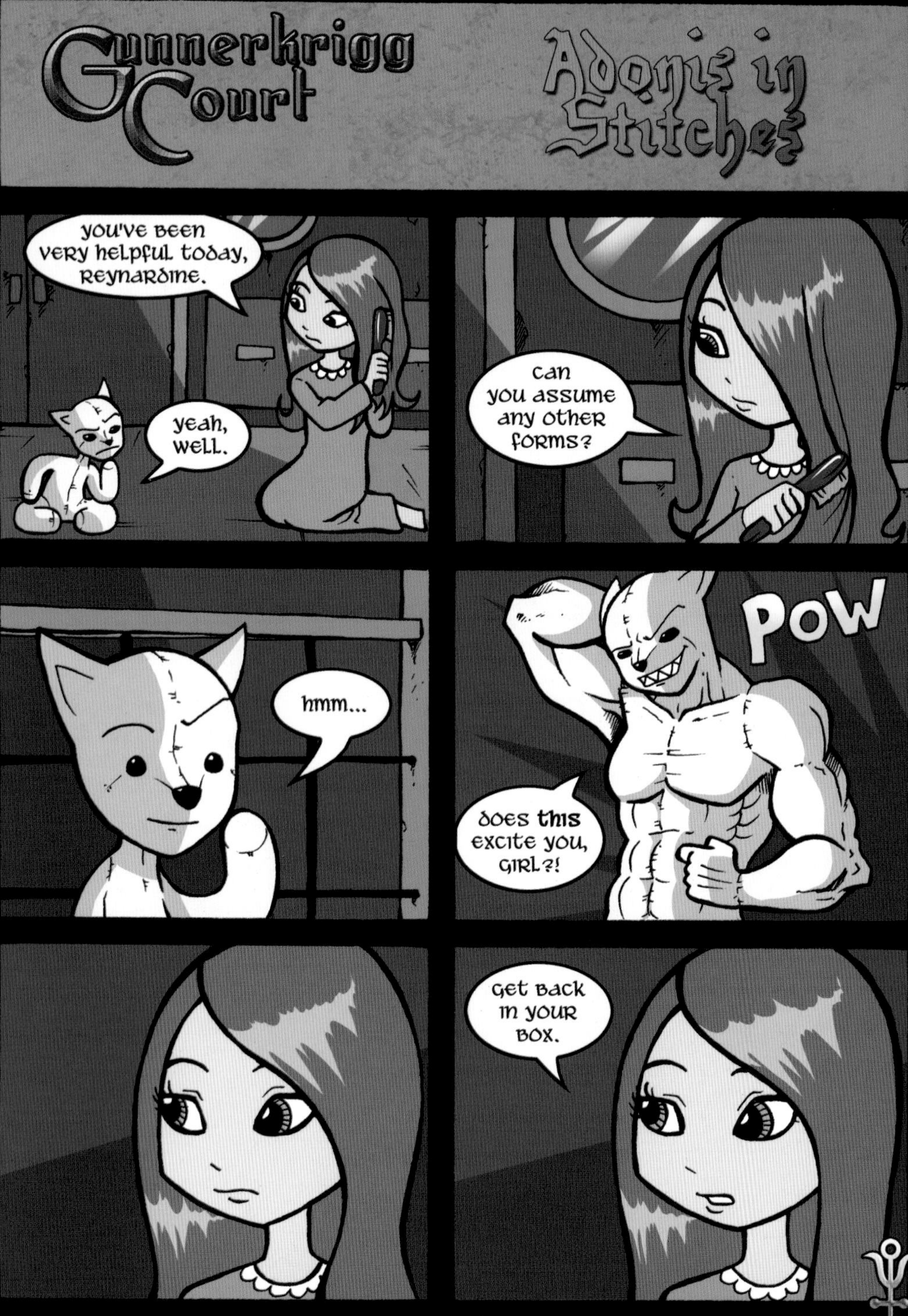
Gunnerkrigg Court
Adonis in Stitches
you've been very helpful today, Reynardine.
yeah, well.
can you assume any other forms?
hmm...
POW
does this excite you, girl?!
get back in your box.

Gunnerkrigg Court

Chapter 13:

A Week For Kat

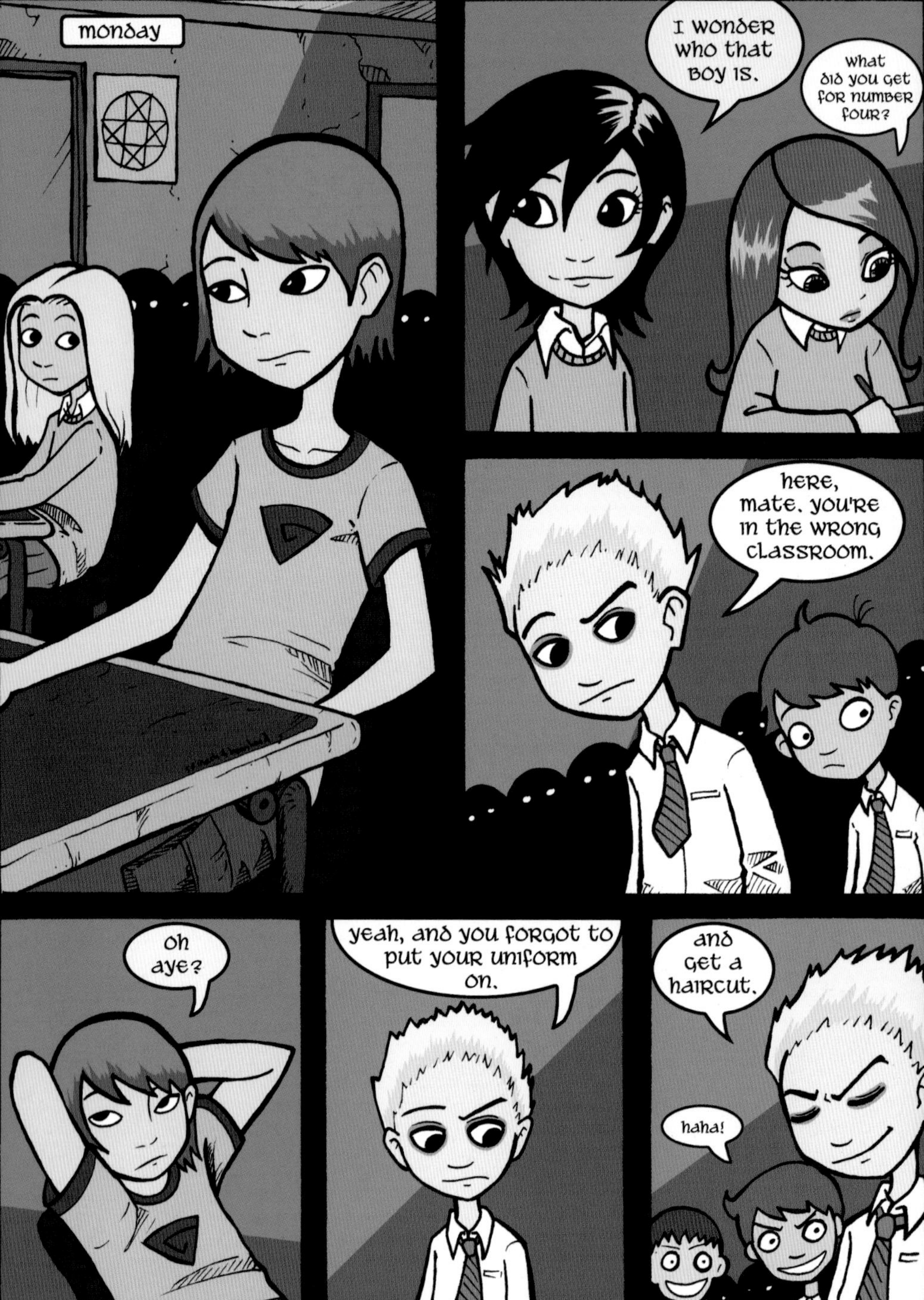
monday
I wonder who that boy is.
what did you get for number four?
here, mate. you're in the wrong classroom.
oh aye?
yeah, and you forgot to put your uniform on.
and get a haircut.
haha!

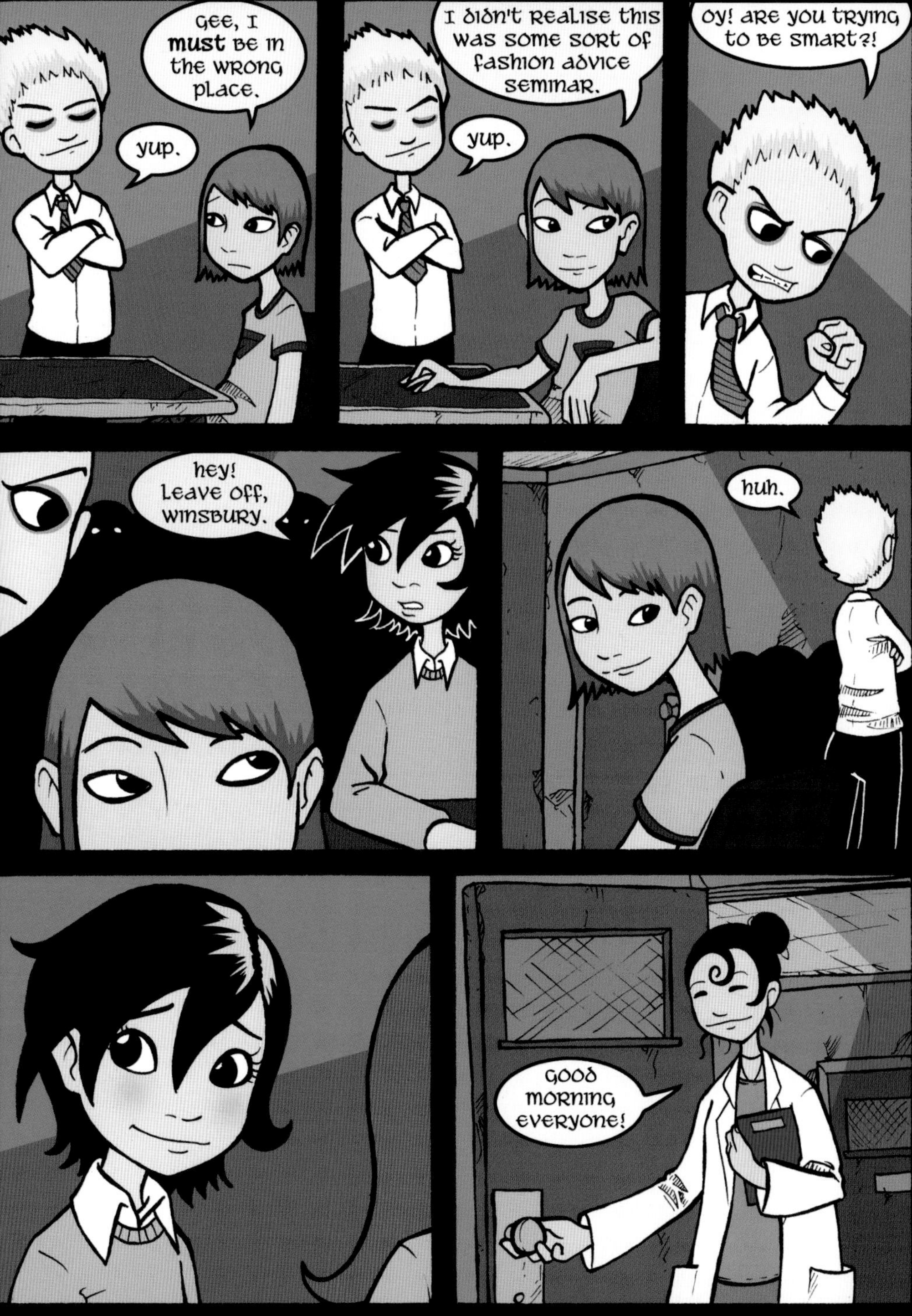
GEE, I **MUST** BE IN THE WRONG PLACE.
YUP.
I DIDN'T REALISE THIS WAS SOME SORT OF FASHION ADVICE SEMINAR.
YUP.
OY! ARE YOU TRYING TO BE SMART?!
HEY! LEAVE OFF, WINSBURY.
HUH.
GOOD MORNING EVERYONE!

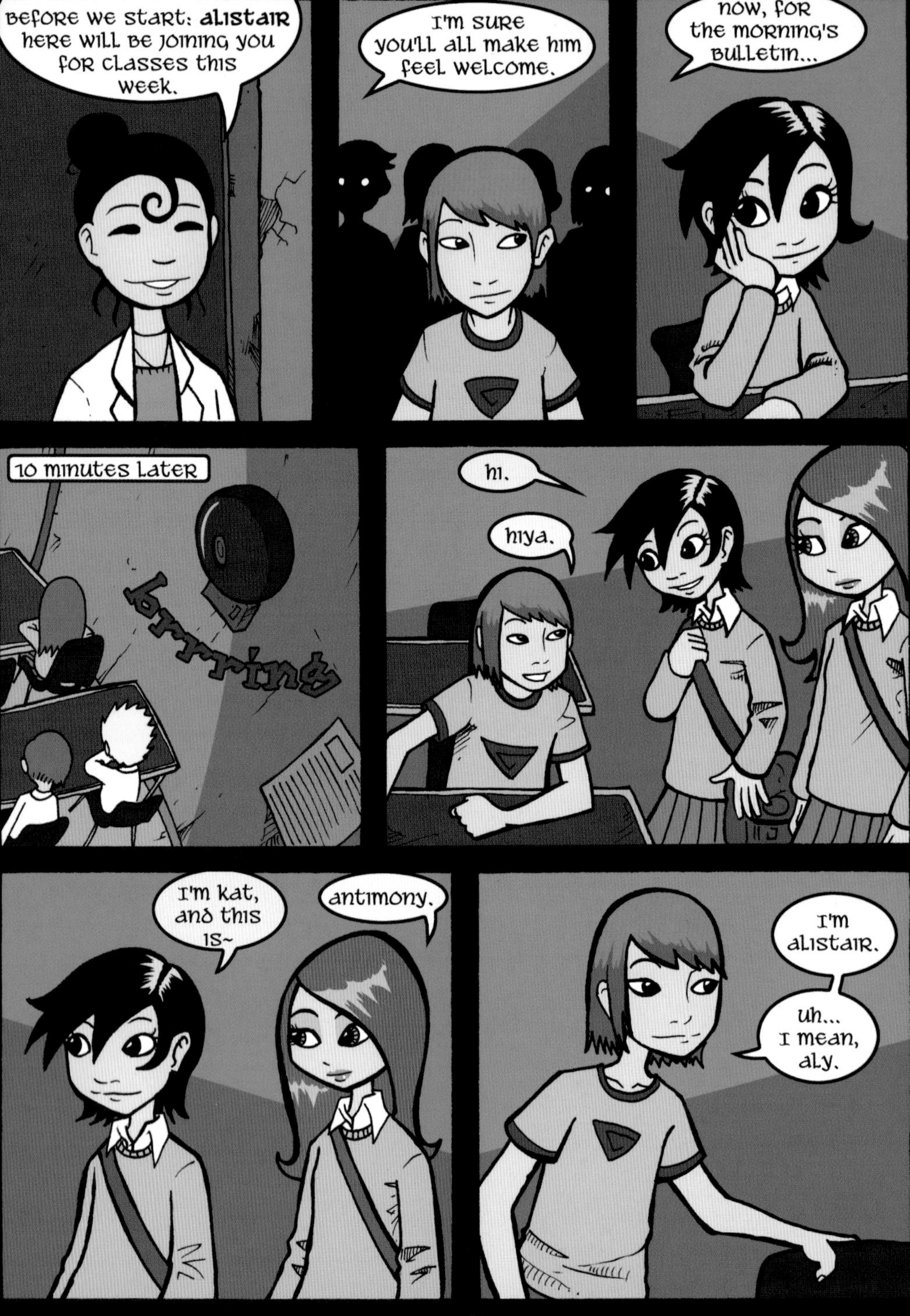
before we start: alistair here will be joining you for classes this week.
I'm sure you'll all make him feel welcome.
now, for the morning's bulletin...
10 minutes later
brrring
hi.
hiya.
I'm kat, and this is~
antimony.
I'm alistair.
uh... I mean, aly.

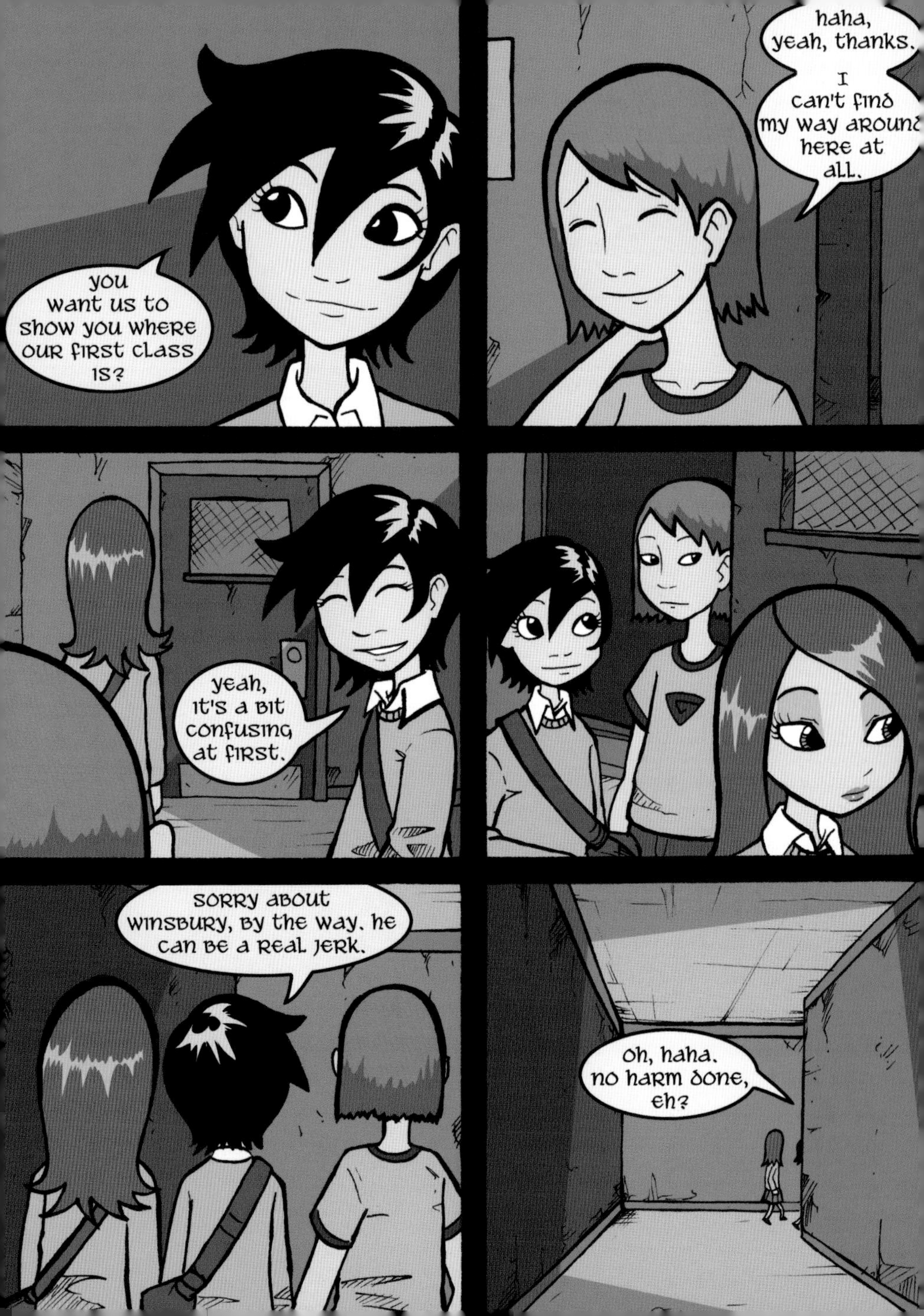
you want us to show you where our first class is?
haha, yeah, thanks.
I can't find my way around here at all.
yeah, it's a bit confusing at first.
sorry about Winsbury, by the way. he can be a real jerk.
oh, haha. no harm done, eh?

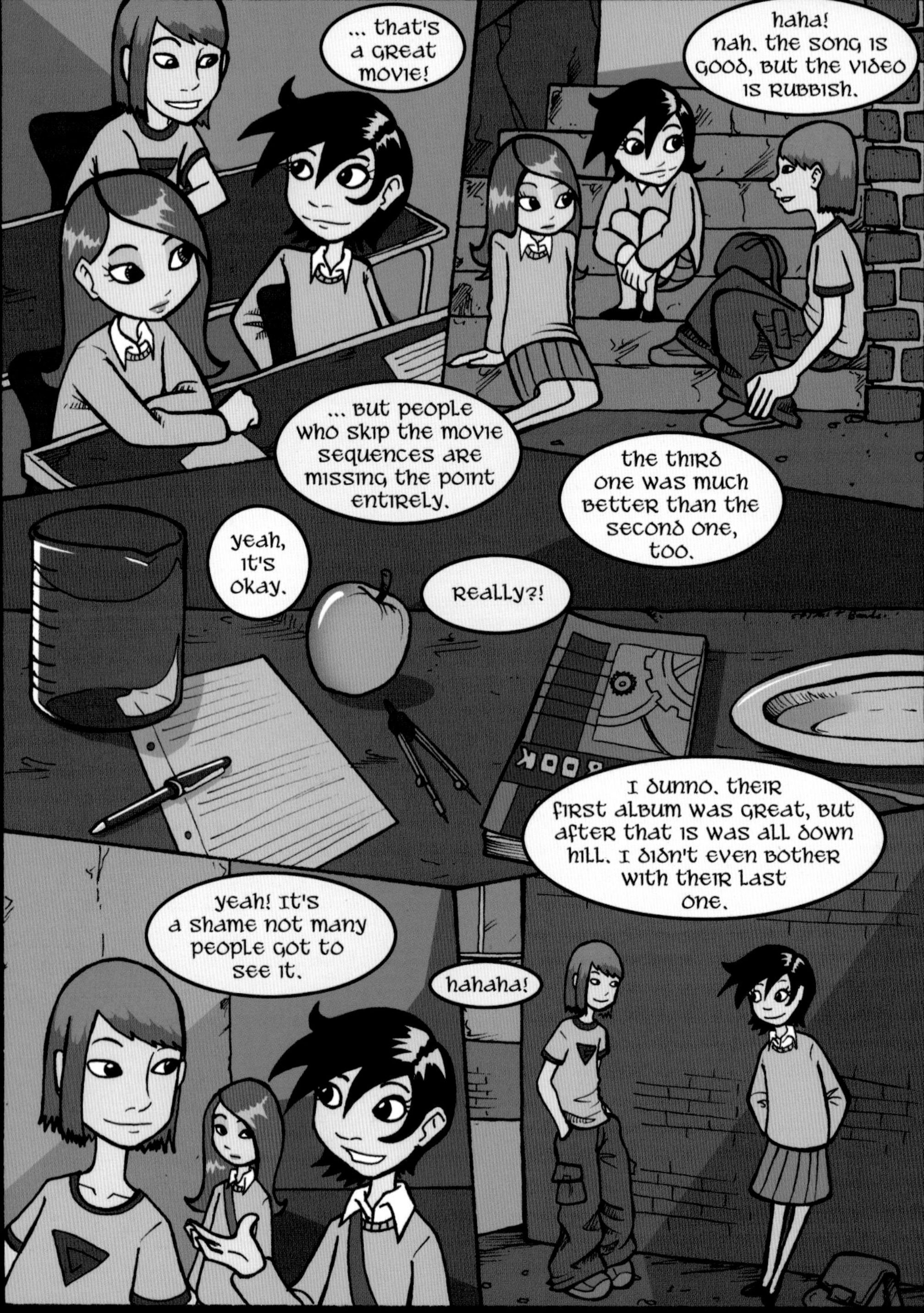
... that's a great movie!
haha! nah. the song is good, but the video is rubbish.
... but people who skip the movie sequences are missing the point entirely.
the third one was much better than the second one, too.
yeah, it's okay.
Really?!
I dunno. their first album was great, but after that is was all down hill. I didn't even bother with their last one.
yeah! It's a shame not many people got to see it.
hahaha!

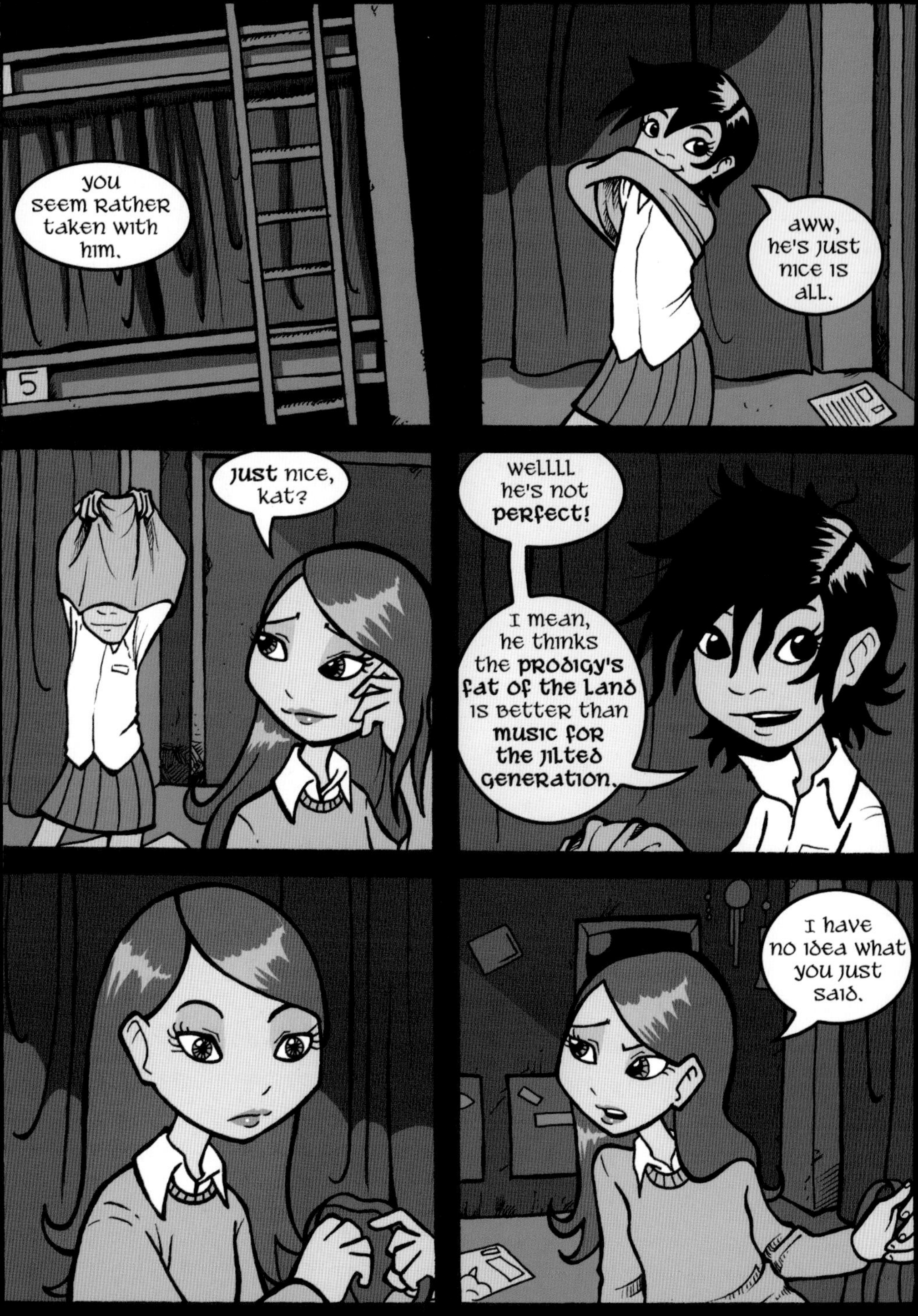
you seem rather taken with him.
aww, he's just nice is all.
just nice, kat?
welllll he's not perfect!
I mean, he thinks the prodigy's fat of the land is better than music for the jilted generation.
I have no idea what you just said.

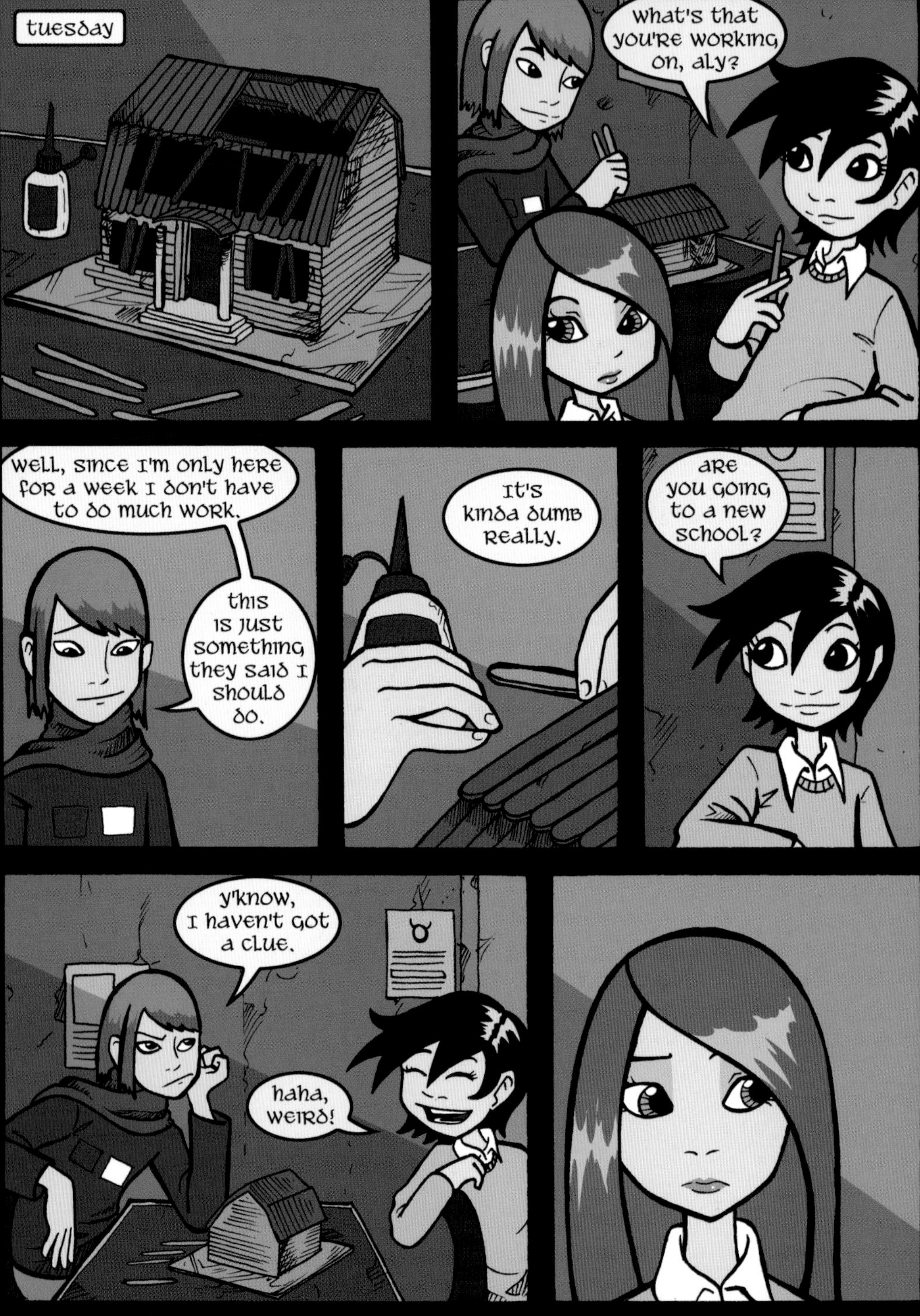
tuesday
what's that you're working on, aly?
well, since I'm only here for a week I don't have to do much work.
this is just something they said I should do.
It's kinda dumb really.
are you going to a new school?
y'know, I haven't got a clue.
haha, weird!

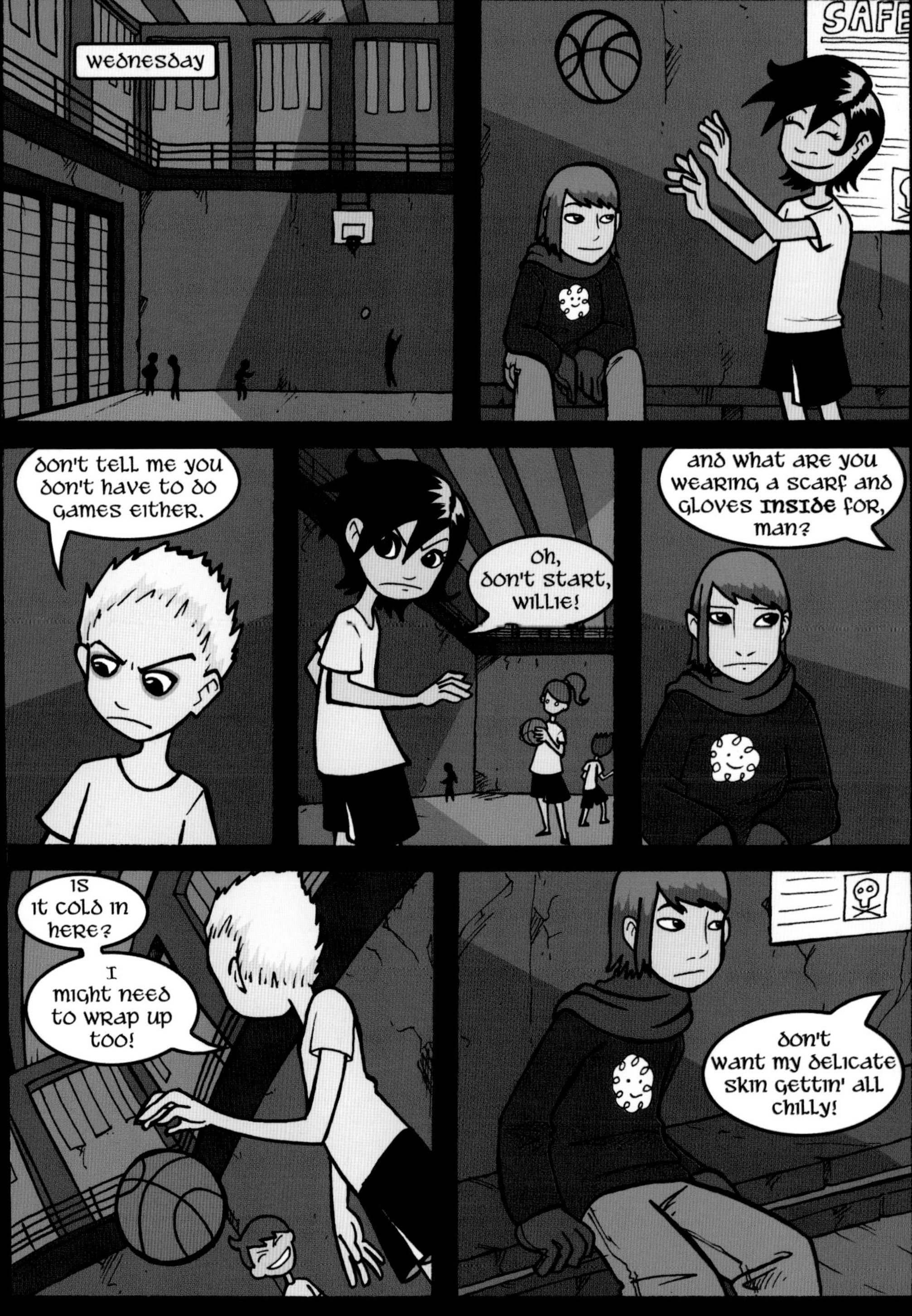
wednesday
SAFE
don't tell me you don't have to do games either.
oh, don't start, willie!
and what are you wearing a scarf and gloves INSIDE for, man?
Is it cold in here?
I might need to wrap up too!
don't want my delicate skin gettin' all chilly!

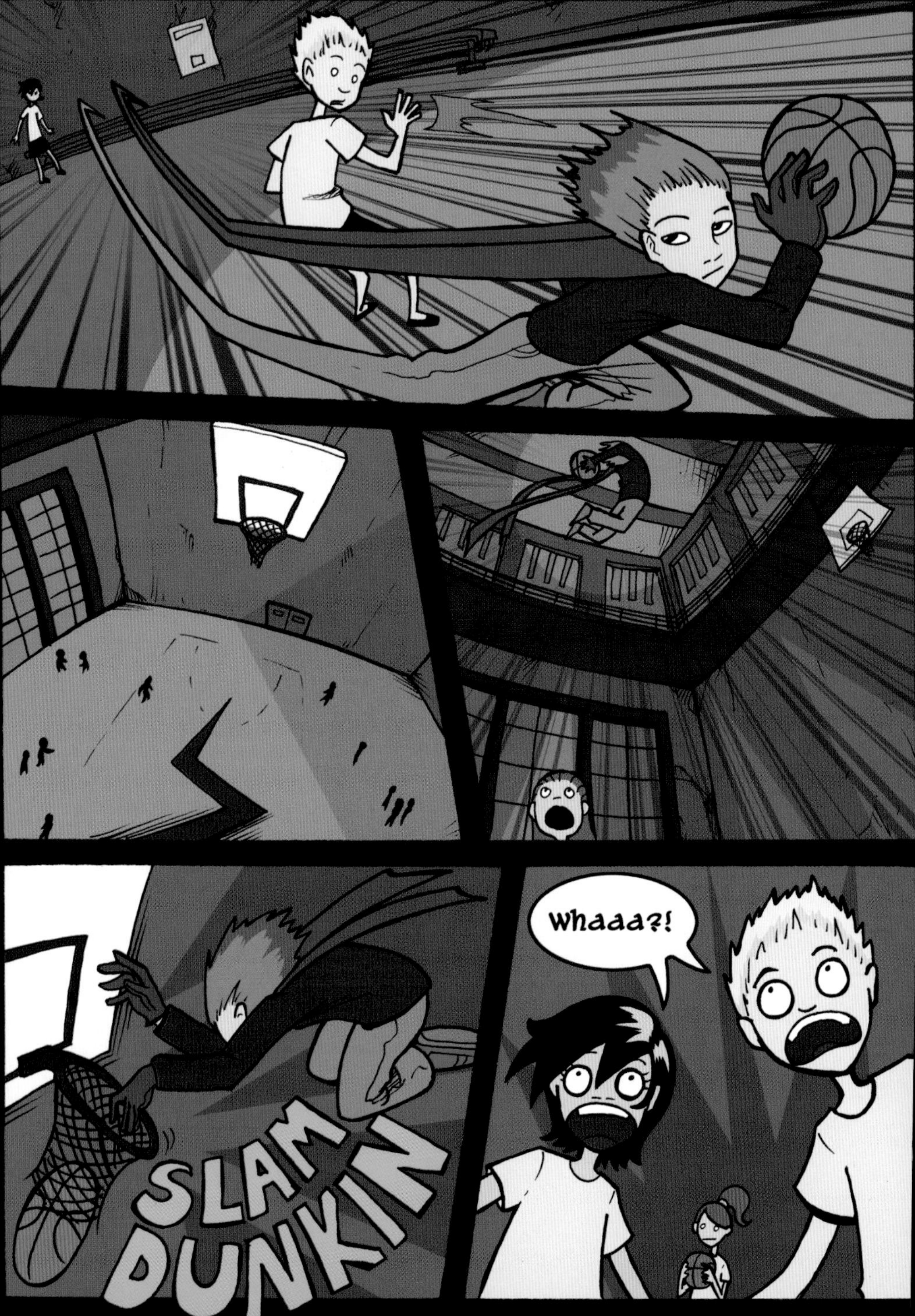
Whaaa?!
SLAM DUNKIN

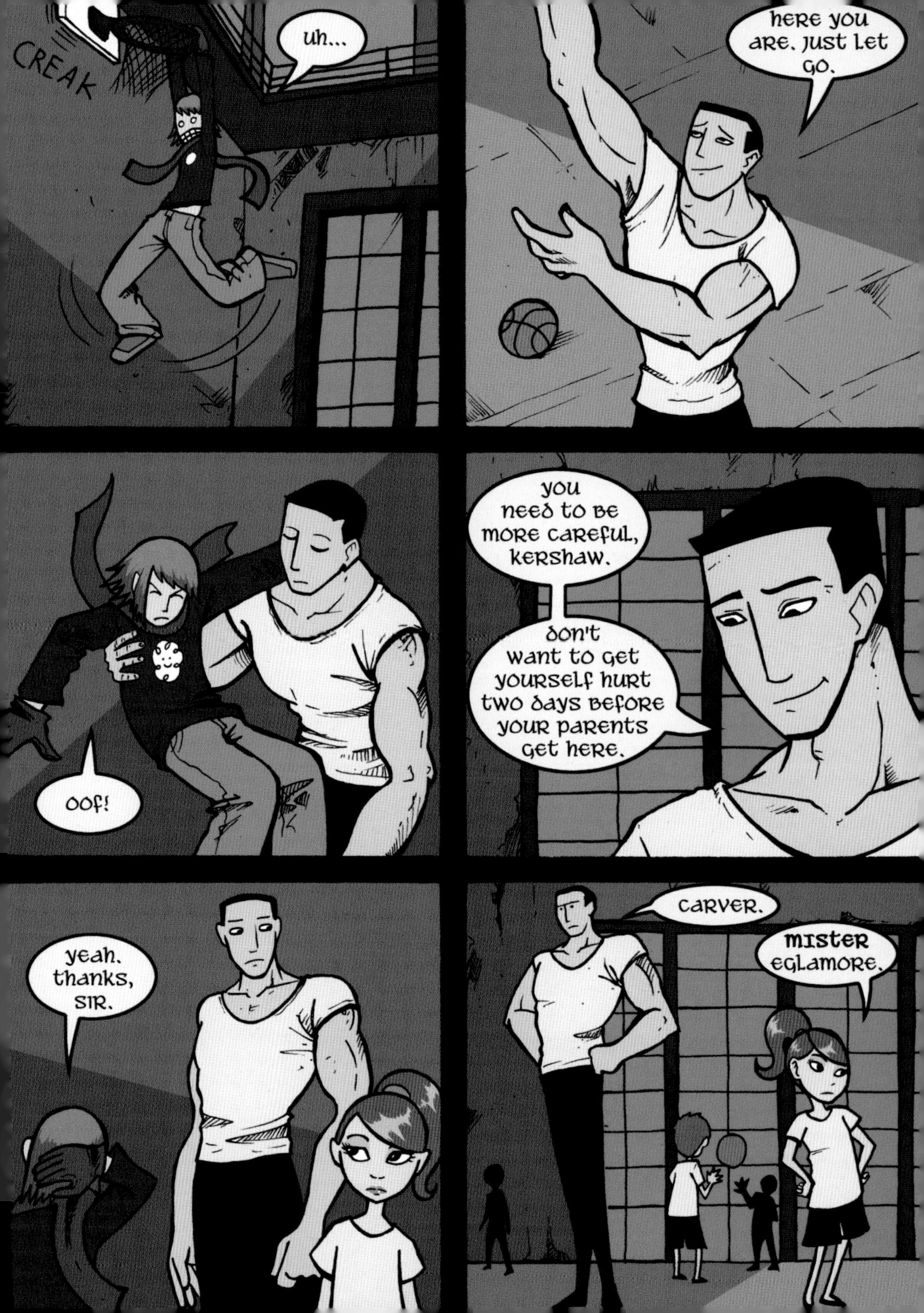
CREAK
uh...
here you are. just let go.
oof!
you need to be more careful, kershaw.
don't want to get yourself hurt two days before your parents get here.
yeah. thanks, sir.
carver.
mister eglamore.

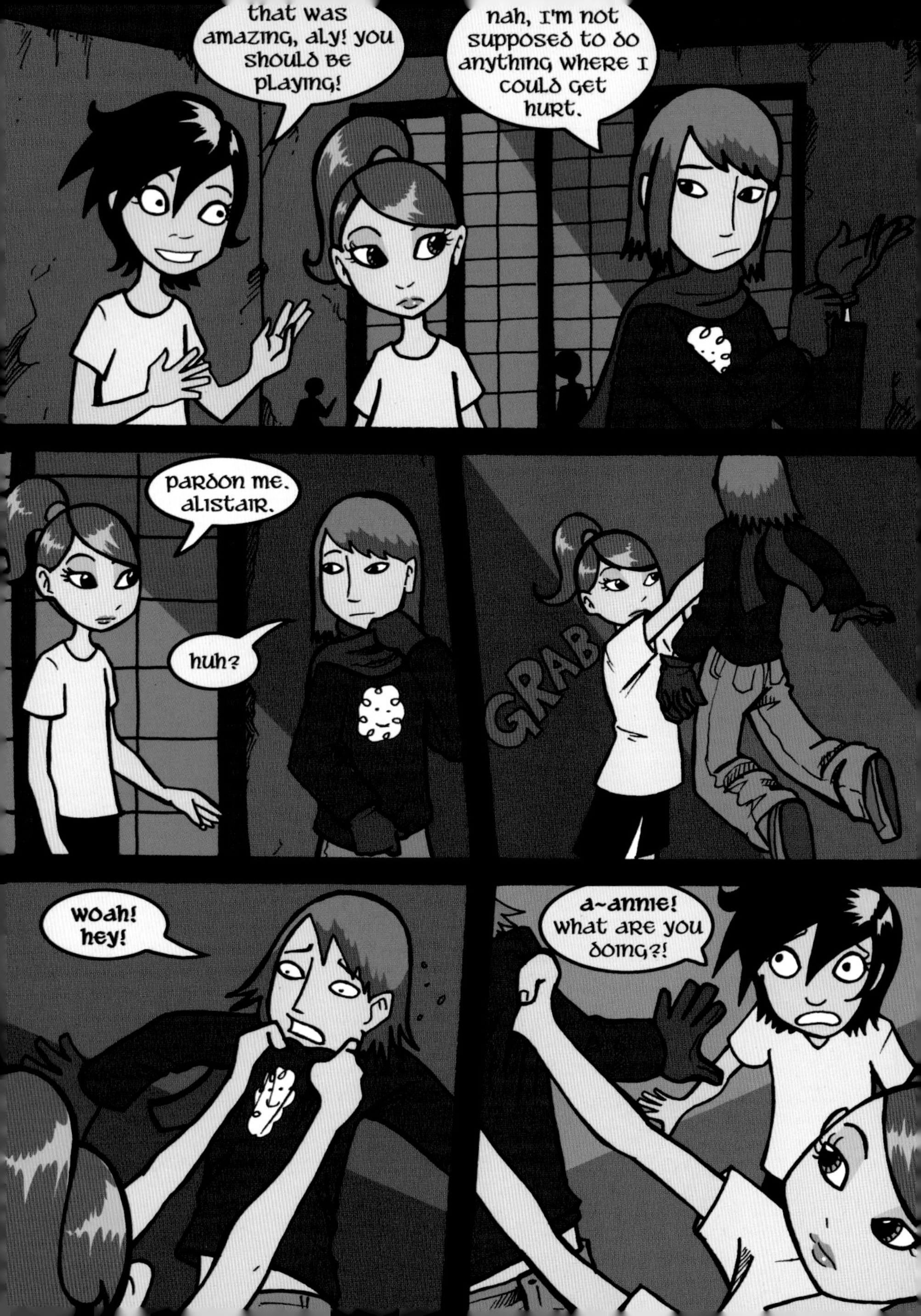
that was amazing, aly! you should be playing!
nah, I'm not supposed to do anything where I could get hurt.
pardon me. alistair.
huh?
GRAB
woah! hey!
a~annie! what are you doing?!

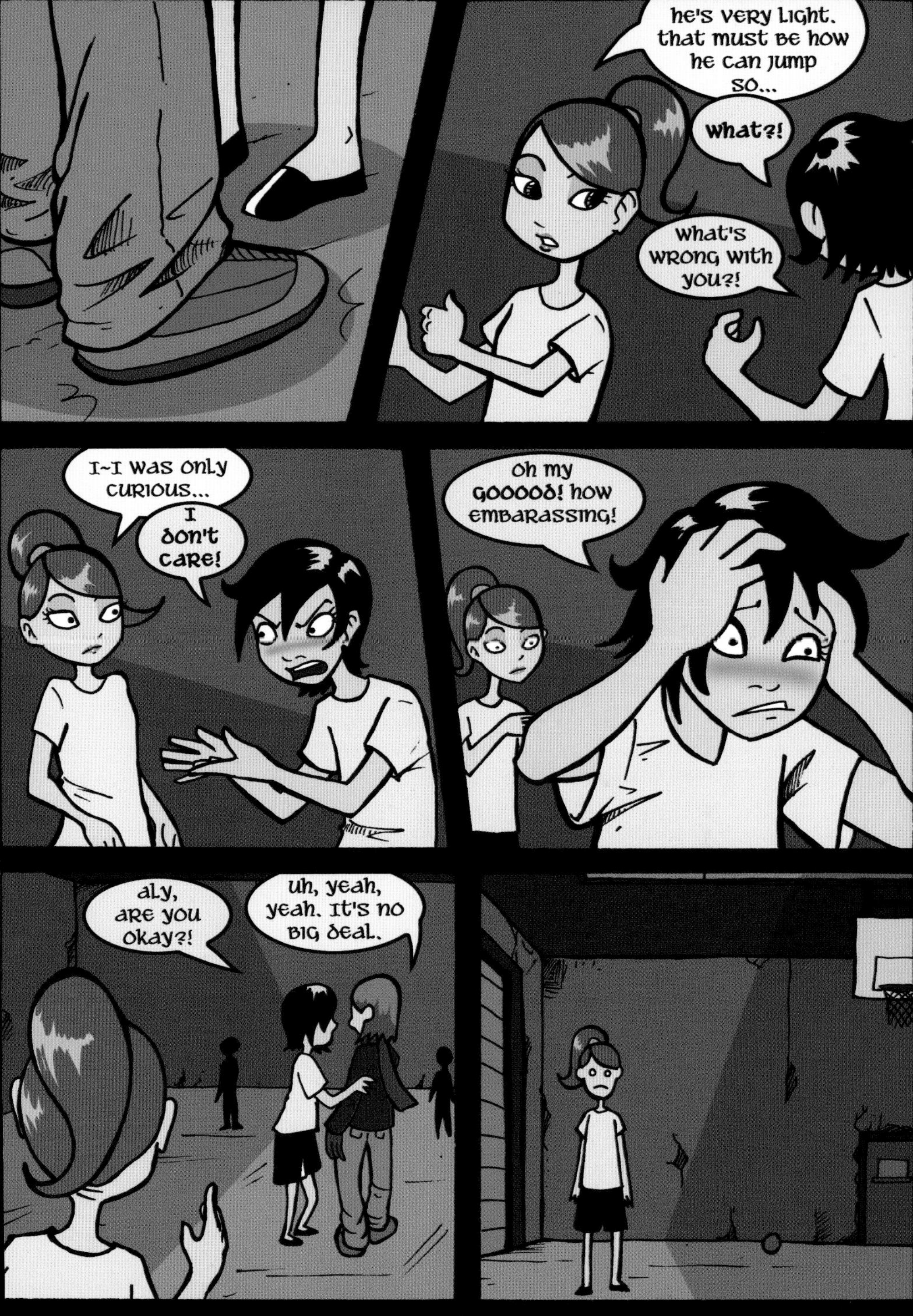
he's very light. that must be how he can jump so...
What?!
What's wrong with you?!
I~I was only curious...
I don't care!
Oh my GOOOOD! how embarassing!
aly, are you okay?!
uh, yeah, yeah. It's no big deal.

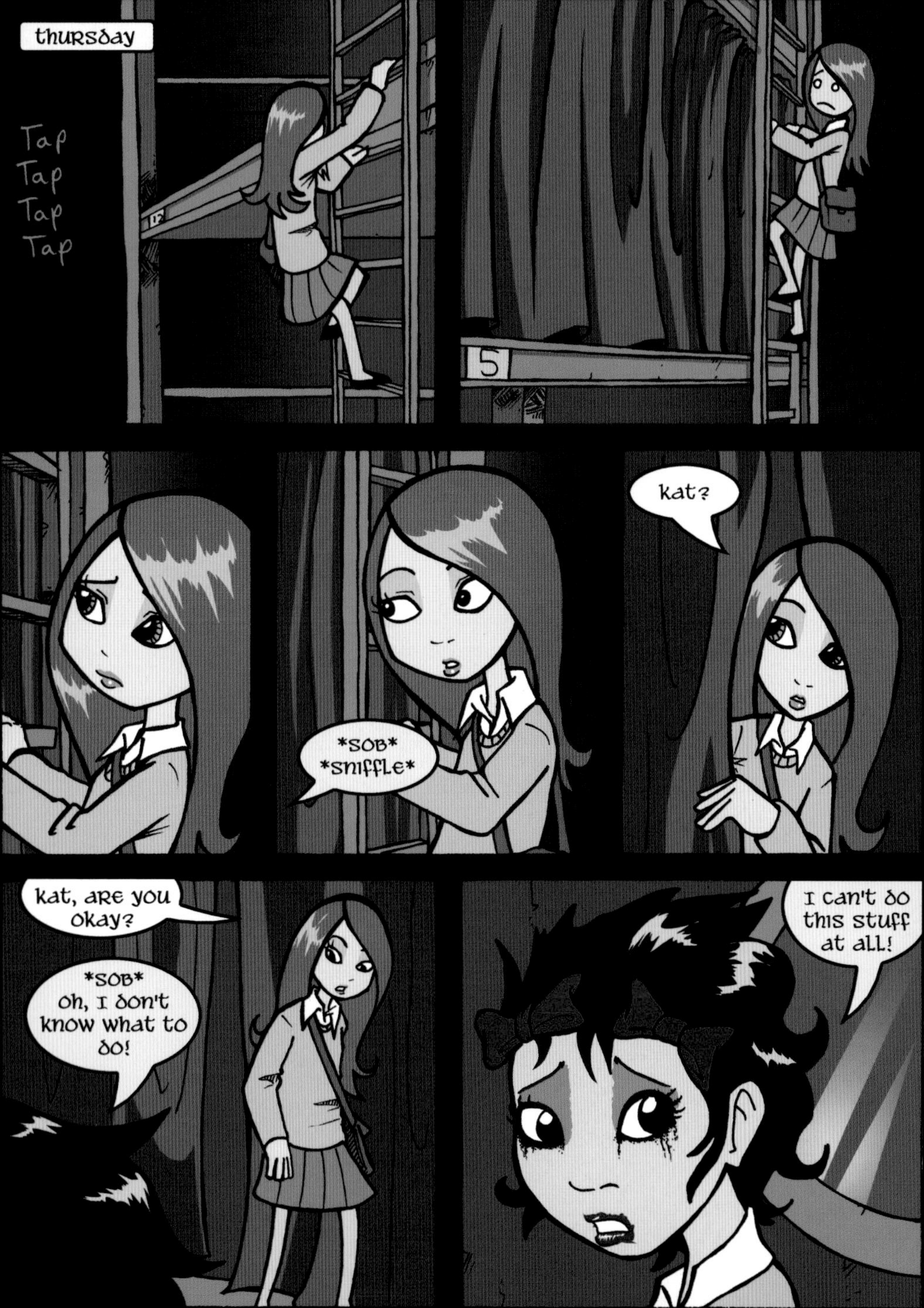
thursday
Tap
Tap
Tap
Tap
SOB *sniffle*
kat?
kat, are you okay?
SOB oh, I don't know what to do!
I can't do this stuff at all!

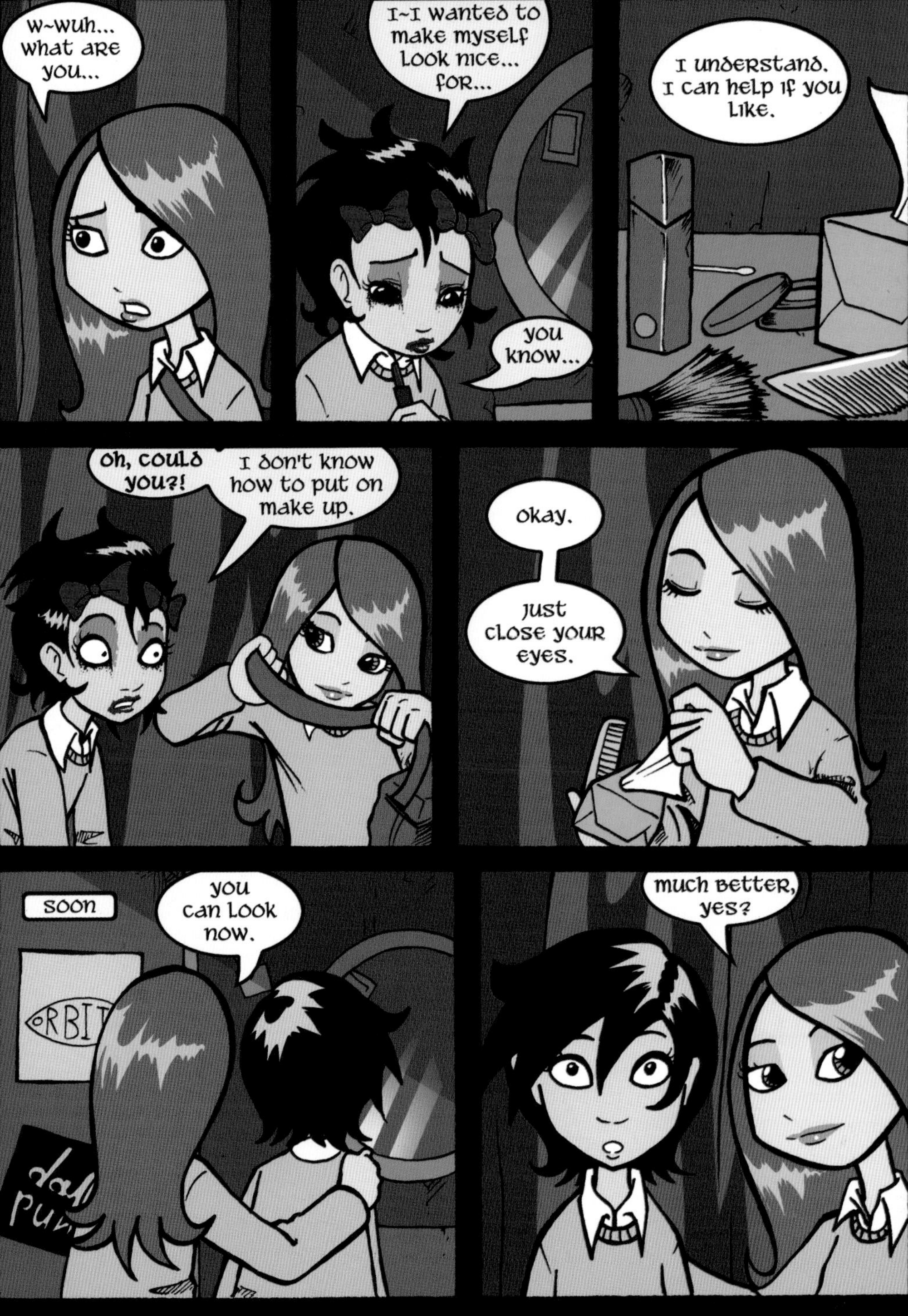
W~WUH... WHAT ARE YOU...
I~I WANTED TO MAKE MYSELF LOOK NICE... FOR...
YOU KNOW...
I UNDERSTAND. I CAN HELP IF YOU LIKE.
OH, COULD YOU?!
I DON'T KNOW HOW TO PUT ON MAKE UP.
OKAY.
JUST CLOSE YOUR EYES.
SOON
YOU CAN LOOK NOW.
ORBIT
MUCH BETTER, YES?

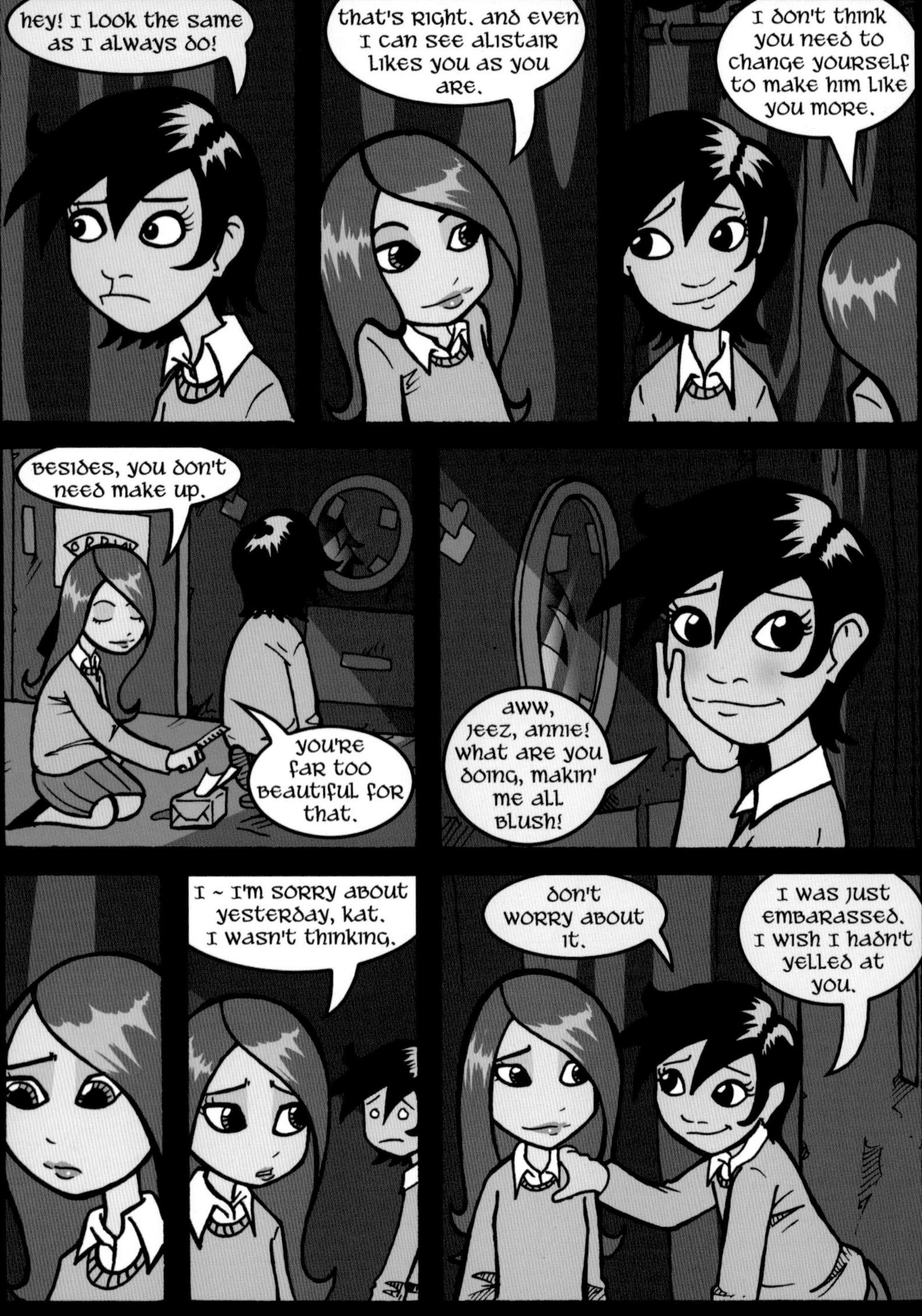
hey! I look the same as I always do!
that's right. and even I can see alistair likes you as you are.
I don't think you need to change yourself to make him like you more.
besides, you don't need make up.
you're far too beautiful for that.
aww, jeez, annie! what are you doing, makin' me all blush!
I ~ I'm sorry about yesterday, kat. I wasn't thinking.
don't worry about it.
I was just embarassed. I wish I hadn't yelled at you.

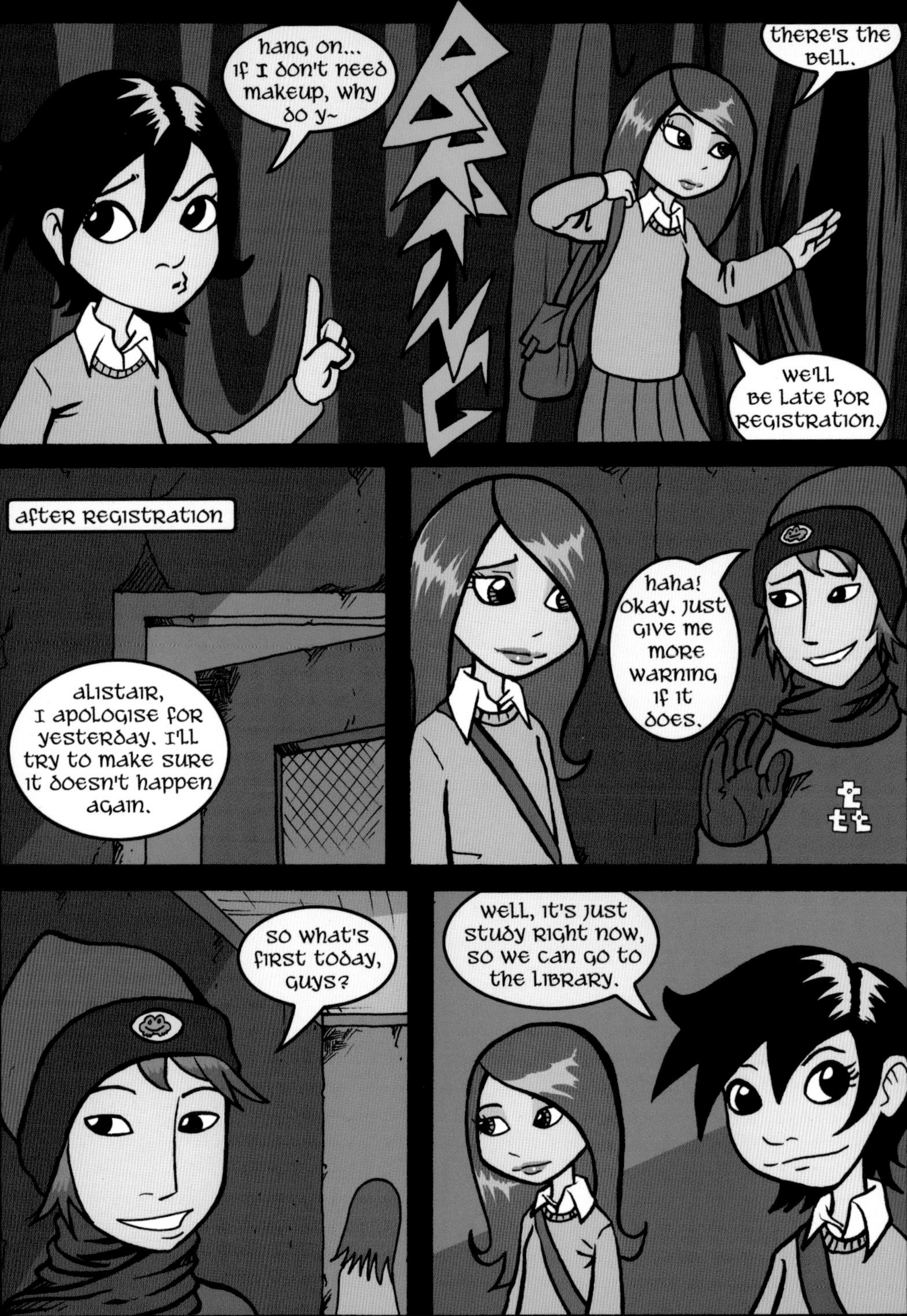
hang on... if I don't need makeup, why do y~
BRRING
there's the bell.
we'll be late for registration.
after registration
alistair, I apologise for yesterday. I'll try to make sure it doesn't happen again.
haha! okay, just give me more warning if it does.
so what's first today, guys?
well, it's just study right now, so we can go to the library.

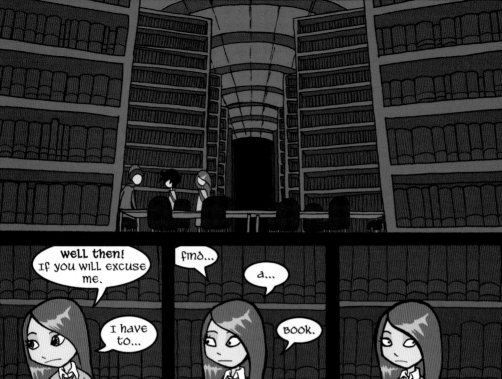

WELL THEN! If you WiLL excuse me.

I have to...

find...

a...

BOOK.

SHE'S NOT VERY SUBTLE, IS SHE?

no.

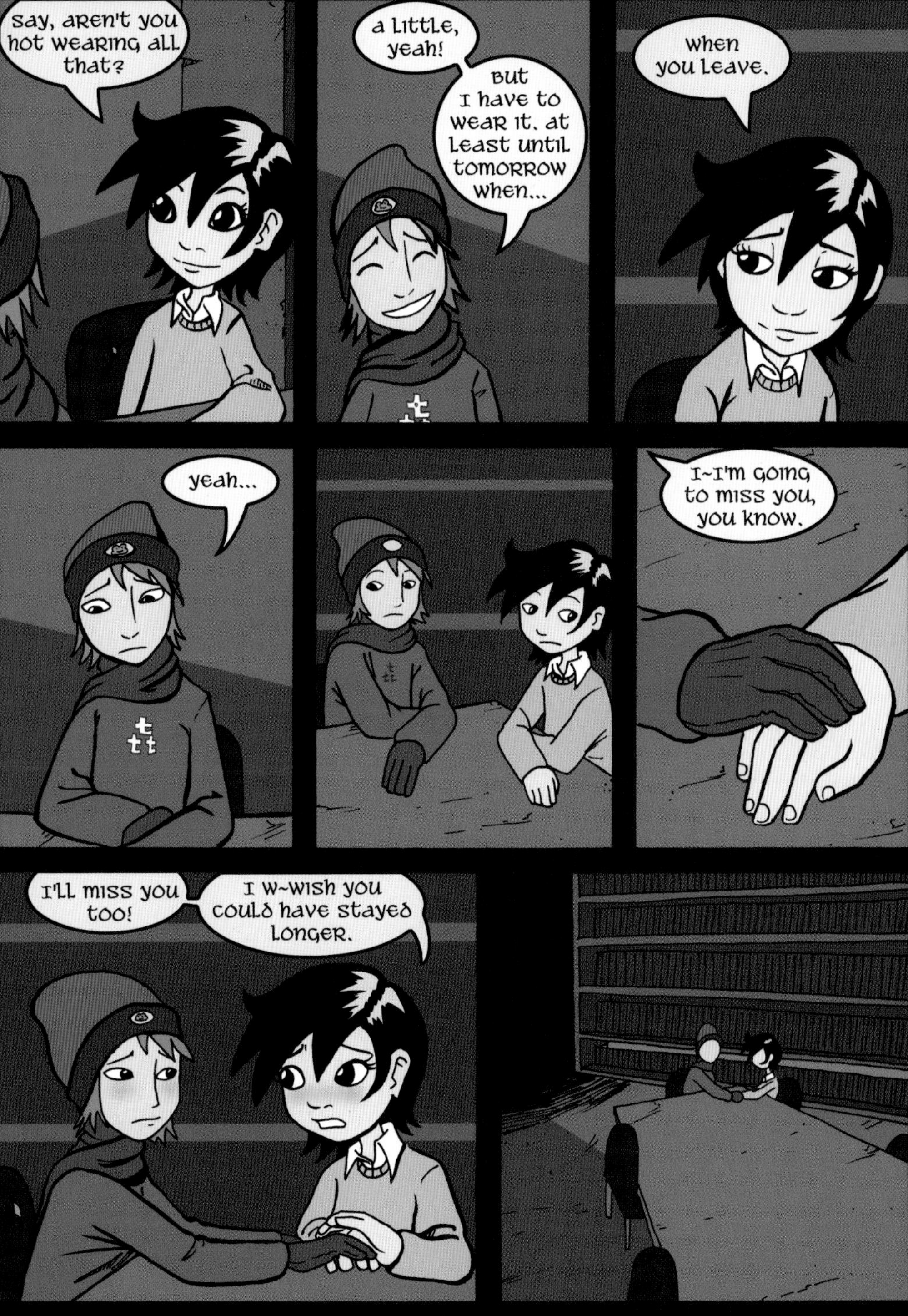
say, aren't you hot wearing all that?
a little, yeah!
But I have to wear it, at least until tomorrow when...
when you leave.
yeah...
I~I'm going to miss you, you know.
I'll miss you too!
I w~wish you could have stayed longer.

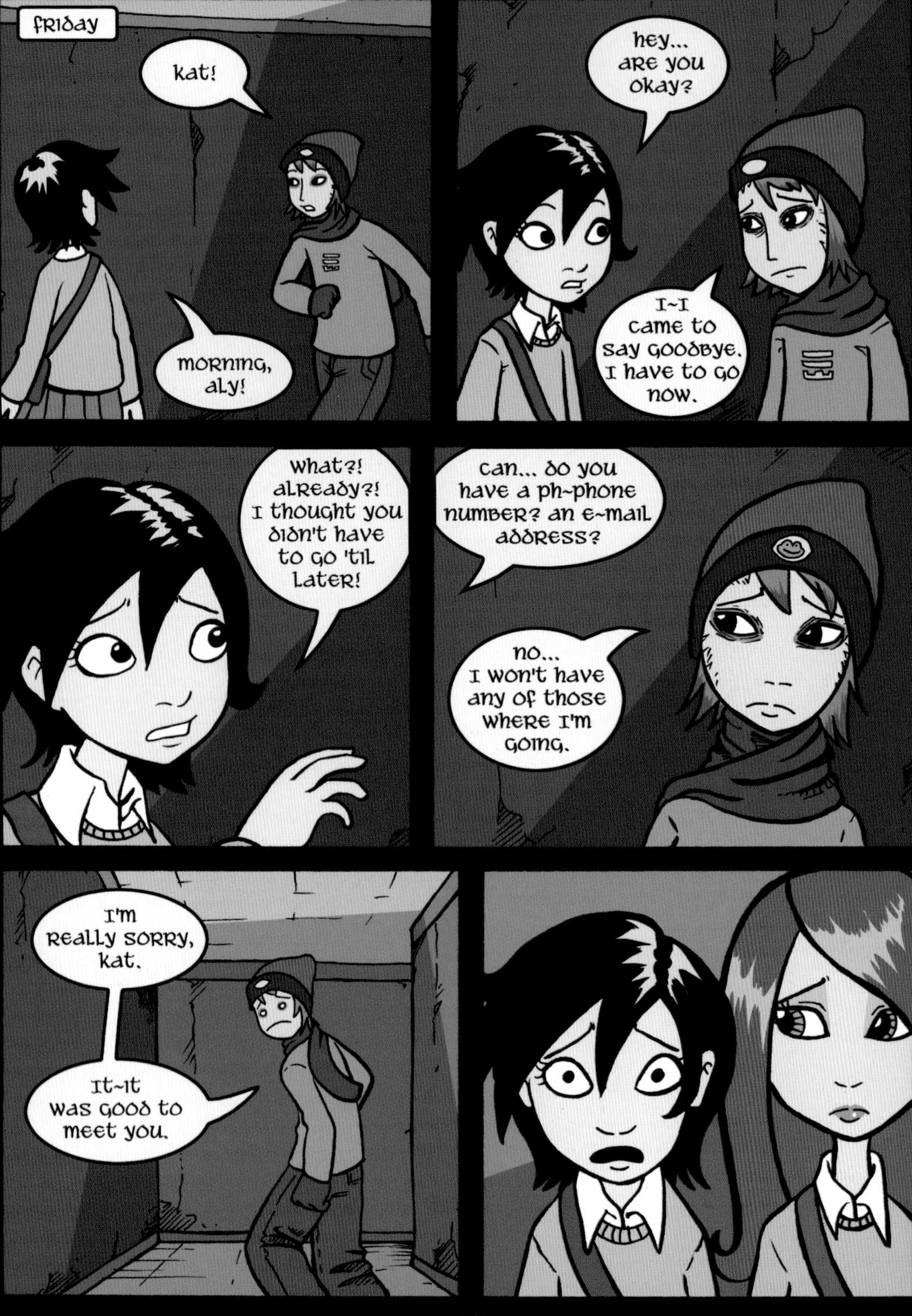
friday
kat!
morning, aly!
hey... are you okay?
I~I came to say goodbye. I have to go now.
what?! already?! I thought you didn't have to go 'til later!
can... do you have a ph~phone number? an e~mail address?
no... I won't have any of those where I'm going.
I'm really sorry, kat.
It~it was good to meet you.

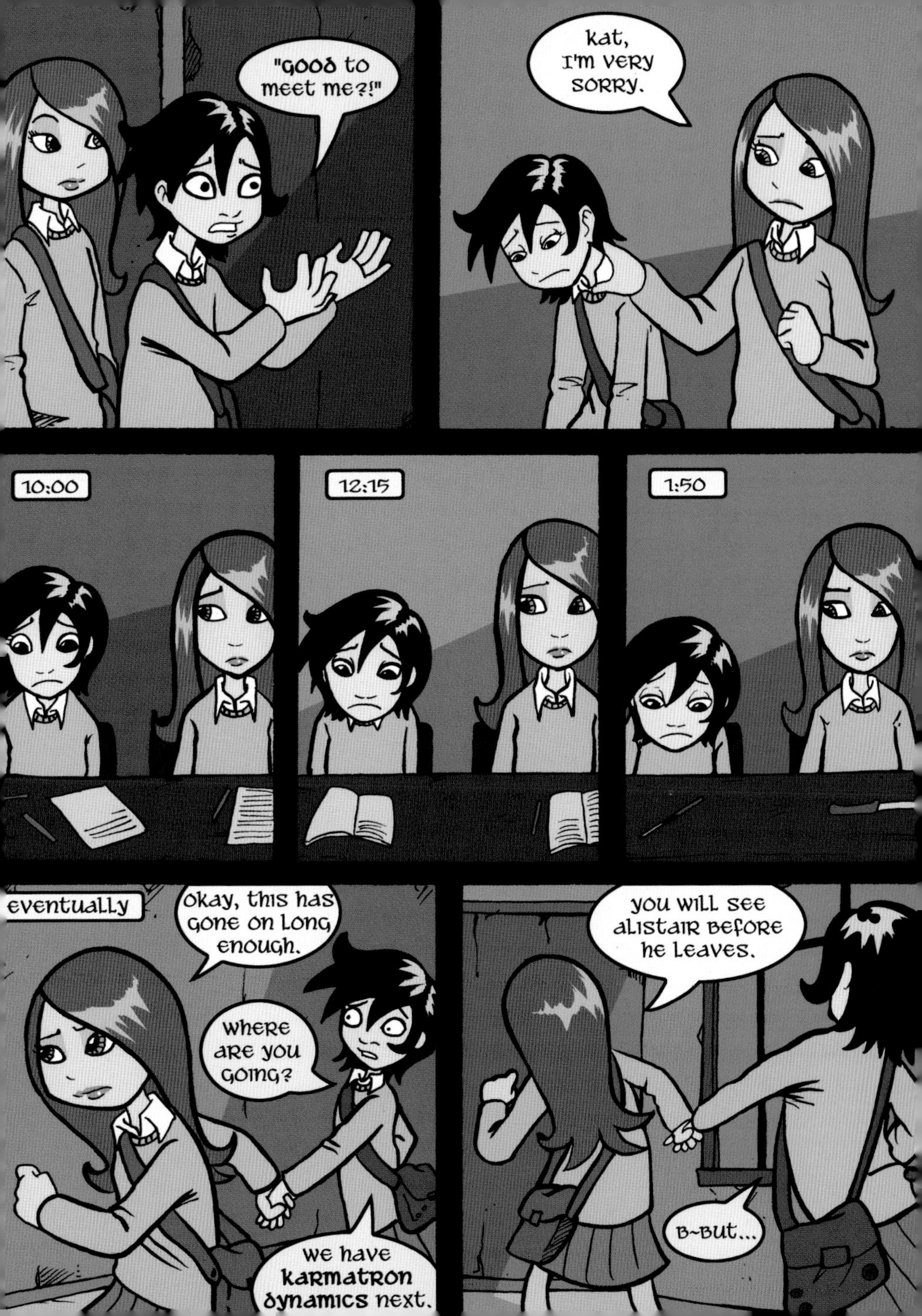
"GOOD to meet me?!"
kat, I'M VERY SORRY.
10:00
12:15
1:50
eventually
Okay, this has gone on long enough.
WHERE ARE YOU GOING?
we have karmatron dynamics next.
YOU WILL SEE alistair BEFORE he Leaves.
B~BUT...

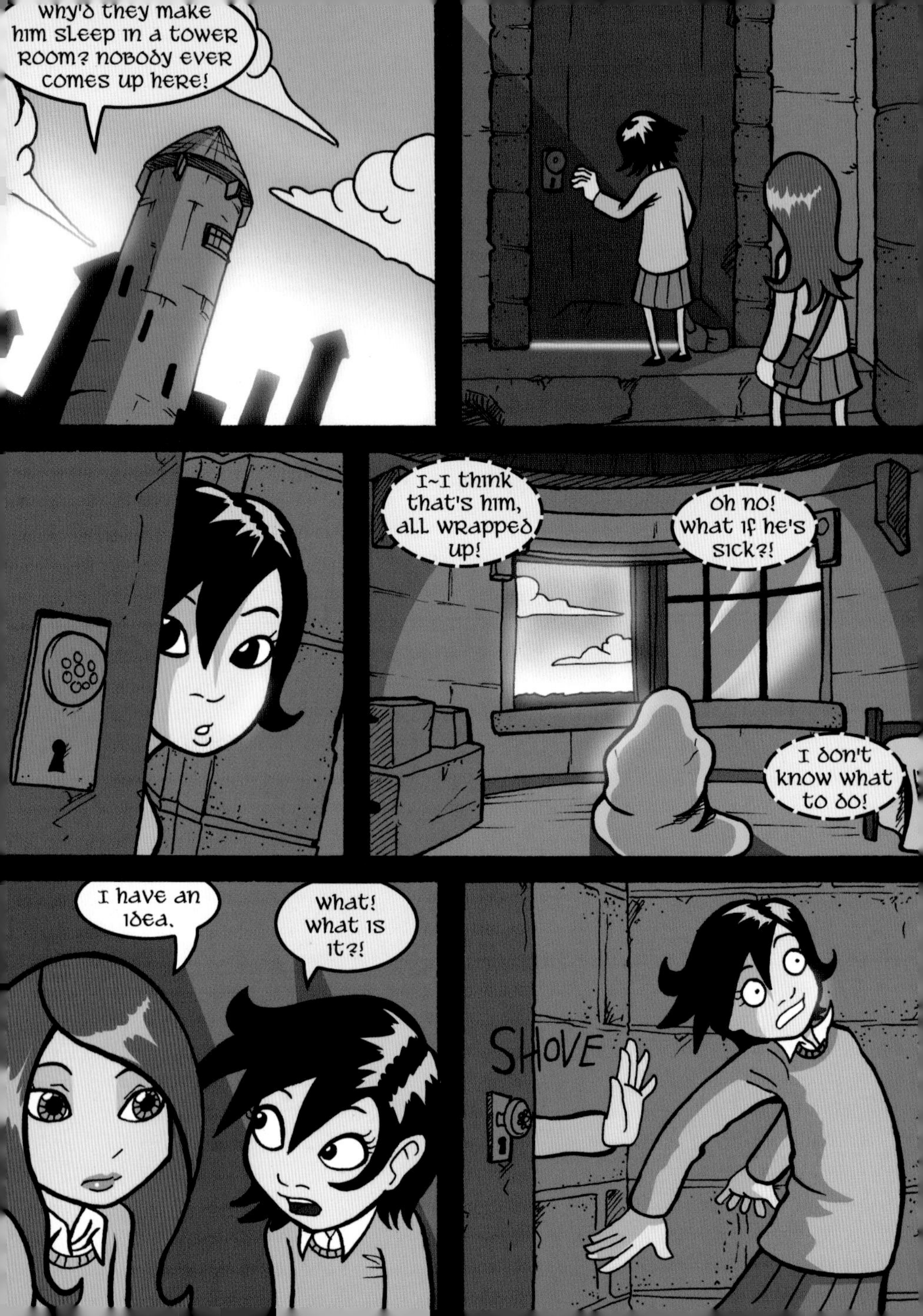
why'd they make him sleep in a tower room? nobody ever comes up here!
I~I think that's him, all wrapped up!
oh no! what if he's sick?!
I don't know what to do!
I have an idea.
what! what is it?!
SHOVE

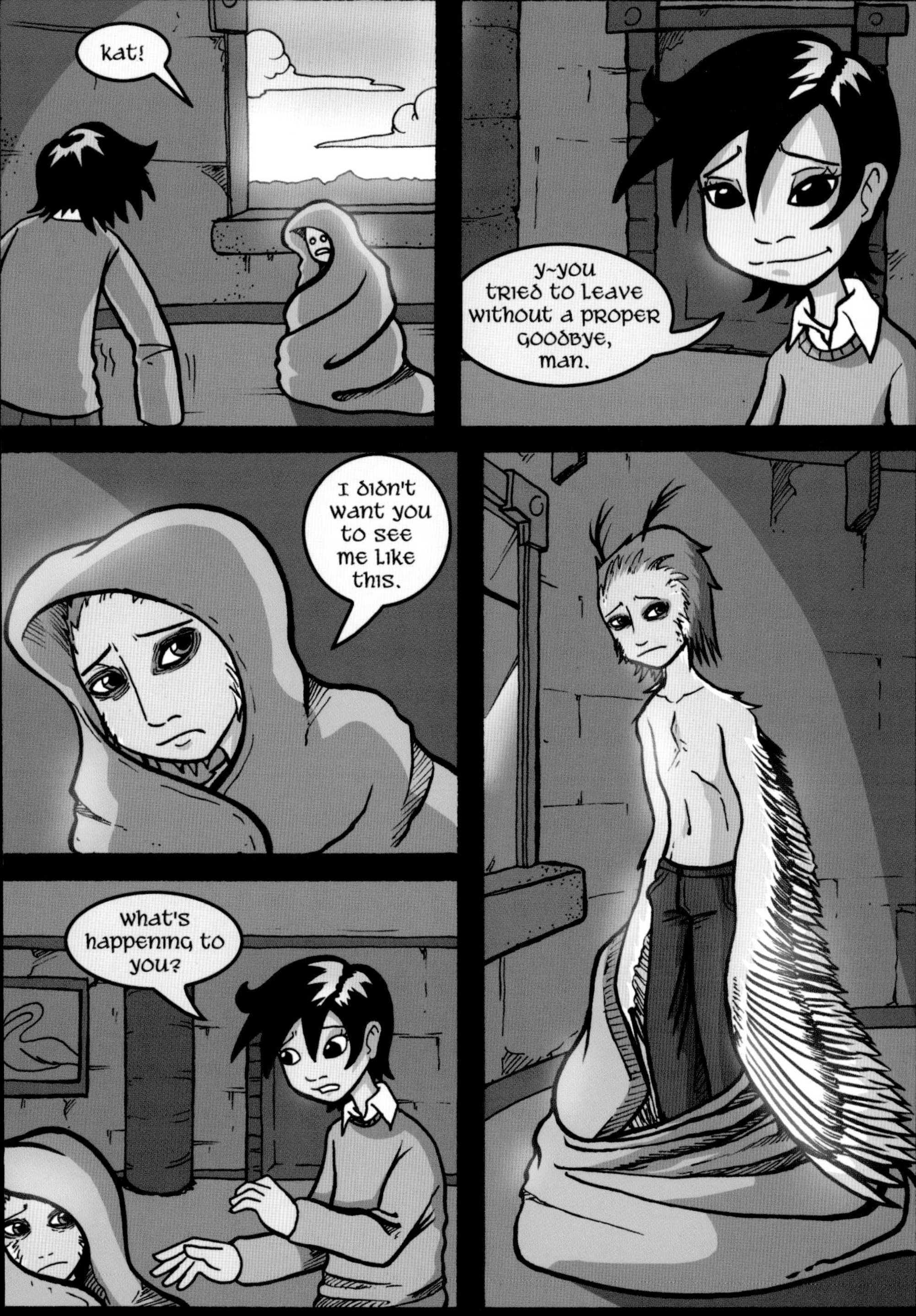
kat!
y~you tried to leave without a proper goodbye, man.
I didn't want you to see me like this.
What's happening to you?

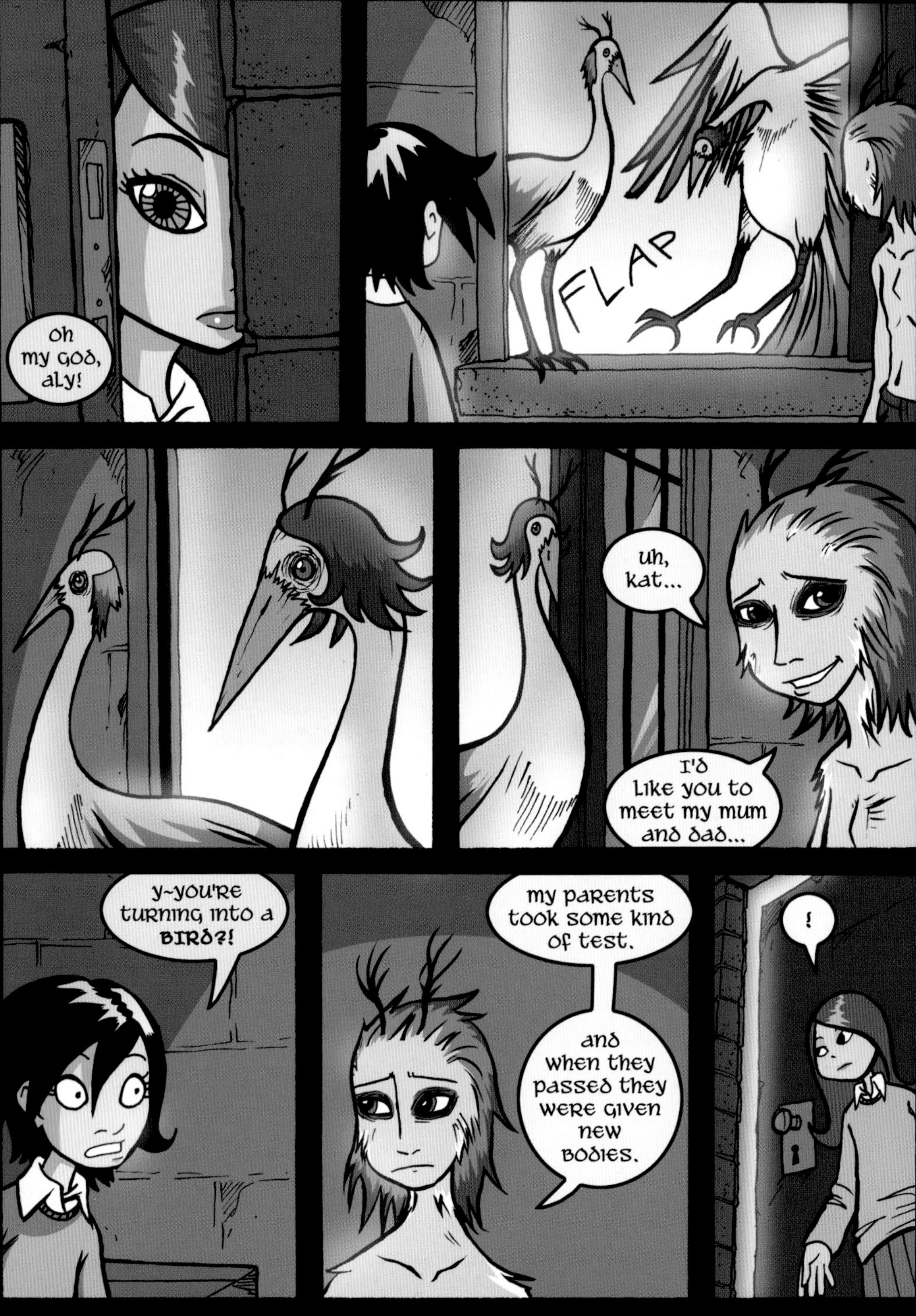
oh my god, aly!
FLAP
uh, kat...
I'd like you to meet my mum and dad...
y~you're turning into a BIRD?!
my parents took some kind of test.
and when they passed they were given new bodies.
!

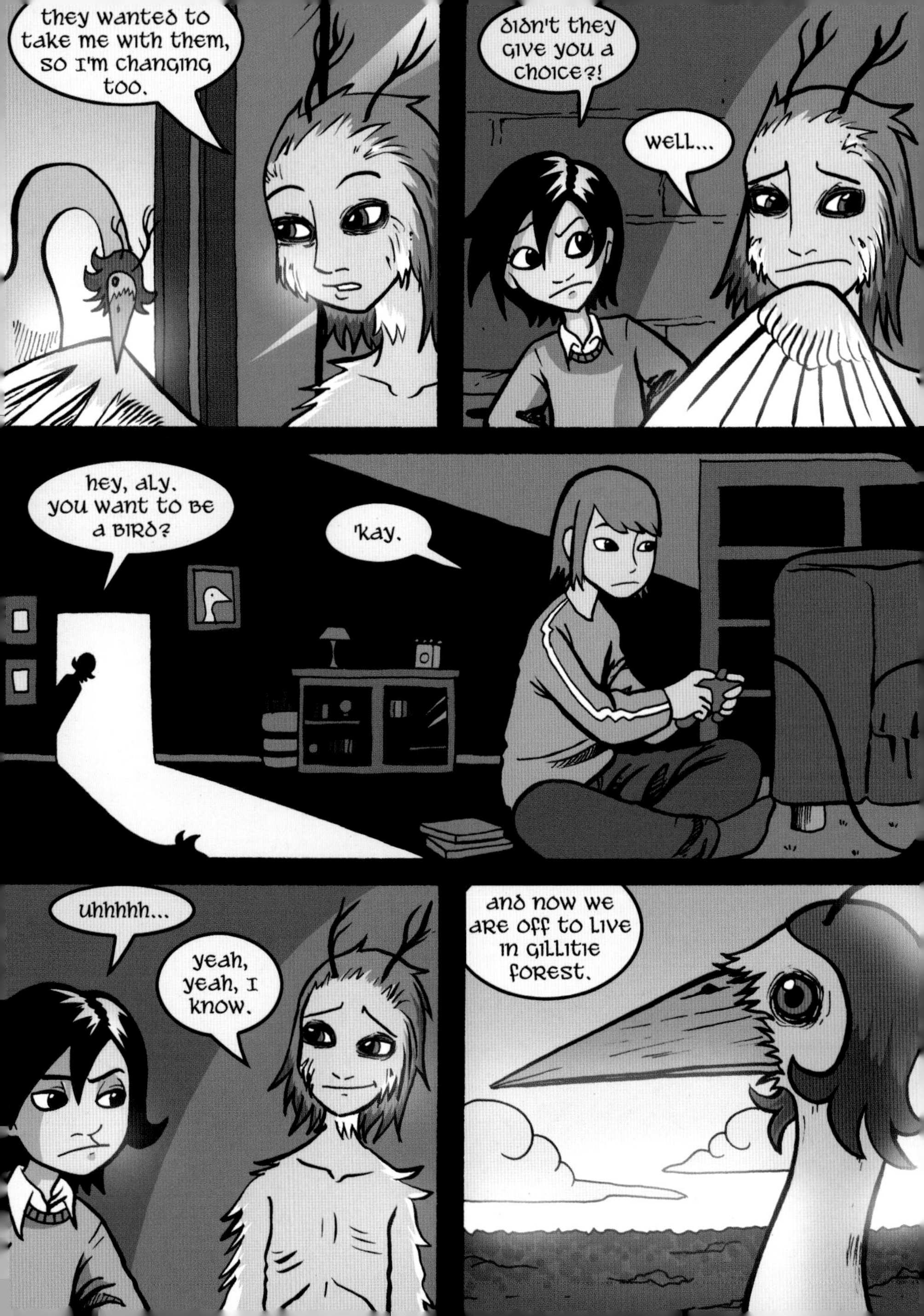
they wanted to take me with them, so I'm changing too.
didn't they give you a choice?!
well...
hey, aly. you want to be a BIRD?
'kay.
uhhhhh...
yeah, yeah, I know.
and now we are off to live in Gillitie forest.

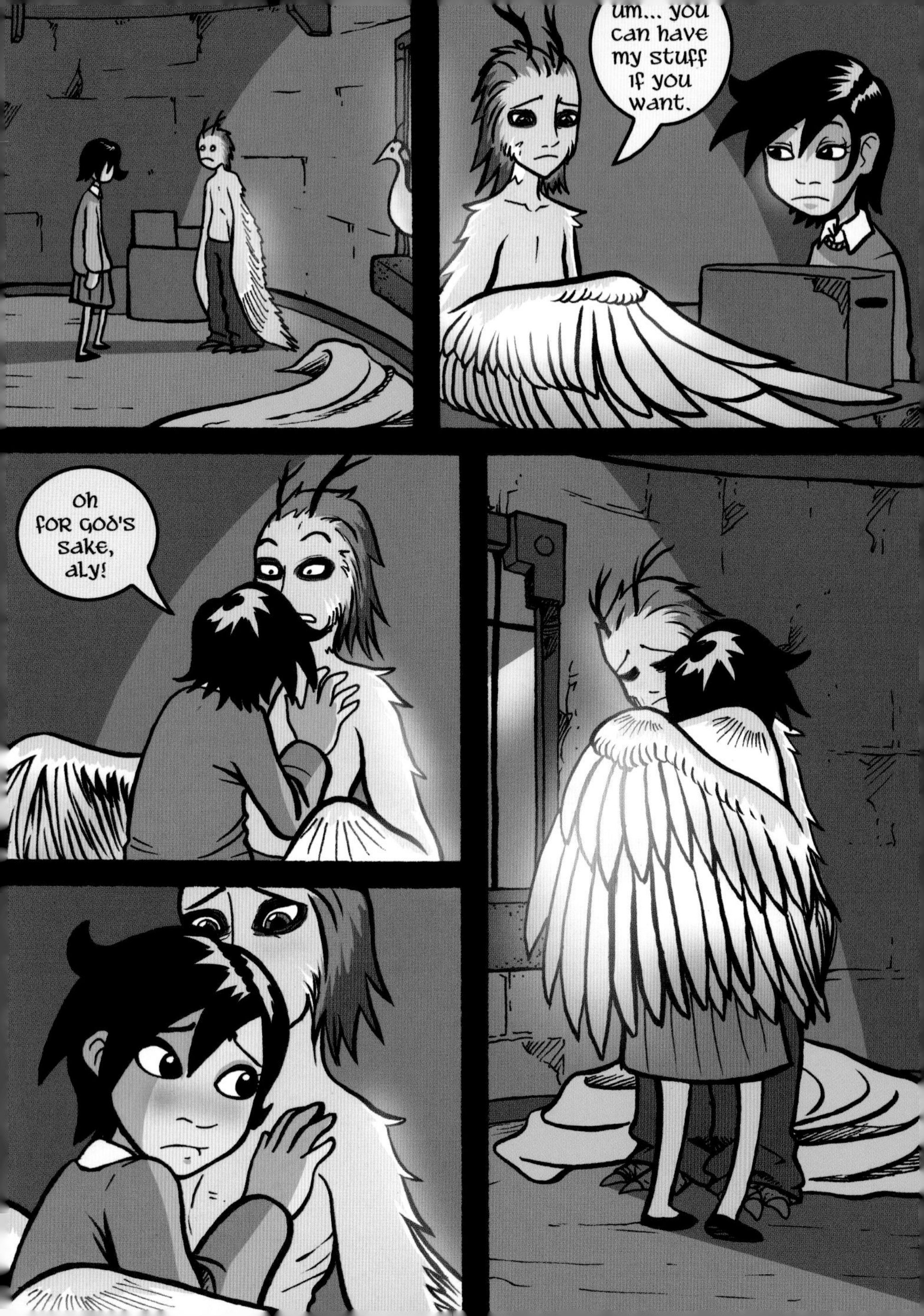
um... you can have my stuff if you want.
Oh for god's sake, aly!

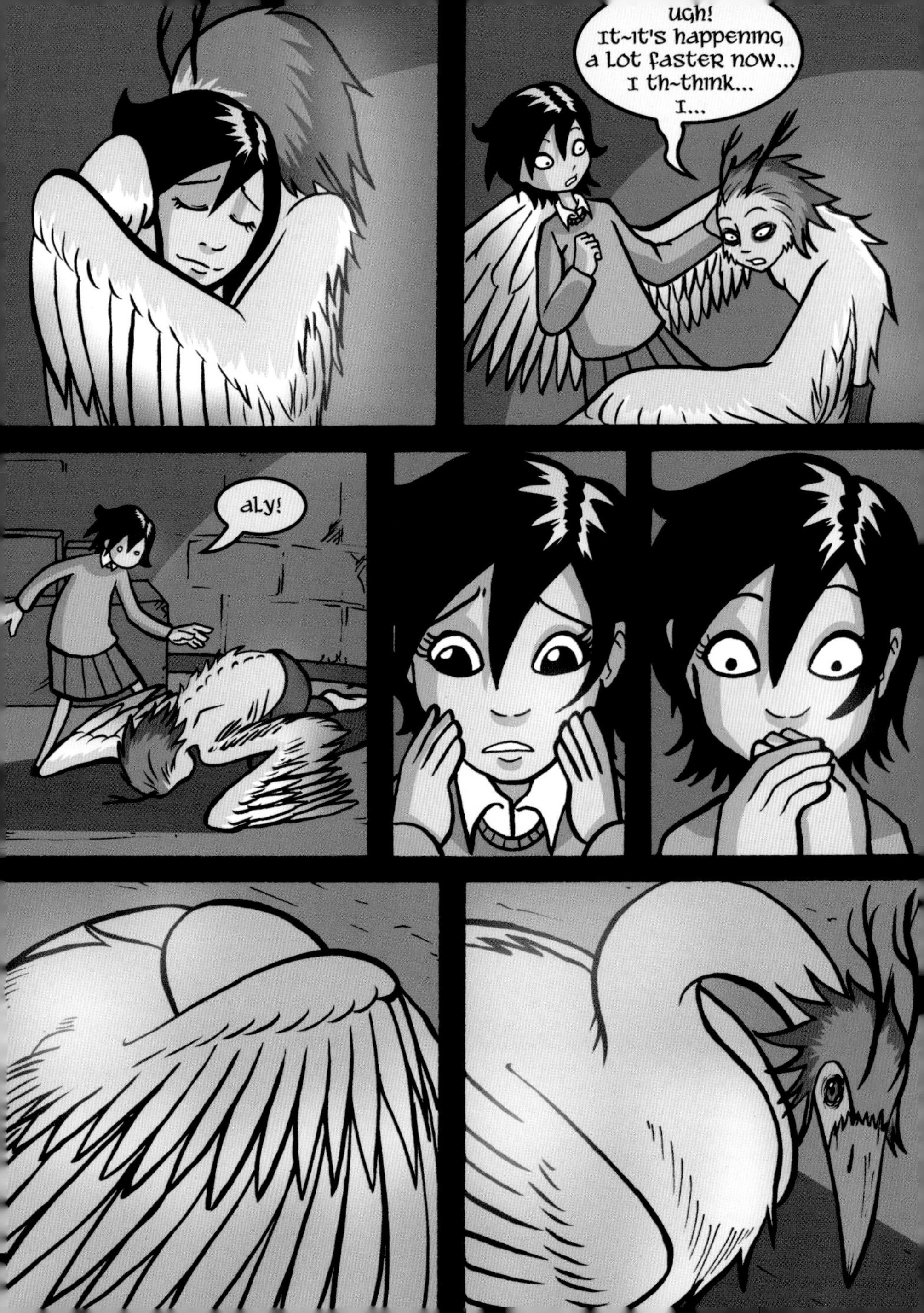
Ugh!
It-it's happening
a lot faster now...
I th-think...
I...
aly!

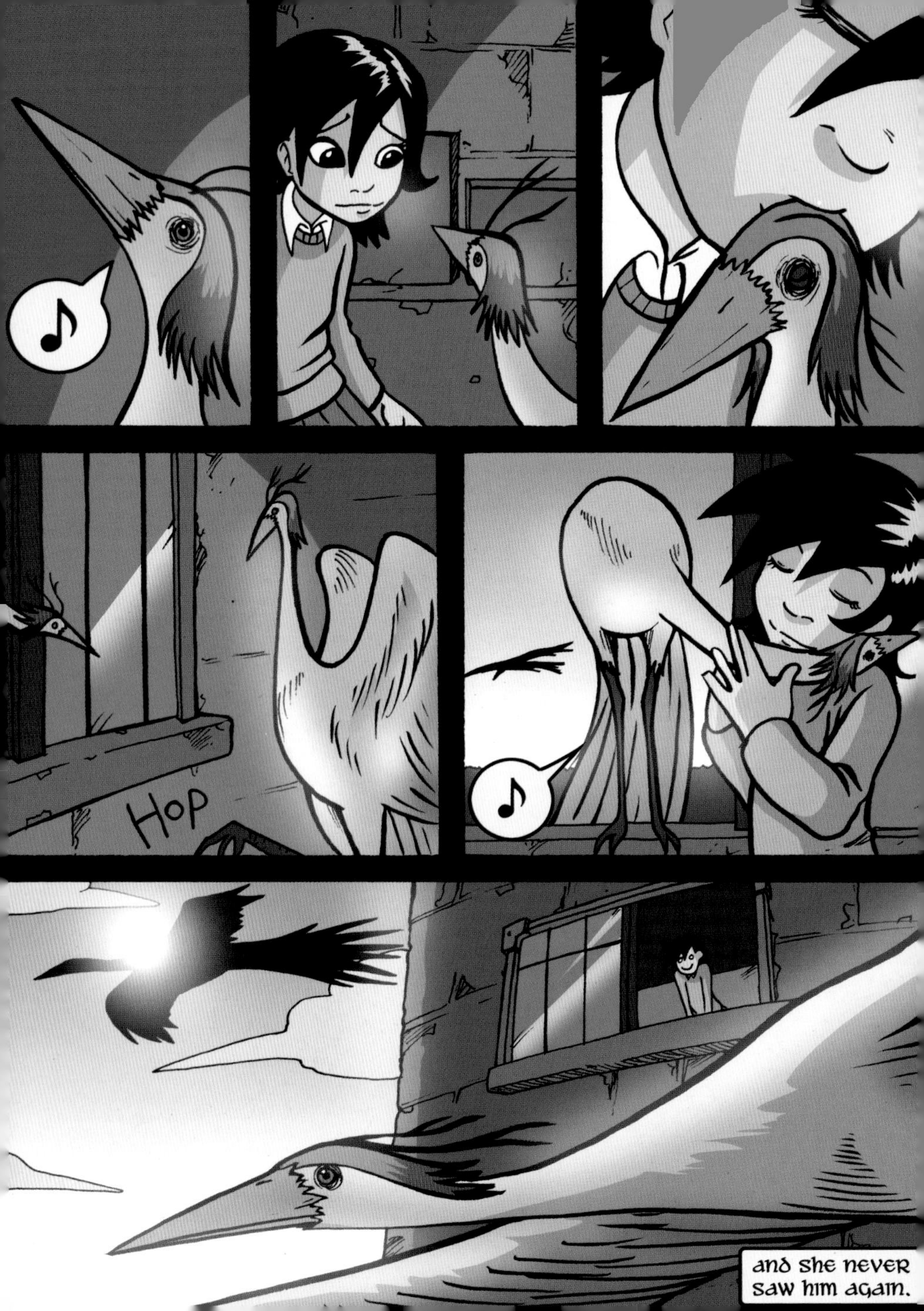
♪
Hop
♪
and she never
saw him again.

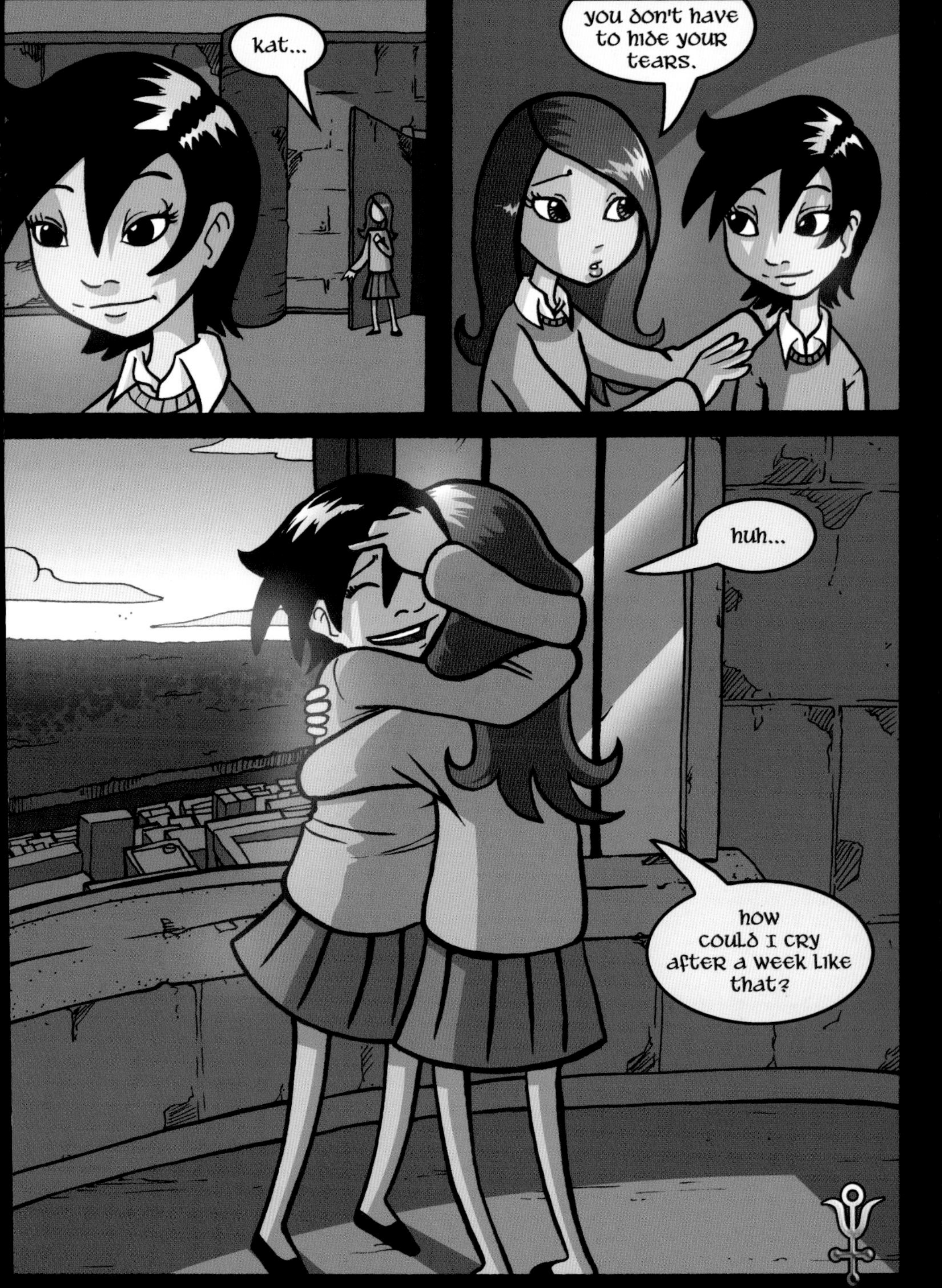
kat...
you don't have to hide your tears.
huh...
how could I cry after a week like that?

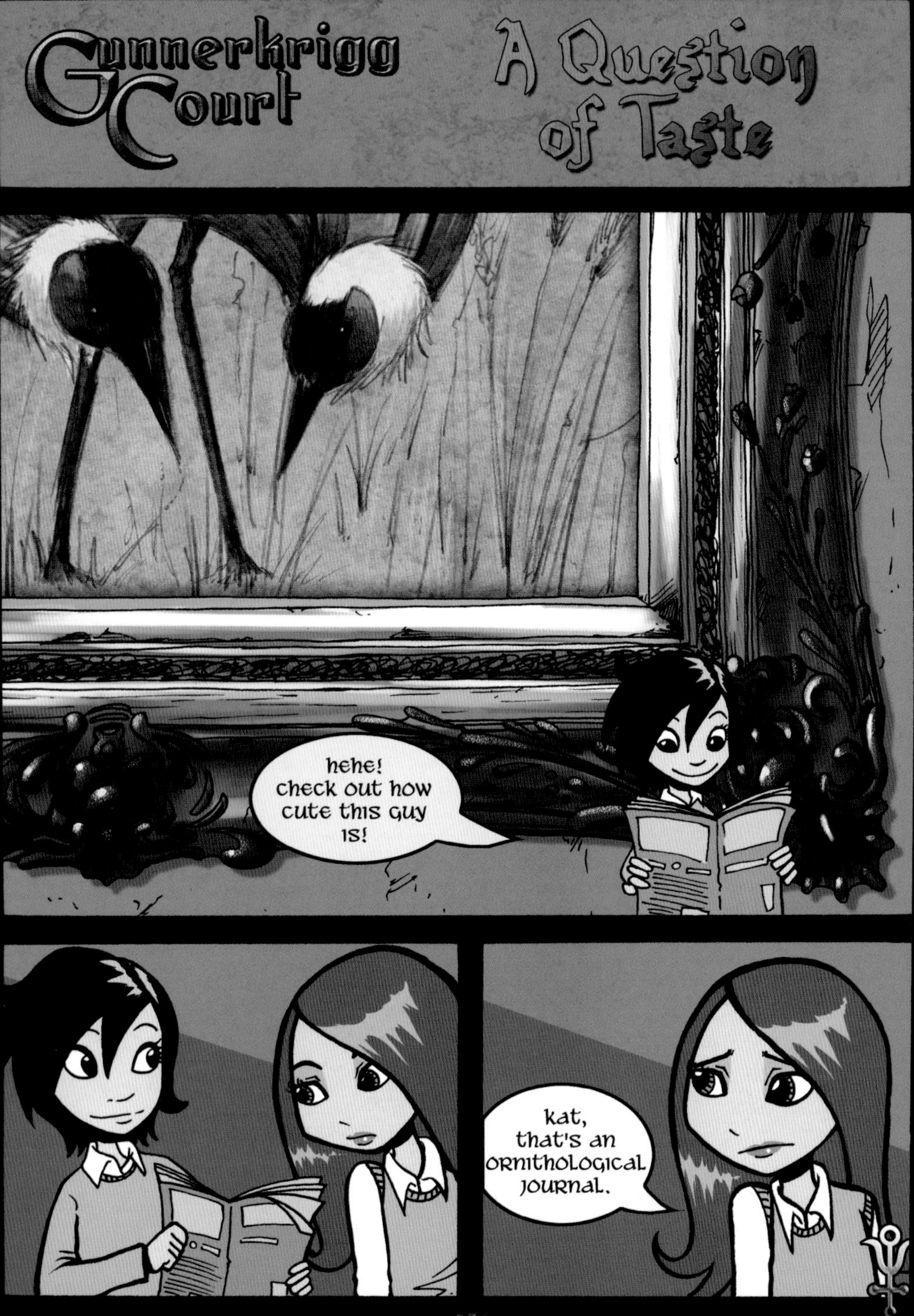
Gunnerkrigg Court
A Question of Taste
hehe! check out how cute this guy is!
kat, that's an ornithological journal.

Gunnerkrigg Court

Chapter 14:

The Fangs Of Summertime

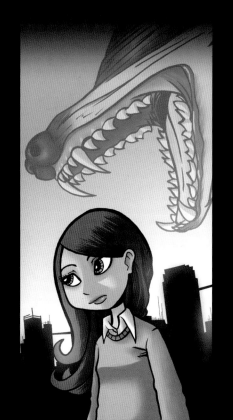

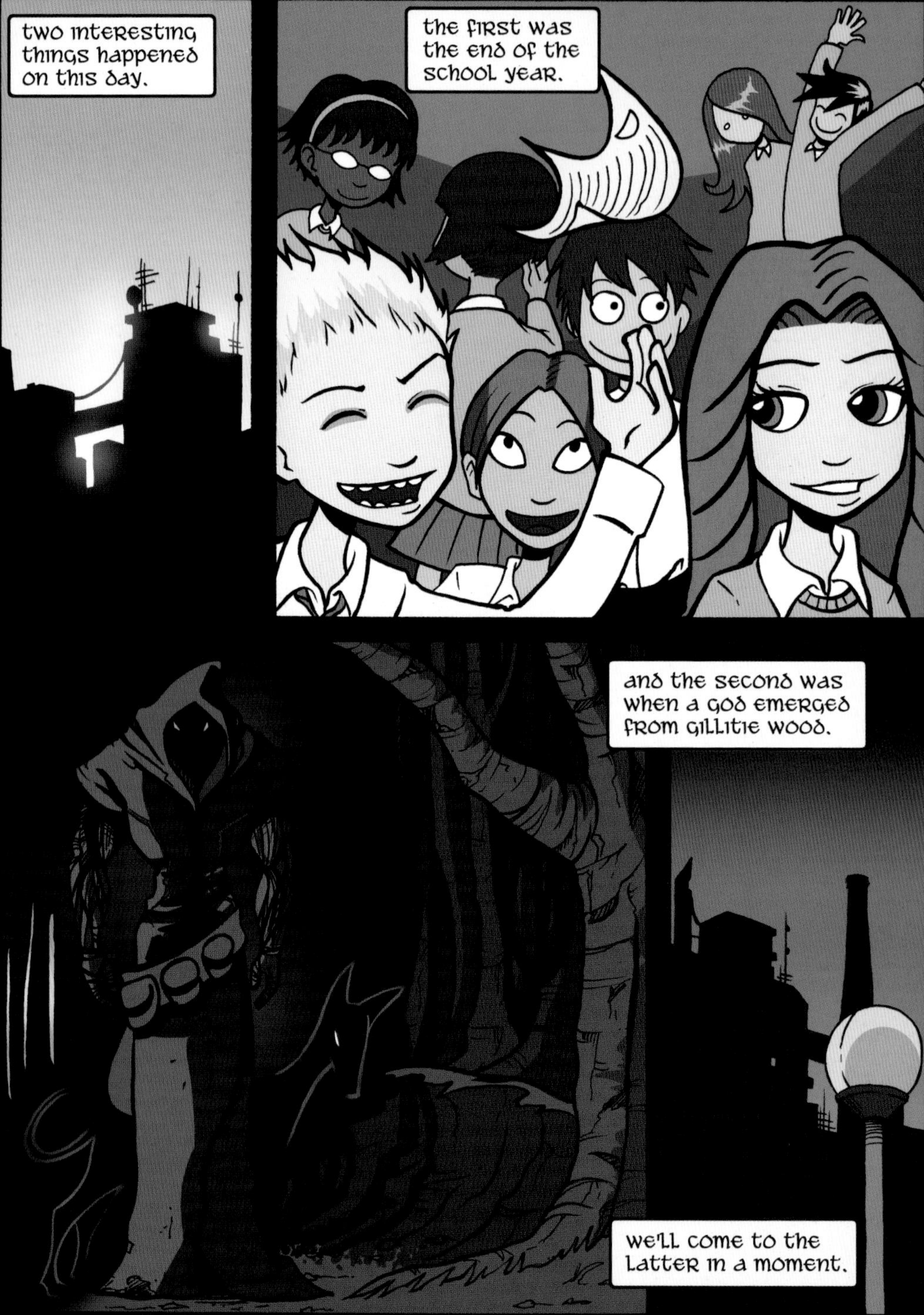
two interesting things happened on this day.
the first was the end of the school year.
and the second was when a god emerged from gillitie wood.
we'll come to the latter in a moment.

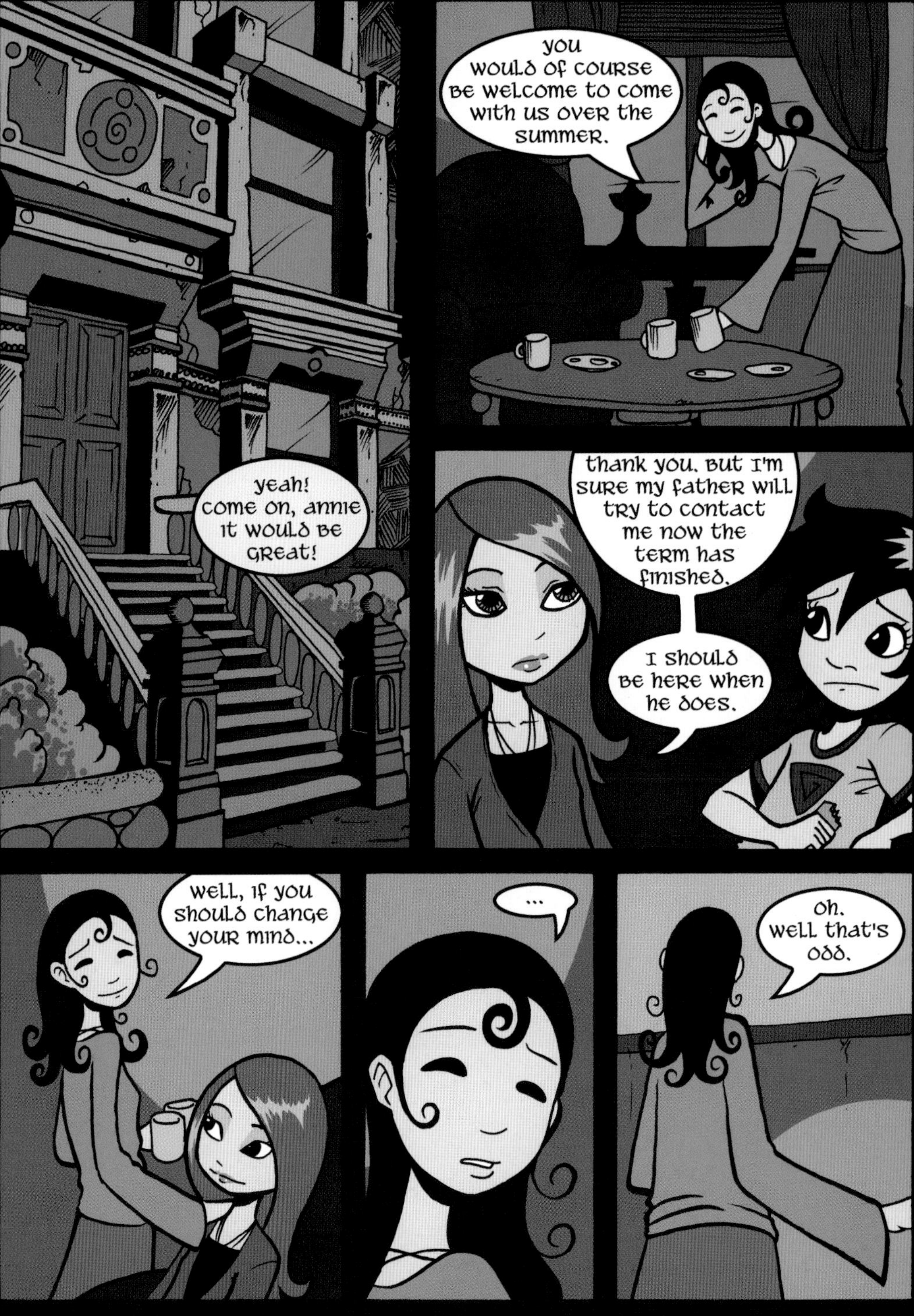
you would of course be welcome to come with us over the summer.
yeah! come on, annie it would be great!
thank you. but I'm sure my father will try to contact me now the term has finished.
I should be here when he does.
well, if you should change your mind...
...
oh. well that's odd.

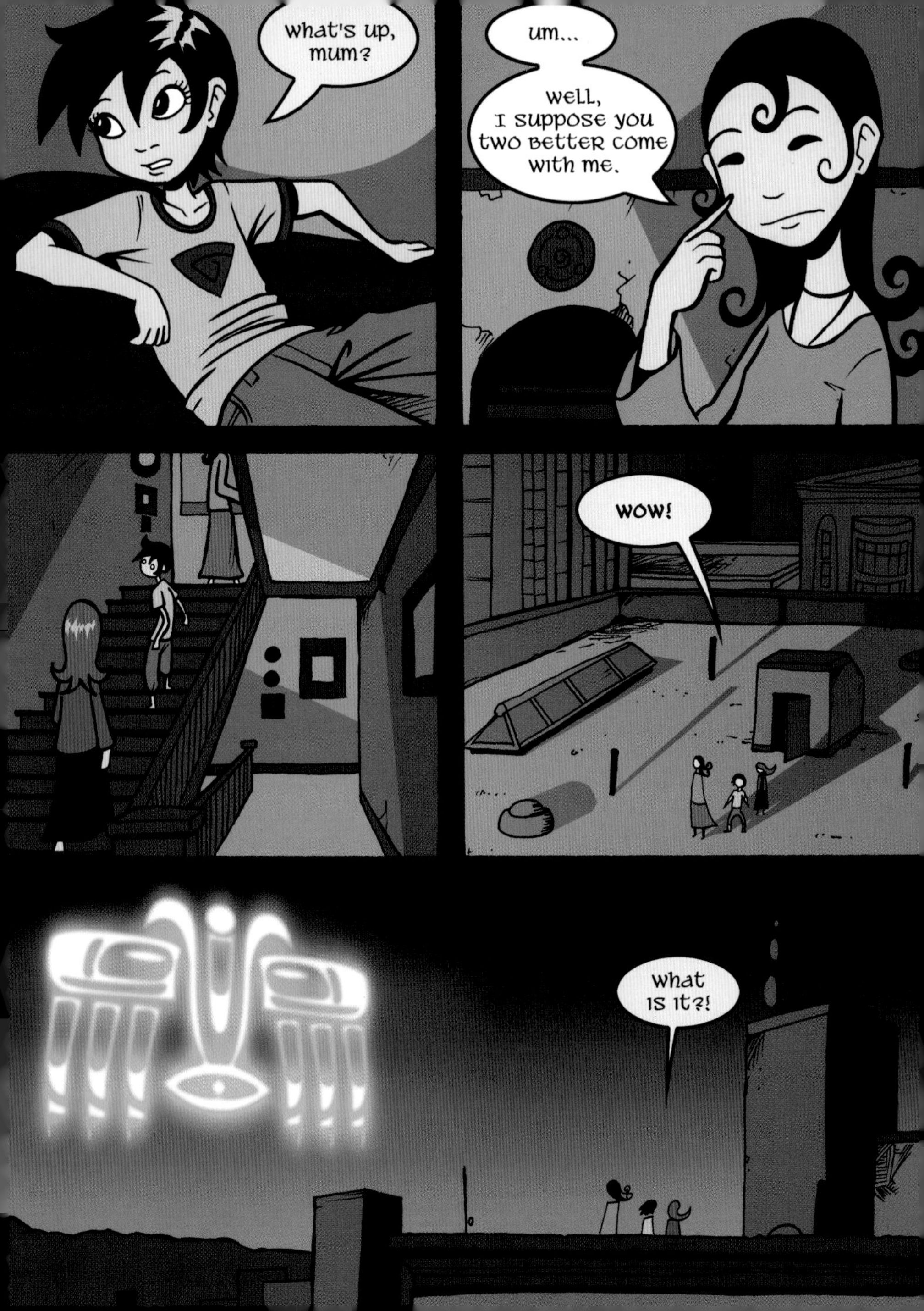
what's up, mum?
um...
well, I suppose you two better come with me.
WOW!
what is it?!

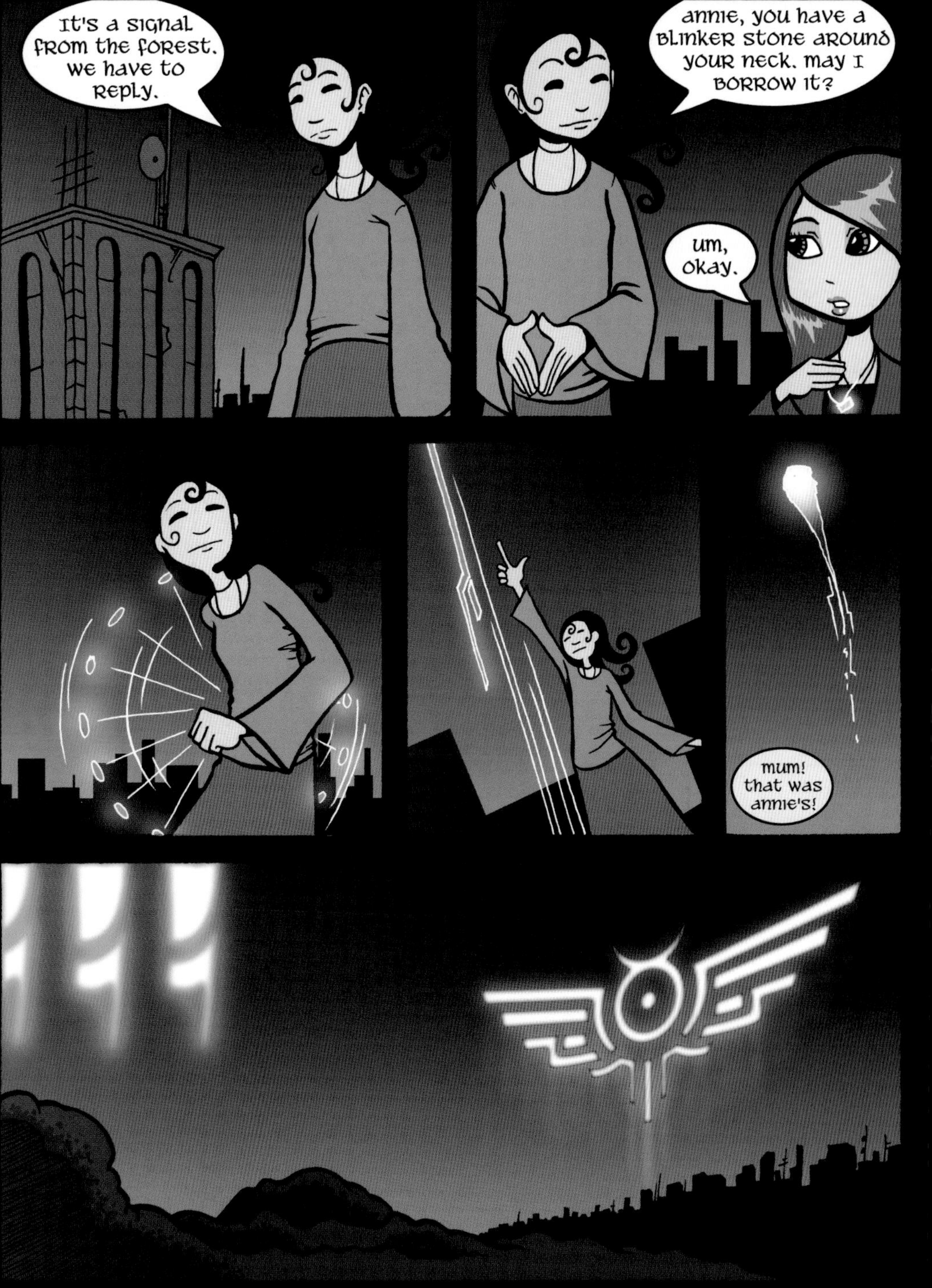
It's a signal from the forest. we have to reply.
annie, you have a blinker stone around your neck. may I borrow it?
um, okay.
mum! that was annie's!

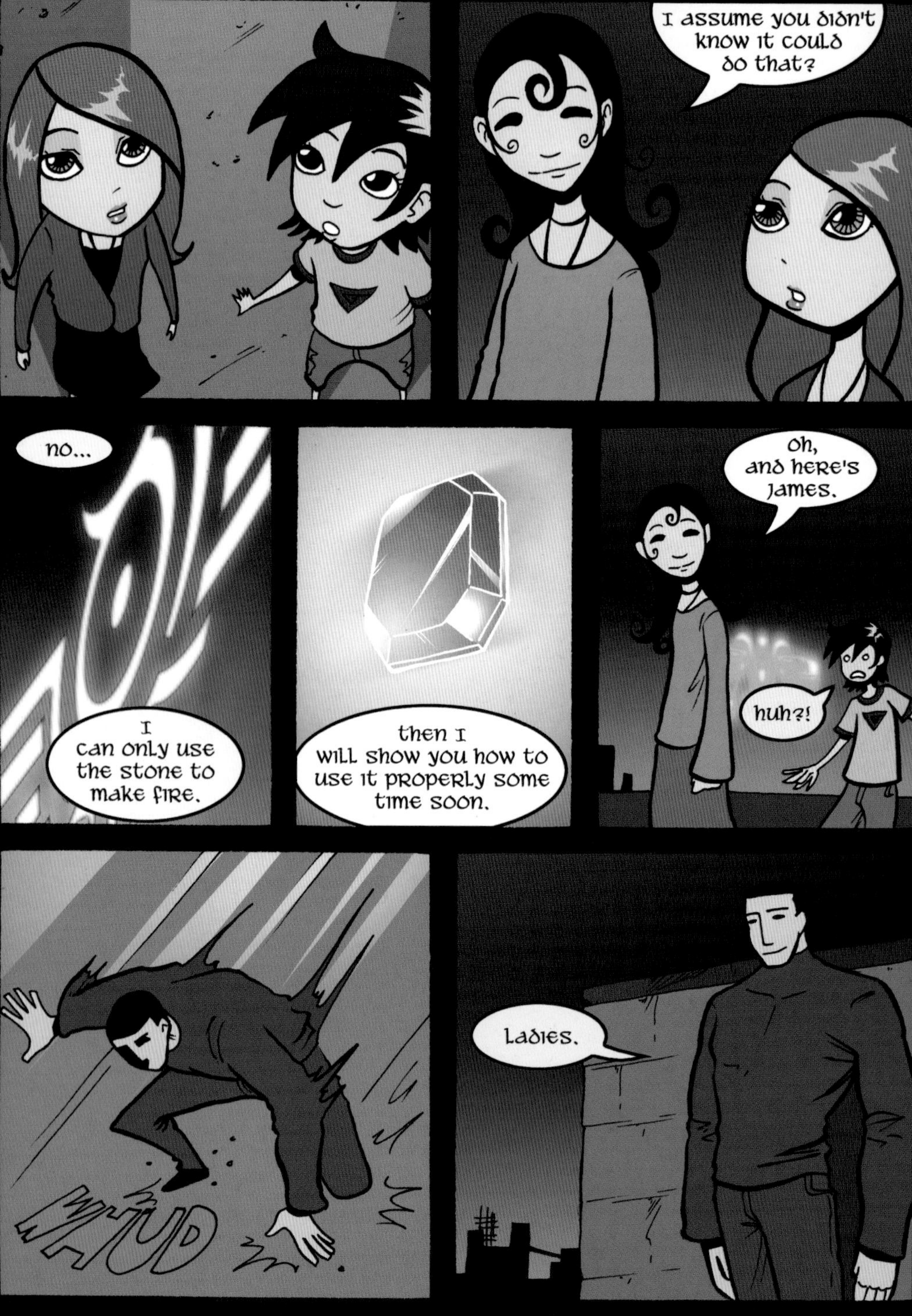
I assume you didn't know it could do that?
no...
I can only use the stone to make fire.
then I will show you how to use it properly some time soon.
oh, and here's James.
huh?!
THUD
Ladies.

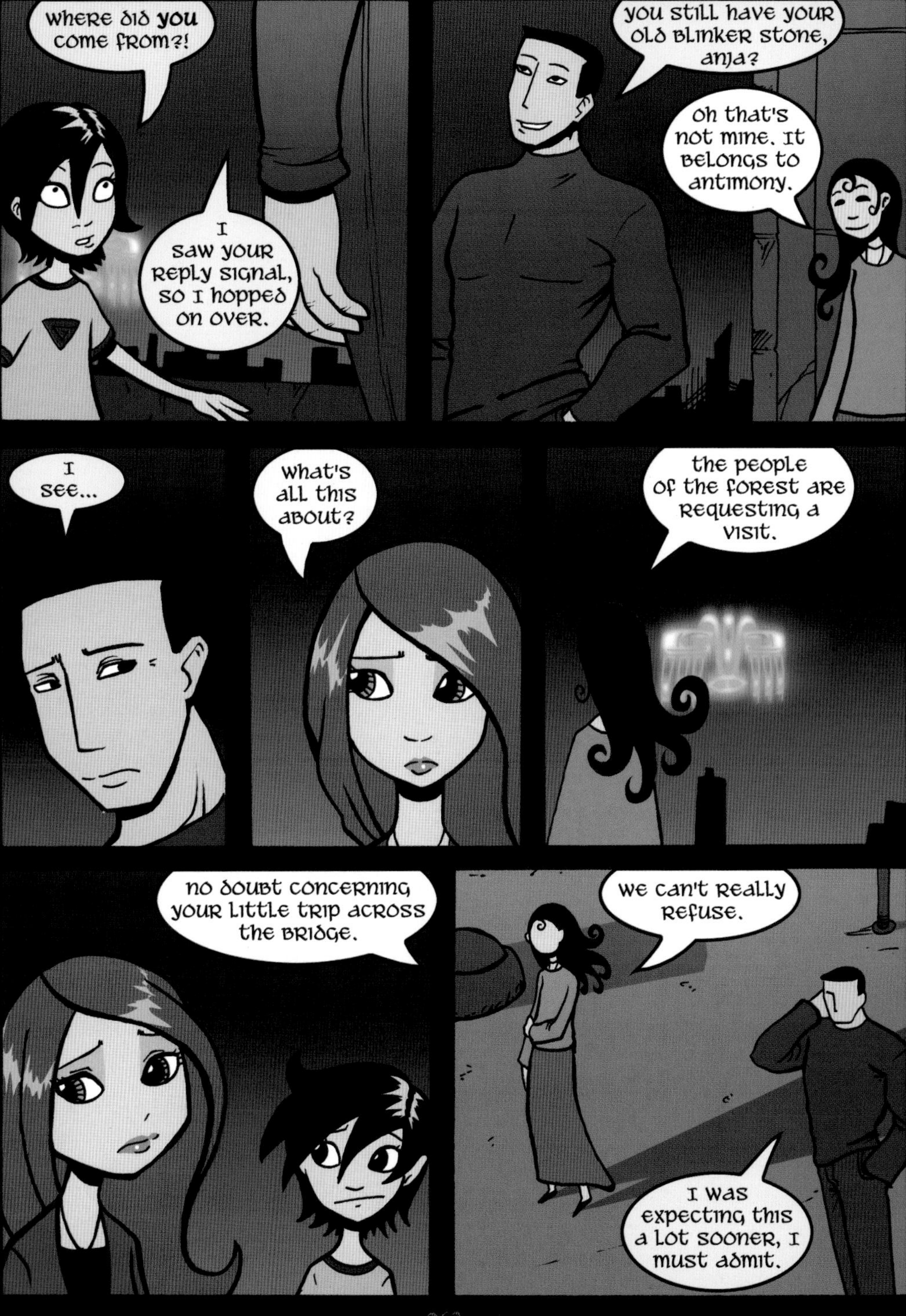
where did you come from?!
I saw your reply signal, so I hopped on over.
you still have your old blinker stone, anja?
oh that's not mine. it belongs to antimony.
I see...
what's all this about?
the people of the forest are requesting a visit.
no doubt concerning your little trip across the bridge.
we can't really refuse.
I was expecting this a lot sooner, I must admit.

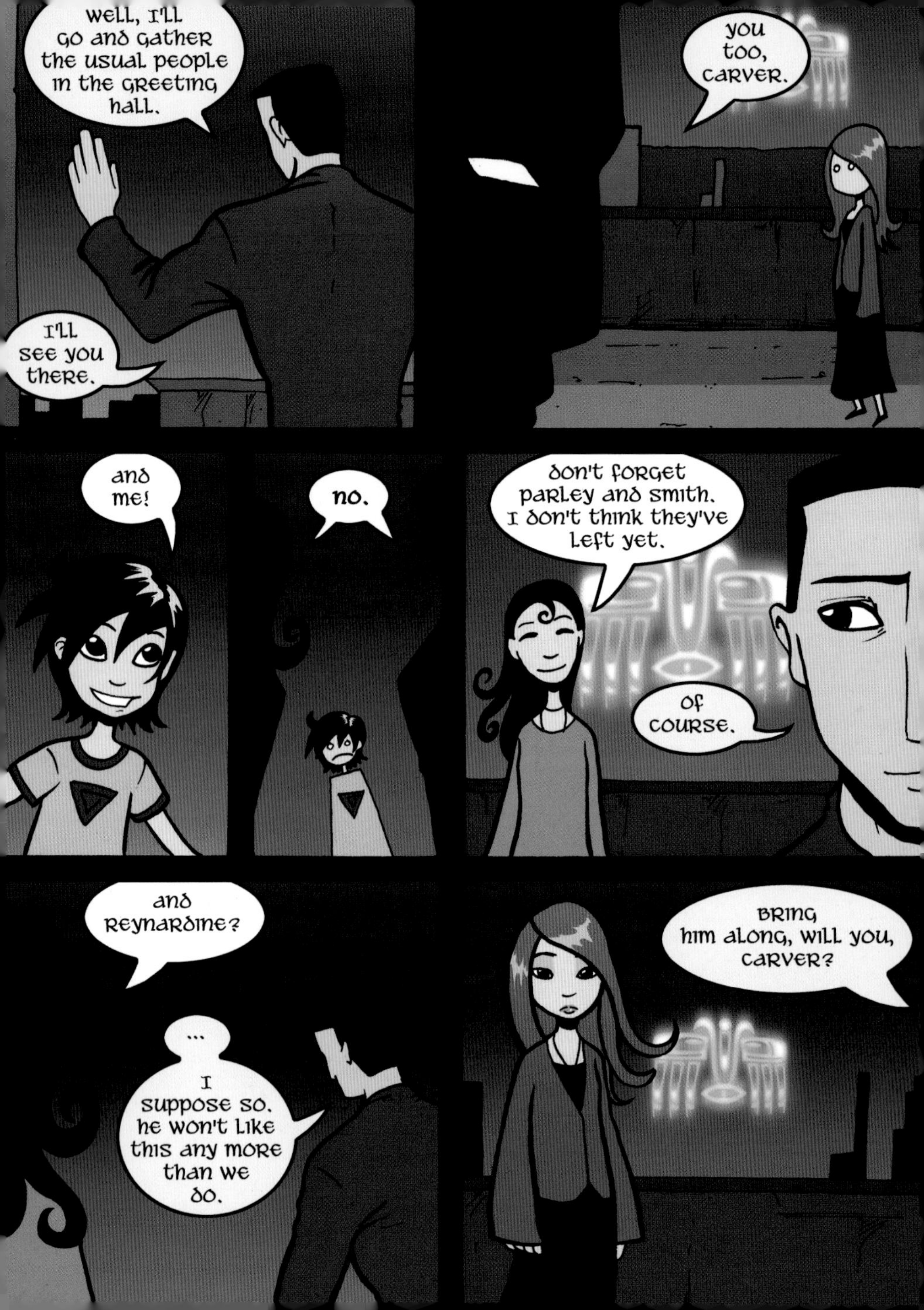
well, I'll go and gather the usual people in the greeting hall.
I'll see you there.
you too, carver.
and me!
no.
don't forget parley and smith. I don't think they've left yet.
of course.
and reynardine?
...
I suppose so. he won't like this any more than we do.
bring him along, will you, carver?

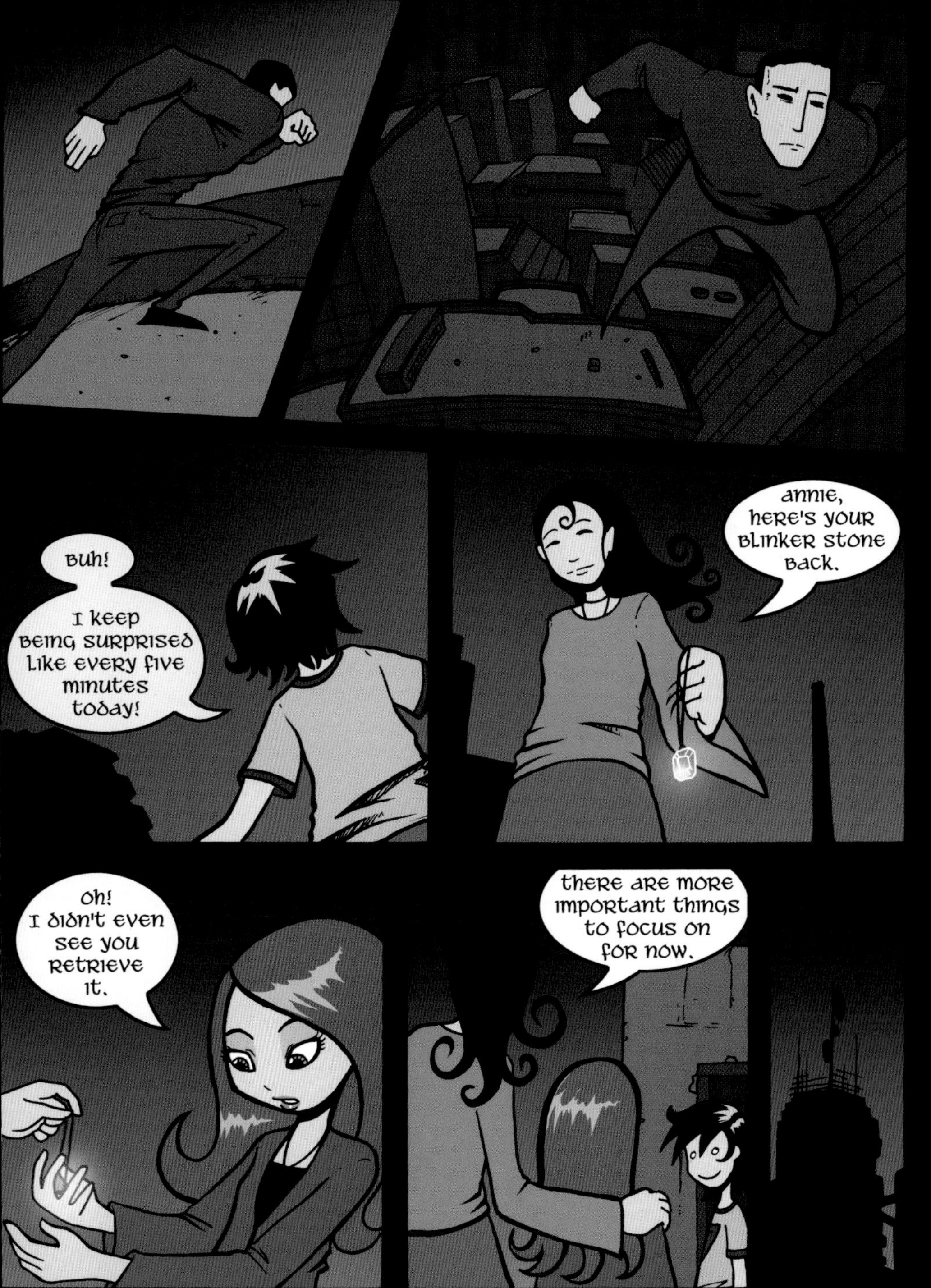
Buh!
I keep being surprised like every five minutes today!
annie, here's your blinker stone back.
oh! I didn't even see you retrieve it.
there are more important things to focus on for now.

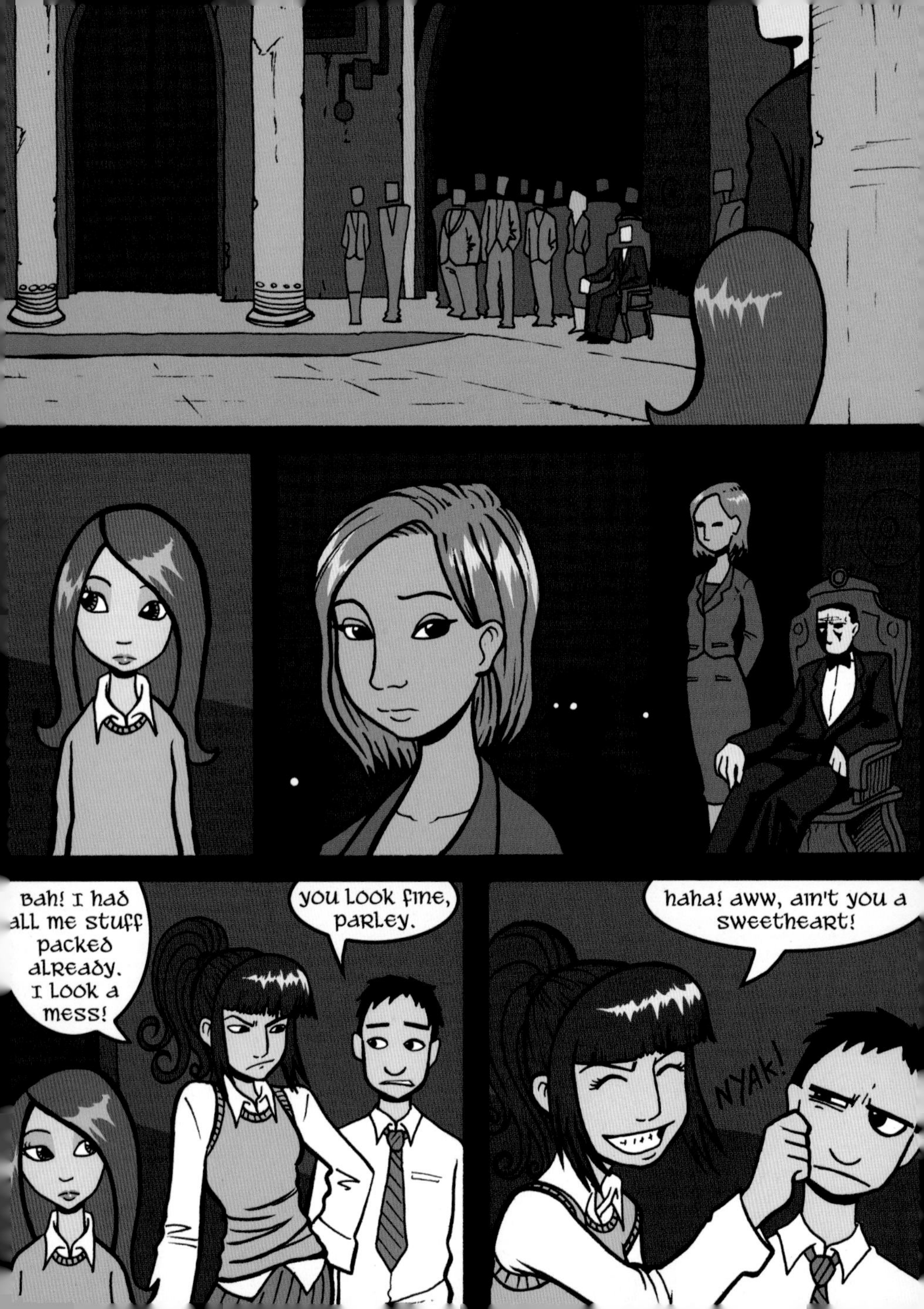
Bah! I had all me stuff packed already. I look a mess!
you look fine, parley.
haha! aww, ain't you a sweetheart!
NYAK!

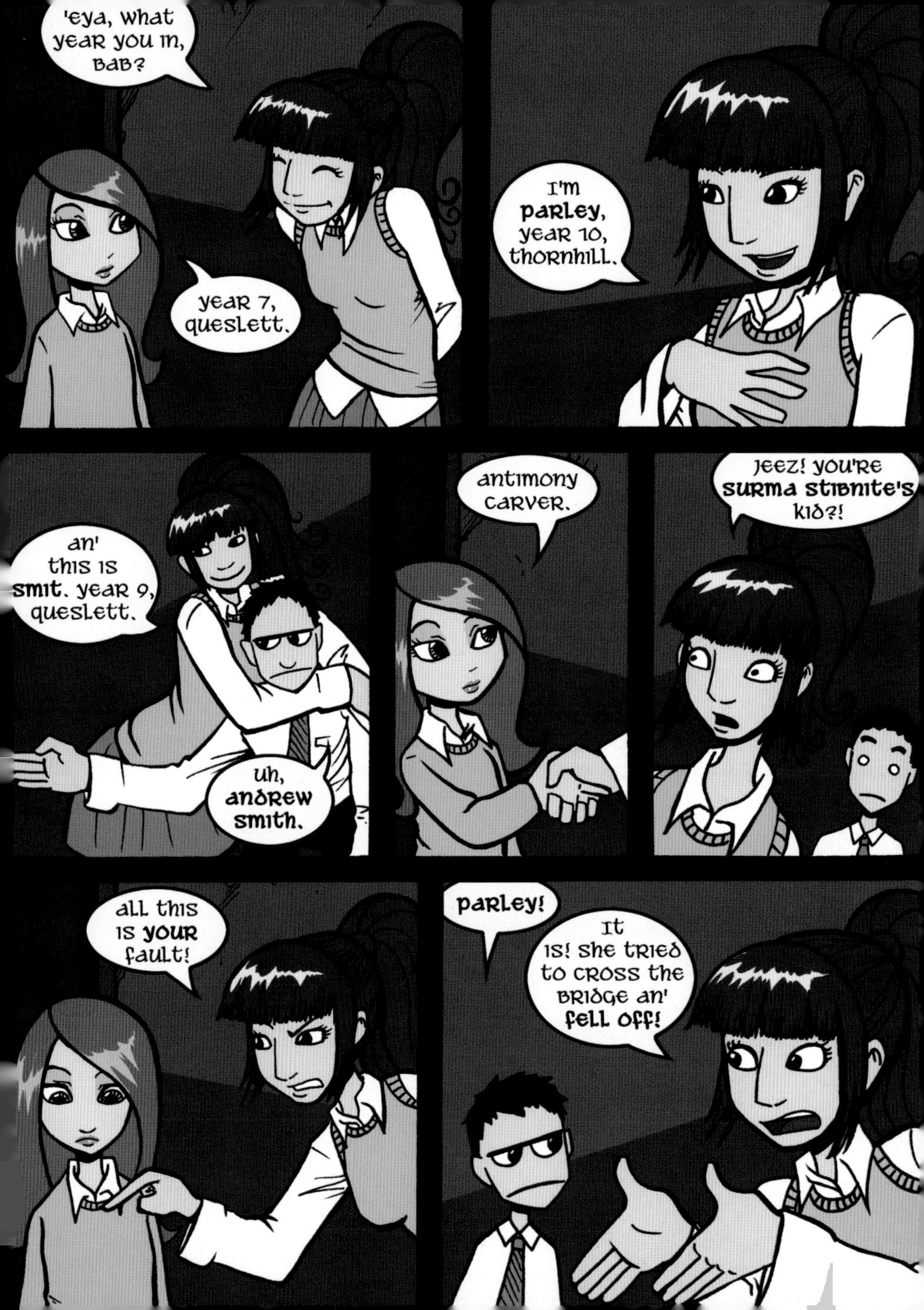
'eya, what year you in, bab?
year 7, queslett.
I'm parley, year 10, thornhill.
an' this is smit. year 9, queslett.
uh, andrew smith.
antimony carver.
jeez! you're surma stibnite's kid?!
all this is your fault!
parley!
it is! she tried to cross the bridge an' fell off!

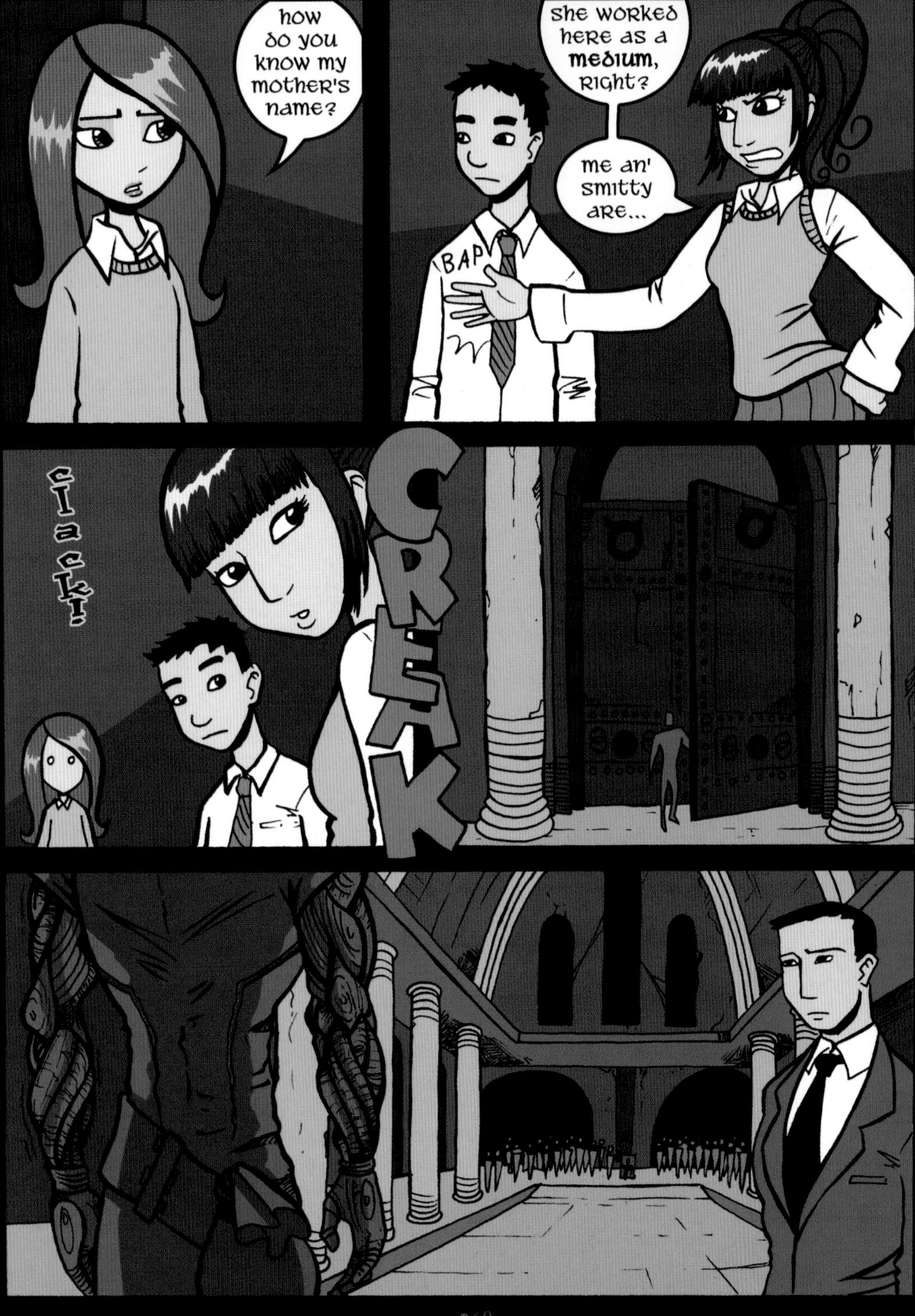
how do you know my mother's name?
she worked here as a medium, right?
me an' smitty are...
BAP
clack!
CREAK

Creak
Creak
IS that you, GENERAL?
what the devil have you done to yourself?

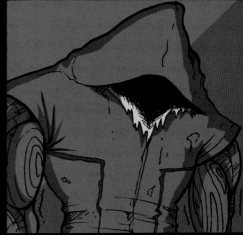

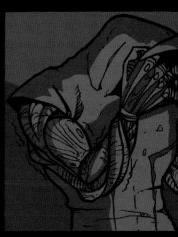

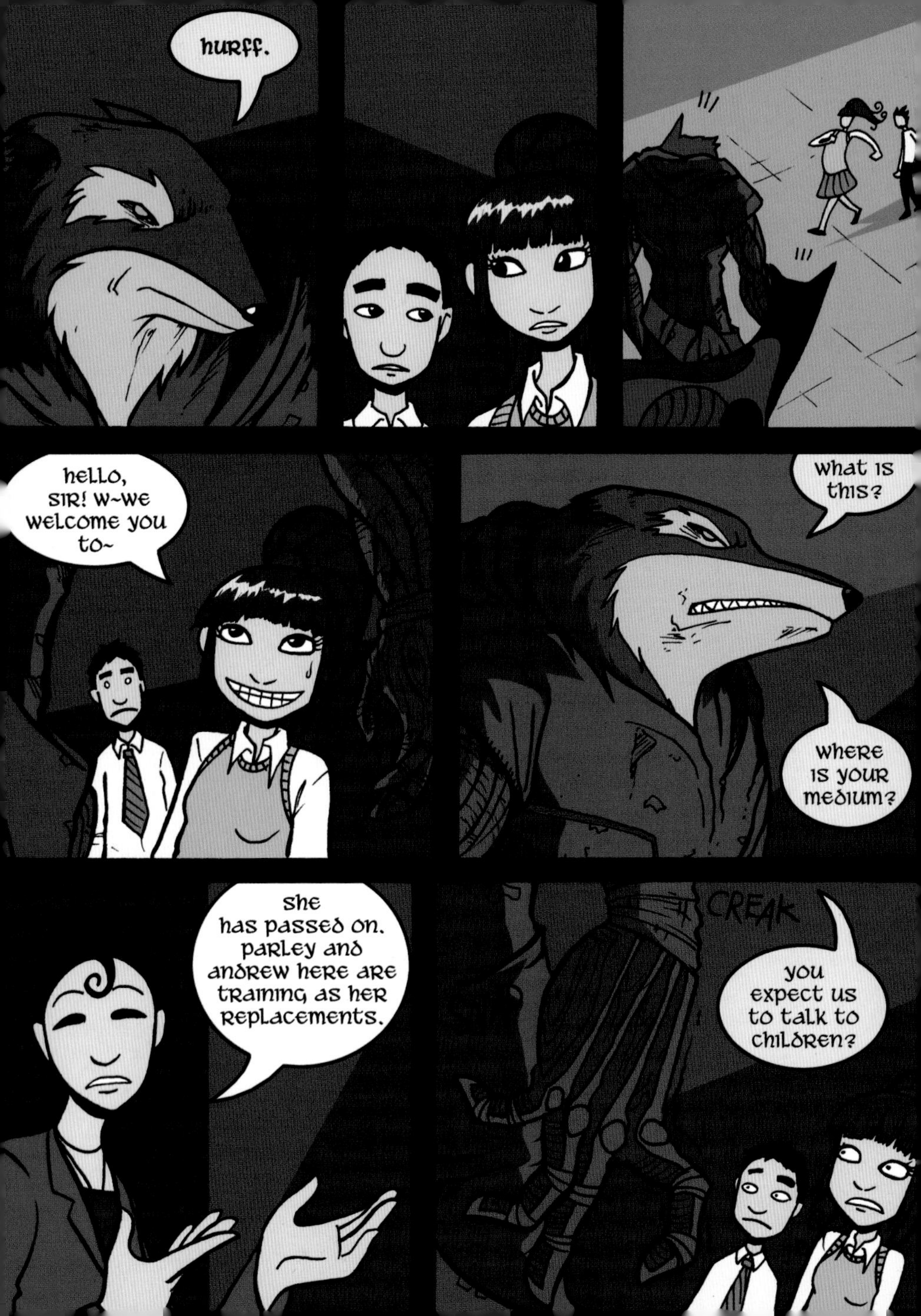
hurff.
hello, sir! w~we welcome you to~
what is this?
where is your medium?
she has passed on. parley and andrew here are training as her replacements.
CREAK
you expect us to talk to children?

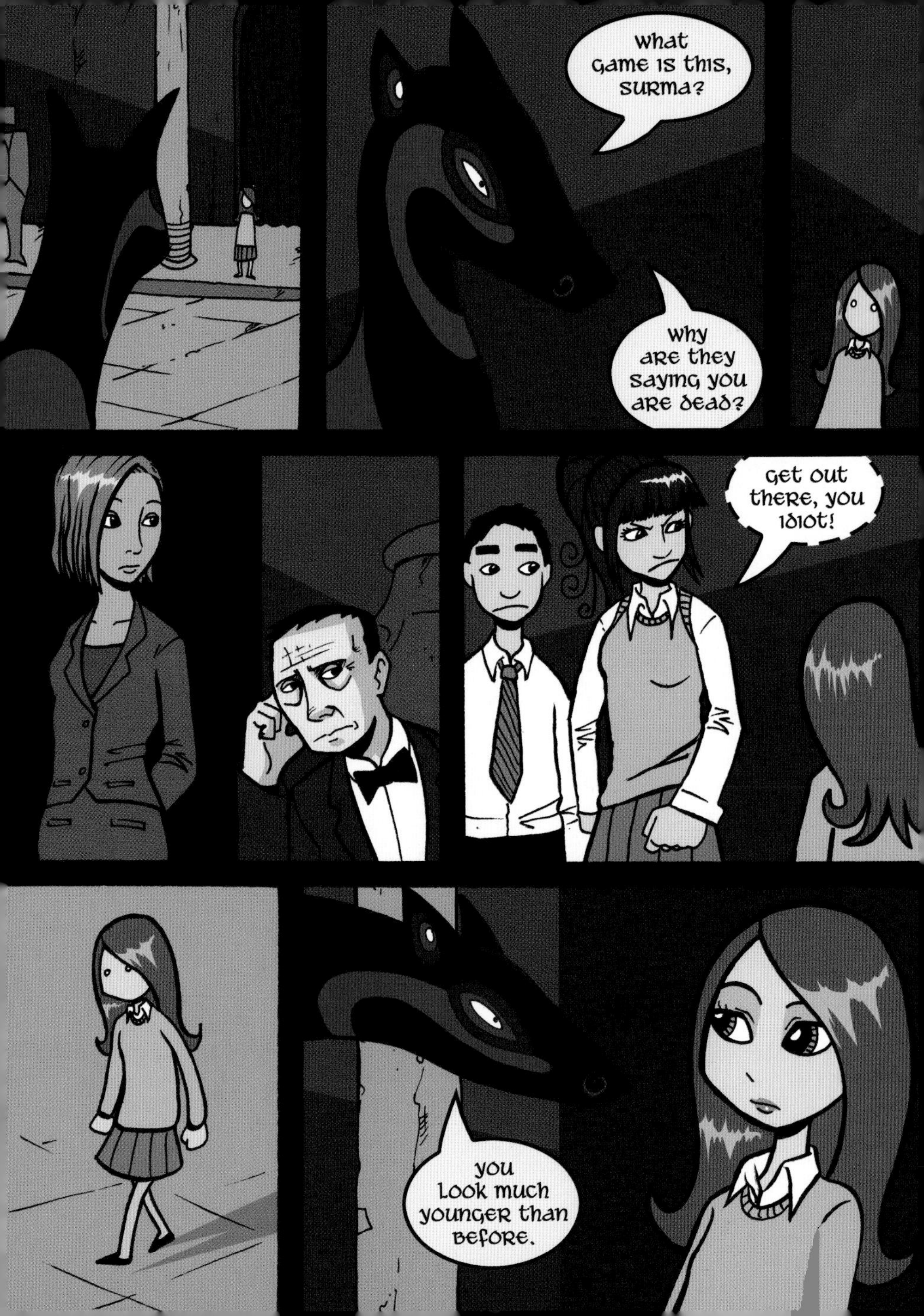
What game is this, Surma?
Why are they saying you are dead?
Get out there, you idiot!
You look much younger than before.

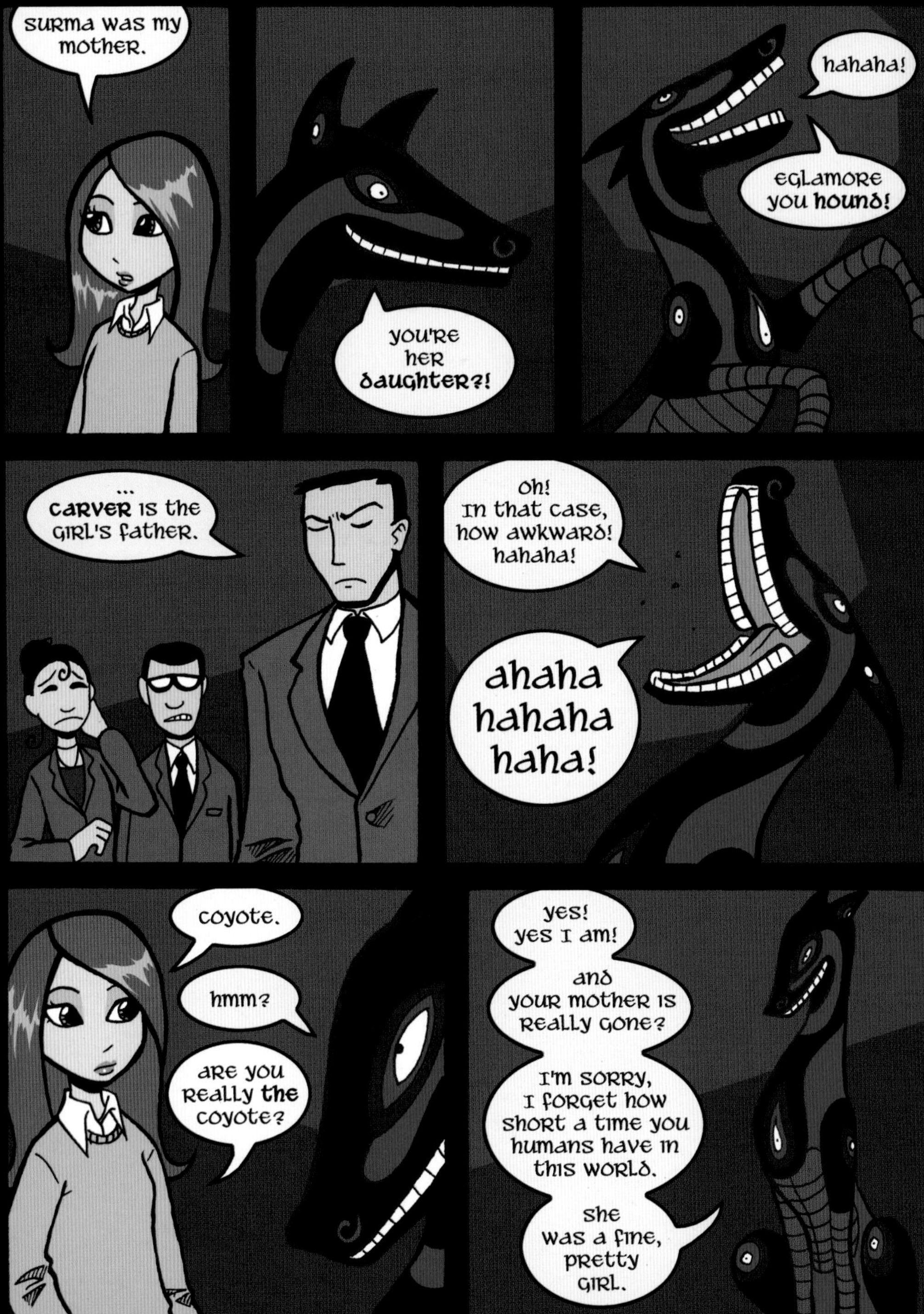
surma was my mother.
you're her **daughter?!**
hahaha!
eglamore you **hound!**
...
carver is the girl's father.
oh! in that case, how awkward! hahaha!
ahaha hahaha haha!
coyote.
hmm?
are you really **the** coyote?
yes! yes I am!
and your mother is really gone?
I'm sorry, I forget how short a time you humans have in this world.
she was a fine, pretty girl.

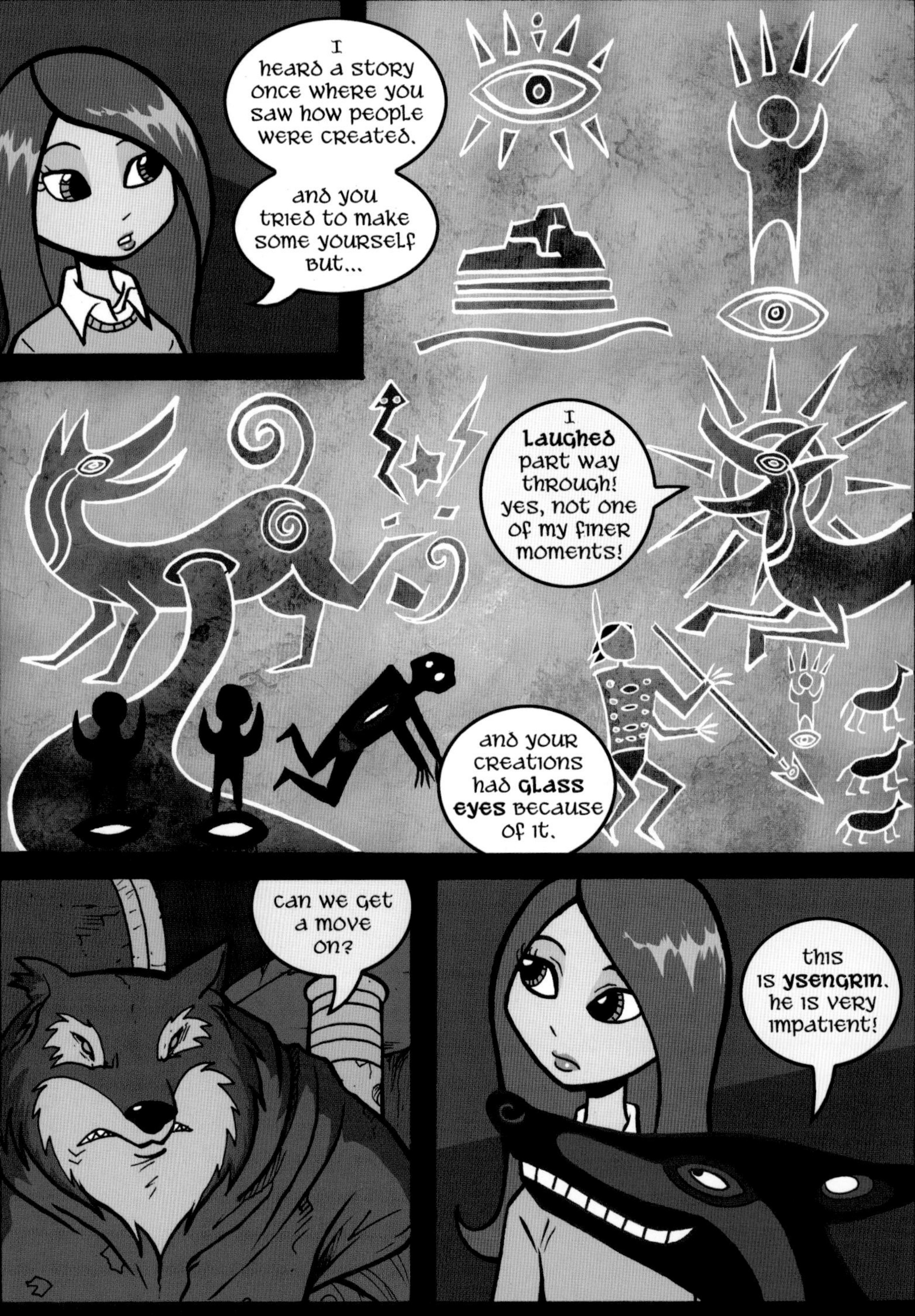
I heard a story once where you saw how people were created.
and you tried to make some yourself but...
I laughed part way through! yes, not one of my finer moments!
and your creations had glass eyes because of it.
can we get a move on?
this is ysengrin. he is very impatient!

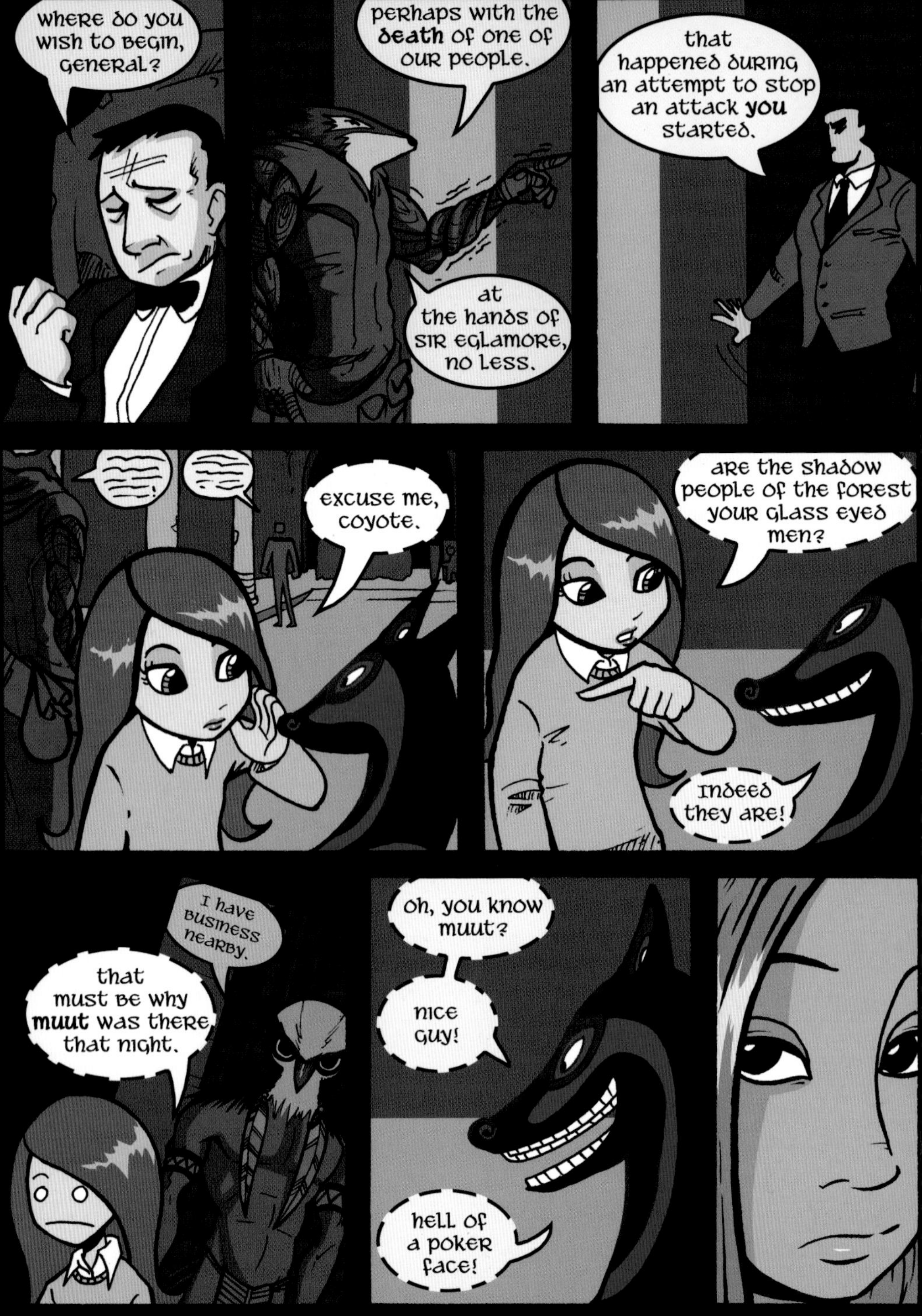
where do you wish to begin, general?
perhaps with the death of one of our people.
at the hands of sir eglamore, no less.
that happened during an attempt to stop an attack you started.
excuse me, coyote.
are the shadow people of the forest your glass eyed men?
indeed they are!
I have business nearby.
that must be why muut was there that night.
oh, you know muut?
nice guy!
hell of a poker face!

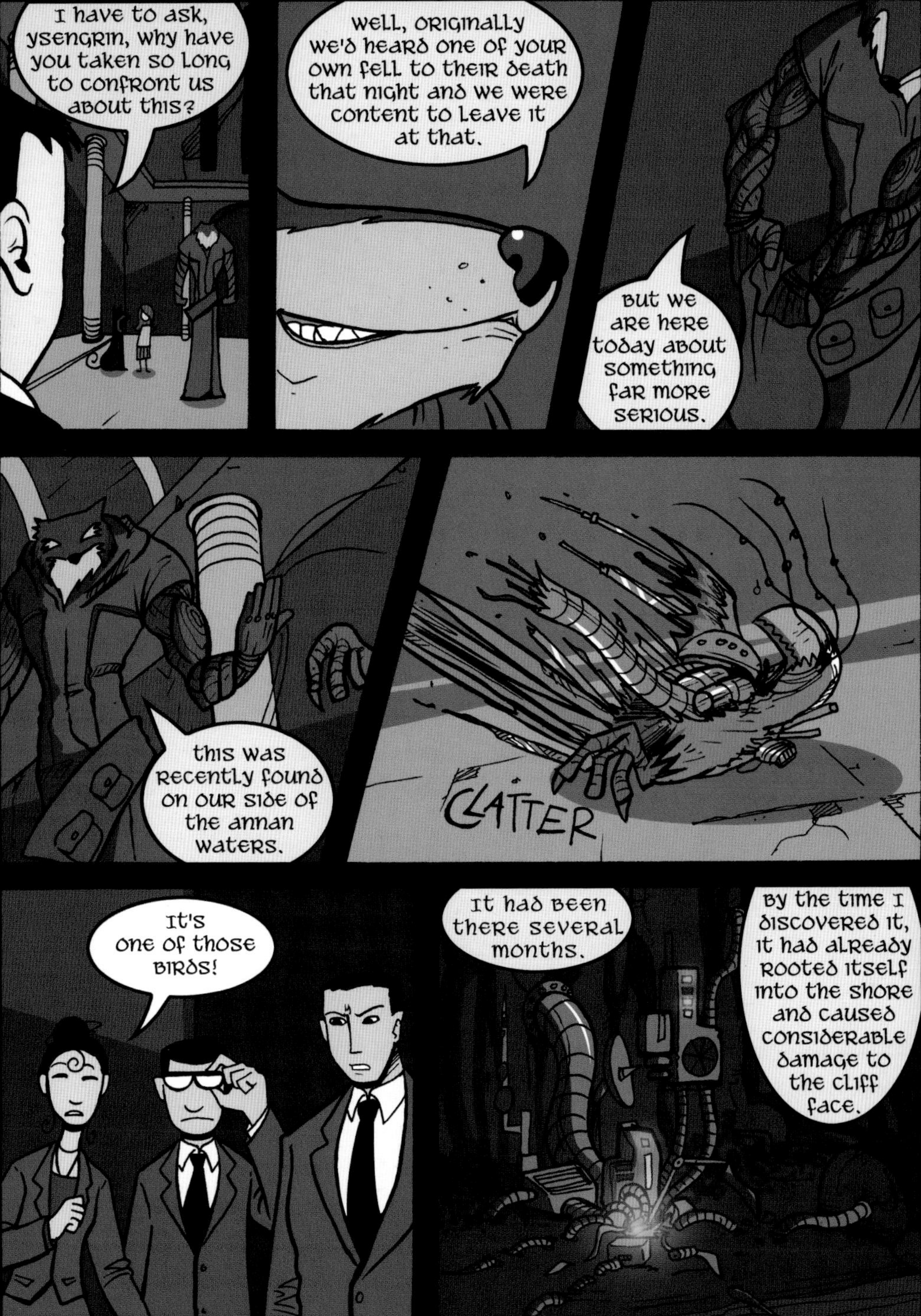
I have to ask, ysengrin, why have you taken so long to confront us about this?
Well, originally we'd heard one of your own fell to their death that night and we were content to leave it at that.
But we are here today about something far more serious.
this was recently found on our side of the annan waters.
CLATTER
It's one of those birds!
It had been there several months.
By the time I discovered it, it had already rooted itself into the shore and caused considerable damage to the cliff face.

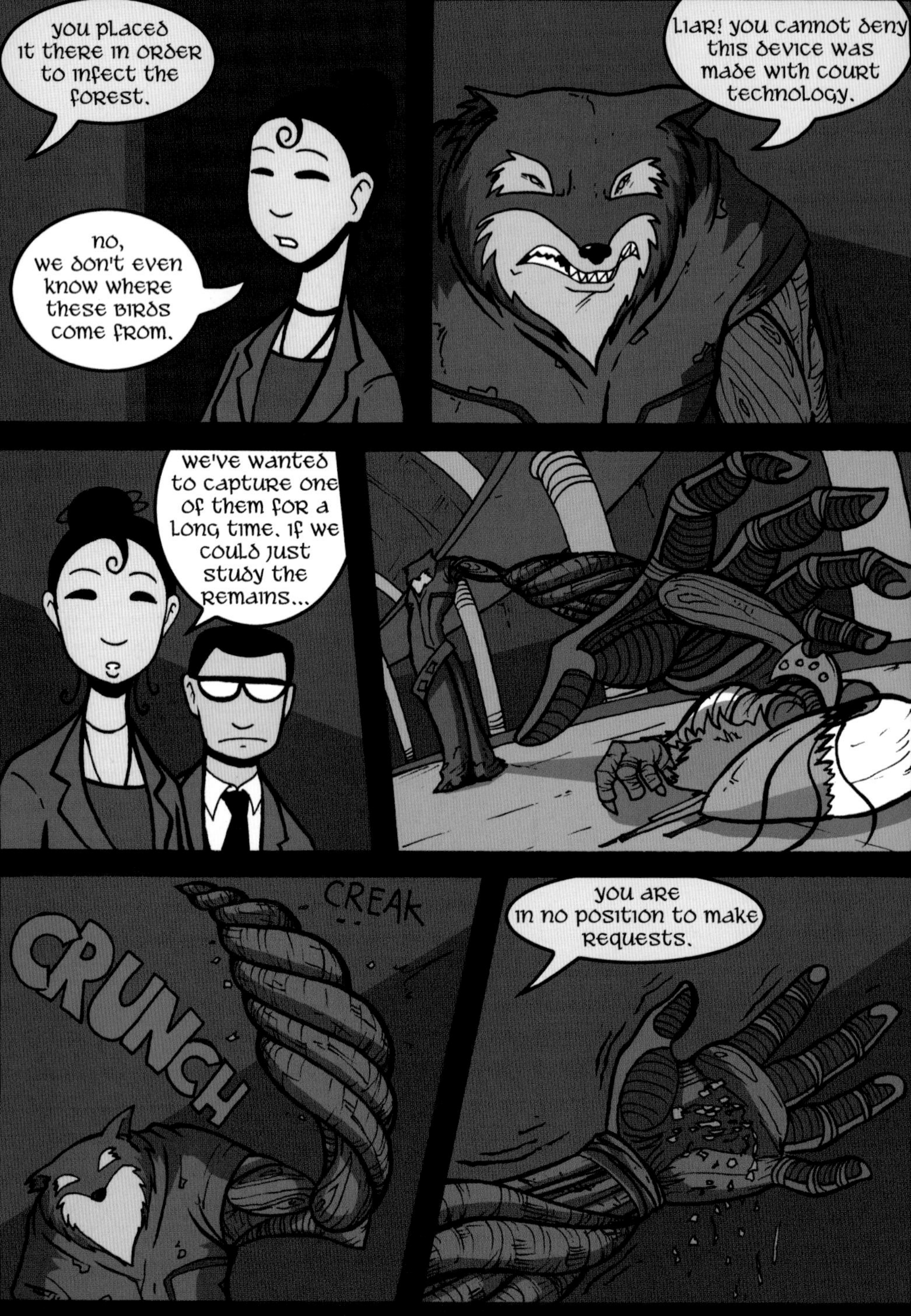
you placed it there in order to infect the forest.
no, we don't even know where these birds come from.
Liar! you cannot deny this device was made with court technology.
we've wanted to capture one of them for a long time. if we could just study the remains...
CRUNCH
CREAK
you are in no position to make requests.

FURTHER MORE, WE HAVE PROOF THAT **ANTHONY CARVER** WAS THE ONE WHO PLANTED THE DEVICE THERE!

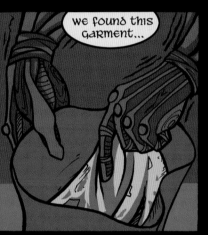

WE FOUND THIS GARMENT...

WHICH BEARS THE NAME a. CARVER!

UM... ACTUALLY, SIR, THAT'S MINE.

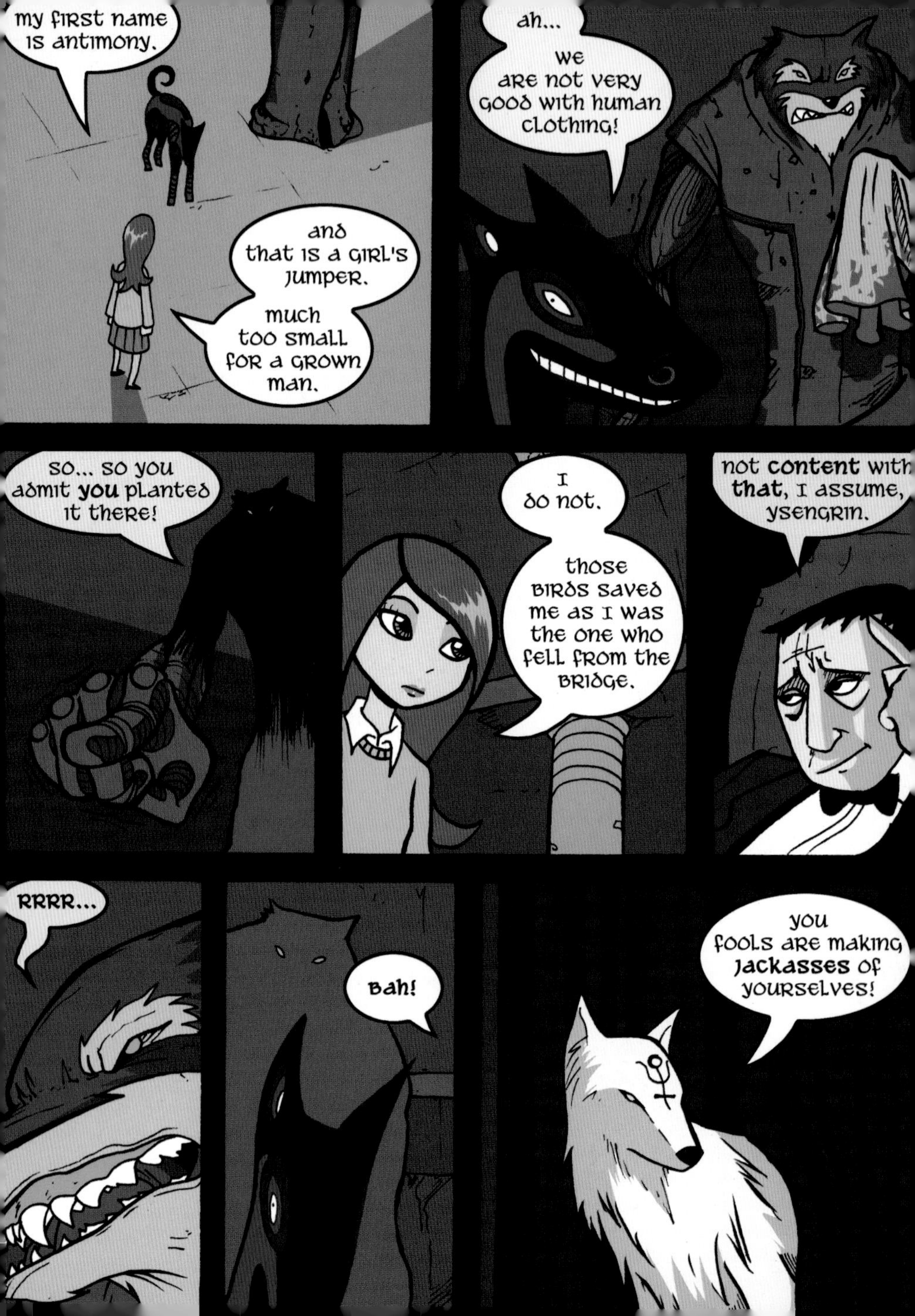
my first name is antimony.
and that is a girl's jumper.
much too small for a grown man.
ah...
we are not very good with human clothing!
so... so you admit you planted it there!
I do not.
those birds saved me as I was the one who fell from the bridge.
not content with that, I assume, ysengrin.
RRRR...
Bah!
you fools are making jackasses of yourselves!

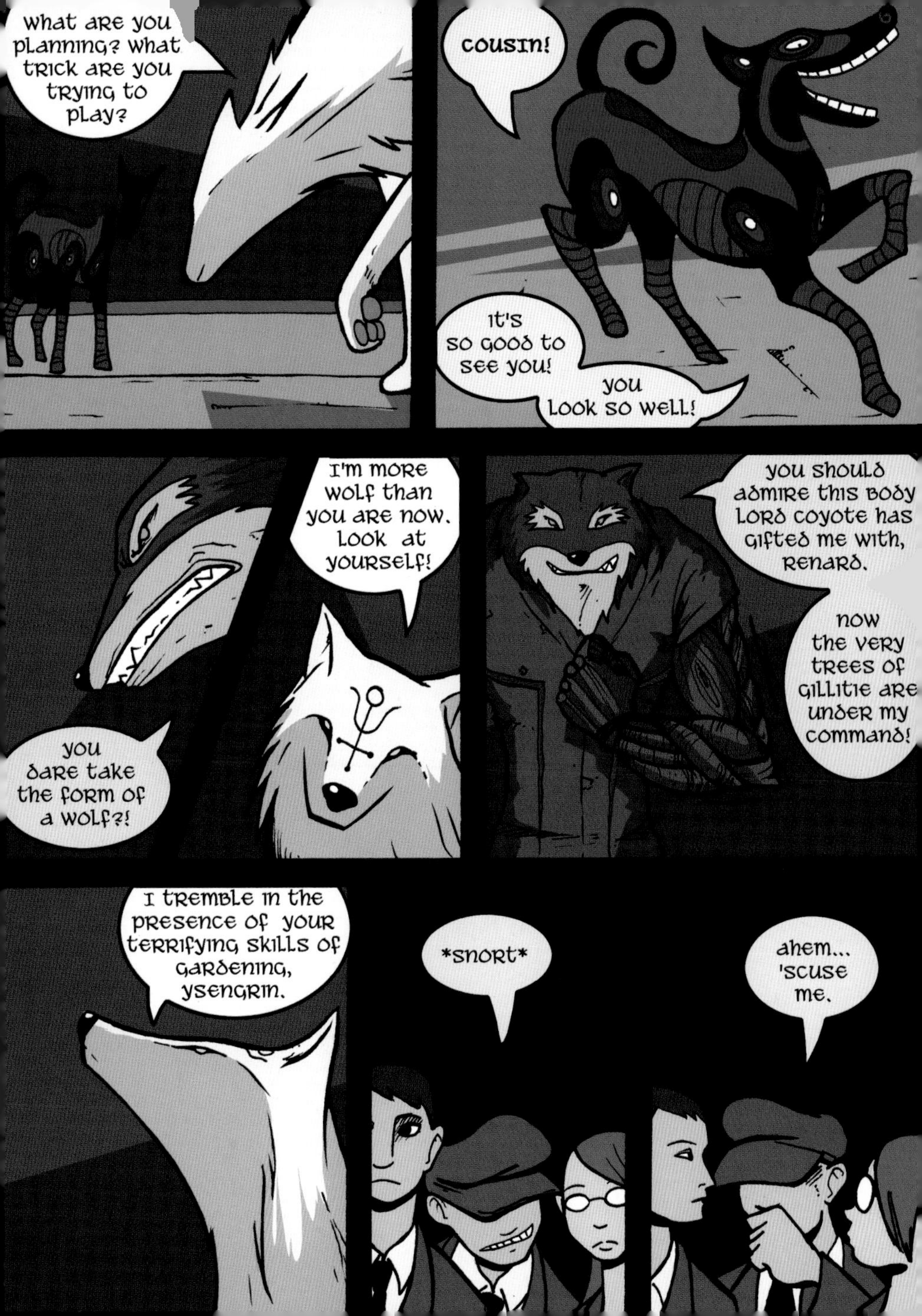
what are you planning? what trick are you trying to play?
cousin!
it's so good to see you!
you look so well!
you dare take the form of a wolf?!
I'm more wolf than you are now. look at yourself!
you should admire this body lord coyote has gifted me with, renard.
now the very trees of gillitie are under my command!
I tremble in the presence of your terrifying skills of gardening, ysengrim.
snort
ahem... 'scuse me.

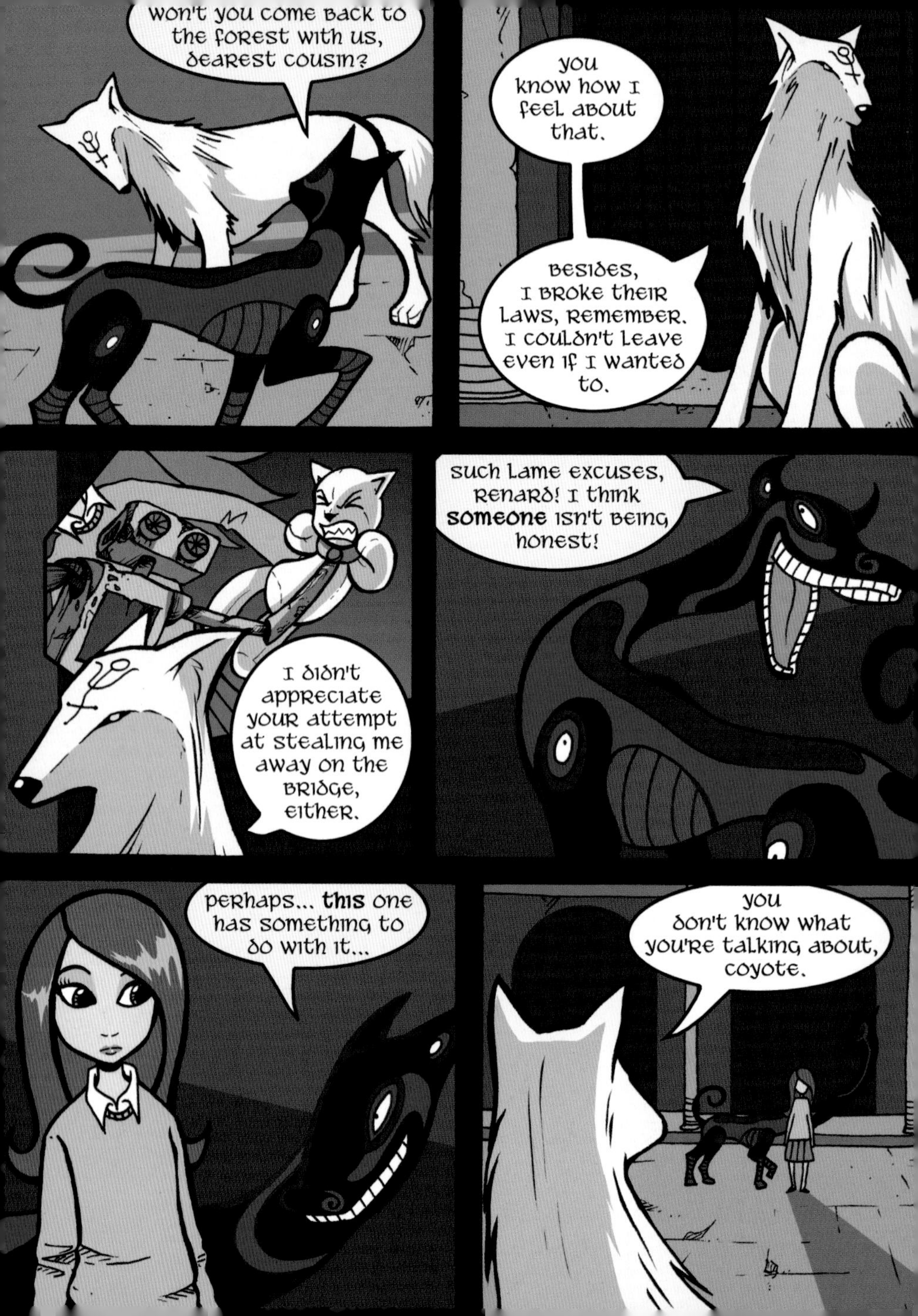
won't you come back to the forest with us, dearest cousin?
you know how I feel about that.
Besides, I broke their laws, remember. I couldn't leave even if I wanted to.
I didn't appreciate your attempt at stealing me away on the bridge, either.
such lame excuses, Renard! I think **someone** isn't being honest!
perhaps... **this** one has something to do with it...
you don't know what you're talking about, coyote.

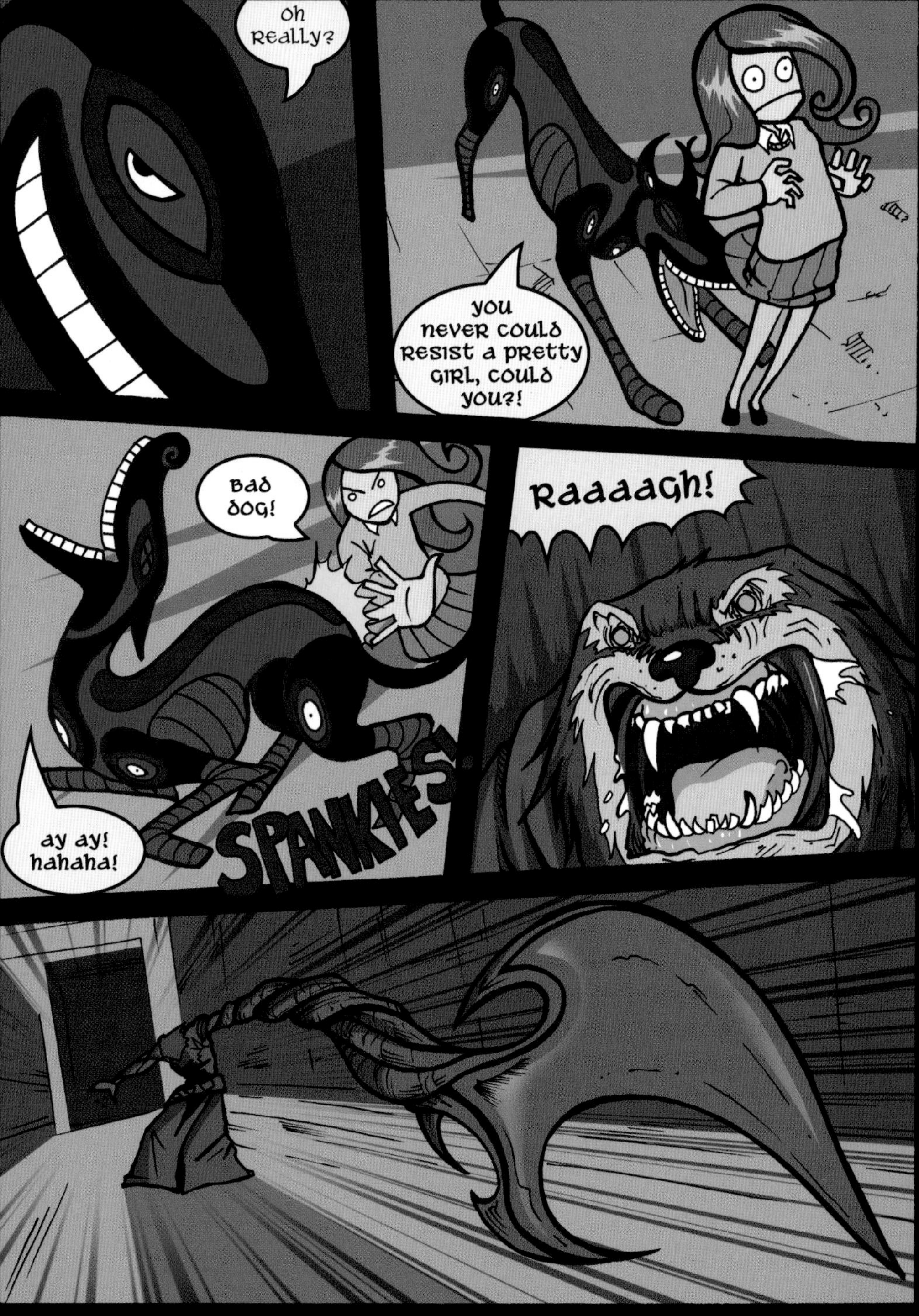
oh Really?
you never could resist a pretty girl, could you?!
Bad dog!
ay ay! hahaha!
SPANKIES!
Raaaagh!

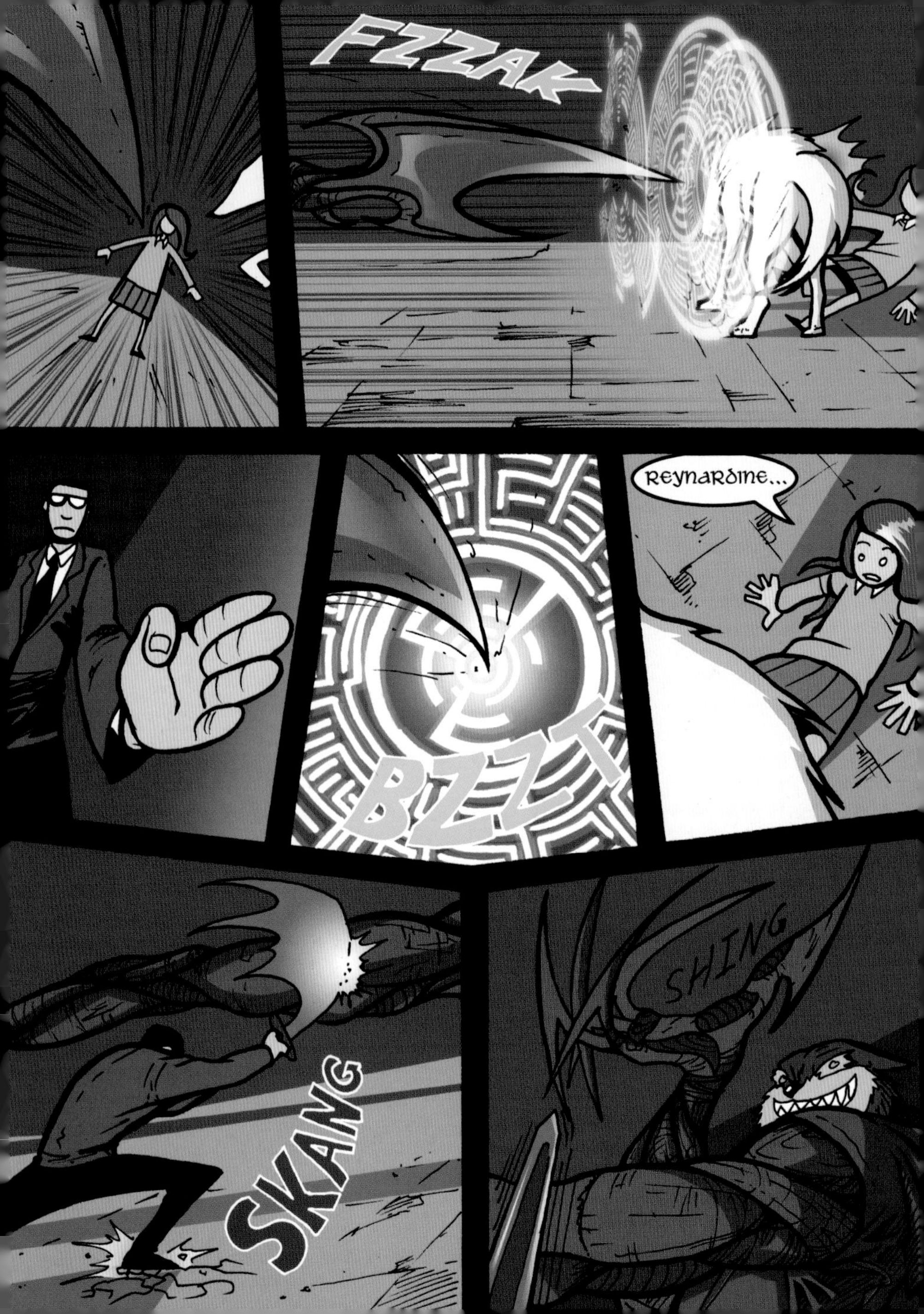
FZZAK
Reynardine...
BZZT
SKANG
SHING

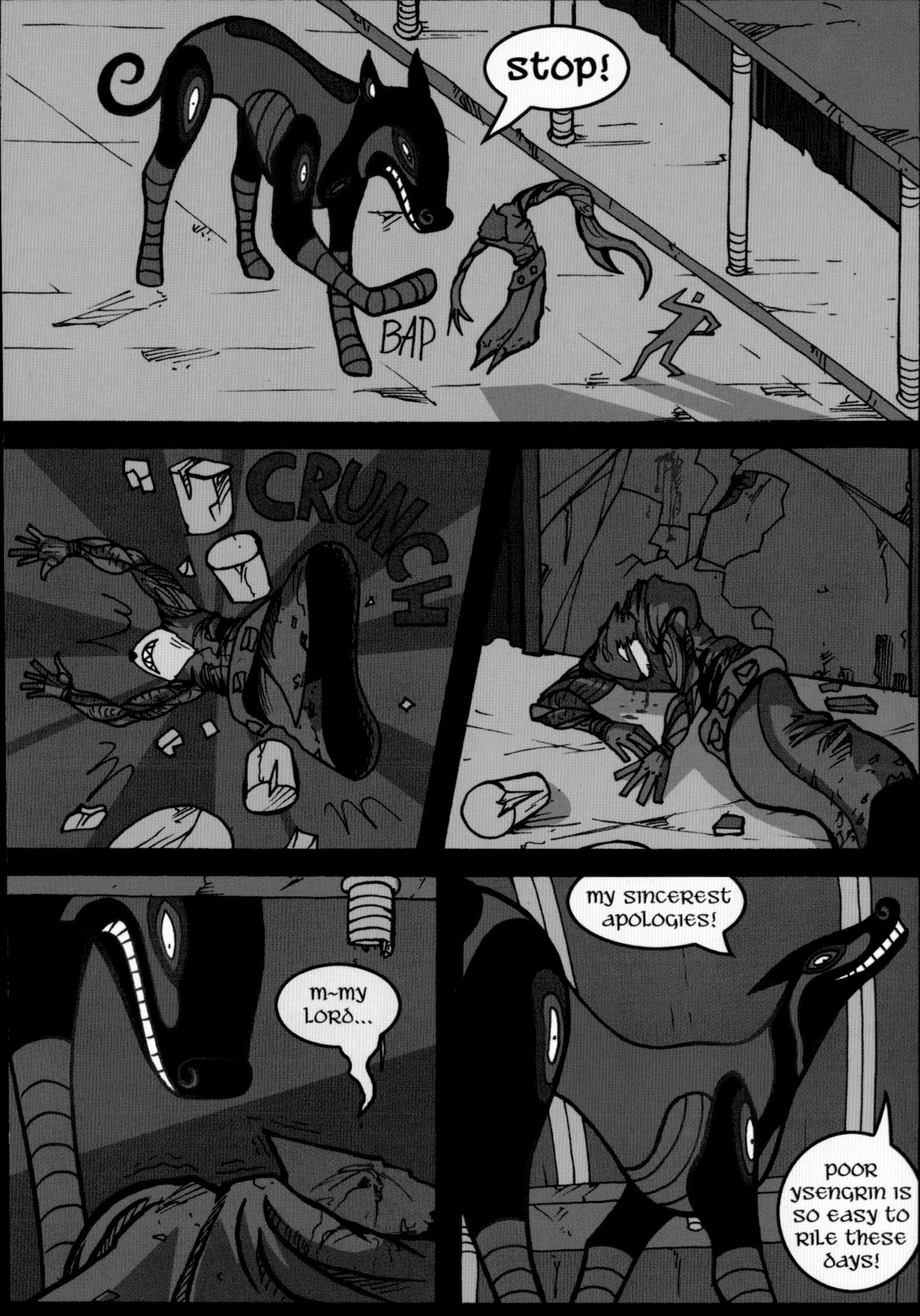
stop!
BAP
CRUNCH
m~my LORD...
my sincerest apologies!
poor ysengrin is so easy to rile these days!

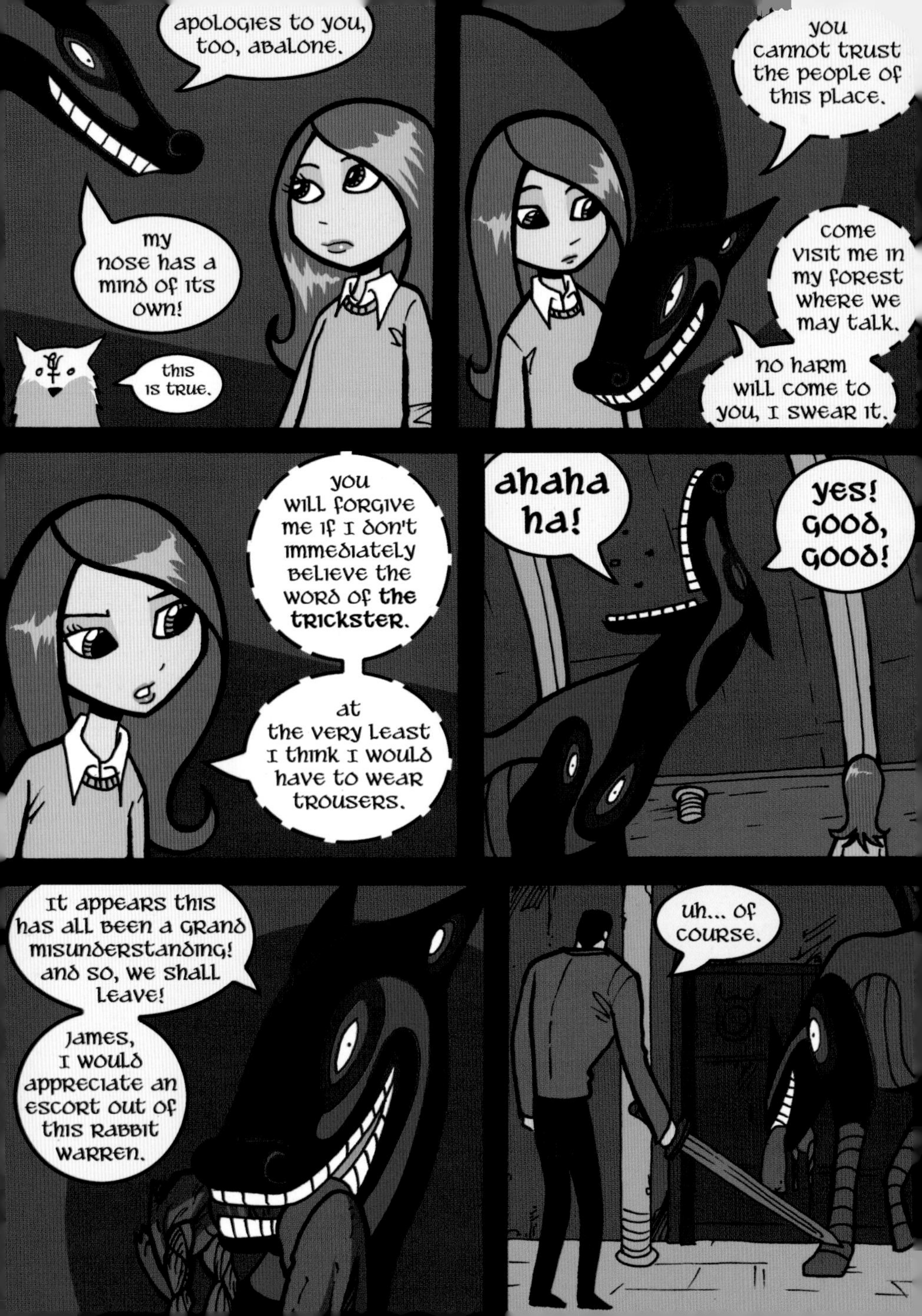
apologies to you, too, abalone.
my nose has a mind of its own!
this is true.
you cannot trust the people of this place.
come visit me in my forest where we may talk.
no harm will come to you, I swear it.
you will forgive me if I don't immediately believe the word of the trickster.
at the very least I think I would have to wear trousers.
ahaha ha!
yes! good, good!
It appears this has all been a grand misunderstanding! and so, we shall leave!
James, I would appreciate an escort out of this rabbit warren.
uh... of course.

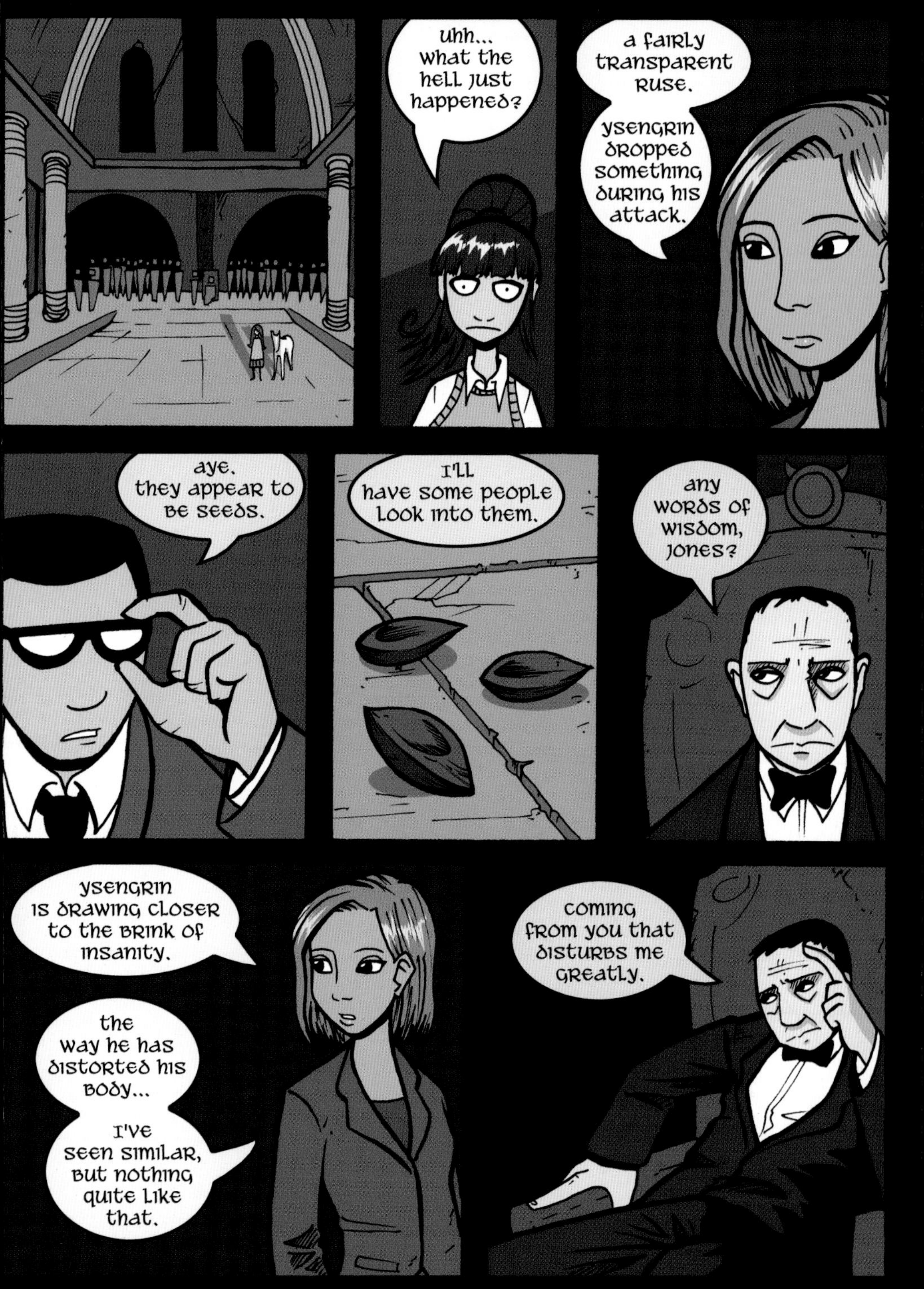
uhh... what the hell just happened?
a fairly transparent ruse.
ysengrin dropped something during his attack.
aye. they appear to be seeds.
I'll have some people look into them.
any words of wisdom, jones?
ysengrin is drawing closer to the brink of insanity.
the way he has distorted his body...
I've seen similar, but nothing quite like that.
coming from you that disturbs me greatly.

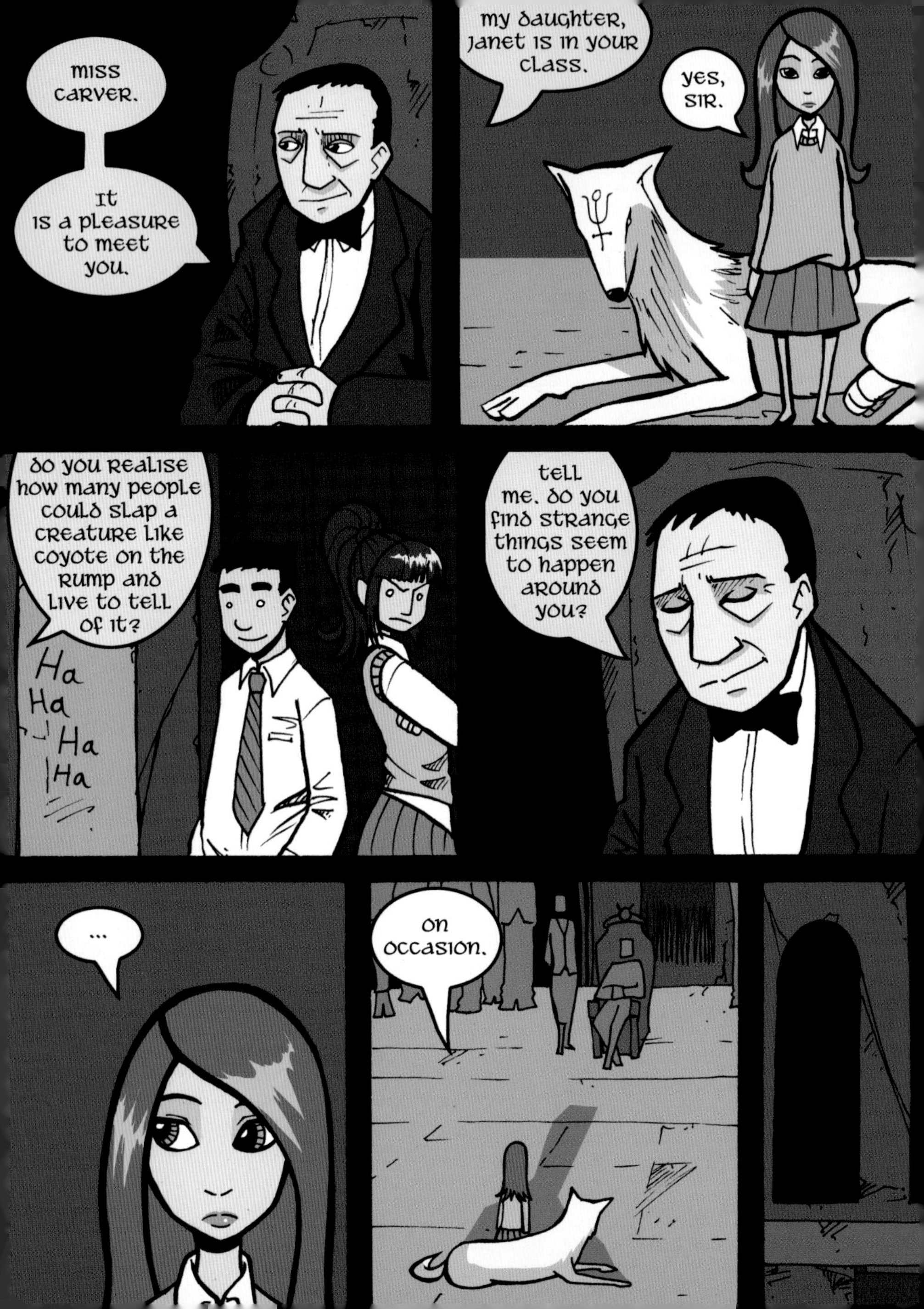

miss carver.
It is a pleasure to meet you.
my daughter, janet is in your class.
yes, sir.
do you realise how many people could slap a creature like coyote on the rump and live to tell of it?
Ha Ha Ha Ha
tell me. do you find strange things seem to happen around you?
...
on occasion.

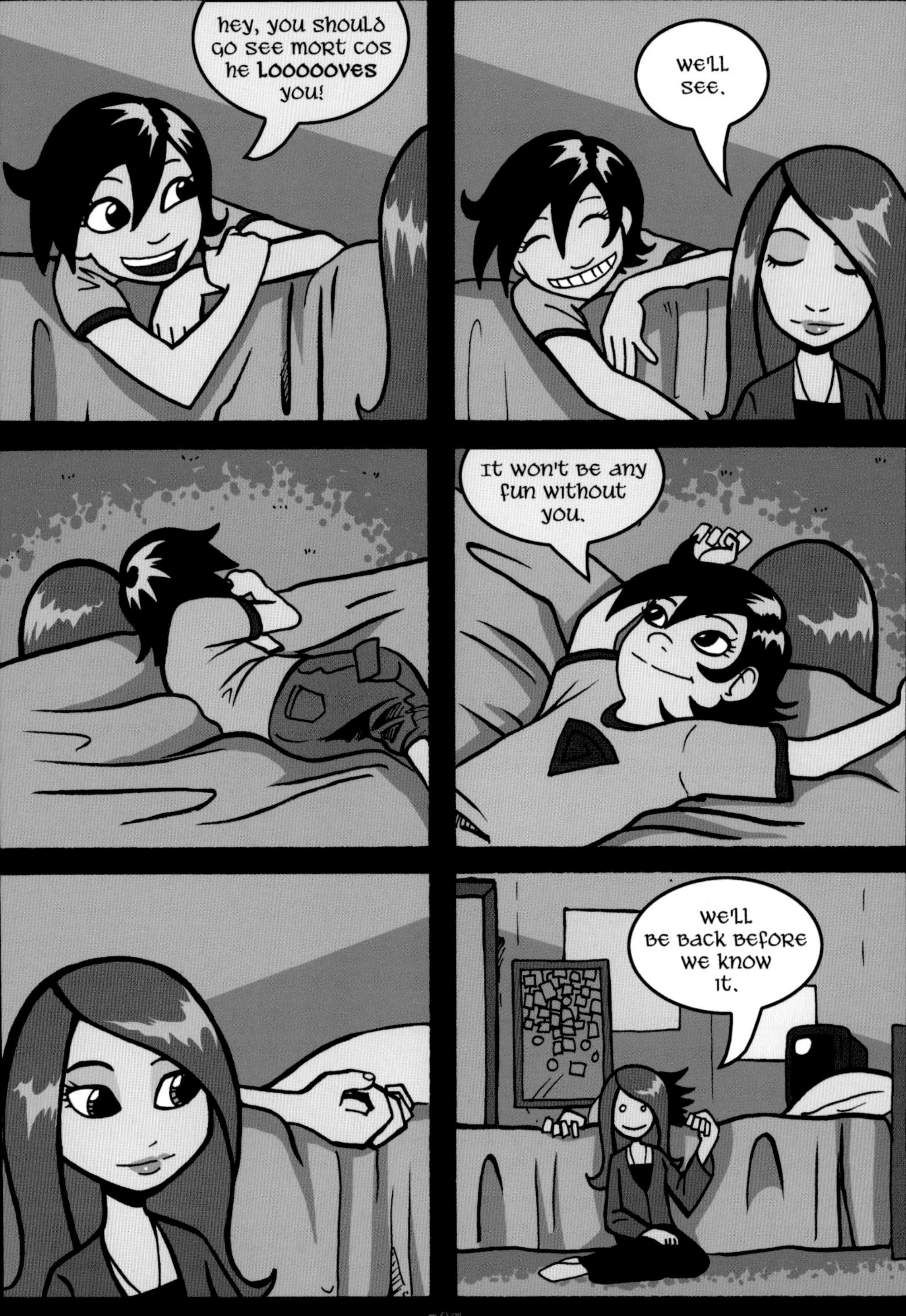
hey, you should go see mort cos he LOOOOOVES you!
we'll see.
It won't be any fun without you.
we'll be back before we know it.

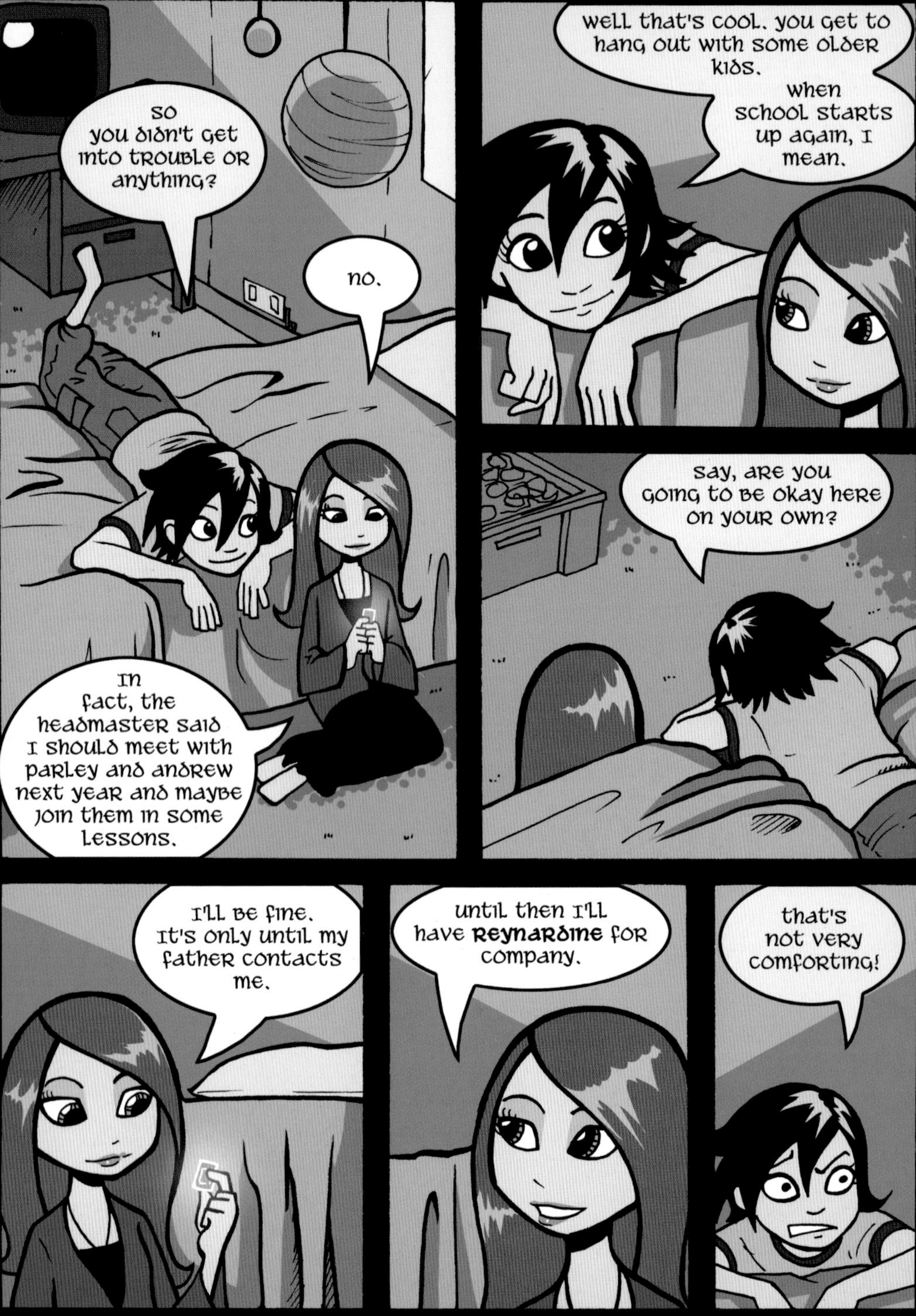
so you didn't get into trouble or anything?
no.
In fact, the headmaster said I should meet with parley and andrew next year and maybe join them in some lessons.
well that's cool. you get to hang out with some older kids.
when school starts up again, I mean.
say, are you going to be okay here on your own?
I'll be fine. It's only until my father contacts me.
until then I'll have **Reynardine** for company.
that's not very comforting!

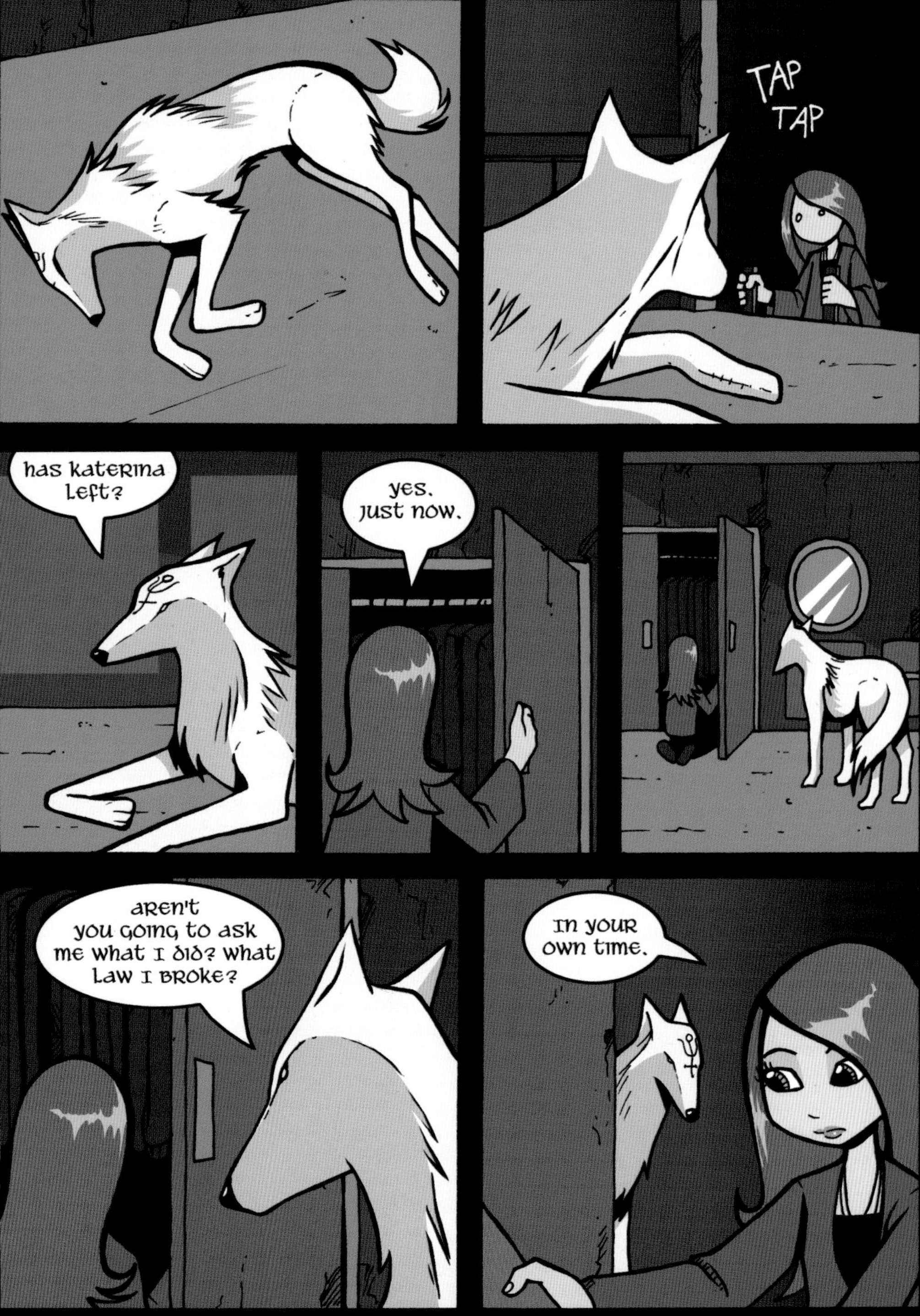
TAP
TAP
has katerina left?
yes. just now.
aren't you going to ask me what I did? what law I broke?
In your own time.

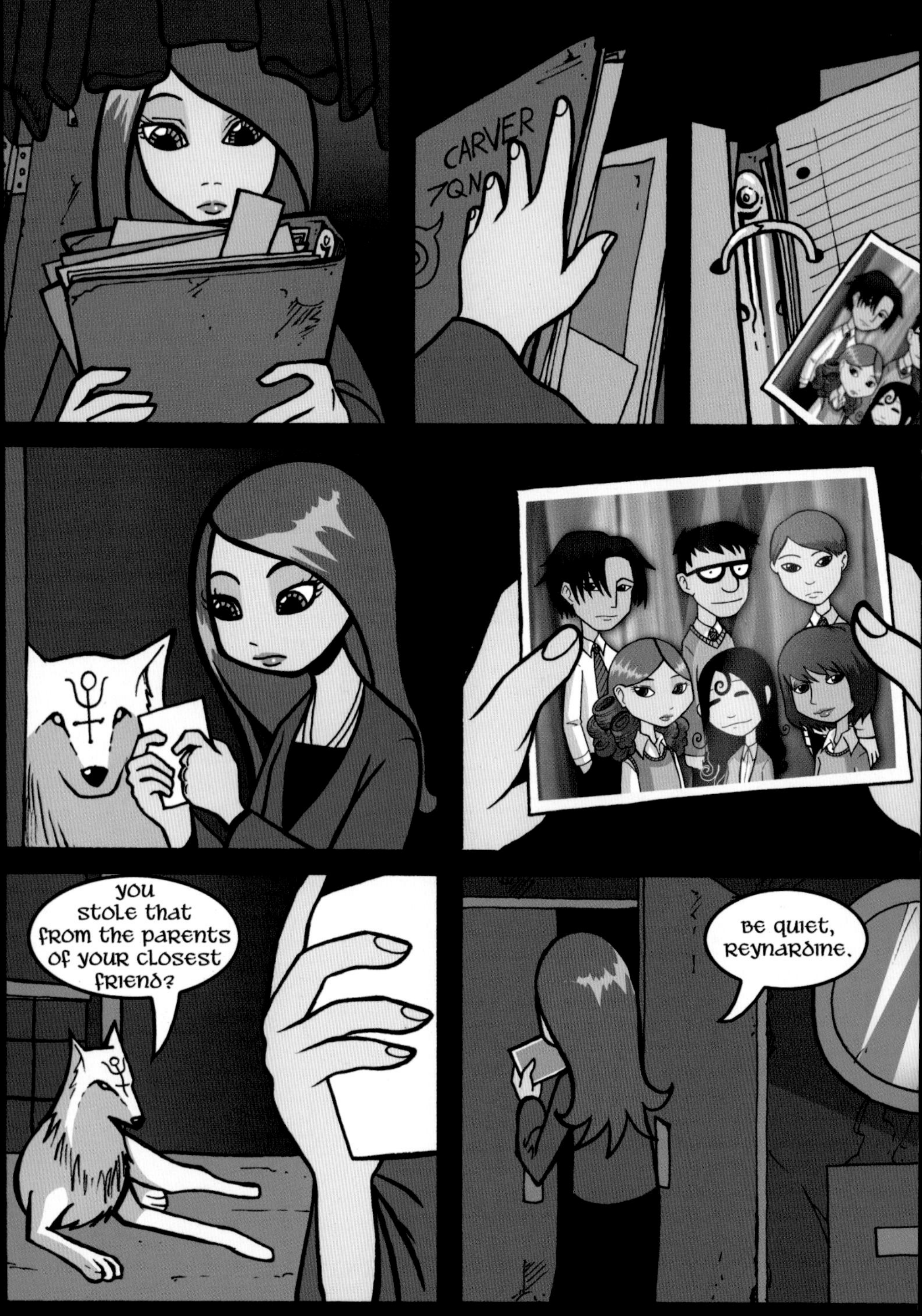
CARVER
7QN
you stole that from the parents of your closest friend?
Be quiet, Reynardine.

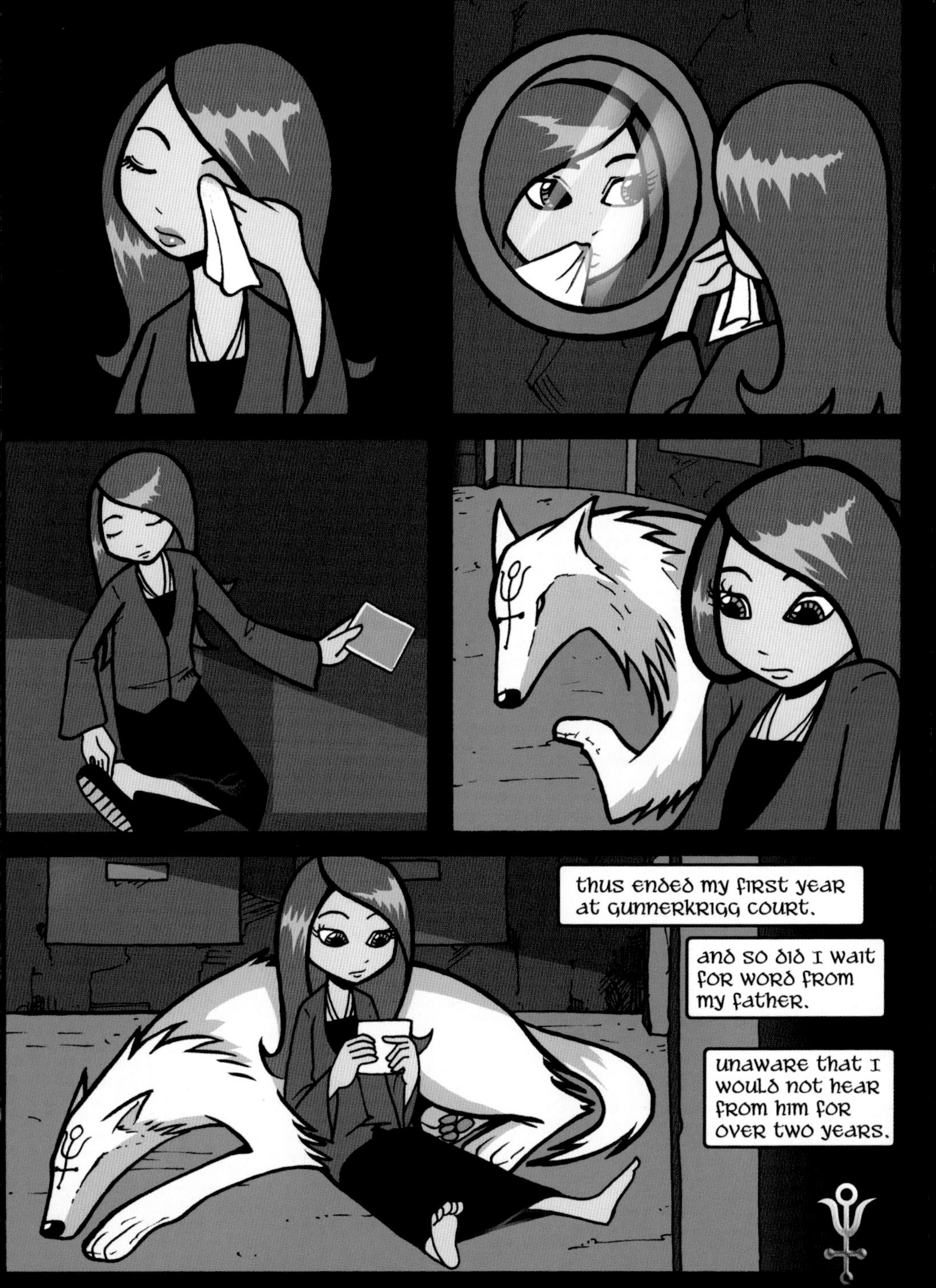
thus ended my first year at gunnerkrigg court.
and so did I wait for word from my father.
unaware that I would not hear from him for over two years.

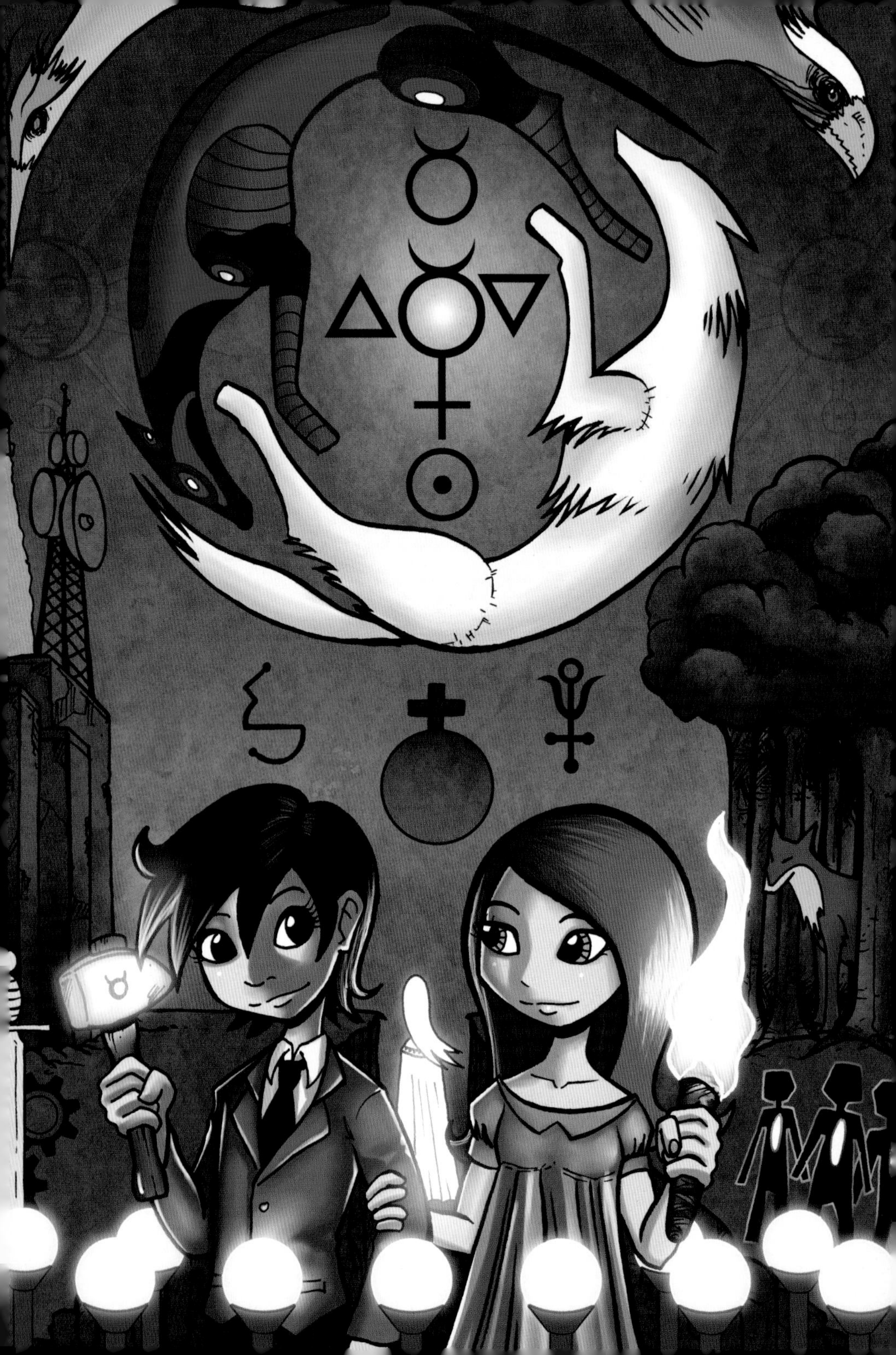

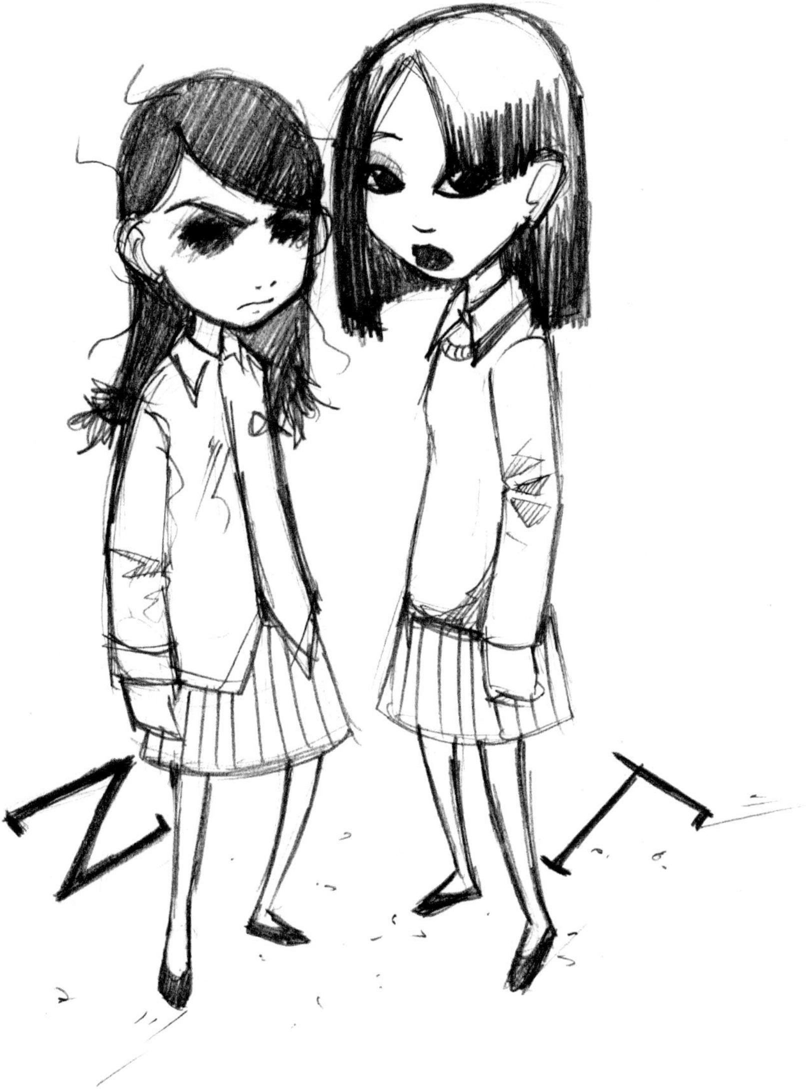

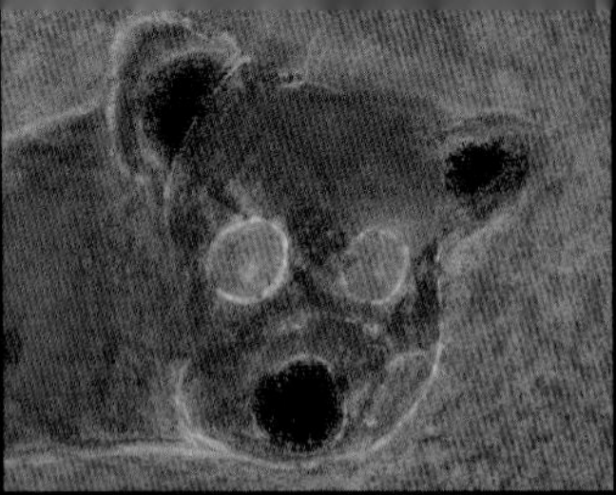

ABOUT THE AUTHOR:

Tom lives in Birmingham, in the United Kingdom. He can be found in one of three places:

1) At work.
2) At home.
3) Waiting for the bus to take him to work, or home.

While waiting patiently for the Travel West Midlands bus service, he has had a lot of time to think about making a book. He is happy to find that this has happened.

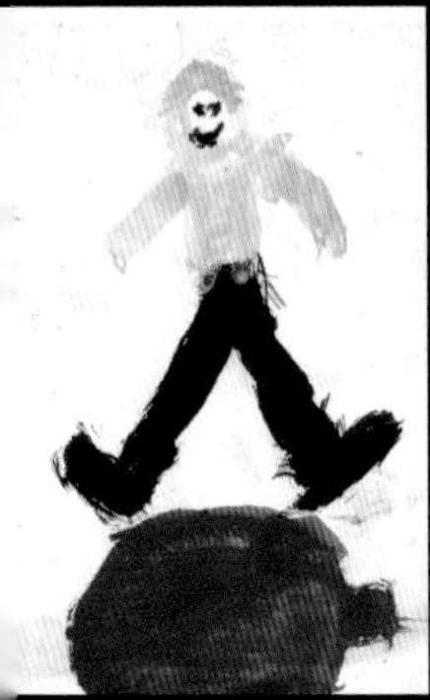

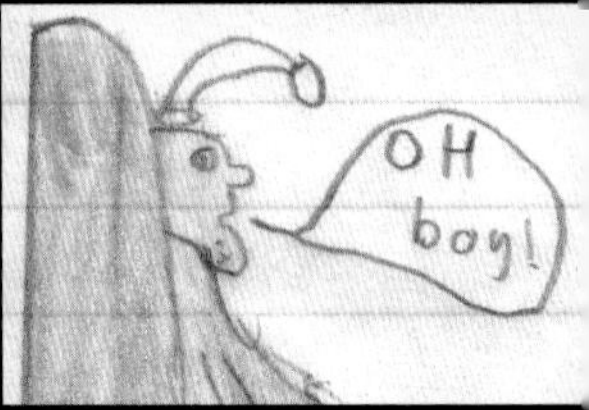
OH boy!

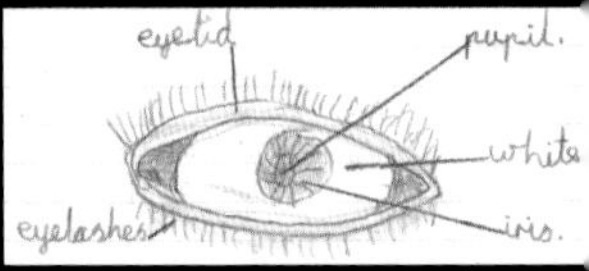
eyelid
pupil.
white
eyelashes
iris.

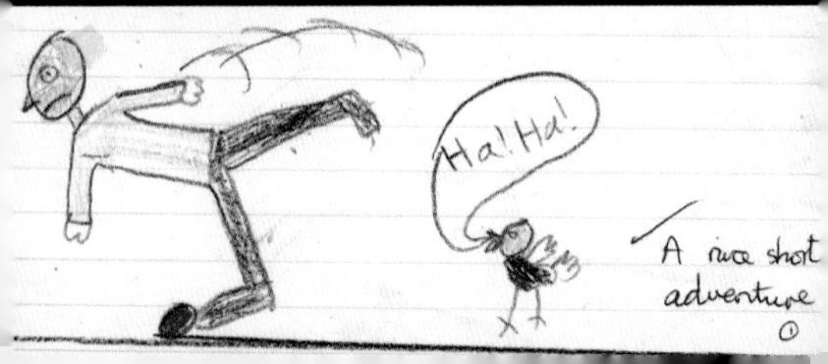
Ha! Ha!
A nice short adventure

Thank you for reading

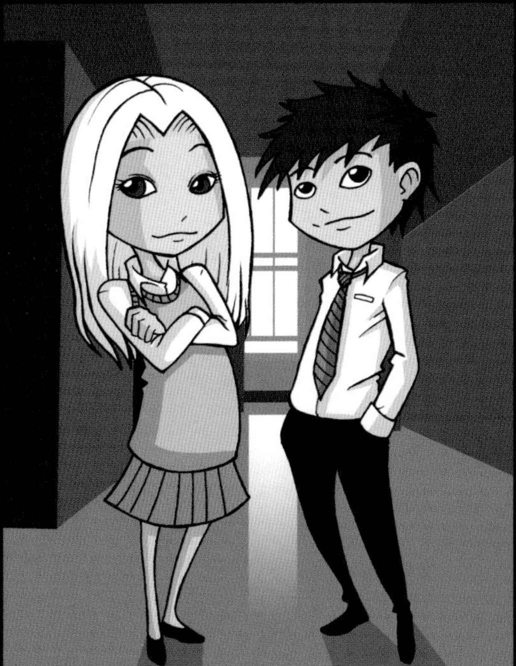

www.gunnerkrigg.com